NEUROPOWER

LEADING WITH NEUROINTELLIGENCE

THIRD EDITION

PETER BUROW

The material contained in this book is not intended as medical advice. If you have a medical issue or illness, consult a qualified physician.

NeuroPower – Leading with NeuroIntelligence

Published by;

Copernicus Publishing Pty Ltd
10 Grosvenor Street, Blackburn North VIC 3130 Australia
PO Box 125, Balwyn North VIC 3104 Australia
Ph +61 3 9017 3162
Fx +61 3 9923 6632

Proofing by Amanda Banhidi
Desktop Publishing by Wade McFarlane

PEOPLE WHO HAVE APPLIED NEUROPOWER TO THE CHALLENGES THEY FACE HAVE THIS TO SAY:

Don't judge a book by its cover, or in the case of this one by its size! When I first saw the NeuroPower book, I was horrified by its size but I quickly learnt that it's actually the modern day version of the holy grail! Understanding Core Beliefs and the emotional resistances that emerge in people's response to change has been invaluable for us. The entire framework gives you such insight into who you are as a leader and how you can influence and inspire your people and stakeholders around you. NeuroPower has enabled us to fast forward strategically and has helped us stay ahead of the curve. Its value to our business comes through at all different levels from formulating strategies to engaging personal relationships – it definitely exceeds the investment.

Sophie Crawford-Jones (Principal, Strategic Sales and Marketing, PricewaterhouseCoopers Australia)

Being a business of nearly 50 psychologists in a very successful consultancy, we are hard to impress on the topic of how to use the mind and brain effectively to enhance performance. Despite this, the NeuroPower team and information not only impressed us, our business is noticeably better as a result. The information was insightful and revolutionary. It has been a long time since I have been this impressed, both professionally and personally.

Jonathan Lincolne (Founder, Sentis Pty Ltd)

Having studied many different psychological and behavioural models and frameworks over the past 40 years, I was impressed by Peter's work in weaving together some of the most significant theorists and writers, from Freud and Jung through to those of Ancient cultures, into one cogent system. NeuroPower is an informed, integrated and - above all - practical model for understanding and facilitating human development. In my experience, it is a powerful asset, not just for practitioners working in therapeutic or counselling contexts, but for anyone who either works with people or is looking for an empowering tool to further their own development.

Dr Daniele Viliunas (Senior Psychiatrist)

The NeuroPower framework is a brilliant system to guide self-development that is insightful, practical and grounded in great science. It is a useful system for those starting out on their journey of self-discovery through to practitioners who will find the system useful within their work.

Dr Sarah Colley PHD (Lecturer and PHD supervisor in organisational psychology, University of Queensland)

Having worked with Peter personally over more than ten years to develop leadership teams in major financial and professional service organisations, I have found NeuroPower to be profoundly insightful, especially in helping clients with motivation, engagement and ensuring their communications hit the mark. In my experience, the insights that the NeuroPower framework brings have been pivotal in helping our client leaders and their teams achieve that elusive top 20 percent of performance.

Tim Rossi (Director, Symphony Leadership)

As a long-time beginner's mind-student of powerful ideas in leadership, culture and neuroscience (which include the wonderful work of Ken Wilber's Integral Model, Beck and Cowan's Spiral Dynamics, Buddhism, Hinduism, Gurdjieff's work on chakras and David Hawkins' masterful use of kinesiology) how I enjoyed this elegantly integrated text of human personality. The road to the integrated selves of acceptance and grace are paved with many a 'self-help' or '10-steps-on-how-to-become-a-CEO-in-90-days' manual. Peter's book, however, is delightfully different and quietly coherent. It appeals to the deliberately disciplined logic in us all whilst at the same time entreating the humble heart within. This is a book that firmly supports the 'how to' of achieving the ultimate goal of leadership: kindness - the ability to see the potential in both ourselves and in the people who work with and for us, so beautifully captured in the Sanskrit greeting of 'Namaste'. As we continue toward our own journey of integration and enlightenment. Peter's instructive and gradually constructive definition of 'potential' becomes more and more intriguing, expansive, playful, and loving.

Katharine McLennan (Head of Global Leadership Academy, QBE Insurance Group Ltd)

I've been using an understanding of the six social cognitive needs to help high performance teams understand their audiences, both internally and externally, for about six years now. In terms of corporate and media engagement, understanding and application, the practical insights of the NeuroPower framework provide a quantum leap in cut-through impact messaging. It provides the tick-tock to my messaging clock.

Warren Clarke (Director, Executive Media Coaching)

There's a certain revelation in truly knowing, accepting and understanding yourself. We're all a key piece of the puzzle and respecting the uniqueness of oneself and others is an empowering way to bring unity, especially to a team. Through the extraordinary depth of research and insights in this book, Peter fast-tracks what most of us take a lifetime to learn – who we are, why we do what we do and what that means for others. Collect, share and leverage that wisdom within a team and suddenly you have a powerhouse of talent capable of driving unlimited outcomes.

Amanda Revis (Group Executive, Human Resources, Suncorp Group)

Thank You

There are many people who have supported the publication of *NeuroPower*.

One of the longest-serving, most dedicated souls has been Wade McFarlane, who has worked tirelessly with me in conducting a staggering amount of field research, theming and analysis to support the development of the framework. Conversely, our newest team member is Amanda Banhidi, who has been a relentless powerhouse of execution driving the completion of this edition.

Anna Byrne and Andrew Burow made a significant contribution as my editorial team on the second edition. They laboured over sentences, diagrams and book structure to significantly enhance comprehension and flow. In the third edition, I'd like to acknowledge Misha Byrne, our resident neuroscientist, for working with me to incorporate the rapid advances of neuroscience (and, in particular, the social cognitive neuroscience that underpins the RELISH method). Zane Harris has also made an important contribution to the commercial application of the RELISH method as he has applied it in numerous leadership teams and coaching assignments across many industries. Using RELISH he is a master at creating high performance teams. And while Zane has been applying NeuroPower to corporate applications, Dr Daniele Viliunas has been applying it as a therapist and working with me to refine the transformation process, integration and wisdom. This has been very helpful indeed.

I would like to acknowledge the significant philosophical contribution made to the NeuroPower framework by both the last living Royal Maya Lenca living treasure, Her Excellency Francisca Romero Guevara, and her grandson Leonel Antonio Chevez. The Maya Lenca insights into integration, the Diamond of Being and the brain's Six Social Cognitive Needs have given the framework the depth and practicality that only wisdom built on more than 10,000 years of learning can bring.

My thanks also goes to Georgia Bailey, Joe Foster, Toni Scoble, Susan Nixon, Angela Whitbread, Tim Rossi, Sophie Crawford-Jones, Lyn Rowland, Darren Ramia-Topp, Warren Clarke, Duncan Amos, Kerrin Edwards, Markus Von der Leuhe, Victoria Wilder, Murray Jorgensen, Andrew Leong and Nathan Taylor for their support. I also want to thank Shelley Evans-Wild for her commitment to building a vibrant community of practice in north Queensland and for her tireless work with schools, community groups and businesses there. It was Shelley's idea to use 'buttons' to represent the social cognitive needs. Finally, my thanks goes to my parents, to my mother, Irene Burow, for her life-long passion for understanding and improving the human condition and my father, Len Burow, for his energy and constant support.

To everybody who has made this book possible, thank you.

Peter Burow
August, 2013

Contents

To download a copy of the following Appendices, Bibliography, About the Author and Index, please visit:

http://neuropowergroup.com/wp2/neuropower-book-appendices/

Tables and Diagrams

The following diagrams are available in the Appendices.

To download the Appendices please visit:
http://neuropowergroup.com/wp2/neuropower-book-appendices/

Chapter 1

NeuroPower –
Leading with NeuroIntelligence

If our brain were so simple we could understand it,
we would be so simple we couldn't.
Lyall Watson

The *NeuroPower* framework offers actionable insight into the complexity of who we are and how we all think, feel and behave in the world. Drawing not only on the latest neuroscientific findings about the brain[1], it also draws on more traditional schools of thought to map a practical pathway for personal and professional development. This approach enables a deep dive into the complex world of how we are shaped by the groups to which we belong - including families, communities and corporate cultures. Leaders in particular find the *NeuroPower* framework a helpful lense to more accurately see how their thoughts, words, emotions and behaviour positively or negatively impact the people they lead.

In striving to understand human consciousness, learning and decision-making broadly there are two different bodies of knowledge (illustrated in Diagram 1.1). The first bundles traditional fields that apply practical insights based on behaviour, but which have had to treat the brain like a black box. This has meant that even in highly researched areas like perception psychology, it's been slow and incremental progress with multiple competing theories and few ways to determine which is most accurate.

---

1   In 2013, U.S. President, Barack Obama, approved the biggest ever investment in neuroscience - rivalling the billions spent on the human genome project. The new area of neuroeconomics, which combines neuroscience (the study of the brain) and behavioural economics (the study of how psychology informs economic decisions), is also booming. Many businesses are using neuroeconomic findings and evolved psychographics to predict and influence consumer behaviour and increase customer intimacy. The commercial world is benefitting from understanding that how people feel and think links to how they behave - including what they choose to purchase. Perhaps even more importantly, applied neuroscience is being used to shape employee experiences in more positive ways, through increased employee engagement, leadership development, cultural change and the building of high performance teams.

Some of the great historic minds such as Jung, Blake and Freud couldn't look inside a working brain, and so had to assume or invent complex models to explain what they heard and saw. Some of these - like Descartes' view that the mind and the body were fused together in the pineal gland - may seem quaint today, and yet many traditional theories have held up remarkably well.

In contrast, the second and more recently emerged body of knowledge is the world of neuroscience. Whereas traditional approaches have been limited to looking at behaviour and working backwards, the benefit of neuroscience has been the growing ability to look inside the black box and start to tease out what's actually going on in someone else's mind. Starting from the most basic level of cells and tiny molecules, neuroscientists are working to build a picture of how the physical structures of our brain support - and sometimes dictate - how, when and why we think and feel what we do. These advances hold the promise of giving us powerful insight into what drives our human experience and the seemingly infinite complexity of human behaviour.

Even now, neuroscience is giving us tools to track not just external markers of your internal state (like sweating, heart rate and breathing changes) but to measure brain

Diagram 1.1 Integrating the Many Different Approaches to Understanding the Human Condition

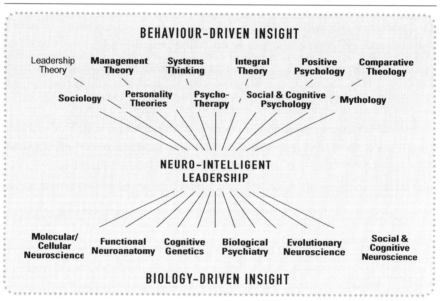

One of my consultants, Misha Byrne, uses the above diagram to illustrate the point that *NeuroPower* draws on both behaviour-driven insight and biology-driven insight to help understand the foundations of human experience, motivation and both personal and professional development.

activity directly and recognise specific words, actions and feelings as they run through your mind.

Unfortunately, however, like all fields, neuroscience has its limitations - some technical, some ideological and some a matter of logistics. For example, even though fMRI and EEG technologies are getting more powerful (allowing us to observe the brain in finer and finer detail), most techniques still have to take us out of our regular environment. Rigorous experimental protocols put hapless university students through long batteries of tests that don't always match up well with the real world. The insights are powerful and valuable, but need discernment to sort the fool's gold (and ambitious claims) from the real gold.

And until recently, the lion's share of research funding has been directed towards understanding and treating medical conditions, so many of our insights have been deficit-focused. (Indeed, just as positive psychology emerged in reaction to the deficit-based focus of most traditional psychological research, we are now just beginning to see strains of growth-focused research coalesce into a coherent school of positive neuroscience.)

Perhaps more importantly, the practice of neuroscience is both rapidly advancing and highly specialised and so practicing researchers are drawn ever deeper into narrowly focused fields - it's hard to build an integrated, practical picture of the brain simply because it's so very, very detailed.[2] No one brain can hold all that information!

Because neuroscience is so highly technical neuroscientists drill down, and relatively few step back and ask 1) How does it all fit together? and 2) How could we use that holistic model to build an integrated approach to managing and getting the most out of our brains?

In this light, *NeuroPower* has been developed to take the powerful and exciting insight that neuroscience is uncovering every day - mindful of its limitations and the occasional fools gold - and integrate it back into the practical and hard-won insights reflected in the many different schools of leadership, management, self-development and interpersonal relationships.

APPLYING THE INSIGHTS OF NEUROSCIENCE THROUGH THE FOUR PRINCIPLES OF NEUROPOWER

Whether you are a leader trying to engage people in your organisation, a therapist looking for ways to engage your clients, a parent wishing to bring the best out in your kids, or you simply want to achieve more in your personal or professional life, understanding how your brain functions—your NeuroIntelligence—can help you better understand yourself and others at every practical level.

---

2   There are, however, notable exceptions, and books like John Ratey's *A User's Guide to the Brain* (Pantheon, 2001). and Dan Siegel's *The Developing Mind: How relationships and the brain interact to shape who we are* (Guilford Press, 2012) make excellent primers on the working state of neuroscience.

To make this digestible, I've broken the content of *NeuroPower* into four sections, each dealing with a key principle or objective.

- **PRINCIPLE #1: Learn the brain's Six Social Cognitive Needs and how to satisfy them for yourself and others.** (Explored in the RELISH Method.)

- **PRINCIPLE #2: Know how to manage your emotional reactivity.** (Explored with a description of the nine Neuro-Limbic Types and the keys to managing them.)

- **PRINCIPLE #3: Know your genius, and when and how to use it.** (Explored with the eight Neuro-Rational Types and their eight Geniuses.)

- **PRINCIPLE #4: Know how to hardwire character and wisdom into your personality.** (Explored with the Inventory of Human Nobility and the four types of Patron Leaders.)

This handbook explores these key principles and how they can be applied in three key areas:

- **Personal Development:** Applying *NeuroPower* to help individuals (yourself or others) grow and develop through the process of integration

- **Leadership Development:** Applying *NeuroPower* to develop your own capability to manage, lead and emotionally engage others

- **Organisational Development:** Applying *NeuroPower* to build organisations that are strategically aligned, agile and responsive, with highly effective marketing and communication that builds trust and aligns the attitudes and behaviours of those receiving the messages with the desired position.

NEUROINTELLIGENCE CAN UNLOCK YOUR 'PHYSIS'

The ancient Greeks had a special word – physis – to describe the drive that compels all living things to grow into all that they can be. Physis is what enables an acorn to become a mighty oak. It also drives humans to become all that they are capable of being. When the force of physis is impeded, it results in mental, emotional and physical frustration.

One objective of the *NeuroPower* framework is to provide a clear road map for directing the inner longing of individuals, teams and organisations to follow the lead of physis towards wholeness and health.

Neuroscience 101

With the development of a range of technologies to study the brain (including e.g. fMRI and EEG) the whole field of neuroscience has exploded in the last decade. It is now regarded as one of the most rapidly advancing areas of scientific research and is helping us understand the complexities of our human behavioural responses.

These have significantly added to our understanding of the brain and how it affects our behaviour. To begin with, here are three foundational insights about the brain to get us started on our learning journey together:

1. **The physical structure of your brain supports and enables your human experience;**

2. **Your brain has two systems—one rational and the other emotional—that drive your decision-making;**

3. **You can change the physical structure of your brain and how you think, emote and behave in life.**

    Let's look at each of these in more detail.

FOUNDATIONAL INSIGHT #1: THE PHYSICAL STRUCTURE OF YOUR BRAIN SUPPORTS AND ENABLES YOUR HUMAN EXPERIENCE

In 1848, American rail worker Phineas Gage was injured in a construction accident, when a tamping iron was forced up through his left cheek bone and out the top of his skull. Amazingly, he survived - but a changed man. The bar had damaged much of his brain's frontal lobe (particularly the left frontal lobe) and while at first doctors thought he had escaped disaster - still able to move, communicate and see through his remaining eye - over time it emerged that his personality had changed significantly. This is often cited as the first concrete example of how different parts of the brain might impact personality. The next 130 years saw medical science collect numerous examples of selective deficits in behaviour, thinking or emotion following damage to specific areas of the brain (in so-called 'lesion studies'). Only in the last three decades or so have new technologies like fMRI, PET and EEG helped us look inside undamaged brains to discover how we function at our best.

Thanks to these technologies, for example, we now know that the parts of the brain damaged in Phineas Gage's accident include areas responsible for many of the abilities that we see as central to what makes us human: our executive functions, including our ability to plan, strategise, reason about what other people are thinking, and - importantly - to control our own behaviour.

This is the part of our brain that has developed most in the last few hundred thousand years. Whereas our ancient ancestors relied almost exclusively on their 'limbic' or emotional brain (Diagram 1.2), allowing their emotions to drive their behaviour e.g. through our 'fight/flight' coping response, today we have more of a choice. Certainly we still have an emotional system - and sometimes it gets the better of us (as you may know from bitter experience). But today, our neocortex—the front-most part of the brain that includes most of the frontal lobes – acts as a control centre. It allows us to observe, interpret and manage our emotional system. Perhaps

Diagram 1.2 Getting Your Bearings in the Brain

a. Key Landmarks

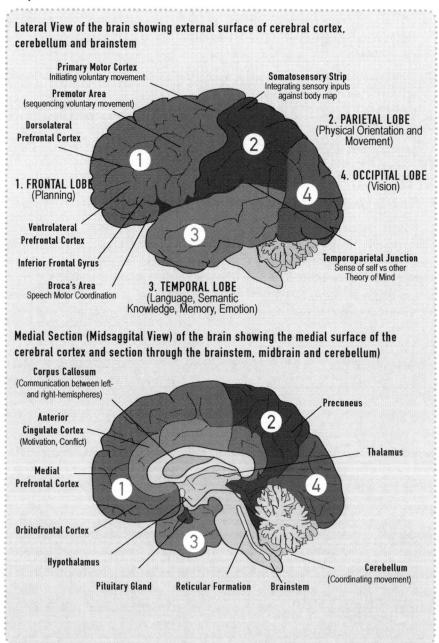

Lateral View of the brain showing external surface of cerebral cortex, cerebellum and brainstem

Primary Motor Cortex
Initiating voluntary movement

Premotor Area
(sequencing voluntary movement)

Dorsolateral
Prefrontal Cortex

Somatosensory Strip
Integrating sensory inputs
against body map

2. PARIETAL LOBE
(Physical Orientation and
Movement)

4. OCCIPITAL LOBE
(Vision)

1. FRONTAL LOBE
(Planning)

Ventrolateral
Prefrontal Cortex

Inferior Frontal Gyrus

Broca's Area
Speech Motor Coordination

3. TEMPORAL LOBE
(Language, Semantic
Knowledge, Memory, Emotion)

Temporoparietal Junction
Sense of self vs other
Theory of Mind

Medial Section (Midsaggital View) of the brain showing the medial surface of the cerebral cortex and section through the brainstem, midbrain and cerebellum)

Corpus Callosum
(Communication between left-
and right-hemispheres)

Anterior
Cingulate Cortex
(Motivation, Conflict)

Medial
Prefrontal Cortex

Orbitofrontal Cortex

Hypothalamus

Pituitary Gland

Reticular Formation

Brainstem

Precuneus

Thalamus

Cerebellum
(Coordinating movement)

b. Directions in the Brain*

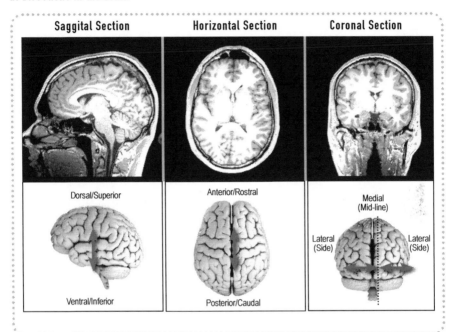

Saggital Section	Horizontal Section	Coronal Section
Dorsal/Superior	Anterior/Rostral	Medial (Mid-line)
		Lateral (Side) — Lateral (Side)
Ventral/Inferior	Posterior/Caudal	

c. Some Important 'Hidden' Structures

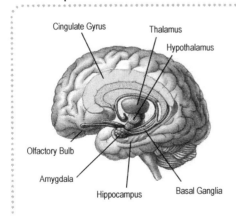

Cingulate Gyrus
Thalamus
Hypothalamus
Olfactory Bulb
Amygdala
Hippocampus
Basal Ganglia

The Limbic System is the name given to a set of connected structures buried within the brain that regulate emotion and memory. These structures directly connect the lower and higher brain functions and influence emotions, visceral responses to those emotions, motivation, mood, and sensations of pain and pleasure. The limbic system is also the name used to distinguish the brain's 'emotional processing' (also sometimes referred to as System 1 or System X) and the brain's 'rational' system (System 2 or System C).

---

*   At the time of printing, a great tutorial for learning the different naming conventions in the brain is available at http://www.getbodysmart.com/ap/nervoussystem/cns/brain/brainviews/tutorial.html.

most importantly - it can help stop us from 'whacking' our boss, even if they are annoying us.

FOUNDATIONAL INSIGHT #2: YOUR BRAIN HAS TWO SYSTEMS-ONE RATIONAL AND THE OTHER EMOTIONAL-THAT DRIVE YOUR DECISION-MAKING

Nobel Laureate Daniel Kahneman (2003), a psychologist from Princeton University, worked with fellow psychologist Amos Tversky in coming to the initially radical conclusion that there are two modes of cognitive functioning that influence behaviour:

- System 1[3] is the intuitive or emotional brain; and
- System 2 is the reasoning or rational brain.

These two systems differ in terms of both speed, flexibility and operation. According to Kahneman:

> [T]he operations of System 1 are typically fast, automatic, effortless, associative, implicit (not available to introspection), and often emotionally charged; they are also governed by habit and are therefore difficult to control or modify. The operations of System 2 are slower, serial, effortful, more likely to be consciously monitored and deliberately controlled; they are also relatively flexible and potentially rule governed. (Kahneman, 2003, p. 698)

As Diagram 1.3 shows, both systems influence our judgements and choices—meaning that how you feel about something is equally as important as what your common sense or reasoning tells you about it. While this may conflict with your sense of yourself as a sensible being who can divorce emotion from the realities of a situation, it probably aligns with your experiences of others' behaviour as occasionally (perhaps often) irrational and emotional.

FOUNDATIONAL INSIGHT #3: YOU CAN CHANGE THE PHYSICAL STRUCTURE OF YOUR BRAIN—AND HOW YOU THINK, EMOTE AND BEHAVE IN LIFE

Our brains are wonderfully complex, adaptive systems that are capable of astounding growth and change—a property referred to as neuroplasticity. This concept has been popularised by books such as Dr Norman Doidge's best-selling *The Brain That Changes Itself* (2007), which includes the almost unbelievable story of a woman born with half a brain that rewired itself to work as a whole. We now know

---

3   The neutral terms 'System 1' and 'System 2' were coined by Stanovich and West (2000).

Diagram 1.3 The Two Systems Involved in Decision-Making

1. Input enters brain and the limbic system reacts emotionally, based on existing Core Beliefs – System 1.

   a. If the situation is not 'out of the ordinary' (or 'novel'), an habitual response is invoked and translates into immediate behaviour.

   b. If the situation *is* novel, then the information moves to System 2. Here it is assessed and matched against the individual's conscious world view and analytical style to reach a decision.

2. The trial decision from System 2 is checked by the limbic system:

   a. If it lines up with past experience (i.e. a similar decision has been made previously and the outcome is familiar) the individual will feel 'comfortable' with the trial decision, which will be embraced and translated into action.

   b. If no similar decision has been made previously and the anticipated outcome is unfamiliar, a feeling of discomfort will arise and the trial decision will then be sent back to System 2 for further thought.

3. This moving between the two systems will continue until a balance is reached and both systems are comfortable with the trial decision. Only then will it be translated into behaviour.

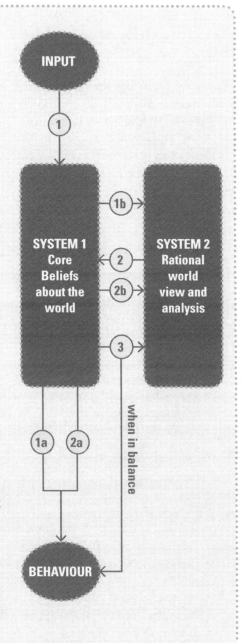

that each time we attempt a new task, our brain creates or strengthens a new neural pathway. Every time we repeat the task, more connections are added and the task becomes easier. Some - like Malcolm Gladwell - have argued that after 10,000 hours of practice, we reach a level of mastery—both practically and neurobiologically—and have built a neural superhighway in our brain. Our brain is then hardwired for that activity.

In the same way, you can also hardwire your brain for certain states, which then translate into personality traits. All it takes is 10,000 hours. Scientifically validated studies bear this out, showing us, for example, that regular meditation practice changes some individuals who spend many hours practising different emotions, such as anger, fear, happiness or anxiety. Others have instead practiced and mastered more conscious, higher-order attributes—we call them Noble Qualities—such as integrity, courage or discernment. Whatever it is that you've focused on will become automatic and this will be reflected in your personality.

The Biology of the Dual-Process Model

In the growing field of social cognitive neuroscience, Kahneman's model has been further developed by Lieberman, Gaunt, Gilbert and Trope (2002). They use the terms 'X-System' and 'C-System' to describe two different types of social cognitive processes:

The X-System

- Reflexive, intuitive processes that are subsymbolic, fast and effortless
- Feels like the reality we experience directly
- Often more perceptual or affective (can be non-conscious)
- Produces a "continuous stream of consciousness that each of us experience[s] as 'the world out there'" (Lieberman et al., 2002, p. 204)
- Includes the ventromedial prefrontal cortex, lateral temporal cortex, amygdala, basal ganglia and dorsal anterior cingulate

The C-System

- Reflective processes that are slow, effortful and based on symbolic logic
- Feels like self-generated thought (typically linguistic)
- Produces "conscious thoughts that we experience as 'reflections on' the stream of consciousness" (Lieberman et al., 2002, p. 204).
- Includes the lateral prefrontal cortex, lateral parietal cortex, medial prefrontal cortex, medial parietal cortex, rostral anterior cingulate and the medial temporal lobes

Six Social Cognitive Needs Underpin Our Human Experience

The Six Social Cognitive Needs (described in this book using the acronym 'RELISH') are the neurobiological building blocks of human personality and human experience. These functional systems, which form the basis of the *NeuroPower* approach, each have a distinct focus of cognitive attention, and specific emotions which give rise to very clear behaviour. We all have access to these six functions but, through conditioning during our early lives, we each develop a preference for certain functions over others, and our favouring of these functions translates into habitual use. The variations in the mix of these functions we habitually use give rise to different personality profiles at different levels of integration (see Diagram 1.5). Each of these personalities has a distinct world view and way of operating in life. Once you understand the six Intelligences you'll be able to explore how the simultaneous accessing of particular combinations of Intelligences predictably gives rise to very different thinking, feeling and behaviour. This becomes the external manifestation of the different aspects (i.e. System 1 and System 2) of human personality. Let's take a closer look at Diagram 1.5 to understand how all the different pieces fit together.

THE SIX INTELLIGENCES

At the bottom of Diagram 1.5 you'll find six coloured buttons. Each relates to a neurobiological functional system or building block of human personality. These are Intelligences which enable the individual to understand and respond to the world.

For linguistic ease, the *NeuroPower* framework has given each of the Intelligences a short-hand descriptor comprising a letter and a number. These reflect the reality that the brain has six different ways in which it processes things, receives information and manifests creatively in the world.

The six Intelligences can therefore be grouped into three pairs of functions as shown in Table 1.4: The Ps (P1 and P2), the Cs (C1 and C2) and the Is (I1 and I2).[4]

Table 1.4 The Six Intelligences

P - Processing	C - Creativity	I - Information Gathering
P1 - Logical sequencing based on experience	C1 - Spontaneous self-expression and adaptation	I1 - Pattern recognition and external data
P2 - Goal-oriented drive and focus	C2 - Visionary downloading of new paradigms	I2 - Empathic attunement and intuition

---

4   Neuroscientists estimate there are more than 600 functional circuits in the brain. Of these, the *NeuroPower* framework identifies just 18 (six sets of three: a thinking, feeling and somatic component of each Intelligence) that have the most significant influence on the manifestation of personality.

Our Biases Towards Each of the Six Intelligences Explain the Diversity of Insight Embedded across Many Professional Tools

Each of us tends to favour one of each pair (e.g. P1 rather than P2) more than the other, and we tend to value some Intelligences but not others. **It's not surprising, therefore, that the myriad of different tools and frameworks of leadership, management, marketing, coaching, personality (and many other fields) focus on achieving some or all of these needs. A cross-section of these tools are mapped out in Table 1.6.** The six Intelligences are helpful in professional practice and personal development because they help us understand why - and in what situations - different tools are effective or ineffective.

More broadly, however, understanding that you need to be highly functioning in all six Intelligences—regardless of whether your focus is individual, career or organisational development—is the first step of your *NeuroPower* awareness.

The easiest way to remember the six Intelligences, and their order, is to remember the acronym RELISH which stands for Relatedness (P1), Expression (C1), Leading the Pack (P2), Interpersonal Connection (I2), Seeing the Facts (I1) and Hope for the Future (C2).

In **Principle #1** of this handbook, we'll be exploring each of the Intelligences in detail, including the neurobiology of each system. For now, let's take a brief look at the characteristics of each of these functions.

P1 | THE AUTOMATIC FUNCTION (R - RELATEDNESS)

P1 Intelligence houses our implicit procedural memory—the parts of our brain that enables us to operate in the absence of conscious attention. This is our 'automatic pilot' mode and the seat of our habitual patterns. Driven by our personal values, this system encodes the rules that we were taught as children and symbolises the part of our mind that thinks as a member of the collective—our family or tribe. P1 is therefore culturally determined and heavily impacted by our family of origin and primary caregivers early in life, although the extent to which these factors continue to influence us are often largely outside our conscious awareness. The P1 Intelligence can also be referred to as 'Relatedness' because the brain loves being part of a group that is cohesive, fair and safe. The evolution and growth of the prefrontal cortex was driven by the need to survive and thrive by remaining secure within our social groups. People define themselves by the groups they belong to and are highly sensitive to social rejection and exclusion.

P1-Related Research Terms in Neuroscience:

Prenatal learning; procedural memory; moral behaviour and moral judgements; fairness; values; self-control; compliance; social inclusion and exclusion (social isolation); ingroup-outgroup; social value orientation; infant attachment; fear-learning; trust; security; certainty vs risk preference; obsessive passion; prevention regulatory focus; 'ought' goals; 'should' goals; extrinsic goal motivation.

Diagram 1.5 The Map of Human Personality

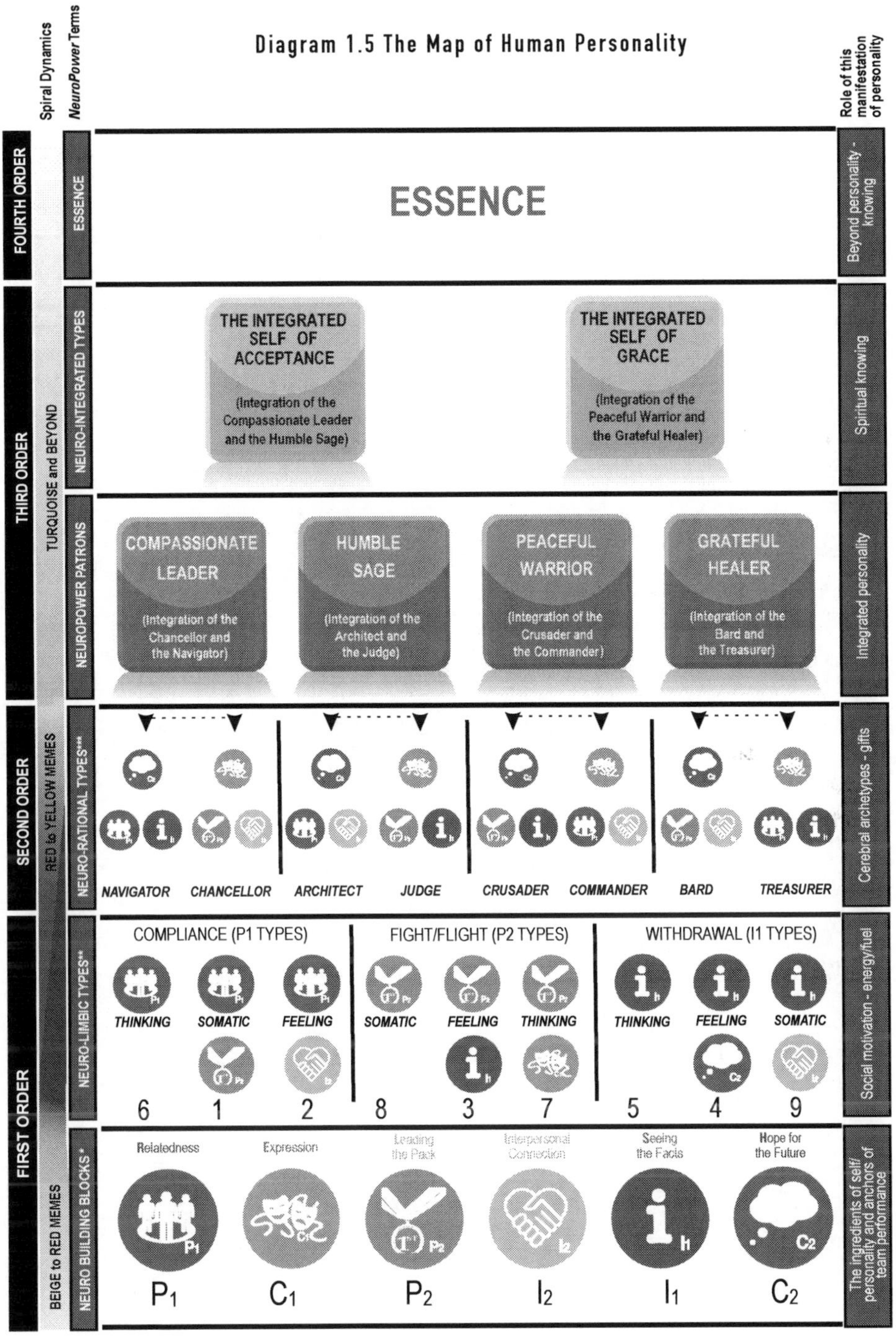

Spiral Dynamics	NeuroPower Terms			Role of this manifestation of personality
FOURTH ORDER	ESSENCE	**ESSENCE**		Beyond personality - knowing
THIRD ORDER TURQUOISE and BEYOND	NEURO-INTEGRATED TYPES	**THE INTEGRATED SELF OF ACCEPTANCE** (Integration of the Compassionate Leader and the Humble Sage)	**THE INTEGRATED SELF OF GRACE** (Integration of the Peaceful Warrior and the Grateful Healer)	Spiritual knowing
	NEUROPOWER PATRONS	**COMPASSIONATE LEADER** (Integration of the Chancellor and the Navigator) **HUMBLE SAGE** (Integration of the Architect and the Judge)	**PEACEFUL WARRIOR** (Integration of the Crusader and the Commander) **GRATEFUL HEALER** (Integration of the Bard and the Treasurer)	Integrated personality

SECOND ORDER — RED to YELLOW MEMES

NEURO-RATIONAL TYPES*** — Cerebral archetypes - gifts

NAVIGATOR   CHANCELLOR   ARCHITECT   JUDGE   CRUSADER   COMMANDER   BARD   TREASURER

FIRST ORDER

NEURO-LIMBIC TYPES** — Social motivation - energy/fuel

COMPLIANCE (P1 TYPES)			FIGHT/FLIGHT (P2 TYPES)			WITHDRAWAL (I1 TYPES)		
THINKING	SOMATIC	FEELING	SOMATIC	FEELING	THINKING	THINKING	FEELING	SOMATIC
6	1	2	8	3	7	5	4	9

NEURO BUILDING BLOCKS* — The ingredients of self: personality and anchors of team performance

BEIGE to RED MEMES

Relatedness	Expression	Leading the Pack	Interpersonal Connection	Seeing the Facts	Hope for the Future
P_1	C_1	P_2	I_2	I_1	C_2

* Also 'Social Cognitive Needs'   ** Also 'Core Beliefs'   *** Also 'Archetypes' or 'Leadership Styles'

Table 1.6 How Contemporary Frameworks Address the Six Social Cognitive Needs

	FRAMEWORK	RELATEDNESS (P1)	EXPRESSION (C1)	LEADING THE PACK (P2)	INTERPERSONAL CONNECTION (I2)	SEEING THE FACTS (I1)	HOPE FOR THE FUTURE (C2)
PERSONALITY	Myers Briggs Type Indicator[1]	Thinking	Extraversion	Feeling	Intuition	Sensing	Introversion
	Herman Brain Dominance Index (HBDI)	Quadrant B	-	-	Quadrant C	Quadrant A	Quadrant D
	Hogan Assessment System[2]	*Low* Ambition, *High* Prudence	*High* Sociability	*High* Ambition, *Low* Prudence	*High* Interpersonal Sensitivity, *Low* Learning Approach	*Low* Interpersonal Sensitivity, *High* Learning Approach	*Low* Sociability
LEADERSHIP FRAMEWORKS	Five Dysfunctions of a Team (Lencioni)	Lack of Trust	Fear of Conflict	Lack of Commitment	Inattention to Results	Avoidance of Accountability	-
	Situational Leadership	Low Directive (S3, S4)	-	High Directive (S1, S2)	High Supportive (S2, S3)	Low Supportive (S1, S4)	-
	S.C.A.R.F (David Rock)	Certainty, Relatedness, Fairness	-	Status, Autonomy	-	-	-
	C.O.R.E (Jan Hills)	Certainty, Equity	-	Options, Reputation	-	-	-
	'Engaged' (Holbeche & Mathews)	Connection, Support	Voice	Scope	-	-	-
PROCESS METHODOLOGIES	Agile Principles	Value	Flexibility, Simplicity	Speed, Teamwork	Collaboration	Continuous Improvement	-
	Agile Practices	Social contract	Stand-ups	Sliders, Progress walls	Co-location, Showcase	Planning poker, Retrospectives	BVCs
	Lean Problem Solving	Define the Problem	Grasp the Situation	Plan, Do	-	Check, Act	Conclusions, Lessons Learned
	Product Management (e.g. Black Blot)	Value proposition/ Unmet needs	Customer segmentation, Pain points	Competitor analysis	Customer personas	Product features matrix	Product roadmap
	Design Thinking (d school)	Focus on human values	Embrace experimentation	Bias towards action	Radical collaboration	Show, don't tell, craft clarity	Be mindful of the process
DEVELOPMENT TOOLS	4Q Integral (Ken Wilber)	Collective	-	Individual	Interior	Exterior	-
	Neuro-Linguistic Programming Techniques	e.g. Anchoring	e.g. Reframing, State Management	e.g. Goal-setting	e.g. Matching & Mirroring	e.g. Chunking Down, Chunking Up, Meta Models	e.g. Shifting Perceptual Positions
	Demartini 7 Areas of Life	Physical, Family, Social	Physical	Physical, Vocational	-	Financial, Mental	Spiritual

1   The MBTI dimensions 'Judging' and 'Perceiving' indicate a preference for either processing (P1/P2) or information (I1/I2), respectively.

2   The 'Adjustment' dimension in the Hogan Assessment System is predominantly Relatedness (P1) with aspects of Hope for the Future (C2). The 'Inquisitive' dimension describes a focus on a creative style, with a bias towards Expression (C1) and elements of Hope for the Future (C2).

C1 | THE EMOTIONAL FUNCTION (E - EXPRESSION)

C1 Intelligence helps us remember what happens to us emotionally so that we keep doing what we enjoy and stop doing what causes us pain. It houses our central emotional position that we develop in early childhood and which, if unquestioned, often dictates the future course of our emotional lives. If the C1 Intelligence is not functioning well, we are destined to repeat the same emotional and behavioural patterns we learned as children. However, when C1 is highly functioning, it fosters spontaneity, experimentation, lateral thinking and fun. The C1 Intelligence can also be referred to as 'Expression' because the brain loves expressing emotions. Unexpressed emotion and activity in the amygdala is related to a significant decrease in cognitive ability and can seriously reduce performance. Labelling emotions appropriately reduces this load. (Labelling is enabling!)

C1-Related Research Terms in Neuroscience:

Emotion regulation; affect labelling; addiction; innovation; dopamine; endorphins; hedonic motivation (pleasure); sexuality; positive affect; emotion reappraisal; extroversion; distraction; ADHD; affective experience; homeostasis; alliesthesia; pleasure paradox; affective neuroscience.

P2 | THE INTERVENTION FUNCTION (L - LEADING THE PACK)

P2 Intelligence enables us to interrupt the habitual process of automatic behaviour and navigate in the external world to get what we individually want or desire. This is the part of the brain that is the seat of motivation, drive and ego. By intervening to break old habits and patterns, P2 enables us to go that extra mile to achieve our goals. It also gives us the energy to aim for what we truly desire. This is the part of your mind that values independence and drives personal accomplishment. The P2 Intelligence can also be referred to as 'Leading the Pack' because the brain loves status and once basic needs have been met, status, recognition and independence are key drivers of satisfaction and must be managed to foster healthy passion rather than unhealthy competition.

P2-Related Research Terms in Neuroscience:

Self-esteem; agency; autonomy; status; social comparison; fight/flight; HPA axis; testosterone; aggression; competition; power; harmonious passion; approach motivation; promotion regulatory focus; 'ideal' goals; 'want' goals; intrinsic goal motivation.

I2 | THE RELATING FUNCTION (I - INTERPERSONAL CONNECTION)

I2 Intelligence is based on several parts of the brain that work together to enable us to empathise with others through attuning to their experiences and 'best guessing' their thoughts and feelings.
This paves the way for genuine heartfelt connection and minimises the amount of needless pain caused by prejudice and misunderstanding. I2 also enables us to connect meaningfully with ourselves and to find what we love in the world—be it a vocation, an activity or others to share the journey. This is the seat of our authenticity and enables us to have lasting and meaningful relationships. The I2 Intelligence can also be referred to as 'Interpersonal Connection' because the brain is naturally focused on connections with other people and needs to feel genuinely understood by others. The brain's mirror neuron system is dedicated to helping us interpret and understand others. This system helps us feel what other people feel and is intrinsically linked to the positive relationships we form with others.

I2-Related Research Terms in Neuroscience:

Empathy; Theory of Mind; mentalising; mindsight; mirror neuron system; default mode network; altruism; generosity; emotional intelligence (EQ); empathising; empathising quotient (EQ); E-S (empathizing–systemizing) theory; oxytocin; pain perception; facial mimicry; synchronicity; autobiographical memory; episodic memory.

I1 | THE OBJECTIVE LEARNING FUNCTION (S - SEEING THE FACTS)

I1 Intelligence draws on our brain's ability to recognise and learn patterns and recall factual information. This includes patterns of behaviour, cause and effect patterns and all forms of data. Our capacity to learn is directly linked to our ability to interpret the information that is available to us in all aspects of life. We are able to do this through our explicit declarative memory—the part of our brain that wants to understand the world through quantifiable fact. The brain loves feedback and having all the information at hand. The I1 Intelligence can also be referred to as 'Seeing the Facts' because the brain is a complex self-regulating machine that adapts constantly to external feedback. The primary source of this feedback is through the eyes and large regions of the brain associated with visual processing. Often we need to see it to believe it and the brain is always looking for continuous feedback.

I1-Related Research Terms in Neuroscience:

Systemising; Systemising Quotient (SQ); E-S theory; explicit semantic memory; spatial memory; 'place cells'; hippocampus; visual discrimination; pattern recognition; feature discrimination; expertise hypothesis of facial recognition; alexithymia; autism; extreme male brain theory; foetal androgen exposure.

C2 | THE OPEN FUNCTION (H - HOPE FOR THE FUTURE)

C2 Intelligence is much more expansive than the other systems. It acts as the modem for the brain, downloading new paradigms, concepts, big picture and fresh vision. It draws on parts of the brain that enable us to be open to a completely new way of looking at things. C2 is also the part of our brain that thinks about tapping into higher consciousness, and is frequently accessed by experienced meditators and strategists. C2 Intelligence can also be referred to as 'Hope for the Future' because the brain loves moving forward based on hope for the future. The brain is an anticipation machine - constantly projecting into the future the consequences of staying on its current path. Importantly, our level of hope is directly linked to our sense of whether our current path will lead to a positive future.

C2-Related Research Terms in Neuroscience:

Neurotheology; spiritual neuroscience; out-of-body; unitary experience; mystical experience or mystical state (including 'timelessness', 'union', 'spacelessness'); alpha-theta state; openness; introversion; prayer *and* health; religion; global precedence; affective forecasting.

As we progress from infancy through childhood, we move through the Intelligences in a sequential order—bottom row, from left to right in Diagram 1.5. Many contemporary psychiatrists have documented this progressive development of self, including Piaget, Erikson, Maslow, Kohlberg and Berne. These, together with two ancient philosophies held by the Maya Lenca and the Indians, are summarised in Table 1.7.

If the development of highly functioning Intelligences is impeded in childhood, there are long-term impacts on the personality of the individual in later life. It also affects their ability to access the capabilities associated with the less developed Intelligences, which will affect their ability to function, both at home and at work. This, in turn, shapes the habitual characteristics that the individual will demonstrate (i.e. their personality).

The Nine Neuro-Limbic Types

In the second row of Diagram 1.5, we start to see how the Intelligences combine to create childlike, emotional personalities. Along the bottom of the row, there are a series of numbers. Each number represents a particular combination of Intelligences (the ones that appear directly above it). These are the personalities that sit in System 1 of our brain and are reactive and emotional. Housed in the more primitive part of our brain, the limbic system, these personalities are essentially habitual patterns that

Table 1.7 Comparative Theories of Development

THEORY OF DEVELOPMENT	RELATEDNESS (P1)	EXPRESSION (C1)	LEADING THE PACK (P2)	INTERPERSONAL CONNECTION (I2)	SEEING THE FACTS (I1)	HOPE FOR THE FUTURE (C2)
Piaget	Sensory-Motor (stages 1 and 2)	Sensory-Motor (stages 3 to 6)	Pre-operational	Pre-operational	Formal operations	Formal operations
Erikson	Trust vs mistrust	Autonomy vs Shame and Doubt	Initiative vs Guilt Industry vs Inferiority Identity vs Role Confusion	Intimacy vs Isolation	Generativity vs Isolation	Integrity vs Despair
Maya Lenca Energetic Symbol	Armadillo	Rabbit	Jaguar	Turtle	Monkey scribe	Eagle
Chakra	Base (Muladhara)	Sacral (Svadhisthana)	Solar Plexus (Manipura)	Heart (Anahata)	Brow (Ajna)	Crown (Sahasrara)
Maslow	Physiology	Safety	Self-esteem	Belonging	Trans-cendence	Trans-cendence
Kohlberg	Punishment/ obedience	Instrumental/ hedonism	Good boy/ nice girl	Law and order	Universalism	Universalism
Berne	Parent	Child	Adult	–	–	–

we've developed in response to our early experiences, a default setting for survival. In *NeuroPower*, we call these the Neuro-Limbic Types (NLTs). At best, the NLTs provide us with the emotional fuel we need to get through life, but hamper us with predictable cognitive biases. At worst, they are reactive, disruptive and cause chaos in our lives. The NLTs are discussed in detail in **Principle #2** of this handbook.

In total there are nine NLTs, each consisting of either one or two of the Intelligences. Each NLT can be broadly described according to how it reacts to stress: by complying, fighting or withdrawing. This relates to whether the type is formed around the P1 Automatic System (which results in *compliance*), the P2 Intervention System (which results in *fighting* or moving against something) or the I1 Objective Learning System (which results in *withdrawal* to reconsider the situation). The impact of these three limbic or emotional reactions on the psychological health of an individual were first quantified in 1945 by the renowned German psychiatrist Karen Horney. These nine personalities can be seen in action in yourself and others. They have been written about extensively in the Enneagram personality system made popular by US researcher and psychologist Helen Palmer (1988, 1995, 1998) and Stanford Professor David Daniels (Daniels et al., 2000). This handbook provides readers with an overview of the nine types rather than an in-depth analysis. This is because many other authors have written excellent material that we would be simply repeating.

We each have access to three of these Neuro-Limbic Types: one compliance type, one fighting type and one withdrawal or flight type. These personalities provide us with our limbic connection to the world and provide the emotional energy or fuel for our more rational, noble Self (see *The Eight Adult Neuro-Rational Types*) to function. When we lose our connection with our Neuro-Limbic Type, we lose our motivation, interest in others and much of our 'gut reaction' to life. Conversely, if we are a slave to them, we lose all human nobility and perceive everyone around us, even those closest to us, as either competition or food.

In Principle #3, *NeuroPower* outlines the specific method required to convert this primitive drive into human nobility. This third principle of *NeuroPower* is

What is the Low Road?

The Neuro-Limbic Types are sometimes described as the Low Road because they are driven by the brain's more primitive limbic system whose function is to keep us alive through quick, automatic responses to the world around us. The structures of the limbic system (including the now popularly infamous amygdala and other parts of the mid-brain basal ganglia) work constantly to scan our environments, filtering out most information and attending only to things that we have learned, through past experience, are most relevant.

When we are under stress and we have a panic response our system floods and the limbic system (our Neuro-Limbic Type) can take over. While a healthy functioning limbic system is critical to our survival, UCLA neuroscientist Matthew Lieberman and others have observed that this system is closed, reflexive, uncontrolled and - largely - unconscious. It also focuses exclusively on self-survival (selfish). So when your limbic system is calling the shots about your behaviour it will tend to be repetitive, narrowly focused and selfish. Philosophers and theologians have historically referred to this as the Low Road.

(Consequently, throughout *NeuroPower* we have referred to an overreliance on the Neuro-Limbic System as the Low Road or the Lower Self.)

In contrast, the brain's rational system (largely seated in the cerebral cortex and in particular the frontal lobe) is more dynamic, responsive, open and creative. While much slower than the limbic system, it is able to recognise and work through complexity to resolve difficult challenges. Our best decisions, therefore, are made when these two systems work together in harmony. Many traditions of meditation (including techniques like yoga) are thought to be beneficial at least in part because they help us practice using the executive functions of the brain's rational system to manage and control the impulses of the emotional system. This then helps us mediate the impulses of the limbic system in the rest of our lives.

a central competency for each human life to master if they are to reach their full potential.

The Eight Adult Neuro-Rational Types[5]

The third row of Diagram 1.5 shows eight combinations of the Intelligences called Neuro-Rational Types (NRTs). Each is made up of three of the Intelligences: one of the Ps, one of the Is and one of the Cs.

Personality at this level manifests when the individual can hold the tension between the P (Processing) and the I (Information) Intelligences and transform this into nobility through the C (Creativity) Intelligence. The Neuro-Rational Types can manifest only when the individual has the ability to **contain** the tensions between the P and I (Intelligences) and unify this through C1 or C2. This takes strength of character because when confronted with a difficult situation it is much easier to disintegrate into one of the Neuro-Limbic Types than to stay in the Neuro-Rational Type and manifest human nobility. This containment requires the use of the large, more evolved part of the brain, the cerebral cortex, rather than the primitive limbic system that gives rise to the Neuro-Limbic Types. The higher levels of human consciousness are accessible only when the individual can access their adult Neuro-Rational Type.[6]

Each Neuro-Rational Type[7] has a way of interpreting the world and has access to a Genius that it can use in their daily life. Knowing and using our Genius is one of the keys to a satisfying life because it results in a flow or optimal experience. While each one of us has a genius, it is only when we discover and apply it that we become a genius. It's also the key to creating wealth in a satisfying way.

All eight Areas of Mastery are needed in teams if they are to perform at an optimum level and avoid blind spots that could impede success. Similarly, the most healthy individuals are able to move flexibly and access Areas of Mastery other than their own.

Each Neuro-Rational Type also has a specific process for moving from one level of consciousness to the next. *NeuroPower* refers to this as transformation through integration. (This is the basis of the NeuroPower Integral Coaching System™.)

---

5 Sometimes referred to as Archetypes.
6 For those well versed in the language of Spiral Dynamics, the Neuro-Limbic Types rarely move the individual beyond the Red meme, whereas the Neuro-Rational Types enable the individual to move up to second-tier consciousness. Each Neuro-Rational Type manifests a different and specific noble quality at each meme. This makes up the comprehensive Map of Human Nobility in Principle #4, Table 20.2.
7 *NeuroPower* gives each of the Neuro-Rational Types names from the Celtic Arthurian Legend. These names are simply tags for generic archetypes and so are not restricted to the Celtic tradition. For a description of the Celtic tradition refer to Appendix 9, The Arthurian Legend.

Each of the eight Neuro-Rational Types has a hidden personality which is made up of three of the six Intelligences not used by the Master (*NeuroPower* refers to this as the individual's Mirror). In Diagram 1.5, each Master and its corresponding Mirror are next to each other. While we are all aware of and are attached to our Master personality, we prefer to keep our Mirror personality hidden because it represents the parts of us that we do not like or accept. The Mirror is usually underdeveloped relative to the Master. As we grow and develop we learn to integrate the viewpoints of both the Master and the Mirror. This enables us to have a more complete and integral understanding of the world.

THE FOUR PATRONS

The fourth row of Diagram 1.5 has four turquoise buttons which represent the four Patron Types. These leaders manifest when the individual has successfully integrated their Master and Mirror. Very rarely do we experience this level of personality, but when we do, it gives us access to an even higher level of consciousness.[8] The term Patron has been borrowed from the ancient Maya Lenca people of Central America who have a similar tiered approach to the manifestation of personality. Like *NeuroPower*, the Maya Lenca system argues that integration is the key to accessing higher levels of consciousness. It is the only system I have found which accurately describes personality at this level of cognitive, emotional and spiritual development. The four Patrons focus not only on living responsibly free, but also on making a difference through a combination of being and doing. The Patron still has internal work to do, however, and this takes the form of integrating the Patron's Mirror.

THE INTEGRATED SELF

When the Patron has integrated its Patron Mirror, one last personality type manifests. These are represented by the two yellow buttons on the very top row of Diagram 1.5. These Neuro-Integrated Types are very rare indeed and when they do manifest they change the world. Jesus Christ and the Buddha are two well known spiritual leaders who *NeuroPower* recognises as falling into this category.

Weaving Ancient Philosophies with Contemporary Science

Dan Siegel, author of *The Developing Mind* (1999), a brilliant and ground-breaking book on neuroscience and human development, made the point that much of his work involved encouraging different university departments to share information. This is because the fields of medicine, neurobiology, psychiatry and psychology

---

8   Spiral Dynamics would refer to this higher level of consciousness as the Turquoise meme.

historically have had no acquaintance with one another's research or conclusions. In the same way that Western scientific schools do not interact, ancient wisdom is often relegated to the school of history and is not seen as relevant to contemporary scientific discussion.

However, ancient cultures like the Celts, the Central American Maya, the Chinese, the Indians and the Tibetans, just to name a few, are rich in insights that can make a substantial contribution to our understanding of developmental psychology, personality and consciousness.

The *NeuroPower* framework explores important insights offered by these traditional cultures and validates elements of these philosophies with cutting-edge neurobiological research.

This text begins the process of distilling the data from the divergent perspectives of science, mythology, medicine and the ancient and primitive oral traditions into an elegant, cohesive and practical system which defines human personality, consciousness and nobility, and can be applied to individual, team and organisational performance.

THE NEUROINTELLIGENCE OF INTEGRAL THEORY

Coincidentally, key research relating to neurobiological functional systems aligns with integral theory as outlined by Ken Wilber (1996). Wilber's *Four Faces of Truth* makes an important link between the world of causality and the higher road of harmony by showing how the integration of four of the Intelligences creates a higher order of awareness. The *Four Faces of Truth* matrix suggests that all living and non-living substance has an interior-exterior dimension. (Neurobiologically, these can be equated to I2 and I1.) It also has an individual-communal dimension (P2 and P1). Wilber argues that along a continuum of complexity, from an individual to a family, to a tribal group, to a nation-state, and to the United Nations, or in the other direction, from an individual to their digestive systems, to each of the organs in the digestive systems all the way down to the sub-atomic particles of the tissues that constitute the organ, there is both an interior-exterior dimension and an individual-communal dimension. For example, a quark, a sub-atomic particle, has an interior-exterior dimension and an individual-communal dimension just as the United Nations has an interior-exterior dimension and an individual-communal dimension. This is certainly true of the brain, where we have one functional system for the communal P1 and one for individual P2, and one system for external I1 and another for internal I2.

To explore this at a deeper level, let us start with a consideration of the interior (I2) and exterior (I1) dimension. This dimension refers to the relationship between the inner world of subjectivity (I2) and the outer world of objectivity (I1). This

Diagram 1.8 Wilber's Four Faces of Truth

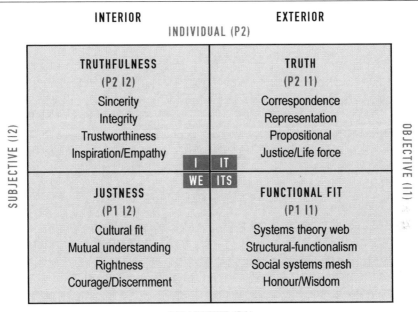

dimension is a fundamental source of tension within many schools of scientific and philosophical thought. The difference is that the interior perspective represents the subjective interpretation of events, whereas the exterior perspective represents the 'rational scientific' approach that bases perception on external and quantifiable details in the external world. We can see this tension in every aspect of life. For example, in the Western theological tradition, we can see the tension in the totally different perspectives of the Christian theologians of St Aquinas and Augustine. St Aquinas argues the existence of God from certain natural facts and then attempts to show that these facts demand an Author. In contrast, Augustine turns attention within, arguing that a subjective and introspective approach reveals the existence of God. If understanding of the world is sought through external sources, material details and empirical observations, it is said to follow the rational path to understanding (I1); if it is sought through interpretive assessment and subjective experience, then it is said to follow the intuitive path to understanding (I2).

The other critical dimension that Wilber describes is the division between individual and communal understanding. This dimension tracks understanding in terms of agency (P2) or communion (P1); that is, understanding can be derived through the experience of individual agency or it can be derived through the experience of collective communion. Along this dimension one can study experience either through the perspective of the individual (P2) or the perspective of the group (P1), the movement of an individual electron (P2) or the understanding of the atom as a whole (P1), the health and functioning of the stomach (P2) or the health and functioning of the entire digestive system (P1).

Neither the dimensions I1/I2 nor P1/P2 are sufficient in themselves to completely understand a situation. What is needed is to combine the two dimensions and the knowledge from the resultant four quadrants (Wilber, 1995). When plotted on a matrix (see Diagram 1.8) four distinct perspectives emerge. Wilber calls these *The Four Faces of Truth*: truthfulness, justice, truth and functional fit.

I, Upper Left Quadrant, Truthfulness: The interior and subjective experiences from an individual perspective place the individual in quadrant I of the matrix. As you read this book, this aspect of your mind will focus on how you, as an individual, are feeling right at this very moment as you begin to understand this knowledge. From this base of truth you may be asking questions like, 'How am I reacting to this knowledge? How am I feeling about this? How is this fitting into my wider life story?' If the ideas have been neither relevant nor appropriate within your life, then they will have no truthfulness for you (I).

WE, Lower Left Quadrant, Justness: The lower left quadrant, the subjective and collective quadrant (WE), comprises, among other things, the fact that the book is written in English. Not only does the book subjectively feel right, but the concepts fit with you and those with whom you are associated. Our collective ability to read and understand the concepts in the book, and to be able to arrive at any assessment as to their personal validity, must be based on a shared cultural perspective that enables these ideas to be communicated. As your mind considers the concepts in this book according to the WE quadrant, you will consider the level of relevance both for yourself and within the broader social groups to which you belong. While these concepts may be useful for you, they may have no cultural fit and so may not represent the collective construct of knowledge that you share with others. Using this face of truth as a filter, the ideas may or may not be fair and reasonable, and if they have no sense of justness about them (WE) they will be rejected.

IT, Upper Right Quadrant, Truth: The aspect of your mind in the exterior-individual quadrant (IT) focuses on the specific knowledge that you are reading here and how you can personally benefit from it. This quadrant would ask, 'What are the concepts that this book has been discussing? Are the frameworks accurate from my understanding? Do they actually represent the truth?' 'How can I use this insight to achieve my goals?' As you study each individual component of the book and assess whether it is accurate, you will make an assessment about the truth of the book (IT). 'Is the concept of the *Four Faces of Truth* itself true?'

ITS, Lower Right Quadrant, Functional Fit: The aspect of your mind in the objective and collective quadrant (ITS) may consider how this concept will fit with all the other ideas discussed within the book. You may be considering the implications of the concept being explored and be wondering how you will form a complete understanding of the *NeuroPower* framework. As you build a complete understanding about how each thought and idea builds into the entire system of integration contained within this book, you will make an assessment of the functional fit of the constituent parts and their collective arrangement (ITS). 'How does the concept of the *Four Faces of Truth* sequentially build towards an understanding of how truth is assessed?'

ADDING CREATIVITY TO THE INTEGRAL MODEL

The *Four Faces of Truth*, however, excludes a very significant neurobiological axis. This additional dimension is centred about the two types of creativity found in the functional systems dedicated to creative expression, C1 and C2. The C1 dimension refers to lateral creativity that is externally focused and gregarious in nature. C1 finds innovative applications and solutions to the problems of life and is referred to in Greek literature as the Dionysian approach from the Greek god Dionysus. The C2 dimension, in contrast, involves adopting a reflective, introverted and visionary approach to resolve issues. Greek mythology refers to this as the Apollonian approach from the Greek god Apollo. When these axes are inserted into Wilber's matrix, each quadrant is broken into halves (shown in Diagram 1.9). These eight segments each perceive a different aspect of truth and describe the eight Neuro-Rational Types.

TRADITIONAL LENSES TO CONTEMPORARY FRAMEWORKS: IS THERE A LINK BETWEEN THE NEUROBIOLOGICAL FUNCTIONAL SYSTEMS AND THE PHILOSOPHY OF CHAKRAS?

Interestingly, several traditional philosophies rooted in thousands of years of behavioural insights have surprisingly clear correlations with some of the emerging insights of neuroscience.

Of the Eastern traditions, the most widely adopted system that falls into this category is the Chakra system. This ancient Indian concept maintains that there are centres of energy throughout the body, called Chakras (sometimes translated as 'wheel' or 'disk'). However, what is of most interest is 1) the clustering of psychosocial issues associated with each Chakra, 2) the recommended personal and social management strategies for each Chakra to maintain healthy individual functioning and 3) the clear sequential relationship between the Chakras (which, some have argued, is also reflected in their development).

These patterns map well to contemporary social and psychological models[9] and to the Six Social Cognitive Needs of the Brain described in the *NeuroPower* framework.

For example, the psychosocial issues typically associated with the Base Chakra (including 'grounding', a sense of personal emotional stability, and your own sense of your 'right to be alive') correlate well with the first phase of many contemporary psychological models of human development - and, more interestingly, with the emerging body of neuroscientific evidence which now suggests that a strong sense of belonging with a community is critical to effective brain function and is laid down early in life. More generally, celebrated Western authors like Maslow have suggested that our needs form a hierarchy ranging from basic needs like food, shelter and survival (the issues concerning the base or first Chakra), through to more evolved needs that centre on self-actualisation (which can be linked back to the higher Chakras).[10]

The benefit of exploring these frameworks is clear; when viewed through the lens of neuroscience, these traditional models can provide additional insight to be tested and perhaps incorporated into contemporary models. For example, one of Europe's mid-twentieth century founding fathers of modern Western psychology, George Ivanovitch Gurdjieff, explored aspects of the Chakra model to tease out the specific feeling (emotional), thinking (cognitive) and physical (somatic) aspects of individual human experience. This well-established trichotomy of thoughts, feelings and behaviours continues throughout modern psychology and into cognitive neuroscience today.

The Chakra system originated in India more than 4000 years ago and was referred to in the ancient literature of the Vedas, the later Upanishads, the Yoga Sutras of Patanjali and in the sixteenth century by an Indian Yogi in a text called the Sat-Chakra-Niupana. Some 4000 years later, we are just beginning now to understand the neural-correlates of this ancient and mythical system.

NEUROPOWER AND THE CENTRAL AMERICAN MAYA LENCA

NeuroPower also uses neurobiological research to validate many of the philosophical beliefs of the ancient Maya Lenca people from eastern El Salvador.

9   We have drawn on pre-eminent Western authors, researchers and practitioners in this area when exploring the building blocks of personality in Principle #1. In particular, Anodea Judith, in her groundbreaking book *Eastern Body, Western Mind*, brought together the Eastern Chakra system and Western developmental psychology. She achieved this by carefully interpreting the Eastern tradition with Western frameworks and the results from her own professional practice.

10   The alignment between the brain's Six Social Cognitive Needs (or ICs) and a range of traditional and contemporary models is outlined in Table 1.7. Each of these relationships are explored more fully in the next six chapters on the brain's Six Social Cognitive Needs.

Diagram 1.9 NeuroPower's Eight Strategic Mindsets

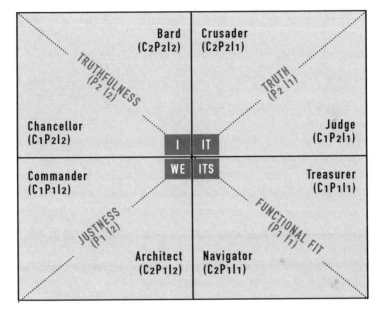

This culture is thought to date back more than 15,000 years and has a highly complex and accurate personality system that they describe as being based on energy. Instead of interpreting our relationship with energy in a framework relating to Chakras, the Maya Lenca describe different kinds of energies. Whereas the Indians see the energy itself as being generic and believe the energy is translated into being useful to the Chakras in the body, the Maya Lenca in Central America see the body as being a powerful antenna with a built-in decoder. For them, rather than the energy being homogenous, there are twenty fundamentally different energies accessed by humans and animals, six of which are instrumental for the creation of personality. Each of these six energies was named after the specific animal which they believed best embodied the energy. This knowledge was taught to each new generation through the oral tradition. These six energies have strong alignment with the Intelligences. For further information on the link between NeuroPower and the Maya Lenca, refer to Appendix 8..

NEUROPOWER AND THE JOURNEY OF INTEGRATION

Each of us has a dominant Neuro-Rational Type, however, the story doesn't end there. Throughout our lives, we can each integrate or disintegrate depending on the choices we make and where we choose to focus our attention. Moving through the process of integration can be described as both simple yet difficult. Each of us can see what we need to do but it means breaking our comfortable pattern of avoidance in order to do it.

In contrast, disintegration is complex yet remarkably easy. In disintegration we misuse our creativity to justify and reframe the situation so that we avoid having to do the hard work of internal awareness, pain and integration. In this way, we cling to our habits, neuroses and entrenched games.

We find the process of integration stressful. We usually make the hard step only when the alternatives—which are to do nothing or to continue on the path of disintegration—are even more painful.

Understanding the processes of integration is essential when leading, managing, coaching, counselling, encouraging or motivating clients, partners, children or friends. We'll explore this in more detail in Principle #3.

FIELD RESEARCH OF THE NEURO-RATIONAL TYPES

The descriptions and insights outlined in the eight Neuro-Rational Types have been based on the author's primary research conducted over the past twenty years. The initial sample consisted of 2,032 Caucasian Australians. To broaden this sample, which primarily consisted of middle-class professionals, further research was conducted with three smaller studies each of 375 respondents of different cultural and socioeconomic backgrounds. This confirmed the validity of the framework of Neuro-Rational Types across age groups, cultures and socioeconomic groups. Since then, from 1991 until present, the findings from the initial sample were depthed through separate studies with a combined sample of more than 20,000 people.

NEUROPOWER AS A MANAGEMENT/LEADERSHIP CONSULTING TOOL

The primary research provided an understanding of the basic propositions, world views, and genius of the eight Master Neuro-Rational Types. From here the *NeuroPower* management consulting team applied the *NeuroPower* framework to a wide range of people-related issues presented by executive teams, coaches, change management consultants, leadership consultants and therapists. This gave us the opportunity to apply the insight in a commercial setting.

With breakthroughs in neurobiology came new insights into functional systems. A further metastudy of these findings in 2006 enabled a correlation to be made between six of the brain's functional systems and the six Intelligences. This enabled *NeuroPower* to be born.

NEUROPOWER: THE INTERDISCIPLINARY SPECIALIST

A central focus throughout the development process has been to ensure that the *NeuroPower* framework integrates the insights from many different, historically fragmented disciplines. This enables the individual to embrace prior learning, experiences, frameworks, models or approaches, and place them into one dynamic system.

YOUR TASK: CONVERTING INSIGHT INTO ACTION (OR 'HOW TO USE THIS BOOK')

Before we start exploring the components of *NeuroPower* in detail, it may be helpful to consider how you want to apply the framework in your life. Having a clear idea of how you intend to use the information—be it with yourself, your team or your organisation— will help focus your mind on the parts that are most relevant to you and ensure that you convert your new found insight into action.

Depending on your own personal objectives in learning about *NeuroPower*, this book can be used in a number of different ways. Firstly, because the Handbook presents the material in a structured and logical way, you can read it from front to back and each section will build on the previous section. This is how we use the book in our Transformational Leadership and Master Practitioner trainings.

For those, however, who want a snapshot of the *NeuroPower* framework, you can read the *NeuroPower* four principles, the introduction to the four principles and Principle #1 and Principle #4 (without having to read all the personality-specific material) and you will gain a good sense of the system's dynamics.

Finally, if you want to use this book as a reference (like a dictionary of personality), start with the Neuro-Rational Type Test in Appendix 2. This will enable you to type yourself or best-guess somebody else's dominant type and you can turn straight to that personality-specific chapter for further relevant reading. For those of you adopting this last approach, the following outline of the book's structure and the key concepts covered in each section may be useful.

As we go through each section, for those who are interested, this book includes some detailed neuroscience behind why people behave the way that they do, including the different neural correlates involved in different responses. If you are new to neuroscience and would like to become more familiar with the different neural structures and how the brain works, you might consider finding a basic neuroanatomy text. One good option, used in many first year neurophysiology courses, is Professor John Pinel's *Biopsychology* (2009).

Overview of this Handbook

THE DEVELOPING SELF

Principle #1: Learn the brain's Six Social Cognitive Needs and how to satisfy them for yourself and others

NeuroPower begins by exploring the development of the six neurobiological functional systems or building blocks of personality (the Intelligences). Physiologically, our bodies and sense of self develop in a sequential process. At each stage of development we learn different insights about the world and develop different personal competencies to respond to the issues that emerge. In growing up we make decisions and assessments about the world based on these skills and insights. Maladaptive or dysfunctional adult behaviour results when one or more of the building blocks of our personality (Intelligences) is not sufficiently integrated. The six developmental steps in childhood that later make up the building blocks of adult personality are described in depth in this section.

CHOOSING THE HIGH ROAD (POWER) OR THE LOW ROAD (FORCE)

Principle #2: Learn how to manage your emotional reactivity

This section introduces readers to the psychopathology of the nine Neuro-Limbic Types (NLTs). These Types provide us with our emotional fuel and are critical to our sense of motivation and engagement, However, it's important that they are integrated with our Neuro-Rational Types (explored in Principle #3), rather than driving us from a place of emotional reactivity. In Principle #2 we explore each of the nine NLTs in detail, including the core emotion at the heart of each Type, predictable triggers of the Type and practical tools for working with and managing each emotional pattern.

Principle #2 also introduces readers to the concept of somatic testing and the revealed relative 'power' of truth. Somatic testing suggests that truth is a graduated scale which moves at best from absolute and sublime truth, which is power-based, life-affirming and constructive, to, at worst, force-based and life-destroying action which has very little truth at all but that enthralls the Lower Self.

YOUR ADULT PERSONALITY

Principle #3: Discover your genius, and when and how to use it

In Principle #3, we look at how we transition from childhood to adulthood by starting to access more than one Intelligence at a time. If you wish to access your *NeuroPower* you need to understand limbic and cognitive systems.

The difference between our developing self (limbic) and our adult personality (cognitive) is significant. It is the difference between being a child chained to causality, and being an adult co-creator in life with the freedom to choose and to determine our own journey.[11] Whether a child makes the leap to adulthood will be partially determined by the integrity with which they have established wholeness within each of their Intelligences.

We also explore the Personality Diamond (Diagram 1.10) which represents the four dynamic aspects of self. The four points correspond with the four distinct expressions of our life force. These are the Higher Non-dual Leader Self, the Lower Limbic Self, and the Master and the Mirror. Each of these four aspects of self has a different perspective of truth and a different role to play.

The **Master** personality, shown on the left-hand side of the diamond, is the aspect of self around which our self-identity is formed. This is who we understand ourselves to be. It represents the gifted part or genius of ourselves of which we are both aware and willing to own. The Master is also the most developed aspect of our personality and has a relatively mature perspective on life.

The **Mirror**, shown on the right-hand side of the diamond, represents all the disowned aspects of self that are not embraced by the Master. The Mirror also controls a great deal of the behaviour of the individual. Since it represents the disowned elements of self, the Mirror has a much younger and less developed level of understanding of the world than the Master. This is explained in more detail in each of the chapters outlining the Neuro-Rational Types and in Appendix 5.

The **Higher Self**, shown at the top of the diamond, represents the Non-dual Leader. When the Non-dual Leader is being expressed, the individual is able to access the wisdom from their Master and Mirror simultaneously. It is a state of self that people often refer to as a 'peak experience'. From this perspective the world is seen to be a place of endless possibility and abundance. The Non-dual Leaders are explored in detail in Principle #4.

The **Lower Self** (or Neuro-Limbic Type), shown at the bottom of the diamond, is the personality which forms when the human body's physical defence mechanisms are triggered. From the perspective of the Lower Self the world is a dangerous and threatening place. The Lower Self is driven by the amygdala in the brain. It is also linked to causality consciousness; that

---

11 Your adult personality (Master) is the gifted part of yourself. It represents a significant part of what it means to be human and enables the various expressions of human nobility. When someone is operating with noble intentions we see in them a glimpse of their true nature. They become capable of making such a significant difference in their own life and in the lives of those around them that, regardless of the specific circumstances of their life, it is a profound experience just to be in their company.

is, life events are interpreted in terms of simple cause and effect and the individual is at the mercy of their environment. Each individual has access to three Neuro-Limbic Types. One provides the limbic fuel for the Master, one provides the limbic fuel for the Mirror and one forces the individual to withdraw so that the Master and Mirror can interact.

The Impact of Adult Consciousness on Personality

Another key concept that is introduced in Principle #1 is the idea of consciousness. As we transition into and live as adults, our consciousness progresses through stages of increasing complexity. Of the many valid models that detail the development of adult consciousness, this *NeuroPower* Handbook describes personality at the different levels using the Spiral Dynamics framework (Beck and Cowan, 1996).

This model describes the progressive levels of complexity through which an individual will move in the course of their life. Interestingly, individuals at the same levels of consciousness are often found to have far more in common than is observed in two people of the same personality at different levels of consciousness.[12]

Having explored the different levels of consciousness, Principle #1 then describes the journey of personal integration required for moving to a higher level. This process enables the individual to develop a 'holon' of integrated knowledge about any experience or event (refer to Appendix 8 to obtain a deeper understanding of holons). Failure to move through this process will result in a partial understanding of the issue at hand, and an inability to resolve related issues or experiences appropriately at that level of consciousness. In this situation, individuals get stuck and cannot resolve the issue. Understanding this integration process enables the individual to grow their awareness and move to the next level. What this looks like for each of the types is explored in more detail in Principle #3.

In my experience, as a coach and a consultant, I have witnessed the most profound changes in people's lives when they increase the amount of time they spend in their gifted Master and Non-dual Leader, expressing human nobility, rather than in the reactive Lower Limbic Self.

In Principle #3 we explore each of the Neuro-Rational Types in detail, including their Area of Mastery, wealth habits, individual processes of integration and disintegration and journey through the Levels of Consciousness. We also see how these personalities

---

12 Consider the difference between two people in a relationship at different levels of consciousness, one of whom is focused on being seen to be successful and having the status symbols of success, while the other is focused on how to build and develop authentic relationships. These two will find it very difficult to understand each other unless they can come to understand their conflicting questions of existence which are more influenced by different levels of consciousness than different personalities. When two people have the same Master personality, if they are operating from different levels of consciousness, they appear to be very different.

Diagram 1.10 The Personality Diamond
(The four manifestations of personality within each individual)

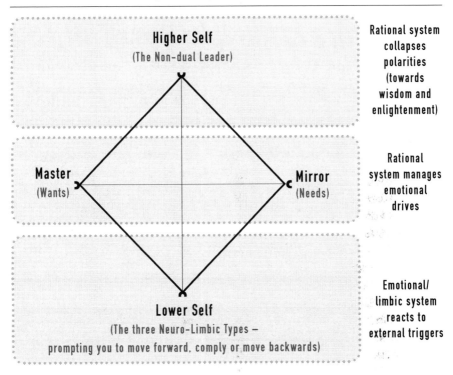

Higher Self
(The Non-dual Leader)

Rational system collapses polarities (towards wisdom and enlightenment)

Master
(Wants)

Mirror
(Needs)

Rational system manages emotional drives

Lower Self
(The three Neuro-Limbic Types –
prompting you to move forward, comply or move backwards)

Emotional/ limbic system reacts to external triggers

reflect the progressive development of human nobility.[13] Every act of greatness and every act that builds and supports humanity is based on human nobility. When you begin to experience your own noble qualities and begin to build them into your daily routine, life takes on entirely new depth, meaning and texture and you will have mastered the Second Principle.[14]

---

13 Human nobility is the human manifestation and practical application of pure essence, spirit, love or God. *NeuroPower* argues that we are given a glimpse of God through the different noble qualities that people manifest at the different levels of consciousness.

14 In developing the *NeuroPower* framework I have drawn upon quantum physics theories, philosophy from the oldest and newest civilisations and the integration of more than fifty mental frameworks, each of which has been carefully selected for the depth of its integration and the level of truth upon which it is based. These have all led to the Map of Human Nobility outlined in Principle #4, Table 20.2.

THE NON-DUAL LEADER
Principle #4: Explore how you can hardwire character and wisdom

Principle #4 takes an in-depth look at the next stage of integration which results in the manifestation of the four Non-dual Leaders. This section describes how Non-dual Leaders use their neocortex to convert internal tension, both theirs and others, into nobility. Principle #4 takes an in-depth look into the four paths of growth for the four Non-dual Leader profiles.

This is followed by several appendices which explore key *NeuroPower* concepts in more detail. These have been summarised as follows:

APPENDIX 1 - HOW THE CORE BELIEFS AND ARCHETYPES WORK TOGETHER

Appendix 1 details and explains the complete roadmap of your personality from Neuro-Limbic Type (Core Beliefs) to Neuro-Rational Type (Archetype) to Patron Leader.

APPENDIX 2 — NEURO-RATIONAL TYPE TEST

Appendix 2 is the Master Profile questionnaire which enables readers to 'best guess' their Master Neuro-Rational Type.

APPENDIX 3 — NEURO-RATIONAL TYPE MATRIX

Appendix 3 is a table that summarises the key attributes of the Master Neuro-Rational Types such as their noble qualities, their personal code of conduct, contribution to the team culture, and first steps of integration or disintegration.

APPENDIX 4 — PROCESS OF INTEGRATION AND (DIS)INTEGRATION

Appendix 4 summarises, for each of the Master Neuro-Rational Types, the steps of integration towards enlightenment and the steps of disintegration towards ignorance and death.

APPENDIX 5 — EXPLORATION OF THE MIRROR

In order to find personal internal harmony and to have full awareness of others' behaviours, it is critical to understand the role and character of both the Mirror and Master. Appendix 5 discusses Dr Fredric Schiffer's research which showed the presence of the Mirror, what can happen when we are blind to our Mirror, and some techniques which enable us to find harmony between our Mirror and Master. This also aligns with the Maya Lenca mythology of the duality of being and it is from here that we have borrowed the term 'Mirror' and key Maya medicine integration techniques.

APPENDIX 6 — INTELLIGENCE COMPATIBILITY MATRIX

Appendix 6 identifies the level of compatibility between different Intelligences. This can assist in identifying the sources of interpersonal conflict.

APPENDIX 7 — THE PATH OF INTEGRATION FOR EACH NEURO-RATIONAL TYPE

Appendix 7 tables the human nobility that each Neuro-Rational Type has access to at the different levels of consciousness.

APPENDIX 8 — NEUROPOWER AND ITS SYNERGY WITH MAYA LENCA PHILOSOPHY OF PERSONALITY, WELLNESS AND ILLNESS

This paper, authored by Leonel Chevez, the grandson of the last remaining Royal Maya Lenca, compares Maya philosophy and mythology with *NeuroPower*.

APPENDIX 9 — THE CELTIC CROSS

Appendix 9 discusses the Celtic Cross, its metaphoric meanings and symbols, and how these relate to the *NeuroPower* framework.

APPENDIX 10 — ONE OF THE GREATEST STORIES EVER TOLD

Appendix 10 tells the story of Camelot, King Arthur and the Round Table. Each character aligns with one of the Neuro-Rational Types. The story shows how the Archetypes act and interact, and how they grow and develop as their life unfolds.

APPENDIX 11 — THE NEUROPOWER ASSUMPTIONS

The *NeuroPower* framework is most effective when used in an environment that is supported by the thirty three *NeuroPower* assumptions. These 33 assumptions provide the philosophical platform for the *NeuroPower* framework.

APPENDIX 12 — APPLYING THE NEUROPOWER INSIGHT TO MAKE YOU A BETTER LEADER

Appendix 12 discusses how applying knowledge of the people's Intelligences and NLTs is critical to good leadership.

APPENDIX 13 — THE NEUROSCIENCE OF THE SIX INTELLIGENCES

Appendix 13 details the neuroscience of each of the six Intelligences in terms of evolutionary social brain function, and somatic, feeling and thinking aspects.

APPENDIX 14 — NEURO-LIMBIC TYPE BODY SHAPES

Appendix 14 depicts how a person's body shape can be linked to their NLT (Diversi, 2006).

APPENDIX 15 – ARTICLE: WHEN GOOD TEAMS MAKE BAD DECISIONS

Complex strategic decisions involving judgement, interpretation and complex trade-offs are at the centre of effective teamwork at senior levels of organisations. Yet leadership teams find it difficult to get it right. Perhaps this is because our brains have developed problem-solving processes that rely heavily on past experiences which significantly bias our beliefs today. This article explains how Cognitive Bias and 'group think' undermine judgement.

APPENDIX 16 – ARTICLE: BUILDING TRUST WITH THE NINE CORE BELIEF TYPES

Becoming a good advisor takes more than having good advice to offer. There are additional skills involved, ones that no one ever teaches you, that are critical to your success. Most importantly, we have learned the hard way that you don't get the chance to employ advisory skills until you can get someone to trust you enough to share their problems with you. No one ever taught us how to do that either. Yet we had to learn it. Somehow. This article explains how to build trust with the nine NLTs (Core Belief Types).

Now that you have a sense of how you plan to use *NeuroPower* in your journey, let's get started.

Principle #1:

Learn the Brain's Six Social Cognitive Needs and How to Satisfy Them for Yourself and Others

Chapter 2

Our First Social Cognitive Need:
RELATEDNESS &
The Automatic Function (P1)

RELATEDNESS (P1) AT A GLANCE

Relatedness is our Brain's First Social Cognitive Need

The brain loves being part of a group that is cohesive, fair and safe. The evolution and growth of the prefrontal cortex was driven by the need to survive and thrive by remaining secure within our social groups. People define themselves by the groups they belong to and are highly sensitive to social rejection and exclusion.

Characteristics of the Relatedness (P1) Functional Network

Process and Logic

STRENGTH	WEAKNESS
Consistent and stable, takes one step at a time	Can be slow to reach an outcome through rigid adherence to process

OPPORTUNITY	THREAT
Can lack prioritisation and enthusiasm - may seem disorganised or disinterested	Can get bogged down or paralysed by obstacles

Management Style

- Ordered and logical thinking
- One step at a time
- Process focused and incremental
- Balanced and even-handed

TRIBAL LOYALTY

P1 THINKING	**P1 FEELING**	**P1 SOMATIC**
Learned logic	Calmness and Stability	Compliance to learned rules

COMMUNICATION STYLE

- Often feels frustrated if others take the discussion off-track - even if it's a beneficial discussion
- Makes a good impartial chairperson or mediator
- Will logically clarify people when they speak, listen for a lack of logic and highlight it
- Will not understand why people are irrationally angry or moody

KEYWORDS INCLUDE

- Logic
- Control
- Order
- One Step at a Time
- Team before Self
- Family

Relatedness (P1) Helps Us to Survive

Relatedness (P1) helps us both as individuals and the group to survive and thrive by motivating and enabling us to learn and comply with specific social roles and understood social rules.

Relatedness & The Automatic Function (P1)

RELATEDNESS: OUR BRAIN'S FIRST SOCIAL NEED

Humans are herd animals. From our earliest ancestors, humans have evolved to be part of groups, not only to satisfy needs for interaction and companionship, but most importantly, in order to ensure our own physical survival. The ones who survived were those who could work together to hunt and gather, warn each other about dangers and maintain knowledge by learning from each other. The infants that instinctively stayed in the middle of the group were safer than those that went wandering.

It is not surprising that neuroscientists have discovered our brains are hardwired to keep us safe within our social groups and are wired to raise the alarm at the mere possibility of social exclusion. Studies in the lab of Professor Matthew Lieberman at UCLA have revealed that experience of social exclusion activates the same regions within the brain that are activated when a person experiences physical pain, with the alarm signals just as strong. The brain's interpretation of social exclusion mirrors its interpretation of physical danger.

From an organisational or community perspective, for leaders looking to build a high performance team, their first task is to make sure that each member of the team feels secure in the value they add to the group. This isn't about being liked, it's about being respected and valued for the contribution a person makes to the group. When team members don't feel safe or are unclear on how they add value, they may resort to playing politics in order to maintain their position in the group. These divisive strategies can destroy group cohesion and dramatically reduce the team's performance.

Within the brain, a diverse range of structures and neuronal networks drive us to satisfy our need for Relatedness. Within the *NeuroPower* framework, this set of structures is called the 'P1 Automatic System' (or sometimes the 'P1 network' or 'P1 function') and gives rise to a particular thinking style referred to as 'P1 Intelligence'. The rest of this chapter explores the characteristics, development and maintenance of this P1 functional network in detail.

THE EVOLUTIONARY SOCIAL BRAIN FUNCTION OF RELATEDNESS (P1)

The P1 system enables the individual to survive through:

- Membership of a community (kinship) through compliance with a specific social role and understood social rules, socially known as moral behaviour (Ciaramelli et al., 2007)

- Movement of behaviour from a conscious action to a habitual response, freeing up mental energy for novel situations requiring creative thought (Saling & Phillips, 2007)

- Control of behaviour in terms of thoughts and physical reactions (Lieberman & Eisenberger, 2004)

- Sequencing events and behaviours (Ratey, 2002)

- The sense that we are the author and controller of our actions (Frith, 2002)

BUILDING BELONGING IS A PRIORITY FOR LEADERS

Our brains are wired to enable us to survive by becoming valued members of groups. Members of these tribes tend to put a premium on leaders that are willing to do what is right to protect follower's interests. This is a key role of leadership in all environments although what is in the best interests of the team members changes according to the type of group. Leadership, therefore, is contextual to the work of the group. That is to say, the role of the leader changes depending on the role of the group. In all groups, the effectiveness of the teamwork is directly proportional to the importance of the work needing to be done by a team. If there is no work to be done by the team, there will be no teamwork. From this perspective, the greatest single priority for a leader is to establish the critical nature of the team's work and clarify, from team members, the role they need the leader to play to enable the team to deliver on this work. Nowhere is this more evident than in the military and other uniformed organisations where the life and death of team members is largely determined by the decisions made by leadership. In these organisations it quickly becomes evident just how important it is that team members can trust that the leader will play their role in keeping team members safe. This is critical to team performance.

In teams, before this trust is established, team members display both aggressive and passive aggressive behaviour as they jostle for power and influence for personal gain and security.

In their groundbreaking book *Leadership in Dangerous Situations*, authors Patrick Sweeney, Michael Matthews and Paul Lester (2011) articulate it like this: "To risk their lives and safety, first responders must firmly believe in their leaders, know those leaders care for them, and have confidence that they can make good decisions quickly. This unique set of skills is called dangerous context leadership. Understanding how to operate and inspire in extreme circumstances greatly strengthens any organisation whether military or civilian."

This underpins the idea that of all the social cognitive needs held by both teams

and individuals, the most foundational is trust. Trust between leaders and their followers and between members of the group is only achieved when group members feel they are valued by, and belong to, the group. The neural correlates of this social cognitive need link to some of the earliest functional networks established in the infant human brain. Research published by the Society for Personality and Social Psychology (Shnabel et al., 2013) and reported by the Scientific American showed that when ethnic minority students felt they didn't belong to their cohort, their cognitive capacity was significantly compromised. By increasing their feeling of belonging, these under-performing students were able to lift their academic performance by a massive 70 percent over three years. These findings suggest that 'reminders of relational connections boost one's ability to perform well academically'.

As babies we are hardwired from before the dawn of consciousness to do what it takes to belong to a group because, at the most primitive level, group belonging means individual survival.

Recognising the Characteristics of Relatedness (P1)

P1 mental processing has distinct features: it is logical and strives to be objective, analytical and impersonal. It follows accepted procedures, thinks one step at a time, and displays intellectual, emotional and physical control. P1 urges us to obey the desire for calm, social order and structure. P1 is in time (rather than through time), steady, focused and in the present. 'What next?' is the cognitive question of P1.

When accessed, P1 feels grounded. The pace of P1 is measured, even, slow, steady and unhurried. Music to access P1 is a march or a steady beat.

The primary fears assessed by P1 are related to issues that could logically challenge physical survival, abandonment by the group, loss of physical order, tribal conflict or individual selfishness that could threaten the tribe. The primary strengths of P1 are related to tribal/family identity, bonding and the tribal honour code, as well as tribal support and loyalty that give the individual a sense of safety and connection to the physical world.

Early neurobiological research linked many of the characteristics of P1 with the 'dorsal pathway' on the left side of the brain, the left prefrontal cortex and the implicit memory systems that are established immediately following birth (Siegel, 1999). In particular, the rigidity of P1 rules correlates with the formation and characteristics of implicit memory.

Brains with highly functioning P1 have three elements that integrate to deliver a greater sense of stability, security and belonging. The thinking function incorporates learned logic, the feeling state centres around a sense of calmness and belonging, and somatically P1 relates to behavioural compliance with tribal authority or, in contemporary cultures, with the 'rules' of society.

Without an integrated P1, the individual may never experience true contentment or belonging.

From an evolutionary perspective, the social cognitive role of P1 is to maintain the survival of the tribe. This means when an individual accesses the P1 function there is a focus on minimising intra-tribal conflict. The P1 injunction is that conflict within the tribe threatens survival and must therefore be removed. There are three ways individuals respond to the issues around the maintenance of tribal rules. Firstly, they can focus on ensuring rule compliance and playing the role of enforcer; secondly, they can focus on maintaining the social order through strong connection with and loyalty to the leader (or if they are the leader, demanding loyalty from others) or finally, they can ensure the tribe is aware of any danger facing it so that it can prepare for the worst.

The first step of adult integration involves taking tribal rules from the unconscious implicit memory and carefully and consciously examining which are relevant and which need to be discarded. Emotional patterns, world views, rituals, interpersonal relationship rules, spiritual beliefs and even food intake all fall into tribal or family patterns and need examination and re-interpretation.

P1 THINKING — LOGIC, MORAL REASONING, FAIRNESS AND SECURITY

The thinking style associated with P1 is logic. Logic enables the brain to apply previously learned rules of cause and effect to predict the future consequences of current behaviour. As such, P1 thinking draws heavily on brain structures associated with working memory (frontal lobe), mathematical reasoning (frontal and parietal lobes) and socially driven self control (frontal lobes, particularly the lateral prefrontal cortex[1]).

The focus of P1 thinking is to help maintain stability in our external environment (including our social environment). P1 thinking is primarily focused on avoiding disruption to the status quo through compliance with social rules, roles and expectations and has been linked to increased activity in the right prefrontal cortex (Amodio et al., 2004). It provides our motivation to follow rules to avoid being 'in trouble' and experiencing others' anger. It is also the same circuit that motivates us to follow the rules or decisions of our own, that we have etched into our memories after experiencing fear. This 'prevention regulatory focus' has been associated with increased activity in the

---

1   Recent reviews suggest that when we comply with and apply 'if-then' rules recently given to us by others (P1 thinking) these rules are represented in more lateral areas of the prefrontal cortex (Berkman & Lieberman in Moskowitz & Grant, 2009). When these rules are repeated over time, they then become progressively embedded into implicit procedural memory, mediated by both the orbitofrontal cortex and subcortical structures including for example, the basal ganglia (Pascual-Leone et al., 1996; Saling & Phillips, 2007).

Social Pain and Social Cognitive Neuroscience

It hurts to be excluded - and around 10 years ago, there was already a large amount of psychological and social sciences research to indicate that feeling left out can lead to anxiety, depression and self-esteem issues. But focusing on social inclusion was still regarded by many in business as a 'soft' topic that didn't apply to the corporate world.

Then, in 2003, Naomi Eisenberger and Matthew Lieberman at UCLA published a powerful study looking at what happens in the brain when we are excluded.

They found that when you are excluded from a group - even in a simple computer game as part of a lab experiment - the same parts of your brain are activated as if we are in physical pain.

This study sparked a whole series of studies over the following decade and in many ways marks the beginning of the field of social cognitive neuroscience, which seeks to explore and understand human experience based on the foundation observation that our brains are hardwired to think and operate in groups.

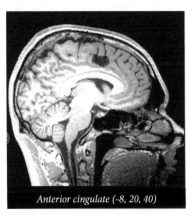

Anterior cingulate (-8, 20, 40)

The anterior cingulate cortex (ACC), indicated here on a structural scan of one of our team member's brains, acts as a 'conflict detector' in the brain and, among other things, is highly sensitive to signs of social exclusion.

precuneus and posterior cingulate cortex (Strauman et al., 2013). A key aspect of this is an aversion to risk and uncertainty, linked to activity in the dorsal medial prefrontal cortex (dMPFC; Xue et al., 2009).[2] P1 thinking is slower, repetitive and more conservative compared to P2 thinking (Crowe & Tory Higgins (1997).

Moral reasoning, which helps us understand and apply moral rules also seems to be linked strongly to activity in both the frontal lobes and areas surrounding the temporoparietal junction (TPJ); Moll et al., 2005). However, more recent research suggests that these different areas are playing quite different roles. Whereas simple moral judgements based on social norms (Relatedness - P1) draw heavily on the

2   Xue et al. (2009) found that the dMPFC was activated whenever we make risky decisions, especially if individuals have a bias towards avoiding risk. Conversely, a positive preference for risk (dominant P2) correlated parametrically with increased activation in the ventral MPFC.

ventromedial prefrontal cortex, the more posterior areas like the TPJ (which is an important part of the brain for integrating complex social information and theory of mind[3]) get called on when there is no clear answer and we need to simulate multiple options and consider their impact on other people before we reach a decision (FeldmanHall, Mobbs & Dalgleish, 2013).

Following on from work done in Professor Matthew Lieberman's lab at UCLA, we also know that the dorsal anterior cingulate, which acts like the brain's 'error detector', is quick to respond at signs of social exclusion.

P1 FEELING - SOCIAL ACCEPTANCE/REJECTION

The feeling states associated with P1 range from positive emotions associated with social acceptance and belonging to feelings of loneliness or panic if isolated from the group. The main neurotransmitters for brain chemicals associated with the P1 system are serotonin, corticotrophin-releasing hormone (CRH) and endorphins

Several groundbreaking studies over the last decade have shown that when an individual's safety within the group is challenged, they typically respond with high levels of distress, anxiety and anger. These correspond with activation in the brain's emotional or limbic system, including those areas associated with the experience of physical pain (Lieberman & Eisenberger, 2004).

In 1998, affective neuroscientist, Jaak Panksepp described in detail a neurobiological mechanism for the emotional experience for this kind of 'FEAR' or 'PANIC', which he observed as common to all mammals. He called it the FEAR Circuit. This circuit spans from the temporal lobe to the anterior and medial hypothalamus through to the lower brainstem and spinal cord. The circuit's temporal lobe includes the central and lateral areas of the amygdala. The circuit's lower brainstem areas include the periventricular gray substance of the diencephalon and mesencephalon and connects to specific autonomic and behavioural output components of the lower brainstem and spinal cord.

Interestingly, the neurochemical mechanisms that help regulate the P1 system are similar to those that are targeted by modern psychiatric drugs used to treat anxiety. GABA receptors are one of the brain's most widespread 'braking mechanisms' (like the brakes in your car) and are found on the surface of neurons throughout the brain and particularly in the cerebral cortex. When GABA binds to GABA receptors it opens channels that allow chloride ions to flow into neurons, which slows down their firing. GABA receptors are highly expressed throughout most of the brain areas that support the P1 system. They exist from the cerebral cortex, right down along the

---

3   These abilities are discussed more in the I2 thinking (Seeing the Facts) section in Chapter 5.

nucleus reticularis, pontis caudalis, the periaqueductal gray and substantia nigra, and continue to the anterior and medial hypothalamus, the ventral amygdalofugal pathway, and the central amygdala. In healthy brains, GABA receptors are activated to inhibit the P1 system to modulate the level of fear or anxiety we experience in daily life. One widespread treatment for anxiety disorders is the use of benzodiazepines (BZs), which enhance the activity of GABA and GABA receptors. Effectively, BZs help hyperpolarise the neuronal fear message carriers to suppress fear. Interestingly, another 'natural' drug - alcohol - also directly activates GABA receptors to sedate the brain.

GABA is the brain's most common inhibitory neurotransmitter and is just one decarboxylation step away from glutamate, the most common excitatory neurotransmitter, and investigations into neuroplasticity suggest that glutamate is a probable excitatory neurotransmitter for this circuit and mediates the learning of fears (Panksepp, 1998).

P1 SOMATIC - HABITUAL BEHAVIOUR

The P1 somatic circuit involves our implicit procedural memory which enables us to complete tasks without needing to give them conscious attention. This is the part of the brain involved when activities become second-nature or habitual.

Our understanding of P1 implicit memory was significantly driven by the case of HM, a young man who underwent radical brain surgery in 1953 in an attempt to treat intractable epilepsy. Unfortunately, the surgery (which removed most of his hippocampus, parahippocampal gyrus and amygdala) had unforeseen consequences.

HM was unable to form new long-term explicit memories and also suffered from temporally graded retrograde amnesia – he could not remember most events in the three to four days before the surgery and some events up to 11 years before then. However, he was able to form new long-term procedural memories, such as motor skills, despite not being able to remember them. HM's personal tragedy was the first evidence that different types of memory involve different parts of the brain. Subsequent research on HM until his death in 2008 enabled scientists to use fMRI to explore his intact implicit procedural memory, particularly in the motor regions of the brain. On 2 December 2009, the Brain Observatory at the University of California, San Diego began an unprecedented anatomical study that aims to create a complete microscopic survey of HM's entire brain. This may well provide further insights about the neurological basis of HM's historical memory impairment, and assist us in gaining an even better understanding of the neural correlates of implicit procedural memory.

P1 and the Link Between Politics and Riding a Bicycle

According to social cognitive neuroscientists, political thinking and bike riding have more in common that you might think. It seems that both involve flexing a common set of mental 'muscles' that support the development and expression of habits (i.e. P1 patterns). Lieberman, Scheiber and Ochsner (2003) identified three common characteristics of habitual behaviours that suggest parallels between the political thinking and cycling:

(1) Both can become routinized and automatic with behavioral repetition.

(2) Once formed, these behaviors are difficult to explain. Just as it is difficult to consciously access and describe the coordinated movements that underlie riding a bike, the bases for decision-making in many domains become less accessible to conscious inspection over time.

(3) We have imperfect introspective access to the mechanisms supporting habitual behaviors; hence, we can lose sight of the forces that trigger and guide their automatic expression. Indeed, decades of social-psychological research have revealed many ways in which thoughts, preferences, and attitudes are influenced by subtle contextual factors, prior habitual thought patterns, and current mood... Similarly, many factors that shape the way we ride a bike—including tire size and inflation, handlebar position, weather, and terrain—can change how we ride, but may do so without any blip on our conscious radar (p. 682).

The link between the two activities is that both involve the implicit procedural memory of the P1 Intelligence.

The Development of Healthy Relatedness (P1)

RELATEDNESS (P1) IS HARDWIRED TO PROMOTE THE CHILD'S SURVIVAL

In the middle of the twentieth century a psychoanalyst and psychiatrist, John Bowlby, turned to animal behaviour studies to develop an idea that profoundly challenged the traditional analytic views of child development (Bowlby, 1969; George and Solomon, 1996). He argued that the nature of the relationship with a child's primary caregiver becomes internalised within the child and, for the infant's lifetime, will determine the degree to which it feels safe, worthy and secure. This breakthrough resulted in a shift in the care of institutionalised children throughout the Western world. (From this time on these children were assigned specific individuals to care for them rather than whoever was available.)

Bowlby's insights were appropriate from a neuroscientific perspective, because the P1 system emerges in the developmental period from the womb to about twelve months. This is the pre-ego stage. The infant is totally dependent and so their identity is merged primarily with their mother and with their environment. The basic needs of infancy are the instinctual needs for survival: holding and nurturing, food and physical comfort, continuity and safety. If the mother is healthy and happy and the environment is safe and nourishing, the child can be expected to emerge with a healthy, strong and integrated P1.

Importantly, the strength of the bond developed between the child and the mother in the first twelve months powerfully shapes the child's brain and has a lasting impact on the nature of the child's P1. Amazingly, researchers have also found that the P1 network can be influenced even before the child is born. For example, Anthony DeCasper (University of North Carolina, Greensboro), has demonstrated that our attachment through voice recognition begins before we are born. In the now famous 'Cat in the Hat' experiment, mothers read to their unborn children in the weeks before birth. After birth, most of these children sucked faster and more enthusiastically when they heard their mothers voice rather than that of a stranger. This suggests that they remembered the sound of their mother's voice from in utero. Once born, the level of emotional synchrony developed within mother-infant pairs during their first year is predictive of the infant's level of self-control (P1) at two years, even after taking into account temperament, IQ and maternal style (Feldman, Greenbaum and Yirmiya, 1999).

The P1 functional network is developed during the stage referred to by German psychologist and psychoanalyst, Erik Erikson as the Trust versus Mistrust stage.

If the infant develops a sense of trust that their needs will be met by their primary caregivers, as they grow they will typically trust the world and himself or herself. With a healthy P1, the child can confidently move on to the next phase of exploring

Attachment Provides a Secure Base

Repeated experiences of treatment by parents become encoded in implicit memory as expectations and then as mental models or schemata of attachment, which serve to help the child feel an internal awareness of what Bowlby referred to as a 'secure base' in the world (Bowlby, 1969, 1988). These neurally encoded representations serve as the core of the social brain. While the development of attachment schemata occurs predominately in children, adults continue to manifest attachment throughout their life span (Parkes, Stevenson-Hinde & Marris, 1991). Particularly under periods of stress an adult will monitor the whereabouts of a few selected 'attachment figures' and seek them out as sources of comfort, advice and strength.

The Importance of Eye Contact

Eye contact is a powerful medium through which a parent translates their internal world to the child. As a child gradually moves away from their parent, they will check back visually to see the expression on a parent's face. If the parent appears calm, then the child will feel confident to explore further, whereas a frightened look will decrease exploration. The process through which the parent's internal world is automatically transferred to the child is referred to as social referencing (Gunnar and Stone, 1984).

the world, confident that it is a safe place to be (Sigelman and Rider, 2006).

As discussed before, many of the attributes of the P1 Intelligence arise from its developmental process. Bowlby's proposition in the late 1960s has since been extensively studied and given rise to the field of *Attachment Theory*, which explores the complex relationship between an infant and its caregivers, and the ramifications of that relationship on the infant's future development. Even from before birth, Attachment Theory argues that our interpersonal experiences become organised into schemas (or basic templates) for attachment (Bowlby, 1969) that form implicit procedural memories incorporating sensory, motor, affective and cognitive memories. These attachment schemas direct our attention by providing ongoing and often unconscious input about dangerous situations. Furthermore, the interactions with attachment figures contribute to the organisation and integration of neural networks that give the child the capacity for self-regulation (Siegel, 1999).

Mary Ainsworth, a professor in developmental psychology at the University of Virginia, collaborated with Bowlby at the Tavistock Clinic in the 1950s (Bowlby, 1969; Bretherton, 1992). Her idea was to study mother-infant interactions over the first year of life, and then to place the child within situations that would trigger their attachment system. This was achieved by bringing each mother-infant pair into a laboratory setting. At various times in the twenty-minute procedure, the infant stayed with the mother, with the mother and a stranger, with only the stranger, and then on its own for up to three minutes. Her theory was that separating a one-year-old from their attachment figure within a strange environment should activate the infant's responses to separation. Ainsworth found that the infants' behaviour at reunion fell into specific patterns of response that reflected how securely the infant was attached to its mother (Ainsworth et al., 1978) and that these categories corresponded to the independently performed home observation ratings for the year prior to the laboratory assessment. This laboratory measure is called the Ainsworth or Infant-Strange Situation (Ainsworth et al., 1978). Ainsworth's Baltimore study has been replicated throughout the world with consistent results.

Another study that explores the P1 social cognitive need through the lens of infant attachment was conducted using a process called the Adult Attachment Interview (AAI) (George and Solomon, 1996). The AAI is a 'narrative assessment of the interviewee's state of mind with respect to attachment' (Main and Goldwyn, 1998; Main, 1995; Hesse, 1999). The AAI is undertaken by an interviewer asking open-ended questions about an adult's childhood relationships and experiences. Their responses enable researchers to conduct a linguistic analysis of the coherence of the narrative's organisation and presentation (Hesse, 1999). The categories that result from research with the AAI, correlate with the results of both in-home observations of mother-child dyads and of the Infant-Strange Situation. The AAI reflects an ingrained state of mind within the interviewee that has a significant impact on later character and archetype development.

Of all available measures – including intellectual functioning, personality assessments, and socioeconomic factors – the AAI is the most robust predictor of how effectively infants have become attached to their parents (van Ijzendoorn, 1992, 1995; Sagi et al., 1994; Hesse, 1999). To contextualise the rates of attachment security, it has been found that in low-risk, non-clinical populations, 55-65 percent of infants are securely attached (Ainsworth et al., 1978).

A wide range of attachment studies have found that by 12 months old, a child will have formed deeply encoded attachments with its parents. The nature of these attachments results in significant differences in behaviour when the child is around its mother or father (Siegel, 1999). By 18 months, the child's brain will have developed explicit memory. It is thought that this enables the child to bring forward in its mind the sensory image of the parent in order to help calm and regulate its emotional state (Schore, 1994; Hofer,

Infant P1 Injunctions Can Impact Our Adult Lives

We all have absolute P1 injunctions that we unconsciously apply to the way we live our lives. ('**Always** eat everything on your plate,' for example.) Many of these deeply held practices come from our earliest experiences. With repeated feedback, the infant's brain detects similarities and differences across experiences. From these comparative processes, the infant makes generalised representations that are encoded within the brain. These generalisations form the basis of prototypal 'mental models' that help the child to interpret present experiences and to anticipate future ones. These mental models are important because they allow the brain to act as an 'anticipation machine', constantly scanning the environment, trying to determine what will come next and to avoid pain (Freyd, 1987). In many cases they also provide a level of certainty that save us from learning everything from first principles every time.

1994). If the child is securely attached, they will be calmed by an image of their parent; if the attachment is insecure, they are likely to be anxious, distant or fearful. In adult life this reaction is often projected onto mother and father figures, authority figures and leaders.

Infants seek proximity to their attachment figures because this provides them with a sense of security. Bonding activity, such as proximity seeking, cooing, cuddling or gazing into the eyes, between a mother and an infant involves a biochemical cascade (including the secretion of oxytocin, prolactin, endorphins and dopamine) that not only produces positive and rewarding feelings in the pair but also stimulates the structural development of the brain (Panksepp, 1998; Schore, 1994). The release of these opiates serves to strongly reinforce and shape preferences from early in life (Kehoe and Blass, 1989). These chemicals help us feel safe and relaxed, which are two emotional hallmarks of a well-functioning P1. When naltrexone, a drug that blocks the effect of many endogenous opioids released through attachment activity, was administered to infant primates their clinging behaviour increased (Kalin, Shelton and Lynn, 1995). This same effect has been demonstrated in rodents (Panksepp, Nelson and Siviy, 1994) and also in dogs (as measured by increases in tail wagging) (Knowles, Conner and Panksepp, 1989). As children grow they internalise their relationships with their attachment figures. This process is facilitated by release of these opioids, which reinforce the network of visceral, motor, sensory and emotional memories that will be evoked in times of stress and can support the ability to regulate emotion.

PHYSICALITY AND A SENSE OF SAFETY HELP BUILD RELATEDNESS

Infants sense the world through their body. Johnson (1987) suggests that it is the experience which our bodies provide that forms the internal basis for meaning and reasoning. He even argues that the physical experiences of the body provide an orientation for mental processing.

Various studies have suggested that physical touch may also have a significant influence on the establishment of stress modulating functions in adulthood (Meaney et al., 1989; Plotsky and Meaney, 1993). Research has shown that rats stroked and nurtured during infancy show more open field activity (i.e. are more inclined to explore new environments; Levine, Haltmeyer, Karas and Denenberg, 1967), increased gene expression and higher levels of stress inhibitors in the hippocampi than control rats that are not handled (Meaney et al., 1989, 2000). These changes remained well into the rats' lives, indicating that the early establishment of these physiological setpoints relating to the individual's ability to emotionally cope with life's stresses and surprises may continue over a lifetime.[4]

4   More recently, researchers have shown that when female rats are stressed by isolation before mating, their offspring are also affected, showing blunted neurohormonal responses to painful physical stimuli (Pisu et al., 2013). This and many other studies are now starting

What is Implicit Memory?

The manifestation of P1 links the individual with their implicit memories from childhood. These implicit memories provide a structured and understandable explanation of the world around us in the form of behavioural, perceptual and emotional learning (Bauer, 1996; Schachter, 1996; Emde, 1990; Fivush and Hudson, 1990). Since this implicit memory is encoded within parts of the brain that do not require conscious processing during retrieval (Bauer, 1996; Schachter, 1996; Emde, 1990; Fivush and Hudson, 1990) the individual accessing P1 may be unaware that they are accessing models of reality based on a child's understanding. Consequently, when the adult is enforcing P1 rules, it is the equivalent of enforcing a view of reality which is seen as 'ultimate truth' and as timeless. Any threat to these mental models triggers unconscious defence mechanisms within the body.

Unfortunately, it is often forgotten that the body has an intelligence of its own and that touch is essential to calm young children. As a result, children who are raised without touch and other somatic expressions of reassurance and safety can develop a dissociation between mind and body, focusing only on the intellectual need for safety but never experiencing a sense of security. As adults, these individuals are often highly anxious. Until the child learns how and when to focus their attention on their somatic P1 they will feel unsafe in the world.

High-functioning somatic P1 can be actively developed through tailored physical exercise. One example of a yoga exercise to access and balance P1 is aptly called 'planting the stump', which involves steady and strong movements. The exercise starts by planting your feet firmly on the ground and imagining wrapping your arms around a huge vertical log and heaving it down while simultaneously exhaling with a 'huh'. Exercises like this are designed to evoke and strengthen the mind's ability to access somatic P1.

Tribal Beliefs (P1) Have Strengths and Weaknesses

The P1 Intelligence enables the individual to apply faith, a belief in community, and control, to maintain a sense of stability. When somebody is accessing P1 they assess others by asking themselves, 'Do you look, smell or sound like those of my tribe?' P1 asks 'who?', 'when?', 'how?' and 'what?' but never 'why?' The role of this

to show us that in addition to our own environment and the DNA that makes up our genes, our parents' lives may also directly influence basic aspects of our temperament and our own experience.

Intelligence is to not challenge the wisdom of the tribe.

The infant is born into a family from which it absorbs the collective consciousness and willpower as it absorbs the family's strengths and weaknesses, beliefs, superstitions and fears. These influences can be both positive and negative. Later in life, an important integration task is to contextualise this implicit tribal world in their current life. This involves moving beyond literal implicit thinking to symbolic explicit thinking.

The beliefs of the tribe form the emerging child's world view; the world is either safe or dangerous, abundant or poverty stricken, educated or ignorant, a place to take from or to give to. Tribal power protects the tribe from damaging external influences (just as the immune system does for the body). There is a sense of power in sharing and acting on the beliefs of the family or community. The consequences of such actions can be either for the greater good or they can be destructive or vengeful. One downside to this social immunity is that no individual takes responsibility for their own actions. At a trial the perpetrator of P1 violence will claim they were only doing what was 'right'.

It is a task of adult P1 integration to become conscious of actions which are prompted by unconscious, outdated family or tribal beliefs. We need to take responsibility for our own behaviour and not excuse it with 'tribal reasoning'. We need to re-examine our family beliefs in the light of our current context, insight, responsibility and values. It is important for our physical and mental health to include in our examination beliefs about our life expectancy, the time we should retire, where we should live, whether to save or spend and even where to invest our money.

If our conscious plans are unconsciously based on family or tribal beliefs, our assumptions can prevent us from changing and expanding our horizons. Adult maturity involves breaking belief patterns that have limited relevance but still have a seemingly inexplicable power over us.

LOYALTY, HONOUR AND JUSTICE — THE UPSIDE OF ATTACHMENT

As we have explored, the human infant has an inbuilt system within the brain that influences and organises emotional, motivational and memory processes with respect to significant caregiving figures. At the most basic level these systems increase the chances of the infant's survival. Neurologically, attachment establishes an interpersonal relationship that helps the immature brain of the infant to use the mature functions of the parent's brain to organise its own processes (Hofer, 1994).

From the healthy family or tribe the developing child learns the virtue of Tribal Loyalty. This virtue is important to the health and security of both the tribe and the individual members. Tribal Loyalty is the human bond in the family or group which ensures reliability, especially in a crisis. It implies keeping one's word and acting with integrity, and imbues strength, dignity and pride in oneself, which is a good basis for further development.

The child learns to trust society and to respect themselves, and so see the world as a trustworthy place. Of course, if the child sees in its family a lack of commitment and respect, they will grow up with this code of (mis)behaviour.

In this way, tribal justice is learned in the family or tribe. This, too, is specific to the tribe. The tribe's justice might dictate, 'Do unto others as you would be done by', or it might say 'an eye for an eye'. We see this noticeably in international relations, where a whole nation will call for aggression in the name of justice.

Exploring and understanding implicit junctions and P1 tribal reasoning can help an outsider make sense of what seems to be strange or illogical in an individual or a group. It can also help you as an individual to free yourself from unconstructive patterns of behaviour that are based on tribal logic rather than contextual insight based on your own personal wisdom.

EMOTIONS RELATED TO FOLLOWING RULES

While the tribal rules are being followed, the person accessing P1 feels safe, grounded, cheerful, certain and self-confident. They appear calm, unhurried and controlled. These emotions stem from the groundedness and certainty of the tribe or family. It is important to remember that rule following is essential for the survival of the tribe. The impulse to survive is instinctual; it is built into the brain and tells the infant that to defend itself it must connect to its environment.

Our P1 emotional state often changes according to whether the tribal rules are being upheld. If the rules are broken, the emotion changes to anger, self-righteousness, rule-bound intolerance and a need to control.

However, when the P1 individual is relaxed and confident that their rules are being upheld, P1 can feel free to be sanguine and tolerant.

P1 RULE FOLLOWING AT WORK

At its best, P1 Intelligence fosters consistency and stability. However, at its extreme, P1 Intelligence can become a weakness, entrenching us into inflexibility and a need to control at the first sign of instability or conflict. Conflict triggers P1 into personal and group control, using the childhood family as its source of rules.

As the individual matures, rule-following behaviour is extended from the family to work, where the rules are the accepted practices of the organisation. Here, individuals high in P1 assume that 'If only everyone would follow the rules we would be fine.' Conflict within the tribe or organisation is seen by P1 as a threat to the tribe's survival and so the person accessing somatic P1 will naturally try to control the situation by demanding everyone follow the rules.

Organisational culture is so embedded in employees' P1 that P1-driven behaviour resembles something Dr Herbert Spiegel, leading New York psychiatrist and author, calls a 'Compulsive Triad', which is not dissimilar to an individual who has been hypnotised.

This Compulsive Triad has three characteristics:

1. *The individual commits an act resulting from post-hypnotic suggestion* (i.e. we do things because the cultural environment cues us to do so);

2. *The individual has amnesia to the signal that triggers the action* (i.e. we are not aware of these cues); and

3. *The individual shows post-event rationalisation of the act* (i.e. when challenged, we recruit the brain's reasoning and narrative-making areas to reconstruct a justification for our behaviour).

In this way it is often virtually impossible for culturally hypnotised employees to see the culture of their own organisation or check whether it is helping achieve corporate objectives - but it is much easier to see the culture of another organisation and the apparent hypnotism acted out by others.

When confronted with tasks without structure or procedure, P1 encourages behaviour that either freezes – not knowing where to start – or mindlessly follows instructions even when they are clearly failing to deliver their intended outcomes.[5]

Furthermore, P1 completes tasks one at a time, so will not want to start a new task before completing the existing one. This can be an issue when the new task has a higher priority for the needs of the workplace.

P1 appears calm and dispassionate, excellent for settling down others. But P1's lack of passion and a lack of contextual prioritising can be misinterpreted by others as a lack of interest or commitment.

People who rely heavily on their P1 function have an opportunity for growth if they are able to learn how not to get bogged down or paralysed by obstacles that fall outside the solutions provided by precedent.

P1'S INFLUENCE ON OTHER INTELLIGENCES AND ROLES

P1 rules may include those determining how an individual expresses the other Intelligences. P1 rules dictate when it is appropriate to use C1, P2, I2, I1 and C2. For example, in some cultures (P1), self-expression (C1) is not encouraged; in others (such as Australia) it is promoted almost to excess. In this way P1 has a disproportionately large influence on the formation of the infant's personality. This blurs the distinction between nature and nurture when considering how our Neuro-

---

5   Throughout more than twenty years of working with middle managers right up to senior executives, I consistently hear complaints from team leaders complaining that 'I am the only one doing the thinking' or 'My team act like children - everything needs to be constantly supervised.' These are classic signs of a team that has collapsed into P1-driven compliance (obsessive passion). This obsessive passion stands in stark contrast to what social researcher Robert J. Vallerand (2003) described as harmonious passion, where an individual is achieving their own objectives with a sense of autonomy and control. These are discussed more in Chapter 4 on the social need of Leading the Pack (P2).

P1 Affect and Social Standing

Serotonin, a chemical in the brain that is linked with the absence of anxiety, seems to be critical to the functioning of P1. Male monkeys who have made it to the leadership position in their tribe show increased serotonin in the left prefrontal lobes and a corresponding lift in mood. In contrast, monkeys who are still fighting to get to the leadership position (and higher in Leading the Pack (P2), *discussed in Chapter 4*) show decreased levels of serotonin in the left prefrontal lobes and experience much higher levels of stress (Siegel, 1999).

Limbic Type personalities are formed.[6]

Poorly Functioning P1 and Neurotic Compliance

Our research suggests that approximately 30 percent of the population default to accessing their P1 rules in a crisis. If their P1 is functioning poorly, this can lead quickly from crisis into personal neurosis. In her book, *Our Inner Conflicts* (1945), Dr Karen Horney gives a detailed description of the traits of co-dependent neurotic patients she treated as a psychiatrist. She also explains the thinking which produced their behaviour, which she classifies as *moving towards* people. People such as these clients have compulsive, neurotic needs for affection and approval, especially the need to be important to a special partner, who they expect will make them happy. This need is indiscriminate; they disregard their own feelings, desires and discrimination regarding the worth of the other, seeing only what they have in common. Indeed, they see everyone as 'nice'.

These needs arise from the person's world view; they see themselves as helpless in a hostile world, and so they seek affection from someone who they hope will protect and guide them. The person most attractive to them is usually therefore the most aggressive one.

Horney (1945) argues that this neurotic behaviour arises directly from a person's inner conflict. For the compliant type of person with a poorly functioning P1, she sees the inner conflict as having a distinct dynamic. Firstly, the person denies their need for affection, approval and acceptance. This denial is a way of dealing with their fear of becoming vulnerable or emotionally involved with others. This disconnection inevitably leads to a profoundly selfish, aggressive and 'egocentric' world view, which directly conflicts with their belief that they are loving, giving

---

6   For more detail on Neuro-Limbic Types, see Principle #2.

and affectionate people who turn themselves inside out to love whatever the cost. Finally, unaware of this internal conflict they look outside themselves for resolution. Believing that all their frenetic demands for attention and approval is authentic love and affection, the neurotically compliant type develops three dysfunctional characteristics.

Poorly Functioning P1 Thinking

The first set of characteristics initially appear to be endearing. They display sensitivity to the needs of others (especially when the needs are similar to their own), and self-denial and compliance, which they justify as unselfishness. This need is also undiscriminating. However, denying their own feelings and judgement (which may tell them that the people they pursue are untrustworthy), they make themselves believe everyone is 'nice'. This sets them up for disappointment when they become victims, which in turn fosters more insecurity.

Poorly Functioning P1 Somatic

The second set of characteristics associated with the person with a poorly functioning P1 are related to an attitude of appeasement – peace at any price. This person is too afraid and too 'nice' to show egotism, aggression or even assertion, too 'nice' to steal the limelight or compete, or even to follow their own selfish goals. They are self-effacing and sweet to everyone. If conflict arises, they avoid attack by becoming conciliatory and apologetic, and will even take the blame themselves, rather than accuse others. Once again they deny their own feelings of innocence, criticism, resentment or aggression since these are 'bad qualities'. All this appeasing is designed to draw fire away from themselves. In practice, they are setting themselves up for exploitation.

Poorly Functioning P1 Feeling

The third set of characteristics relate to a sense of worthlessness and helplessness. The neurotic person is so self-effacing and dependent on others that they are unable to enjoy their own company or their own pursuits (this is often accompanied by a poorly functioning P2 – we will look at that Intelligence later). They sense themselves as empty, as having nothing inside them. They feel weak and helpless, which becomes a self-fulfilling prophecy. They also use this stance to stave off attack, along the lines of, 'You wouldn't hurt or desert/blame/not love poor little helpless me!'

As well as feeling helpless, Horney argued that this person has a pervading sense of their own inferiority and incompetence, even in areas of obvious competence. Around aggressive or arrogant people they feel even more stupid. We have seen how childhood abuse sets people up for feelings of low self-esteem. As a result of their belief that they are worthless, such a person depends on others for their feelings of self-worth. Their self-esteem, therefore, see-saws with the feedback they get from others. Worse, any criticism or rejection by others is seen as a disaster and the poor 'victim' will turn themselves inside out to regain the person's regard. Of course this neurotic's attitudes of self-abasement and consequent insecurity and dependence on others invites exploitation and makes them particularly vulnerable when others do exploit them or even simply fail to give them all the support, appreciation and affection they crave.

It is important to remember that although we suppress unwanted emotions, they are still there and surface in subconscious behaviour. Therefore, while this neurotic type of person suppresses their inevitable feelings of egotism and self-will – their criticism, resentment, aggression and so on – these feelings are still manifested, but usually in ways which are acceptable to this person's strict code of P1 behaviour. So they will, for example, make demands out of helplessness, or control out of 'love'. Repressed anger may surface as irritability or temper tantrums, or if totally denied may affect the person's health. Occasional lapses of temper can be justified, of course, because as we have seen, the person's self-abasement and dependence can invite abuse.

Horney's research explains that the neurotic's 'good' behaviour is motivated by a desire either to avoid hostility or to avoid their need to excel[7]. In some cases, if they let others exploit them, they may be motivated by a reactive fear of their own capacity to exploit others themselves.

The sad thing about the neurotic with a poorly functioning P1 is that they mistake their compliant, affectionate feelings – which are really based on need – as real love.

They never realise how excessive and egocentric their constant demands are, and how controlling they can be in their loving. Yet for them love is everything. Nothing has meaning without it.

The reality is that because of the irrational and compulsive nature of the neurotic's drive, this 'love' which can never be satisfied becomes the sole focus of the person's attention.

There is a strange logic in the reasoning of the neurotically compliant person's world view. Love as an attachment answers all their conscious and unconscious needs: the need to like and be liked; the need to dominate (in the guise of love); the need to use their initiative and work off their aggression (on behalf of the other and so for a 'good' cause); even the need to excel (in the lover's eyes) without the stress of being out in front; and above all, the need not to have to be assertive (after all, the beloved should know what they need), or to defend themselves (because the beloved will love them for their helplessness and protect them).

All this, of course, is a vain hope. At best they will find a co-dependent

---

7   This drive is part of the Leading the Pack (P2) social cognitive need, described in Chapter 4.

relationship, which is intrinsically unhealthy anyway. Usually they remain unaware of their neurosis, and their relationships end in great pain. Feeling that they are nothing when they are alone, solitary pursuits are meaningless. This person seeks love or, if desperate, sexual intimacy, yet in reality they remain detached; they are afraid of being emotionally involved (Horney, 1945).

The only way out for the compulsively compliant person is first of all to recognise their inner conflict – their repressed attributes of aggression and even destructiveness, their egocentricity (the repressed P2 Intelligence) and 'victim' mentality versus their kindness and caring thoughtfulness for others. They need to be aware and observe the polarities, and hold them, both 'good' and 'bad' in their awareness – not with a view to resolving the conflict, but to reconcile the two opposite intentions, to accept them and live with them and the energy they generate.

From Cradle to Grave: The Impact of P1 Over a Lifetime

How can rules embedded in the P1 Intelligence so young have such a strong impact on adult life? I have found one of the most effective lenses to help understand this is an approach which first became popular in the mid 1970s, called Transactional Analysis or TA. In 1976, Thomas Harris published the book *I'm OK You're OK* , which popularised the Transactional Analysis school of thought that had been developed by renowned New York Freudian psychiatrist, Dr Eric Berne. In many ways this book was one of the first attempts to translate insights from neuroscience into a practical interpretation of internal conflicts and lived experience.

In his book, published long before neuroscientists had access to today's sophisticated fMRI brain imaging technologies, Harris argued that there is an information highway that connects the left prefrontal lobe (which early evidence suggested was linked to P1) and the right temporal lobe (which had been linked to immediate emotional experience). This, was how he explained the observation that family rules stored in the P1 Intelligence don't feel to the individual like an injunction or a memory from the past; instead, they feel as if they are happening right here, right now. He then proposed that scripting, dreams or direct downloading, and experience feel equally immediate and real because they are experienced through parts of the right temporal lobe that are focused on the present moment. To explore this a little deeper, it is useful to have a high level of understanding of the principles of the theory of Transactional Analysis.

In his clinical work, psychiatrist and author Dr Eric Berne observed that every person carries inside them three parts (or aspects of themselves) that seem to emerge quite separately in real time as the person interacts with others. As Harris (1976) explains:

*[A]s you watch and listen to people you can see them change before
your eyes. It is a total kind of change. There are simultaneous changes
in facial expression, vocabulary, gestures, posture and body functions,
which may cause the face to flush, the heart to pound, or the breathing
to become rapid ...*

*Changes from one state to another are apparent in manner,
appearance, words, and gestures... Continual observation has
supported the assumption that these three states exist in all people.
It is as if in each person there is the same little person he was when
he was three years old. There are also within him his own parents.
These are recordings in the brain as actual experiences of internal
and external events, the most significant of which happened during
the first five years of life. There is a third state, different from these
two. The first two are called Parent and Child, and the third, Adult.*

*These states of being are not roles but psychological realities. Berne says
that Parent, Adult, and Child are not concepts like superego, ego, and id
but phenomenological realities. The state is produced by the playback of
recorded data of events in the past, involving real people, real times, real
places, real decisions and real feelings. (pp. 16-18)*

This concept has direct relevance to three of the Intelligences. Briefly, the Parent
state is the articulation of P1. The Child state is the articulation of C1 and the Adult is
the articulation of the adult Neuro-Rational Type[8] (which starts to emerge as the child
individuates and develops their P2 Intelligence). Harris explains the P1 Parent in more
depth:

*The Parent is a huge collection of recordings in the brain of imposed,
unquestioned external events perceived by a person between birth and
age five (a taught concept of life).*

*The name Parent is most descriptive of this data inasmuch as the most
significant 'tapes' are those provided by the example and pronouncements
of a person's own parents or parent substitutes. Everything the child saw
his parents do and everything he heard them say is recorded in the Parent.
Everyone has a Parent and each Parent is specific for every person, being
the recording of that set of early experiences unique to him. Interestingly*

8   The Neuro-Rational Types are our higher order, conscious personalities that form when we
     access three Intelligences simultaneously (a phenomenon known as parallel processing).
     This gives rise to a unique world view and Area of Mastery that is invaluable in the team
     context. For more detail about the Neuro-Rational Types, see Principle # 2.

the data was recorded straight without editing. (1976, pp. 18-19)

The child takes in all the information uncritically because he or she is too young, too dependent and does not possess the language skills to be able to analyse, edit or explain its meaning critically.

Harris continues:

> *In the Parent are recorded all the admonitions and rules and laws that the child heard from his parents and saw in their living. They range all the way from the earliest parental communications, interpreted non-verbally through tone of voice, facial expression, cuddling or non-cuddling, to the more elaborate verbal rules or regulations espoused by the parents as the little person became able to understand words. In this set of recordings are the thousands of 'nos' directed at the toddler, the directed 'don'ts' that bombarded him. They are recorded as the truth from the source of all security, the people who are six feet tall. A time when it is important to a two foot tall child that he please and obey them. It is a permanent recording. A person cannot erase it. It is available for replay throughout life. This replay is a powerful influence throughout life. These examples – coercing, forcing, sometimes permissive but more often restrictive – are rigidly internalised as a voluminous set of data essential to the individual's survival in the setting of a group, beginning with the family, and extending throughout life in a succession of groups necessary to life.*
>
> (1976, pp. 19-21)

However, when the recording in the Parent is inconsistent, as when the child's parent says one thing and does the opposite, or when the two parents disagree in their rules, and the recording is discordant, the child becomes confused or fearful. In these cases the P1 is weakened or fragmented, and the rules in this area will not be a strong positive influence in the person's life (Harris, 1976).

Included in the vast amount of Parent data are all the 'how to' instructions: how to hit a nail, eat soup, shake hands or pretend no one's at home. This data is useful as long as it is relevant to the real world of the person. It is our task as adults to take another look at and sift through these instructions for relevance to our current world view.

Throughout life, whenever a person consciously focuses on something, the brain lays down memories as vivid, specific and detailed as a video tape recording, often stored in the unconscious mind. These memories are stored in the temporal cortex, which is the part of the brain used when the person is making meaning of current events. That's why past events can impact on the meaning given to present events. The memory is complete and intact even if the person is unaware of and unable to

Do Babies Pick Up Stress?

An infant will experience trauma if they are separated from parents, looking into the eyes of a depressed mother, or are in a household with a high level of marital tension (Cogill, Caplan, Alexandra, Robson and Kumar, 1986; Lupien et al., 2009). This was discovered by monitoring the chemical changes within an infant's body that indicate a stress response (Gunnar, 1992).

More recently, neuroimaging studies have confirmed that even when asleep, infants' brains showed distinct patterns of activity corresponding to different emotional tones and that tension at home has a lasting impact on brain responses. Compared with babies raised in healthy homes, infants in high-conflict homes (as reported by their mothers) had a greater response to angry voices in brain regions involved in stress and emotion regulation — the rostral anterior cingulated cortex, the caudate, the thalamus and the hypothalamus (Graham et al., 2013). Children from chronically high-conflict families have less gray and white matter in the anterior cingulate cortex (an important area for social cognition and regulating our stress responses), and this reduction predicted poorer performance on spatial memory tasks (Hanson et al., 2012).

voluntarily recall it. Amazingly, these memories can be involuntarily evoked at any time by stimuli such as sound, sight or smell.

For example, if the event was recorded when the person was five years old, if it is later triggered, they relive the event as a five-year-old. This means they simultaneously experience the past event together with the current event with all the feelings of the five-year-old. For that moment, the person is back in the original event with exactly the same feelings they had at the time the brain recorded it. Further, the person gives the event the same meaning as they did when the tape was laid down. So when accessing P1, the reason the rules seem vital is because the event relating to the source of the rules feels as if it is happening in real time – right now (Harris, 1976).

P1 AND TRANSACTIONAL ANALYSIS (TA)

Transactional Analysis (TA) also provides a useful and accurate model for analysing our interactions with others. Harris (1976) outlines Berne's definition of TA as follows:

The unit of social intercourse is called a transaction. If two or more

The Attachment Window

The repeated activation of specific neuronal pathways creates, reinforces and strengthens connections between groups of neurons and consequently macro systems within the brain. Neurons that do not get activated are not reinforced and can eventually die away completely.

Researchers learned early on that there are critical periods in development, like 'windows of opportunity', during which our environment has a vital impact on the development of specific functions. For instance, when kittens are raised in an environment that gives them no exposure to horizontal lines within a specific critical period of their development, then their visual cortex does not develop the capacity to process such visual input later in life (Hubel, 1967). Similarly, infants who are not exposed to any spoken language are dramatically impaired in their ability to acquire normal linguistic functions after the first few years of life (Schuman, 1997).

In a similar way, infants who have poor or absent attachment relationships (such as an infant in an orphanage that lacks sufficient staff so that attachments do not develop) before the end of their third year of life may find it extremely difficult to form attachments later in life and ever feel secure (Bowlby, 1988; Colin, 1996).

people encounter each other.... Sooner or later one of them will speak, or give some indication of acknowledging the presence of others. This is called the transactional stimulus. Then another person will say or do something which is in some way related to the stimulus, and that is called a transactional response.

Transactional Analysis is the method of examining this one transaction wherein 'I do something and you do something back' and determining which part of the multiple-natured individual is being activated.

As we have seen, the three parts of the individual are the Parent (P1), the Child (C1), and the Adult (the Neuro-Rational Type).[9] It is a useful exercise to analyse our

9   In some cases, however, the individual's narrative about themselves is focused not around their Neuro-Rational Type but rather on their more reactive selves. When this happens, the Adult part of the self is more likely to reflect the individual's P2 Intelligence than their Neuro-Rational Type, and the content of this P2 reaction will depend on how the individual unconsciously balanced the competing needs and scripting of their Parent and Child selves. Regardless of how sophisticated this management strategy was, a key developmental step

incidents of conflict by using TA. In this way we can discern when we lapse into our Parent (P1) or our Child (C1) or are accessing our Adult.

TRAUMAS AND ABUSE IN INFANCY CAN IMPACT P1 DEVELOPMENT

If the infant's basic needs are not met – if they are not nurtured and nourished and they don't feel safe – the child will have a sense that the world is hostile and not to be trusted. This can negatively impact on subsequent stages of their development.

Childhood traumas such as abuse, accidents or even illnesses can damage a formerly highly functioning P1, since the child's survival is threatened.

Early traumatic experiences also impact on biochemical levels and neuroanatomical networking. Prenatal stress may result in permanent alterations in dopamine activity and cerebral lateralisation, making infants more susceptible to anxiety and limiting their functioning well into adulthood (Field et al., 1988). This can create a tendency to dissociate and disconnect various elements of processing, and a bias towards unintegrated information processing across conscious awareness, sensation, affect and behaviour. General dissociative defence mechanisms result in an aberrant organisation of neural networks of memory. If the child is frightened, it results in deficits of affect regulation, attachment and executive functioning (van der Kolk et al., 1996). The malfunctioning of these interdependent mental systems results in many disorders. Compulsive disorders related to eating or gambling, borderline personality disorder, and self-harm can all reflect complex adaptation to infant trauma (Saxe et al., 1994; van der Kolk et al., 1996).

Judith (1996) argues that the survival instinct is part of being human and that when an infant's needs are satisfied, they can develop a well-functioning P1. In this situation, their survival instinct, instead of putting their senses on red-alert, will retreat into the background of their consciousness.

However, when the developing infant's survival instinct is constantly threatened, as happens when they live in a violent or chaotic environment, their P1 is damaged. Hence they grow up with a pervasive sense of insecurity. They may have recurring issues related to survival, such as housing, work, health or money. Judith's research suggests that the following traumas suffered in childhood can affect the individual's development, even into adulthood:

Birth traumas: There is a whole generation of people for whom the birth experience was traumatic. Born under glaring lights, they were immediately separated from their mother for the first week of life, except for the brief periods of feeding. Worse, baby boys were circumcised without being anaesthetised.

---

for the individual involves shifting from a reactive 'Adult' position (which is emotional and driven by the limbic system) to the more considered, rational and mature world view of their Neuro-Rational Type.

Children who experienced a traumatic birth almost always have increased P1-related issues, such as being more likely to cry, being needy and having various health issues. If the parent does not respond to the pleas and cries from the child, the child may not learn to invite the positive support it needs.

Incubators: If an infant is put into an incubator from birth they are denied the mother's touching and suckling. This can result in an adult feeling a sense of distance and isolation in relation to others.

Abandonment: Physical or emotional abandonment influences the infant's survival. A child needs the mother's touch. Institutionalised babies who have been deprived of touch often die. However, any separation from parents is traumatic for a young child, especially if it is for more than a day or so. A lengthy time in hospital, long holidays or divorce can be traumatic, especially if the child does not receive extra attention. Similarly, adopted babies are abandoned for a time and the new parents should give them more than the usual amount of care to compensate.

Abandonment in the formative years often creates an over-reliance on P1, with the individual overcompensating by clinging to security, food, loved ones or routine. The person will cling to money or an unsatisfactory situation for fear of being alone or desperate. Without trust in life, they fear change. For others, abandonment as a child causes them to abandon themselves as adults. For instance, they abandon a course, a project, or even their body, forgetting to care for it. Abandonment can also be seen as including neglect, which often results in an inability to trust others or treat oneself well.

Feeding difficulties: Poor nourishment or difficulty with breast feeding or eating can have a lasting impact. It can result in adult problems with food, allergies, addictions or avoidance, or digestive problems. It can also cause wider nourishment issues such as lack of partaking in friendships or intellectual or creative stimulation.

Physical abuse: Since the abuse usually comes from the home, physical abuse leads to the child living in fear. This can stimulate stress hormones, which in turn may lead the child to become addicted to abnormally high levels of these hormones in order to overcome the numbness from the body. In extreme cases, the person may become accident-prone or create crises in order to feel the familiar pain, sense of stress and chemical response.

Accidents, surgeries and illnesses: These traumatic events can seriously damage a previously highly functioning P1. They can cause problems with P1 issues such as sleeping, eating, concentrating and persevering or even sitting still, or may lead to an unconscious but pervasive sense of fear.

Inherited traumas: These can be passed unconsciously from parents to their children through injunctions or the child's vicarious experience of the parent's responses to the world. Hence, even though they have not experienced the traumas directly, the children can grow up with pervasive insecurity or lack a sense of trust in the world.

Depressed parents: Chronically stressed or depressed mothers give birth to depressed children. Tiffany Field and colleagues found that infants of mothers who were depressed during the baby's first year of life demonstrate biochemical, physiological and behavioural dysregulation. These infants show more neurophysiological and behavioural signs of stress and depression, including greater activation in their right frontal lobes, higher heart rates, higher levels of norepinephrine, lower vagal tone, and higher cortisol levels (Field, 1997; Field et al., 1988).

THE LEGACY OF TRAUMAS AND ABUSES

Doctors and counsellors are constantly working with unhappy or dysfunctional people damaged by childhood traumas or abuses. Judith (1996) offers a compelling list of P1-related issues that arise from poorly functioning P1:

- **Poor boundaries (P1 Feeling):** One general effect is an inability to create appropriate boundaries – to know, for example, when one has had enough food, or drink, or time with another person. The person is unable to leave, because

The Impact of Poorly Functioning P1

Impulsive behaviours and thoughts, disconnected from self-reflective processes, often serve the purpose of avoiding awareness of unaddressed feelings and needs (Miller, Alvarez and Miller, 1990). For those with poorly functioning P1, the experience of the inner world is paired with discomfort, sadness, isolation and shame from a time before conscious awareness. Psychologist Louis Cozolino (2002) describes imperfect attachment formation as resulting in individuals with an inability to be alone. These adults come to therapy with reports of despair and emptiness unconnected to any event, and often is despite a seemingly successful life. Their lives show patterns of insecure attachments, based on achievement, which of course, had to be continually increased. Constant activity meant they never relaxed. Time alone or unoccupied allowed the return of uneasy feelings, so they kept themselves distracted by busyness.

they never had enough closeness as a child and they are still trying to fill the gap. Co-dependence is another example of an inability to set appropriate boundaries.

- A second general effect of childhood trauma is a mind-body split (**P1 Thinking**). The mind concentrates on intellectual, creative or imaginative engagement and does not listen to the body or the person's own emotions. Consequently the individual ignores their own needs, often while experiencing an ongoing sense that something is wrong.

- A third general effect of a damaged P1 is to make **the body an object (P1 Somatic)** alienated from the self. In this case the body is seen as a thing to be mastered and controlled, to be shaped even as an ornament, rather than a living expression of who we are.

Early trauma results in the adult questioning the value of life. This cynicism extends to their attitude to accepted norms and values.

The key underlying theme, however, for all P1 issues is a sense of fear or terror. This is the antithesis of highly functioning P1, which provides the individual with a sense of safety and security. If a person is living amidst danger or impoverishment, they must be constantly vigilant. If this state continues over time, it is likely to affect the stressed person's health, resulting in such ailments as high blood pressure, insomnia, chronic fatigue or problems with heart, stomach, adrenal glands and their immune system (Judith, 1996).

ISSUES WITH P1 FUNCTIONING

Poorly functioning P1 is caused by either insufficient or excessive use of the Intelligence:

Under-reliance on P1: A person with a deficiency or under-reliance on P1 is not much interested in their body. They are primarily focused on activities of their mind – fantasies, dreams, knowledge or spirituality. Consequently they may have little interest in daily life, including grooming, hygiene or dress, and are likely to be restless and have difficulty concentrating. Their mind is often not present in the here and now. In short, they have a mind-body split. This person will benefit from grounding exercises.

Over-reliance on P1: A person with excess or over-reliance on P1 likes routine to the point of being so afraid of change that they are inflexible. They are interested in security, possessions and incremental financial gain. They are likely to be interested in their appearance and meticulous in habits and grooming. In their thinking they prefer to focus on the concrete rather than abstract ideas. They are likely to have strict boundaries. This person will benefit from physical movement, such as dancing, swimming or yoga.

Further insight can be gathered by identifying which component of the Intelligence the individual relies on to excess: the somatic, feeling or thinking aspects.[10]

Somatic Over-Reliance on P1: Those who have an over-reliance on somatic P1 tend to obsess about doing things the way they have always been done. This is linked to implicit procedural memory and is largely outside conscious awareness.

Feeling Over-Reliance on P1: Those who have a high degree of focus on the feeling aspect of P1 concentrate on being accepted within the group and focus on drawing the group together in a way that maintains the current power structure. This individual can be particularly obsessed with bonding with and looking after the leader of the tribe.

Thinking Over-Reliance on P1: If an individual focuses more on thinking P1 than the feeling or somatic aspects, they can become obsessed with the risks facing the group. This can lead to paranoia and anxiety and is accompanied by heightened awareness of the internal social politics of the group. The combination of these two characteristics often results in the development of sophisticated but nonetheless spurious conspiracy theories.

Strengthening your Relatedness (P1) as an Adult
REVISITING OUR ANCESTRAL BASE

The P1 Intelligence, our first stage of development, is grounded firmly in our roots, which my ancestral heritage, the Celts, associated with the element earth. Our roots are our family or our tribe, which give us nurture and care. Also, according to many traditional cultures, we are rooted in the earth, which gives us sustenance and shelter. These constitute our primary needs for survival. As we grow up, in order to develop autonomy and the free will to follow our own goals, we feel the need to distance ourselves from our family. For some people, there needs to be a time of complete separation.

However, although we may believe we have severed ourselves from our roots, they are still there in our unconscious and this can affect our behaviour. We need to bring our roots into our conscious awareness, to uncover and examine our past and reclaim our ancestral base in order to again feel the groundedness of the tribe.

Grounding brings us into the here and now and connects us to the environment, giving us focus and strength. Judith's (1996) research found that the basic rights of

---

10 Each of these reflects a particular Neuro-Limbic Type; the One, Two and Six respectively. These relate to *NeuroPower* Principle # 2 and are explored in detail in Principle #2.

P1 are the right to be here and to have what we need for survival. We need to reclaim our right to be here, to learn to ground ourselves and to nourish ourselves if we are to do the work of reclaiming our roots.

A significant finding of the Adult Attachment Interview (AAI) is that exposure to trauma or loss during childhood is not the key determining factor in attachment. What does appear to matter more critically is the coherence of the narrative created. This strongly suggests that the processing, working through and integration of childhood experiences is the most significant variable in a parent's ability to provide a safe haven for their children. It is through this *earned autonomy*, by a parent healing their own wounds, that the transmitting of negative attachment patterns is stopped from one generation to the next (Siegel, 1999).

Judith suggests that it is important to realise that with the security and grounding that P1 gives, comes the acceptance of our own personal limitations and the strength of family or community.

CREATING A HIGHLY FUNCTIONING P1

Diagram 2.1 shows the three aspects of P1 that require integration so that true Tribal Loyalty can form.

Due to family upbringing, socialisation, genetic disposition or individual tendencies, you may have a thinking, feeling or somatic understanding of P1 rather than a highly functioning P1 that shows on all three aspects.

Compare your own experience with Diagram 2.1. Which aspects of P1 are you more aware of – the thinking, feeling or somatic? Is there one that you tend to focus on above the other two?

- The P1 somatic element is expressed in even, measured movements and a strong sense of physical *grounding* or being present.
- The P1 feeling element involves a sense of contentment and pride.
- The P1 thinking element is one of logic and sequential thinking, overriding unacceptable social responses, and anticipating and managing risk for the tribe.

INTEGRATION TASK

It is the task of the adult to examine and update their P1 data file. However, when the rules given by the child's parents were reinforced with words such as 'never' and 'always', and accompanied by a high degree of intensity, it may be too uncomfortable and stressful for the person to revisit them. In this case, the imperatives may persist long after the rules have become archaic, resulting either in prejudices, or quirky or compulsive adult behaviour.

When you have an over-reaction to an event it could be that you have triggered some unresolved event from childhood. You may need to examine these unconscious P1 beliefs

Diagram 2.1 Healthy P1 Intelligence — Noble Quality: Tribal Loyalty

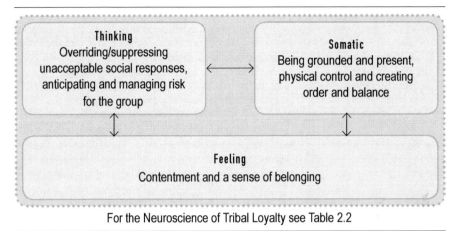

Thinking		Somatic
Overriding/suppressing unacceptable social responses, anticipating and managing risk for the group	⟷	Being grounded and present, physical control and creating order and balance

Feeling
Contentment and a sense of belonging

For the Neuroscience of Tribal Loyalty see Table 2.2

from the adult experience of your conscious Neuro-Rational Type.[11]

According to Myss (1996), key questions to ask yourself are:

- 'Do these rules all hold water and are they aligned with my new level of awareness?'

- 'Where are these rules coming from?'

- 'Are they coming from my parents, or history, or are they relevant now?'

In first-order consciousness the whole personality forms around one or two Intelligences. When P1 is at the lowest level of consciousness, rules are to be taken literally and obeyed, not interpreted. At second-order consciousness (i.e. from the perspective of your Neuro-Rational Type), the objective is to contextualise the P1 Intelligence, not ignore it or let it run rampant.

The task of integrating P1 involves embracing your family heritage and unifying it with your chosen life path. Whenever you feel unreasonably aggressive, it is advisable to consider whether someone is breaking your family or tribal rules. Whenever you experience that unmistakable sense of knowing something is absolutely right, beware! The source may well be unexamined family rules.

---

11 To explore your Neuro-Rational Type, see Principle #3.

Table 2.2 The Neuroscience of Tribal Loyalty

The table below details the Neuroscience of P1. Refer to Appendix 13 for more details.

Somatic Aspect	Feeling Aspect	Thinking Aspect
• Embedding learned rules into implict (unconscious) procedural memory (orbitofrontal cortex, dorsolateral prefrontal cortex and striatum; Pascual-Leone et al., 1996; Saling & Phillips, 2007)	• Feelings of loneliness or panic if isolated from the group (either physically or socially) (dorsal anterior cingulate cortex and anterior insula; pituitary-induced increases in cortisol and progesterone (Eisenberger & Lieberman, 2004; Brown et al., 2009)	• Suppressing/ disrupting unwanted cognitive, affective or behavioural responses (frontal cortex and left prefrontal cortex)
• Automatic habitual response without thought (ACC, posterior rostral cingulate zone and dorsolateral prefrontal cortex)	• Aversion to risk and uncertainty (dorsal prefrontal cortex; Xue et al., 2009)	• Applying 'if-then' rules given to us by others (lateral prefrontal cortex; Berkman & Lieberman in Moskowitz & Grant, 2009)
• Coordination of smooth, timed and rhythmic movements (primary motor cortex, basal ganglia)	• Preference for fairness (midbrain dopaminergic reward regions; Tabibna & Lieberman, 2007)	• Focusing on 'ought' goals based on social roles and expectations (precuneus and posterior cingulate cortex, in particular right prefrontal cortex; Strauman et al., 2013; Amodio et al., 2004)
• Selection and coordination of movements (basal ganglia)	• Homeostasis/Neutrality – maintained by serotonin; influenced by e.g. valium and other anti-anxiety drugs which increase the ability of GABA inhibitory neurons to prevent excitatory transmission (sent by the cortex to settle down the amygdala)	
• Making associations that may promote our survival (anterior insula and orbitofrontal cortex)	• Positive emotions associated with social acceptance and belonging – through endorphins (opium-like hormones that stimulate well-being; Eisenberger, 2008)	• Applying simple moral rules to determine socially appropriate behaviour (ventromedial prefrontal cortex; Moll et al., 2005; FeldmanHalll, Mobbs & Dalgleish, 2013)
• Priming, conditioning and skill-learning (striatum, cerebellum and brainstem)	• Emotion is felt by the body, monitored by brain areas placed at several levels of the central nervous system (e.g. singular cortices, hypothalamus, tegmentum) and interpreted by the cortex (lateral and polar parts of frontal lobe). Activity in the prefrontal cortex increases and decreases respectively with feelings of acceptance and rejection	
• Somatic markers – access to information about the best way forward based on past experience, focusing on safety (circuits linking posterior sensory cortices, temporal and parietal regions with prefrontal circuits)		

Highly Functioning P1 in Adult Life

The noble quality of Tribal Loyalty requires the integration of the thinking aspect of cultural logic, the feeling aspect of calmness and the somatic aspect of physical strength and control.[12] This sense of Tribal Loyalty is critical in teams and is a key characteristic of High Performance Teams.

Tribal Loyalty arises from a sense of membership of a tribal group or community. This is expressed when the individual identifies with and feels a sense of obligation to the common good of the tribe. This will include a sense of the individual's own good, but will stretch beyond the self and encompass the interests of others in the group.

An individual with these strengths has a strong sense of duty, works for the good of the group rather than for personal gain, is loyal to the tribe or collective, and can be trusted to pull his or her weight. This capability will be expressed through active involvement in civic affairs in the community. This noble quality embraces public interest over self-interest.

There are three elements of Tribal Loyalty:

1. **Social responsibility** to members of the 'tribe': An orientation to helping others even when there is nothing to be gained from them.

2. **Loyalty:** An unwavering commitment to and a bond of trust with the members of the group.

3. **Team work:** An ability to work with others in a group for a common purpose – to collaborate and cooperate.

Aristotle, writing in ancient Greece about small city-states comprised mostly of related individuals, describes this Tribal Loyalty as a network of friends bound together by the pursuit of a common good. According to Aristotle:

> *The man who is isolated – who is unable to share in the benefits of political association, or has no need to share because he is already self-sufficient – is no part of the polis, and must therefore be either a beast or a god.*

Embedded in this noble quality there is a sense of reciprocity, an implicit understanding that if the community cares about an individual, that individual will respond by respecting the cultural norms and adhering to the common good of the community. Eccles and Gootman (2002) found empirical evidence to support the importance of loyalty with troubled youth whose expression of the noble quality

---

12 Peterson and Seligman's meta-study of the most widely influential traditions of thought and religion in human history found Tribal Loyalty to be a significant human strength (Peterson and Seligman, 2004).

positively changed their personal behaviour towards their community.

HOW P1 TRIBAL LOYALTY MEETS THE NOBILITY CRITERIA

Tribal Loyalty can answer key questions of existence related to the right of the individual to live. This noble quality also enables the individual to accept that their own survival is no more important than the survival of their family. The individual learns how to be valued for who they are, their heritage, their family's future and the unconditional love that this commitment brings.

Tribal Loyalty is appealing to express. Individuals yearn to be a valued member of their family and the community. To be unconditionally loved by family members and to be able to contribute rates highly on life satisfaction surveys. Individuals report that using loyalty to resolve an internal tension has a paradigm shift impact on their lives.

When leaders are able to create an environment in which Tribal Loyalty flourishes, team members feel safe, secure and committed to a team on which they know they can rely. This is the first characteristic of a High Performance Team.

I got support from this community and I decided to chip in,
to help my community change with the times.
If you don't serve your community,
then you don't plow anything back.

Sam Nzima,
a South African freedom fighter

P1 Toolbox

THE IMPORTANCE OF P1 IN BUILDING HIGH PERFORMANCE TEAMS

P1 Tribal Loyalty, ensures the survival of the organisation even at the cost of personal autonomy or individual status.

When Tribal Loyalty is absent, individuals in the team think only of themselves. In the absence of highly functioning P1, personal agendas replace organisational aspirations and objectives. The workplace becomes a 'dog eat dog' world – every person for themselves, preoccupied with watching their own backs. No one is safe and the survival of the organisation is threatened.

However, when P1 is functioning highly in the organisation, team members think beyond their own personal survival to provide genuine help to others in the team. In this way, standards of organisational welfare are established and individuals can feel secure in the knowledge that they are safe and valued.

Leaders looking to increase the functioning of P1 in their team can increase Tribal Loyalty by applying the following P1 techniques and tools.

P1 QUESTIONS FOR PERSONAL DEVELOPMENT AND SELF REFLECTION

The best high performing teams are made up of individuals who have focused on their own personal development. The following questions can be used as a starting point for those leaders looking to improve their P1.

In this exercise, you can survey how rules functioned in your family's life. Many of these rules will be implicit (i.e. not top of mind). Your task is to recall them and then, if necessary, update them.

1. Make a list of five rules, spoken or unspoken, that you remember from your childhood and adolescence.

2. Write your responses to these rules, giving examples or recounting vivid incidents:

    a. Who made the rules in your family?
    b. How were the rules enforced?
    c. How easy or hard was it to change the rules?
    d. How were you affected by your family's rules as a child? How have you either kept them or changed them as an adult?

3. Write directly and simply whatever message you most want to convey about trust, hope, and possibility to the child you were somewhere between birth and three. Notice and express whatever you feel as you write, and finish with some comments and reflections about the short message you've written.

4. How important is control to you? (Do you thrive on chaos?)

5. Was your family life chaotic and out-of-control, fairly stable and orderly, or overly controlled and rigid?

6. Did you learn as a child that keeping control of a situation was one way to be safe? Explain.

7. Has your family life stance about control worked well for you?

P1 TOOL #1:
DEVELOP YOUR TEAM'S VALUE PROPOSITION

HOW THIS RELATES TO P1

If there is no shared understanding of the value of your team, members are not secure that the team, as a group, will survive. This results in limited commitment. Conversely, when the value of the team is clear and shared, team members feel the team's future is secure and are willing and wanting to commit to achieving the team's objectives.

PROCESS

1. Write a **list of the benefits** – technical, economic, service and social benefits – that your team brings to your customers (virtual or actual customers).

2. **Classify each benefit** as either a:

   a. **Point of parity:** Elements that have essentially the same performance or functionality as those of the next best alternative (i.e. your closest competitors);

   b. **Point of difference:** Elements that make your offering either superior or inferior to the next best alternative; or

   c. **Point of contention:** Elements about which there might be some debate about how your performance or functionality compares with the next best alternative. You might see it as a point of difference in your favour, but your customers might see it as a point of parity. The reverse may also be true.

3. If necessary, conduct an **opinion audit** to validate your initial assessment regarding how your team compares with others.

4. Once you've consolidated your team's value proposition (VP) (based on your main points of difference), you may need to conduct **shareholder research** in your key target markets to assess whether your team's VP resonates with others and is commercially appealing. Review and revise the team VP as necessary.

5. Use this VP as the basis for communication with all stakeholders. **Review the ongoing appropriateness** of your team's VP at least every six months.

P1 Tool # 1

DOS

✓ Do be prepared to use the VP development process as an opportunity for review. Chances are, if you don't have clear points of differences between your team and others, your commercial viability may be uncertain. Use the process to think laterally about how you might expand your operations to increase points of difference hat matter to your internal or external customers.

DON'TS

✗ Don't assume either that your customers will automatically presume the benefits of your team, or that it will be enough simply to state the benefits. This may work sometimes, but the gold standard you should aim for is to demonstrate to your internal or external customers how you offer superior value compared to the next best alternative.

P1 TOOL #2:
CLARIFY EACH TEAM MEMBER'S ROLE AND GIVE FEEDBACK ON HOW THEY ARE GOING

HOW THIS RELATES TO P1

If the individual has poor attachment, this exercise enables them to feel they have a legitimate right to be a member of the team - and that they are valued for the role they play.

PROCESS

1. **Identify the format of the meeting** – decide whether you will conduct individual one-on-one meetings, or review with the wider team as a whole.

2. **Prepare for the meeting**:

   a. **Schedule the meeting** with the employee(s). Allocate between one hour and two and a half hours, depending upon your observations of how things have been going and how much clarification is needed.

   b. **Arrange a venue**. Make sure there's enough room for comfort, and that you'll have access to a whiteboard and flip chart.

   c. Inform the employee that in preparation for the review, they'll need to conduct an **employee self-assessment of their work performance** and bring with them a list of the things that they would like to either keep doing, stop doing and start doing in relation to their job (a 'Keep, Stop, Start').

   d. **Review the employee's role and responsibilities document**. If there isn't one, write one so that you can bring it with you to the meeting.

   e. Based on both their role document and your observations, prepare your own **Keep, Stop, Start** suggestions.

3. **Conduct the meeting**. Use the roles and responsibilities document and the Keep, Stop, Starts (yours and theirs) as a starting point for the discussion. The aim of the meeting is to ensure that there is mutual clarity about what is expected of the employee, how they are currently tracking against those expectations, what needs to change for them to fulfil their role and responsibilities and how that performance can be tracked. Make sure that you provide positive feedback about their performance (include those items in the 'Keep' list) as well as areas for improvement. By the end of the meeting, there should be agreement about all aspects of the employee's role and a documented action plan for making any necessary changes moving forward.

P1 Tool #2

4. **Set a date for review**. When you inform the employee of the review date, simultaneously provide them with a copy of the record from the review session.

5. **Track progress** to ensure that there are no holes in the process (i.e. the individual team member's performance is not being impeded by other external factors).

DOS

✓ Do use the employee's roles and responsibilities document to highlight any ways in which they are not performing their role.

✓ Do use the review meeting as an opportunity to explore the hidden talents and aspirations of your staff.

✓ Do consider conducting a skills audit if you are concerned about competency levels. You might also consider this option if you suspect the employee is overqualified by their current position, and may contribute more value in another role.

DON'TS

✗ Don't use hearsay comments as the basis for negative feedback. Either comment from first-hand experience or investigate all issues thoroughly before raising them with the employee.

✗ Don't allow the aspirations of the employee to become the focus of the meeting. Although it's helpful information for you to have as their leader (particularly if they have a specific plan for moving either sideways or upwards), the aim of the session is for them to leave with clarity about what's expected of them now, not where they'd like to be in the future.

P1 TOOL #3:
DEVELOP YOUR OWN LEADERSHIP CODE OF CONDUCT

HOW THIS RELATES TO P1

Every member of your team comes from a different family background with different rules. It is important to have one set of explicit rules encoded in a code of conduct to create a sense of tribal loyalty and minimise unnecessary conflict. Start with your own code of conduct as a leader and then facilitate a session to create one for the team.

PROCESS

1. **Write a list of your strengths and weaknesses.** Then write a paragraph summarising your **signature gift** and how you use it in daily life.

2. Write a list of your **top 10 current key objectives**.

3. **Identify your six key leadership behaviours** – the qualities you want to establish as foundational attributes of your leadership style.

4. **Link your leadership behaviours to the achievement of your objectives**. Use the following sentence construction: 'I will ... (behaviour) ... so that ... (outcome)...'. For example, 'I will focus my attention and keep the end goal in mind so that I can reduce my wasted time and complete my Tax Return by July 7'. This creates a very clear cause and effect statement with results that can be measured.

   Make sure that all your leadership behaviours link to your objectives. Although there may be many other 'nice' qualities that you want to embody, they don't belong on this list. As a team leader, you need to learn how to be both a person of character and a yielder of great results – and your Leadership Code of Conduct needs to reflect both.

5. **Focus on cultivating these qualities** over the next three months. Place your Leadership Code of Conduct in a prominent place – somewhere that you'll see it a number of times each day (e.g. noticeboard, ruler insert in a filofax, screensaver on your computer or mobile). Continually review the extent to which you are embodying these qualities in daily interactions and remind yourself that they are the key to helping you achieve your objectives.

DOS

✓ Do see your six key behaviours as the life principles you've chosen as your 'true north'.

✓ Do remember that, as the saying goes, *'If you're not achieving your own objectives, you're probably achieving someone else's.'*

DON'TS

✗ Don't rush this process. Make sure you give yourself enough time to identify the six key qualities that genuinely reflect the leader you want to be.

✗ Don't forget about your Code of Conduct once it's written. Review it on a daily basis, and constantly self-assess how well you measure up against the standard you've set for yourself. Develop strategies for how you could incorporate these qualities more fully into your daily life.

KEY RELATEDNESS QUESTIONS FOR BUILDING A HIGH PERFORMANCE TEAM

1. What is the purpose of your team? What value does it add to the business?

2. How does your team interact with the rest of the organisation?

3. What is your own role within the team? How do you contribute to the team?

4. If the team is to deliver its work, what role do you want your leader to play? What should s/he keep doing, stop doing, start doing?

5. For the team to deliver on its purpose, what ground rules do you need to have in place for working together? What needs to go in the team's Code of Conduct?

6. How will you keep each other accountable and provide feedback on behaviour that is outside of the Code of Conduct? How might this work on a practical level?

Key P1 Questions for High Performance Teams

THE IDEA IN ACTION

ORGANISATIONAL CASE STUDY #1: STATE HEALTH HAND HYGIENE PROJECT

The Task: To improve compliance by health workers with hand hygiene practice.

Recap:

In 2007, an Australian state health department wanted to address the serious threat that health-associated infections posed to hospital patients. Micro-organisms are readily transmitted on the hands of health care workers. In Australia alone, health officials estimate that up to 7000 people die annually from hand hygiene-related infections in hospitals. The economic burden is also considerable, costing millions each year.

Hand hygiene has been proven to substantially reduce transmission of micro-organisms. However, despite well-established guidelines, compliance throughout the world with hygiene standards is concerningly low. International and national health agencies have been grappling with how to deal with the issue for some time, and few interventions have had any impact whatsoever, despite both European and US hospitals and governments spending tens of millions of dollars on communications, incentives, closed circuit TV and education.

Since research demonstrated that the hand hygiene issue centred around human behaviour, one state health department decided on an innovative, behaviour-changing approach using the *NeuroPower* framework to drive the solution. Working with the *NeuroPower* Consulting Team, the department implemented a behaviour change program called Clean Hands are LifeSavers that engaged the health workers and increased compliance from 18% to 60%. A key driver of this behaviour change involved effectively addressing each of the six Intelligences in the correct sequence. How these progressive steps were taken is outlined in the Organisational Toolbox Case Study at the end of each Intelligence chapter.

Action: Create Safety and Security in the Hospital Environment

Attitudes to hand washing are culturally determined on one level but also heavily impacted by the individual's primary caregivers in their early life. *NeuroPower* consultants undertook extensive research with doctors, nurses and other health workers to determine their core views and values about hand hygiene and uncovered the resistance strategies being used by different profiles.

To implement the program, we embarked on establishing Hand Hygiene LifeSavers in each hospital. Their key role was to be on the front line making sure all their colleagues – doctors, nurses, orderlies or caterers – adhered to their specialised roles as guardians of the community's health. The LifeSavers ensured everyone agreed to the code of conduct that was expected of them around safety and security in the hospital environment.

ORGANISATIONAL CASE STUDY #2: MERCHANT BANK EQUITY DERIVATIVES LEADERSHIP TEAM

The Task: Improve employee engagement and tangible business performance.

Recap:

In 2006, at the height of the financial boom, one of Australia's leading equity derivatives teams was operating in an environment that was fast-paced, demanding and with a high level of stress. In order to handle large volumes of work in a very volatile market, the team needed to be highly functional and collaborative. Growth was nearly 200 percent over the previous year so the enormous strain was evident. This was mainly caused by a leadership team in crisis.

The Leadership Team was fractured, non-collaborative and driven by their own individual agendas. There was both a lack of respect and a lack of honesty between members which led to highly reactive responses and conflict. The broader team could see this occurring and they felt they were part of a warring tribe with all the insecurities that brought.

NeuroPower consultants devised a program which focused on addressing the splintered Leadership Team. The intervention involved a series of group structured processes which were embedded by individual coaching sessions.

Action: Repairing and Embedding P1

The first task was to repair the fractured P1 in the Leadership Team. To set the stage, a Leadership Team Code of Conduct was developed and agreed upon to establish the rules the team would play by – how they would treat each other and interact as a group.

The most powerful session followed – Role Clarification. Much of the interpersonal conflict came from the confusion around overlapping roles and responsibilities within the Team. This workshop had been scheduled for two hours but was extended to a whole day because the members found it so invaluable. It was during this session that the Team relaxed, opened up and began to work together in a more harmonious manner. By day's end, there was an expanded sense of safety and openness as the P1 had been repaired and stabilised.

Chapter 3

Our Second Social Cognitive Need:
EXPRESSION &
The Emotional Function (C1)

EXPRESSION (C1) AT A GLANCE

Expression is our Brain's Second Social Cognitive Need

The brain loves expressing emotions. Unexpressed emotion and activity in the amygdala is related to a significant decrease in cognitive ability and can seriously reduce individual and team performance. Labelling emotions appropriately reduces this load.

Characteristics of the Expression (C1) Functional Network

Spontaneity and Innovation

STRENGTH	WEAKNESS
Open to new experiences and ideas	Easily bored; tactical rather than strategic

OPPORTUNITY	THREAT
Recognising that new doesn't mean better; learning to endure pain	Can become easily bored, distracted or manic

Management Style

- Great for adapting concepts and designs
- Innovative and can think on the run
- Can frustrate with too many new ideas

SPONTANEITY

C1 THINKING	C1 FEELING	C1 SOMATIC
Brainstorming and innovation	Excitement, fun and extroversion	Body sensations, pleasure and fun

COMMUNICATION STYLE

- Witty and humorous
- Conversational and tangential (easily side-tracked)
- Loves brainstorming
- Highly animated
- Loves interacting with others
- Playful

KEYWORDS INCLUDE

- Flexibility
- Spontaneity
- Laughter
- New ideas
- Child-like and Playful
- Self-Expression

Expression (C1) Helps Us to Survive

Expression (C1) helps us both as individuals and the group to survive and thrive by motivating and enabling us to move rapidly towards pleasant (constructive) experiences and away from painful (unconstructive) experiences.

Expression &
The Emotional Function (C1)

EXPRESSION: OUR BRAIN'S SECOND SOCIAL NEED EXPLAINED

Our emotions - and expressing them to others - seem to be core to our human experience. We become excited when things improve and frustrated when things just won't change, anxious when things are uncertain and self-righteous when we feel we're being unfairly criticised. These emotions colour our experience, and the more intense the emotion, the more driven we seem to let others know about it! (Those people who thrive on expressing their emotions to others are usually referred to as 'extroverts'.) Now neuroscience is confirming that emotions are central to our lives because they are powerful tools that our brain - through Expression (C1) - uses to keep us alive and help us thrive.

Our understanding of emotions has come a long way since Cicero, Seneca and the Roman Stoic thinkers described the 'perturbatio' (their word for emotions), which they believed distracted us from our virtues, caused our suffering and were to be avoided at all costs (Schmitter, 2010). Instead, we now know that emotions are core to how we make sense of the world and - when functioning appropriately - the emotional system is the brain's way of giving us rapid access to our past experiences - both positive and negative. The brain's limbic system[1] is the seat of our emotional experience. It constantly scans the environment and our internal state to help us notice the 'important stuff' and filter out everything else. As a rapid decision-making system, our emotions help us move towards pleasant, positive experiences and away from painful, negative experiences.

When we feel emotional, whether it is a positive or negative emotion, our bodies become flooded with neurochemicals that change our breathing, heart-rate and muscle responses. In the brain, these neurochemicals affect what we can remember,

---

1   In the past, emotional processing was thought to be supported by contiguous structures in a dedicated 'limbic lobe', but contemporary neuroscience evidence now points to a more loosely connected set of structures within the midbrain, described as the 'limbic system'. The limbic system includes some popularly known brain areas including the amygdala (which pop culture frequently, though inaccurately, describes as the 'fear' part of the brain. It is shown in research to perform a primary role in the processing of memory, decision-making, and emotional reactions) and the hippocampus (associated with memory formation and consolidation) as well as other less well known but important structures such as the areas closely associated with our experience of pain like the insula and dorsal anterior cingulate cortex (dACC). Areas like the striatum, rich with cells producing dopamine, play a crucial role in the experience of pleasure and reward, while the ventral tegmental area and periaqueductal gray are thought to be critical to our behavioural responses to emotionally charged experiences.

Table 3.1: At a Glance – The Benefits of Healthy C1 Expression

Five reasons to develop C1 Expression for yourself and others	
1. Effectively labelling emotions in the moment can reduce their intensity.	Lieberman et al.,(2011)
2. In contrast, unexpressed, intense emotions significantly reduce cognitive performance by shifting activity from the frontal lobes to lower-level emotional parts of the brain.	Oei et al.,(2012)
3. Expressive flexibility is an important contributor to personal resilience over time.	Westphal, Seivert and Bonanno (2010)
4. Self-expression activates the mid-brain dopamine reward system and can in itself be rewarding and motivating.	Tamir & Mitchell (2012)
5. Emotional states have a strong impact on creativity and innovation, particularly for individuals high in C1 (extroverts)	Stafford, Ng, Moore and Bard (2010)

how we perceive the outside world and how we process information. In times like these it is all too easy to find yourself carried away by instinctive emotional responses because our emotions prepare our bodies to run when we are afraid, fight when we are angry and rest and heal when we are relaxed.

Although strong emotional reactions were critical to the survival of our ancestors, they create a lot of conflict and can often be disruptive. Workplaces often expect employees to try to eliminate, suppress or ignore their emotional responses. But neuroscience research is now confirming that this is exactly the wrong approach if you're looking to create high performance in yourself and in others.

Studies conducted by Matthew Lieberman at UCLA show that being asked to control our emotional responses (what he calls 'masking') can dramatically reduce performance on even simple cognitive and physical tasks. When we ask individuals to 'control their emotions' at work instead of expressing them constructively, we force them to use parts of their frontal lobes (the 'higher thinking' part of the brain) to keep the brain's emotional system under control so they can focus on the task at hand (Anticevic et al., 2010). This competing challenge significantly reduces the brain's available capacity for complex thinking.

Perhaps, even more importantly, unacknowledged or unexpressed emotions can bias our performance. Emotions have the powerful ability to shape what we perceive, what we remember, and how we interpret and respond to the world. For example, anxiety leads us to be more pessimistic when making judgements about the future, whereas anger makes us more optimistic so that we downplay risks (Lerner & Keltner, 2000). This means that, when unexamined and unexpressed, our emotions drive cognitive biases. As individuals, our judgements are clouded by emotions, and in teams their collective pact leads to flawed decision-making.[2]

So what's the alternative? Studies by Lieberman and others show that one highly constructive way to manage our emotions is not only to become aware of them but also to find the right word to describe them. This approach (called 'labelling') leads to big decreases in activity in the amygdala (the brain's 'danger detector'). This in turn reduces the intensity of the emotion so we can get a better grip on the situation. While there are many useful tools and techniques for building your personal emotional awareness, a key role of leadership is to create a culture that fosters healthy emotional expression.

In high-risk environments, expression can mean the difference between life and death

Effective leaders are able to create an environment where emotions can be expressed. In their book *Leadership in Dangerous Situations,* authors Patrick Sweeney, Michael Matthews & Paul Lester (2011) make the compelling point:

> "Strong cohesive bonds between members serve to form an effective social support network within an organisation. Support networks are important in assisting group members in managing stress because they provide a forum to voice concerns, receive guidance, and get information about how to more effectively manage problems. Thus, support networks enhance members' perceptions of their ability to handle dangerous situations and also to formulate realistic expectations of the demands involved, which helps members manage stress."

EXPRESSION, FLEXIBILITY AND FUN – THE CHALLENGE FOR LEADERS

From a community or organisational perspective, to build effective teams, leaders need to understand that emotional responses are an inevitable part of working in teams. If team members are emotionally triggered by each other or by external inputs but are unable to express this within the group in a constructive way, their agility, creativity and overall mental capacity for completing complex tasks will diminish. As a leader, creating a culture that enables the team to identify and label their emotions appropriately can liberate a surprising amount of enthusiasm and creativity that will then fuel their performance.

---

2   In Principle Two, we explore each of the nine patterns of emotion (the nine Neuro-Limbic Types) and the core bias associated with each one.

SET POINTS DEFINE OUR CHARACTER BY RETURNING THE BRAIN TO EMOTIONAL HOMEOSTASIS (ALLIESTHESIA)

Our brain has a simple operating principle which goes something like this: what has got us here, will keep us here. This simple principle is informed through past emotional experience. This primitive system is in the brains of most of the more advanced living things because it underpins learning, adaption and agility which are important to survival. Creatures without this aspect of adaption intergenerationally adhere to the principles of natural selection but the species requires mutation and multiple generations to achieve what more advanced brains can do with surprising speed.

Each of the social cognitive needs has a set point based on repeated experience which is rewarded by the C1 system (emotional alliesthesic homeostasis). For example, if during the consolidation of the P1 system, the child has positive attachment, feels comfortable with their caregiver and experiences many of the positive feelings associated with belonging and self value this encodes in the child's brain as reality. In this way, when the child feels wanted, supported, loved and connected, the brain will release a reward to reassure the baby that it is on the right path. Later in life the child will not always experience this sense of belonging in every group they are members of, however, their brain will let them know that this is the exception rather than the rule and the individual will do whatever it takes to become a trusted and valued member of the team knowing that this is how it 'should be'. Conversely a child that has poor attachment, that has never really felt they belonged or was valued, may experience anxiety, rejection and isolation. If this state is experienced for a long enough time it moves from being a state into being a trait. The brain treats our own emotional traits as set points that need to be maintained for survival. In the brain of this child, anxiety, rejection and isolation become the 'norm' and represent the world,

Diagram 3.2 The Functional Neural Architecture of Emotional Labelling

Directing attention to the affective response Dorsomedial Prefrontal Cortex	Categorising the response (Verbalising) Ventrolateral Prefrontal Cortex	CONSCIOUS INTERPRETATION
Intensity of the emotion Limbic regions, including the anterior insula, amygdala		EMOTION

Based on Satpute, Shu, Weber, Roy & Ochsner, (2012)

Talking – Even When You Don't Feel Like It

Research in Professor Matthew Lieberman's lab at UCLA has confirmed something that we all seem to get wrong: talking about unpleasant feelings makes us feel better. Lieberman and his team have found that accurately labelling both positive and negative emotions dampens their intensity by reducing amygdala-related responses, but that even when we experience this directly, we keep on mistakenly believing that talking about negative emotions will make us feel worse (Lieberman et al., 2007, 2011).

Lieberman's research indicates the positive impact of labelling comes when parts of the frontal lobe (including the ventrolateral prefrontal cortex (VLPFC) and the ventromedial PFC) increase their activation and help to interpret and reduce activation in the amygdala and other emotional areas of the brain. This lines up with a number of other studies into emotional reappraisal which similarly found that reappraising our emotions increases prefrontal activity and reduces limbic activity and emotional distress (Ochsner & Gross, 2005).

Applying this insight, researchers at Oxford have recently shown that training smokers to be aware of their cravings (through mindfulness practices) when they see images of smoking successfully reduced their cravings, and that this corresponded with a decrease in activity in craving-related regions of the brain (particularly the subgenual anterior cingulate cortex; sgACC) and reduced the functional connectivity between the sgACC and other craving-related regions in the brain (Westbrook et al., 2013).

Such studies reinforce the powerful impact awareness of activity of the emotional system has on the frontal lobe's ability to manage our emotions and, therefore, associated behaviour.

---

as it actually is for them. Every time they feel this pattern of emotions the brain will reward them with a mix of positive neurotransmitters the predominant of which is dopamine. Rewards like this feel as if everything is right with the world – "I am on track. This is right." So for this poorly attached child, the world feels right when he or she is anxious, feeling rejected and isolated. This emotional alliesthesic set point becomes a homing system, a script or a repeating pattern which is encoded into the individual's sense of self and emotional identity. This process is true for all six of the social cognitive needs and explains how character traits emerge. **The unusual aspect of this process is that in this way the brain has the ability to sometimes make us feel good about feeling bad if feeling bad is our set point.** There are two other important characteristics of this reward system that it's useful to understand:

Firstly, the brain does not establish an emotional set point according to what is right or wrong but rather according to the number of times you have experienced that emotion. In this way the brain can reward the individual for things that are not healthy. This explains why we keep following patterns of behaviour that are plainly no longer serving us.

Emotional alliesthesic homeostasis (C1) means that depressed people are rewarded for being depressed, angry people feel good about exploding and strange people feel good about demonstrating behaviour that is strange.

C1 is the system that rewards us for maintaining the status quo by reliving the same emotions again and again. Our C1 also does one more thing. It rewards us for expressing these emotions, which we do through a rehearsed narrative or story. To explore this space further, therefore, we need to look at the nature of self-expression, its benefits and explore further the evolutionary benefits of emotion itself.

Within the brain, a diverse range of structures and neuronal networks help us satisfy our need for Expression. Within the *NeuroPower* framework, this set of structures is called the 'C1 Emotional System' (or sometimes the 'C1 network' or 'C1 function') and gives rise to a particular thinking style referred to as 'C1 Intelligence'.

THE EVOLUTIONARY SOCIAL BRAIN FUNCTION OF C1

The C1 system enables an individual to survive through:

- Aversive motivation (pain) or getting away from hedonically unpleasant experiences of food, recreational drugs, sex and the like (Esch & Stefano, 2004).

- Motivation to repeat constructive activities. Natural rewarding activities are necessary for survival and appetitive motivation ('pleasure'), usually governing beneficial biological behaviours like eating, sex and reproduction, and behaviour directed towards hedonic or pleasurable processes. Social contacts can further facilitate the positive effects exerted by pleasurable experiences (Esch & Stefano, 2004).

- Adaptation to novel situations by thinking laterally or creatively, using creativity to problem-solve and resolve conflict with others.

- Maintaining positive expectations for the future (Klein, 2006).

- The experience of pleasure, the state of feeling happiness and satisfaction resulting from an experience that one enjoys (Esch & Stefano, 2004).

- The experience of extraversion and subjective well-being (Pavot et al., 1990).

- Satisfaction of the body returning to homeostatic conditions ('sensory alliesthesia'; Burgdorf & Panksepp, 2006).

Recognising the Characteristics of Expression (C1)

Thomas Edison, whose mind was very high in the Expression (C1) function, is famous for having once explained, "I'm not discouraged, because every wrong attempt discarded is another step forward."

This seemingly inexhaustible energy to try something new, to give it another go in a different way, is characteristic of the C1 function at work. Levels of motivation are at their peak when new ideas and solutions are being sought, new people are being met or new experiences are at hand. They love anything new, fun or novel. This extroverted, emotional, associative part of the brain also gives our brain the ability to create unusual, previously unthought of 'creative' ideas which, in Edward de Bono's language, would be thought of as lateral thinking or practical creativity. C1 most often plays out as a 'hands on' practical creation of new things, adaptability and an ability to change course mid-way.

C1 THINKING

On a daily basis we use this C1 kind of creativity when we think outside the square to solve problems. In this process, we integrate feelings of freedom, play and novelty-seeking with the hands-on touching of objects and curiosity about how things work in practice. Added to this is a fluidity of focus, which canvasses a spectrum of disparate thoughts then selects one for the task at hand.

C1 Thinking is nicely described by Dr Joel Robertson[3], who observes that thinking related to excitement, risk-taking, sex, gambling, fear, anxiety, frightening scenarios or stories, or concerns about a challenging or difficult future is all linked to the release of dopamine in the brain. How we experience each of these is bundled up in the mental frameworks that each of us use to describe the relationship between us and the world. These manifest in the layered and complex thoughts, behaviours and emotions that make up our core beliefs about the world. According to Robertson, this system of core beliefs determines the individual's baseline chemistry and, to a large extent, establishes a range of automatic behaviours or even addictions. This is because if the individual believes that he or she is under any kind of threat their dopamine levels will be raised.

This also works in reverse; if we have a particular view about the world and dopamine is linked to rewarding the brain for returning to a homeostatic set point, any well-worn narrative will result in the release of dopamine. Either way – if we respond to stress in a way that has become habitual, we will be chemically and therefore emotionally reassured and even rewarded with the release of dopamine. That's why so many counterproductive core beliefs are so difficult to change.

---

3   Dr Joel Robertson is an internationally acclaimed clinician, lecturer, consultant, author and director of the Robertson Institute in the USA, which provides neurochemical evaluations and treatment techniques for corporations, athletes and mental health facilities.

C1 FEELING

C1 is characterised by a great sense of extroversion and spontaneity, which is facilitated by both the expression of feelings and emotions and fluid, flexible and fluent movement of mind, body and emotions. When accessing C1, individuals experience a range of characteristics including rapidly changing moods; a sense of freedom from boundaries and from rules; a seeking for pleasure, play and novelty; a sense of adventure and engagement in the real world; a fascination with the here and now; and a focus on exploring the world through the senses. There is a sense of timelessness and of playing with whatever is at hand. Add to this the creative life force and the stage is set for the individual to adapt whatever they find to make a new plaything. This is the cradle of a practical kind of creativity using lateral thinking.

C1 SOMATIC

C1 intelligence is the domain of spontaneous emotional expression in the physical world. Individuals high in C1 tend to have a wide range of expressions, move quickly, smile, laugh, cry and express their emotions facially and using gestures.

Equally, the C1 system is highly influenced by the emotional expressions of others in the immediate surroundings, mediated by our emotional reactivity to our own bodily states. For example, studies have found that simulating a frown (negative) or a smile (positive) using simple facial exercises creates negative and positive biases in interpreting otherwise neutral data (Larsen, Kasimatis and Frey, 1992). Neurologist Antonio Damasio (1994) argued that these arose because our brains recognise our body states as 'somatic markers' which it interprets to judge our emotional state. In particular, he argued, muscle changes in our limbs and faces send information directly to the brain and are represented in the somatosensory cortex, and are very sensitive components of emotional reactions. Meanwhile, less clearly defined - but arguably more intense - bodily responses in the viscera (such as the stomach, intestines, heart and lungs) are registered in the orbitofrontal cortex and related areas. These bodily responses are the C1 somatic markers of our emotional experience.

The correlation between how the physical body is feeling and how we're thinking is very clear to the C1-dominated brain. Hollywood is a testimony to being able to change people's mood and thinking through the use of explicitly expressed emotion. The old truism 'Smile and the world smiles with you', encapsulates the C1 somatic obsession with using emotion to actively frame the way messages are interpreted and the ways others perceive experiences.

Those high in C1 are highly aware of how expressed emotion directly shapes their emotional state: they dance to happy music to raise their mood, find humorous videos to diffuse tension, and their faces tend to default back to looking for physical expressions of fun and interaction. For those low in C1, this bodily feedback also occurs but largely without awareness (Porges, Donssard-Roosevelt and Maiti, 1994; Ehlers, Margraf, Roth, Barr and Birbaumer, 1988).

Highly Functioning Expression (C1) has Both Strengths and Weaknesses

Those who enjoy accessing their C1 are energised by brainstorming new ideas and are practical, quick-witted, energetic, adaptable, flexible thinkers who hop from one idea to another. These strengths are inevitably accompanied by inherent weaknesses, ranging from a short attention span through to a strong discomfort with negative emotions (either personally or in others). The lesson to learn for those high in C1 is that life is more than an addiction to fun, novelty, change and fast movement.

Expression (C1) and Childhood Development

In the Relatedness (P1) chapter, we looked at the issue of attachment and how the pattern of a child's emotional relationship with its primary caregiver at age one has significant predictive power for their future relationships (Ainsworth et al., 1978). Specifically, this relationship determines how the child sees the world (i.e. whether it is safe or not) and whether they are entitled to be in it. Attachment also affects the development of the C1 Intelligence by shaping how the child views themselves and others. This becomes their central emotional position (i.e. I'm OK, Not OK; You're OK, Not OK) (Harris, 1976). These are described in Table 3.1.

The same interactions that stimulated excitement, exhilaration and brain growth within an infant during its first year of life now include information on the recognition of disapproval and disappointment. During early socialising experiences, disapproval and disappointment reflect a loss of connection with the attachment figure, which is a powerful socialising experience given the primal requirement of staying connected for personal survival. Prolonged and repeated experiences result in physiological dysregulation and produce a negative result for the development of networks that affect regulation and attachment located within the medial prefrontal areas (Schore, 1994). In other words, the C1 Intelligence can be damaged from these very early experiences which later can have a very negative impact on adult personality.

Several key developmental theories have explored how Expression (C1) matures in early life.

In 1990, Henry Wellman proposed that at about two years of age a child's theory of mind first takes shape as a desire psychology (Sigelman and Rider, 2006). At this age toddlers communicate what they want and justify their own behaviour and the behaviour of others based on this (Sigelman and Rider, 2006).

According to Judith (1996), the emergence of C1 occurs within the child between six and twenty-four months. Developmentally, this aligns with Freud's oral stage, Piaget's sensory-motor stage and Kohlberg's Instrumental Hedonism stage. Developmental psychology assumes that there are specific facets of the child to be developed at each stage and specific knowledge to learn. It also assumes that the strength of the emerging facet for each stage depends on how effectively the work has been done in the preceding stage.

From a neurological perspective, the early emotional environment (C1) of an infant may become imprinted within the human brain through the shaping of their narrative and, in turn, their neural networks, and by establishing biochemical setpoints for circuitry dedicated to memory, emotion and attachment. These structures and processes then serve as the infrastructure for later-developing intellectual skills (I1), affect regulation, attachment (I2) and the sense of self (P2) (Schore, 1994; Siegel, 1999).

Neurobiologist Joseph (1996) refers to implicit memories relating to early childhood experiences as our human 'childlike central core'. This reflects the C1 Intelligence, which encapsulates the individual's C1 central emotional position, involving their emotional core beliefs about themselves.

To determine the strength of the attachment script, the AAI (Adult Attachment Interview as discussed in P1) was administered to parents when their children were at different ages: in utero; at the same time as the Strange Situation interaction (age one) and five years later (when the child is six) (Fonagy et al., 1991; van Ijzendoorn, 1995). In each situation the AAI was associated with the specific classification of the infant-parent attachment. This means that the findings from the AAI are strong, seem to be stable across time, and have predictive power even before an infant is born. Even when the child reaches late adolescence, the classifications made in the Strange Situation interactions generally remain predictive of AAI classifications (Benoit and Parker, 1994; Main, 1995; van Ijzendoorn, 1995; van Ijzendoorn and Bakermans-Kranenburg, 1996; Hesse, 1999). This suggests that the central emotional position encoded in the C1 Intelligence is stable and predictive into adulthood.

While an infant will have a different attachment pattern with different caregivers, and so may have different central emotional positions, it seems the primary caregiver exerts the strongest influence over the adult's narrative and attachment status (van Ijzendoorn and Bakermans-Kranenburg, 1996). This supports Berne's theory that men inherit their C1 (child ego state) from their mothers. Why women tend to inherit their C1 (child ego state) from their fathers is still unclear.

EXPRESSION (C1) PROBLEMS AT SCHOOL

In training for creative problem-solving, many teachers in Western schools have trained children to develop this flexibility and fluency of thought with lateral thinking exercises. Unfortunately, the rest of the time these same teachers often chastise and 'correct' their naturally C1-dominant students for being off task, not concentrating,

Table 3.3: The table below shows the Emotional Positions manifested in childhood and corresponding adult behaviour, based on Ainsworth et al.'s (1978) Strange Situation experiments

Emotional Position Expressed In Childhood Behaviour	Emotional Position Expressed In Adult Behaviour	Central Emotional Position	Response to Psychosocial Challenge Test
Secure The infant will explore the room and toys with interest during pre-separation. Displays signs of missing parent during separation with frequent crying by the second separation. Infant has an obvious preference for parent over stranger. Greets parent actively, typically initiating physical contact. By the second reunion the infant will maintain contact but will then settle and return to play.	**Secure/Autonomous** Coherent and collaborative discussion. Valuing their attachment, but appears objective regarding any particular event/relationship. Description and evaluation of attachment-related experiences is consistent, regardless of whether experiences are favourable or unfavourable.	I'm OK. You're OK.	• **Low** level of reported stress • **Moderate** HPA response (ACTH and cortisol); • **High** level of oxytocin release
Avoidant The infant fails to cry on separation, then actively avoids and ignores parent on reunion (for example, turning away, leaning out of arms when picked up, moving away). Little or no proximity or contact seeking, and no anger or distress. Response to parent appears very unemotional. The infant focuses on toys or environment throughout the procedure.	**Dismissing** Lacks coherence. They dismiss attachment-related experiences and relationships. They use normalising descriptions ('fine', 'nice' and 'typical mum') with generic statements invalidated through specific episodic recall. There is a tendency to have very brief statements of childhood.	I'm OK. You're not OK.	• **Moderate** level of reported stress • **High** HPA response (ACTH and cortisol); • **Moderate** level of oxytocin release
Resistant or ambivalent May be wary or distressed even before parent leaves. The infant explores very little, is preoccupied throughout procedure, and may seem angry or passive. Fails to settle and take comfort in parent on reunion, and usually continues to focus on parent and cry. Infant does not return to exploration after reunion.	**Preoccupied** No coherence. They will be preoccupied with past attachment relationships/experiences, and will appear angry, fearful or passive. Their sentences are often long, grammatically entangled, or containing vague phrases ('and so on').	I'm not OK. You're OK.	• **Moderate** level of reported stress • **Moderate** HPA response (ACTH and cortisol); • **Low** level of oxytocin release
Disorganised or disorientated Infant shows disorganised and/or disorientated behaviours in the parent's presence. This suggests a temporary collapse of behavioural strategies. For instance, infant may pause with a trance-like expression, with hands raised in the air; may rise up at their parent's entrance, then they fall prone and huddled on the floor; or may cling to their parent while bawling and leaning away with their gaze averted. Otherwise the infant will fit within the other three categories.	**Unresolved/Disorganised** While discussing abuse or loss within the attachment they will show surprising lapses in the monitoring of reasoning or discourse. This may be through a sudden belief that the person who is being spoken of is still alive in the physical sense even though they have been dead for years, or that this attachment figure was killed as a result of a childhood thought. They may lapse into prolonged silence or eulogistic speech. They will otherwise ordinarily fit within the other categories.	I'm not OK. You're not OK.	• **High** level of reported stress • **Suppressed** HPA response (ACTH and cortisol); • **Moderate** level of oxytocin release

Note: This table is adapted from Hesse (1999). The descriptions of infant classification (secure, avoidant, resistant or ambivalent) are summarised from Ainsworth et al. (1978) while the descriptions of the disorganised or disorientated category is summarised from Main and Solomon (1990). The descriptions of adult attachment classification system are summarised from Main, Kaplan and Cassidy (1985) and from Main and Goldwyn (1984, 1998). The descriptions of the central emotional positions are from Harris (1976). Responses to the Psychosocial Challenge Test are from Pierrehumbert et al., (2012).

making smart comments or 'fooling around'. Indeed, children whose C1 is highly activated and who have an understimulated brainstem are often labelled as having Attention Deficit Disorder (ADD) or Attention Deficit Hyperactivity Disorder (ADHD) and given drugs to calm them, such as Ritalin (a drug which stimulates the brain so the child doesn't need to use C1 to keep themselves awake).

As they mature and C1 Intelligence is mediated by the development of other Intelligences, these children usually learn to balance and moderate their tendency to create chaos, but C1 is still a powerful force which can be creative, light-hearted, vivacious and witty. However, this childish C1 energy is so pleasurable that it can become addictive, even when the child grows into an adult. After all, who wants to be serious and take responsibility when life can be so much fun? This may be why the C1 inner child within us refuses to grow up, continues to run towards pleasure and avoid pain, and may prefer not to take responsibility throughout our lives.

THE IMPORTANCE OF NARRATIVE

One of the most powerful ways parents and caregivers shape the brains of the children they have in their care is wrapped up in the way they make sense of the events the child experiences.

The way in which parents construct narrative descriptions of events creates scripts by shaping their children's sense of self and the world (Ochs and Capps, 2001). This is because the self is a combination of learning and memory, reflective of, and constantly being influenced by, social interactions (Cacioppo and Berntson, 1992). Narrative is important in establishing our sense of self because storytelling is the primary method for integrating activity in a sequential and meaningful manner (Oatley, 1992). Narratives are a means of explaining behaviour and defining both the social and private selves. They are emotionally meaningful, causally linked sequences of actions and consequences that help in the organisation, maintenance and evaluation of behaviour (Fivush, 1994). They also serve to educate children in the tales, myths and legends of their families and cultures (Howard, 1991; Malinowski, 1984).

As the child begins to verbalise, parents and children work together to co-construct the child's narrative. Miller and Sperry's (1988) research showed that when the child is around two-and-a-half, co-construction of narrative descriptions of events occurs at the rate of 2.2 per hour in everyday conversation. This dialogue helps the child form their C1 emotional life script.

C1 Expression and the Facebook Effect

Have you ever wondered why social networking sites like Facebook are so addictive? Recent research from Harvard provides some insight into why sharing so much of our personal lives can be so satisfying.

On the one hand, there's the positive reinforcement we get from our friends every time they 'like' something we've shared. But in addition, recent evidence suggests that the act of sharing may itself be an instant reward.

Researchers Tamir and Mitchell (2012) recently reported that expressing your own opinions activates dopamine-related reward systems in the brain. As part of a range of experiments, they offered participants small cash rewards for answering easy, factual questions based on things they observed, or lower rewards for offering their own views about a subject. To their surprise, more than two thirds of the time participants chose smaller rewards for talking about themselves, even when it meant a smaller financial reward. *"Just as monkeys are willing to forgo juice rewards to view dominant groupmates and college students are willing to give up money to view attractive members of the opposite sex, our participants were willing to forgo money to think and talk about themselves,"* the researchers wrote.

In a separate experiment, Tamir and Mitchell used fMRI to observe the brains of their participants. They found that when participants were disclosing their own attitudes they had significantly greater activation in the nucleus accumbens and the ventral tegmental area (both part of the dopaminergic reward system) than when they were evaluating other people's opinions.

Little surprise, then, that platforms like Facebook have unleashed an avalanche of sharing. It looks more than likely that each post we make and photo we share gives us another hit of one of the brain's favourite drugs.

DEVELOPING AN EMOTIONAL IDENTITY[4]

C1 enables us to feel and emotionally connect to the world. Piaget observed that young children learn this at the sensory-motor stage of development when the body first starts accessing the C1 Intelligence. This is when the child is beginning to separate from, and move independently of, its mother and connect to the outer world. Since children at this age have not yet developed language, they have no ability to name the

---

4   An in-depth analysis of the nine emotional identities (Neuro-Limbic Types) that form during the sensory-motor stage is outlined in the second section of this book (Principle #2).

things they sense, and consequently cannot categorise or reason about them. They explore their world by sensing and expressing emotion through their bodies. At this age, the child's focus is on seeking pleasure, avoiding pain and acquiring knowledge of the world (Harris and Butterworth, 2002).

If all goes well, the little person will integrate the cognitive, emotional and physical aspects of C1 and will be able to feel, know and validate what they want. They will also decide how they feel about the world (based on scripting embedded in their P1), including whether it is a place of pain to be avoided or pleasure to be embraced. Further, the child will know whether or not they have valid needs and desires, which can be gratified without guilt (Judith, 1996).

From the C1 stage the child's emotional identity emerges. Reality is felt and translated through the senses, and since the child has no sense of time, now is forever. As a result, their many experiences combine to form the dominant sense of reality.

To cement this belief about themselves and the world, the child receives explicit training and implicit teaching through modelling. The impact of this interaction is boosted by face-to-face interactions which activate an infant's sympathetic nervous system and increase oxygen consumption and energy metabolism. High levels of C1 activity correlate with increased production and availability of norepinephrine, endorphins and dopamine, serving to enhance the infant's energy and enjoyment (Schore, 1997). Once embedded in the C1 Intelligence, this results in what psychologist Eric Berne called a 'life script'.

> *A script is an ongoing life plan formed in early childhood under parental pressure. It is the psychological force which propels the person toward his destiny, regardless of whether he fights it or says it is his own free*

Diagram 3.4 Healthy C1 Intelligence – Noble Quality: Spontaneity

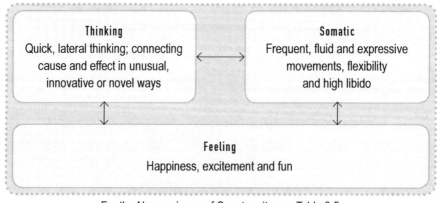

Thinking
Quick, lateral thinking; connecting cause and effect in unusual, innovative or novel ways

Somatic
Frequent, fluid and expressive movements, flexibility and high libido

Feeling
Happiness, excitement and fun

For the Neuroscience of Spontaneity see Table 3.5

Table 3.5 The Neuroscience of Spontaneity

The table below details the Neuroscience of C1. Refer to Appendix 13 for more details.

Somatic Aspect	Feeling Aspect	Thinking Aspect
• Increases in **skin temperature, dampness** and the rate at which blood pulses, as well as trembling fingers	• Dominated by **dopamine**, but also affected by oxytocin and beta-endorphone	• **Cheerfulness and optimism** (left prefrontal cortex)
• **Relaxation of muscles and increased flexibility**	• The dopamine pathway to the nucleus accumbens:	• **Positive emotional/ arousal states**, including those induced by taste, sight, touch and sound (orbital frontal cortex, prefrontal and cingulate cortices, the nucleus accumbens and its mesolimbic projection, the lateral hypothalamus, the ventral pallidum and the brainstem, especially the parabrachial nucleus)
• **Slight tensing of zygomatic muscle** (which pulls the mouth upward), **contraction of the orbicularis oculi muscle** ('crow's feet') and **relaxation of the corrugator supercilii** (responsible for expressions of disgust, sadness and fear)	– 'The Pleasure Pathway' can be activated by amphetamines (e.g. cocaine, crack, heroin, opium etc.) (tegmentum-nucleus accumbens). Anticipation of pleasure ultimately leads to addiction	
• **High activity in the midbrain:** including processing impulses from the brainstem and sending instructions to the muscles (cerebellum), releasing emotional excitement (diencephalon) and conversion of emotions to plans and actions (prefrontal cortex)	– Stimulation also leads to the sudden onset of mirth	• **Decrease in amygdala activation** with positive arousal-inducing stimuli (such as music, odour, self-generated positive arousal and male/ female orgasm)
	• Emotion is **felt by the body, monitored** by brain areas placed at several levels of the central nervous system (e.g. cingulate cortices, hypothalamus, ventral tegmentum) and **interpreted by the cortex** (lateral and polar parts of frontal lobe). Activity in the prefrontal cortex increases with feelings of anticipation	• **Divergent or creative thinking** (increased complexity of brain activity in the frontal cortex)
• **Activation of the 'pleasure and pain centres'** linked to the limbic system (cingulate gyrus, hippocampus, dentate gyrus, amygdala, hypothalamus, septal area and thalamus)		
• **Somatic markers** – access to information about the best way forward based on previous experience (circuits linking posterior sensory cortices, temporal and parietal regions with prefrontal circuits)	• The anticipation of an **eminent and highly predictable reward** elicits positive feelings	

will. A real person may be defined as one who acts spontaneously in a rational and trustworthy way with decent consideration for others. One who follows a formula is a not-real, or unreal, person ... these seem to constitute the bulk of humanity. (Berne, 1975, p. 32)

In describing those who follow scripts, Berne uses the image of a player sitting at a pianola, pedalling for all he is worth, believing he is autonomous, but really just following a set piece. Every so often he will improvise, but most of the time he plays out the script. As we have seen, the child has no way of reasoning about events that happen to and around them in their early family life so they lay down these life scripts uncritically.

[By the end of the nursing period] *the child already has certain convictions about himself and the people around him, especially his parents. These convictions are likely to stay with him the rest of his life, and may be summarized as follows: (1) I'm OK or; (2) I'm not OK; (3) You're OK or; (4) You're not OK. On the basis of these he makes his life decision. 'It's a good world, some day I'll make it a better one' – through science, service, poetry, or music. 'It's a bad world. Some day I'll kill myself' – or kill someone else, go crazy, or withdraw. Perhaps it's a mediocre world, where you do what you have to do and have fun in between; or a tough world, where you make good by putting on a white collar and shuffling other people's papers; or a hard world, where you sweep or bend or deal, or wiggle or fight for a living; or a dreary world, where you sit in a bar hoping; or a futile world, where you give up.* (Berne, 1975, pp. 84-85)

However, these scripts can be augmented or revised later through reasoning or experience. Berne (1975) explains that though they 'are usually based on childlike illusions which may persist throughout a whole lifetime ... in more sensitive, perceptive, and intelligent people these illusions dissolve one by one' (p. 26) as the person is faced by life's crises and deals with them according to their own judgement. These crises can include 'the adolescent reappraisal of parents; the protests, often bizarre, of middle age; and the emergence of philosophy after that' (Berne, 1975, p. 26).

C1 IS THE EMOTIONAL CHILD STATE

You will recall from our discussion of P1 that parents' rules and data are embedded in the memory of the child exactly as the little person hears them and sees them. As the parents' data is being observed, heard and recorded, the child is simultaneously recording internal events as their individual responses to what is perceived.

The Importance of Self-Expression

C1 enables you to take in new ideas, think conceptually and work collaboratively in an innovative and spontaneous way. However, when we are emotionally charged, our brain becomes 'full' of emotion and prevents our C1 from fully functioning. The key to getting back on track is to vent some of the emotions that are clogging up the system. This self-expression is like turning on a tap that is connected to an over-pressurised pipe system – it releases the pressure and enables the ideas and creativity to flow freely once more.

Harris (1976) makes a good point:

> It is this seeing and hearing and feeling and understanding body of data which we define as the Child. Since the little person has no vocabulary during the most critical of his early experiences, most of his reactions are feelings. (pp. 24-25)

Harris' research shows that these feelings are generally positive.

> However, for most children of loving and well-intentioned parents there is also much positive data recorded. Creativity, curiosity, the desire to explore and know, the urges to touch and feel and experience, and the recordings of the glorious, pristine feelings of first discoveries. In the child are recorded the countless, grand a-ha experiences, the firsts in the life of the small person. (1976, p. 27)

The *feelings* that accompany all of these delightful experiences are recorded as emotional memories in the C1 Intelligence, and include the many delicious feelings of the happy, carefree child. Importantly, this happy child can re-emerge at any time in the grown person's transactions.

The OK, not OK world view of our C1 child ego remains with us throughout life and it can emerge any time we feel helpless or overwhelmed by life's circumstances. Harris explains:

> As in the case of the Parent, the Child is a state into which a person may be transferred at almost any time in his current transactions. There are many things that can happen to us today which create the situation of childhood and bring on the same feelings we felt then. Frequently we may find ourselves in situations where we are faced with impossible alternatives, where we find ourselves in a corner,

either actually or in the way we see it. These 'hook the child' as we say, and cause a replay of the original feelings of frustration, rejection, or abandonment, and we relive a latter day version of the small Child's primary depression. Therefore, when a person is in the grip of feelings, we say his Child has taken over. When his anger dominates his reason, we say his Child is in command. (1976, p. 26)

If we prefer C1 to the C2 Intelligence (which we will explore in due course), we may habitually want to seek pleasure and avoid pain. This is the C1 Child – the life of the party, the seductive lover, the cute little girl, the charmer; all are accepted and sometimes encouraged in our culture.

But children are not always charming. In this situation, the Child's negative feelings far outweigh the positive. When they do not get their way, they usually throw a tantrum; even senior executives do this when they are accessing C1 in a Child state and have their wants thwarted. They rant, and rave and yell, and I have even seen some stamp their feet! Sometimes they bully, or scream, or become helpless and cry or wail. Others pout and sulk. All this behaviour reflects the inner Child (C1) wanting to avoid pain and responsibility, and trying to exert power over others to get their own way. For example:

> **Example one:** You are at a dinner party. The lady of the house (your hostess) has cooked a dish containing herbs she knows her husband dislikes but does it anyway. When they are served, the husband demands very loudly, 'What's this got in it? It tastes mouldy! It's disgusting! etc.' He gets a win when all the guests stop eating and push their plates away.

> **Example two:** A conversation becomes too dull (C1 cannot bear slow, ponderous talk) or too depressing, as in someone's heartfelt sad story. The person accessing C1 takes control by simply and blatantly changing the topic (e.g. 'Did you hear the great news about ...').

INTEGRATING C1 INTO THE OTHER INTELLIGENCES

If the child's needs are felt, expressed and met, the person will grow up with the capacity to feel and gratify their own emotional needs and fulfil the desires of their own soul. As the child grows they pass through each of the Intelligences, and at every stage, the C1 Intelligence interacts with a specific emotional need to be met.

The needs of each stage are as follows: P1 needs control (we have already explained how the family meets this need of belonging, security and control); C1 needs fun; P2 needs achievement and recognition; I2 needs connection and love; I1 needs to learn and experience new things; and C2 needs freedom.

Well-functioning C1 will help the individual to meet each of these needs in turn. The members of the family, the source of P1, interact with the little child and teach them to have appropriate expression of emotions. At the emergence of P2, C1 emotions fuel the passion to achieve. Next, C1 gives the emerging I2 Intelligence the courage to connect with others. Then, C1's energy and love of novelty spur on the developing I1 Intelligence to seek out new knowledge and experiences. Finally, C1's free Child gives C2 the freedom to dream and so develop.

Poorly Functioning C1

If the child's needs are not heard, acknowledged or gratified, the C1 Intelligence will not develop strongly. In fact, the grown adult may find it difficult or even impossible to understand their own emotional needs, and so may operate some or much of the time with a child-like level of emotional maturity. The adult following a Child script may depend on family, spouse, partner or friends to tell them what they need, how they should feel and what they should do. The dependent person relies on someone else to look after them. Hence, they plead and charm, wheedle, cry, or throw tantrums to ensure this happens. If the C1 script is unpleasant, it will often be suppressed and pushed out of conscious awareness.

As well as not knowing what they need, an individual with poorly functioning C1 does not understand the link between external stimulus and internal emotional gratification. In this case if they like something, they will often assume more is better, and that even more is even better. This is the genesis of the addictive personality that has an inability to gauge limits.

OVER-RELIANCE ON C1

If you have an over-reliance on C1, you are likely to be conscious of your feelings but express them as a child. The task of integration is to learn to recognise and express your feelings when appropriate, using an Adult mode of communication. Be mindful that our feelings often spring from the scripting of our little Child and so may no longer be relevant to the current situation. Make sure you consciously filter for whether the feelings are appropriate.[5]

Whenever you catch yourself acting like a child, remind yourself that you have the option to behave as an adult instead. It is important to listen to your own transactions and practise Transactional Analysis.

UNDER-RELIANCE ON C1

Those with a poor awareness of their C1 have difficulty recognising their emotions (their core belief types) and often ignore their body sensations altogether. They may

---

5   This is done by accessing your Neuro-Rational Type. For more detail, see Principle #3.

deny them or explain them away, especially if their family scripting says, for example, 'It's bad to get angry' or 'Crying is a sign of weakness'.

Even so, their emotions will still be there, buried in the individual's mind and body, ready to ambush them. These feelings will either come out inappropriately (such as through a petulant sulk), or will be buried so deep that they remain unrecognised and unresolved, until they ultimately affect the individual's health and sense of wellness.

SEXUALITY

Judith (1996) argues that the C1 Intelligence also gives the child a healthy sense of their own body, as they are handled and touched with love and respect. At this age, this bodily pleasure is not associated with good or bad, right or wrong. From here the child can develop a healthy positive sexuality, which Judith aptly calls 'the connecting force that unites and delights' (p. 123). From this libido issues the creation of new life and of procreation. This powerful life force is also associated with a general creativity, of new ideas, and of self-expression.

Creating a Highly Functioning C1

Compare your own experience with what you have learned about C1. Which aspects of your C1 are you aware of? Is there one that you tend to focus on above the other two?

- The C1 somatic element relates to fast and constant physical movements and a heightened sense of libido.

- The C1 feeling element involves happiness, excitement, and the sensation of fun.

- The C1 thinking element focuses on creating multiple options and scenarios. It is about brainstorming.

Diagram 3.2 shows the three aspects of C1 that require integration for the C1 Intelligence to function optimally. While every individual is different, our research suggests that the majority of the population experiences C1 as somatic (i.e. as fast movement and high libido).

To integrate these three aspects, you first need to recognise and acknowledge your body sensations and feelings, be they anger, hurt, fear, envy, guilt, etc. and reconcile them with the meaning you give them and how you think about them.

Begin this process by paying attention to your body. Your voice will provide clear give-away signs if you are in the Child state: a bully roars; a tantrum is full of screams or yells; and a helpless child has a high whining voice. Your body also reflects your emotion; bullying stance, stamping feet, frowning face, pouting lips, seductive looks and smiles, pleading eyes, and coy shoulders are all indicators of different emotions. Once you notice any of these (or other) physical characteristics, stop and ask yourself what are you feeling and how you interpret these feelings.

Emotions are instinctual, unconscious reactions to life, telling us to move and to be fluid. When feelings are habitually ignored or controlled, the body becomes the opposite of fluid and flexible and moving – it becomes stiff and rigid. Habitually unacknowledged anger, for instance, not only makes you stubborn, passive-aggressive and inflexible in your attitudes, but also gives you a rigid jaw, and stiffness in your neck and shoulders. If you hold your anger in long enough it will become painful. So if you develop a stiff neck and shoulders you could ask yourself, 'What am I angry about?' There are two parts to the work you can do to resolve the body pain. One part is to think it through and the other is to move the body. This will help you access your C1 Intelligence and process the emotion that underlies the pain.

YOUR EMOTIONAL SCRIPT

Every family has spoken or explicit rules about expressing emotions. When you were very small, before you could evaluate critically, scripts for emotions were laid down in your memory as you listened to your family and interacted with them. The following exercises will help you investigate your emotional life script. Start by considering anger.

Write a short response to each of the following questions. It can be a sentence, a recollection of an event, a poem, a conversation – however you choose to answer.

a. When someone in your family was angry, how did you know? How did you feel? Was the anger acknowledged? What was the family's response? Did they respond positively? Did the family try to acknowledge it, control it, ignore it, punish it, or was there an all-out fight?

b. Do you remember a time when you felt angry? Did you express your anger? How did you express your anger? How did your family respond? How did that make you feel? Was the conflict resolved?

c. Write a new script for yourself about expressing anger. Now that you have considered anger, go through the same exercise with sadness, fear, guilt, joy, pleasure, sexuality and envy.

The following methodology can be helpful in accessing and integrating the C1 Intelligence.

1. The first step is to recognise the feeling. If you need to, give yourself permission to have the feeling.

2. Acknowledge the emotion and the meaning you give the feeling.

3. Consider the appropriateness of the feeling. If it appears inappropriately strong, it could be you are reliving a past unresolved event.

4. Express your feeling in an adult way to the person involved.

5. If the person is no longer living, one strategy is to write them a letter.

6. Tidy everything up: There may be restitution for you to make if you have hurt someone, or there may be someone you can forgive.

After doing the thinking work, complete the integration work by moving your body to release the emotions – massage and/or exercise will release the frozen parts of the body, restore your wholeness and health, and facilitate increased functioning in your C1 Intelligence.

C1 AND PROJECTION

Projection, a common psychological phenomenon, can also result from poorly functioning C1. An individual who has an under-reliance on C1 and is, for example, unconsciously angry, may be overtly polite while noticing how stubborn, terse and obviously angry others around them are. Projection leads us to notice and criticise in others what we cannot acknowledge in ourselves.

Well-functioning C1 operates under the mantra of 'honour one another'. To do this for others first we need to honour the entirety of ourselves, including our poorly functioning C1. Only then will we have the capacity to accept and respect others. A key component of honouring one another is a sense of fair play. While societal rules are derived from P1, a sense of personal ethics and morals for the individual springs from C1. As these develop, we learn to forgo the need to control, manage ourselves in relationships, and devote time to enjoying life.

Highly Functioning C1 in Adult Life

The first-order noble quality of Spontaneity requires the integration of lateral thinking, childlike feelings and the somatic aspect of kinaesthetic appreciation and pleasure.

Spontaneity[6] enables an individual to generate creative solutions to the various problems they encounter at both home and work. When expressing this noble quality, individuals tend to be independent, nonconformist, unconventional, even bohemian, and are likely to have wide interests, greater openness to new experiences and more conspicuous behavioural and cognitive flexibility (Feist, 1998). The noble quality also

---

6   Peterson and Seligman's meta-study of the most widely influential traditions of thought and religion in human history found spontaneity to be a significant human strength (Peterson and Seligman, 2004).

fosters a certain risk-taking boldness. William James (1890) saw ingenious creativity as an evolutionary tendency because it fostered exploring. Since attention is a limited resource, James suggested that individuals who are curious tend to focus on stimuli fostering excitement or personal meaning. The noble quality of Spontaneity involves a definite attraction to novel stimuli. This is adaptive because it increases the individual's knowledge of the world. Spontaneity is also a fun-loving noble quality that experiences life through the pleasures of the physical body. Strongly associated with humour and the Dionysian pursuit of all earthly things that can be enjoyed by the body, C1 Spontaneity is never stumped for options and can brainstorm solutions quickly and effortlessly.

This noble quality actively seeks novel and exciting experiences to elevate stimulation. This often requires a willingness to endure high levels of risk (for example, rejection when meeting new people, and high-risk sports activity) to obtain the benefits of trying something new. Spontaneity also embraces the childlike capacity to see life as a uniquely pleasurable physical experience that only being alive in human form can bring.

HOW C1 SPONTANEITY MEETS THE NOBILITY CRITERIA

Spontaneity answers questions related to the right of the individual to experience physical pleasure. This noble quality enables the individual to discover that they have the right to independently enjoy their life and their body and can build relationships of integrity while doing it. This noble quality is linked to what the German philosopher Nietzsche called the Dionysian man who is transformed through earthly pleasures.

Spontaneity brings value to the community by facilitating ingenious creativity and enabling the community to solve problems. This creates a sense of fun, right here, right now, and manifests in celebrations, parties, community theatre and comedy.

Being Spontaneous is appealing. Individuals yearn to relax, let their hair down and have fun. Hormonally we 'need' laughter as a medicine to release endorphins and to break free from our reactive selves[7] and reduce stress. Individuals report that using Spontaneity to resolve an internal tension has a paradigm shift impact on their lives.

In teams, Spontaneity leads to ingenious creativity which enables the team to be innovative, agile and able to respond adaptively to changing situations.

---

7   The nine reactive personalities, or Neuro-Limbic Types, are explored in Principle #2.

I will tell you something. I love friends, I want more friends. I love smiles. That is a fact. How to develop smiles? There are a variety of smiles. Some smiles are sarcastic. Some smiles are artificial - diplomatic smiles. These smiles do not produce satisfaction, but rather fear or suspicion. But a genuine smile gives us hope, freshness. If we want a genuine smile,
then first we must produce the basis for a smile to come.

14th Dalai Lama

C1 Toolbox

THE IMPORTANCE OF C1 IN BUILDING HIGH PERFORMANCE TEAMS

The emergent cultural impact of C1 is Spontaneity, which enables the organisation to be agile and constructively solve problems as they arise in the course of daily business.

When Spontaneity is absent or suppressed, problems, pessimism and negativity escalate. In the absence of highly functioning C1, workplaces and teams experience low productivity and minimal engagement. Interpersonal conflicts remain unacknowledged and unaddressed, creating either an environment in which everyone feels stifled or a quagmire of emotional tension. Far from bringing joy to employee's lives, work is not a pleasant place to be.

However, when there is highly functioning C1 in the organisation, team members feel comfortable expressing themselves and are able to deal with any potential interpersonal issues constructively. This facilitates the agility of the team and its capacity to think creatively in solving problems that inevitably arise. The team is filled with a sense of optimism – right here, right now! – which is reflected in a fun and lighthearted work environment.

Leaders looking to improve the function of C1 in their team can increase Spontaneity by applying the C1 Tools.

C1 QUESTIONS FOR PERSONAL DEVELOPMENT

The best high performing teams are made up of individuals who have focused on their own personal development. The following questions can be used as a starting point for those leaders looking to improve their C1.

Write a short response to each of the following questions. It can be a sentence, a recollection of an event, a poem, a conversation – however you choose to answer.

1. What do you really enjoy doing?

2. How did your family enjoy themselves?

3. Did you enjoy the same things as your family?

4. What makes you laugh?

5. How much were you encouraged to express your feelings when you were growing up?

6. How did your parents respond to you when you expressed negative emotions? Did the family try to acknowledge it, control it, ignore it, punish it, or was there an all-out fight? How may that still be influencing you today?

7. Do you remember a time when you expressed yourself and it was not accepted well?

8. What did you do?

9. How did your family deal with issues around sexuality?

10. When there was emotional conflict, how did your family resolve it?

11. How did that make you feel?

12. How effectively was the conflict resolved?

13. How can you increase the amount of fun you have in your life?

C1 TOOL #1:
ACTIVELY FOSTER INNOVATION

PROCESS

1. **Identify sources of creativity** – There are many different areas of your business that creative solutions can come from:

   - **Employees:** are the ones who handle the day-to-day problems and are best placed to spot opportunities for devising better ways of doing things
   - **Customers:** listen carefully and explore their comments as they often give good feedback
   - **Relationships with suppliers:** many suppliers are also looking for mutual benefit
   - **Competitors:** gather intelligence on what your competitors are doing

2. **Set an example yourself** – Realise that staff need a space to chat, think and have sessions to explore different ideas in different ways. Encourage new ideas consistently, discuss all the ideas in an open forum, welcome new explorations and different directions. Be willing to think outside the box and not just the way you've always done things.

3. **Foster a climate of creativity** – Provide a sense of dynamism rather than 'quiet time' and provide a feeling of interest and mutual respect when people interact. Create an atmosphere of enthusiasm, open-mindedness and commitment in which conflicting ideas are used positively.

4. **Use techniques for creativity** – Brainstorming involves spontaneous discussion in the search for new ideas and is invaluable in generating large numbers of ideas (See C1 Tool #3). Employee suggestion schemes also gather great ideas but the key to success is to offer feedback and rewards to contributors so that employees realise that management listens and values the ideas. Focus groups can also explore a particular topic in depth and are good for developing related ideas.

5. **Become a team member** – Challenge others in the way they do things, and encourage them to challenge you.

6. **Build in breathing space** – If you want people to be creative, you can't expect them to be 'doing' all the time. Trust people with space and time and generally they will come up with the goods.

7. **Work out inexpensive pilots** – It is important to try out ideas that seem to be promising but be aware that some of these ideas may need significant investment. Work out how to pilot such ideas on a smaller scale so that you can get feedback on how they can be further developed.

8. **Feedback and reward** – Let employees know how their suggestions are being implemented and the results being achieved because this encourages them to be forthcoming with further ideas. Feedback should be constructive, supportive and should cover all the ideas they have contributed

DOS

✓ Have a customer focus in order to produce goods and services that people want now or may want in the future

✓ Encourage trials and experiments, and use failure to move forwards, not backwards

✓ Weigh up the importance of different ideas whether they be good or bad

DON'TS

✗ Don't accept that good ideas are the privilege of a few

✗ Don't accept that all conflict is negative

✗ Don't accept that creativity takes a second place to order and routine

C1 TOOL #2:
MAKE EMOTIONAL CONFLICT A BUSINESS AS USUAL PROCESS

HOW THIS RELATES TO C1

Spontaneity only occurs when individuals are free to express themselves. This expression, however, can cause conflict within the team that can negatively impact performance if the team doesn't know how to manage it. The Pinch Crunch model is a highly effective way for teams to effectively manage the conflict that free expression engenders.

INTRODUCTION TO THE PINCH CRUNCH MODEL

The key to managing conflict is to understand how to respond rather than react to Pinches. A Pinch is a signal of the possibility of an impending disruption; it describes a sense of loss of freedom within one's current role and translates into a range of emotions including anger, frustration, hurt and shame, just to name a few (for detailed information on the nine Pinch points refer to Principle 2). If not addressed, an emotional Pinch is likely to become a Crunch – a major disruption.

If the renegotiation of expectations is raised at the point in the relationship when one of the members feels a Pinch, the parties have more choice and more control over the situation. It is important that people learn to detect Pinches before Crunches develop so that they can be managed before a full on emotional hijack takes place and the individuals either withdraw from the process, maliciously comply or attack each other.

PROCESS

1. Identify your own Pinch point.
2. Identify what happens when this Pinch turns into a Crunch.
3. Have a discussion with every key member in your team about what your and their Pinch point is.
4. Explore what happens when their Pinch turns into a Crunch.
5. Create a contract with every key member in your team that outlines what causes a Pinch for you, how that can be dissolved, and what takes the Pinch to a Crunch and how that can be dissolved.

DOS

✓ Do be honest about your Pinch
✓ Understand how you feel when the Pinch turns into a Crunch
✓ Be aware of what makes other people Pinch
✓ Agree with them on how together, if a Pinch does happen, it can be resolved

DON'TS

✗ Don't assume that other's Pinch and Crunch is the same as yours
✗ Don't intentionally trigger people into a Pinch
✗ Don't turn the Pinch into a Crunch

C1 TOOL #3:
USE BRAINSTORMING TO DRIVE INNOVATION

THERE ARE FIVE STEPS TO BRAINSTORMING

1. **Set directions**. Describe the situation and define the problem. Help people to understand the problem to be solved and clarify the objectives. Focus on productive objectives and keep group on track. Spend time deciding on what criteria the final solution will need to address.

2. Encourage everyone to say whatever comes into their mind about possible solutions to the problem. **Encourage outside-the-box thinking**. *Challenge assumptions*. Be creative. Go crazy. *Think outside the box*. Sometimes the wildest ideas lead to great ones. The wilder the ideas the better. Step out of your shoes to surface new insights. ('What if you were a cat, or a film scenario writer – how would you solve the problem?'). *Encourage active listening*.

3. **Record and display each idea**. To avoid misunderstanding, make sure each idea is complete – don't use one-word descriptions. Don't edit.

4. **Apply the 80/20 rule and shift thinking styles to select the best ideas**. Look through your list of ideas and circle the 20% that will yield 80% of the results you are looking for. Encourage full-spectrum thinking.

5. **Prioritise the ideas** by evaluating them against the criteria established at the beginning of the session.

DOS

✓ Involve everyone. Encourage everyone to contribute. Control dominating participants. Celebrate diversity. Use different techniques to draw ideas from the group.

✓ Encourage cross-fertilisation. Build on each other. Let others' ideas take you somewhere else. Combine, synergise, and improve upon ideas.

✓ Suspend judgement. No ideas are bad ideas. All ideas are good ideas. (Actually, a minority opinion offered during group decision-making often stimulates more innovative solutions to problem.)

DON'TS

✗ Don't overlook the obvious – the obvious solution is sometimes the best.

✗ Don't fear repetitions. At different moments you see with different eyes. During discussion, afterwards you may find that duplicate ideas are actually different, or that they may trigger different responses.

✗ Don't stop and discuss. Go for quantity, not quality. Keep the momentum going.

KEY EXPRESSION QUESTIONS FOR BUILDING A HIGH PERFORMANCE TEAM

1. How well does your team deal with conflicting points of view?

2. How good is your team at expressing their emotions to each other?

3. How does the team manage the conflict that inevitably comes from expressing emotions?

4. How good are you as a team at being creative and innovative when working together and solving problems?

5. How often does your team encourage new ideas and approaches? How often do you stretch yourselves to try something novel or different?

6. How do you have fun as a team? How could you inject more of this?

NeuroPower Case Study

NEUROPOWER CASE STUDY

ORGANISATIONAL CASE STUDY #1: STATE HEALTH HAND HYGIENE PROJECT

The Task: To improve compliance by health workers with hand hygiene practice.

Recap:

In 2007, an Australian state health department wanted to address the serious threat that health-associated infections posed to hospital patients. Micro-organisms are readily transmitted on the hands of health care workers. In Australia alone, health officials estimate that up to 7000 people die annually from hand hygiene-related infections in hospitals. The economic burden is also considerable, costing millions each year.

Hand hygiene has been proven to substantially reduce transmission of micro-organisms. However, despite well-established guidelines, compliance throughout the world with hygiene standards is disconcertingly low. International and national health agencies have been grappling with how to deal with the issue for some time, and few interventions have had any impact whatsoever, despite both European and US hospitals and governments spending tens of millions of dollars on communications, incentives, closed circuit TV and education.

Since research demonstrated that the hand hygiene issue centred around human behaviour, one state health department decided on an innovative, behaviour-changing approach using the NeuroPower framework to drive the solution. Working with the NeuroPower Consulting Team, the department implemented a behaviour change program called Clean Hands are LifeSavers that engaged the health workers and increased compliance from 18% to 60%. A key driver of this behaviour change involved effectively addressing each of the six Intelligences in the correct sequence. How these progressive steps were taken is outlined in the Organisational Toolbox Case Study at the end of each Intelligence chapter.

Having already: Created safety and security in the hospital environment by embedding values through a code of conduct

Step 2: Empower People to Express Themselves Spontaneously and Creatively
Historically, programs developed and delivered elsewhere in Australia failed to improve compliance greatly despite pouring millions of dollars into impressive (and expensive) marketing materials.

NeuroPower's approach was to encourage each ward in every hospital to work collaboratively to solve the issue. We showed the LifeSavers how to engage the health workers themselves in the creation and production of communications and marketing materials to support the campaign. As a result, every ward across the state came up with its own individual approach with events, posters, competitions and other inventive ideas for getting the hand hygiene message across.

ORGANISATIONAL CASE STUDY #2: MERCHANT BANK EQUITY DERIVATIVES LEADERSHIP TEAM

The Task: Improve employee engagement and tangible business performance

Recap:

In 2006, at the height of the financial boom, one of Australia's leading equity derivatives teams was operating in an environment that was fast-paced, demanding and with a high level of stress. In order to handle large volumes of work in a very volatile market, the team needed to be highly functional and collaborative. Growth was nearly 200 per cent over the previous year so the enormous strain was evident. This was mainly caused by a Leadership Team in crisis.

The Leadership Team was fractured, non-collaborative and driven by their own individual agendas. There was both a lack of respect and a lack of honesty between members which led to highly reactive responses and conflict. The broader team could see this occurring and they felt they were part of a warring tribe with all the insecurities that brought.

NeuroPower consultants devised a program which focused on addressing the splintered Leadership Team. The intervention involved a series of group structured processes which were embedded by individual coaching sessions.

Having already: Created role clarity

Step 2: Empowering People to Express Themselves using C1

Once the team environment became safe, the next step was to ensure the Leadership Team had permission to express themselves honestly, be creative and use out-of-the-box thinking with no fear. We looked at the Core Belief profiles of the group members (these are the profiles embedded in C1) which revealed each individual's world view and how they interacted with others in the workplace. For many members, the fact that people saw the world differently was a revelation. A key aspect of this session was the Pinch/Crunch model which looked at the resistance strategies and emotional reactions the various Core Belief profiles have and how this underlies all conflict. We helped them develop ways to deal with conflict in this volatile and challenging environment.

Chapter 4

Our Third Social Cognitive Need:
LEADING THE PACK &
The Intervention Function (P2)

LEADING THE PACK (P2) AT A GLANCE

Leading the Pack is our Brain's Third Social Cognitive Need

The brain is competitive and loves status. Once basic needs have been met, money itself has little influence on happiness. Instead, status, recognition and independence are key drivers of motivation and satisfaction and must be managed to foster healthy passion rather than unhealthy competition.

Characteristics of the Leading the Pack (P2) Functional Network

Action and Passion

STRENGTH	WEAKNESS
Committed and focused on doing whatever it takes to achieve the outcome	Can cut corners and ignore processes to achieve the outcome

OPPORTUNITY	THREAT
To detach from their overattachment to outcomes	Can burn out

Management Style

- High energy and passionate
- Results-focused and able to make quick decisions
- Can be argumentative or aggressive

VITALITY

P2 THINKING

Personal goals
and priorities

P2 FEELING

Passion
and drive

P2 SOMATIC

Physical
strength

COMMUNICATION STYLE

- Can often push the conversation in one direction
- Can be totally insensitive to others not in line with their ideas
- Can be very passionate about a cause or topic
- Will talk over others and will not keep to set timeframes unless they believe they should
- Can be bombastic or rude
- Very persuasive and energetic

KEYWORDS INCLUDE

- Passion
- Success
- Drive
- Achievement
- Goals

Leading the Pack (P2) Helps Us to Survive

Leading the Pack (P2) helps both individuals and the group to survive and thrive by motivating and enabling us to break past patterns, challenge the status quo and apply passion to drive towards better outcomes.

Leading the Pack &
The Intervention Function (P2)

LEADING THE PACK: OUR BRAIN'S THIRD SOCIAL NEED

In Chapter 1, we introduced a foundational social need - Relatedness (P1) - which drives us to learn the rules of the groups to which we belong and to then apply them. Relatedness (P1) encourages us to blend into the group and promote our own survival by helping the *group* to sustain itself (using historical knowledge embedded in the group's culture). It encourages us to learn our place in the group and stay there. And yet on a daily basis many of us seem to push back against this Relatedness and the group. Rather than maintaining the status quo, we challenge ourselves and the group and drive towards achieving personal goals that help us differentiate ourselves as individuals. We want to be better than the rest, we want to 'lead the pack' and be respected for it in at least one area. As with Relatedness (P1), this drive to be Leading the Pack (P2) has deep roots in our evolution.

Within the brain, a diverse range of structures and neuronal networks help us satisfy our need for Leading the Pack. Within the *NeuroPower* framework, this set of structures is called the 'P2 Intervention System' (or sometimes the 'P2 network' or 'P2 function') and when we emphasise this social need, we give rise to a particular thinking style referred to as 'P2 Intelligence'. The rest of this chapter explores the P2 Intervention System in detail.

No matter how much some of us deny it, all humans are competitive. We see it on full display- in schools, stadiums, bars and workplaces around the world. Whether we're athletes, spectators, workplace leaders or followers, our brains are constantly comparing ourselves to others. For our ancestors, those at the 'top of the tree' in the group had first choice of food and mates, giving us a definite incentive to reach for the top (Jordan, Sivanathan & Galinsky, 2011). Now, many generations later, social cues about status, recognition and independence can have a powerful impact on our brains. For example, brain imaging studies have shown that praise activates the same reward areas of the brain (the caudate and putamen) as money rewards - and that these areas are highly sensitive even to small changes in your status (Izuma et al., 2008; Zink et al., 2008). The value of money itself seems to diminish when we know someone else is earning more, with less internal reward activity in the brain (Fliessbach et al., 2007). And David Rock[1], who first coined the

---

1   David Rock's SCARF model draws on neuroscience and other research to effectively explore the impact of social dynamics on workplaces. Within this model, the elements of 'Status' and 'Autonomy' align well with the social need of Leading the Pack (P2). In addition, Rock's 'Certainty', 'Relatedness' and 'Fairness' each describe aspects of the P1 Intelligence (Relatedness) within the *NeuroPower* framework.

term NeuroLeadership, has highlighted Japanese research showing that when we see others outperforming us in things that we value then the challenge to our sense of status and self-esteem activates a threat response in the anterior cingulate cortex. Needless to say, the resulting emotional response can be quite unconstructive (Takeushi et al., 2008).

Performance-driven tasks can lead to stress responses when we know that we are being assessed by others, but - importantly - psychology and neuroscience research suggests that our ability to cope depends heavily on our sense of control over the situation; the more autonomy and control we have, the easier it is to cope (Dickersen & Kemeny, 2008). In fact, in 2012, Gary Sherman and his colleagues at Harvard Business School found that amongst senior military and government leaders, individuals who *felt* they had more power showed consistently lower levels of the stress hormone cortisol. And the benefits don't just extend to the individual. Research out of Stanford has shown that giving someone a greater sense of control over their situation increases their optimism and self-esteem, and leads to greater task-related activity and effort (Fast et al., 2009).

Both organisational and neuroscience research point to the benefits of supporting and encouraging this drive (Leading the Pack) for individuals and teams. Driven by greater activity in the left frontal lobe, individuals high in Leading the Pack focus more on achieving the goals of the organisation, show tenacity in the face of early failures and can generate more options (Amodio et al., 2004; Crowe & Higgins, 1997; Markovits et al., 2008; Mehta & Josephs, 2006). And yet, when over-emphasised and misdirected, the drive of P2 can lead to divisive competition and aggression (McAndrew, 2009).

THE P2 CHALLENGE FOR LEADERS

So how can leaders keep 'P2' in their teams within the healthy zone and motivate their teams to brilliant performance? Firstly, as we mentioned earlier, building evidence from research conducted by people such as Dr Caroline Zink and highlighted by authors such as Daniel Pink, show that status, recognition and independence are key drivers of motivation and performance and in many cases have a greater long-term effect than money. In a family, community, team or corporate environment, we all have a need to be personally successful and to be recognised. Leaders can create this in three ways. Firstly, to build energy and drive, leaders need to identify different markers of excellence so that each member of the team has an area in which they Lead the Pack.

Secondly, they need to recognise that central to the P2 system in the brain are two areas, the orbitofrontal cortex and the anterior cingulate cortex, which together work to constantly assess the relationship between what you're doing and the rewards that you are getting. The question they ask: *"Is this course of action still bringing me sufficient reward or do I need to change my behaviour?"* When working with individuals high in P2, leaders need to keep a keen eye on the effort-reward ratio for both the individual and the team as a whole as it works towards its goals.

Finally, to drive high performance, leaders must align individual aspirations and motivation with the team's goals and have the ability to redirect individual competitiveness towards shared competitive advantage.

THE EVOLUTIONARY SOCIAL BRAIN FUNCTION OF P2

The P2 Intelligence enables the individual to survive through:

1. Goal-directed behaviour and independent action (Berkman & Lieberman, 2009)

2. Motivation and drive that keeps the mind and behaviour focused on the achievement of purposeful goals – including those that may involve competition with other members of the group for individual reward. Specifically, this involves attention, motor control, response inhibition and progress monitoring (Decety et al., 2004)

3. Prioritisation of options so that the individual can achieve the greatest benefit with minimum cognitive, somatic or emotional effort (Walton et al., 2006)

4. A sense of urgency and independence; a sense of willpower and ego .

Recognising the Characteristics of Leading the Pack (P2)

The P2 Intelligence gives the mind willpower that drives enthusiastic behaviour aimed at success. P2 is a very high-energy function, and individuals with highly functioning P2 are skilled at energising, striving, convincing and debating. Many of the world's most powerful leaders have highly developed P2.

However, the P2 Intelligence can also drive a person to be so intent on performing and achieving that they become exclusively task-oriented. When this happens they often bully or play favourites because they see people only as a means to achieving their own success and rise to power.

From an Eastern perspective, Judith (1996) argues that in our physical body P2 is associated with the solar plexus or 'the gut'. The childhood development of this Intelligence follows on from that of C1, the pleasure instinct. From the safety of the family (P1) and awareness of their own individuality and emotions (C1), a young person with well-functioning P1 and C1 will develop the motivation to act independently and to address the challenge of P2: to realise their separateness, to establish their autonomy and to establish the right to act. As the child rises to these challenges and begins to take risks, they develop

P2 in the Brain[*]

Research has revealed that several parts of the brain support the P2 system:

- The left medial prefrontal cortex (PFC) and in particular the orbital PFC, which performs executive functions (Schore, 1994) mediates both the reward value of voluntary actions and calculates the magnitude of reward or punishment values (O'Doherty et al., 2001; Rolls, 2000; Tremblay & Schultz, 1999; Watanabe, 1996). This part of the brain is sensitive to the size of our gains and losses and assesses whether there is enough in it for us to undertake a task (Xue et al., 2009).

- More generally, the medial PFC is consistently implicated when we make evaluations about ourselves (Saxe & Haushofer, 2008), and when we reflect upon our personal goals and aspirations (P2 Thinking; Johnson et al., 2006).[†]

- The anterior cingulate cortex contains many neuron pathways that are also recruited to help process the costs and benefits of different courses of action. Activity in individual neurons in this area predicts whether an individual will choose to compete for a larger reward or settle for a smaller reward without having to compete (Walton & Baudonnat, 2012).

- The insula (in particular the right insula) is strongly implicated in having a sense of agency (Sperduti et al., 2011) and the precuneus (located on the medial surface of the parietal lobe) is associated with first-perspective taking (Cavanna & Trimble, 2006).[‡]

---

[*]   Both P1 and P2 can be seen as describing different motivations that produce behaviours. Those behaviours and actions are supported by an extensive set of structures in the somatosensory and motor areas of the brain (including, for example, the primary and supplementary motor areas. Here we focus on brain areas supporting characteristics that distinguish P2 (achievement-focused action, a sense of agency, assessment of status, social competition) from P1 (obligation-focused action, motivation to comply with externally directed rules and behaviours, assessment of safety and security).

[†]   By contrast, recent reviews suggest that applying 'if-then' rules given to us by others (P1 thinking) seem to be represented in more lateral areas of the PFC (Berkman & Lieberman in Moskowitz & Grant, 2009).

[‡]   Interestingly, however, the precuneus has also repeatedly been implicated in both self-related processes (such as recognising your arms and legs as your own) and other-related processes (such as the ability to recognise actions caused by others, and a focus on duties and obligations; Cavanna & Trimble, 2006; Farrer & Frith, 2002; Mitchell et al., 2009).

Searching for the 'Self' in the Brain

Where are 'you' in your brain? Answering that in any one brain imaging study has many challenges. But as technology increases in speed and capacity, researchers are now combining data collected over years of brain imaging studies to examine similarities between thousands of brains simultaneously - and some, like researchers from the NeuroImaging Data Access Group, have begun sharing this database online to the public.[§]

The images below show the results of an automated, computer-based meta-analysis of 206 different studies that each explored different brain processes involving our sense of 'self'. Each blue dot shows a location where one of these tasks involved greater activation when study participants had to perform tasks that involved thinking about or making decisions related to themselves.

The pattern of activations across all these different studies suggests that processing about the 'self' involves activity predominantly in the left medial prefrontal cortex (which sits just above the eyes) and another midline area further back in the left precuneus. These areas are part of what has become known as the midline default mode system which seems to be critical for understanding our own (and others) internal states.

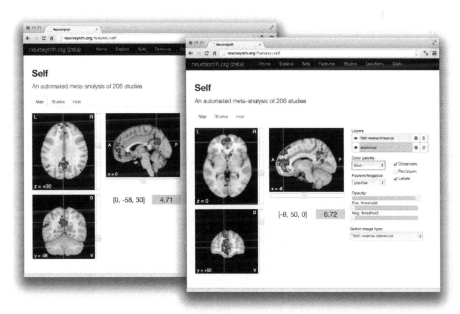

§   At the time of printing, this searchable database of comparisons has been made available at www.neurosynth.org

their own individual willpower.

Research focused on the neuroscience of 'promotion-focused' regulatory styles and goal-approach behaviours indicate that P2 is linked to activation in the left prefrontal cortex (Amodio et al., 2004; Eddington et al., 2007; 2009) as well as left and right precuneus and the anterior cingulate cortex (Strauman et al., 2013).

The Development of Leading the Pack (P2)

THE EMERGENCE OF THE EGO

The strengths of P2 include:

- Self-esteem
- Self-respect
- Self-discipline
- Ambition

- A willingness to take risks in order to achieve goals
- Drive
- High energy

The P2 Intelligence relates to the ego, which Jung proposed is made up of the individual's conscious perceptions, memories and thoughts and is responsible for the individual's sense of personal success.

The focus of this Intelligence is on individual action. High functioning P2 reflects the development of a person's autonomy and the ability to take responsibility for themselves. Without this independence, they will act like a victim, blaming others for events in their life, while believing they have no power to influence the direction their life takes. Those with high functioning P2 act in a way that reflects their strong sense of self, even if this risks the disapproval of others or conflicts with the values or beliefs of the tribe.

THE DEVELOPMENT OF AN EGO IDENTITY

During the P1 stage, the child identifies with their body and internalises society's rules. Freud would refer to P1 as the *superego*. As they develop their C1 Intelligence they identify with their emotions and needs – what Freud would refer to as the *id*. The focus of P1 is the internal unconscious world, while C1 focuses on the conscious external world. According to Freud, the child then develops their ego, which consists of the conscious elements of the self. Thus P2 acts as the communicator between the unconscious and conscious parts of self. As the P2 Intelligence develops, the focus shifts from how we relate to others to how we relate to ourselves.

During the P2 stage the child needs to learn to direct the impulses and emotions from P1 and C1 into goal-aligned behaviour. The focus of the ego is self-definition, but the tribe moderates it. As the child develops their ego they step out and take risks. According to the response of the tribe, the more acceptable parts of the individual become the first ingredients for what will later become their conscious personality profile (i.e. their Master[2]). The parts that are rejected by the significant people in the tribe are also rejected by the child's ego and sent into the unconscious. These aspects of the self are the first ingredients for what will later become their unconscious second-order personality profile (also known as their Mirror). This aspect of self, while denied by the person, is quite obvious to those around them, especially during times of stress.

The P2 Intelligence is linked with the hippocampus (in the medial temporal lobe) and the orbitofrontal cortex. The development of these areas allows the child to have 'explicit' memories where they are aware that they are remembering something (Squire & Zola-Morgan, 1991; Perner & Ruffman, 1995; Tulving, 1993; Schachter et al., 1996).

The development of the P2 Intelligence may begin to occur as early as the second year of life. During this sensitive period a 'cognitive mapper' develops (Edelman, 1992; Bauer, 1996). Thought to be located within the hippocampus, this mapper enables the child to recall the order in which events occur. This allows the child to develop a sense of time and sequencing. The child comes to expect what typically comes first and what comes next in a specific circumstance. For example, consider the passionate reaction displayed by a toddler to a visitor sitting in the 'wrong' chair for the family dinner. This hippocampal development is associated with the capacity to generate the spatial representational maps for the locations of things in the world. Loss of hippocampal functioning in rats, for example, leads to loss of memory for running a maze (Squire, 1987).

This cognitive mapper allows the brain to create a four-dimensional sense of the self in the world across time. The ability to link reward with actions through time is particularly important for the development of actions based on positive reinforcement, such as those associated with P2 (Siegel, 1999).

Highly functioning P2 will act as a force that encourages self-expression, rather than one that produces guilt and a feeling that the individual is confined to behaving in certain approved ways. Keeping this in perspective can enable us to have a strong will, while simultaneously transcending it.

Aggression from significant adults for 'bad' behaviour can result in the child developing low self-esteem. This leaves no room for taking risks that may result in further mistakes. The risk-averse ego instead loses power and relies on external success and the approval of others in order to feel good. On the other hand, if the significant adults can support risk-taking and moderate the child's behaviour without shaming, the child will develop a healthy self-esteem (Judith, 1996).

---

2   For more information about the Master and Mirror personalities, and the Neuro-Rational Types, see Principle 3.

'Asian Brains' vs 'Western Brains'

Do cultural differences show up in the brain? Researchers describing themselves as 'cultural neuroscientists' have been exploring this question in recent years, using brain imaging techiques to try to explain interesting differences between Western and Asian styles of thinking.

For example, culturally speaking, anthropologists have observed that individuals in Western cultures tend to have a strong focus on the self (individualistic), and Asian cultures tend to place comparatively more emphasis on family and social groups (collectivist). One easy demonstration of this in the lab is that American individuals are much better at recognising and remembering adjectives related to themselves than those relating to family or strangers; Chinese individuals, on the other hand, seem to remember descriptions of themselves and of their family equally well.

To explain this, cultural neuroscientists looked at brain activity when performing this kind of task. They have found that the ventromedial PFC (a key area for awareness of the 'self') was activated by viewing descriptions of the self for both Americans and Chinese participants, but that the Chinese *also* had activity in this area when viewing descriptions of their family members (Zhu et al., 2007; Han & Northoff, 2012).

As UCLA-based researcher, Dr Meghan Meyer (2009), observes:

> *Taken together, these divergent findings fit with each cultures' conceptualization of the individual — independent in Western-European/American cultures, and intertwined with others in your environment in East-Asian cultures. Of course, this research should not be used to over-generalize differences in thinking across cultures. Indeed, there is also a great deal of research highlighting the commonalities in cognition across cultures. That said, acknowledging the subtle differences may help people in contemporary society — which is increasingly culturally diverse — appreciate the nuances in thought and behavior among the people we come across in our day to day lives.*

Willpower has Both Strengths and Weaknesses

POWER

It is clear when we spend time around people with highly functioning P2 that they are powerful individuals. Our society promotes power over (force), but when an individual with developed P2 becomes more evolved, their power is more akin to the original Latin meaning, which is 'to be able'. This most commonly takes the form of physical power, but also relates to the ability to cause change. To be empowered is to be able to determine our own destiny, to risk and take responsibility for the outcome, to learn from and correct mistakes, and to change our behaviour accordingly.

People with a highly functioning P2 are confident in their own personal opinions. During their development, the child forms opinions and develops the confidence to express them. If the tribe supports this independence, they will grow up to become passionate, persuasive and powerful. With self-confidence, these people can express their individuality while appreciating the opinions and beliefs of others. Respecting both themselves and others, they will willingly cooperate and contribute to their community.

P2 provides us with the means to break through the glass ceiling of performance to be and do whatever it is that we really want. As psychiatrist Dr Brenda Davies (1998) suggests, if your ship hasn't come in yet, use your P2 to take you out to meet it.

However, P2 also has a dark side. With excess P2, individuals can act as insensitive weapons, potentially marring or destroying relationships and the self-esteem of others.

Myss (1996) insightfully outlines the natural evolution of P2 as involving four stages, each of which can take just a short time, months, or years. Each stage challenges the person's character, ethics, morality and self-respect. (This is the same process undertaken by teams as they develop a sense of team identity and compete in the market.)

The first stage is **rebellion**. It starts with an act of revolution or several minor rebellions. This establishes the person's separateness from group authority and signifies they have sufficient inner strength to 'stand their ground' and live according to their own examined values and beliefs. In teams, this is also known as *Forming* and involves establishing the team's separation from the rest of the world. This gives the team permission to operate as a separate unit.

The second stage of P2 evolution is **involution**. The person calls on their 'guts' or internal fortitude to do the internal work of dealing with the consequences of their choices and actions. They acquire the skills of self-inquiry and finding insight, and therefore develop faith in their ability to act in a way that honours themselves. This includes releasing the past and accepting themselves and is like dying to self in order to be reborn. In teams, this phase is also known as *Storming* and reflects a realisation that the team possesses the skills and knowledge needed to get the job done; that is, that it does not need to rely on anyone outside the team.

At this stage, it is important to acknowledge that it takes strength to withdraw from the authority of a group norm. If your spirit is strong enough to go against your support network, it has the potential to change your life. If we look our fears in the face, they will be overcome. As individuals, it is at this stage that bad childhood memories can be used to make good choices as an adult.

The third stage of P2 evolution is a period of **narcissism**, when the person develops the personal strength to create an image of themselves regardless of tribal criticism. Their newly formed self-esteem gives them a strength, stamina and the ability to follow their 'gut' instincts. The individual now feels free to be guided in their choices by more than reasoning; their 'gut' feelings warn them, then direct them towards personal power and encourage them to take control of their life. In teams, this equates with a period of *Norming* in which a team gains a sense that it can compete in the market and deliver on KPIs. The team creates its own sense of true north, through performance management and the celebration of success.

The fourth stage is **evolution**. A person needs to like themselves, or they will continue to attract situations that reinforce their low self-esteem. As they face sequential challenges, they gain strength to make wiser choices – choices which enhance their spirit rather than drain their power. Eventually the person gains a high level of self-esteem and spiritual power and can be whoever they wish. They are empowered to maintain their principles, dignity and passion without compromise, whatever the odds. In teams, this final phase of P2 evolution is called *Performing*; the team is empowered and every member does whatever it takes to smash through glass ceilings.

P2-DRIVEN PERSON AT WORK

The P2-driven person at work is a competitive, formidable powerhouse. A mind with highly developed P2 is a study in proactivity. These individuals set their goals and use their initiative to make things happen, taking responsibility for their own circumstances. This is no helpless victim!

Whereas a P1-driven person is not ego-centred but instead focused on the ways of the team and will cooperate with workmates, the P2-driven person is egocentric and strives to achieve as an individual.

It is a common perceptual bias for those with highly developed P2 to consistently overestimate their control over an outcome and to underestimate the role of chance or factors beyond their control (Taylor & Brown, 1988; Langer, 1978).

It is not the *doing* but the *completing* that holds pleasure for the P2 Intelligence. Work is a means of enhancing their own rise to stardom or to look the strongest

Childhood Experience of Shame
Damages P2 Intelligence

During early infancy, the vast majority of parent-child interactions are positive, affectionate and playful. Due to the very limited skills and mobility of the infant, he or she will tend to stay in close proximity to the caretaker, who provides for the child's bodily and emotional needs. As the helpless infant grows into an exploring toddler, the parent's role expands to include protecting the infant from the many domestic risks of life, like stairwells, cars and the vagaries of pets. As the parent's role increases they begin to say 'No!' on an almost constant basis from the beginning of the second year (Rothbart, Taylor & Tucker, 1989). Now the state of acceptance and attunement with the attachment figure begins to be conditional on specific behaviour. Shame, arising from this loss of attunement, is a powerful inhibitory emotion and a primary means of social control (Schore, 1991). Shame effectively truncates the positive emotions generated within reciprocal interactions through activation of dopaminergic and opioid systems – systems that build the brain and increase tolerance for higher levels of positive affect and arousal. During the second year of life, studies have found that the eyes and facial expressions come to be used to inhibit toddler activities. Looks of disapproval or disgust from an adult, while their infant is in a state of arousal, result in the experience of shame (Schore, 1994). This is in sharp contrast to early infancy where the mutual gaze between attachment figure and child is a primary mechanism for promoting brain growth and organisation.

and the best. Therefore, the P2-driven team member often presents as the most efficient, tireless and achieving member of the team. In this space, there is no time for friendship or play for self or others unless useful to their rise to power or prestige (Horney, 1945).

Of course, there is a price to pay for this self-forgetfulness and denial of feelings. Judith (1996) argues that the gut feelings of our solar plexus are the source of P2. Their domain is in dealing with action as well as integrity and righteousness. The emotions of the gut include anger, rage, jealousy, resentment and guilt. Repressing any of these can cause diseases such as cancer, digestive problems, diabetes, obesity, problems with the pancreas or gall bladder, fatigue, depression and even despair (Judith, 1996).

Poorly Functioning P2 and Ego-Centric Behaviour

Poorly functioning P2 manifests in low levels of energy, passion and self-discipline, and a weak will and ego. The person will be passive, avoiding risks and confrontation by following the rules. They appear to please but resent the demands of others, and yet lack the will to manage their own lives. These individuals do not take responsibility for their situation but blame others. They may have goals, but lack the self-discipline, perseverance and will to bring them to fruition. These people can become passive-aggressive or detached. Shy and withdrawn, they can appear cold. How was this character formed? We can look back to childhood to find the answer.

When the child starts to act according to their own volition, and takes risks to 'do their own thing' independent of directions of their elders, they are working with the emergence of P2. If they are to develop a highly functioning P2, they need guidance without stifling their ego. Of course, the world is not full of wise parents, and so many children fail to effectively develop their ego. This can happen in any number of poor parenting approaches including overindulgence, under-attention, too high expectations, parentification, excess control or sexual over-stimulation (Judith, 1996).

UNDER-RELIANCE ON P2

Not all children grow up with a highly functioning P2. Judith (1996) argues that children with poorly functioning P2 have usually been the victims of inconsistent parental discipline. This parenting approach teaches the child that taking on new or risky things will result in punishment rather than support and guidance. Operating from a space of fear, the child therefore learns to follow the rules without question and not stray into the unknown. Children who have been abused may also interpret their experience as punishment, which can similarly affect the development of the P2 Intelligence. In an attempt to compensate for being 'bad', they continue restricting themselves and feeling unworthy of the reward of pleasure and happiness even into adulthood (Judith, 1996).

The demon at this stage of development is shame. When a child is shamed, their power is destroyed and their ego development is impeded. This involves shaming not only of their ego but also their instincts, which are part of their identity from P1 and C1. As the child tries to control their instincts with their thoughts, their instincts are denied and driven into their unconscious. But of course this isn't the end; their instincts break out in bad behaviour, such as bursts of temper, passive-aggression or procrastination.

From the perspective of the individual, shame is somehow atoned by self-punishment or suffering. The person punishes themselves with misery and failure,

When More is Never Enough

Cozolino (2002) describes the behaviour of minds totally focused on P2 as being manic. This pattern of behaviour involves engaging in constantly escalating levels of activity in order to avoid facing the difficult personal questions that the P2-driven mind has repressed.

and will continue to do so all their life unless they focus on developing their P2 self-esteem. The task of integration is to embrace their P2 and give themselves permission to act on their own behalf.

OVER-RELIANCE ON P2

Some people grow up with an over-reliance on P2. This manifests somatically in high anxiety (hypertension), which makes the person overcharged with energy or hyperactive. Their muscles are tense and their stomach becomes acidic. Because their core self is undernourished, they need to bolster their false self with the approval of others.

This is achieved through constant activity and trying to over-achieve. Indeed, these individuals do not feel alive without this frenetic activity. Their ironclad will appears powerful but is brittle and fragile; when challenged, they retreat out of fear or react with anger. They may also become obsessed with getting everything right.

These people are obsessed with having power over themselves and others. Some people who over-rely on P2 put great energy into pushing their own bodies, treating them like machines in order to look and perform well (thereby bolstering their ego). These people are well advised to find a balance between listening to their body and achieving. At the extreme, people who rely excessively on P2 become like robots. Their ego comprises no body or spirit, only will, and activity. They are what they do and achieve, and are just one small step from abusing their power. This is the dominator, or the bully, who needs to win at all costs – to have power over rather than power *with* others (Judith, 1996).

Karen Horney (1945) suggests that excessive P2 leads to neurotic thinking and behaviour. This can be experienced to some extent by any person with a strongly developed P2 Intelligence, especially if their reactive personality (i.e. Neuro-Limbic Type or Core Belief) is dominated by P2.

To this person, life follows the Darwinian theory of survival of the fittest, where everyone is fighting for survival. Life is seen as a struggle and you have to fight to win. This aggressive type, therefore, 'moves against' people, rejecting compliance or neutrality as foolhardy. Instead, they proactively go out to face the 'enemy' (although this is usually accompanied by a smile or a greeting). These individuals are constantly alert to the fighting strengths of everyone they meet because, of course, they feel they need to be prepared. The demon of P2 is fear and is usually the unrecognised motivation for action. This fear is completely ego-based, usually involving fear of rejection, not looking good or criticism.

However, at the heart of all P2 fear is the fear of death. Facing death, heartbreak or even depression causes panic in the ego-focused individual who relies excessively on P2. In contrast, an individual who prefers the P1 Intelligence feels part of the tribe and can usually accept death as part of life, believing, 'When I die, the tribe or family lives on and I'll leave a legacy if there's time.' However, the P2 ego thinks, 'I'm an individual. When I die nothing survives.'

The P2-driven mind works very hard to overcome its fears and does its best to hide these fears from others, because to show it will weaken their competitive edge. Horney (1945) explains that while aggressive and innately fearful, a P2-dominated person often appears to be a 'good fellow'. In reality, their feelings are a combination of genuine benevolence, pretence and a neurotic need for approval (to bolster their fragile ego). Because of their innate fear about survival, raw P2 has a great need to control, either directly or indirectly. This can take the form of overt use of power or indirect manipulation. In the latter case, the individual may choose to be the power behind the throne while sadistically pursuing their own goals.

Individuals who over-rely on P2 are driven by an endless need to succeed. Success for them means not just a pass, but to surpass the competition. They crave prestige and recognition, as this external affirmation makes them feel strong and powerful. Of course, they can never feel satisfied. They always feel insecure because of their innate belief that the world is dangerous. Therefore, they become and wish to appear hard or tough, giving the message, 'I'm no pushover.'

Unfortunately, in their drive to win at all costs, these people exploit, outsmart and use others. Whenever they form a new relationship they are asking themselves, 'What's in it for me?' This can mar their close relationships as well, as they will choose a life partner who will bring them success, power, prestige, contacts or ideas. Love is often considered to be soft or weak.

There is a basic persona versus authenticity conflict for the P2-driven person: whether to ignore or repress their feelings, or alternatively to allow their feelings, show their vulnerability and allow an opening for their enemies to attack.

A person driven by raw P2 can be deceptive. When they interact they appear to be uninhibited because they express their viewpoint with confidence and passion; they say what they want and clearly express any anger. However, because they are inhibited in their emotional world, they have a diminished capacity for friendship, love, affection, sympathy and understanding. All of these feelings are rejected

How Autonomy and Learned Helplessness Relate to the P2 Function

Psychologist Fritz Perls, who founded the Gestalt movement, moved the concept of aggression from the Freudian concept of a purely destructive force to a concept closer to its original root which is 'to reach out'. He wished to re-establish its true biological function, which is not senseless discharge but rather application of one's will to bring about desirable changes in one's environment (Perls, 1969).

In contrast, the psychological condition, termed 'learned helplessness', that results in clinical depression occurs when individuals do not believe they have any influence on their circumstances and lack control over the conditions of their life (Maier & Seligman, 1976; Overmier & Seligman, 1967; Seligman, 1975; Seligman & Maier, 1967).

Interestingly, recent neuroscience research shows that this learned helplessness may be linked to decreased activity in the left prefrontal cortex (PFC). The left medial orbital PFC is usually activated when we focus on the achievement of positive goals, but individuals with major depressive disorder showed much less activity in this region, even when primed to focus on personal goals (Eddington et al., 2009).

and seen as sloppy sentimentality with no positive impact on the achievement of results. The P2-driven person can therefore send mixed messages; while they may appear friendly and confident and express 'safe' feelings, they must appear strong in order to appear successful.

The inner conflict for neurotic P2 is the need to combat all softer feelings because emotions will weaken their ability to fight in a hostile world. Even more challenging is the need to fight the enemy within, which is their desire to be sympathetic and caring. If they do repress their feelings and their desire to be 'good' or compliant, they can become more compulsively aggressive (Horney, 1945). It is important to remember that we all have the potential for aggression, but when we are not neurotic we can integrate this into our conscious personality profile (i.e. Neuro-Rational Type) and so moderate it. Thus, we can let our Master lead us out of our fear.

Individuals who have an over-reliance on P2 somatic, feeling or thinking circuits can be described as follows[3]:

3 Each of these reflects a particular Neuro-Limbic Type; the Eight, Three and Seven

Unhealthy Narcissism

Narcissists crave others' admiration more than their love. These people are often innovators and compelled to perform, not because they are working to a high internal standard of excellence but because they want the benefits and accolades that performance bestows. They take the freedom to follow their goals aggressively, irrespective of the cost to and effect on others. In stressful times, narcissistic managers can appear attractive, but only because they have the fight to push through plans that bring radical change (Goleman, 2006, p. 119).

Somatic Over-reliance on P2: If there is an over-reliance on P2 somatic, the individual focuses on feats of strength, physical power and exacting revenge. Using the self-justifying reframe of having a lust for life, they do everything in excess.

Feeling Over-reliance P2: With an over-reliance of P2 feeling, the individual becomes obsessed with success, approval and looking good in everybody's eyes.

Thinking Over-reliance P2: If there is an over-reliance on P2 thinking, the individual focuses on reframing everything so it is positive, motivated by a desire to avoid emotional pain (either their own or that of others).

THE IMPORTANCE OF WILLPOWER

The experience of shame can break a child's will. Any kind of shaming can crush the child's emerging P2, especially if it is related to behaviour they are too young to manage. Shaming includes child abuse, both verbal or physical. At this early stage the child's ego is fragile and grows to include a sense of shame because they believe their 'self' (as opposed to their behaviour) is bad. These children can grow up to believe they will fail at anything they put their hand to, and their lives often become self-fulfilling prophecies.

Receiving insufficient attention can also break a child's will. Some parents mean well but are just too busy to pay attention to what the child feels or wants. They give the child no choices, so provide no chance to develop a sense of will. The child then grows up with a sense of powerlessness and resignation. To compensate for their sense of loss, the child (and later the adult until the deficit is resolved) may become passive-aggressive and resentful, or swing the other way and become a violent bully. Lacking the will, power and freedom of P2 to create their own destiny, they must rely on their other

respectively. These relate to *NeuroPower* Principle #2.

Intelligences to run their life. Under-stimulation can also break a child's will, potentially inducing the child to grow up troubled by fatigue, low energy, a sense of emptiness and low libido (Judith, 1996).

Conversely, an overindulged child learns that any behaviour is accepted without restraint. They grow up with an inflated ego, feeling inferior or superior according to their unrealistic expectations, and lacking the self-confidence and limits to discover their own power. If a child is pushed beyond an appropriate level by supportive parents with very high expectations they can develop a sense of inadequacy, with their achievements never being enough. They too will grow up with low self-esteem and may ultimately specialise in failure, regardless of ability.

Some children are parentified and given work or sex roles that are far beyond their age and ability. They can also emerge with a sense of inadequacy and inferiority and are set up for failure.

A child's will can be broken as a result of over-controlling parents. This child submits but still has inner conflicts between their will (inner resistance) and outer compliance. My experience supports Judith's (1996) research that shows that when these children grow up they become reliable, hard working, eager to please and enduring during a crisis. However, in my experience these same adults are often quietly passive-aggressive and likely to sabotage the work environment.

The Difference between Shame and Guilt

Schore (1994) differentiates between shame and guilt. Guilt occurs later in development and is related to unacceptable behaviour, whereas shame is an emotion about the self that becomes internalised before there is an ability to differentiate between one's behaviour and self. Physiologically, shame is represented in a rapid transition from a positive to a negative affective state and from sympathetic to parasympathetic dominance. This shift occurs when the child has an expectation of attunement in a positive state, only to find disapproval and misattunement in the face of the attachment figure (Schore, 1994). Prolonged and repeated shame states result in physiological dysregulation and negatively impact the development of networks of affect regulation and attachment centred in medial prefrontal areas (Schore, 1994). Since shame is a powerful, preverbal and physiologically-based organising principle, the overuse of shame in the process of parenting can predispose a child to developmental psychopathology related to affect regulation and identity (Schore, 1994).

Sexual over-stimulation can also break the will of a child. Physical abuse that overloads the sensory system can cause a heightened resistance to intrusion to develop. Judith (1996) observes insightfully that this can grow into hypersensitivity to other intense sensory stimulations, such as noise, colour or emotions. These children may also attempt to discharge their excess energy through hyperactivity (Judith, 1996).

In summary, if the child risks acting autonomously and the parents respond with shaming, punishment or control, the child becomes either compliant (remaining in P1) or rebellious (over-relying on P2). Either way, they fail to develop an appropriately functioning P2, and lose their ability to match the appropriate P2 response with a problem requiring the application of willpower. Complaining about a situation is the manifestation of a poorly developed P2. Protest and rebellion are reactive positions and stem from repressed P2. A well-functioning P2 is instead proactive and provides the individual with the ability to make their own luck.

Building Your Willpower (P2) as an Adult

DEVELOPING YOUR WILLPOWER

If you wish to strengthen your willpower, you need to develop the courage to take risks and work outside your comfort zone.

If you have learned to habitually follow orders, your weak will is prey to the manipulation of others. Obeying orders without question relinquishes your own sense of responsibility, and so sells a piece of yourself in the process. An alternative is to try to find your own true will. Ask yourself, 'What would I do if there was nothing I was supposed to do?' Then action becomes future-focused and goal-centred. This sounds simple but it requires willpower and the effective management of emotions.

Acknowledge your innate power and decide what you really want. Exercise your will to direct your life with thought, self-discipline and passion, and then apply this willpower to ensure you remain honest and sensitive to yourself and others.

DEVELOPING P2

Poorly developed P2 or an over-reliance on P1 can cause illnesses related to issues of self-responsibility, self-esteem, fear of rejection or an over-sensitivity to criticism. It may also be difficult for an individual who is low in P2 to develop the power, energy and willpower they need to achieve success. Working through the following list of excellent actions suggested by Myss (1996) can build ego strength:

- Build your body health and fitness with a good diet and aerobic exercise.
- Engage in activities you enjoy.
- Plan in your schedule to engage in these activities regularly.

- Meet challenges and difficulties one at a time.
- Start small and build your will and power.
- Set long-term goals: a master plan plus a plan for a routine to include your goals. Then follow the plan, meeting the challenges and difficulties that naturally arise.
- Confront others when necessary.
- Risk new ventures. Each time you meet a challenge, you will gain power and confidence.
- Give up playing safe. Take risks and grow your ego strength.
- Work on your anger, both past (from enduring bad situations) and current.
- Attack the demon shame.
- Engage in an inner dialogue between your caring adult self and your abused child. Give your child permission to rebel against the rules you don't agree with.

HEALING P2 OVER-RELIANCE

If you have an over-reliance on P2 you will have more energy in your system than it can handle. Therefore, it needs to be discharged or rerouted. The following exercise (adapted from suggestions by Judith (1997) and Davies (1998)) can help.

- First, relax. Sit still and let go of control.
- Then do either a guided meditation, Feldenkrais or yoga. A hyperactive person will probably find it easier to start with yoga or Feldenkrais – at least they are active.
- Give yourself regular downtime. That is, take time to do nothing. Just be. You are, after all, a human being, not a human doing.
- As you relax, integrate your body, mind and emotions. Let your internal observer state be aware of your submerged emotions. Listen to your gut feelings.
- Then align your thinking with your relaxed emotions. Understand, respect and accept your feelings. Consider their relevance and appropriateness to the current situation then decide on and monitor your actions.

CREATING A HIGHLY FUNCTIONING P2

Compare your own experience with what you have learned about the P2 Intelligence. What are the aspects of your P2 of which you are aware? Is there one that you tend to focus on above the other two?

- The P2 somatic circuit is high energy and moves towards creating new rules that right injustice for the old rules.

- The P2 thinking circuit experiences high levels of enthusiasm, optimism and excitement.

- The P2 feeling circuit focuses on end results and the means of attaining them.

Diagram 4.1 shows the three aspects of P2 that require integration so that true Vitality can form.

The task involved in creating highly functioning P2 is to integrate the thinking aspect of enthusiasm, personal values and prioritising options, the somatic aspect of passion and justice, and the feeling aspect of moving towards goals. You may start by examining your values and beliefs and the degree to which they align with your feelings as well as your actions.

AFFIRMATIONS

If you are unaccustomed to it, putting your P2 willpower into play with confidence may feel as if you are unreasonably trusting the unknown. This may feel dangerous. If this is the case, some find that repeating the following affirmations inspired by Myss (1996) can help develop P2 functioning:

- I welcome opportunities to live in the power of the universe, to be self-expressed in my actions, and to fulfil my highest potential.

- I am powerful and I am worthy.

- I am responsible for myself, my life, my health, my welfare and my behaviour.

- I am open to receive prosperity in all its forms.

Diagram 4.1 Healthy P2 Intelligence — Noble Quality: Vitality

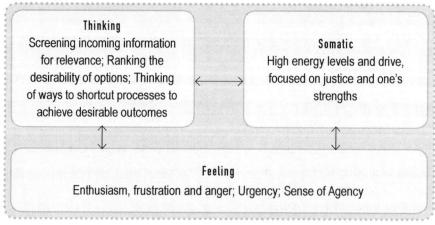

Thinking
Screening incoming information for relevance; Ranking the desirability of options; Thinking of ways to shortcut processes to achieve desirable outcomes

Somatic
High energy levels and drive, focused on justice and one's strengths

Feeling
Enthusiasm, frustration and anger; Urgency; Sense of Agency

For the Neuroscience of Vitality see Table 4.2

Table 4.2 The Neuroscience of Vitality

The table below details the Neuroscience of P2. Refer to Appendix 13 for more details.

Somatic Aspect	Feeling Aspect	Thinking Aspect
• Motor control through recruitment of P1 motor areas (primary motor cortex, supplementary motor area, premotor cortex, cerebellum and basal ganglia) • Sense of 'self' (integrated in the precuneus and supported by somatosensory areas in the parietal lobe) that orientates us in physical space and time essential to our ability to interact with the physical world (e.g. prevents us bumping into things; orientation association area), filtering out redundant sensory information (e.g. to navigate a crowded railway station; lateral prefrontal cortex)	• High motivation to succeed (left putamen and caudate nucleus, orbitofrontal cortex and the insula, medial prefrontal cortex for social feedback) • Anger and frustration (left orbital cortex, right anterior cingulate cortex affective division, bilateral anterior temporal poles) • Sense of power, perception of strength (leading to dominating behaviour) (testosterone, cortisol and adrenaline) • Urgency or impatience (adrenaline and testosterone) • A sense of what action to take to be successful (through somatic markers relating to success) • Feelings of elation following success or dejection following failure (associated respectively with increases and decreases in activity in the left prefrontal cortex monitored by the cingulate cortices, hypothalamus, tegmentum and interpreted by lateral and polar parts of the cortex in the frontal lobe)	• Ability to focus attention of goal-relevant information (lateral prefrontal cortex), including the ability to focus the mind to single-pointed attention (prefrontal cortex) in contemplative disciplines often developed through mantras, chanting, images and repetitive movement • Intrinsically driven, achievement focused, goal-directed behaviour (both physical and psychological; medial prefrontal cortex) • Filtering of redundant thoughts (prefrontal cortex) (i.e. elements not related to the achievement of the identified goal) enables us to focus on the issue at hand and come up with an appropriate plan of action

Highly Functioning P2 in Adult Life

The first-order noble quality of Vitality[4] requires the integration of the thinking aspect of prioritisation, the feeling aspect of goal-oriented passion and enthusiasm, and the somatic aspect of physically moving towards achieving specific objectives even if it is frightening.

A primary contributor to Vitality is the exercising of will to achieve objectives and specific results. As the vital individual attains and reaches their goals, they experience a sense of success, achievement, and of having the capability to achieve greater objectives (Tracy, 2004).

Vitality refers to feeling alive; the very word is derived from vita, or 'life'. While Vitality is related to being energetic and passionate, Vitality entails only energy experienced as positive and available to the self (Nix, Ryan, Manly & Deci, 1999). Someone who is tense, angry or jittery may be energised but not imbued with the noble quality of Vitality.

Individuals with a high level of Vitality strongly endorse the following statements:

1. *I feel alive and vital.*

2. *I have energy and spirit.*

3. *I nearly always feel awake and alert.*

4. *I feel energised.*

5. *I rarely feel worn out.*

Vitality is an activated positive emotion, which means personal energy is directed towards the attainment of goals. As such, it is different from happiness or contentment, which are undirected.

HOW P2 VITALITY MEETS THE NOBILITY CRITERIA

Vitality answers questions related to the right of the individual to personally achieve and make the world a better place for themselves and others. This noble quality enables the individual to discover that they have the right to be who they want to be. This is linked to the desire to make things better, to be committed and to stake life itself on an outcome.

Vitality brings value to the community by enabling it to complete projects on time, to strive, to compete and to constantly improve in every aspect of community life. It helps focus the individual on achieving their best and reaching their potential. This in turn enables the community to compete in the wider world.

---

4   Peterson & Seligman's meta-study of the most widely influential traditions of thought and religion in human history found Vitality to be a significant human strength (Peterson & Seligman, 2004).

Vitality fosters the sense that, 'Yes, we CAN do this' which is a fundamental aspect of improving community life.

Vitality describes a dynamic aspect of well-being marked by the subjective experience of energy and aliveness (Ryan & Frederick, 1997). Individuals report that using Vitality to resolve an internal tension has a paradigm shift impact on their lives.

In high performance teams, Vitality gives team members confidence in the ability of the team to achieve its goals, exceed expectations and compete against the rest of the world.

P2 Toolbox

THE IMPORTANCE OF P2 IN BUILDING HIGH PERFORMANCE TEAMS

The emergent cultural impact of P2 is Vitality, which enables the organisation to complete projects on time, to strive, to compete and to constantly improve in every aspect towards organisational objectives.

When Vitality is absent in the organisation engagement is low, challenges are passed up, deadlines are missed and opportunities disappear. Without Vitality, personal productivity declines along with a sense of achievement and satisfaction for work.

When there is highly functioning P2 in the organisation there is also a focus on the individual achieving their best and reaching their potential. This in turn enables the organisation to compete with greater effectiveness

Leaders looking to increase the function of P2 in their team can increase Vitality by applying the P2 tools.

P2 QUESTIONS FOR PERSONAL DEVELOPMENT AND SELF REFLECTION

The best high performing teams are made up of individuals who have focused on their own personal development. The following questions can be used as a starting point for those leaders looking to improve their P2.

1. What do you believe about yourself? Do you like and respect yourself? (A healthy P2 has a healthy ego.)

2. Do you trust your ability to make good choices? Describe a time when you forgave yourself when you made a mistake or fell short of your own goals and expectations.

3. What do you want to be famous for having achieved?

4. Have you developed the skill of self inquiry - have you learnt to trust your own insights, and do they help you to act in ways that honour yourself and others? Explain.

5. Do you believe you can make the world a better place? How?

6. Do you often need the others' approval in order to feel good? Explore why this is or isn't so.

7. Do you live according to your own objectives or are you more influenced by others' expectations? When you achieve your objectives do you need another's praise before you feel good about it or able to affirm yourself? Explore this.

8. When you have strong feelings, explore how you are able to express them in ways that respect yourself and others.

9. What is your greatest fear? Is it a fear of failure or of offending others? (When your inner observer notes this, it is valuable to ask yourself if this is appropriate now, or is it a replay of disapproval expressed by others in your childhood?)

10. Do your actions align with your values and principles as well as your feelings?

11. Can you stand up for yourself, and respect yourself and keep your principles, whatever the odds?

12. How do you manage power? Is it power over (force) or an enabling power?

13. What do you feel highly motivated about in life right now?

14. Can you forgive yourself when you make mistakes or fall short of your own goals and expectations or are you plagued by guilt or shame?

P2 TOOL #1:
REFINE YOUR COMPETITIVE STRATEGY

HOW THIS RELATES TO P2

P2 gives the individual the energy required to win. Your competitive strategy will fuel this energy by enabling all team members to work together and agree on an approach. This keeps the P2 function focused on team success rather than individual success achieved at the expense of the team.

PROCESS

1. **Schedule a Strategy Review Workshop** with key thought leaders within your team/ organisation.

2. **Conduct a SWOT analysis** by getting the workshop group to list the team's Strengths, Weaknesses, Opportunities and Threats given its current positioning and existing strategy. (Depending on the size of the group, you may like to split the workshop into smaller tables, then combine the responses to one group analysis). While it is critical that the workshop group drives the process and analysis, make sure that you have given this some thought yourself in advance (so that you can keep things moving with suggestions of your own where needed). You may even like to have some relevant figures and data to share. Another good option is to send each participant details on the SWOT analysis as a pre-workshop exercise, so they will have the chance both to think it through and to informally consult colleagues in advance of the workshop.

3. **Introduce the work of Michael Porter** (1998). Many will be familiar with Porter's work, which is still as useful today as it was when introduced in the 1980s. He identified five competitive forces that affect profitability:

   a. **The entry of new competitors.** New competitors necessitate some competitive response which will inevitably use resources and reduce profits.

   b. **The threat of substitutes.** If there are viable alternatives to your product or service in the marketplace, the prices you can charge will be limited.

   c. **The bargaining power of buyers.** If customers have bargaining power, they will use it. This will reduce profit margins.

   d. **The bargaining power of suppliers.** Given power over you, suppliers will increase their prices and adversely affect your profitability.

   e. **The rivalry among existing competitors.** Competition leads to the need to invest in marketing or Research and Development, or to price reductions.

Explain that the collective strength of these five forces determines the ability of firms in an industry to earn, on average, rates of return on investment in excess of the cost of capital (Porter, 1998).

4. **Assess the existing strategy** based on the extent to which it either currently addresses each of the forces or has the flexibility to do so as needed. Is the organisation/your team currently at the whim of one or more of these forces or is it taking proactive steps to strengthen its competitive edge in the current market? Where possible, relate this analysis back to the SWOT conducted at the start of the session.

5. **Finalise an Action Plan moving forward.** This may involve seeking further information, tweaking the strategy or contacting key stakeholders (internally or externally) to action any changes. The important outcome is to emerge from the workshop with clarity about both how the strategy needs to change to stay competitive and who is responsible for the identified actions moving forward.

DOS

✓ Do set aside enough time to finalise the Action Plan – there's no point spending the day working out what's missing from the existing approach if you don't direct that toward the practical goal of actioning the insights

DON'TS

✗ Don't allow the discussion to get bogged down – focus on the end goal of getting shared clarity about the benefits and weaknesses of the strategy and what needs to change

P2 TOOL #2:
DYNAMISE YOUR GROUP

HOW THIS RELATES TO P2

P2 drops when goals are too distant (there is no urgency) or complex. This tool will lift P2 by simplifying and clarifying the goals and creating a clear deadline (compelling event).

PROCESS

1. **Identify a key new project or operation** (e.g. new product launch or initiative) that can be used as a vehicle around which to dynamise the team.

2. **Assemble a Tiger Team** — a special team to focus on the new project/operation. Find the ablest people and place them under highly motivated, effective leadership that will encourage sub-leadership.

3. **Brief the Tiger Team**

   a. Introduce yourself (if appropriate) and explain the purpose of the team and the project. Emphasise that the group has been put together for a specific purpose/project, and that the particular skills of each individual member are fundamental to the success of the project.

   b. Highlight the team's freedom in choosing how to approach the challenge, emphasising that creativity and innovation are encouraged.

   c. Outline the value of the team and make sure that everyone is clear on their role in achieving these objectives. If possible, identify 'the competition' – whether it is last year's figures, another section within the organisation or an external rival. This will set a benchmark for the team's performance.

   d. Express confidence in the people present and emphasise group/team working and cohesion.

   e. Emphasise that the team's efforts will be fully supported, including outlining the resources that are available to them.

   f. Express confidence in and optimism about the group's ability.

4. **Hold regular meetings** to ensure the team stays focused. Make sure there is clarity about what has been achieved and how much more needs to be done. Use these times to reinforce motivation and purpose, as well as to review progress.

5. **Continue to recruit new talent**, particularly as gaps in the skills base become apparent throughout the project. Encourage the group to be proactive in identifying potential new talent and areas in which they could valuably contribute.

P2 Tool # 2

DOS

✓ Make your authority clear, but make sure that the group feels that it also has autonomous power to act. For the group to be dynamised, team members will need to feel a sense of urgency in tackling the challenges that arise.

✓ Be positive and enthusiastic – your energy with inspire confidence and encourage your group to follow your example.

DON'TS

✗ Don't allow the process to be stagnated by 'how things have been done in the past'. Encourage the group to look forwards, not backwards, and to forge its own path towards the end goal.

✗ Don't forget that the ultimate objective is for the group to drive the project. You can be firm about your expectations, but make sure that the energy for the process is coming from the team itself.

P2 TOOL #3:
EFFECTIVELY MANAGE PLATEAUED PERFORMERS

HOW THIS RELATES TO P2

When an individual's P2 drops to counterproductive levels it can be due to a range of issues. Many of these have been outlined in the text. Your role as a leader is to work with the individual to find what has worked in the past and what can be introduced into the current situation to restimulate the P2 function.

PROCESS

1. **Scope the plateau.**

   a. **Diagnose the plateau.** A plateau is an emerging process that doesn't happen overnight. To qualify as a Plateaued Performer, the employee would have been plateaued for at least a year, perhaps two. They are also likely to have been in the same job or department for some time. Ask yourself whether the employee's productivity has declined consistently or sporadically. Have you observed a slackening in interest and commitment? Has the person's behaviour deviated from the norm? Or are they simply not interested in improving?

   b. **Characterise the plateau.** Use the individual's attitude or level of activity to characterise the type of plateau involved. Potential categories include:

      - **Passive:** Low in energy and activity and trapped in personal inaction.
      - **Productive:** Plenty of energy and activity, but the busy-ness is not translating into effectiveness.
      - **Partial:** Concentrates on one small area of responsibility, valiantly keeping a personal spark alive in the absence of prospects for promotion or challenge.
      - **Pleasant:** Happy with the status quo, doing the job well enough, in a comfortable groove but wanting neither challenges nor risks, and showing no desire to improve. Different strategies will be appropriate depending upon the nature of the plateau.

   c. **Get to know the person properly.** Try to understand what makes the plateaued performer tick. Ask about outside interests, whether there's anything stressful happening at home and whether they're content to stay where they are (e.g. an earlier failure to get a promotion had a demotivating effect). Try to find out from the person what their personal and professional ambitions are. Only by knowing the plateaued performer as a person can you hope to improve matters.

2. **Identify the core problem.** Using all the detail obtained in scoping the plateau, be as specific as you can in outlining its root causes. Some of these will be within the control of the individual but others may not.

Examples of causes for the plateau may include:

    a. The company has not offered a stimulating environment

    b. The person feels written off by you or another superior

    c. It's a long time since the person has been given a new challenge

    d. Colleagues are largely ignoring the person

    e. Problems at home

While there may be many contributing factors, lack of stimulus is likely to feature prominently.

3. **Find out what has worked for them in the past.** By exploring with the employee times in their work history when they have been motivated you can discuss how some of the characteristics of the external environment and their approach can be reintroduced into the current situation.

4. **Work with the individual to develop an Action Plan moving forward.** This will necessarily depend on the individual circumstances, but the solution usually involves providing a new stimulus. This might include: introducing a new challenge within the individual's existing responsibilities; assigning the person to work on a special team or project; or suggesting a sideways shift to a new position within the company. Make sure the plateaued performer has ownership of the Action Plan and understands that they need to take responsibility for their own future.

5. **Continue to show interest, and give support and positive feedback.** While you need to emphasise the plateaued performer's responsibilities, make it clear that they have your support. A plateaued performer may show a short-term improvement and then sink back again. Show continuing interest without being too obtrusive, and be prepared to intervene where needed.

6. **Follow up if there is no improvement.** It is important to recognise that some performers will stay on a plateau. Although you will have some surprising successes, you won't succeed every time. If you can't raise a particular staff member's sights after several attempts, take advantage of the opportunity to alert them that their behaviour is likely to be unsatisfactory to the organisation sooner or later and might risk dismissal.

DOS

✓ Do make identification and support for plateaued performers company policy.

✓ Do assume that something can be done.

✓ Do get to know the person as well as you can and identify what is holding him or her back.

✓ Do remember throughout the process that the employee is not yet a problem – so don't treat them like one! Your only aim is to see if and how they can rise off the plateau.

DON'TS

✗ Don't start with negative assumptions.

✗ Don't underestimate the potential disadvantages of handling the situation poorly.

✗ Don't assume that plateaued performers are incompetent. Often they simply can't channel their energies or abilities into productive performance.

✗ Don't give up too easily.

KEY LEADING THE PACK QUESTIONS FOR BUILDING A HIGH PERFORMANCE TEAM

1. What would you like your team to be famous for?

2. What most motivates you about your role in the team?

3. What do you believe to be the team's greatest strength? How can the team leverage from this strength?

4. As a team, when have you been successful in the past? How might we use the same techniques to deliver in the future?

5. Do you have something against which to benchmark your performance as a team? How do you know when you are doing an excellent job?

6. How do you celebrate success as a team? What is your philosophy towards recognition and reward?

Key P2 Questions for High Performance Teams

NEUROPOWER CASE STUDY

ORGANISATIONAL CASE STUDY #1: STATE HEALTH HAND HYGIENE PROJECT

The Task: To improve compliance by health workers with hand hygiene practice.

Recap:

In 2007, an Australian state health department wanted to address the serious threat that health-associated infections posed to hospital patients. Micro-organisms are readily transmitted on the hands of health care workers. In Australia alone, health officials estimate that up to 7000 people die annually from hand hygiene-related infections in hospitals. The economic burden is also considerable, costing millions each year.

Hand hygiene has been proven to substantially reduce transmission of micro-organisms. However, despite well-established guidelines, compliance throughout the world with hygiene standards is disconcertingly low. International and national health agencies have been grappling with how to deal with the issue for some time, and few interventions have had any impact whatsoever, despite both European and US hospitals and governments spending tens of millions of dollars on communications, incentives, closed circuit TV and education.

Since research demonstrated that the hand hygiene issue centred around human behaviour, one state health department decided on an innovative, behaviour-changing approach using the *NeuroPower* framework to drive the solution. Working with the *NeuroPower* Consulting Team, the department implemented a behaviour change program called Clean Hands are LifeSavers that engaged the health workers and increased compliance from 18% to 60%. A key driver of this behaviour change involved effectively addressing each of the six Intelligences in the correct sequence. How these progressive steps were taken is outlined in the Organisational Toolbox Case Study at the end of each Intelligence chapter.

Having already:
- Created safety and security in the hospital environment by embedding values through a code of conduct
- Empowered spontaneity and self-expression through collaboration and the development of creative promotional materials

Step 3: Get action happening, establish key goals and motivate by celebrating wins

LifeSavers were encouraged to get action happening and keep motivation high by celebrating wins within each hospital. Wards were encouraged to compete with each other to find creative approaches to keeping hand hygiene top-of-mind so posters, events, barbecues, film tickets and other motivating offers were used. As well, internal observers were sent periodically to watch the health-workers at their tasks, completing a statistical survey on hand-held recording devices. Results from each ward were then posted around the hospital, indicating the results in graphic form. The teams in these wards were then rewarded with the kudos of being most successful.

ORGANISATIONAL CASE STUDY #2: MERCHANT BANK EQUITY DERIVATIVES LEADERSHIP TEAM

The Task: Improve employee engagement and tangible business performance

Recap:

In 2006, at the height of the financial boom, one of Australia's leading equity derivatives teams was operating in an environment that was fast-paced, demanding and with a high level of stress. In order to handle large volumes of work in a very volatile market, the team needed to be highly functional and collaborative. Growth was nearly 200 per cent over the previous year so the enormous strain was evident. This was mainly caused by a leadership team in crisis.

The Leadership Team was fractured, non-collaborative and driven by their own individual agendas. There was both a lack of respect and a lack of honesty between members which led to highly reactive responses and conflict. The broader team could see this occurring and they felt they were part of a warring tribe with all the insecurities that brought.

NeuroPower consultants devised a program which focused on addressing the splintered leadership team. The intervention involved a series of group structured processes which were embedded by individual coaching sessions.

Having already:
- Created role clarity
- Empowered people's self-expression

Step 3: Encouraging Healthy Egos and Passion for Work Through P2

The Equity Team Leaders all had enormous passion for their work and strong ego development. The work here was to show that healthy ego development was fine but they needed to know when to reduce their drive for the betterment of the whole team.

It was important to set clear team goals so the group identified six key competencies they wished to focus on during the intervention and developed 360 degree questions which linked to their performance review. This was an overt way to make the team accountable as a group while offering the end game of individual reward for success.

Chapter 5
Our Fourth Social Cognitive Need:
INTERPERSONAL CONNECTION &
The Relating Function (I2)

INTERPERSONAL CONNECTION (I2) AT A GLANCE

Interpersonal Connection is our Brain's Third Social Cognitive Need

The brain is naturally focused on connecting with and understanding others, and needs to feel that you have been genuinely understood. The brain's oxytocin, mirror neuron and default mode networks work overtime to help us interpret and understand others - at times by helping us literally feel what others feel. Our willingness to be generous, to forgive and to 'think together' are linked to how well we feel we understand and connect with someone else.

Characteristics of the Interpersonal Connection (I2) Functional Network

Empathy and Understanding

STRENGTH	WEAKNESS
Can pick up how others are feeling (emotionally intuitive)	Easily swayed by the emotions or people aspects of a situation

OPPORTUNITY	THREAT
Developing objectivity and discernment	Can be swamped by powerful external emotions

Management Style

- Often socio-emotional leaders
- Decision-making based on avoiding pain for others
- May struggle to manage non-performers

EMPATHY

I2 THINKING

Theory
of mind

I2 FEELING

Connection to others
and self

I2 SOMATIC

Emotionally
responsive to the
environment

COMMUNICATION STYLE

- Will be excellent listeners
- Will focus on how people are feeling and responding to work and personal life
- Excellent counsellors/encouragers/affirmers
- Will respond slowly and need time to go away and think about it - conversations can take days to complete

KEYWORDS INCLUDE

- Awareness
- Collaboration
- Empathy
- Generosity
- Connection
- Feeling

Interpersonal Connection (I2) Helps Us to Survive

Interpersonal Connection (I2) helps both individuals and the group to survive and thrive by helping us be aware of our own internal states, and by motivating us to understand, be generous and collaborate with others.

Interpersonal Connection & The Relating Function (I2)

INTERPERSONAL CONNECTION: OUR FOURTH SOCIAL NEED EXPLAINED

Humans have a rare - possibly unique - advantage over other species: our highly sophisticated ability to understand what another person is thinking and how they are feeling (Saxe, 2006). This ability, which is informed by empathy (feeling what others are feeling), prompts us to care for others (children, parents, employees), make sacrifices for others based on generosity and make us sensitive to the impact of our actions on others. These abilities are supported by highly sophisticated (and overlapping) mechanisms in the brain including the mirror neuron network, the default mode network and the oxytocin system, and are intimately linked with our fourth social cognitive need: to understand others and be understood by them (Interpersonal Connection).

WHEN YOU FEEL WHAT I FEEL

A few years ago, European neuroscientists, Dr Peter Their and Dr Giacomo Rizzolatti, discovered that when you see someone hit their finger with a hammer, something fascinating happens in your brain. As you see that person's pain response, your own brain's pain areas fire up as if you're the one who has been hit.[1] This and many other studies in humans and other primates revealed the existence of a so-called 'mirror neuron' system, which together with parts of the frontal and parietal lobes (notably, the temporoparietal junction), form the biological hardware that we use to understand others and empathise with them.[2] This ability to understand others reduces stress responses and promotes generosity with our time and money, so much so that researchers have argued that "Human altruism derives from our readiness to understand each other in terms of their internal thoughts, feelings and desires" (Waytz, Zaki & Mitchell, 2012).

---

1   Notably, this happens even for individuals with medical conditions that prevent them from having ever experienced pain themselves (Danziger et al., 2009).

2   It's worth noting that while the mirror neuron system has been extensively investigated in primates, exploring the full extent - and limitations - of the human mirror neuron system is the subject of substantial ongoing research. This includes, for example, earnest debate about whether the overlapping areas of brain activation between a person's emotional experience and the observation of another's emotion reflect the same neural circuits or different circuits located close to one another (see e.g. Decety, 2010, for a detailed critique). Nonetheless, substantial accumulating evidence from social cognitive neuroscience supports the idea that so called 'mirror neuron' areas of the brain interact with other areas of the brain focused on understanding our own and other's minds (mentalising; Rameson & Lieberman, 2009) to help us form working models of what others are experiencing.

Simultaneously, neuroendocrinologists have shown us that neurochemicals like oxytocin and progesterone increase our motivation to be close to and focus on others (e.g. Schultheiss et al., 2004; Brown et al., 2009).[3] When the brain releases oxytocin, our social anxiety reduces and our affiliative motivation increases, our heart rate starts to respond more adaptively to our social environment and our awareness of social cues and information increases (Bartz et al., 2011; Kemp et al., 2012). This effect also seems to be uniquely social - oxytocin improves our learning when feedback has a social component; it increases generosity when we're playing a game with another human, but not with a computer.

Interestingly, some studies have suggested that oxytocin's impact on generosity also works in reverse. Research from Paul Zak's lab suggests that when we receive generosity from others that is based on trust, it increases our own levels of circulating oxytocin, increases our own prosocial intentions (Zak, Kurzlban & Matzner, 2005). This is important, because it emphasises that Interpersonal Connectedness (I2), rather than just benefiting the recipient, changes our brain chemistry in a way that helps the group as a whole.

Oxytocin was first discovered through its role in childbirth and when new mothers form attachments with their infants, and then sprang into popular consciousness for its role in romantic love. Today, however, researchers have teased out oxytocin's broader ability to focus our attention on others, to improve our understanding of how they are feeling and to promote generosity and forgiveness.[4] As our understanding of this grows, it's now easy to see that this neurobiological system also has a crucial role in day-to-day work life for establishing strong interpersonal connections between people in all aspects of our lives.

---

3   Oxytocin has swept through popular consciousness in the last decade as the now infamous 'love drug' of the brain, with the frenzy going so far that some have even marketed oxytocin-based products as aphrodisiacs and tools for building trust and love. In reality, oxytocin is likely to be far less of a 'quick fix'. Instead, there is building consensus from the research community that oxytocin's primary effects are to increase our awareness of social information, motivate us to connect with others and reduce social anxiety. See Bartz et al., (2011) for some recent insight into this debate.

4   Given the overlap between the effects of oxytocin and the domains of the mirror neuron system and default mode network, you would expect that the two are intricately linked. However, only in the last few years have the first tentative pieces of evidence for this emerged. Perry et al.,(2010), for example, reported that giving healthy adults a dose of oxytocin changed patterns of brain activity near sensorimotor regions recorded using EEG in a pattern that has been linked to mirror neuron activation. This is the first tentative step I have seen in the neuroscience literature linking oxytocin to the mirror neuron system, but I predict that this link will become stronger over the coming years.

'FEELING THE LOVE' AT WORK - THE CHALLENGE FOR LEADERS

Interpersonal Connection (I2), or our ability to understand and connect with others, is a powerful glue that helps keep groups together and reach high performance. It does this in part by helping us manage stresses and conflict through mutual understanding, generosity and forgiveness. In a corporate setting, then, in order to create high performance a leader needs to learn how to create a sense of connection, empathy and dare we say it...even love...within their teams.

Importantly, recent research has confirmed something I have observed for decades, namely, that the brain areas that support Interpersonal Connection (I2) and our understanding of others' *internal states* are very different - and compete with - the parts of the brain that help us understand the physical, external world (Seeing the Facts, or I1; Jack et al., 2013). Of course, many of our leaders and managers have been promoted for their analytical and technical skills, rooted deeply in their ability to master the complexity of their technical profession. While these strengths are critical, brains that run high in Seeing the Facts (I1) often miss the human impact of objectively justified decisions. This one-sided set of information lies at the heart of many costly 'surprises' for corporate leaders, from failed mergers that looked 'good on paper' and product launches that fell flat, through to the valued team member whose 'sudden resignation' significantly impacts the ability to deliver corporate objectives. Without a healthy Interpersonal Connection (I2), our brains simply miss the people information.

To realise the full potential of their teams (as well as their own potential), effective leaders need to learn to meet the team's needs for Interpersonal Connection (I2). Part of this involves the leader working to build their personal awareness of their own internal world. (This challenging task is a core theme of the many Eastern traditions that describe the longest journey in the world as that 'between the head and the heart'.)

Based on my work with organisations around the world, I have found a useful process for building I2 within teams involves team members getting to know each other for their heartfelt passions, strengths and aspirations (rather than their weaknesses). This is important, because understanding the strengths of your colleagues, and the challenges they have faced to build them, fosters an appreciation of the individual, an increased sense of closeness and an increased willingness to tolerate and forgive their foibles. Learning what people are passionate about doing and where they shine the most, reveals hidden areas of strength that become resources for the team. Having a range of different strengths supports the team's diversity. These diverse teams are not always easier to manage but they make better decisions and get better results.

As we have already discussed, several structures and neuronal networks help us satisfy our need for Interpersonal Connection. Within the *NeuroPower* framework, this set of structures is called the 'I2 Relating System' (or sometimes the 'I2 network'

Taking a Closer Look at Mirror Neurons

In the last decade or so, neuroscientists have been trying to understand how human brains make sense of what other people are thinking and feeling. One line of this research has been the investigation of whether 'mirror neurons' in the brain might help us understand others (giving rise to an understanding of their intentions and, perhaps, empathy) by matching their actions and experience back to our own bodies.

Using single-cell recording techniques, early research found individual 'mirror neurons within the premotor areas of a primate's frontal cortex that fire *both* when it performs a specific task (such as grasping an object with a hand) *and also* when it sees another primate or the experimenter engage in the same behaviour (Jeannerod, Arbib, Rizzolatti, & Sakata, 1995; Gallese, Fadiga, Fogassi & Rizzolatti, 1996). Since then, these mirror neurons have been discovered in several areas of the brain, including some in motor areas responsible for controlling, and, it seems, interpreting eye gaze and attention (I2 Thinking; Shepherd et al., 2009).

A range of studies have also attempted to extend these findings to humans and indicated that - as with primates - there are specific areas of the human brain (described by some as the parieto-frontal mirror system) that are strongly activated by both taking specific goal-directed actions and observing those same actions being taken by others (reviewed in Fogassi & Rizzolatti, 2013). Interestingly, the response of these brain areas to an action seems to depend on the context and intention being the same for the actions and there is some evidence that our unconscious body responses may also have mirror-like qualities (I2 Somatic).

To understand the link between mirror neurons and empathy, some have argued that observing the facial expressions, gestures and posture of another individual will activate similar sensory-motor circuits in an observer. Supporting this, Cattaneo et al., (2007) found that a muscle which we use to open our mouths is activated when we reach for food to eat and when we see someone else reach for food to eat, but not when we see someone else reach for food to put it away. These motor systems, in turn, are presumed to activate in the observer networks of emotion associated with such actions. For example, observing a sad child makes us reflectively frown, tilt our heads and make soothing gestures. It is thought that this is one means by which the gap between the sender and the receiver is bridged. In this way mirror neurons allow for the possibility of empathic attunement (Wolf, Gales, Shane & Shane, 2000).

or 'I2 function') and gives rise to a particular thinking style referred to as 'I2 Intelligence'. The rest of this chapter explores the I2 Relating System in detail.

THE EVOLUTIONARY SOCIAL BRAIN FUNCTION OF I2

The I2 system enables an individual to:

1. Survive through understanding and empathising with others, and through connection and loving friends and family.

2. Empathise with others and provide support and comfort during both good and bad times (attachment).

3. Best guess how others will react through Theory of Mind – being able to guess what somebody else is thinking about you and others. This can be described as a process by which most healthy human adults:

   a) attribute unobservable mental states to others (and under certain circumstances, to the self); and

   b) integrate these attributed states into a single coherent model that can be used to explain and predict the target's behaviour and experiences (Saxe & Wexler, 2005).

4. Form lasting and meaningful relationships through romantic (pair bonding) and maternal love (Dêbiec, 2007).

Recognising the Characteristics of Interpersonal Connection (I2)

The purpose of I2 is to connect with, understand others and attune with others. The characteristics of a highly functioning I2 Intelligence include attunement, active listening, love, altruism, peace, balance, trust, generosity, inspiration, dedication, forgiveness, and acceptance of others. These facilitate the noble quality of Empathy.

Empathy is linked with active listening (Rogers & Farzon, 1987). This form of listening involves no value judgements and simply reflects the content of what is being said. Active listening presupposes in the listener an attitude of genuine respect for the other person and an expectation that they have the potential for self-direction. Clinical and research evidence shows that active listening can be expected to produce positive developmental changes in both the listener and the person being listened to (Rogers and Farzon, 1987).

The recipient of active listening receives a respectful, uncritical, sensitive hearing. As a result, they commonly exhibit positive growth in emotional maturity. They listen more openly and carefully to themselves and give more care to expressing their own thoughts and feelings more clearly. They also become more democratic and attentive to others, and are less inclined to be defensive or authoritarian.

Active listening also has a positive effect on groups. When a group of individuals experience attentive and non-judgemental listening, their group discussions tend to become more agreeable and sensitive. Individuals feel their contribution matters and are more likely to see their own ideas more objectively. At a neurobiological level, this settles the amygdala and reduces the experience of stress.

Rogers & Farzon (1987) make the excellent additional point that this active listening can have a profound effect on the listener as they learn to build deep, meaningful and positive relationships by constructively altering their attitudes.

A TRADITIONAL UNDERSTANDING OF THE DYNAMICS OF THE I2 FUNCTION

Most traditional schools of thought and faith argue that connection based on love nourishes our physical, emotional and spiritual bodies. It motivates, controls, inspires and heals us. However, painful experiences of connection can also have a profoundly negative impact on our psychological and physical health. Many of life's challenges result in a lesson on some aspect of love. How we respond often affects our health.

The demon of I2 is sometimes described as grief. Poorly functioning I2 can also bring jealousy, bitterness, grumpiness, anger, hatred, insensitivity, disconnection from others and an inability to forgive oneself or others. Judith (1996) argues that physical malfunctions arising from poorly functioning I2 may include problems with the heart, lungs, thymus, breasts, arms, hands, shoulders or diaphragm. Telltale symptoms include shortness of breath, sunken chest, circulation problems, asthma, immune system deficiency, tension between the shoulder blades and pain in the chest (Judith, 1996)[5].

---

5   After emerging from the twentieth century's rigid focus on rational thinking and research into brain functioning, work by a range of western-trained researchers has begun to reintegrate an awareness of the role our physical heart might play in understanding and sensing emotional experiences (I2). In doing so, they are re-discovering the philosophies of earlier thinkers. In the nineteenth century, for example, William James posited that an emotion is firstly a physical state that then becomes accessorily a perception in the brain. In more recent times, the apparent relationship between heart and brain has led some cardiologists and neurologists to refer to an indivisible 'heart-brain system' (Servan-Schreiber, 2005). Meanwhile, neuroscientist Antonio Damasio (2003) on somatic markers argues that the work of seventeenth century philosopher Baruch Spinoza, which linked mind and body, fits neatly with modern concepts of neurophysiology. The notion that the heart is an independent centre of information, memories, desires and behaviours is also explored by Paul Pearsall in his book *The Heart's Code* (1999), while Californian researchers at the Institute of HeartMath have for over a decade been using neurophysiological measures like EEG and ECG to help understand how once mysterious 'heart-heart' connections might in fact be mediated by the electromagnetic impulses (generated by calcium-mediated contraction) in the tissue of the heart. These researchers are among the first to publish reports that heart rate variability in one person may directly influence

The developmental task for the individual at this stage is to form healthy peer and family relationships. The primary fears associated with I2 are loneliness, commitment, following one's heart, fear of not being able to protect oneself emotionally, emotional weakness and betrayal (Judith, 1996).

SIMULATION THEORY AND THEORY OF MIND

Our ability to empathise with others has recently captured the attention of the neuroscientific world, with two different theories developing about the neural

Diagram 5.1 Some of the Brain Areas Supporting Interpersonal Connection (I2)*

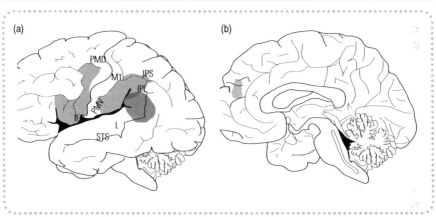

(a) Cortical areas belonging to the parieto-frontal mirror system. Gray shaded regions indicate cortical sectors activated during action observation, that become also active during execution of the same actions. Note that in some studies additional cortical areas (e.g. dorsal premotor cortex and superior parietal lobule) can activate during observation of reaching or body movements. A rostral sector of the superior temporal sulcus also activate during action observation, but not during action execution. IFG, inferior frontal gyrus; IPL, inferior parietal lobule; IPS, intraparietal sulcus; L, lateral sulcus; M1, primary motor cortex; PMD, dorsal premotor cortex; PMV, ventral premotor cortex; SPL, superior parietal lobule; STS, superior temporal sulcus (Adapted from Fogassi and Rizzolatti, 2013). The temporoparietal junction (TPJ, orange), particularly the right TPJ, has been shown to be important for our ability to attributing mental states to others Saxe & Wexler (2005).

(b) Region of dorsomedial prefrontal cortex (DMPFC, green) - known to be important for our ability to 'mentalise' or think about others' mental states. Activity in this region when thinking about other people correlates with altruism as measured by allocation of money and time (Waytz et al., 2012).

* Areas associated with mentalising (I2) as compared to reasoning about inanimate objects (I1) are discussed further in Diagram 6.1 in Chapter 6.

patterns of brain activity in someone nearby, suggesting a possible physical mechanism for interpersonal 'intuition' and empathy.

underpinnings of empathy. The *Simulation Theory* of empathy proposes that we use our own mind as a model in understanding the thoughts and feelings of others. This theory found support in the discovery of the mirror neuron system, which is thought to allow us to vicariously experience the emotional states of others, thus enabling empathetic feelings (Decety & Jackson, 2004). In seeming contrast, *Theory of Mind* research has focused on the role of the medial prefrontal regions, which enable us to consider that what others think, feel and believe, may differ from our own thoughts, feelings and beliefs. The ability to best guess what another person is thinking or feeling is known as mentalising (Frith & Frith, 1999). *Theory of Mind* work suggests that empathy is based on this deduction about another person's experience.

In 2009, social cognitive neuroscientists Lian Rameson and Matthew Lieberman published an outstanding article about the social cognitive neuroscience of empathy, including a concise but comprehensive review of the literature supporting both theories. They suggest that these two models for explaining empathy are not mutually exclusive and may, in fact, provide a more comprehensive understanding of empathy when considered together. Their analysis supports the view that our ability to have Theory of Mind is an indication of how readily we access *I2 thinking*, while the activity of our mirror neurons reflects the strength of our *I2 somatic* functioning.

In considering reactions to upsetting events that are focused on others, Rameson & Lieberman (2009) argue that responses can be either *experiential* (i.e. feeling like you've taken the place of the other person and are in the situation, experiencing it for yourself) or *propositional* (i.e. a controlled cognitive process focusing on the other person's thoughts, feelings or experience). They suggest that while the two modes

I2 and the Right Hemisphere

While the idea of 'lateralisation' itself moves in and out of popularity with the neuroscience community, many of us have traditionally seen I2 characteristics as a '*right*' brain' quality. This was based on evidence that linked the right hemisphere of the brain with empathetic experiences and emotional awareness. The right hemisphere was found to be superior at comprehending emotionally laden language (Searleman, 1977). Emotions in general, and the ability to evaluate emotional facial expressions and visual-spatial abilities, are predominately right-hemisphere processes (Ahern et al., 1991). When damage occurs to the right hemisphere there is an impairment not only in the ability to assess facial gestures, but also in the ability to comprehend other non-verbal aspects of communication such as hand gestures and tone of voice (Blonder, Bowers & Heilman, 1991). This suggests that the right hemisphere plays an important role in I2 functioning.

of processing presumably share some common neural circuitry, each is likely to have a 'unique neural signature' (Rameson & Lieberman, 2009, p. 103). Experiential processing therefore maps very closely onto Simulation Theory, while propositional processing bears striking similarities to *Theory of Mind*. From their perspective, the two modes of processing are complementary rather than contradictory, and may in fact build on each other. For example, seeing a picture of maltreated inmates in a WWII concentration camp may generate an affective response that is magnified by furthering consideration of their circumstances and mental state.

Rameson & Lieberman also note that the two modes of processing are likely to result in qualitatively different motivations and consequent behaviours; experiential processing is likely to engender an affective reaction to the other person's distress that motivates immediate physical engagement, while propositional processing may 'initiate more complex thinking about long-term solutions to problems that might not be immediately gratifying, but might produce systemic changes in the target's situation' (Rameson & Lieberman, 2009, p 103).

Highly Functioning Interpersonal Connection (I2) has Both Strengths and Weaknesses

Bertrand Russell once said, "We know too much and feel too little." Interpersonal Connection (I2) is what helps us to 'feel' and so come to understand ourselves and others' internal states. I2 enables you to empathise and gives you access to your ability to connect with others. I2-dominant minds - sometimes called 'Empathisers' - are sensitive, emotionally aware and naturally focus on others. They easily sense the feeling in a room - including the fears and insecurities of others - and seem to know just how others are feeling in the most difficult situations. Although this ability to empathise is very useful, it can also cause difficulty for the I2-dominant mind.

Most people high in I2 never feel totally confident or in control, and sometimes wonder why they don't seem to be able to be as balanced or consistent as their more 'objective' friends[6]. The primary reason for this is that the I2 function naturally tracks and picks up pain, excitement and pleasure from others - meaning the individual often becomes a passenger on someone else's emotional journey. To function effectively, individuals high in I2 need to learn to detach, and balance their natural empathy for others with an objective perspective on the world.

---

6   Explored in Chapter 6 on Seeing the Facts (I1)

Alexithymia

The inability to consciously experience and describe your own and others feelings (both of which are features of healthy Interpersonal Connectedness (I2)) is referred to as alexithymia. Patients with alexithymia often report being consciously aware that other people have feelings, but not being aware of them themselves. Early research suggested that this condition appears to reflect a lack of transfer or integration of right-hemisphere emotional and somatic information with the linguistic cognitive systems of the left hemisphere (Taylor, 1999), and subsequent studies have shown that alexithymia is linked to reduced activity in the broader network of regions of the brain dedicated to understanding the mental states and emotions of others, including the DLPTF, anterior insula and temporoparietal junction. This alexithymia, which can be interpreted as a deficit in Interpersonal Connection (I2), leads to reduced accuracy in judging others' mental states, reduced awareness of the pain of others and reduced altruism to others (Moriguchi et al., 2006; 2007; FeldmanHall et al., 2013).

Interpersonal Connection (I2) and Childhood Development

COGNITIVE DEVELOPMENT AND I2

The development of the I2 Intelligence aligns with Piaget's pre-operational stage. During this time the child wishes to be judged by their intentions as well as their behaviour. This aligns with Lawrence Kohlberg's 'good boy, nice girl' stage of moral development. At this stage the individual learns to incorporate their cognition with their persona. This also aligns with Erikson's stage of *intimacy versus isolation*, which sees the individual consider whether they are loved and wanted and who they, in turn, wish to love (Sigelman & Rider, 2006).

DEVELOPING A SOCIAL IDENTITY

During childhood, individuals become aware of relationships between their parents and within the family. The child develops a social identity based on family interactions and their place in it, especially the family's response to their behaviour. They become, for example, a good boy or girl, a clown or perhaps a princess expecting attention (Judith, 1996).

As we have seen in our discussion of P1 and C1, the child also internalises family scripts, which they may play out in later life. For example, they respond to criticism by becoming a 'bad boy' or they become quiet and passive-aggressive. A person's family relationships also impact on their behaviour and who they become.

As the child observes their family, imitates gender roles and adopts family patterns, their persona also becomes part of their social identity. They identify with the 'tough' or problem-solving father or self-sacrificing mother. This is when the child learns how to either access or ignore I2. The little boy might be told not to cry, and the little girl not to be a tomboy. This repressed part of them becomes a further ingredient of their unconscious personality (their Mirror[7]).

Finally, the innate conflict that exists between mother and father is resolved by reconciling the differences and loving both equally. This external reconciliation is matched by an internal reconciliation of the perspectives of their same sex parent (embedded in the child's P1) and their opposite sex parent (embedded in the child's C1).

CHILDHOOD DEVELOPMENT

In healthy development, the individual's identity expands to include all previous Intelligences as it embraces I2 in a balanced way. In this case, the ego or P2 expands as

The Role of Parenting in the Development of I2

Children raised in families that discuss people's emotional reactions tend to be more interested in and able to understand others' emotions (Bretherton, 1993; Nelson, 1993). These children also appear to be taught that what they have to say about the contents of their minds is important. Each of these experiences may help to enhance their capacity for emotional regulation (Oppenheim, Nir, Warren & Emde, 1997; Fivush, 1994).

Studies have found significant differences in the manner in which parents help to shape their offspring's narrative processes. Miller & Sperry (1988) suggest that narratives with boys frequently include angry emotions and often reflect autonomy of self and actions. In contrast, girls are guided to create narratives about the self in which their identity is embedded in a social context. They are taught to take responsibility for the feelings of others, which is quintessential I2 development. This may explain why in some *NeuroPower* middle management samples in Australia fewer than 20 percent of the males surveyed have highly functioning I2 compared with 55 percent of the women surveyed.

---

7   For more information about the Mirror, see Principle #3.

it learns to love itself and others; the sense of being grounded in P1 acts as a protector for the I2 heart; and the C1 provides a means for emotional release and embraces the pleasure instinct.

For social acceptance the child needs to control their self-centred instincts of C1 and P2. Judith (1996) argues that if the P2 ego is weak, the child may feel the need to deny their instincts entirely and become a 'good child'. What begins as a conscious behaviour to please a parent can become a lifelong unconscious role.

If this compliance becomes continuous and pervasive, the individual will grow up with an under-reliance on P2, an over-reliance on I2, and a dependence on others to keep them grounded and make them feel happy and successful (Judith, 1996).

On the other hand, a highly functioning I2 will give the person the ability to be altruistic and empathetic, cooperative and friendly while maintaining a healthy sense of self. This enables the individual to strike a balance between maintaining autonomy and deferring to others' needs and wishes.

LOVING AND BEING LOVED

Often people report that they feel as if their I2 Intelligence and heart expand when they fall in love. Judith (1996) explains that they lose their egocentricity and rigidity of thought as they encounter and accommodate their beloved's interests, ideas, values and beliefs.

As well as their thoughts, they share with their beloved their bodies and their innermost self. Furthermore, as they are adored by their beloved, they may sense their own beauty. Being beloved is often the basis for self-acceptance and self-esteem, as we know ourselves more deeply, reflected in the eyes of our beloved. It usually follows that we take pride in ourself – our bodies, homes and our actions, all key aspects of self.

Judith (1996) notes that when we fall out of love we return to the vulnerability of the child, and become immersed again in our past identity. As a result of the pain, we are forced to re-examine ourselves in a new light, and in the process our awareness is raised.

I2 AND BALANCE

Some Eastern philosophers suggested that since the physical heart is positioned in the centre of the body, that the essence of the themes of the spiritual (or psychological) heart (I2) is balance. Judith (1996) argues that balance within the person is a prerequisite for developing meaningful and deep relationships with others rather than forming relationships as a subconscious means to completing oneself.

Love Conquers All

A key aspect of intimate love is devotion or surrender without ego (P2)[8]. This

---

8   Discussed in detail in Chapter 4

requires a balance between devotion to the other and to the self. As we explain later, when devotion is excessive, the devoted one can lose their own self, as they follow only the needs and wishes of the other. This is most likely to happen when their own ego strength (their P2) is poorly functioning. In this situation the individual needs to reconnect with their own needs (C1), take action (P2) and re-establish the balance.

True love demands attunement and empathy, but this must not arise from the lover's own need to be needed. When a person shows attunement with another, they are not necessarily expected to fix problems but rather to understand and empathise with the trials of the other. For this to work we must be self-aware enough to know our own needs, open enough to share with the other at a feeling level, and grounded enough to remain centred in self (Judith, 1996).

Grief

If a person is unaware of or denies their grief, they often shut down their capacity for empathy and feel emptiness inside. When acknowledged, grief can be expressed and healing can follow. When this process is completed, we can be filled with hope and life (Worden, 1983).

Briefly, the person needs 'to go inside' themselves to return to their own groundedness, and from there, gain the ego strength to be healed. (For more detail, see *Healing the Heart (I2) as an Adult* later in this chapter.)

Childhood Traumas and Abuse

The most tragic cause of wounding of the heart occurs in childhood when the young person is at their most impressionable. Judith (1996) argues that common traumas and abuses from which many children in our society suffer include rejection, abandonment, loss, shaming, constant criticism, unacknowledged grief (including parents' grief), parental divorce, death of a loved one, a loveless and cold environment, conditional love, sexual or physical abuse, and betrayal. Abuses to the other Intelligences, particularly P1, C1 and P2 can also affect the functioning of I2.

A defenceless child is totally dependent on their family for nurture and love. Yet if a little child is abused it is usually at the hands of their own family. As a result, instead of the child's emerging I2 integrating the self, this child is separated off from the parts of themselves that are rejected by the parents. The child fails to develop some of their capacity to love and connect and may grow up to view relationships as being static rather than a process. Even their primary relationships may be seen as an afterthought, with the individual living their life as if alone. For them, the I2 space hurts and so they learn to rely on the other Intelligences for meaningful interaction (Judith, 1996).

Feeling Worthless

When a young child is abused by those they love, they often lose their love of life and their natural willingness to connect. They withdraw and 'shut down' their I2 function. Further, they grow to believe they are unlovable, with no validity as a human, and see themselves as nothing special. As we have already seen, the quality of parenting determines the way the developing child ends up seeing and relating to the world. They may become responsible or rebellious, they may expect acceptance or rejection, and so on.

Horney (1945) suggests these individuals look to their partner for a sense of value. However, without self-love and self-acceptance, a partnership will not improve the situation.

Projection

Added to their feelings of worthlessness, the abused child will be likely to project the critical, abusing or rejecting parental characteristics onto others. This is particularly difficult when their life partner is the subject of their projections. Instead of seeing the partner as they are, they see only the behaviour of the critical or abusive parent.

For the adult to break these patterns, they need to spend time, with a skilled listener, unravelling the web of childhood experiences and looking again at their current situation. Some abused children grow up to find partners who continue to abuse them. Because as a little child they could not challenge the situation, they may accept the adult relationship without question, never aware that it is unacceptable, because that is how life has always been for them.

Rejection

Rejection is a powerful form of childhood trauma and abuse that impacts the functioning of I2. To a child it is equivalent to death, and results in self-hatred, because the child identifies with the parent and rejects themselves. In adult life it will be just as traumatic when the person is rejected, especially by a partner, because they will relive the original trauma. When this happens, the solution lies in the individual learning to have attunement with themselves. This enables them to love and accept themselves rather than identify with the partner and their rejection (Judith, 1996).

Poorly Functioning Interpersonal Connectedness (I2)

My observation is that a poorly functioning I2 manifests in the person being withdrawn and antisocial, cold-hearted, critical and judgemental, intolerant, isolated, depressed, disconnected and closed, without empathy, and with narcissistic tendencies.

TRAUMA AND AN UNDER-RELIANCE ON I2

When a child experiences trauma such as abuse, they close their heart and their I2 may remain underdeveloped into adulthood. They are afraid of intimacy in any relationship, because they see only the risk of being hurt again. This can happen for all of us, too, after a lover's rejection. Fortuitously, a highly functioning I2 usually recovers after a time of grief.

Unfortunately, for the wounded person, a poorly functioning I2 results in not only a withdrawal of love, but also in the closure of the channel for receiving love. Therefore, the wounded heart is not open to receive the love of friends or family, and the individual becomes lonely and withdrawn. They may function quite well in day-to-day life but cannot connect meaningfully with others.

Furthermore, because they received no empathy as a child, the wounded heart

Knowing Others, Knowing Myself:
When I2 is Impaired

The prefrontal cortex assists in constructing ideas about the beliefs, intentions and perspectives of others (Goel, Grafman, Sadato & Halletta, 1995; Stuss, Gallup & Alexander, 2001). Damage to this area early in childhood, or in later stages of life, results in deficits in the development of empathic abilities (Dolan, 1999). Damage to the orbitofrontal cortex has been correlated with acquired antisocial personality (Meyers, Berman, Scheibel & Hayman, 1992).

Neuroscience has also helped to demonstrate, through functional imaging studies, the important link between understanding our own emotional states and the states of others. Empathy requires conceptual understanding, emotional attunement, and the ability to regulate one's personal emotional state, and early studies with patients suffering brain injuries suggested that damage to either the dorsolateral or orbitofrontal areas (which are linked to these abilities) impairs different aspects of empathic behaviour (Eslinger, 1998).

Since then, research has shown that individuals with a poor ability to be aware of and describe their own emotional states also show poor ability to understand the mental states of others, and reduced activation in the right medial prefrontal cortex (a key area of the brain associated with mentalising). These 'alexithymic' individuals (literally, to be 'without words for emotions') also struggle to recognise when others are experiencing pain and have reduced activity in the DLPFC as well as reduced responses in parts of the brain to do with our threat response (Moriguchi et al., 2006; 2007).

feels no empathy for themselves or for others. Thus they can be cold and critical or even cruel in response to their own suffering as well as to the suffering of another. A common characteristic of this person is unforgiveness of themselves and others. The person with little empathy holds on to past hurts and nurses their anger.

For the person with an under-reliance on I2, there is an unconscious but very strong fear of intimacy and with good reason, according to their early experiences and reasoning. As a child, they learned from their parents that they were unlovable. Therefore, the adult resists letting anyone too close for fear of exposing their inner self.

Judith (1996) observes that, from time to time throughout life, many adults display both an over-reliance and under-reliance on I2. After deep hurt they will metaphorically close their heart and withdraw for a time; another time they may become co-dependent and metaphorically open their heart too wide, with no barriers, only to be rejected and close down again. The task for us is to observe and be aware of our behaviour and the deeper intention from which it arises.

OVER-RELIANCE ON I2

My experience concurs with Judith's (1996) when she argues that an over-reliance on I2 causes co-dependency, poor boundaries, excessive demands, a tendency to cling, jealousy and a tendency to be excessively sacrificing.

In particular, an over-reliance on I2 Intelligence often centres around manipulation. This is about using the context of love to ease our own pain or compensate for our own incompleteness; that is, using love for our own needs, using another to do what we will not, or avoiding taking responsibility for our own life in some way.

Over-reliance on I2 can create co-dependency – ignoring our own needs to gain love through our apparent helpfulness and care. There is no real love in co-dependency. Not knowing their own needs, the individual focuses only on the needs of the other, hoping for fulfilment by deserving love in return.

However, with this excessive focus on love comes the flip side of insecurity, which manifests in possessiveness, jealousy and excessive demands. Moreover, so needy is the person that it clouds their own awareness and discrimination. Even an abusive relationship may be explained away by wishful thinking. In the end the craving for intensity of connection can have the opposite effect and drive the beloved away, leaving the individual in total isolation.

Healing the Heart (I2) as an Adult

AWAKENING THE AUTHENTIC SELF

Developing a highly functioning balanced I2 involves knowing our authentic self apart from the dictates of the tribe. Once a person on the I2 journey has entered into this stage of development they may return to the tribe for comfort, but it will no longer be able to fulfil this role. They are now on a different journey within themselves. The questions they ask themselves at this time are related to their own personal desires, strengths, weaknesses, emotions and needs.

Myss (1996) explains that whereas the task during the P2 phase of the journey is for a person to learn to love themselves in relation to the achievement of their own goals (such as the acquisition of material possessions or the climbing of the ladder of success), the I2 journey is about loving themselves in relation to having the courage to listen to their own heart.

Our culture is only recently beginning to embrace I2's needs in marriage. Individuals are beginning to have a strong sense of self when they enter marriage. There is also an emerging expectation that partners will give mutual support not only on a physical level, but also on an emotional, psychological and intellectual level. For many, I2 has resulted in transforming the marriage into a partnership (Myss, 1996).

SELF-LOVE

Before we can form a healthy love relationship with another, we must first love ourselves. Self-love arises from self-awareness, knowing what we need, wish, fear and hope and where our boundaries lie. When we honour ourselves we respect, understand and care for self.

Thomas Moore (1994) advises that an effective method of self-discovery is to neither judge nor change, but simply to witness the self. In so doing, we realise our own sacredness, the divinity in us. This process of self-examination will heal the heart and balance our psyche.

It is through self-reflection that we can do the work of integration of our body, mind and emotions. The I2 stage is the time to heal the heart by working through past hurts, memories and unresolved emotions.

HEALING I2 WITH SELF-ACCEPTANCE

Self-love is the medicine that heals the I2 function. But due to painful events that were supposedly in the context of love, we may be unclear about what true love looks like. So what is love that heals the heart? Acceptance. You must acknowledge all that you are and all that you are not and embrace, honour and respect all of it. To do this thoroughly Judith (1996) suggests the following exercise.

1. Create a four-column table.

2. In the first column, list each part of who you are or the roles you play. For example, you might be the nurturer, parent, friend, protector, critic, carer, inspirer, achiever and hurting child.

3. In the second column add a few words describing how you see that part of yourself. For example, you may see your parent as judgemental, angry and protective, and your achiever as obedient, cute, often lazy but intelligent.

4. Now take some time to consider each specific part listed – to honour, respect and acknowledge that part. Consider how realistic its desires are, how well those desires have been met, and what can be done to make that part whole.

5. Consider which parts relate to other parts. For example, the hurting child may be related to your role in the workplace. Your protector may want to protect the hurting child. Use the third column to draw lines to indicate the relationships and describe them in the fourth column.

6. If you become aware that you would like some of your internal relationships to improve, write a script outlining how you would like the relationship to develop between the two parts of self. Keep going until they come to some resolution.

DEALING WITH GRIEF

We grieve when we lose someone or something dear to us. It is a truism that with the person we lose we also lose some part of ourselves. For example, when we lose a lover, we may temporarily lose the tender part or the playful, sexual part of ourselves. The task is to reclaim and reconnect with the lost part of ourselves rather than fixate on the person lost.

Judith (1996) suggests the following excellent reflection process for healing. To do this reflection, answer the following questions and note the answers in your journal.

Question 1. How was this person special to me?

Question 2. What did this person give that was otherwise missing in me?

Question 3. What parts of me did I especially show to them? What does that part need now? Have I lost contact with that part of myself?

Question 4. What does that part of myself need in order to re-open itself to be healed?

DEALING WITH EMOTIONAL MEMORIES

When we look inside ourselves and listen to our heart, many of us find a 'wounded child'. Many of us also discover this child has had a surprising and unwanted amount of power and influence over our lives. While our heart is unhealed we continue to live in the past. When we are hurt, we close our heart not only to the one who hurt us, but also to everyone else. The same result occurs if we are ashamed of our behaviour and cannot forgive ourselves. Healing can only take place when we can find attunement with the other and ourselves.

Critical to the process of healing is the process of reconsidering our emotional memories, which starts with self-love and forgiveness. We need to open ourselves to the healing power of love and act out the love and attunement of I2.

Many support groups and churches, although intending to help, inadvertently encourage people to see themselves as victims, not responsible for doing anything about their own lives and what has 'happened' to them. The intention of such support groups is to provide a context of unconditional love to work through issues and heal the wounds of abuse, personal violations and injustices. However, to heal the child within's wounds, Myss (1996) points out that the outcome is often that many remain trapped in these warm, caring groups, seeing themselves as needing their wounds in order to receive the love they crave from the group. They then embrace their wound as part of their identity and so do not move on to a new life. Instead of the wound being embraced as a bridge to a new life, it unfortunately becomes an integral part of the new self.

THE POWER OF FORGIVENESS

For self-forgiveness, the victim needs to forgive and embrace the perpetrator, which in some cases includes themselves. Many sensitive individuals beat themselves up long after an event for which they feel ashamed or disappointed. Forgiveness requires heart-felt attunement and empathising with the perpetrator, their intentions, environment, constraints and culture. This requires a separation of the perpetrator's basic essence from their action. Empathising with the perpetrator does not condone their actions, but it does provide the opening for the heart to forgive and heal.

If you want to forgive but you find it is too hard right now, you may find the following exercises recommended by Judith (1996) to be helpful. The first exercise relates to forgiving yourself in order to improve the functioning of your I2 Intelligence.

1. **List the events**
Identify the events for which you have not been able to forgive yourself.

2. **Recreate the events**
For each event, recreate what happened that led to the action.

3. **Identify the parts**
For each event, identify which part of you was acting, for example, the unique child, the unloved spouse, or oppressed teenager.

4. **Understanding**
Relive the feeling and actions of each event to truly understand what was happening.

5. **Attunement**
Listen to that part of yourself with attunement. Consider what it needed and what it was looking for. Consider how you would feel if you saw someone else doing what you did – if you can apply attunement with them then you can apply attunement with yourself.

6. **Forgiveness**
Forgive yourself. Tell that part of yourself, 'I forgive you. I know you were only meaning to ...' If that part of yourself still has not fulfilled what it was looking for at the time, suggest other, more productive, ways of meeting those needs.

FORGIVING OTHERS

This second exercise relates to forgiving others in order to heal the heart.

1. **List the events**
Identify your wounds, perhaps with the help of a therapist or insightful friend.

2. **Identify your benefits**
Ask yourself what you gain by keeping the wound open. Rather than say, 'Something's not right in my life,' say, 'Now I have a job to do.' Perhaps you are demanding of others that they make your life go the way you want it to. Perhaps you are letting your wounds fester and giving yourself permission to act negatively to avoid taking responsibility for your life. Letting the wound fester may mean becoming powerful or avoiding domination. This may take the form of being right, making someone else wrong, and acting as their judge and master. You may be using grumpiness to blackmail another into doing something your way. Perhaps you are being grumpy as a means of communicating what you want without being vulnerable and taking any of the risks involved by asking verbally.

3. **Consider the message**

   Access your I2 to ask yourself the question, 'What is the message behind this hurt and unforgiveness?' Sometimes our hearts hurt, prolonging the wound, as a means of carrying a message. Perhaps you have been violated in some way and your heart is merely meaning to emphatically communicate, 'Don't do that!' Letting your heart release its message often helps in letting go. Use this opportunity to really understand the message of your I2 Intelligence.

4. **Empathise**

   Empathise with your perpetrator. Imagine the series of events that led up to the wound. Consider the valid needs of your perpetrator. Recreate the event as they would have experienced it.

5. **Identify the cost of keeping the wound open**

   Being a victim costs. Look at the costs to your health, energy levels, and your effectiveness. Holding hurt against another is comparable to taking a poisonous pill and expecting someone else to die. Holding hurt hurts you. It affects your health. It consumes your attention. It also impacts your effectiveness in interacting with others. Look at the impact on your ability to express and receive love. Empathise with others about how holding your unforgiveness affects them. You can expect it to be detrimental to others even if they have been too polite to say so. Be clear that you have chosen to be this way by choosing to hold your unforgiveness. It is a reaction from your heart, having a significantly detrimental effect on your own heart and those of others. Identifying the cost provides the fuel for your heart to forgive.

6. **Forgive**

   Once you know that your unforgiveness is about you and your benefits, and that it may merely represent a message, that it costs your heart, and costs others' hearts, you may be ready to forgive and let go. If you decide to talk it through with your perpetrator, either face-to-face or by letter, be sure to focus on forgiving rather than blaming. Create a space which completes your spirit, and does not cause yet another message of anger through you being accusational about the issue.

7. **Think love**

   Live with gratitude and love and, most importantly, live in the present moment.

UNDERSTAND WHAT LOVE IS

Love is a feeling, but it is sustained by a daily commitment to act in loving and caring ways. Judith (1996) offers the following excellent fantasy to help you be present to what love is. Fantasy helps reprogram the heart through a succession of developmental stages.

> *In fantasy, we can imagine our ideal mum, dad or lover. We can imagine how they would speak to us, what they would do for us. In the fantasy, it is important to let the feelings fully permeate the body. [Completely drench your body and your memories in this feeling.] It is often helpful to begin this fantasy imagining ourselves at a young age and gradually growing up with this feeling present. How would it have felt at three years old to have had this kind of support and love? How would it have felt to go to school if you had had this kind of love? How would it have felt going through puberty? Would you walk, talk, or reach out differently? What would college have been like? How would your marriage or your relationship to your children be different?*
>
> (Judith, 1996, p. 291)

I2 is our doorway to love, connection and empathy. The most important thing to remember is always to keep a balance between love and respect for yourself, and love and respect for others.

AFFIRMATIONS

Judith (1996) offers the following affirmations to be used to increase the strength of our I2:

- I love myself and am worthy of my love.
- I love to know that I am worthy of loving myself and others.
- The source of love is unending.
- I live in empathy, forgiveness and acceptance of others.

SUMMARY OF HEALING PRACTICES

According to Myss (1996), the following list identifies some practices which may help to further develop your I2 Intelligence:

- Arm exercises involving reaching out and taking in
- Self-examination and psychotherapy – examine your assumptions about your relationships
- Exercises of emotional release – be complete with others and yourself

- Forgiveness when appropriate
- Inner child work
- Co-dependence work
- Self-acceptance

CREATING A HIGHLY FUNCTIONING I2

Compare your own experience with what you have learned about the I2 Intelligence. Which aspects of I2 are you aware of? Do you focus on one above the other two?

- The I2 somatic element is the physical sensation of being connected with another person or being emotionally responsive to the environment (facilitated by mirror neurons).

- The I2 feeling element is love, generosity and compassion. It involves a sense of attunement and a desire to connect with other people. It also involves feeling what they are feeling within yourself.

- The I2 thinking element involves cognitively understanding what other people are feeling through accurate theory of mind.

Diagram 5.2 shows the three aspects of I2 that require integration so that true Empathy can form.

In integrating this Intelligence the adult needs to align the thinking aspect of Theory of Mind, the feeling aspects of love and compassion, and the somatic aspect of feeling connected to others.

First, focus on awareness of your own emotions and body sensations, be they positive, such as love, attunement and connection, or painful, such as grief, sadness or hurt. To begin, focus on your body. I2 sensations are felt in the chest, around the heart. For some people it is obvious – they place their hands on their heart or they open their arms to open the heart or they may mirror the facial expression of the other person. The task of your conscious self is to observe these somatic sensations, understand them and express them appropriately.

The I2 Intelligence mirrors in you what another person is feeling. This is not your own emotion; it is focused on the other person. This may be attunement (authentic connection) or love, joy or light-heartedness. Above all, there is a sense of connection with the other. If you have well-developed I2, you will be aware of these feelings and will usually express them as appropriate. However, if your I2 is poorly functioning, you will probably not be conscious of this aspect of communication, focusing more

Diagram 5.2 Healthy I2 Intelligence — Noble Quality: Empathy

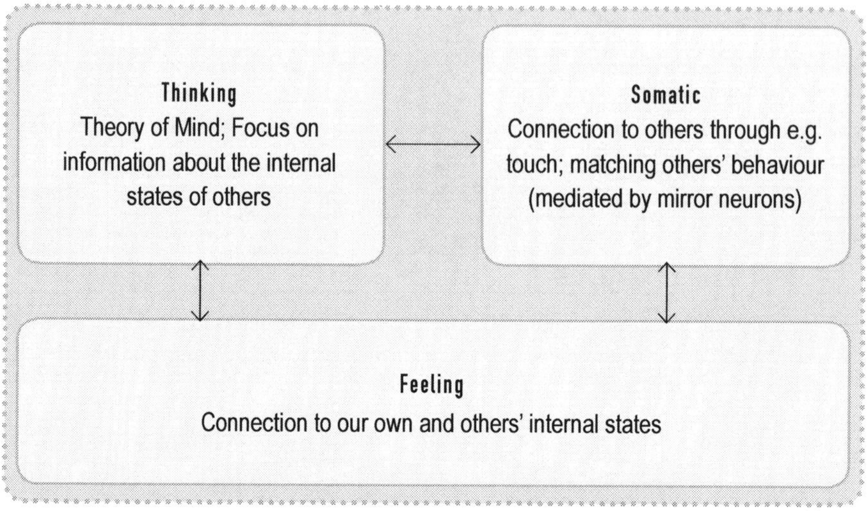

Thinking
Theory of Mind; Focus on information about the internal states of others

Somatic
Connection to others through e.g. touch; matching others' behaviour (mediated by mirror neurons)

Feeling
Connection to our own and others' internal states

For the Neuroscience of Spontaneity see Table 5.3

on the content of the interaction – the argument or the data. However, you may still pick up the feelings and will file the information away into your subconscious mind. Later you may have a 'gut feeling' about the person. It is important to listen to it as it is telling your conscious self what you saw about the person's feelings.

One of the tasks of integrating the three aspects of I2 is to cognitively monitor your feelings and sensations. A person who has highly developed I2 can find themselves overwhelmed by the feelings of others that they 'pick up' from their environment, or they may allow themselves to be controlled by their aesthetic response to their surroundings. The cognitive task is to assess the appropriateness of your response and use 'self talk' to monitor it. Consciously attend to and honour the feelings, then make an executive decision about your response.

I2 is a valuable part of your personality. It can help you connect with others and understand the feelings of both yourself and others. But it is very quiet, maybe unconscious, and so can be ignored when the P1 or P2 Intelligences are busy on a task. The task of integration for your conscious self is to pay attention to the aspect of I2 that 'speaks' to you, however quietly, and integrate it with the other two aspects, so that your responses of feeling, bodily sensation and understanding are unified and whole.

Table 5.3 The Neuroscience of Empathy

The table below details the Neuroscience of I2. Refer to Appendix 13 for more details.

Somatic Aspect	Feeling Aspect	Thinking Aspect
• **Maternal Love** (orbitofrontal cortex, periaqueductal gray, anterior insula, dorsal and ventralateral parts of the putamen)	• **Happy, motherly, joyful, warm, love, calm, excited** (areas rich in oxytocin and vasopressin receptors – both produced in the hypothalamus and stored in the pituitary)	• **Theory of Mind** – the assessment of other people's intentions and emotions (right temporoparietal junction, left temporoparietal junction, posterior cingulate and the medial prefrontal cortex)
• **Attachment** and pair bonding (the medial insula, anterior cingulate, hippocampus and parts of the striatum and nucleus accumbens)	• **Love and attachment – both romantic and maternal** (neurohypophysical peptides, oxytocin and vasopressin, dopamine also released by the hypothalamus)	• **Romantic love** (activation of the frontal, parietal and middle temporal cortices) anterior cingulate cortex, ventral caudate nucleus, insula, striatum (consisting of putamen, caudate nucleus, globus pallidus), central periaqueductal gray and the hippocampus
• **Mirror Neurons** (prefrontal cortex and Broca's area) give us the ability to have mindsight or empathetic attunement – Fire when another individual is observed engaging in a specific behaviour - their facial expressions and posture are thought to activate similar sensory-motor circuits in the observer – This is thought to generate the emotions that result in a sense of empathy	• **Love** – associated with a deactivation of regions commonly associated with negative emotions and social judgement and a decrease in serotonin levels • Many of these responses are activated by the visual system when we **see the face of a loved one** (cerebral cortex, orbitofrontal cortex, anterior cingulate, cerebellum, insula, posterior hippocampus, caudate nucleus and putamen)	• When viewing images of loved ones, the amygdala and parts of both the parietal cortex and temporal lobe – **parts of the brain commonly associated with negative emotions – are deactivated** (middle temporal cortex, occipital parietal junction, temporal pole and lateral prefrontal cortex) elements not related to the achievement of the identified goal) – enables us to focus on the issue at hand and come up with an appropriate plan of action
• **Spindle Neurons** (anterior paracingulate cortex and orbitofrontal cortex)	• **Generosity** (oxytocin) – treatment with oxytocin leads to greater 'liberality in giving' in tasks that require splitting of money	

Highly Functioning I2 in Adult Life

The first-order noble quality of Empathy requires integration of the thinking aspect of intuition, the feeling aspect of love, and the somatic aspect of being emotionally responsive and connective to others.[9] Empathy represents the ability to understand and manage people and to act wisely in human relationships. This noble quality enables the individual to:

1. Accurately empathise with the feelings of other individuals;

2. Interpret the motivations behind the individual behaviours of themselves and others;

3. Understand the likely emotional impact of their own emotional behaviour on others in various situations and actively manage their own behaviour to ensure the best outcome; and

4. Understand emotional concepts and meanings and the links between emotions and relationships.

People with this noble quality enjoy spending quality time with their close friends and are able to monitor the social 'pulse'. They also have the ability to know what to say in difficult, sensitive or emotionally charged moments. Their focus is on building and maintaining honest relationships through authentic connection.

HOW I2 EMPATHY MEETS THE NOBILITY CRITERIA

The first-order noble quality of Empathy answers questions related to the right of the individual to love and be loved. This noble quality enables the individual to discover that they have the right to connect with others and give and receive unconditional love. This noble quality is linked to the desire to authentically connect to others and be 'true' to oneself.

Empathy brings value to the community in three ways. It enables the community to learn to interact in a civilised and sensitive way, and to minimise the amount of needless pain caused by insensitivity. It fosters the idea that community members can be honest and open and form strong ties with other community members based on love rather than simply family or tribal membership. Empathy can also calm another's amygdala, reducing their experience of stress and allowing the space for their more noble qualities to show.

---

9 Peterson & Seligman's meta-study of the most widely influential traditions of thought and religion in human history found emotional and social intelligence to be a significant human strength (Peterson & Seligman, 2004).

It feels good to empathise. Emotional connection created through the noble quality of Empathy describes a key aspect of well-being marked by the subjective experience of connectivity and love (Ryan & Frederick, 1997). Individuals report that using emotional connection to resolve an internal tension has a paradigm shift impact on their lives.

In high performance teams, Empathy ensures that the team feels connected and listened to. Secure in the knowledge that they are cared for by others in the team, each member is able to bring their own love and passion to the work of the group..

I2 Toolbox

THE IMPORTANCE OF I2 IN BUILDING HIGH PERFORMANCE TEAMS

The emergent cultural impact of I2 is Empathy, which enables the organisation to learn to interact in a civilised and sensitive way, and to minimise the amount of needless pain caused by prejudice and misunderstanding.

When Empathy is absent respect for the individual declines. Behaviours are expressed that cause pain in the workplace, uncaringness, dishonesty and disconnection fragments teams.

However, when there is a highly functioning I2 in the organisation, staff at all levels can be honest and open and form strong ties with other staff members based on understanding.

Leaders looking to improve the function of I2 in their team can increase Empathy by applying the I2 tools.

I2 QUESTIONS FOR PERSONAL DEVELOPMENT AND SELF REFLECTION

The best high performing teams are made up of individuals who have focused on their own personal development. The following questions can be used as a starting point for those leaders looking to improve their I2.

1. Who in life provides you with the opportunity to express your ability to love?

2. Who in life do you provide the opportunity to express their ability to love?

3. How do you show love?

4. How is the way you express your love sometimes mistaken?

5. If there is one aspect of love you can't express what would it be?

6. How well do you connect with others?

7. What is one thing you can do to manage your I2 Intelligence?

8. Who do you know who connects well with others and who demonstrates they understand the world view and motivations of others?

9. Is it possible to have one of these people mentor you so that you can further develop your I2?

I2 TOOL #1:
ENSURE ALL AGREEMENTS ARE WIN-WIN

PROCESS

1. **Familiarise yourself with the concepts outlined by Stephen Covey** in his book, *The 7 Habits of Highly Effective People* (1989), focusing particularly on Habit 4: Think Win/Win: Principles of Mutual Benefit.

2. **Ensure you understand the Six Paradigms of Human Interaction:**
   - **Win.** People who hold a win paradigm think only of getting what they want. Although they don't necessarily want others to lose, they are personally set on winning. They think independently in interdependent situations, without sensitivity or awareness of others. *Characteristics of the paradigm:* Appeals to individuals who are self-centred, think 'me first', don't really care about the outcome for the other person and have a 'Scarcity Mentality'.
   - **Lose-Lose.** People with this paradigm are low on both courage and consideration. They envy and criticise others, put both themselves and others down and are usually highly dependent.

     Characteristics of the paradigm: Ends up with nobody benefiting (i.e. 'no win'). This is the long-term result of win-lose, lose-win or win.
   - **Lose-Win.** People who choose to lose and let others win show high consideration for others, but lack the courage to express and act on their feelings and beliefs. They are easily intimidated and tend to borrow strength from acceptance and popularity.

     Characteristics of the paradigm: Appeals to individuals who voice no standards, no demands and no expectations of others. These people are quick to please or appease and tend to bury their feelings.
   - **Win-Lose.** People with this mindset are concerned with themselves at the expense of others. Like those with a win paradigm, they want to win – but unlike those with a Win approach, they also actively want others to lose. These people see their success as being achieved at the expense or exclusion of another's success. They are driven by comparison, competition, position and power.

     Characteristics of the paradigm: Very common scripting for most people – the authoritarian approach. The individual uses position, power, credentials, possessions or personality to achieve the desired 'win'.
   - **Win-Win.** People with this paradigm choose to win themselves and to ensure that others also practice win-win. They take the time to search for solutions that will satisfy their objectives and simultaneously satisfy others.

     Characteristics of the paradigm: Involves seeking mutual benefit – is cooperative, not competitive. Appeals to individuals who listen more, stay in communication longer and communicate with greater courage.

- **Win-Win or No Deal.** This is the highest form of win-win. People who adopt this paradigm seek first for win-win, but if no acceptable solution can be reached, they agree to disagree agreeably.

  Characteristics of the paradigm: Allows each party to say no – the highest form of win-win. This is also the most realistic at the beginning of a relationship or business deal.

3. **Do a quick self-audit.** Which paradigm do you adopt in most of your interactions? What does this reflect about your leadership style? How does this mindset affect the achievement of your objectives, both as an individual and for the team?

4. **Explore the four dimensions of Win-Win.** These are: (1) Character; (2) Relationships; (3) Agreements; and (4) Systems and Processes. The Win-Win Exercises on the following page will provide you with a starting point for developing Win-Win Character and Relationships. For more information refer to Stephen Covey's original materials.

5. **Develop an Action Plan for shifting your paradigm to Win-Win.** Based on the outcome of your reflections, develop a three-month Action Plan for developing Win-Win Character and Relationships. Include conducting a workshop with your team to introduce them to the win-win paradigm and foster discussion about how this mindset can be cultivated in the team.

DOS

✓ Do give yourself time to work through enough of your own feelings about the win-win paradigm before introducing it to your team. While you don't need to be a committed convert, it helps if you see value in and benefits of the win-win approach. If you don't, and you try to introduce the concept to your team, they'll pick up on the incongruence between what you're saying and how you really feel.

DON'TS

✗ Don't be disheartened if shifting your mindset seems like a big task. Early in life, we each learn to base our self-worth on comparisons and competition, and tend to think about our success as resulting from someone else's failure. As you work with the exercises, you'll uncover your own personal unconscious script about the nature of power and success in the world. This underpins how you approach life in general. If you can successfully shift your view to win-win, you're therefore likely to find that it impacts more than just your business interactions. So it's well worth persevering!

Win-Win Exercise: Developing Win-Win Character

Your character communicates your deepest beliefs and values. A win-win leader possesses three character traits:

- **Integrity** – The quality of being true to their feelings, values and commitments
- **Maturity** – The ability to express their ideas and feelings with courage and consideration for the ideas and feelings of others
- **Abundance Mentality** – The belief that there is plenty for everyone

The combination of these three traits builds trustworthiness.

Instructions

1. For each of the three characteristics, give yourself a score out of 10 for the extent to which you embody this trait (0 = not at all, 10 = innate to you 100% of the time).

2. Now give yourself a score out of 10 for each for where you would like to shift that to over the next month. Don't automatically assume that the answer will be 10 – make sure that your response both reflects your genuine desire and is realistic.

3. Resolve to focus on bridging the gap over the next month. Start by listing five things that you can action immediately to develop in these three areas.

Our ability to adopt a win-win approach in life reflects our ability to respond to situations with a high degree of both courage and consideration for others. The character traits of integrity, maturity and abundance provide a strong foundation for responding in this way.

1. How would you rate yourself in terms of your courage and consideration of others? Place a dot in the Matrix to show where you think you sit at the moment.

2. Consider the following scenario:

   You're lunching with your boss and a client at a local café. You're pressed for time (you need to be back at the office in 15 minutes) but the place is crowded and service is extremely slow. It's been 15 minutes since the waiter brought your boss's and client's orders, and they've almost finished eating. When the waiter finally brings your meal, it's not the one you ordered.

   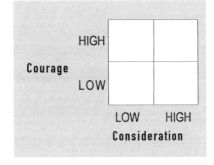

   For each box in the Matrix above, write a sentence about how a person with that approach (e.g. low courage, low consideration) would respond to the situation.

3. Based on your responses to Question 2, create a name for each box of the Matrix that best describes the approach of someone in the quadrant. For example, you might decide to call those with high courage and low consideration the 'Temper Tantrum' or 'Cause a Scene' group.

Win-Win Relationships

Win-win relationships build high trust between individuals. In the same way that regular deposits in a bank build interest, deposits in the 'Emotional Bank Account' lead to a relationship that flourishes with high interpersonal value.

1. The list below outlines the key skills required to establish win-win relationships. Give yourself a score out of 10 for each according to the frequency with which you demonstrate this capability (0 = never, 10 = all the time).

#	Integrity, maturity, and abundance mentality (Win-Win) Relationship Skill	Score
	How often do I:	
1	Demonstrate consistent actions that convince people I have a well-earned reputation for honesty, integrity and loyalty. My actions are consistent with my behaviour, decisions and position	
2	Believe in the best of other people	
3	Share information to help others understand my position, behaviour and decisions	
4	Communicate clear expectations	
5	Seek others' ideas	
6	Listen with empathy to the ideas of others when they are shared	
7	Provide accurate, timely and honest communications	
8	Treat people with respect and respond to their needs	
9	Respond to the needs of others in my team	
10	Focus on the positive but provide constructive feedback on areas for improvement	

2. Add up your scores and divide by 10 to get your average score for your win-win relationship skills. As a leader, you should be aiming for at least a score of 8, if not higher.

3. Identify the three areas in which you rated yourself as performing most poorly.

4. Reflect on how the absence of these skills is impacting your team, your interpersonal relationships and the effectiveness of your leadership. List some examples of recent instances that are in theme with these skills. What was the outcome of these interactions or events? How might things have ended differently if your win-win relationship skills were more highly developed?

I2 TOOL #2:
COMMUNICATING EFFECTIVELY WITH GROUPS

PROCESS

1. **Schedule your face-to-face communication.** The nature of verbal communications can vary greatly, from large formal team briefings to casual encounters between two or three colleagues from different departments. However, the effectiveness of all communications and the extent to which they build and strengthen relationships is greatly affected by factors that affect the dynamic of the group. In scheduling your face-to-face communication, ensure that you:

    a. **Invite the right people.** Group communication works best when the people present have a legitimate reason for being there, have something to contribute and have an interest in the outcome. This often involves making sure there is P1 clarity about the value people add by being at the meeting (for more information about creating P1, see the P1 Toolbox).

    b. **Invite the right number of people.** For most group discussion, five is recognised as the optimum number for debate and decision-making. In a group of this size, members can adopt different roles and a single member can be in the minority without undue pressure to conform. However, making sure the right people are there always takes priority over number considerations.

    c. **Set a time limit.** Even for informal encounters, this demonstrates sensitivity to the pressures on other people's time. You also need to be realistic about what you can expect to achieve within the group given its representation.

2. **Define the purpose of the communication and facilitate introductions.** These P1 actions are critical to ensuring a stable foundation for the discussion – even the most highly skilled I2 communication and active listening abilities become irrelevant if people are busy wondering why they're even there. Is this a meeting to take decisions, a briefing session to impart information or a brainstorming session to generate new ideas? Who are the people in the room, why are they there and what are they each expected to contribute? Make sure you define your own contributions as well as your authority for making them (either as a function of your position or with vested authority on behalf of someone else). Once you've articulated these things, if your expectations turn out to be unrealistic, allow people to leave or, if appropriate, suggest alternative members to join the group. Make sure you apply good active listening skills in determining that the right people are in the room for the right reasons.

3. **Be rational but open-minded during the session.** Groups work effectively only if participants – including you as leader – are open to listening to new points of view and receiving new information. While it's important that you take up a clear position on

issues, be willing to listen to others' positions and be prepared to change your mind. If you do shift your position, explain why.

4. **Demonstrate good I2 communication skills.** There are many different communication techniques and rules that you may wish to adopt. The following are particularly critical in group discussions:

   a. **Practice active listening.** As you facilitate the group, demonstrate that you've heard what others have been saying by linking your comments to the contributions already made. Where possible, clarify areas of support for the arguments of individual team members or identify potential areas of disagreement or overlap between different points of view.

   b. **Make good use of non-verbal communication.** Make eye contact with each member of the group with a view to connecting with each of them as you do so. Use non-threatening but positive body language and convey an impression of calm and confidence. Use gestures to reinforce your key messages and non-verbal signals to convey attitudes and expressions. Also make sure that you pay attention to other people's non-verbal signals: are you irritating or patronising them?

   c. **Stay calm and don't argue.** Even if you believe the group is taking the 'wrong' decision, stay calm and don't become emotional in defence of your own ideas. Emphasise points of agreement and minimise areas of disagreement with a view to finding a way forward.

   d. **Avoid personal attacks.** The key to effective group communication is mutual respect. If you believe someone is wrong, criticise the idea, not the person. The impact of your criticism can be increased by making it more palatable; preface it with a word of support or agreement on a related topic. Other things to focus on include:

      i. Avoid being too negative, even if someone is deliberately putting forward unhelpful ideas;

      ii. Resist the temptation to allocate blame for previous mistakes or failures – otherwise the group dynamics will break down; and

      iii. Remember that while group members may be competing to present individual positions, you are co-operating to find an overall solution.

5. **Bring the communication to a conclusion.** Review what you were hoping to achieve out of the communication and whether it has been achieved in the session. Articulate the decision and review any action statement so that attendees have the opportunity to express any concern about the final outcome. Make sure you translate this into written form as soon as possible after the meeting and make sure that everyone involved has a copy (including interested parties not present).

DOS

✓ Do be aware of the reference points of other group members: how are they viewing the issue (i.e. apply Theory of Mind to determine what they're thinking and feeling) and what barriers will their views create that impede you achieving your own objectives

✓ Do take part in any discussion with a genuinely open mind. Remember good listening skills are critical

✓ Do be aware of the dangers of unconscious domination. If you as leader always give an opinion first, it is possible the others may: be unduly influenced from the start; be liable to think it's all sewn up and that they are only required to react, not contribute; or get into the habit of not thinking for themselves

DON'TS

✗ Don't dominate the discussion because you are convinced of the merits of your own argument and oblivious to others

✗ Don't bring your own prejudices to the group and assume that certain staff members will react in a certain way

✗ Don't allow 'group think' – the process whereby everyone ends up agreeing by default, usually on what they think the leader wants to hear

✗ Define your contribution in terms of meeting the group's objectives and stick to your position unless you are genuinely convinced by other member's arguments

I2 TOOL #3:

BUILD ACTIVE LISTENING IN YOUR TEAM

PROCESS

1. **Self-assess your own active listening skills.** Complete the Active Listening Exercise on the following page, paying particular attention to the follow up reflection questions.

2. **Ask colleagues to provide you with feedback about your active listening skills.** Identify at least two colleagues who have worked closely with you and whose opinions you value and trust. It's also important that you feel comfortable receiving constructive feedback from the people you choose. Provide each colleague with a copy of Questions 1, 2 and 3 of the Active Listening Exercise. For each skill listed, ask them to rate you (according to the instructions) by asking themselves the question: 'In conversations with others, including me, how often does [your name] ... [insert skill]'.

3. **Compare the assessments.** Look for any discrepancies in scores, particularly any skills for which you gave yourself a high score, while others did not. Have an informal chat with your colleague - show them your self-assessment and ask for further comments about why they scored you as they did. This is your chance to have the benefit of their insights about how you might improve. It is not an opportunity to explain to them why they were wrong/misguided/harsh/foolish in their scoring.

4. **Identify five key skills for improvement over the next month.** Set aside some private time to consider your active listening skills. Consider which skills need to be prioritised first – and make sure you take into account the feedback you received from your colleagues, your own reflections from Questions 4 and 5 of the Active Listening Exercise and the particular circumstances of your position. Identify five key active listening skills that you intend to focus on improving over the next month. Develop an Action Plan for how you intend to achieve this goal.

5. **Take your team through the same process.** Schedule a team-building session and start by explaining the critical importance of empathy to team performance. (You may like to use the introduction to the I2 Toolbox as a thought starter.) Invite each team member to follow the process you've already undertaken – first completing the Active Listening Exercise, getting at least one other colleague to assess them, discussing the results with their colleague, identifying their priority areas for improvement and developing an Active Listening Action Plan. Then bring the group together for a discussion about the insights they gained from the exercise, particularly how the group's listening skills have been affecting team performance. Make sure you link the active listening principles back to any key projects or objectives to 'make it real' for the team. You should be able to cover this in 2-3 hours, depending on the how many colleagues each person asks to assess them (1-2) and the amount of time you want to give to discussion.

DOS

✓ Do give some thought to who you want to ask for feedback. If you can, resist the temptation to invite only people you get along with for comment. Often it's with the people we find challenging that we allow our listening skills to remain unused. This is a great opportunity to challenge yourself to be a good listener even with those you violently disagree with/dislike. If you can master those conversations, your chances of making active listening an innate part of your leadership style will increase dramatically

DON'TS

✗ Don't be devastated if the results show that you're not as good a listener as you thought you were. Most of us aren't. This is a good opportunity to identify areas for improvement so that you can become the excellent listener that you want to be. Also, remember that this is one person's perception, so extract the helpful feedback without taking it too much to heart

Active Listening Exercise

1. The following list details the skills of a good listener. Give yourself a score out of 10 for each according to the frequency with which you demonstrate this capability (0 = never, 10 = always).

#	Good Listening Skill	Score
	In conversations with others, how often do I:	
1	Probe for clarification	
2	Listen for unvoiced emotions (i.e. how the other person is feeling, even if they're not expressing it overtly)	
3	Listen for the story	
4	Summarise what has been said	
5	Empathise	
6	Listen for what's different and new about the narrative, not what's familiar	
7	Take the other person's story seriously (i.e. not say things like, 'You shouldn't worry about that')	
8	Look for hidden assumptions underlying the story	
9	Let the other person 'get it all out of their system'	
10	Ask the other person, 'How do you feel about that?'	
11	Keep asking for more detail to help me understand	
12	Get rid of distractions while listening (e.g. turn off the mobile phone, don't multi-task by reading emails at the same time etc.)	
13	Focus on hearing the other person's version of events first	
14	Let the other person tell their story their way	
15	Try to stand in the other person's shoes, at least while I'm listening	
16	Ask how I might be of help to the other person	
17	Ask the other person what they've thought of before sharing my own thoughts	

#	Good Listening Skill	Score
18	Make it seem as if the other person is the only thing that matters and that I have all the time in the world	
19	Look at (not stare at) the other person as they're speaking	
20	Look for congruity (or incongruity) between what the individual says and how he or she gestures and postures	
21	Encourage by nodding my head or giving a small smile	
22	Control my own body movements (i.e. no moving around, shaking legs, fiddling with paper clips, etc.)	

2. The second list below details the skills of a poor listener. Give yourself a score out of 10 for each according to the frequency with which you demonstrate this capability. However, this time 0 = always, 10 = never.

#	Poor Listening Skill	Score
	In conversations with others, how often do I:	
1	Interrupt or respond too soon	
2	Match the other person's points (e.g. 'Oh yes, I had something like that happen to me. It all started when…')	
3	Editorialise while the other person is mid-stream (e.g. 'Well, that option is a non-starter')	
4	Jump to conclusions or judgments	
5	Ask closed-ended questions for no reason	
6	Give my own opinion before asking the other person for their thoughts about the situation	
7	Try to solve the problem too quickly	
8	Take calls or interruptions in the course of client meeting	

3. Add up both sets of scores and divide by 30 to get your average score for your active listening skills. As a leader, you should be aiming for at least a score of 8, if not higher.

4. Identify the lowest five areas in which you rated yourself as performing relatively poorly.

5. Reflect on how these skills are impacting your team, your interpersonal relationships and the effectiveness of your leadership. List some examples of when you can remember yourself doing or not doing these things in conversations (depending on whether you've identified absent good listening skills or the presence of poor listening skills as areas of concern). Then describe the outcome of the interaction and include reflections on how the listening skill may have affected that result.

KEY INTERPERSONAL CONNECTION QUESTIONS FOR BUILDING A HIGH PERFORMANCE TEAM

1. How well do you know each of the other members of the team?

2. In your opinion, how committed are you as a team to ensuring each team member feels heard and understood by other members of the team?

3. How aware are you of the strengths of the other members in your team?

4. How well do you feel your strengths are utilised within the team?

5. As a team, how do you support each other during challenging times?

6. What can you do to facilitate more connection within the team?

Key 12 Questions for High Performance Teams

NeuroPower Case Study

ORGANISATIONAL CASE STUDY #1: STATE HEALTH HAND HYGIENE PROJECT

The Task: To improve compliance by health workers with hand hygiene practice.

Recap:

In 2007, an Australian state health department wanted to address the serious threat that health-associated infections posed to hospital patients. Micro-organisms are readily transmitted on the hands of health care workers. In Australia alone, health officials estimate that up to 7000 people die annually from hand hygiene-related infections in hospitals. The economic burden is also considerable, costing millions each year.

Hand hygiene has been proven to substantially reduce transmission of micro-organisms. However, despite well-established guidelines, compliance throughout the world with hygiene standards is disconcertingly low. International and national health agencies have been grappling with how to deal with the issue for some time, and few interventions have had any impact whatsoever, despite both European and US hospitals and governments spending tens of millions of dollars on communications, incentives, closed circuit TV and education.

Since research demonstrated that the hand hygiene issue centred around human behaviour, one state health department decided on an innovative, behaviour-changing approach using the *NeuroPower* framework to drive the solution. Working with the *NeuroPower* Consulting Team, the department implemented a behaviour change program called Clean Hands are LifeSavers that engaged the health workers and increased compliance from 18% to 60%. A key driver of this behaviour change involved effectively addressing each of the six Intelligences in the correct sequence. How these progressive steps were taken is outlined in the Organisational Toolbox Case Study at the end of each Intelligence chapter.

Having already:

- Created safety and security in the hospital environment by embedding values through a code of conduct
- Empowered spontaneity and self-expression through collaboration and the development of creative promotional materials
- Kick started action and motivation through establishment of goals and the celebration of quick wins

Step 4: Encourage empathy and connection

Most health workers, especially the nursing staff, are very high in empathy (I2). Part of the issue with infectious transmission rests in the fact that many health workers use touch to reassure patients or had a belief that washing hands after each patient made the environment too scientific. Health workers were trained not to rush and to spend time listening to patients and their family and friends, and to engage in other compassionate activity other than touch.

ORGANISATIONAL CASE STUDY #2: MERCHANT BANK EQUITY DERIVATIVES LEADERSHIP TEAM

The Task: Improve employee engagement and tangible business performance

Recap:

In 2006, at the height of the financial boom, one of Australia's leading equity derivatives teams was operating in an environment that was fast-paced, demanding and with a high level of stress. In order to handle large volumes of work in a very volatile market, the team needed to be highly functional and collaborative. Growth was nearly 200 percent over the previous year so the enormous strain was evident. This was mainly caused by a leadership team in crisis.

The Leadership Team was fractured, non-collaborative and driven by their own individual agendas. There was both a lack of respect and a lack of honesty between members which led to highly reactive responses and conflict. The broader team could see this occurring and they felt they were part of a warring tribe with all the insecurities that brought.

NeuroPower consultants devised a program which focused on addressing the splintered leadership team. The intervention involved a series of group structured processes which were embedded by individual coaching sessions.

Having already:

- Created role clarity
- Empowered people's self-expression
- Encouraged healthy egos and passion for work

Step 4: Developing Teamwork and Leadership Capabilities through an expanded I2

A key workshop focused on the Signature Strength or Gift of each team member. The group was introduced to the eight Neuro-Rational Types (Principle 3) that exist in a healthy and high performing team and what unique qualities and capabilities each profile brought to the group. By the end of the session, the team could see each of their colleagues in a different light, and there was a sense of combined effort and excellence that eased the task ahead. The team displayed an expanded sense of themselves as being leaders that were unified and connected and with the right qualities to lead the whole Equity Team to high performance.

Chapter 6

Our Fifth Social Cognitive Need:
SEEING THE FACTS &
The Objective Learning Function (I1)

SEEING THE FACTS (I1) AT A GLANCE

Seeing the Facts is our Brain's Fifth Social Cognitive Need

The brain looks for constant feedback and needs to have all the information at hand.
The brain is a complex, self-regulating machine that adapts constantly to external feedback - much of it visual. Of all the senses, the human brain is heavily invested in perceiving, processing and remembering information, particularly visual information. We need to 'see it to believe it'.

Characteristics of the Seeing the Facts (I1) Functional Network

Data and Facts

STRENGTH	WEAKNESS
Focuses on the detail and works with quantitative information	Can disregard the human element when making decisions

OPPORTUNITY	THREAT
To get comfortable with processing qualitative information	Can be rendered useless when faced with ambiguity

Management Style

- Will want to base all discussions and decisions on data and evidence
- Will assess others on their depth of field-specific knowledge
- May forget to consider the people side of things

LOVE OF LEARNING

I1 THINKING

Pattern Recognition, Explicit Semantic Memory

I1 FEELING

Curiosity, Emotional Connection with Objects

I1 SOMATIC

Withdrawal and Objectification

COMMUNICATION STYLE

- Tends to have an excellent vocabulary
- Tends to listen for interesting or new facts
- Values facts (objectivity) over feelings
- Often oblivious to how people are feeling or to any hidden agendas
- Can talk facts all day and not resolve issues
- Will want to see the evidence for themselves

KEYWORDS INCLUDE

- Evidence
- Data
- Truth
- Facts
- Pattern recognition
- Objectivity

Seeing the Facts (I1) Helps Us to Survive

Seeing the Facts (I1) helps both individuals and the group to survive and thrive by helping them see the world as it is (rather than how they would like it to be), track progress and make detached decisions based on reality.

Seeing the Facts & The Objective Learning Function (I1)

SEEING THE FACTS: OUR FIFTH SOCIAL NEED EXPLAINED

In Chapter 5, we looked at our need for Interpersonal Connection (I2), which is supported by the brain's sophisticated ability to understand what others are thinking and feel what others are feeling. Our Interpersonal Connection (I2) - sometimes described as our ability to empathise - motivates us to connect with other people, understand them and respond appropriately to this social stream of information[1].

But - as any structural engineer will tell you - **feelings alone can't build a bridge**. Sometimes we need to get the facts right; near enough is not good enough.

Luckily, our brains are exquisitely wired to perceive and respond to the external, physical world, particularly by interpreting and understanding the world through what we see (Seeing the Facts - I1). Sight is extraordinarily difficult. It takes many thousands of calculations for a computer to detect even basic visual shapes, and yet we find it easy. This is because an extraordinary amount - over 50% - of the brain is dedicated to visual processing, pattern recognition and object classification. Over 70% of all your sensory receptors are in your eyes[2], and while most of us hardly think about the millions of visual inputs our brains are piecing together or filtering out every second, a range of findings from neuroscience, social science and communication research have confirmed that the ability to 'see' something is strongly linked to your ability to understand and remember it. For example, simple diagrams on medicine labels increase our ability to understand them by 25% compared to text alone (Dowse & Ehlers, 2005). Being able to see something for yourself increases audience comprehension rates by one third, compared to just hearing it.

---

1   This ability to connect and empathise is hardwired, and at times hard to overcome. In fact, our natural tendency to try to understand the mental states of other living things (whether human or another animal) is so strong that at times we mistakenly attribute mental states and intention to inanimate objects - from computers that 'refuse to cooperate' through to the relationships that some people form with their cars or other precious belongings!

2   Whereas dogs, rats and many other vertebrates have brains with large olfactory bulbs dedicated to discriminating between smells, the human brain has instead invested its resources into visual perception (our ability to see). Interestingly, though, while the human olfactory bulb is a relatively small organ, it has retained its strong and direct links to the amygdala and other parts of the limbic system, which some neuroscientists suggest is why particular odours (like the smell of smoke, for example) have the ability to influence body physiology and evoke strong emotional memories.

Of all the Six Social Needs and their associated systems in the brain, Seeing the Facts (I1) is perhaps the most thoroughly researched. With access to brain imaging technologies, researchers have observed that the data the brain needs about people (Empathy, I2) and the data the brain needs about the physical world (Seeing the Facts, I1) not only belong to two separate systems but also compete for dominance in the brain. Jack et al., (2012) looked at brain activity when people were performing a 'mechanical' reasoning task based on factual knowledge about the physical world (Seeing the Facts, I1) and a 'social' reasoning task based on understanding and predicting what and how people feel (Interpersonal Connection, I2). They found that the network of brain regions activated by the I1 task was suppressed by the I2-related task, and vice versa. This finding was particularly relevant for researchers trying to understand the biological basis of autism, who have similarly found that healthy adult brains have both a tendency to empathise (your empathy quotient, or EQ) and a tendency to think analytically or systemise (your systemising quotient, or SQ) and that the stronger your tendency to systemise (high SQ), the lower your empathy (EQ) (Goldenfeld et al, 2005)[3].

One other insight into our objective learning function (I1) comes from Cambridge University, where researchers have found that people who are good at maintaining precise memories have more folds in specific areas of their frontal lobes; those of us with less pronounced folds seem to be much more likely to confuse things we have experienced with things we have imagined or felt (Simons, 2013).

The I1-driven motivation to 'systemise' (by focusing on observable patterns in the physical world to understand how systems work) is critical to many of the technical fields that are required in modern organisations. Fields built on mathematics and physical sciences rely heavily on people with a high systemising quotient (SQ), and science, engineering and computing faculties have a significant over-representation of 'systemisers' compared to the humanities (Focquaert et al, 2007). Systemisers (high in Seeing the Facts - I1) tend to have more activity in areas of the frontal lobe dedicated to focusing on fine detail and filtering out distractions as well as much more activity in areas dedicated to integrating sensory inputs (Billington, Baron-Cohen & Bor, 2008)[4]. At a structural level, their brains have much more myelinated nerve connections ('white matter') in areas of the brain linked to the external attention system (Takeuchi et al, 2013).

3　This line of research has helped contextualise autism by showing that it is the combination of both very high SQ *and* very low EQ that gives rise to a clinical diagnosis of autism; in reality, each of us sits on the SQ spectrum and the EQ spectrum.

4　By contrast, empathisers show more activity in social-processing areas of the brain, including mirror neuron areas such as the left inferior frontal gyrus and inferior parietal lobule, and in temporal areas involved in perspective taking and autobiographical memory (Focquaert, Steven-Wheeler et al, 2010).

Diagram 6.1 Physics vs Friends – The Competition Between Analytical (I1) and Empathic (I2) Systems in the Brain

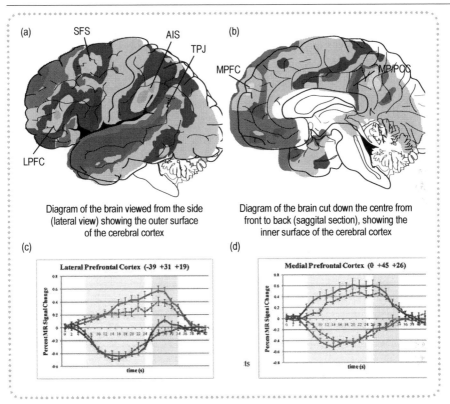

Diagram of the brain viewed from the side (lateral view) showing the outer surface of the cerebral cortex

Diagram of the brain cut down the centre from front to back (saggital section), showing the inner surface of the cerebral cortex

Jack et al., (2013) investigated whether mechanical reasoning (i.e. solving problems based on inanimate physical objects; I1) and social reasoning (i.e. using information about people to understand their thinking and/or predict their behaviour; I2) might recruit different areas in the brain. Their research revealed two distinct patterns of brain activation for these two different types of reasoning and, fascinatingly, showed that the areas involved turn 'on' or 'off' for these two different tasks. What they called the 'mechanical reasoning' areas (I1) increase in activity when we're thinking about the external physical world and then turn off when we start thinking about people's internal states (and vice versa for social areas). *(a,b)* On the diagrams above[1]*, cool colours (purple, blue, cyan, green) activate more for mechanical than social reasoning. Warm colours (pink, red, orange, yellow) activate more for social than mechanical reasoning. Bright colours (orange, yellow, cyan, green) identify areas which were significantly above the rest for one type of task and significantly below the rest for the other. *(c,d)* Tracking the activity of specific areas in the brain reveals activation or deactivation for mechanical (blue lines) and social tasks (red lines). The two examples provided are the lateral prefrontal cortex (LPFC) and medial prefrontal cortex (MPFC), which are more involved during mechanical and social reasoning tasks, respectively. Other activation centres linked to mechanical reasoning (I1) included the superior frontal sulcus (SFS) and anterior intraparietal sulcus (AIS). Activation centres linked to social reasoning (I2) included the temporoparietal junction (TPJ) and medial parietal/posterior cingulate (MP/PC).

---

*   For illustration purposes, the diagram above presents an artist's approximation of reported activation areas from one side only. Detailed, bi-hemispheric maps of brain activation are reported in Jack et al., (2013), (p. 390) Figure 3.

TRACKING PROGRESS: THE BRAIN'S CONSTANT QUEST

The brain is a complex self-regulating machine that adapts constantly to external feedback.[5]

For teams to achieve peak performance each team member's brain needs external, verifiable measures that track the team's progress. These measures need to be simple enough that team members can understand them. Very few teams do this well, because they either fail to keep track of key measures of progress or, alternatively, they measure anything and everything to the point where no one is able to effectively decipher the information in real-time. We call this paralysis by analysis. The simple idea is that tracking progress enables the individual and the team to evaluate the effectiveness of the strategy and tap into the brain's natural ability to respond to feedback in real-time, adapting the strategy with incremental changes along the way. Without an ability to see progress, motivation quickly diminishes.

Within the brain, a diverse range of structures and neuronal networks help us satisfy our need for Seeing the Facts. Within the *NeuroPower* framework, this set of structures is called the 'I1 Objective Learning System' (or sometimes the 'I1 network' or 'I1 function') and gives rise to a particular thinking style referred to as 'I1 Intelligence'. The rest of this chapter explores the I1 Objective System in detail.

THE EVOLUTIONARY SOCIAL BRAIN FUNCTION OF I1

The I1 system enables the individual to survive through:

1. The recognition of objects and recall of information associated with them (Creem and Proffitt, 2001);

2. Communication within the individual internally and externally with others through language;

3. Learning new things about the world and the formation of declarative memory; and

4. The ability to identify patterns in: behaviour (both one's own and others'); the seasons; dangerous situations; and opportunities.

Recognising the Characteristics of Seeing the Facts (I1)

---

5 One example of this is apparent in the fascinating clinical discipline of neurofeedback, where your brain trains itself into more constructive patterns through real-time visual feedback.

The I1 Intelligence relates to the mind's ability to see patterns and remember facts. I1 involves the psychological ability to stand outside our beliefs and attitudes by focusing on the objective facts and the data of the world. The I1 function enables the mind to process data quickly. The attributes and characteristics of I1 suggest that it is linked strongly with the left hippocampal area and involves the explicit semantic memory system.

The I1 Intelligence loves learning and experiencing life. It gives rise to curiosity that fosters an increased understanding of the external world as it actually is. However, I1 will often be oblivious to hidden agendas and has limited ability to handle ambiguity.

I1 has three elements that require integration. The cognitive thinking aspect focuses on data, learning and pattern recognition. The feeling aspect centres on a sense of curiosity and unique connection with objects, and the somatic behavioural aspect is typified by withdrawal and focusing the eyes.

The factual, data recall aspect of I1 is usually the aspect that is most conscious. This may be because it is this aspect of I1 that is supported, encouraged and developed through formal education. The purpose of I1 is to objectively review our world without judgement or emotional subjectivity. Through these objective perceptions we are able to establish a starting point from which to rechart our next step to help us reach our goals. In the corporate context, this is reflected in the tracking of lead and lag indicators.

Seeing the Facts (I1) has Both Strengths and Weaknesses

Objectivity and a motivation to seek external, validated data are critical to effective decision-making in many fields. Many organisations recognise this and dedicate significant resources to tracking progress using a diverse range of overlapping (and at times contradictory) measures. It is important to recognise that an **overemphasis** on Seeing the Facts, either personally or organisationally, is largely unconstructive for two reasons. The first is that the I1 system alone is not a decision-making system. An overemphasis on I1 manifests as a feeling of 'lacking the data' to make a decision. This leads to an obsession to keep collecting more and more information, instead of synthesising and learning. The second is that the I1 system encourages the brain to focus purely on objective data and largely ignores the human element of most situations. When Seeing the Facts (I1) is overemphasised, many of the positive aspects of Interpersonal Connection (I2) suffer, including the ability to understand other people's thoughts and feelings. This leads to astonishingly bad predictions about what others will do - and when not managed it leads to relationship-damaging decisions.

The Development of a Healthy Objective Perspective (I1)

While a rudimentary I1 circuit develops in most children from as early as two years of age, it only becomes high-functioning as the young person learns to think symbolically and abstractly. In Jean Piaget's developmental model, this occurs during the period of Formal Operations, usually beginning around age twelve. This is when the child begins to think as a scientist, and to reason and philosophise about life. As the child begins to think in abstract concepts and symbols, they start to develop an objective (rather than personal) understanding of the world.

Up until this point in the development journey, the progressive development of the Intelligences has made the following contributions to the individual's identity:

- P1 brings understanding of physical identity as we identify with the body and its needs and abilities, as well as the physical world. It is orientated towards self-preservation.

- C1 develops our emotional identity and life script as the feeling sensations of the physical body are transformed into value-oriented meaning. The drive here is towards self-gratification.

- P2 develops a sense of our autonomous, separate awareness. The primary concern here is with self-definition (ego).

- I2 focuses on our social identity where the ego identity expands to include relationships with others. The quality of this identity is towards self-acceptance, which is essential for acceptance of others.

The I1 Intelligence enables the adolescent to objectively create a sense of personal identity that is separate and removed from the other Intelligences. It can be an aspirational identity based on what the individual likes the look of in others.

COMMUNICATING OUR PERSONAL IDENTITY

Developmentally, the onset of I1 in the teenage years ushers in the idea that we communicate who we are (I2 social identity) with objects (I1) that tell our story for us. In ancient societies this may have been with small, culturally defined objects like earrings, headpieces or bangles. In modern society, we have added thousands of other fashion items and objects to the list. What the teenager wears, the phone they have, the websites they visit, the car they drive, the shoes they wear, the style of haircut etc. are all external symbols of the individual's inner world. They also describe the individual's place in the external world through value-laden objects. This signposting continues through life with the partner you choose (or don't), the holidays you enjoy (snapshots), the suburb you choose to live in and your ever-changing fashion sense.

Regardless of our personal I2/I1 dominance, we all 'believe' the validity of our internal world (I2) once it manifests in external reality (I1). We signpost who we aspire to be, which in turn educates and reinforces this emerging us to ourselves and those we meet. Most recently, the channel of choice in the west is quickly becoming social media options like Facebook that help us clearly encode our sense of ourselves in an I1 reality.

I1 AND EXPLICIT SEMANTIC MEMORY

I1 enables the brain to remember facts. It governs and records the specific, factual and objective memory of an event. This is the library in which we store the images that we link with experience. Unfortunately, these images are not automatically linked with the correct emotional memory of the event centred in I2.

Consider, for example, a memory for a fact, such as the French word for table. Your explicit semantic memory (I1) describes the objective memory of the details. (How is it spelt? Is the noun masculine or feminine?) On the other hand, there may also be an emotive memory such as the memory of sitting at the French table while you were spending last summer at the seaside with Auntie Flo, including how you felt about it (I2). For a memory to be consolidated, I1 and I2 must be consciously reconciled. This is only possible if there is communication between the hippocampus

Comparing I1 and I2 Memory Systems

There are two distinct forms of explicit memory. While the explicit autobiographical memory system correlates with I2, it is the semantic memory (or the memory for facts) that relates to I1. I1 is the mind's ability to perceive patterns, focusing on the facts and the data of the world – the semantic memory function of the brain (Wheeler, Stuss and Tulving, 1997). Our memory for facts (I1 semantic memory) is functionally different from our memory of self across time (I2 subjective memory). I1 memory allows for propositional representations – symbols of external or internal facts that can be assessed as 'true' or 'false'. I1 recall has been found to involve a dominance of left over right hippocampal activation. Further, the perceptual, objective representations of the I1 function have been found to involve the visual cortex that processes information on the basis of pattern recognition. This sensory cortex makes links between different patterns and identifies any 'match' with past experiences. For example, when reviewing a document, it links the specific perceptions of a set of angles with the conclusion that they represent a 'table'.

and the outer region of the cortex.

The fact that the emotion (I2) and object (I1) are not linked unless the hippocampus is engaged creates a distinct problem. As described earlier in this chapter (e.g. Diagram 6.1), individuals tend to use either I1 or I2 at any one time. Unless we integrate the two, the correlation between our emotional response (I2) and the object (I1) that causes it will remain low. If your I1 Intelligence functions more highly than your I2 Intelligence, you may be aware of an object but not the emotion it causes within you. If your I1 is not functioning as well, you will probably be aware of your emotions, but not the object in your environment that is causing them. When the image or memory of an event is disconnected from the rest of the experience, the energy that is split off from it becomes a false image and we become sincerely confused.

Poorly Functioning (I1)

The strength of I1 is to recognise patterns. The process of learning occurs as patterns reveal the identity of a thing, what it is, what it is for, and how to relate to it. But too often we look at something only until we recognise the pattern and then we stop. This point is often when the amygdala makes an inaccurate and often irrelevant emotive connection to the pattern.[6]

Since visual memory is strongly linked with our somatic, or physical experience, it follows that abuses to any of the Intelligences – to the body, the emotions, one's autonomy, one's heart, or freedom of expression – will affect I1. Any abuses to P1, C1, P2 and I2 will therefore become embedded within the body's defensive mechanism – the limbic system, particularly the amygdala. Part of our more primitive centre for interpreting our environmental stimuli, the amygdala's primary function is to scan the environment for potentially hostile inputs and to arrive at an immediate response. This is a role that it plays in all animals. In humans it performs the same function of interpreting hostile events and determining whether to fight (engage P2), to comply (engage P1) with the threat, or to withdraw completely from the situation (engage I1).

The amygdala prompts us to action by chemically inducing emotion. It effectively mediates our library of emotional memories. As the 'librarian' for emotional memory, the amygdala scans experience, comparing what is happening now with what happened in the past.[7] Its method of comparison is associative:

---

6   Often the first step of therapy is to challenge unconscious associations that have formed between the object and the emotion. The realignment of these is an important first step of awareness.

7   In reality, the amygdala is much closer to a guerilla leader, military general and arms trader all rolled into one. It is constantly scanning for risk and rapidly marshalling the troops to head off any threat (however small).

The Impact of Priming on Memory

The divided attention phenomenon reveals an important aspect of memory priming. Experiences must be concentrated on and be a focal point of awareness for them to be consciously recalled in the laboratory. This phenomenon can be tested when a subject is asked to pay attention to only one ear while listening to two auditory lists on a set of headphones. (An example of the two lists may be that one discusses a list of politicians while the other is a list of zoo animals.) When the subject is asked to repeat what it was that they heard in the focally attended ear (say, the right) then they will have excellent recall about the zoo animals. When they are then asked what they heard in the left ear, subjects typically state that they have little recall. When the subjects are then asked to fill in the blank spaces on partially spelled words from the list of words spoken into the left ear, they are statistically more likely to fill in the correct word over subjects who were given a different list. This is a clear example of indirect recall, a measure of implicit memory. The subject's brain has encoded the politicians' names implicitly and so their brain is 'primed' to bring up a politician's name when given a cue. Subjects may have no conscious recall of what they heard, or even a sense that what they are writing is a reflection of a list that they heard or something that they have experienced. While implicit memory is intact, without focal attention, experience does not become encoded explicitly (Schachter, 1992).

when a key element of a present situation is similar to the past, it identifies a 'match' and responds accordingly. Therefore, what something reminds us of will be more important than what it actually 'is', and only one part of an identity is needed to evoke the whole memory. So the amygdala will make connections between things that merely have similar striking features (Epstein, 1994). These associations will represent inaccurate linkages, as they will be based on partial matches and incomplete assessments. We therefore need high functioning I1 to see the entirety of a situation or event, and identify a more complete reality.

ILLUSIONS

When we suffer from an illusion, our attention is fixated on a specific image or outcome we desire. We do not focus on reality, but instead on how we think the present situation should be.

These incorrect associations could be referred to as illusions. An illusion is bound up in the static nature of the amygdala's emotional associations with objects. The

The Trick to Selective Attention

People tend to engage in what psychologists call *belief perseverance*, which is our tendency to see only facts that support our beliefs and ignore those that contradict them (Lord, Ross & Lepper, 1979). This tendency helps us hold on to a world that has, thus far, led to our personal survival (Janoff-Bulman, 1992). However, this confirmation bias can also justify maintaining the status quo long after it has ceased to be constructive. The development of a well-functioning I1 allows for the perception and acceptance of objective truth – even if these facts do not support our beliefs.

more we are attached to an illusion, the more energy we need to invest.

The illusion can become either an obsession or a delusion. When they become obsessions, our perceptions fixate on obtaining a desired outcome. We focus an unusual amount of energy on one particular issue, often to the exclusion of others that are more important.

A delusion is a total misconception of a situation. I once worked with a chairman of a large public company whose father had been a much liked and enthusiastic Presbyterian minister. The chairman lived under the illusion that he was a charismatic preacher just like his father had been. Suffering under this delusion, he was unable to see the reality of his situation, which was really quite the opposite. Despite the best efforts of those around him to help him see things as they were, his perception kept him imprisoned in repetitive cycles of appalling speeches which ultimately led him to losing his appointment as chairman.

TRAUMA AND ABUSE

As we have seen in previous chapters, childhood traumas can affect the development of well-functioning Intelligences. When the child is laying down their memories of family, traumatic memories can impair the developing I1. Judith (1996) argues that this results in adult repression or dissociation. In an effort to shut out the unhappy feelings associated with a memory, we can repress it, close down our perception and limit what we see. This reflects an under-reliance on I1. An alternative is to dissociate from it; in other words, shut down our feelings about the experience and so limit our ability to make sense of it. This results in an over-reliance on I1, at the expense of I2 feelings.

Judith (1996) relays the story of Tom who could recall many incidents of abuse from his childhood, but he completely dissociated himself (and his feelings) from them. In his successive unhappy relationships, he could not 'see' the impact his words and actions had on his partners because he could not feel them. Judith (1996) reports that although a talented, elegant man, 'he had a streak of coldness in his relationships that made one shudder'. He had developed total reliance on I1 and his I2 had atrophied.

An individual's ability to see what they do not want to see can also be impacted if, as a child, they saw something and were told the situation was not as they saw it. For example, if a child sees parents being abusive and is told they come from a family who love one another dearly, this creates a contradiction which may end in illusion. The child does not trust their observations and so their I1 does not develop.

Judith (1996) cites another cause of psychological blindness – childhood shaming. This causes the young child to turn their eyes inward, to ensure there are no more faults to be accused of. Hence, the child does not learn to look outward to see how others are feeling.

DETACHMENT AND I1

The I1 Intelligence enables us to detach from subjective perceptions and see the truth in a situation. Detachment involves stilling your internal fear-driven voices until no external influences have authority over your sense of objectivity. In a healthy sense, this is the realisation that no one person or group of people can dictate reality.

The capacity for detachment is linked to the pattern recognition capacity of I1. With detachment comes the awareness that all things end at the appropriate time and all things begin at the appropriate time. This means that the individual does not hold on to emotional bonds past the point where they are constructive. Detachment also prevents others from having emotional power over you.

Detachment is vital in order to appreciate the truth of revealed patterns removed from their social or cultural form. But if taken too far, and if the entire personality is built around the behaviour of I1, neurosis can occur.

OVER-RELIANCE ON I1

Karen Horney (1945) describes the thinking and behaviour of the adult whose excessive I1 has made them neurotic. She suggests that life, for those over-reliant on I1, is lived like the zombies of Haitian lore. Revived from death through witchcraft, they function like live people, but there is no real life in them. What all detached (excessively I1) minds have in common is their capacity to look at themselves with an objective view. They have an 'on-looker's' attitude towards themselves and towards life in general. They effectively 'move away' from people. This contrasts with the other types identified by Horney: the aggressive (P2) types 'move against', while the compliant (P1) types 'move towards' people.

The goals of the detached person are negative: they want to remain uninvolved, not to need anybody, not to allow others to intrude on or influence them. The underlying and driving end of the detached person is a need for utter independence. From this comes a drive towards self-sufficiency and a withdrawing from people to gain privacy.

Privacy

I1-dominated individuals have an inner need to put emotional distance between themselves and others. They do not want to get emotionally involved with others in any way, whether in love, fight, cooperation or competition. They draw around themselves a kind of magic circle, which no one may penetrate. While they may appear to get along with people at a superficial level, this is only because they are not really relating to others at all. The compulsive character of the need shows up in their reaction of anxiety when the world intrudes on them. They may dislike sharing any experience because the other person may disturb them. Even when they interact with others, their real enjoyment only comes later, in retrospect as they privately review the experience.

Self-Sufficiency

For the mind with an over-reliance on I1, all needs and qualities are applied to support their desire to not get involved. Among the most striking is a need for self-sufficiency. A more precarious way to maintain self-sufficiency is by consciously or unconsciously restricting one's needs. The underlying principle is never to become so attached to anybody or anything that that person or thing becomes indispensable.

Neurotically detached people avoid competition, prestige and success. They are inclined to restrict their eating, drinking and living habits and keep them on a scale that will not require them to spend too much time or energy earning the money to pay for them. They may insist on acquiring their knowledge first hand; rather than take what others have said, they will want to see or hear for themselves.

Neurotic Superiority

All neurotic tendencies have a need for superiority as a motivating factor and are umbilically linked to the maintenance of the neurosis. Detached people want the uniqueness within themselves to be recognised without any effort on their part. Their hidden greatness should be felt without them having to make a move. A sense of their own uniqueness is an outgrowth of their desire to feel separate and distinct from others.

Emotions

For the neurotic person controlled by I1, there is a general tendency to suppress all feeling, even to deny its existence. This pertains primarily to feelings towards others and applies to both love and hate. Any strong emotion would bring them either closer to others or into conflict with them.

This can even extend beyond the sphere of human relationships, motivated by the desire to maintain self-sufficiency. Any desire, interest or enjoyment that might make the detached person dependent upon others is viewed as treachery from within and may be checked on that account. Any threat of dependence will cause them to withdraw emotionally.

The more the emotions are checked, the more likely it is that emphasis will be placed upon intelligence. The expectation then will be that everything can be solved by sheer power of intellect, as if mere knowledge of one's own problems is sufficient to cure them, or as if information alone could cure all the troubles of the world (Horney, 1945).

Judith (1996) argues that an over-reliance on I1 can induce the following additional issues:

- Hallucinations;
- Illusions;
- Difficulty concentrating; and
- Nightmares.

When there is an over-reliance on I1, the individual is likely to have poor discernment as they are overly bombarded with data input. As they focus on everything, they focus on nothing in particular. This happens when energy is withdrawn from the P1, C1, P2 or I2, and the individual is left without the capacity to discern and sort through the images they perceive. The effect can range from 'mild neurotic annoyance to full-blown psychosis' (Judith, 1996).

An over-reliance on I1 somatic, feelings or thinking will result in the following[8]:

Somatic over-reliance on I1: An over-reliance on the I1 somatic aspect fosters an individual's love of exploring things kinesthetically, taking things apart with their hands to see how they work, understanding complex things but only through physical interaction.

---

8   Each of these three situations reflects a particular Neuro-Limbic Type; the Nine, Four and Five respectively. The Neuro-Limbic Types relate to NeuroPower Principle #2.

Feeling over-reliance on I1: An individual with an over-reliance on the I1 feeling aspect of the Intelligence emotionally connects with objects of perceived beauty or significance.

Thinking over-reliance on I1: An over-reliance on the I1 thinking aspect of the Intelligence creates compulsive observers who get easily overwhelmed, who want to watch and analyse rather than play in the game of life.

All of these reactions are different from the problems that occur if the I1 function is not sufficiently developed.

UNDER-RELIANCE ON I1

An under-reliance on I1 Intelligence prohibits people from following through on the ideas that they have. They appear to be surrounded by plans that never quite come to completion. Physically, the area most affected by poorly functioning I1 is eyesight and the person may suffer from eyestrain, conjunctivitis, poor sight or even blindness. Headaches and migraines may occur and there may be difficulties with memory (Judith, 1996).

The following issues may also result from an under-reliance on I1:

- Insensitivity to self and others;
- Believing there is only one true way/reality;
- Poor memory (because the mind is busy with repressed memory);
- Denial (cannot see what is really going on);
- An inability to learn from life's lessons; and
- An inability to link cause and effect.

CLARITY

As the objective and pattern recognition capacity of I1 is developed, we can see more of ourselves and more deeply into the behavioural patterns of the people around us. As we expand our internal picture into a larger, more comprehensive world view, we inevitably begin to create a clear picture of what is happening. This is the counterpart to illusion.

Clarity arises when we extricate ourselves from the social and cultural patterns of behaviour which we have adopted and develop a plan and purpose for ourselves. With a well-functioning I1 we can be clear about the patterns of our life.

Diagram 6.2 Healthy I1 Intelligence — Noble Quality: Love of Learning

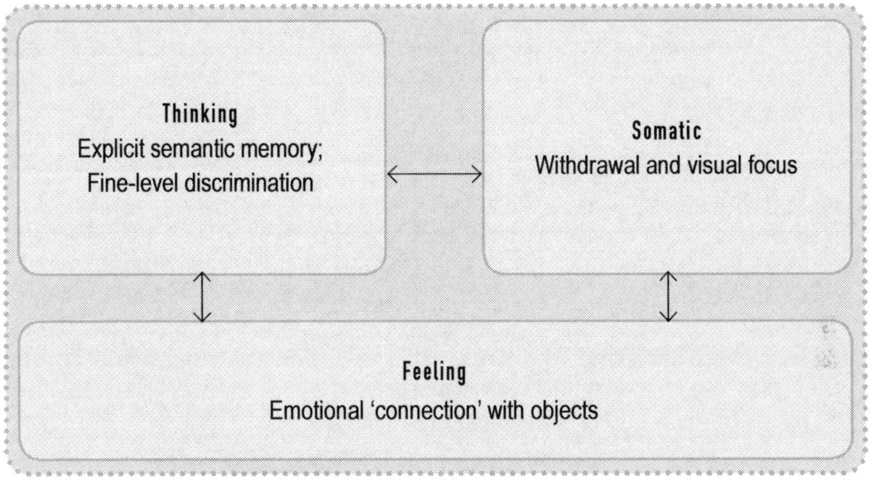

For the Neuroscience of the Love of Learning see Table 6.3

Developing Healthy Objectivity (I1)

The following exercise can help develop your I1.

Look up from this page and closely scrutinise the room that you are in. Look at the walls, look at the furnishings of the room and see them as they actually are - not just as a 'wall' or 'desk'. Now try sketching an object that caught your attention. Notice the difference between what you think the object looks like and what it really looks like. This is the gap between your I1 representation of the object and the object itself.

CREATING A HIGHLY FUNCTIONING I1

Compare your own experience with what you have learned about the I1 Intelligence. Which aspects of I1 are you aware of? Is there one aspect (thinking, feeling or somatic) that you tend to focus on above the other two?

Diagram 6.2 shows the three aspects of I1 that require integration so that true Love of Learning can emerge.

- The I1 somatic element is withdrawal and visual focus.

- The I1 feeling element involves forming our emotional link with objects.

- The I1 thinking element involves consciously perceiving patterns, as well as short term and working memory.

Table 6.3 The Neuroscience of the Love of Learning

The table below details the Neuroscience of I1. Refer to Appendix 13 for more details.

Thinking	Feeling	Somatic
• **Object discrimination** (inferior temporal lobe) • Initial **processing of visual information** and distribution to specialised cortical areas for further processing (visual cortex and hippocampus) • **Semantic, phonological and syntactic verbal fluency** (Broca's areas etc.) • Other relevant structures: posterior parietal lobe, medial temporal cortex, prefrontal cortex (including the hippocampus and parahippocampal cortex), parietal cortex, middle temporal area, medial superior temporal area and posterior parietal cortex)	• **Fascination** – intense interest and a love of learning (midbrain dopaminergic regions) • **Withdrawal – wanting to move back to get perspective and look or watch from a safe place** (amygdala fear response) • **Feelings of either fascination and interest or boredom** (associated respectively with increases and decreases in activity in the prefrontal cortex – monitored by the singular cortices, hypothalamus, tegmentum and interpreted by lateral and polar parts of the cortex in the frontal lobe)	• **Working memory** (prefrontal cortex) • **Medium-term memories (i.e. less than a few years old)** (hippocampus) • **Long-term memories** (frontal lobe)

If you tend to prefer the I2 to the I1 Intelligence, you are still likely to feel curious and be able to work with data. However, there is always the risk that you will ignore objective data in favour of paying attention to the people and environment around you. In this case, to develop your I1 ask yourself, 'What are the facts of the situation?' 'What is the objective reality here?' Accept the validity of the insight provided by the I1 Intelligence. Nurture your curiosity, recall facts and look for repeated patterns in your life. Being able to detach, withdraw and focus is a valuable quality. Encourage this part of you to grow, honour it and integrate it into your personality.

AFFIRMATIONS

The following affirmations can help to build the power of your I1:

- I am clear.
- I am open to my own wisdom and clarity.
- I see things as they actually are.
- I see the repeating patterns in my life.
- I can see.

Highly Functioning I1 in Adult Life

The first-order noble quality of a Love of Learning requires integration of the thinking aspect of pattern recognition and a focus on data, the feeling aspect, and the somatic aspect of withdrawal.[9] This noble quality includes the process of finding content that may or may not result in immediate achievement or any immediate benefit. Instead, the purpose is the discovery of information and knowledge for its own sake (Harackiewicz, Barron & Elliot, 1998). Over time, an individual with this noble quality will develop a deeper or wider knowledge of their subject matter and will be in an ideal position to coach, train or mentor others on the subject. The noble quality of a Love of Learning, strongly correlates with being open-minded to new or confronting data, which means that teams are able to operate with a much broader knowledge base. This noble quality seeks to find, store, retrieve and understand data. It will enjoy categorising information and cross-referencing it with data from other sources.

Experimental studies have found that acquiring specific knowledge evokes curiosity, which is the desire for further information (Loewenstein, 1994). It can also be an orientation towards investigating specific objects, events and problems to understand them better. A Love of Learning improves the individual's ability to recognise patterns of behaviour, seasonal patterns, social patterns – in fact, the patterns in any set of data.

HOW I1 LOVE OF LEARNING MEETS THE NOBILITY CRITERIA

The noble quality of the Love of Learning can answer the individual's current questions of existence in two ways. It answers the questions we all have about understanding how the world works and the true nature of cause and effect. It is

---

9   Peterson & Seligman's meta-study of the most widely influential traditions of thought and religion in human history described Love of Learning as a general disposition towards new information and the search for more content on any particular topic. This was found to be a significant human strength (Peterson & Seligman, 2004).

also central to answering questions about the true nature of the natural, emotional, material, spiritual and metaphysical worlds.

The Love of Learning brings value to the community. A Love of Learning enables the community to develop the ability to see the patterns in the data, to then understand the natural cycles of trading, wealth creation, war strategy, farming, technology and patterns of individual and group behaviour. A Love of Learning also fosters the idea that community members can learn how the world works and maximise their strengths, minimise their weaknesses, and predict future patterns and prepare for them. This noble quality allows for the passing of hard-won knowledge from generation to generation.

The Love of Learning evokes highly positive feelings in the process of acquiring new knowledge, satisfying curiosity, building on existing knowledge and/or learning something completely new (Krapp & Fink, 1992). Individuals report that experiencing a Love of Learning to resolve an internal tension has a paradigm shift impact on their lives.

In teams, a Love of Learning ensures that the team is constantly acquiring new knowledge and can continue to refine its approach based on these insights. This ensures that the high performance team remains competitive in a fast-paced, constantly changing market.

I1 Toolbox

THE IMPORTANCE OF I1 IN BUILDING HIGH PERFORMANCE TEAMS

The emergent cultural impact of I1 is A Love of Learning, which enables the organisation to develop the ability to see the patterns in the data of everyday business.

When A Love of Learning is absent the organisation fails to assess the meaning of information being generated daily, ignorance about the business escalates and denial of the organisation's true status grows.

However, when there is a culture with an effective I1, the organisation can learn how the business works and maximise its strengths, minimise its weaknesses, predict future patterns and prepare for them.

Leaders looking to increase the functioning of I1 in their teams can apply these I1 tools.

I1 QUESTIONS FOR PERSONAL DEVELOPMENT

The best high performing teams are made up of individuals who have focused on their own personal development. The following questions can be used as a starting point for those leaders looking to improve their I1 function.

1. What attitudes do you have that disempower you that may need to be updated?

2. What beliefs do you continue to accept that you know are not true?

3. What negative behavioural patterns continually surface in your relationships with others?

4. Are you judgemental? If so, what situations or relationships tend to bring out that tendency in you? Re-examine the information on which you have based these judgements to ensure their accuracy.

5. Do you give yourself excuses for behaving in unproductive ways? On what data are your excuses based?

6. What new topic areas do you need to learn about to realise your life goals?

7. How would you describe your learning style?

8. If there was one topic that you could learn more about that would have a positive impact on the quality of your life, what would it be?

9. Are you comfortable thinking about your life in impersonal terms?

10. What beliefs and attitudes would you like to change in yourself? Are you willing to make a commitment to making those changes? Are you frightened of the changes that might occur in your life should you openly embrace a conscious lifestyle?

11. Is curiosity a driver for your acquisition of data? Are there occasions when this has driven you to actions which did not honour you or another person? Do you manage this curiosity in a conscious, noble way?

12. When you think about it, have there been occasions when you have allowed avarice to control your behaviour? Could you have used the cognitive part of your I1 to assess the reality of the situation and advise the feeling part of yourself so that your behaviour became integrated with the reality you saw?

13. Do you recall feeling a sense of detachment at times during your life? Let the thinking aspect of your I1 re-examine the situational patterns to see the reality – were there times when this was entirely appropriate? Were there times when this was a reaction to something negative in your environment? Was this a way of collapsing into the tension instead of dealing creatively with the situation?

I1 TOOL #1:
CREATE A 'LEARNING LAB' TEAM CULTURE BY EMBRACING DOUBLE-LOOP LEARNING

PROCESS

1. **Assess the current learning culture** in your team by deciding which of the following the current culture is based on:

   a. **Single-loop learning** (i.e. the detection and correction of organisational error that permits the organisation to carry on its present policies and achieve its current objectives); or

   b. **Double-loop learning** (i.e. where organisational error is detected and corrected in ways that involve the modification of underlying norms, policies and objectives).

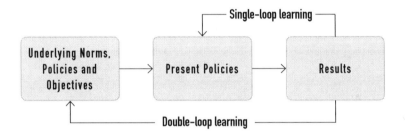

2. **Review the literature on organisational learning models,** including Argyris & Schön's seminal text, Organisational Learning (1995). Make sure you're aware of current thinking about different learning models, and if possible find case studies and examples that are relevant to your industry. You need to be able to demonstrate the benefits of double-loop learning.

3. **Schedule a series of workshops** with key thought leaders in your organisation. Introduce them to the concept of different learning models and present the case for the importance of double-loop learning for the organisation to achieve its strategic objectives. Facilitate discussion about the organisation's current position, desired position and what needs to be done to bridge the gap.

4. **Create an action list for creating a learning lab culture.** Make sure that by the conclusion of the workshop sessions there is clarity about steps that need to be taken moving forward. Examples may include developing new systems for obtaining information, scheduling regular sessions for reviewing systems, policies and practices in light of new data or creating opportunities for learning to be shared and embedded

within the team. The 'Keep, Stop, Start' technique may be a useful strategy to conclude the workshop. Have the team agree on a list of things that they need to keep doing, stop doing and start doing in order to create a learning lab culture.

5. **Follow through on the action list.**

DOS

✓ Do continue to explore ways in which you can embed a learning culture within your team

✓ Do encourage the team to think laterally about how the systems could be improved to encourage double-loop learning. This may involve wider reform than you first anticipate. At this point, it's helpful to remind the team that, as Gary Hamel (described by *Fortune* as the world's leading expert on business strategy) notes, *"If your organisation has not yet mastered double-loop learning, it is already a dinosaur. No one can doubt that organisational learning is the ultimate competitive advantage."*

DON'TS

✗ Don't be disheartened if the team finds the exercise challenging. Deutero-learning (the process of inquiring into a learning system by which an organisation detects and corrects its errors) offers even greater challenges than mastering double-loop learning. While it can be tricky for the team to get its head around, it's central to the contemporary concept of the learning organisation, and well worth the effort

I1 TOOL #2:
MAKE, IDENTIFY AND TRACK YOUR LAG AND LEAD INDICATORS AND USE THIS TO DRIVE STRATEGY (KAPLAN & NORTON'S BALANCED SCORECARD)

PROCESS

1. **Prepare** for the development of your organisation's Balanced Scorecard by:

   a. *Making the team/organisation aware of the scorecard initiative.* Ensure that the purpose of the balanced scorecard is clear (i.e. to provide a balanced view of the organisation's performance with a view to continual improvement). Highlight that the process should not affect the ability of the team to get on with its work; and

   b. *Clearly defining the corporate strategy* and ensuring that the team is familiar with the key issues. Make sure there is clarity about:

      i. the strategy;

      ii. the key objectives or goals to achieve the strategy; and

      iii. the three or four critical success factors fundamental to achieving each major objective or goal.

2. **Identify the key measures of successful goal attainment.** These should be linked to specific strategic goals, and there should be no more than 15-20 key measures in total – significantly fewer may not result in a balanced view, significantly more may result in an unwieldy process that includes non-critical issues. Suggestions from Robert Kaplan & David Norton (who developed the Balanced Scorecard approach) appear below (Kaplan and Norton, 1996), but it's important that your organisation determines its own strategic goals and activities to be measured.

Goals	Measures
Financial (Shareholder) perspective Increased profitability, growth, increased returns on assets	Cash-flows, cost reduction, economic value added, gross margins, profitability, return on capital/equity/investment/sales, revenue growth, working capital, turnover
Customer perspective New customer acquisition, retention satisfaction	Market share, customer service, customer satisfaction, number of new/retained/lost customers, customer profitability, number of complaints, delivery time, quality performance, response time
Internal perspective Improved core competencies, improved critical technologies, streamlined processes, better employee morale	Efficiency improvements, development of leads/cycle times, reduced unit costs, reduced waste, amount of recycled waste, improved sourcing/supplier delivery, employee morale and satisfaction, internal audit standards, number of employee suggestions, sales per employee

I1 Tool # 2

Goals (cont.)	Measures (cont.)
Innovation and learning perspective New product development, continuous improvement, training of employees	Number of new products and percentage of sales from these, number of employees receiving training, training hours per employee, number of strategic skills learned, alignment of personal goals with the scorecard

In order to finalise your organisation's objectives and measures, you may need to conduct further discussions, interviews or workshops throughout the wider business. Ensure that the finalised implementation plan includes setting targets, rates or other criteria for each of the measures, as well as defining how, when and where they should be recorded.

3. **Implement the system and track the results.** Produce an implementation plan and communicate it to the staff. Ensure that employees have a clear line of sight between their individual Key Performance Indicators (KPIs) and the organisation's KPIs.

4. **Identify the key lead and lag indicators.** This is the step that is often overlooked. As a team, identify the lead indicators that result in the lag indicators. Often, as unlikely as it sounds, teams have no real understanding of how these two align. These interdependencies must drive the corporate strategy and are the true, proprietary I1 insights.

5. **Publish the results.** Decide in advance:

   a. Who will receive the specifics of the data (e.g. senior management, divisional/ departmental heads/all staff);

   b. How much information to make available (i.e. the complete body of data available or whether to circulate partial information on a need-to-know basis); and

   c. How the results can be best publicised (e.g. through meetings, newsletters, organisation's intranet etc).

6. **Use the results to drive improvements.** Measurement is not an end in itself it simply highlights areas (e.g. management, operations, procedures, processes) that need strengthening. Taking action on the information you obtain is as important as the data itself.

DOS

✓ Do define your goals clearly

✓ Do select measures that focus on the critical success factors of each goal

✓ Do limit yourself to a manageable number of measures

✓ Do reassure staff about the purpose of the scorecard

✓ Do review the system at the end of the first cycle, taking care to assess the quality of information gathered and the success of subsequent actions. Modify the system if required

DON'TS

✗ Don't simply use the Kaplan & Norton approach suggested as your measures - take the time to reflect on what will be most appropriate for your organisation

✗ Don't over-measure your organisation

✗ Don't allow the measurement process to interfere with employees' ability to get on with the job

I1 TOOL #3:
LEVERAGE FROM YOUR TEAM'S INTELLECTUAL CAPITAL

PROCESS

1. **Schedule a workshop** with key thought leaders in your organisation to focus on how the business can optimise its intellectual capital. Make sure the room has a whiteboard, flip charts (for smaller group working) and enough space for the people attending.

2. **Prepare for the workshop** by reviewing and collating information about the current use of intellectual capital within the organisation. Use any statistics or data available to you to achieve a good understanding of the organisation's current performance across the three areas that comprise intellectual capital:

   a. *Human capital:* The knowledge residing in the heads of employees that is relevant to the purpose of the organisation. Human capital is formed and deployed when more of the time and talent of employees is devoted to activities that result in innovation that drives strategic performance. This occurs either when the organisation uses more of what people know, or when people know more that is useful to the organisation. Unleashing human capital requires the organisation to minimise mindless tasks, meaningless paperwork and unproductive infighting.

   b. *Customer capital:* The value of a business' ongoing relationship with its clients/customers. Indicators of customer capital include market share, customer retention, defection rates and profit per customer. This is often the worst managed intangible asset—many organisations don't even have clarity about who their customers are.

   c. *Structural capital:* The knowledge retained by the organisation. It belongs to the business as a whole and can be reproduced or shared—this includes technologies, inventions, publications and business processes.

Prepare a briefing sheet/brief presentation if needed.

3. **Introduce the concept of leveraging from intellectual capital.** At the start of the workshop, explain the reason for the workshop, the benefit of reviewing how the team uses its intellectual capital and the story behind your interest in the exercise. Introduce the different types of intellectual capital (see above) to the team and acquaint them with the nine principles for managing intellectual capital:

   a. Companies don't own human and customer capital. Only by recognising the shared nature of these assets can a company manage and profit from them.

   b. To create usable human capital, a company needs to foster teamwork, communities of practice and other social forms of learning.

   c. Organisational wealth is created around skills and talents that are proprietary and scarce. Companies must recognise that people with these talents are assets to invest in.

d. Structural assets are the easiest to manage but those that customers care least about.

e. Organisations need to move from amassing knowledge 'just in case' to having information that customers need ready to hand.

f. Information and knowledge can and should substitute for expensive physical and financial assets.

g. Every company should re-analyse its own industry to see what information is most crucial.

h. Organisations should focus on the flow of information, not the flow of materials.

i. Human, structural and customer capital work together. It is not enough to invest in people, systems and customers separately.

4. Get the group to assess the organisation's use of intellectual capital by:

a. Conducting a SWOT analysis (strengths, weaknesses, opportunities, threats) regarding the organisation's intellectual capital;

b. Identifying the key existing sources of human, customer and structural capital;

c. Scoring the organisation's current utilisation of these resources;

d. Setting a target for desired usage; and

e. Identifying key actions to bridge the gap.

Operationalise the action plan that emerges from the workshop.

DOS

✓ Do use the information you gathered in preparation for the workshop to guide the discussion. However, make sure that you build on the reflections of the group about the organisation's ability to leverage from its intellectual capital

DON'TS

✗ Don't forget to consult widely across the organisation in your preparations. This will ensure that you bring comprehensive and valid data to the workshop

KEY SEEING THE FACTS QUESTIONS FOR BUILDING A HIGH PERFORMANCE TEAM

1. How good are you as a team at taking the learnings from results and using them to update your strategy and approach?

2. How well do you as a team use information and data to track trends and anticipate changes to the way the strategy needs to be executed?

3. How well does the team share knowledge between team members?

4. How effectively does the team document decisions and make sure that they are implemented?

5. Are there information silos within the team and how could they be broken down?

6. Are there any skills you need to learn that would allow you to better work as a team to deliver on your strategy?

NeuroPower Case Study

ORGANISATIONAL CASE STUDY #1: STATE HEALTH HAND HYGIENE PROJECT

The Task: To improve compliance by health workers with hand hygiene practice.

Recap:

In 2007, an Australian state health department wanted to address the serious threat that health-associated infections posed to hospital patients. Micro-organisms are readily transmitted on the hands of health care workers. In Australia alone, health officials estimate that up to 7000 people die annually from hand hygiene-related infections in hospitals. The economic burden is also considerable, costing millions each year.

Hand hygiene has been proven to substantially reduce transmission of micro-organisms. However, despite well-established guidelines, compliance throughout the world with hygiene standards is disconcertingly low. International and national health agencies have been grappling with how to deal with the issue for some time, and few interventions have had any impact whatsoever, despite both European and US hospitals and governments spending tens of millions of dollars on communications, incentives, closed circuit TV and education.

Since research demonstrated that the hand hygiene issue centred around human behaviour, one state health department decided on an innovative, behaviour-changing approach using the *NeuroPower* framework to drive the solution. Working with the *NeuroPower* Consulting Team, the department implemented a behaviour change program called Clean Hands are LifeSavers that engaged the health workers and increased compliance from 18% to 60%. A key driver of this behaviour change involved effectively addressing each of the six Intelligences in the correct sequence. How these progressive steps were taken is outlined in the Organisational Toolbox Case Study at the end of each Intelligence chapter.

Having already

- Created safety and security in the hospital environment by embedding values through a code of conduct
- Empowered spontaneity and self-expression through collaboration and the development of creative promotional materials
- Kick started action and motivation through establishment of goals and the celebration of quick wins
- Encouraged empathy and connection through active listening and team building

Step 5: Maintain the flow of information

Hand-held recording devices, which observers used to gather factual data about hand hygiene, were implemented to track the results of the each ward's progress. These results were communicated throughout each hospital and throughout the state, thereby providing everyone with up-to-date information about progress, maintaining interest in compliance and embedding the behaviour.

ORGANISATIONAL CASE STUDY #2: MERCHANT BANK EQUITY DERIVATIVES LEADERSHIP TEAM

The Task: Improve employee engagement and tangible business performance

Recap:

In 2006, at the height of the financial boom, one of Australia's leading equity derivatives teams was operating in an environment that was fast-paced, demanding and with a high level of stress. In order to handle large volumes of work in a very volatile market, the team needed to be highly functional and collaborative. Growth was nearly 200 per cent over the previous year so the enormous strain was evident. This was mainly caused by a leadership team in crisis.

The Leadership Team was fractured, non-collaborative and driven by their own individual agendas. There was both a lack of respect and a lack of honesty between members which led to highly reactive responses and conflict. The broader team could see this occurring and they felt they were part of a warring tribe with all the insecurities that brought.

NeuroPower consultants devised a program which focused on addressing the splintered leadership team. The intervention involved a series of group structured processes which were embedded by individual coaching sessions.

Having already:
- Created role clarity
- Empowered people's self-expression
- Encouraged healthy egos and passion for work
- Developed teamwork and leadership capabilities through an expanded I2

Step 5: Create a Learning Lab Culture through Driving Excellence in I1

The Equity Derivatives Team operated in a fast-paced and volatile market where speed of response was based on the power of the information received. The right information at the right time was key to their success on a daily basis. During this part of the intervention, more emphasis was placed on maintaining a good flow of information and sharing results. Before the intervention began, the Back Office – the technical engine of the group – had felt under-valued and under pressure. Now their expertise and importance was brought to the fore, as the Team learned the power of the Learning Lab Culture where every team member has crucial information and insight that can be shared with the group. This was achieved by conducting a series of three intellectual capital workshops and coaching sessions where double-loop learning was culturally embedded in the team's approach.

Chapter 7

Our Sixth Social Cognitive Need:
HOPE FOR THE FUTURE &
The Open Function (C2)

HOPE FOR THE FUTURE (C2) AT A GLANCE

Hope for the Future is our Brain's Sixth Social Cognitive Need

The brain loves moving forward based on hope for the future. The brain is an anticipation machine - constantly projecting into the future the consequences of staying on its current path. Importantly, our level of hope is directly linked to our sense of whether our current path will lead to a positive future, which is highly influenced by how well the first six needs are being met.

Characteristics of the Hope for the Future (C2) Functional Network

Future Vision

STRENGTH	WEAKNESS
Able to see the future and take a long-term perspective	Attachment to particular future

OPPORTUNITY	THREAT
Being present and expressing emotions instead of focusing on abstract principles	Can be too abstract to the point where others struggle to understand

Management Style

- Great at painting a new vision
- Motivates by drawing others into the vision
- Sensitive and often reluctant to share
- Can accurately anticipate difficulties further down the track

WONDER

C2 THINKING

Paradigm-shifting visions

C2 FEELING

Appreciation and Awe

C2 SOMATIC

Daydreaming, meditation and/or prayer

COMMUNICATION STYLE

- Has creativity that is visionary and has a clear sense
  of the future
- Describes future events
- Conceptualises things

KEYWORDS INCLUDE

- Imagine
- Vision
- Future
- Possibility
- What could be

Hope for the Future (C2) Helps Us to Survive

Hope for the Future (C2) helps both individuals and the group to survive and thrive by helping us look past the immediate reality and envisage a different future. It draws on our ability to completely re-imagine a situation - almost like downloading a whole new vision.

Hope for the Future & The Open Function (C2)

HOPE FOR THE FUTURE: OUR BRAIN'S SIXTH SOCIAL NEED EXPLAINED

The brain is an anticipation machine - constantly projecting into the future the consequences of staying on its current path. Our brain actively creates a future image of what our current actions or trends are leading towards. In this way, our level of hope is directly linked to our sense of whether our current path will lead to a positive future. Vision is the end result of a current trajectory. We call vision a lag indicator rather than a lead indicator. If, as a leader, you have been able to effectively implement the previous five steps then your team will naturally be more optimistic and hopeful about their future and being a part of your team.

Whether from a community or organisational perspective, in order for a team to have vision for the future, leaders must effectively implement the previous five steps and show their team that by continuing along their current trajectory, a positive future state exists.

EVOLUTIONARY FUNCTION OF C2

The neurocircuitry of C2 is not yet well understood, but we see that **the C2 intelligence enables the individual to 'download' new ideas, paradigms or concepts.** These reflect a fundamentally changing world that requires a new map of understanding. C2 is a difficult system to chart and neuroscience is still not clear about exactly how the C2 Intelligence works. fMRI research on the neural pathways linked to meditation, as well as some research in 'mystical experiences' (MEs) provide useful first steps of insight into how the C2 system may function.

Recognising the Characteristics of Hope for the Future (C2)

Joseph Conrad once said, 'Only in men's imagination does every truth find an effective and undeniable existence. Imagination, not invention, is the supreme master of art as life.'

The C2 function also enables the brain to connect our spiritual nature with our physical experience. This often manifests as the human drive to experience an intimate relationship with a 'greater, other or the divine'. To the secular mind, C2 gives access to a sense of awe and wonder at the physical world, from the immensity of the cosmos to the interdependencies of the physical world that at times seem too complex for any one mind to comprehend and almost too perfectly balanced to be plausible.

The Neural Correlates of Mystical Experiences (MEs)

Researchers in the field of neurotheology, or spiritual neuroscience, have undertaken studies revealing that MEs (involving altered states of consciousness such as a sense of timelessness and spacelessness, a dissolution of fear and self-consciousness, or feelings of oneness with the universe) are associated with complex patterns of activity in the brain. These studies are beginning to give us insight into the workings of the C2 system.

One particularly influential researcher in this area, Mario Beauregard, worked with a group of Carmelite nuns who had altogether spent over 210,000 hours in prayer and who reported having an 'intense union with God'. As they relived their most intense ME in an MRI scanner, Beauregard observed a complex network of regions being activated, including the right middle temporal cortex (giving the subjective impression of contacting a spiritual reality), the insula (integrating representations of external sensory experience and internal somatic state), the caudate nucleus (facilitating feelings of joy and unconditional love) and the left medial prefrontal cortex (gaining conscious metacognitions of one's emotions).

This pattern of activity seems consistent with the complex and multidimensional nature of MEs as described by those who experience them - with potential neural correlates for reports of changes in perception (e.g. visual mental imagery), cognition (e.g. representations about the self) and emotion (e.g. peace, joy, unconditional love). Interestingly, they also align broadly with some of the findings of other researchers such as Nataraja, who have looked at the impact of certain forms of meditation practice on the brain (explored in detail in Appendix 13).

Studies like these inevitably lead to questions about the nature of the universe itself. For example, when an individual reports a sense of 'spacelessness', is that directly caused by reduced activity in areas of the brain linked to the physical body? Or is the reduced activity a product of a transcendent metaphysical experience? Unfortunately, as with many brain imaging studies, the causal relationship is very difficult to establish and so it may be sometime before neuroscience - or any other discipline - can give us a clear answer to satisfy our I1 system (Seeing the Facts).

Fortunately, however, the strong positive benefits associated with more 'transcendent' forms of meditation - independent of spiritual belief - confirm that the C2 system is accessible for both those who believe in a higher power and those who don't.

A mind with an over-reliance on C2 can be interpreted as 'dreamy'. The person can appear as though they are 'on another planet', or they are constantly distracted. In fact, if an individual relies heavily on C2, their personal reality may well be somewhere completely different from the existing reality.

C2 has three elements that require integration. The visionary (cognitive) aspect focuses on finding entirely new possibilities and creatively bringing about a whole new paradigm. This is the creative function we use when we visualise new and abstract ideas. The emotional aspect centres around a sense of inspiration, transcendence, nirvana or awe. The somatic aspect is typified by a melancholic lamenting of the world that is, since it cannot match the world that could be, almost like a wistful wondering.

Of all the Intelligences, C2 is the one that is least understood from a functional perspective; even with recent advances in neuroscience, we are still not quite sure how it works. Our best current insights about C2 come from studies of meditation. In Appendix 2, you'll find excerpts from Dr Nataraja's book *A Blissful Brain* (2009), which explores the experience of meditation from both subjective and objective perspectives (i.e. from the point of view of both the meditator and a neuroscientist observing the activity in the meditator's brain. If C2 and meditation are of interest to

C2 Activity and its Possible Link to the Parietal Lobes

Albert Einstein, the quintessential absent-minded professor who did poorly in maths classes during his adolescence, became renowned for solving complex problems of mathematics and physics using visual imagery. Many of his intuitive theories have been proven to be accurate with the development of more sophisticated technology and space exploration. In a post mortem examination of his brain, it was revealed that there were differences in the inferior parietal area in the ratio of neurons to glia cells when compared to other areas of his brain and two control subjects (Diamond, Scheibel, Murphy & Harvey, 1985). Diamond and her compatriots (Diamond, Krech & Rosenweig, 1966) suggested that these lower ratios represented the capacity for higher levels of neuronal activity. Another research group concluded that Einstein's brain differed from ninety-one other brains only in the size of the inferior parietal lobe (Witelson, Kigar & Harvey, 1999). This is particularly interesting given that Einstein often reported that he arrived at the answers to complex mathematical questions based on vague mental images and bodily sensations rather than empirical logic, suggesting that the parietal lobes may play a key role in the C2 Intelligence.

C2 and Out-of-Body Experiences

Dr Olaf Blanke and colleagues observed that stimulating a patient's angular gyrus of the right cortex resulted in an out-of-body experience. Their patient described the experience thus: 'I see myself lying in bed, from above.' Blanke interpreted this as being the region in the brain where the visual system and the self-awareness system overlap (Blanke, Ortigue, Landix & Seeck, 2002, pp. 269-280, 419).

This suggests that an individual can perceive two realities simultaneously and that this ability can be deliberately switched on in the brain.

you, Dr Nataraja's book is fascinating and well worth a read.

The purpose of this Intelligence is to provide direction through future-centred visioning. What blocks the use of C2 is an attachment or fixed insistence on one idea, concept, notion or vision. Judith (1996) argues that physical problems arising from an unbalanced C2 include comas, migraines, brain tumours, amnesia and cognitive delusions. The developmental task of the individual at this stage is to assimilate knowledge and to develop wisdom (Judith, 1996).

The primary fears of C2 are related to spiritual issues such as the 'dark night of the soul', spiritual abandonment, loss of identity, or loss of connection (Myss, 1996).

C2 ACTS AS THE BRAIN'S 'WIFI' — READY TO DOWNLOAD NEW IDEAS OR PARADIGMS

One fascinating idea posited by Dr David Hawkins, author of *Power versus Force* (2005), is the proposition that there exists a unified consciousness that is external to time and space and encapsulates all the knowledge and experience of life. Chaos theory suggests that the universe does not follow a linear, cause and effect Newtonian model. Rather, all elements of the universe are interrelated and in a fashion independent of time and space.

Hawkins refers to physicist David Bohm's description of the universe as being holographic with an invisible *implicit* ('enfolded') and a manifest *explicit* ('unfolded') order. **This means that while the universe appears to be unfolding in a linear manner from our perspective in time, this may not be the case.** Time is the manner in which the implicit reality becomes explicit reality. For example, a person driving through a forest can see only the road ahead of them. But the satellite in space beaming to their GPS receiver has a view of the terrain. C2 is like every individual's personal GPS unit. Hawkins' field of consciousness stands external to time and is accessible through the C2 function of the mind.

Our capacity to download information from this storehouse of knowledge is dependent upon the effective functioning of our C2. Using Hawkins' language, it acts as the bridge between this universal field of consciousness and our own personal consciousness. In the commercial context, this is the part of the brain that enables us to envision revolutionary new ideas that provide a giant leap forward (e.g. the shift from typewriter to computers). Without highly functioning C2, teams have no sense of what lies ahead and no appreciation of non-linear inter-dependencies. This means that they are constantly forced to be tactical, rather than strategic, and are always one step behind the competition. Judith (1996) describes C2 as a doorway between the individual consciousness and the universal consciousness.

Using C2 Intelligence feels a bit like the wireless connection (WIFI) on your laptop or mobile phone that allows you to download the information available on the internet. Accessing C2 is about expanding our personal perspective so that it can embrace a much larger truth. The work to be done with C2 is to examine our belief systems, for they are the windows through which we see the world and this view informs and ultimately determines our view of reality. The awakened C2 can act to constantly reprogram and upgrade the 'map room' that runs our life.[1]

Christian theology argues that, with God's help, man is able to see 'dreams and visions'. Eric Jantsch's (1975) theory of the evolution of human consciousness argues that as we evolve we have a greater awareness of and reliance on C2. He outlined three distinct systems of human consciousness: the *rational*, the *mythical*, and the *evolutionary*.

The *rational system* is where knowledge comes through science and other logical, empirical means. This mode of thinking focuses on observation and acting upon the observations. The method of inquiry that dominates is characterised by *I-it* relationships —subject to object. We do things to *it* and observe *its* reaction. (This relates to the I1 thinking function.)

The *mythical system* moves from observation to experience. The collection of data gathered at the rational level now assembles itself into an intuitive whole, a complete gestalt that involves mind and body simultaneously. Inquiry moves to *I* and *You* as subject embraces subject. This type of inquiry gives us what Jantsch terms as 'a sense of systemic existence'.

The *evolutionary system* is an expansion into the universal mind, the union with the divine and the all-inclusive state of being where system boundaries have

---

1   The term 'map room' was first introduced to me by Dr Moishe Perl, an internationally recognised authority in the field of clinical neurofeedback. Neurofeedback techniques that work with C2 put the individual in a highly suggestible state by taking the brain down to the alpha-theta state (8-10Hz). They call this the map room because in this semi-conscious state the individual can reprogram many of their unconstructive beliefs about themselves and their world.

C2, Psilocybin and Mystical Experiences

Individuals with high C2 system sometimes describe themselves as having feelings of no boundaries between self and others, belonging to a larger state of consciousness, unity to all things, and feelings of peace and intense happiness. Interestingly, these feelings are exactly what individuals using specific cognition-altering psychotropic drugs have reported. In fact, these substances have been used in religions throughout history and across the world to initiate C2 experiences such as mystical states of consciousness and communication with the spirit world. The Aztecs, Rig Veda and Native American cultures each used plants such as the morning glory vine, magic mushrooms, and the peyote cactus for their active compounds (e.g. mescaline, psilocybin and psilocin).

In the last few decades, despite the strong negative connotations also associated with western drug-users (many of which were established with US President Richard Nixon's war on drugs), some published research suggests these substances can provide users with both mystical experiences (MEs) and long-term improvements in well-being.

In one Harvard study, participants received either the psychedelic substance psilocybin or a placebo prior to a Good Friday church service. Nearly all the participants in the psilocybin group reported ME experiences, whereas those in the control group experienced nothing unusual. In a similar experiment, conducted at John Hopkins University, participants were given either psilocybin or a placebo and told to close their eyes and direct their attention inward. Two thirds of participants in the psilocybin group experienced feelings of enhanced well-being and satisfaction and rated it as either the best experience in their life or in the top five. What is astounding is these feelings were ongoing and still apparent at two months and fourteen months after the experiment was conducted. Although these substances are often thought of as mind expanding, they in fact cause brain activity to decrease in the brain's most dense areas. These dense hubs are what constrain our experience and filter out information that's irrelevant to our biological survival. It is through deactivation of these areas that people can experience the mind at large.

So while this book is not actively encouraging its readers to engage in psychedelic use, it is important to note that access to the C2 system, even for a short period of time, can have a substantial and profound positive impact on people's well-being.

dissolved and re-formed to a greater and deeper whole. Inquiry moves to *I* and *We* as the *I* now includes all that is encompassed in the universal consciousness. There is no *We* without an *I*. Consequently, to the spiritually inclined, embracing the use of C2 is not to abandon the sense of personal awareness, but to realise that divine consciousness is part of that personal awareness (Judith, 1996).

They would argue that to connect with the divine, we need to give up our attachment to the rational system of thought when it is unable to give us a deeper meaning to life's themes. Evolutionary inquiry gives us a sense of direction.

C2 AND INSPIRATION

Some Eastern traditions suggest that C2 operates as a two-way channel of inspiration from the universe. It is the source of creativity and vision. This in turn inspires ideas and plans from which come actions and experiences. The C2 Intelligence provides us with an opportunity for transcendence, for expansion of consciousness to awakening (Judith, 1996).

For Christians, Jews and Muslims, the purpose of C2 is to merge with divine consciousness and realise our individual true nature – that we are children of the divine seeking our way home. Not only is the purpose to contact the divine, but also to manifest divinity in our bodies and actions on a daily basis and so transform the world as a consequence of our relationship with God (Myss, 1996, p. 267).

The Development of Hope for the Future (C2)

The development of the C2 Intelligence for an individual is not age specific since it develops in different ways from the moment of birth until the day we die. The development of C2 is primarily about learning, building on and adding meaning and wisdom to our previous understandings and beliefs, and our ability to think independently (Judith, 1996).

Though this is a process that occurs throughout our life, it is well known that it is in late adolescence that we start asking questions about the meaning of life. This is the dawning of idealism and spirituality for many young people.

C2 AND I1 DIFFERENCES

The development of C2 moves from the search for knowledge in I1 ('This is who I am in the greater scheme of things') to a shift beyond the ego, with a search for meaning that asks the bigger questions about life, such as 'What does it all mean?'

C2 gives meaning to the images already in the memory and incorporates them into an ever-growing body of understanding about why the world works the way it does.

BEWARE OF ATTACHMENT

Judith (1996) makes the interesting point that one downside of an underactive C2 network is the kind of unhelpful 'attachment' referred to in Buddhist teachings. Development through the first five Intelligences demands a degree of attachment to outcome as we navigate increasing responsibilities to the people we love, our own goals and our commitments. And we should honour our attachment to these things; they are necessary for a balanced life.

However, we can become so attached to certain relationships, desires, outcomes or belief systems that we shut down our C2 in a desire to control our life circumstances. This denies the belief that the universe is conspiring to help us, and closes us to new possibilities.

Another form of attachment is avoidance, which is really attachment to *not* having something, in order to avoid facing some issue which makes us feel inadequate.

By focusing outward on the attachment and closing down our use of C2, we lose the chance to grow. Judith suggests we need to turn our attention inward and examine ourselves to identify both the reason for our attachment and our underlying needs, and then meet those needs. This is usually about facing something or letting something go, and it is usually an issue of our ego (our P2). We need to let go and trust the universe if we wish to awaken our C2 and live at a higher level of consciousness. If you rarely access your C2, it is as if you don't get updates to your operating system, and thus live on old paradigms.

TRAUMAS AND ABUSES

Abuses to C2 tend to be subtle, but with profound impacts. They can occur at any age and in many different ways.

The inquisitive nature of children, with their burning desire to understand the world that surrounds them, sets the development of their personal belief systems. If the curiosity of a child is stifled, the child may either make up the information or they stop asking questions. In either case the searching stops and their C2 ceases to draw in new ideas, visions and future possibilities so it shuts down. But in the busy modern world of today's children, bombarded as they are by technology and a focus on outcomes like maths and reading scores, there is little time for simple daydreaming and letting the mind imagine.

In a similar manner, poor education can damage the development of C2. C2 needs encouragement, time, a stress-free environment, and a chance to be expressed. When this is not provided, the functioning of the C2 Intelligence can be affected.

Judith (1996) also strongly argues that unpleasant spiritual experiences in Christian churches which focus more on sin and shaming than on love and respect of the individual developing young person, will also shut down a child's C2, and so,

The Power of Visualisation

Neuroscience has shown that visualising an activity is almost as powerful as actually doing it when it comes to the formation of new neural networks. In a neuroplasticity experiment involving piano playing, those who mentally rehearsed a five-fingered keyboard exercise demonstrated similar reorganisation of their motor outputs as those who physically practiced the movements (Pascual-Leone, 1995). This suggests that visualisation of motor activities changes neural circuitry and may be used to acquire skills more rapidly with reduced physical practice. This technique is now commonly used by athletes looking to enhance their performance.

ironically, therefore, blocking their access to the divine.

Poorly Functioning C2

OVER-RELIANCE ON C2

Having an over-reliance on C2 is quite common as individuals withdraw into their heads to avoid feelings and to distance themselves from worldly demands, or to avoid emotions or the sensations of the body. Judith (1996) notes that, in general, excessive C2 leads to a loss of discrimination. This reliance tends to have a number of manifestations:

- Intellectualisation;
- Spiritual obsession;
- Confusion;
- Dissociation from the body; and
- Fixation on one paradigm or vision.

Intellectualisation is a particularly common result, with constant thinking and analysing typifying this type of individual. Such individuals overdevelop their intellect at the cost of their other aspects of self, in order to escape the more difficult issues of life. However, knowledge for its own sake is useless without wisdom and insight that the C2 Intelligence brings.

Spirituality can also be used as an escape route from the demands of the other Intelligences, and spiritual obsession is another common consequence of an over-reliance on C2. This may be expressed as 'Bible bashing', 'guru chasing' or through

Diagram 7.1 Healthy C2 Intelligence — Noble Quality: Wonder

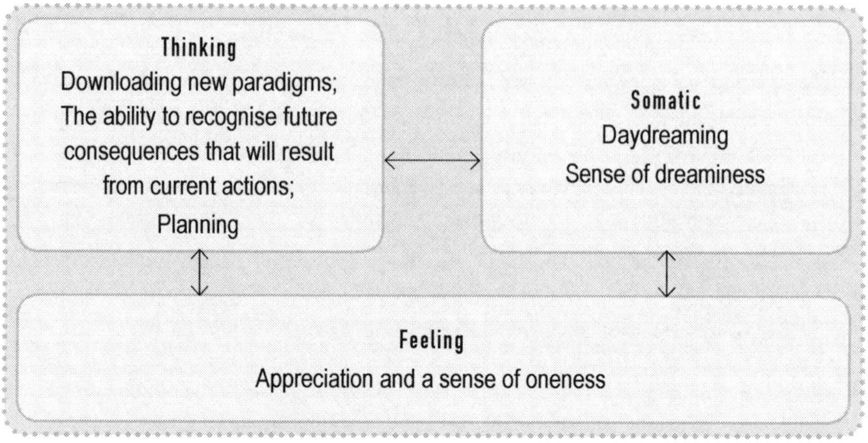

Thinking
Downloading new paradigms;
The ability to recognise future
consequences that will result
from current actions;
Planning

Somatic
Daydreaming
Sense of dreaminess

Feeling
Appreciation and a sense of oneness

vows of poverty, chastity and obedience. Whatever the form, this is often merely another attachment that prevents the growth of the individual (except, of course, if it is sensibly applied in ways which help the person evolve).

Another result of excessive use of C2 can be psychosis. Psychotic disturbances are characterised by a break from reality and from the grounded aspects of the other Intelligences. They are manifested as a lack of predictable patterns, with voices, hallucinations and delusional beliefs (Judith, 1996).

UNDER-RELIANCE ON C2

According to Judith (1996), poorly functioning C2 can manifest in the following patterns:

Fixation: The opposite of infinite knowledge is fixation, where only one point of view is accepted. As their mind is closed to new information, the person may become a sceptical 'know it all'.

A need to be right: Being right supports the sense that we know everything and bolsters our ego as it provides a (delusional) sense of superiority.

Belief in limitations: Being convinced that there is no possibility of a situation being remedied is a form of C2 deficiency. These beliefs will then become a self-fulfilling prophecy.

The general characteristics of an individual with poorly functioning C2 are:

- Spiritual scepticism;

- An inability to take on new concepts that fall outside the current paradigm;

- Out-of-date belief systems;

- An over-reliance on other Intelligences in life without the mediating and conceptualising function of C2; and

- An inability to imagine the future or how reality could be different.

C2 AND PARADIGMS

As we have seen, C2 assigns ultimate meaning to all areas of our life and the meanings we give to our experiences in life eventually construct for us a coherent belief system. In turn, this belief system, based on the past, impacts how we interpret all future experiences and the decisions we make. The world in which we live, therefore, both causes our reality and is caused by it[2].

We can easily identify our level of consciousness by looking at the world we have created for ourselves. There is no point trying to help people change their life if they do not also change their belief system. In order to awaken our consciousness, we need to examine every belief system in our life.

If our C2 is poorly functioning, we will be guided by our Dionysian needs (C1) to move towards pleasure and away from pain, by our P1 family rules, our P2 ego or our I2 desire to connect. There is no unifying Apollonian paradigm. When we are trying to solve a problem, if we use first-order thinking, we stay within the paradigm without being aware the paradigm exists. If we use second-order thinking, we are aware and see that we are working to a paradigm (that is, we see closer to the reality of our life). When we are using third-order thinking, not only do we understand our paradigm, we also develop our awareness and change our paradigm, and so transform it into more productive action. The C2 Intelligence gives us access to second- and third-order thinking.

Reintegrating Wonder (C2) as an Adult

EXERCISE ONE[3]

Imagine you are an eagle flying through your own life. What does it look like from above? How does it appear from the removed perspective? What issues do you see in the horizon of your life? When I was working with accountants I would instruct them to visualise themselves flying through the city and looking into the windows of their potential clients to see if they could see any new work opportunities – this system yielded millions of dollars worth of new work for them. In the same way you

---

2   This concept, which is based on insights emerging from quantum physics paradigms, is explored in more detail in Principle 3.

3   I have used this simple exercise to improve the C2 function of accounting directors in one of Australia's largest accounting and management practices. It had dramatic and profitable results.

can look at your life through the C2 function for new opportunities and options.

EXERCISE TWO

This exercise is suggested by author Brian Tracy. According to Tracy (2004), the development of C2 is about creating a future orientation and forming a habit of idealisation. Idealisation involves taking your thoughts off the present situation and imagining a perfect future for yourself, your business, your finances or your relationships. It involves practising 'back from the future' thinking. This is about projecting forward into the future the ideal results that you desire and imagining what it would look like in every way. You then look back to the present and ask yourself, 'What would I have to do, starting today, to create the ideal future that I desire?' This process is articulated in a more structured way in C2 Tools #1 and #3.

CREATING A HIGHLY FUNCTIONING C2

Consider your own experience in light of what you have learned about the C2 Intelligence. Are you aware of C2 thinking, feeling and somatic in your life? Is there one that you tend to focus on above the other two?

- The C2 somatic behaviours include dreaminess, light-headedness and having a straight back.

- The C2 feeling element involves a sense of appreciation and oneness with the universe.

- The C2 thinking element involves a strong capacity to visualise images and events.

Diagram 7.1 shows the three aspects of C2 that require integration so that a unified Intelligence can form.

The task of integration of C2 is to relax the body, quieten the mind's visioning of egocentric plans and strategies, and tune into a sense of Wonder and appreciation of the mystery and miracles of life. This allows you to 'let go and let God', trusting that the universe is conspiring to bless you.

While every individual is different, the majority of the population is most familiar with the feeling aspect of C2.

AFFIRMATIONS

Judith (1996) suggests the following affirmations can help you increase the functioning of your C2:

- Divinity resides within.

- I am open to new ideas.

- Information I need comes to me.

- The world is my teacher.

- I am guided by a higher power.

- I am guided by inner wisdom.

- I am open to God's wisdom.

Highly Functioning C2 in Adult Life

The first-order noble quality of Wonder requires the thinking aspect of creative vision, the feeling aspect of appreciation, and the somatic aspect of daydreaming, meditation or prayer[4]. This noble quality is described by Plotinus (205-270 AD), the founder of Neoplatonism, as when 'the soul finds joy in contemplating beauty, for it sees in works of art a hint of the divinity that it (the soul) shares'.

The behavioural manifestations of Wonder are subtle, because appreciation, awe, and responses to beauty and excellence often involve passive receptivity and stillness (Frijda, 1986). This appreciation is likely to be associated with certain physiological symptoms such as goose bumps, tears or even a lump in the throat. This noble quality of Wonder fosters a desire to improve the self and strive for the greater good (Keltner & Haidt, 2003). Abraham Maslow (1964) focused on the importance of this noble quality and identified character traits that are commonly associated with it. When this first-tier noble quality is manifested:

1. Perception is relatively ego transcending, self-forgetful, unselfish and more object-centred than ego-centred;

2. The world is seen as beautiful, good, desirable and worthwhile, even as evil and suffering are recognised and accepted as part of the world; and

3. Cognition is much more passive, receptive and humble. The person is more ready to listen and much more able to hear.

It is from this noble quality that the Greek idea of divine creativity arises. The Greeks believed that muses (of poetry, tragedy, comedy, music, dance, astrology and history) bestowed creativity upon certain individuals. This creativity is able to

---

4   Peterson & Seligman's meta-study of the most widely influential traditions of thought and religion in human history found that appreciation represented a consistent aspiration across cultures and through time. They identified appreciation as a strength because it enables self-transcendence (and its associated loss of ego, and increased openness to others) (Peterson & Seligman, 2004).

flow through the noble quality of Wonder. Plato referred to this style of thinking as Apollonian transcendence. Jung refers to this noble quality as the Transcendent function.

HOW C2 WONDER MEETS THE NOBILITY CRITERIA

The noble quality of Wonder provides the individual with a sense of perspective about where they fit into the world. This noble quality is central to answering questions about how the individual communicates with their Maker and future paces[5] to anticipate what lies ahead.

Wonder brings value to the community. It enables the community to join together to appreciate the world in which they live and work. Wonder fosters the idea that community members can celebrate their involvement in a world that is beyond the control of their ego.

There is a yearning to act in accordance with the noble quality of Wonder. When it is expressed it is often associated with a paradigm shift. Being in awe or experiencing Wonder creates a space of perceiving a world that is beautiful, good, desirable and worthwhile. When in Wonder, the individual transcends ego, is self-forgetting, unselfish, and enters a state of flow. Individuals report that using Wonder to resolve an internal tension has a paradigm shift impact on their lives because cognitive resistance is reduced, and individuals are more ready to listen and much more able to hear.

In teams, Wonder enables us to look beyond the status quo and create a new reality that fundamentally improves the position of the business.

---

5   Future pacing is an NLP methodology which comes naturally to those high in C2.

C2 Toolbox

THE IMPORTANCE OF C2 IN BUILDING HIGH PERFORMANCE TEAMS

The emergent cultural impact of C2 is Wonder, which enables the organisation to join together to appreciate the world in which they live and work.

When Wonder is absent from an organisation, its existence and activity is mundane, perfunctionary and without true appreciation.

However, when there is highly functioning C2 in the organisation, staff members can celebrate their involvement in a world that is beyond the control of their ego.

Leaders looking to improve the effectiveness of C2 in their team can increase Wonder by applying the C2 tools.

C2 QUESTIONS FOR PERSONAL DEVELOPMENT

The best high performing teams are made up of individuals who have focused on their own personal development. The following questions can be used as a starting point for those leaders looking to improve their C2.

1. How and from where do you seek guidance when all your solutions have failed?

2. If that source of guidance were to respond, what answers to your questions would you most fear?

3. What is your concept of God (Grand Organising Design)? Is there such a thing?

4. Do you complain to others more than you express your gratitude? Explain.

5. Do you tend to wish for specific things rather than show appreciation? Explain.

6. Are you devoted to a particular spiritual path? If not, what spiritual path best reflects your world view?

7. Are you waiting for life, your parents, friends or family to send you an explanation for your painful experiences? If so, list those experiences.

8. How would your life change if suddenly all your questions were answered?

9. How would your life change if you spoke to God and the answer you received was, "I have no intention of giving you insight into your questions at this point in your life"?

10. How do you explain sudden flashes of insight? What are they?

11. Have you started and stopped a meditation or spiritual practice? If so, what were the reasons that you failed to maintain it?

12. What spiritual truths are you aware of that you do not live by? List them.

13. Are you afraid of a closer spiritual connection to something greater because of the change that it might trigger in your life?

C2 TOOL #1:
CREATE THE FUTURE YOU WANT

C2 VISIONING

The C2 Intelligence is accessed when the brain settles into an Alpha-Theta state. The below experience enables you to achieve this relaxed state.

PROCESS

1. **Set aside the time** for a personal planning session an hour is a good start. The ideal time from a physiological perspective is during the evening at a time when you usually feel relaxed but not yet sleepy this is a good indication that your brain is in a state that will support the C2 exercise. If that's not possible, and you need to take time during the day, arrange things so that you don't have to go rushing off to another meeting or event straight away.

2. **Choose your venue.** Environment can have a big impact on how our brain functions, and certain environmental cues make it easier to access the different intelligence circuits. If you've scheduled your session during the day, the ideal location for C2 planning is outside, in an open expanse with a view (preferably on top of a hill). At night time, when you're likely to be inside, it's better to have soft ambient light rather than bright fluorescent lights overhead. Of course, it may not be possible for you to coordinate this. Even so, it's still a good idea to introduce a change of scenery – you'll find it easier to think outside the square if you take yourself out of your usual environment.

3. **Prepare** for your session by making sure you won't be interrupted. This includes turning off phones and letting family and others know that you won't be available during the hour. Also make sure that you have supplies of water, paper, pencil etc. Once that's all taken care of, take a few minutes to settle into wherever you've decided to conduct your session. Sometimes it takes a while to switch from 'go-go-go' mode to a more reflective, relaxed space. Make sure you've changed gear before you start the actual exercise.

4. **Visualise your ideal future.** The focus of the exercise is on projecting forward into the future the results that you desire and imagining what it would look like in every way. Where do you want to be in five, ten, twenty years? What are you doing? What are you focusing on? How are you feeling? What do you notice about this future reality?

5. **Work your way backwards to the present.** As you imagine every detail of that future, look back to the present and ask yourself, 'What would I have to do, starting today, to create the ideal future that I desire?' Use the insights that arrive to create an action list and begin working towards that future reality.

DOS

✓ Do allow your mind to wander, provided it's broadly on track. While there's certainly a fine line between getting distracted and thinking freely, it's often by following seemingly unrelated tangents when contemplating the future that brainwaves about how to create a radically different future reality will arrive.

DON'TS

✗ Don't forget to write down the important things! The C2 space feels quite dreamy, and much like dreams – people often forget the insights they've gained as they 'wake up again' and their brain shifts back into 'normal operating mode'.

C2 TOOL #2:
UNDERTAKE SCENARIO PLANNING TO CREATE A NEW FUTURE

PROCESS

1. **Schedule a two-day scenario planning workshop.** It is important to hold the workshop offsite to signal the difference from routine work. A two-day residential format allows optimum reflection and absorption time. Make sure that the venue is a light and airy environment, preferably in a location that is elevated and surrounded by greenery. (These environmental factors will affect the capacity of the brain to access C2.)

   In positioning the event and its purpose for your people, prepare a briefing sheet about the concept of scenario planning: imagining potential qualitatively different futures and using these forecasts to improve the quality of decision-making. Explain the importance of scenario planning to your business, and how it can be invaluably used to:
   - Stimulate debate about the organisation's options moving forward;
   - Develop a strategy that is resilient against several futures;
   - Test existing business plans against potential futures; and
   - Anticipate futures as an aid to decision-making.

2. **Identify future scenarios.** Many organisations are shifting focus from developing new scenarios towards using and tailoring existing scenarios. Explore whether your organisation has existing scenarios that may be appropriately modified. If not, your leadership team will need to take one to two days to develop scenarios based on existing information. This can also be a valuable exercise in exploring shared perceptions. You may wish to research current trends more quantitatively to provide a platform for developing your scenarios. Alternatively, consultants may be employed to fulfil this role.

3. **Develop the agenda for the two-day scenario workshop.** This is likely to be specific to your industry, organisation and your people's familiarity with the exercise of scenario planning. However, a broad template (involving both plenary sessions, workshops and break out sessions into smaller working groups) might look like:

Day One	
Plenary	Purpose of the workshop. Briefing on current trends – positive and negative
Groups	Discuss effect of positive and negative trends on the organisation. Report findings back to group. Identification of which trends are certain and which uncertain, and the degree to which they would impact the organisation.
Workshop	Articulation of key scenarios taking each of the most likely/high impact positive and negative trends and chart the impact on the organisation. From this identify the top six scenarios.
Groups	Explore strategies and tactics to make the most of the positive trends and turn the negative trends into the organisation's advantage.
Groups	Report back and discuss strategies.

C2 Tool #2

Day Two	
Groups	Explore non-linear dependencies and ways that each strategy/tactic can be refined.
Workshop	Explore what the organisation needs to focus on short/medium/long-term.
Groups	Develop timeline for action.
Workshop	Report back to group. Plan actions moving forward.

4. **Conduct the workshop.** Make sure there's plenty of time for debate and discussion, and allow the groups lots of breaks to have unrestricted discussion time. Remember, part of the purpose of scenario planning is to enable your people to think beyond the current status quo. You need to be prepared for them to think outside the square and supportive of them when it happens.

5. **Make the most of the scenario planning.** Most people who work with scenarios find it to be stimulating and enjoyable, and are keen to incorporate the insights when they return to work. The success of the next stage will depend on:

   a. Deciding what problem the scenarios are intended to help solve. You need to ask: *What are the crucial questions facing the organisation, the ones that, seven years in the future, we'll wish we'd know the answer to seven years ago (i.e. now)?*

   b. Exploiting the scenarios that explore areas of uncertainty, rather than falling into the trap of focusing only on close-to-home and internal problems.

   c. Incorporating the scenarios into BAU decision-making by using them to stimulate project-based debate, developing strategies, testing business plans and anticipating future developments.

DOS

✓ Do make sure that the timescale for the scenarios is longer than the budget or planning cycle of the organisation – a longer time-scale is easier to work to as many defining trends will have run their course and be largely resolved at that future time, whereas in the medium-term current complexities are often still unresolved and confusing

✓ Do make sure that the scenario effort is given high enough status by making sure the workshop is offsite and ensuring high level sponsors and management feedback

DON'TS

✗ Don't simply adopt the budget or planning cycle of the organisation as the time frame for the scenarios, it needs to be longer. There are two reasons for this:
(1) A longer time-scale is easier to work with than medium-term, as many defining trends will already be clear and current complexities are often still confusing in the medium-term; and
(2) Many of the people at the session are unlikely to be in their current position at the end of this longer time frame. This gives them the freedom to think outside the square without feeling hampered by personal interest/implications

C2 TOOL #3:
VISUALISE IDEAL OUTCOMES

PROCESS

1. **Identify the event or activity.** It may be a big upcoming presentation, a team meeting where you need to introduce a new concept or a challenging one-on-one meeting that you need to have with a subordinate or peer.

2. **Set aside uninterrupted time in a quiet environment.** Environment can have a big impact on how our brain functions, and certain environmental cues make it easier to access the different intelligence circuits (see point # 2 in C2 Tool #2). In order to make the most of your time, make sure others know not to interrupt you.

3. **Visualise the setting for the future event.** The focus here is to imagine the event if it were to go absolutely perfectly from your perspective. The more detail you can see as you're visualising the event, the better. What does the room look like? Who else is there? How do they seem? What can you hear? Most people find it easiest to do this (and the rest of the process) with their eyes closed – simply closing your eyes slows the pace of your brainwaves, making it easier to access a brain state that is conducive to the slower C2 space.

4. **Focus on visualising yourself as the event proceeds.** Once you can see the setting clearly in your mind, visualise the event as it proceeds – again focusing on things going according to your ideal plan. Make sure you focus on how you're feeling and what you're thinking, as much as on what you're actually doing. For example, if you were to apply this technique to a presentation, you might visualise yourself arriving on time, feeling calm, collected and prepared. You see yourself conversing easily with other attendees, comfortable in the knowledge that you're ready for the show to start. As it gets closer to the time to present, you're feeling excited and enthusiastic about being there. The technology all runs smoothly and you visualise yourself presenting at your very best – 10 out of 10. When people ask questions, you see yourself giving great answers that both give them the information they need and enable you to weave in your message and support your argument. At the end, people congratulate and thank you for a fantastic presentation, and the key business objectives of the event are achieved. This is very different from imagining – or fearing (which often has much the same effect emotionally and physically) – yourself arriving late, frantic, unprepared, anxious and nervous about the presentation, grappling with technology that doesn't work, not having answers to questions people ask and, at the end of all that, not achieving the outcomes you need to with the presentation! By focusing on the former, you set up a different expectation in your mind and cue your body to respond differently to the same

stimulus. For example, a question from the audience is an opportunity to reinforce and embed your argument, not an interruption to be feared. This sets up a fundamentally different self-created expectation about the future event.

5. **Repeat the visualisation process.** Once you've imagined the event in its entirety, visualise it again... and again... and again. As you repeat the process, more and more neural networks are created around that particular activity, thus fundamentally changing the structure of your brain. The more you are able to see yourself performing successfully, the more likely it is that your brain will get on board and help you along the way – all because you've created a superhighway in your brain that's leading the way towards a successful outcome.

DOS

✓ Do give yourself the space to imagine things going perfectly. While realistically there may be hiccups in the plan, the focus of this exercise is to concentrate on the positive to influence how you feel about the event. If you find it particularly challenging to imagine an event with any difficulties, you may like to focus instead on how you respond to these problems – taking them all in your stride, working calmly to find solutions and not letting them upset your equilibrium.

DON'TS

✗ Don't underestimate the power of this exercise. Visualisation is a common technique used by top athletes to improve their performance, and has been shown to affect the neural networks in the brain. It's powerful stuff and definitely has applications in the commercial world.

KEY HOPE FOR THE FUTURE QUESTIONS FOR BUILDING A HIGH PERFORMANCE TEAM

The C2 system runs at a much slower pace than the other circuits and involves the brain downloading an entirely new paradigm/operating system. This really involves the brain stopping searching frantically for answers to questions and instead creating the space so that they can arrive.

Therefore, rather than focusing on a lot of different questions, it's better for teams looking to enhance their C2 functioning to ponder just a few key questions and see where the answers naturally take them.

If the team successfully delivers on its value proposition over the next few years, consider the ideal future outcomes in the following areas:

1. What will the style and quality of teamwork be like?

2. What will the team have achieved?

3. What will internal and external stakeholders have to say about the team?

4. What will the team be doing differently?

NeuroPower Case Study

ORGANISATIONAL CASE STUDY #1: STATE HEALTH HAND HYGIENE PROJECT

The Task: To improve compliance by health workers with hand hygiene practice.

Recap:

In 2007, an Australian state health department wanted to address the serious threat that health-associated infections posed to hospital patients. Micro-organisms are readily transmitted on the hands of health care workers. In Australia alone, health officials estimate that up to 7000 people die annually from hand hygiene-related infections in hospitals. The economic burden is also considerable, costing millions each year.

Hand hygiene has been proven to substantially reduce transmission of micro-organisms. However, despite well-established guidelines, compliance throughout the world with hygiene standards is disconcertingly low. International and national health agencies have been grappling with how to deal with the issue for some time, and few interventions have had any impact whatsoever, despite both European and US hospitals and governments spending tens of millions of dollars on communications, incentives, closed circuit TV and education.

Since research demonstrated that the hand hygiene issue centred around human behaviour, one state health department decided on an innovative, behaviour-changing approach using the NeuroPower framework to drive the solution. Working with the NeuroPower Consulting Team, the department implemented a behaviour change program called Clean Hands are LifeSavers that engaged the health workers and increased compliance from 18% to 60%. A key driver of this behaviour change involved effectively addressing each of the six Intelligences in the correct sequence. How these progressive steps were taken is outlined in the Organisational Toolbox Case Study at the end of each Intelligence chapter.

Having already:

- Created safety and security in the hospital environment by embedding values through a code of conduct
- Empowered spontaneity and self-expression through collaboration and the development of creative promotional materials
- Kick started action and motivation through establishment of goals and the celebration of quick wins
- Encouraged empathy and connection through active listening and team building
- Maintained the flow of information through data tracking and communication

Step 6: Create hope for the future and a new vision of success

With the advent of more infectious diseases entering the community as a result of global travel, NeuroPower ensured that the LifeSavers encourage health workers to keep the future in mind at all times so the community does not get ravaged by outbreaks. Hand hygiene has become more urgent than ever and has to be kept top of mind with new programs and a fresh approach being implemented on a regular basis.

ORGANISATIONAL CASE STUDY #2: MERCHANT BANK EQUITY DERIVATIVES LEADERSHIP TEAM

The Task: Improve employee engagement and tangible business performance

Recap:

In 2006, at the height of the financial boom, one of Australia's leading equity derivatives teams was operating in an environment that was fast-paced, demanding and with a high level of stress. In order to handle large volumes of work in a very volatile market, the team needed to be highly functional and collaborative. Growth was nearly 200 per cent over the previous year so the enormous strain was evident. This was mainly caused by a leadership team in crisis.

The Leadership Team was fractured, non-collaborative and driven by their own individual agendas. There was both a lack of respect and a lack of honesty between members which led to highly reactive responses and conflict. The broader team could see this occurring and they felt they were part of a warring tribe with all the insecurities that brought.

NeuroPower consultants devised a program which focused on addressing the splintered leadership team. The intervention involved a series of group structured processes which were embedded by individual coaching sessions.

Having already:

- Created role clarity
- Empowered people's self-expression
- Encouraged healthy egos and passion for work
- Developed teamwork and leadership capabilities through an expanded I2
- Created a learning lab culture through driving excellence in I1

Step 6: Celebrate Success and Scenario Plan for a new Future using C2

As the end of the financial year loomed, the Team was now well on track to reach their financial goals and reap the rewards in terms of bonuses which were linked to their performance. The Team held a celebratory event and invited the Bank's top executives to witness the fast turnaround which had unleashed enormous energy and passion and had tangible business performance results. Employee satisfaction had been raised from 54 to 94 percent in just four months. The head of the Team saw they had a new vision for success and began scenario planning for the coming year with his leadership group.

Chapter 8

Leading From the Front with the Six Intelligences

For those of you who are business leaders, your world is complex. There are always time-critical problems to solve, budgets to achieve, stakeholders to manage and external market dynamics to anticipate. And amidst all of this, there's a team of people–your team–looking to you to guide, lead and help them succeed. From my work with leaders at all levels, I've observed a consistent pattern. Effective leaders are able to focus simultaneously on two fronts: firstly on how they, as leaders, can manage themselves –their own energy levels, enthusiasm and sanity; and secondly on empowering and motivating their teams by creating the conditions required to enable them to perform at exceptionally high levels.

The key to these two seemingly distinct tasks is essentially the same. Both require that the six Intelligences are functioning at a high level, modelled by you as a leader and within your team. To recap in a nutshell, we know from neuroscience that each of the Intelligences represents a distinct human need that exists regardless of the external environment. Interestingly, when times are good and there is plenty of money, these needs tend to get met easily (or at least the fact that the Intelligences aren't functioning well seems on the surface to be less of an issue). When times are tough and stress levels increase, however, these needs become much harder to satisfy, and the poor functioning Intelligences within the teams have a much more obvious impact on team output. The reassuring news is that when these needs are met, and the unconscious preoccupation with satisfying something that we can't always put our finger on is resolved, team members and teams are able to perform at exceptionally high levels. By accessing the six noble qualities that we've looked at (Tribal Loyalty, Spontaneity, Vitality, Empathy, Love of Learning and Wonder), they become secure, innovative, motivated, passionate, realistic and optimistic–the six foundational characteristics of High Performance Teams.

In this chapter, we review how to apply the six Intelligences in teams. If you want to be a successful leader you will need to learn how to meet these six needs and create these characteristics in your team, regardless of the external circumstances and dynamics. How you do this will vary according to your situation, but somehow—if you are going to create a High Performance Team—you will need to develop these very specific capabilities. You also need to know which of the Intelligences are foundational to the others. In other words, these needs present in a definite order—address the right needs in the wrong order and you will still fail. The previous chapters have provided you with a lot of detail about each of the Intelligences, including their evolutionary social function, their characteristics, how they form, what we know about the brain activity that enables them to function and the implications of different levels of functioning, both for individuals and for the team. The Toolboxes have provided you with practical insights about how to strengthen each of the Intelligences for personal, career and organisational development. Let's recap the order and the themes of each Intelligence at a topline level to ensure that you understand the entire process of creating High Performance Teams in a nutshell. We'll do this by recapping each of the Intelligences as a key leadership capability that you need to master.

The Six Capabilities you need to learn how to address as a leader if you are going to lead effectively and drive team performance

CAPABILITY #1: LEARN HOW TO CREATE SAFETY AND SECURITY

Your first task is to create a sense of security. If you don't do this, you and your team will constantly be in 'emergency mode'. When you feel insecure your brain activity moves from your cerebral cortex (the big modern brain) to your limbic system (your primitive survival brain). In this mode, everyone else is considered to be competition or food. You cannot build teams when all team members are competing with everyone else to survive. You need to learn how to help your people feel safe and know that the environment around them is secure—regardless of whatever external factors may be at play. Focus on encouraging a collaborative and unified team effort—very much in the theme of 'One for All and All for One'. This is the noble quality of Tribal Loyalty. For example, remind your team that making budget is not just an issue for the sales people; it's a 'whole of organisation problem' that needs to be tackled together requiring input from all levels. Give your people ownership of the key problems the organisation is facing and allow them to develop solutions together. Because you're looking to create calm and balance, this phase needs to be done at a slow, 'one step at a time' pace for the group, so the team has time to consider the ideas fully.

In Chapter 2, we looked at the themes that underlie the functioning of the P1 Intelligence, and provided you with tools to enable you as a leader to:

1. Clarify each team member's role and give feedback about how they are going;

2. Develop you team's Value Proposition; and

3. Develop leadership Codes of Conduct, both for yourself as an individual and for your team.

CAPABILITY #2: LEARN HOW TO EMPOWER YOUR PEOPLE TO EXPRESS THEMSELVES BY TURNING EMOTIONS INTO WORDS

It may sound counter-intuitive to **encourage moaning from your team**, but the rationale is deeply rooted in brain science. In Chapter 3, we looked at the importance of self-expression in enabling individuals to take in new ideas, to think conceptually and to work collaboratively. All these abilities are facilitated by the right side of the brain, which easily becomes 'full' of emotion when we're emotionally charged. This prevents the full functioning of this Intelligence. So, as a leader, you need to help your team unblock or empty their system by turning emotions into words.

At the first step you have already enabled your team to feel safe and secure and to understand, respect and value each individual's role within the group. With this in place they will begin to take on a more collaborative approach to solving the problems at hand and access the innovation that is characteristic of High Performance Teams. It is at this point you will need to learn how to encourage them to express how they are feeling about everything—their role, their KPIs, the role of the team in the organisation, even the stresses and disappointments they're facing. It is only by allowing your team to fully articulate how they're feeling that a truly resourceful space will arise and make way for effective solutions to emerge from their problem solving. This engenders creative spontaneity. But remember, as people express themselves, conflict increases. This means that as a leader you will need to upskill your team members on how to effectively manage this conflict.

In Chapter 3, we looked at the themes that underlie the functioning of the C1 Intelligence, and provided you with tools to enable you as a leader to:

1. Actively foster creativity;

2. Make conflict a business-as-usual activity (by using the Pinch Crunch model to establish a way to manage emotional expression); and

3. Use brainstorming to drive innovation.

CAPABILITY #3: LEARN HOW TO MOTIVATE BY IDENTIFYING, DELIVERING AND CELEBRATING QUICK WINS

With clear roles, lively discussion and enthusiasm starting to build, the team is now ready for some focus. Here, your role as a leader is to take your team through a process of identifying the three or four key objectives it can achieve that are on strategy. You need to **create urgency and focus resources on kicking a few high profile goals**. The key is to ensure that each individual's ego, drive, motivation and sense of competition are focused on achieving for the team, rather than for themselves as an individual at the expense of the team. Once the team starts to feel that by working together it can achieve whatever it focuses on, you will have mastered the capability of motivation and invoked the noble quality of Vitality in the team.

In Chapter 4, we looked at the themes that underlie the functioning of the P2 Intelligence, and provided you with tools to enable you as a leader to:

1. Develop a competitive strategy for your team;

2. Dynamise the group; and

3. Effectively manage any plateaued performers.

CAPABILITY #4: LEARN HOW TO FACILITATE EMPATHY THROUGH ACTIVE LISTENING

We all have a need to feel heard and understood. Feeling emotionally connected to those with whom we work not only has a significant impact on our enjoyment of daily life, it can also be a pivotal factor in performance—both our own and the team's. In the face of major challenges, both internal and external, bonds between individuals can be critical in determining the resilience and responsiveness of a group. When team members enjoy strong interpersonal connections, they're able to support each other through tough times and together find the heart to persevere. This is the noble quality of Empathy. In the absence of these bonds, teams often become fractured and performance drops.

The key for you as a leader is to **learn and model the noble art of active listening to drive win-win outcomes**. When you encourage team members to listen to each other and try to see situations from another's point of view, you promote the development of Empathy within the team. Even when it's all smooth sailing, this can mean the difference between a team that merely performs and one that excels. Leaders that have mastered the capability of empathy create teams that are cohesive, connected and have a culture of empowerment and support (rather than politics and white-anting). These characteristics enable team members to work seamlessly together to achieve exceptional win-win outcomes.

In Chapter 5, we looked at the themes that underlie the functioning of the I2 Intelligence, and provided you with tools to enable you as a leader to:

1. Build active listening in your team;

2. Communicate effectively with groups; and

3. Ensure all agreements are win-win.

CAPABILITY #5: LEARN HOW TO GET INFORMATION FLOWING—LEAD AND LAG INDICATORS

Your role as a leader is now to **ensure everyone is working from accurate data** about how they are performing, both individually and as a team. This involves invoking the noble quality of Love of Learning, so that data and information is valued and used to drive team performance. To master this capability you as a leader need to understand the difference between lead and lag indicators and their impact on strategy development. As we explored in Chapter 6, lead indicators are inputs, lag indicators are outputs and both are needed to ensure team strategies are effective. As a leader, you need to understand how to identify and then share lead and lag information so that the team is a living, learning group—not a collection of automatons following an inaccurate strategy.

In Chapter 6, we looked at the themes that underlie the functioning of the I1 Intelligence, and provided you with tools to enable you as a leader to:

1. Create a 'learning lab' team culture;

2. Identify and track your lead and lag indicators and use this to drive strategy; and

3. Leverage from your team's intellectual capital.

CAPABILITY #6: LEARN HOW TO CREATE HOPE FOR THE FUTURE

In the brain, there is no chemical difference between anticipation and anxiety. The only difference between these profoundly different emotions is our perception of what is going to happen in the future. Anxiety is a feeling of future dread. Anticipation is an expectation of something positive happening in the future. Your job as a leader is to **transform anxiety into anticipation by creating a sense that somehow something positive is coming up**. This is a capability that all the great leaders have mastered. It encourages the team to access their own C2 Intelligence to vision how a different future for the team could be created, through revolutionary ideas, paradigm shifts and strategic thinking. At this stage, your role as a leader is critical, because your ability to create a sense of anticipation (rather than anxiety) about the future will determine whether your team is forward-thinking, optimistic and eager to face the challenges that the future brings or is quietly dreading the next meeting.

In Chapter 7, we looked at the themes that underlie the functioning of the C2 Intelligence, and provided you with tools to enable you as a leader to:

1. Create the future you want through visualisation;

2. Undertake scenario planning to create a new future for the team; and

3. Visualise and focus on ideal outcomes.

When these six capabilities are mastered by leaders and the six Intelligences are fully functioning in teams, the results are breathtaking. Team members work seamlessly together to achieve outstanding results and the success and impact of the team, as a whole, far exceeds anything that could have been achieved by just one or two of the team members working in isolation.

Creating high performance teams is not a simple task. It takes commitment, time, energy and internal fortitude from you as a leader and commitment from the team members. However, it's well worth the effort. Your team will achieve exceptional outcomes, your people will feel engaged, motivated, fulfilled, self-actualised and optimistic about the future. And, of course, so will you.

Principle #2:

Know How to Manage Your Emotional Reactivity

Key Concepts in this Section

The low road of Neuro-Limbic Types:

- Perfectionists

- Helpers

- Achievers

- Artists

- Analysts

- Loyal Sceptics

- Epicures

- The Boss

- Peacemakers

Chapter 9

Exploring Your System 1 Emotional Reactivity

Life is nasty, brutish and short
(Thomas Hobbes, 17th Century English philosopher)

The world in which we live is wonderfully complex. But it is far too rich with stimuli to fully assess and weigh up each and every decision. Instead, our brains have adopted perceptual short cuts that act as filters and provide easy ways of reducing the complexity down to manageable chunks of data. These filters are encoded in nine emotions that enable us to quickly access relevant data and come to a fast decision. These emotions draw on our cognitive ability by accessing one or two of the Intelligences together. These combinations make up the nine Neuro-Limbic Types and are represented in the second row of Diagram 1.5. This is a raw level of personality, and the characteristics of each type are relatively predictable. The helpful thing about the Neuro-Limbic Types is that they not only significantly simplify our decision-making processes, but also provide us with our emotional motivation. Unfortunately, they do also hamper us with cognitive biases and can lead us to make decisions based on inaccurate or partial interpretations of situations – which can often end in unhelpful outcomes.

You may remember from Chapter 1 that your brain has two systems – one rational and the other emotional – that influence our decision-making and consequent behaviour (see Diagram 1.3). These systems differ in terms of speed, flexibility and operation. The Neuro-Limbic Types reflect System 1, the intuitive, emotional brain, and are found in the more primitive part of the brain – the limbic system. This is the part of your brain that enables you to make fast, automatic, effortless determinations, without conscious thought and based only on what you have experienced in the past. The perceptual filters that our Neuro-Limbic Type uses to interpret the world are referred to as Core Beliefs. Governed as they are by habit, these Core Beliefs are difficult to modify. This reactive, automatic system differs greatly from the more considered, rational decision-making of System 2, which is driven by our Neuro-Rational Type (or Archetype). We'll explore that more complex level of personality in Principle #3.

Reflecting the reality that the decision-making of System 1 is driven by our emotional brain, the nine Neuro-Limbic Types[1] arise from nine separate internal motivations. While each of us has a tendency towards one or other of these nine profiles (our temperament), each profile forms around a signature emotion. While the emotion itself will typically be of a short but intense duration, each temperament will have a typical mood that colours its perceptions and behaviours. For example, an individual in a 'bad' mood is far more likely to become angry about an issue or occurrence that happens in the course of a day, than an individual who is in a 'happy' mood. If the individual Neuro-Limbic Type is formed around anger, they will start recognising issues to justify/trigger their anger in their environment. After the amygdala has alerted the brain and the focus of attention has narrowed, the individual uses the neocortex to justify feelings and expressions of feelings (this is known as a self-justifying reframe).

The degree to which an individual's behaviour aligns with a Neuro-Limbic Type will be determined by the degree to which the individual has allowed the tension in their environment to dictate their mood. The degree to which they do not cognitively assess their decision-making process will indicate the degree to which they use Core Beliefs to make their world simpler. The psychologist Richard Wenzlaff (1993) states, "Thoughts are associated in the mind not just by content, but by mood. People have what amounts to a set of bad-mood thoughts that come to mind more readily when they are feeling down." In a series of experiments volunteers were told heart-wrenching scenarios of tragedy and were then asked to try to distract themselves with other thoughts. Volunteers who were already depressed would try to distract themselves with other distressing thoughts whereas more cheerful individuals would attempt to distract themselves with more positive mental images.

The chemicals that drive the emotions that cause the manifestation of Neuro-Limbic Types are generated in the brain in the amygdala. The amygdala is part of our more primitive centre for interpreting our environmental stimuli. The primary function of the amygdala is to scan the environment for potentially hostile inputs and to arrive at an immediate response. Its role is to interpret hostile events and determine whether to fight, to run away, or to comply with the threat (fight, flight or freeze).

Consider a dog's response to an angry owner who is threatening to hit it. A dog's

---

1   This falls within an ancient Sufi profiling system called the Enneagram which accurately tracks the emotional and force-based responses of people. This system has been written about extensively by US psychologist Helen Palmer.

OFC is the Channel for the Archetype to Manage the Amygdala's Emotional Reactivity

Our Neuro-Rational Types, which are housed in System 2 of the brain, have a number of ways of managing the amygdala. One of these is the Orbital Frontal Cortex (OFC). The OFC maintains an overseeing management role over the amygdala's often antisocial emotional urges. Patients with lesions in these inhibitory circuits commonly lose the power to, for example, stop themselves from mimicking another's angry face; they may do socially embarrassing and tasteless three-year-old-style funny toilet jokes, greet a total stranger with a kiss or reveal embarrassingly far too much. Without this OFC emotional guard, they interact childishly with their unruly amygdala having free rein. Similarly, some war veterans with dysfunctional OFCs are incapable of reasonably assessing stimuli and are panicked by a gunshot on TV or a car backfiring (Beer et al., 2006).

amygdala presents it with three responses. The dog can either fight, it can run away, or it can crawl on its belly and fawn. In the case of humans, there are still only three general responses to perceived threats, but for humans there are three different ways to fight, three to run away and three to comply. These nine approaches give rise to the Neuro-Limbic Types.

The reason that the amygdala plays such a powerful role in interpreting and evaluating our environment is because of its purpose in our personal survival. Since it prompts us to action through chemically inducing emotion[2], it acts as a storehouse of all emotional memory. All passion and emotion depends on the amygdala as it stores emotional associations. One young man who had his amygdala surgically removed (to control severe seizures) became completely uninterested in other people. While he was capable of conversation, he no longer recognised close friends, relatives, or even his own mother (Joseph, 1993: Siegel, 1999). Without an amygdala he seemed to have lost all recognition of feeling, as well as any feeling about feeling. Further, animals that have had their amygdala removed or severed lack fear or rage, and lose the urge to compete or cooperate.

Research by neuroscientist Joseph LeDoux explains how the amygdala can take control over what we do even as the thinking brain (the neocortex) is still coming to a decision. Incoming signals from the senses allow the amygdala to scan every experience for trouble. The amygdala evaluates every moment, 'Is this something

---

2 The root of the word emotion is in the Latin verb 'to move' with the prefix 'e-' to connote 'move away' suggesting that there is a tendency to act implicitly in every emotion.

Diagram 9.1 Flight or Fight Response

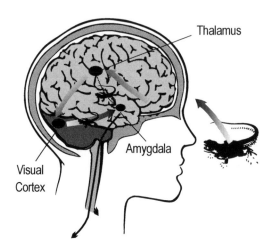

Heart rate and blood pressure increase.
Large muscles prepare for quick action.

that I hate? That hurts me? Something I fear?' If the answer is 'Yes,' the amygdala will react instantaneously, transmitting a message of crisis to all parts of the brain.

Psychologists refer to these perceived threats as 'stressors'. If the amygdala interprets a stressor as something to be feared, then it will trigger the secretion of the body's fight-or-flight hormones, mobilise the centres for movement and activate the cardiovascular system, the muscles and the gut (Kagan, 1994). LeDoux's research reveals that the amygdala receives some direct inputs from the senses and the amygdala can start reacting before the inputs are even registered in the neocortex.

The interval between what triggers an emotion and its eruption can be virtually instantaneous. The chemical states, or emotions, that the amygdala creates to handle stressors are the key to understanding Core Beliefs. They represent the emotions that the amygdala has triggered to deal with a specific stimulus in the environment. Since these chemicals are not removed completely from the system, they represent moods that can last for much longer periods of time than needed and that will predispose the person to act in set ways to the stimuli.

Neuro-Limbic Types form with a tendency to express one emotion because the chemicals that the brain uses to create a physical response to the environment are the same that potently embed the event in memory (Cahill, L., et al., 1994). Therefore, what has caused a strong reaction in the past is most likely to draw a reaction in the future. These responses become habitual and hardwired into the brain because neurons that fire together, wire together.

The neocortex interprets the emotion produced by the amygdala in three ways:[3]

---

3   These align with the traditional heart, head and body cardinal points outlined in the Enneagram

1. Attention, which plays out as a focus on relationships

2. Security, which plays out as a focus on intellectual answers

3. Individual autonomy, which plays out as a focus on physical issues.

Interestingly, psychiatrist Karen Horney breaks the types into social behaviour types. She identified three fundamental ways in which people interact in a social setting. This work was based on the earlier work of Sigmund Freud on how people attempt to resolve their internal conflicts. These three styles represent the social approach of the Neuro-Limbic Types and the manner in which they externalise their inner conflicts.

The three basic approaches are:

- **Moving against types:** Assertive about resolving their internal conflicts in the external domain. These types are ego-oriented and ego-expansive and they respond to stress or difficulty by building up, reinforcing or inflating their egos. (These three types are centred on P2.)

- **Moving towards types:** Compliant by needing to be of service to other people. These types respond to stressors by complying in the belief that this will remove the perceived stressors. (These three types are centred on P1.)

- **Moving away from types:** Withdrawal from social interactions and from issues that threaten the broad issues about which they are focused. These types respond to stress by withdrawing into an internal world. (These three types are centred on I1.)

These three categories represent three ways people respond to stressors and seek to answer the inner cries of their amygdala and its warnings of danger. Knowing these Hornevarian type reactions and behaviours is very useful when predicting how individuals will react to situations and seek to 'resolve' their amygdala's chemical alerts.

FROM STATE TO TRAIT — HOW STRESS INFLUENCES OUR NEURAL CHEMISTRY

Over a decade ago, Perry, Pollard, Blakley, Baker & Vigilante looked at the effect of childhood trauma on the emotional, behavioural, cognitive, social and physical functioning of the brain, including how it can "... dramatically alter the child's trajectory into and throughout adult life" (Perry et al., 1995, p. 273). They identified two major response patterns to threat: the hyperarousal continuum (which encompasses defensive and *fight or flight* response behaviours) and the dissociation continuum (which encompasses the freeze or surrender responses). These responses activate the different intelligence centres that we've already associated with the Hornevarian type reactions and behaviours:

- **Defensive,** *fight or flight* **responses** reflect the engagement of the P2 circuit
- **Initial freeze or alarm responses** reflect the engagement of the P1 circuit
- **Dissociative surrender responses** reflect the engagement of the I1 circuit.

Our responses to stressful situations, therefore, depend on the perceived level of threat. "When threatened, a human will engage specific adaptive mental and physical responses. Increasing threat alters mental state, style of thinking (cognition) and physiology (e.g. increased heart rate, muscle tone, rate of respiration). As the individual moves along the threat continuum [from alarm (P1) through to fear (P2) and terror (I1)] different areas of the brain control and orchestrate mental and physical functioning. The more threatened the individual, the more 'primitive' (or regressed) becomes the style of thinking and behaviour" (Perry et al., 1995, p. 274).

So, as the perceived level of threat increases, causing the individual to move along the threat continuum, the brain naturally recruits different intelligence centres as part of its survival strategy. With the initial, relatively low level threat, the individual is alarmed but complies, reflecting the engagement of the P1 system. As the threat increases to a moderate fear-inducing level, the individual accesses their P2 system, either fighting back or fleeing (depending on the circumstances). However, when this proves unsuccessful, the individual reaches a level of terror and withdraws completely. In a child, this final stage can manifest in "numbing, fainting or even mini-psychosis" (Perry et al., 1995, p. 274).

Diagram 9.2 shows these progressive stages of alarm, fear and terror and maps the neuroscience of the response to threat.

THE P1 SYSTEM SOUNDS THE ALARM

4. The P1 motor and the P2 attention systems are well interconnected with the amygdala and the structures of the limbic system, which regulates emotions and conditioned emotional learning (Ratey, 2001, p. 165).

5. When there is an emergency, corticotrophin releasing hormone (CRH), the brain's own stress hormone, is released, which heightens anxiety and vigilance (P1) and the parasympathetic nervous system briefly freezes all behaviour (including silencing normal physiological processes like the heartbeat). This precedes sympathetic nervous system activation (including adrenaline release), and hormonal release from the pituitary gland (Ratey, 2001, p. 172). How the

Diagram 9.2 The Progressive Stages of Alarm, Fear and Terror

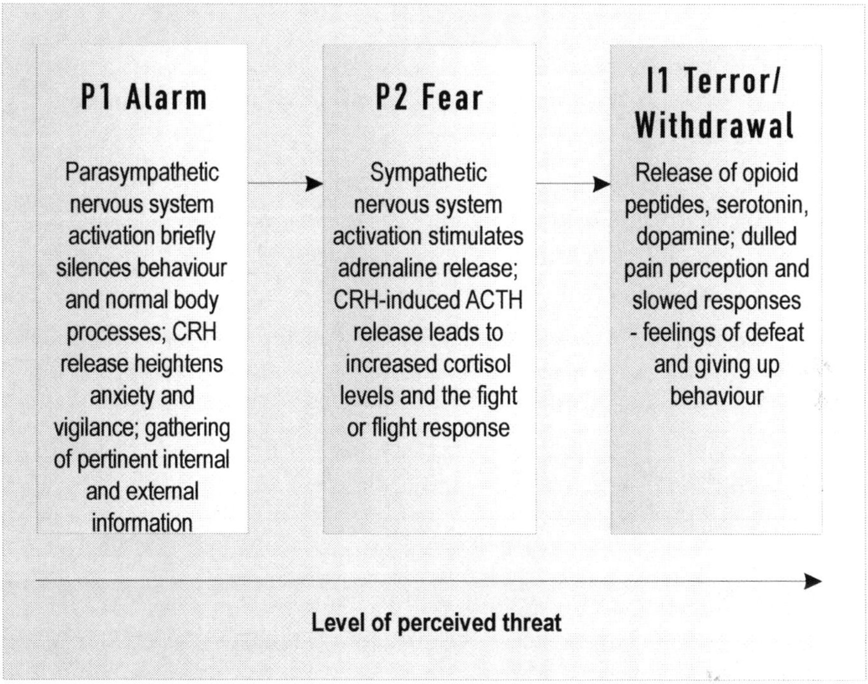

P1 Alarm	P2 Fear	I1 Terror/ Withdrawal
Parasympathetic nervous system activation briefly silences behaviour and normal body processes; CRH release heightens anxiety and vigilance; gathering of pertinent internal and external information	Sympathetic nervous system activation stimulates adrenaline release; CRH-induced ACTH release leads to increased cortisol levels and the fight or flight response	Release of opioid peptides, serotonin, dopamine; dulled pain perception and slowed responses - feelings of defeat and giving up behaviour

Level of perceived threat

individual then responds to a threat will be largely influenced by their history.

Those with a well-developed P1 threat response spend more time evaluating in their parasympathetic response to gather more information before they react.

THE P2 SYSTEM ACTIVATES THE 'FIGHT OR FLIGHT' RESPONSE

1. CRH released during the P1 alarm phase increases the secretion of adrenocorticotrophic hormone (ACTH) from the pituitary gland into the blood, promoting the release of catecholamines and glucocorticoids that mobilise the body's energy reserves for fight or flight. (Perry et al., 1995; Ratey, 2001, pp. 171-173).

2. "When the threat is perceived to materialise there is activation of the complex set of centrally controlled peripheral autonomic nervous system, the immune system, and the hypothalamic-pituitary axis with the concomitant peripheral release of ACTH and cortisol and other stress-response neural systems in the brain. The key mediator of the fight/flight response is the locus coeruleus

Mediating the Amygdala Fear Response

While the threat continuum involves the fear-based activation of P1, P2 and I1 circuits, research suggests that the other ICs may in fact reduce the amygdala fear response.

Brain imaging studies reveal that positive affect-inducing stimuli (i.e. stimuli that increase activation of the C1 circuit) such as music, odours, self-generated positive affect, and male/female orgasm decrease amygdala activation (Burgdorf and Panskepp, 2006).

Similarly, oxytocin, the principle neurotransmitter of the I2 system, reduces stress and amygdala activation triggered by an exposure to social fear signals. It also attenuates the functional connectivity between the amygdala and the brain stem structures that are involved in mediating autonomic fear responses. This suggests that oxytocin may facilitate prosocial attitudes in humans by calming fear (Debiec, 2007; Zak et al., 2007).

(LC). This bilateral grouping of norepinephrine-containing neurons originates in the pons, a more primitive, regulatory part of the brain, and sends diverse axonal projections to virtually all major brain regions enabling its function as a general regulator of noradrenergic tone and activity. The ventral tegmental nucleus (VTN) also plays a role in regulating the sympathetic nuclei in the pons/medulla" (Perry et al., 1995).

3. "If you encounter a threatening person in the street, the sympathetic nervous system ('fight or flight' response) kicks into action, driving your heart rate and breathing rate up, slowing down any unessential bodily processes, such as digestion, and dilating your pupils" (Nataraja, 2008, pp. 60-61).

Those with a well-developed P2 threat response will be quick to spring into action, moving towards or away from whatever is causing the stress.

THE I1 SYSTEM PROMPTS WITHDRAWAL

1. In addition to a fight or flight ('arousal') response to stress, Perry et al., (1995, p. 280) observe an alternative threat response set, which they characterise as dissociative. This reaction is associated with the release of opioid peptides, serotonin and even dopamine, dulling pain perception and slowing responses. The individual associates this reaction with a sense of 'defeat' or 'giving up' behaviour.

2. Depression can be linked to the removal of energy and the desire for the organism to remove itself from the immediate environment. A most striking example was Bejjani's observation of sudden onset of depression by stimulating midline diencephalic structures near the subthalamic nuclei (Burgdorf & Panksepp, 2006, p. 177).

3. In the brain, sadness seems to be related to an increase in activity in the left amygdala and the right frontal cortex and a decrease in activity in the right amygdala and the left prefrontal cortex. Damasio identified intense sadness as being related to the anterior cingulate (now increasingly recognised as an area important to the experience of all emotions), the bed-nucleus of the stria terminalis, the ventral septal and dorsal preoptic areas, the dorsomedial thalamus and the periaqueductal grey (PAG) of the brain stem (Damasio, 2000; for schematic, see Panksepp, 2003).

Those with a well-developed I1 threat response may acquiesce in the face of threats, opting to withdraw in order to regroup and re-evaluate (reconstruct their narrative).

STATES BECOME TRAITS – HOW YOUR NEURO-LIMBIC TYPE DEVELOPS

According to Perry et al., repeated experience of these threat-driven 'states' leads to their potentiation and the emergence of 'traits'. This is the practical reality of the concept of neural plasticity. "The more frequently a certain pattern of neural activation occurs, the more indelible the internal representation. Experience thus creates a processing template through which all new input is filtered" (Perry et al., 1995, p. 275). In this way, the state becomes a trait.

Therefore, based on our early experiences, we each develop a dominant survival response that centres around one of Perry et al.'s three response patterns. This means that when faced with a stressful situation, each of us has a predisposition to either comply, fight/flee or withdraw.

This reflects our dominant Neuro-Limbic Type (NLT), and each of the nine NLTs can therefore be classed according to where they sit along the continuum:

Dominant Intelligence	Threat Continuum (Perry et al., 1995)	Neuro-Limbic Types
P1 Compliance	Freeze or alarm responses	NLT1 – The Perfectionists NLT2 – The Helpers NLT6 – The Loyal Sceptics
P2 Fight/Flight	Defensive and fight or flight responses	NLT3 – The Achievers NLT7 – The Epicures NLT8 – The Boss
I1 Withdrawal	Dissociative surrender response	NLT4 – The Artists NLT5 – The Analysts NLT9 – The Peacemakers

Interestingly, the Byrne Theory links Perry et al.'s work with understandings from developmental psychology about how early environments impact on psychosocial development (A. Byrne, personal communication, May 24, 2009). It posits that the level of stress in the early family environment may determine a predisposition to a particular response pattern. For example, if you grew up in a family with a low level of stress, you're likely to have a compliant response pattern (i.e. a P1 NLT). Moderate and high levels of stress, in turn, would predispose you respectively to either a fight or flight response (i.e. a P2 NLT) or a withdrawal response pattern (i.e. an I1 NLT).

This theory also helps explain why people seem to vary in terms of their abilities to cope with external stressors. It makes sense that naturally withdrawn types (i.e. NLTs 4, 5 and 9), who grew up in high stress environments, would require a much greater level of external stress to stimulate them than a compliant type (i.e. a NLT 1, 2 or 6), who is accustomed to a much lower stress environment. This may explain why some people are attracted to high intensity, high stress jobs (e.g. trauma, emergency, high risk tactical operations), while others prefer more predictable, low stress workplaces.

YOUR BRAIN'S GEAR BOX

Perry et al.'s work highlights the amazing ability of the brain to adapt in order to achieve its primarily evolutionary purpose – keeping us alive. Although the methods and strategies employed may vary according to the position along the threat continuum (as well as the specifics of the particular NLT) may vary, each is designed to achieve this key objective. This begs the question: surely there are situations where a fight/flight response would be more appropriate than a compliant or a withdrawn one, and vice versa? And what does that mean for our Neuro-Limbic Personalities?

Although we each have one NLT that we tend to collapse into most frequently, we in fact have access to three NLTs: one that we use to comply, one that we use to fight or flee and one that enables us to withdraw and rewrite our narrative about the world. In a way, this is the gear box of our brain; these three personalities are what enable us to Park (i.e. Freeze/Comply), go Forward (i.e. Fight/Flight) and Reverse (Withdraw). The extent to which we are able to access all three points of our triad reflects our level of integration at the limbic level, and often contributes to our success in the world (i.e. how well we drive our car). Imagine a car that could only reverse, but not park or go forward. Or one that can only drive forward, but is incapable of parking or reversing. Not a very practical vehicle! In the same way, we need to be able to access all three points of our triad so that we can drive through life most effectively. Another way of describing this is dynamic equilibrium; we need to have an appropriate balance between all three gears so that we can respond appropriately and flexibly to the situations in which we find ourselves. Our ability to do this also determines whether we are able to access limbic wisdom in our later years (see Chapter 21).

There are three different limbic triads, each with a specific theme or focus that shapes our world view and often determines how we behave. People often report that they 'get' other people from the same limbic triad as themselves, even if they have a different dominant NLT. This is because, effectively, they are the same type, viewing and sorting the world through the same thematic filter. Collectively, we refer to the three triads as:

- The *Idealist* Triad (which focuses on the creation of the ideal past, present and future);

Diagram 9.3 The Brain's Gearbox

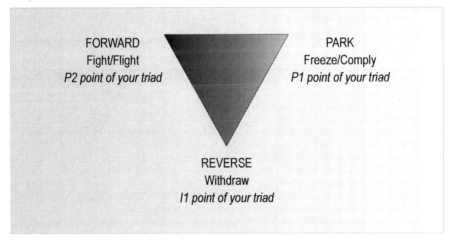

FORWARD
Fight/Flight
P2 point of your triad

PARK
Freeze/Comply
P1 point of your triad

REVERSE
Withdraw
I1 point of your triad

- The *Power* Triad (which focuses on helping those in power, amassing power or accumulating powerful information); and

- The *Groupies* Triad (which focuses on the achievements of the group, protecting the group from risk and maintaining group harmony).

Each NLT therefore reflects a specific point of focus within the theme of the triad.

THE AMYGDALA AND THE NEOCORTEX

While all the Neuro-Limbic Types are motivated by fear (as indicated by Perry et al.'s (1995) *Threat Continuum*), each NLT is based around a particular key emotion. When people are first introduced to the Neuro-Limbic Types, they sometimes see aspects of themselves in a number of NLTs. This reflects the fact that each NLT represents a particular survival strategy, the operation of which is associated with a core, very human emotion. However, while you may have experienced any number, perhaps even all, of these emotions, there will only be a few that you default to or use habitually. These are the emotions that you specialise in.

We'll look at the key emotions of the Neuro-Limbic Types as we look at each Type in detail. Before we do, however, it's important to understand that emotions can arise from either the amygdala (the reactive part of the brain) or the neocortex (the thinking part of the brain). The neocortex allows us to comprehend what our senses perceive. Therefore, it is the centre of thought. It adds to a feeling what we think about it – while we may feel fear because of a certain object, the neocortex allows us

Diagram 9.4 NLT Focus Points

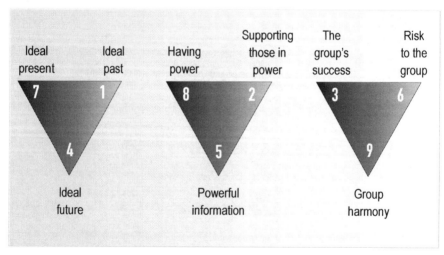

to think and reason why we have that fear. It allows for the subtlety and complexity in emotional life such as the ability to have feelings about our feelings. It also explains the wider variety of responses that humans can have with their environment than animals, since we have so much more thinking capacity – the human brain is roughly triple the size of our nearest evolutionary relatives.

The emotions that arise in the neocortex can be contextualised and understood. It is a more deliberate emotional route, as we are typically aware of the thoughts that lead to it. This is clearly demonstrated in an actor's capacity to cry on demand by thinking about sad memories. The actor is consciously aware that they are focusing on elements in their environment (namely, their brain) that will generate a specific response. The emotional experiences of our neocortex are capable of being assessed, evaluated and revised.

In contrast to this controlled perception of the environment, emotions generated out of the amygdala are very strong and have clear physical consequences. Chemicals are released into the body in order to deal with the environment; these are then interpreted as emotions. All strong and reactive emotions are impulses to action since they chemically prime the body to be prepared to take specific actions. For example, when someone is angry, blood flows to the hands, which would make it easier to strike an opponent or to pick up a weapon. Also, the heart rate increases and a rush of hormones, like adrenaline, generates a strong pulse of energy to help the body deal with the emergency. When the emotion of fear occurs, blood goes to the large skeletal muscles, such as the legs, making it easier to fight or flee. Circuits in the brain's emotional centres trigger a flood of hormones that put the body on general alert, making it edgy and ready for action, and forcing attention to fixate on the threat at hand.

UNCONSCIOUS

LeDoux has observed that we can form emotional reactions and memories unconsciously (LeDoux, 1998: Siegal, 1999). The amygdala can house memories and response repertoires that we enact without quite realising why we do so because the

---

NLTs and Behaviour

Darwin believed that having emotions such as fear, anger and joy involved taking a predisposition to act in a mode of freeze or flee, fight or embrace respectively. At a neural level, brain imaging studies now support this paradigm. Any emotion we feel evokes in us the associated impulse to act (Goleman, 2006, p. 61).

---

neocortex can be completely bypassed. Emotional preferences and interpretation can arise from this unthinking part of the brain, the amygdala. This means we can have formed emotional responses to stimuli we are not consciously aware of. We will never question an association we do not know we have made.

SPEEDY BUT INACCURATE ASSESSMENTS

The emotional associations made in the amygdala represent the central core of the formation of evoked sets and Core Beliefs. As the repository for emotional memory, the amygdala scans experience, comparing what is happening now with what happened in the past. Its method of comparison is associative: when a key element of a present situation is similar to the past, it can call it a 'match' and will respond accordingly. Therefore, what something reminds us of will be more important than what it 'is' and it needs only one part of an identity to evoke the whole memory. So the amygdala will make connections between things that merely have similar striking features (Siegel, 1999). These associations will represent inaccurate linkages, because they will be based on partial matches and incomplete assessments. Since the emotional intensity of these associations is not brought into the rational mind for consideration, the accuracy of these associations is not questioned. Therefore, they act as subconscious filters that alter perceptions and set priorities on a purely subconscious level.

Core Beliefs are inaccurate because the circuitry of the amygdala can become engaged in generating a response before all the information about a situation has been assessed. This occurs because the amygdala is primed to ensure survival – and this requires fast responses to threatening environments. When survival depends on recognising danger and responding to it immediately, the analysis of the neocortex may take vital seconds that the individual doesn't have. While most people face few, if any, situations in which this survival reaction is necessary for survival, nevertheless, we all have it hardwired into our brains.

ASSESSMENTS BASED ON NEURO-LIMBIC TYPES ARE FIXED

The emotional connections that the brain makes are fixed in that as the amygdala scans the environment for stressors, it makes connections to events and situations it considers to be similar to past occasions. So when an event seems similar to an emotionally charged memory, the amygdala responds by triggering the feelings that went with that event. This leads to disproportionate reactions to symbols, statements or events that trigger the amygdala's fight/flight/comply mechanism.

Part of the response to a stressful situation is to reshuffle memory and options for action so that those most relevant are at the top of the hierarchy and so more readily enacted. This makes emotional states self-justifying, with a set of perceptions and 'proofs' all their own. That is, each chemical reaction is state-based and so only information that supports it is recognised. This is to a certain extent due to the fact that the amygdala does not have a great deal of connection with the rest of the brain. Therefore, it remembers/looks only at information that supports its position (in the present or in the past) and minimises other information (Wenzlaff, 1993).

CERTAINTY OF CORE BELIEFS

Not only do Core Beliefs simplify and filter the environment, they also provide an enormous sense of clarity and 'rightness'. As the emotion or chemical state grows stronger, so too does categorical thinking and clear mindedness. As the amygdala releases chemicals that focus on the perceived threat, this threat becomes the centre of attention, and so it tends to grow clearer and more absolute. This can be best illustrated with a survival situation. Imagine a rabbit being hunted by a dog. The rabbit's senses focus on seeking a means of escape, so its eyes will dilate, and it will enter what feels like a heightened level of awareness. This physical state will allow it to better sense the danger, and run faster to get away from that danger. This means that data that is irrelevant to the rabbit being chased – like 'that looks like nice grass to eat' which is not pertinent if the rabbit dies – will be ignored.

UNCONVERTED, YOUR NEURO-LIMBIC TYPE WILL PROBABLY KILL YOU – EVENTUALLY

Each Neuro-Limbic Type is based around a different set of chemical states that the amygdala releases. The NLTs represent temperaments with a strong tendency to experience certain emotions. This means that a range of chemicals is continually inundating the body, with long-term side effects.

Let us return to our chased rabbit. The perception of a dangerous or frightening situation causes the release of chemicals, called neurotransmitters, from the pituitary gland. These chemicals will have an impact on many tissues in the rabbit's body, but most notably the adrenal glands. Consequently, in the short term the rabbit's respiratory rate increases, its eyes dilate, and its blood sugar levels soar. If these chemicals are maintained for a long period of time, they affect the rabbit negatively.

The restriction of blood supply to 'non-essential' areas leads to their deterioration, and the exhaustion of the liver's energy stores (required to maintain the heightened state of awareness) and this can lead to a starvation of body tissues that is lethal. In rabbits this leads to 'Shock Disease' where the rabbit's body collapses after being exposed to stressful circumstances for a prolonged period of time.

A similar process of deterioration occurs in humans. Different chemicals released by the amygdala will influence the likelihood of different diseases affecting the individual. Currently there is considerable work being done by neurobiologists,

The Neurobiology of a Gut Feeling Driven by the Neuro-Limbic Type

Goleman discusses a Patient X who suffered two strokes destroying the connections between his eyes and the rest of the brain's system for sight in the visual cortex. This meant his eyes could receive signals but his brain could not even acknowledge them. This gave him the experience of being completely blind.

When Patient X was presented with shapes such as circles and squares he did not know what his eyes were seeing. But when he was presented with faces with emotions such as happiness or anger, he guessed the expressed emotions at a rate significantly better than chance.

The usual pathway we use where all the senses first enter the brain runs from the eyes to the thalamus, and then to the visual cortex. Brain scans of Patient X while guessing the faces' emotions indicated he was using a second pathway. This pathway sends information directly from the thalamus to the amygdala which then draws emotional interpretation from the non-verbal message such as a frown, or a change in posture or tone of voice. This may take microseconds, potentially happening before we are aware of what we are seeing.

The amygdala has a high sensitivity for such non-verbals, but it is not directly wired to the speech centres. That means when we register a feeling, signals from our brain circuits do not alert the verbal areas where words can express what we know. We register feelings by mimicking that emotion in our own bodies. So Patient X was not seeing the emotions on the faces so much as feeling them, a condition called *affective blindsight* (Goleman, 2006, p. 15).

Patient X gave us insight to what we all have. This has the impact of *priming*. For example, I may meet someone; neurolimbically, with my affective blindsight, that person may look or feel a little like my father. So without even being aware of it, my experience is primed in a way such that I am looking for attributes like my father. The question is, do you ever challenge the priming that your amygdala has provided you?

like Dan Siegel, to determine the correlations between the amygdala's activation and cognitive, emotional and somatic health.

There are nine Neuro-Limbic Types which are discussed together with some sobering tales of how notable historical figures have wreaked havoc on themselves and others as they have become entrenched in their neuro-limbic reaction. We have sourced the stories from Greene & Elffers (1998), *48 Laws of Power*, which chronicles some of history's most notorious monsters and who perhaps unintentionally, in *Star Wars* terms, embraced the *dark side*.

The Nine Neuro-Limbic Types — a Primitive Expression of Humanity

NEURO-LIMBIC TYPE ONE — PERFECTIONISTS

Neuro-Limbic Type One (NLT1) has a strong need to be considered a 'good person' and their emotional drivers are to do what is perceived as right and good in their community. They live by extremely high personal standards of excellence, and expect others to do so as well. The NLT1 personality

SOMATIC

focuses on living the one right way. This stems from an assumption that there is one ultimately correct solution for every situation. NLT1s are dedicated to this one right way as a statement of character, regardless of how attractive other ways might be. They also seek to improve themselves and others since they want to be right and to justify their position in order to be beyond criticism and reproach.

The reason that they have high standards is because they feel that they must gain a sense of worthiness (love) through being good, correcting error and being responsible. NLT1 is a compliant profile since it seeks affirmation through being good, correcting error and being responsible. This means that they seek to embody socially acceptable standards and behaviours. They seek autonomy through strict adherence to the social rules, and through imposing them on other people (P1 enforced by P2).

EMOTIONAL STATE

The NLT1 is formed when the amygdala's emergency chemicals are justified in the neocortex using P1 and P2. In this state the NLT1 believes anger is present because nothing is as it should be. This is a dilemma since anger itself is bad and must be avoided by the 'good boy' or 'good girl'. Ones do not acknowledge their own resentment until they are absolutely certain that they are in the right and then they express their anger as self-righteous indignation. This self-righteous anger is often an externalisation of their preoccupation with being correct so that they can avoid guilt or self-criticism. Therefore, a NLT1's anger is typically focused on violations of standards.

Since the NLT1 is focused on being and doing 'the right thing' they will react to what they perceive as being wrong. Their focus is on being right, particularly compared to other people, which gives them a sense that they are 'better than' others. When a NLT1 walks into a room, they may subconsciously think, 'This place is so sloppy and disorganised. If I were in charge, things would not be such a mess.' Because they are seeking approval for having done the 'right thing', anything that is perceived to be 'wrong' will represent an irritant that MUST be removed. Further, their focus on creating order will bring anything that is out of order into stark relief. Once the source of chaos is removed or corrected, then all will be 'right' and they can feel affirmed or secure.

AS A CHILD

As children, the NLT1s remember being punished for bad or impulsive behaviour. They learnt that to control impulsive behaviour, especially expressions of anger, would please their parents. NLT1s believed that such control could make them appear good boys or good girls in the eyes of their parents. Therefore the child sought to be affirmed and commended for being good, correcting error and meeting the demands of their critical mind. As a child, the NLT1 came to the conclusion that people are not accepted for whom they are but for their behaviour. Any behaviour, thought or emotion that is judged inappropriate is bad and should be punished within themselves and within others. For example, in the eyes of a child, anger seems to rise to almost murderous proportions and so no expression of anger is possible (Palmer, 1988).

AT THEIR WORST

At their worst the NLT1 is a hyper-critical, self-righteous individual fixated on adhering to the rules regardless of the situation or circumstance. They can be incapable of giving praise or appreciation for anything or anyone – since nothing ever reaches perfection. At their worst the greatest compliment that a NLT1 can give is, 'There was nothing that I could criticise in the work that you did."

BODY SHAPE

The NLT1 is an even shape. The vast majority of them are a thin shape; however, even overweight Ones have excess fat distributed in an even fashion. Regardless of body weight, the face of a One is elongated and thin. Although lean, they are not muscular or toned (Diversi, 2006).

Cognitive Bias in Action:

HOW SOMEONE CAN BE SINCERELY WRONG WITH THIS NEURO-LIMBIC TYPE

Greene & Elffers (1998, pp. 393-394) tell the story of Thomas Cromwell who was absolutely certain of what needed to be done. He was determined to break up the power and wealth of the Catholic Church, making way for the Protestant Church, in as short a time as possible. While his certainty may have been seen as religious faith and fervour, it actually came from his chemical disposition. Since his decision was chemically driven, he ignored the fact that his speedy reforms would cause pain and resentment. He calculated that these feelings would fade away quickly.

In 1534 Thomas Cromwell was given the position of being the King's secretary. This was due to his support of King Henry VIII of England when he was determined to separate his throne from the Roman Catholic Church. In that very same year Cromwell laid the foundation of his program of religious conversion by undertaking a complete survey of the churches and monasteries of England and of the wealth that they had accumulated over the centuries. The result was far more riches than he had imagined.

Cromwell was convinced there was widespread corruption in the English monasteries; they abused their power and exploited the people they supposedly served. He started seizing the holdings of each monastery and dismantling it, with the Parliament's support. While he was doing this, he also began to impose Protestantism (the old P1 rules) on the people of England. He did this by introducing reforms in religious ritual and punishing those who remained with the Catholic process. The latter he labelled heretics.

'Wrapped in his self-righteousness, he failed to appreciate how horrified Britons were as churches were demolished, images of the Madonna and saints were broken in pieces, stained-glass windows were smashed, and the churches' treasures were confiscated. Without the monasteries, which had previously supported the poor, these people started flooding onto the streets. As further indication of his intolerance, Cromwell levied high taxes to pay for his ecclesiastical reforms, so certain was he that he knew the right way to go' (Greene & Elffers, 1998, pp. 393-394).

In June of 1540, Cromwell was arrested on charges that he was a Protestant extremist and a heretic. As a consequence he was sent to the Tower of London and was executed within six weeks. There was a very large and enthusiastic crowd who watched his execution.

NEURO-LIMBIC TYPE TWO — HELPERS

The Neuro-Limbic Type Two (NLT2) has a strong need to be perceived as a 'loving person' and so their focus of attention goes to meeting the needs and desires of people with power. They are constantly thinking, 'Will I be liked by the leader?' Since they focus on achieving a 'Yes' answer, they will

FEELING

seek to develop a deep emotional connection with the powerful to satisfy their needs for love and affection. They focus on the approval of powerful others by meeting their need and becoming indispensable to them.

NLT2s are adept at manoeuvring other people into liking them. They live with an assumption that almost anyone or anything can become available to them with the right approach or the proper amount of subtly applied special attention. They are a compliant profile because they suppress their own desires to focus on the needs of others. Their own needs become subordinated to the needs of others. They seek to earn the respect they crave.

EMOTIONAL STATE

The NLT2 is formed when the amygdala's emergency chemicals are interpreted in the neocortex using P1 and I2. In this state the NLT2 feels the emotion of pride. In relationships pride manifests through being the favourite, the trusted confidant of the person they are in a relationship with. This is pride because they become attractive by adjusting their personal focus and taking on their partner's interests, tastes and preferences. This gives them pride in feeling indispensable and at being important to the success of others.

To the NLT2, other people appear very needy and they take a great deal of pride in meeting the needs of others. Frequently, the NLT2 has repressed their own needs, and has projected them onto others. Therefore, they will be especially attracted to either inspiring/powerful people (all the better to meet their personal needs), or to those in obvious need (so their 'value' is more obvious).

When a NLT2 walks into a room, they tend to subconsciously think, 'These poor people! I wish I had time to give everyone my attention. They look troubled— they need my help!' By approaching people from a position of being the loving person who gives their concern and service to others, NLT2s have a sense of being 'better than' others. Since they tend to repress their own desires to better satisfy the needs of others, they become highly dependent on other people to meet their repressed desires. Any threat to their relationships, or any perceived depreciation of important connections, causes the NLT2 considerable stress.

AS A CHILD

As children they usually experienced a deep love and attention from one or both of their parents. In order to continue the flow of this love, the NLT2 developed the habit of anticipating the needs and desires of powerful others in their life and also of presenting themselves as being helpful and giving. Another scenario may have been that a parent had significant physical and emotional needs that were met by the child. As a consequence, the child sought to have his or her own needs for love and affirmation met by meeting those of powerful others. The world view that they adopted was that their needs could only be met through the agency of powerful others. Their survival strategy is to please others and to protect their sensitive connections to powerful agencies (Palmer, 1988).

AT THEIR WORST

When the emotion of pride becomes all consuming then the NLT2 not only avoids their own needs but ceases to be aware that they have any needs at all. The NLT2 is more easily able to recognise the needs of their spouse, family or of the person they are with rather than see their own. This often involves them transferring their own needs onto other people. For example if a NLT2 were cold, they may ask someone else, "Are you cold?" rather than recognising that they themselves are cold. This creates a manipulative tendency where the NLT2 uses the feelings and needs of others to get their own needs fulfilled. Another downside of this tendency is that frequently the help that the NLT2 offers is not the help that is desired or required.

BODY SHAPE

The NLT2 is a feminine and curvaceous shape. Their face and body is plump and soft. They store excess fat in buttocks and hips and around their chest in men and breasts in women. They have a definable waist regardless of how overweight they are. They like food and love preparing food for others or going out for a nice meal (Diversi, 2006).

Cognitive Bias in Action:
HOW SOMEONE CAN BE SINCERELY WRONG WITH THIS NEURO-LIMBIC TYPE

Greene & Elffers (1998, pp. 137-140) tell the story of Muhammad, who was driven by NLT2. A massive empire was founded in the early part of the thirteenth century by Muhammad, the shah of Khwarem. This empire had as its capital Samarkand, incorporating modern Turkey and parts of Afghanistan. The shah formed a powerful and well-trained army, and his fighting forces could number 200,000 warriors within days. But his temporal powers eventually led to his downfall.

After he had consolidated his power Muhammad received an emissary from a new tribal leader to the east, Genghis Khan, in 1219. Khan gave Muhammad many gifts representing the finest goods from his small but quickly growing Mongol empire. It was the desire of Genghis Khan to re-open the Silk Route to Europe and he suggested that this could be shared with Muhammad, along with a promise of peace between the two empires.

In his pride, Muhammad refused to acknowledge the man he saw as an upstart from the East, who, it seemed to him, was extremely arrogant to try to talk as an equal to one so clearly his superior. Muhammad completely ignored Khan's offer. So Genghis attempted diplomacy once again. On this occasion he sent a caravan with over one hundred camels carrying the most costly possessions garnered from his plunder of China. Before the caravan reached Muhammad, Inalchik, the governor of a nearby region, killed the leaders and took the booty.

Genghis Khan was sure that this must have been some sort of mistake and that Inalchik must have acted without Muhammad's direction. So the long-suffering Genghis Khan sent yet another mission to Muhammad. This time he reiterated his offer and asked that the governor be punished. Refusing to see his own need for peace, Muhammad himself had one of the ambassadors executed and the other two had their heads shaved, a terrible insult to a Mongol warrior.

Having failed at diplomacy, Khan sent a message to Muhammad: 'You have chosen war. What will happen will happen, and what it is to be we know not; only God knows' (Greene & Elffers, 1998, p. 139). In 1220 he attacked Inalchik's province and quickly seized the capital where he executed the captured governor by having molten silver poured into his eyes and ears.

In the course of the next few years, Genghis Khan was able to utterly defeat Muhammad's army, surround Samarkand and then seize it. Muhammad fled, and a year later died, his vast empire broken and destroyed. Genghis Khan was sole master of Samarkand, the Silk Route and most of northern Asia. All this happened because of Muhammad's pride that refused to recognise his own need for peace.

NEURO-LIMBIC TYPE THREE — ACHIEVERS

The Neuro-Limbic Type Three (NLT3) desires to be seen as a 'successful person' and so they tend to focus on achievement, on image and on what they produce. They seek to be seen as successful through a single-minded pursuit of an objective, through hard work, efficiency

FEELING

and competition. Looking good and the image of appearing successful are as important as success itself. They are focused on high-profile achievement. They will avoid failing at all costs.

The NLT3 assumes that people receive love and approval by achieving success, and they are rewarded by what they do and what they are perceived to have. Therefore, they are highly motivated and energetic at achieving their goals, and they constantly focus on the work that needs to be done. Their own positive self-esteem is based on personal productivity and winning. The NLT3 is an assertive profile in that it demands the attention and respect that it craves in social settings.

EMOTIONAL STATE

The NLT3 is formed when the chemicals produced in the amygdala are interpreted through the neocortex using I1 and P2.

The emotional state of the NLT3 is deceit. This involves maintaining an image of success in the eyes of others, and this image is more important than substance. The image of being a successful person can be tailored to suit what is most successful in different situations. Since they are always changing themselves to be consistent with the most successful image of whatever group or individual they are with, they deceive themselves and others. This can be expressed as 'just putting a little spin on the facts' or using charm and self-promotion. The NLT3 is an assertive profile because it moves against others and, in the face of stress, will expand their sense of self. To as great a degree as possible, NLT3s will find subtle ways to get positive regard from others so they will feel like the centre of the room, as if to say, 'Look at what I have achieved. Look at me and affirm my value.' The feeling is that anything meaningful that occurs in a social setting occurs because of them.

AS A CHILD

As children, NLT3s were generally affirmed and loved for what they achieved and what they produced rather than for who they were as a person. They came to the conclusion that projecting the image of success and achievement would attain recognition and praise. Therefore they learnt to cultivate an image of success, high performance, efficiency and hard work to ensure affirmation and love (Palmer, 1988).

AT THEIR WORST

The deceit of the NLT3 that is most easily seen is self-deceit. However, it is also the deception of others. Since the NLT3 is constantly changing themselves to be consistent with the most successful image of whatever group or individual they are participating with, they deceive themselves and others that they are actually what it is that they are doing. This deceit can manifest itself as simply putting one's best foot forward by just placing a little spin on the facts to sound good, charm or to self-promote. Deceit is a desire for approval measured by material success.

BODY SHAPE

The NLT3 is a tight and rigid shape. They are often quite strict with their diet and how they appear to be eating. They can over-exercise and under-eat to control their body composition. When they put on weight, they do so around their abdomen. They are often following low carbohydrate diets, which results in lowered awareness of how strong their P2 is. They are critical of their body shape, even if it is quite acceptable. Threes often feel that if they change their external appearance, their internal conflict will disappear (Diversi, 2006).

Cognitive Bias in Action:
HOW SOMEONE CAN BE SINCERELY WRONG WITH THIS NEURO-LIMBIC TYPE

Another story told by Greene & Elffers (1998, pp. 37-58) is of Thomas Edison, a prime example of NLT3. Much of Edison's fame was generated from the work and brains of others. A perfect example of how he stole the spotlight from others was the case of the Serbian scientist Nikola Tesla. As a young man, hired by Edison, Tesla worked like a slave on Edison's dynamo project. Tesla eventually offered to redesign the dynamos completely.

Edison was certain this could not be done, at least in the short term. He did not share these thoughts with Tesla; rather, he offered him fifty thousand dollars upon completion.

Nikola Tesla worked even harder than before and after only a year he had radically improved the dynamos, to a fully automated version. While Edison was very pleased with the improvements, he broke his promise, telling the young Serb, 'Tesla, you do not understand our American humour!' (Greene & Elffers, 1998, p. 57) Instead of the money, Edison offered him a small raise. But Edison was very pleased with the improvements and proceeded to take complete credit for their invention.

Tesla passionately pursued the creation of an alternative-current system (AC) for electricity. Thomas Edison felt that the existing direct-current system (DC) was all that was needed and so he not only refused to support Tesla's research but also tried to sabotage his work. When Tesla appeared to have succeeded in creating a system based on alternating current (AC), Edison became furious. Edison set out to try and ruin Tesla's reputation and to also discredit the AC system. He made it appear inherently unsafe and claimed that Tesla was irresponsible for promoting it.

It is known that to do this Thomas Edison captured all kinds of pets and proceeded to electrocute them with an AC current. When this wasn't enough, in 1890 he arranged for New York State prison authorities to organise the world's first execution by electrocution, using an AC current. Unfortunately, all of Edison's experiments had been conducted on small creatures and so the charge used on the man was too weak, and he was subjected to extreme pain rather than death. The prisoner had to be executed in a different way. It was a totally dreadful event and almost ruined Edison's reputation.

On another occasion, Edison was offered the Nobel prize for his inventions. When he found that he would need to share the prize and the spotlight with Tesla he said, 'I would rather no prize, than to share a prize with him!' And so his need to be the centre of attention made him turn down the Nobel prize.

Edison once stated that 'he did not need to be a mathematician since he could always hire one' (Greene & Elffers, 1998, p 58). He was skilful at being a businessman and at being a publicist but not as an inventor or scientist. His fame came from his need to be in the spotlight at any cost – even if it meant cheating, lying and stealing the ideas of other inventors.

NEURO-LIMBIC TYPE FOUR — ARTISTS

The Neuro-Limbic Type Four (NLT4) is a 'unique person' and focuses on being special and un-ordinary. They are absorbed in an emotional world. So emotional connection and relationships are important to the NLT4s, and they value highly the expression of authentic feelings. The NLT4 focuses on living a unique and extraordinary life, and they tend to long for the unobtainable, whatever that may be.

FEELING

The reason that NLT4s are drawn to deep connections is that they feel that they need to keep searching for an ideal love or for perfect circumstances to make them complete. The underlying assumption is that there is more to life than merely the ordinary. This means that they will be sensitive to emotions and feelings in others, and that they will experience intense feelings, from great joy to depression.

The NLT4s are a socially withdrawing profile because they tend to hide themselves in the hope that someone will discover and appreciate their uniqueness. While they want attention, they withdraw from social settings with the hope that someone will seek them out and appreciate them for being the unique creature that they feel themselves to be.

EMOTIONAL STATE

The NLT4 is formed when the chemicals released by the amygdala are interpreted through the neocortex through I1 and C2. This gives rise to the emotion of envy because they feel they have been denied the feelings of contentment and fulfilment that other people appear to experience. This envy fuels a search for the objects and status that supposedly make people satisfied. It also creates a cycle of desire, acquisition, disappointment and rejection as the NLT4 pulls for the unobtainable and pushes away when it comes within reach. This envy will arise in comparison to others, in competition with people for approval or through rivalry with those who claim the recognition that they want.

The NLT4 is focused on being unique and special, and responds to stress by moving away from engagement with the world and into an 'inner space' in their imagination. Their focus is on what is not in their lives: people who have disappointed them, let them down or left them; and on being slighted, rejected or abandoned. When a NLT4 enters a room, their sense of self is, 'I am not part of what is going on. I am not like these other people. I do not fit in.' They will then reinforce this position by being standoffish and aloof or acting in a detached fashion.

AS A CHILD

As children, the NLT4 experienced a deep personal loss or disconnection from a significant relationship. In the majority of instances, this would have been with the loss of parental love. This loss is a source of deep longing by the child who romanticises and idealises this unique relationship, while continually experiencing the melancholy of its loss. Some NLT4s report that as a result of a childhood sickness they were 'kept in cotton wool' and felt disconnected from relationships with their peers and siblings. As a result the child learnt to idealise and romanticise their relationships while longing for that ideal and unique relationship (Palmer, 1988).

AT THEIR WORST

At their worst the NLT4 will be completely driven by their envy. This results in a constant awareness that others have what is missing in their own life since envy manifests as dissatisfaction with one's current status in comparison with others. Envy can also manifest as an awareness of what else there is in the world that the NLT4 would like or need. Often it is accompanied by a sense of personal flaws or lacking. At their worst, the NLT4 will experience intense competition for approval and the symbols that represent it. This will have been observed in their seeking attention through beauty, drama, creative acts, unique perspectives and wilful behaviour. It will also be accompanied by rapidly changing mood swings, bouts of self-pity and dramatic expressions of anger.

BODY SHAPE

The NLT4's Intelligence Circuits are located in the head. Consequently, the NLT4 has little awareness of their body. They are either extremely thin or quite overweight. Keeping at either of these extremes allows the NLT4 to further satisfy their desire for uniqueness. Their face is shaped like an upside down triangle when they are thin, or big and round if they carry more weight (Diversi, 2006).

Cognitive Bias in Action:

HOW SOMEONE CAN BE SINCERELY WRONG WITH THIS NEURO-LIMBIC TYPE

Greene & Elffers (1998, pp. 55-79) tell a story, which exemplifies this profile, of Marie Gilbert of Ireland who arrived in Paris in the 1840s in order to make her fortune as a dancer and performer. Changing her name to Lola Montez she asserted that she was a flamenco dancer from Spain. Unfortunately for Lola her career languished and by 1845, in order to survive, she became a courtesan and quickly became one of the more successful in Paris.

There was only one man with enough influence and power to save Lola's dancing career—Alexandre Dujarier, the owner and operator of the largest circulating newspaper in France. Giving in to her envy for what she did not have, Lola was determined to woo and conquer Alexandre. To this end she investigated his habits, discovering that he habitually rode every day. A horse rider herself, Lola contrived to ride with him. From then on they rode together and eventually shared the same apartment.

Their happiness was complete. But only for a while, since envy can never be satisfied. Lola Montez began to resurrect her dancing career, with the help of Dujarier. Dujarier claimed that he would marry her in the spring. However, he was completely unaware that Lola had eloped at age nineteen with an Englishman, and had not divorced. Dujarier's life started to fall apart. His business fortunes turned against him and he lost his friends.

Lola began to see things in a new light. She was used to being pampered and showered with gifts. Why should a special person like her live such a dull life with an ordinary man? On the night of their very first quarrel, Dujarier attended a party alone. There he insulted an influential drama critic, Jean-Baptiste Rosemond de Beauvallon. The very next morning Beauvallon, one of the best pistol shots in France, challenged Dujarier to a duel. While Dujarier attempted to apologise, Beauvallon refused to accept and Alexandre Dujarier was shot and killed.

In a state of high melancholy, Lola left Paris.

In 1846 Lola Montez arrived in Munich, where she was determined to conquer King Ludwig of Bavaria. Again her envy caused her to look for the most powerful individual who could supply her needs. She set about her investigations and soon found that the best way to Ludwig was through his aide-de-camp, Count Otto von Rechberg, a flirtatious man. On a day when the count was having breakfast at an outdoor café, Lola rode by on her horse and was 'accidentally' thrown from the saddle at the feet of Rechberg. The count offered his assistance to the distressed Lola and quickly became ensnared by her. Rechberg promised to set up Lola with Ludwig.

An audience was arranged between the king and Lola, but when she arrived to meet him she could hear the king saying he was far too busy to entertain a favour-seeking foreigner. Refusing to be denied her catch, Lola thrust aside the sentries barring the king's presence and brazenly entered the room. In the process the front of her dress 'somehow' became ripped and to the astonishment of all, Lola's bare breasts were blatantly exposed. The king granted her an audience. Fifty-five hours later Lola began her career in Bavaria; while the reviews were terrible, Ludwig was undeterred and arranged more performances.

Ludwig described himself as being 'bewitched' by Lola. And while he had a reputation for being a miser, and he was not given to flights of fancy, he soon began to bestow all manner of gifts onto Lola and started to write poetry about her. Having conquered the most powerful man in the country, Lola began to lose her sense of proportion and started to act in a manner that made the Bavarian commoners despise her.

The very Bavarians who had previously loved their King began to show signs of outward disrespect towards him. Regardless, Lola was given the title of countess and she began to try her hand at politics, giving Ludwig advice on policy. Hers was the most powerful voice in the kingdom and she treated all the other ministers with complete contempt. Consequently, the once peaceful land erupted into riot. Bavaria was virtually in the grip of civil war, and students everywhere were chanting 'Raus mit Lola!'—*Out with Lola!*

Ludwig was forced to order Lola to leave Bavaria in February of 1848. For more than five weeks the Bavarians poured out their wrath against their formerly admired King. By March, Ludwig was forced to abdicate.

Lola then moved to England. Seeking respectability she was determined to capture George Trafford Heald, who had an army career and influential parents. This was despite still being legally married. While George was more than ten years younger than Lola he quickly fell under her spell and they married in 1849. Unfortunately, Lola was soon arrested on charges of bigamy, since she still had not divorced her first young husband. Rather than face trial Lola skipped bail and fled with Heald to Spain. Their time together was tempestuous, and they frequently quarrelled. On one occasion, Lola slashed George with a knife. In the end Lola thrust him away from her. This again indicates Lola's habit of creating drama for the sake of intensity, at someone else's expense. When George Heald came back to England he had no position in the army and was no longer welcome in society. So he moved to Portugal and lived in poverty until he died in a drunken boating accident.

By 1853, Lola was living in California where she married a man named Pat Hull. Again she experienced a stormy relationship until she finally left Hull for someone else. Hull also ended up depressed and alcoholic, and died of alcoholism four years later.

When she was forty-one, Lola gave away all her clothes, finery and possessions and turned to God. She began to tour America as a lecturer on religious topics. She dressed all in white and wore a headgear that was like a halo. Lola Montez died two years after she began lecturing, in 1861. As readers can see, there is no resolution or growth in the Neuro-Limbic Types. Lola had one strategy – to seek out what she felt she did not have—but all the money, power and beauty in the world could not scratch the itch created by the NLT4.

NEURO-LIMBIC TYPE FIVE — ANALYSTS

THINKING

The Neuro-Limbic Type Five (NLT5) is the 'wise person' who is highly observant and reflective. They use their observing and thinking as a way of ensuring an emotional separation from others and relationships. NLT5s tend to have a lifelong attachment to knowledge and value understanding highly. They have a special attraction to the secret and unexplained. They are described as maintaining an emotional distance from others, protecting their privacy, not getting involved, doing without and getting by on a minimum.

The reason that NLT5s withdraw into intellectualism is because they use this to protect themselves from intrusive demands and from being drained of their resources by becoming private and self-sufficient. The underlying assumption is that resources, both personal and physical, are in short supply. So NLT5s try to preserve their resources by becoming private and self-sufficient, while limiting their desires and accumulating a great deal of personal knowledge. The NLT5 is a withdrawing profile in that it seeks security by withdrawing from people or situations that are perceived as threatening.

EMOTIONAL STATE

The NLT5 is formed when the chemicals released by the amygdala are interpreted by the neocortex through I1. This gives rise to the emotion of avarice and a belief that there is scarcity in the world. Avarice manifests as a harbouring of resources— money, time, energy, food, the self – or an attention to minimising waste. It is often accompanied by a sense of superiority in getting by with the least of something; for example, the least amount of money spent on food, or the smallest heating bill in the winter. This avarice is not just financial stinginess; it can also be a withholding of time, love or interest. Avarice is the state of having a desire to take everything in, and an unwillingness to let anything go.

AS A CHILD

As children, NLT5s report that they experienced psychic intrusions into their life by adults who demanded too much and returned far too little. These intrusions were such that the child closed down their emotions in self-defence. A second, less common scenario is that the child felt abandoned and so closed down in order to survive (Palmer, 1988). As a result, the child sought to protect itself from these intrusions and feelings of inadequacy through privacy, self sufficiency, limiting desires and accumulating knowledge.

AT THEIR WORST

When they are at their worst the NLT5 is driven by the belief that there is scarcity in the world, wastage and a limited amount of resources. They respond with avarice which manifests as a harbouring of resources whatever they are: Money, time, energy, food, the self or an attention to minimising waste. There is often a sense of superiority associated with getting by with the least amount of something: the least heat in winter, the least spent on food and so on. They can become dominated by the need to hoard resources, either to avoid being controlled by others or to be used as power over others. At their worst, the NLT5 will follow a period of being generous which is designed to create dependence, with periods of stinginess and withholding.

BODY SHAPE

The Intelligence Circuit of the NLT5 is located in the head. As they detach themselves from others they also detach themselves from their body. They tend to skip meals and find this quite rewarding as they save money in doing this. A NLT5 is generally tall, thin with long limbs and a long torso (Diversi, 2006).

Cognitive Bias in Action:

HOW SOMEONE CAN BE SINCERELY WRONG WITH THIS NEURO-LIMBIC TYPE

Greene & Elffers (1998, pp. 337-338) tell the tale of the Duke and Duchess of Marlborough who lived in the early 18th Century, and who were highly esteemed by the English aristocracy of the day.

The Duke, having succeeded against the French, was considered to be one of England's greatest generals. Queen Anne rewarded him after the battle of Blenheim with a plot of land and resources to build himself a great palace. The project was awarded to John Vanbrugh, a young and flamboyant architect and dramatist, who intended to design a magnificent monument to the owner's brilliance and power. It would include grand features such as seen in the most extravagant houses in Europe. Right from the start there was absolutely no way to please the Duchess. She thought that the architect was wasting money on needless embellishments; all she wanted was for the palace to be completed as soon as possible for as little money as possible. This shows avarice.

The Duchess proceeded to interrogate Vanbrugh and his workmen over absolutely every detail. She was obsessed with the pettiest of issues; even though the government was paying for the palace she insisted on counting absolutely every penny. She justified this behaviour by using the excuse that she was saving the family fortune. Eventually, her penny-pinching attitude and controlling behaviour caused the Queen to lose patience and dismiss her from the court. On exit, the Duchess, driven by her meanness, stripped the apartment of every frill and fixture, right down to the doorknobs.

As the project slowly progressed, she made life miserable for all the workmen who had to bear her abuse for every stone that was used.

While the Duke only wanted to have his beautiful construction completed, his wife was so entrenched in meanness and control that the workers had to sue her to be paid. In the end the poor old man never got to sleep in his bed, as he died before his palace was finished. After the Duke's death, it was found that the obsession of the Duchess was unfounded. He had a large estate.

NEURO-LIMBIC TYPE SIX – LOYAL SCEPTICS

The Neuro-Limbic Type Six (NLT6) is the 'loyal person' in that they see themselves as being loyal, dutiful, and doing what they ought to do. They seek relationships with others or with organisations that can protect them and to which they can respond with loyalty and duty. The NLT6 focuses on gaining safety and avoiding harm through constant vigilance, questioning of motives and doubting.

THINKING

The reason that they express loyalty and desire security is that they assume that the world is a dangerous place and that you simply cannot trust other people. Therefore, the focus of attention is on danger and potential threats that must be avoided by constant vigilance and scanning of the environment. The NLT6 is a compliant profile in that they try to obey the internalised rules, principles and dictates that they have learned from childhood. They try to earn the security that they are seeking.

EMOTIONAL STATE

The emotion that dominates the NLT6 is fear and it runs the gamut of flight to fight (or from phobic to counter-phobic). The NLT6 uses P1 to interpret the emotional outputs of the amygdala. The compliant form is referred to as the phobic, and they will be very aware of their fear and will avoid the cause of it. In contrast, the counter-phobic will directly attack the very thing that they fear the most, but they have no awareness of their fear. Both strategies are formed around the emotional state of fear. The NLT6 spends a considerable amount of time preparing for the worst possible disasters, often thinking ahead to the worst-case scenarios and preparing for them. The need for absolute certainty frequently leads them to endless planning and considerable procrastination.

The NLT6 has a sense of being 'better than' other people through their affiliations and social identifications. For example, 'I live in Sydney, which is better than Brisbane and so I am better than people who live in Brisbane.' Since they seek security, they want to earn this security through personal displays of loyalty and displays of the power of their affiliations.

AS A CHILD

As children, NLT6s report that they experienced the world as a dangerous or fearful place. Often it was the result of unpredictable parents or siblings. The danger could have taken an emotional, intellectual or physical form. The child observed that the powerful figures in their world could not be depended on for protection and security. As a result the child sought protection by scanning the environment for danger, through thinking before acting, by doubting self and others and through an augmented imagination (Palmer, 1988).

AT THEIR WORST

The emotions of the NLT6 are manifested through the continuum of phobic to counter-phobic. The flight form of fear, through retreat or through compliance, is the phobic response while the confrontational and anti-authoritarian response is referred to as counter-phobic. While phobic NLT6s may be very present to their fear and seek to avoid it, the counter-phobic NLT6 has absolutely no idea that they are fearful because they attack anything that they fear, flying in the face of the most dangerous situations. At their worst the NLT6 spends a lot of time in preparation for possible disasters. They are often thinking ahead to the worst-case scenario and anticipating it. The need for absolute certainty leads to endless planning and procrastination on the part of the NLT6.

BODY SHAPE

The NLT6 is a soft and relaxed shape that is held low to the ground. Limbs are generally thin in relation to their torso and shoulders are rounded. In men, excess weight is stored in the lower half of the abdominal. As weight increases, limbs tend to remain thin yet the lower abdomen region continues to increase in size. In women, excess weight is stored around the hips. After the lower body, the area around the face is the next place to put on weight (Diversi, 2006).

Cognitive Bias in Action:
HOW SOMEONE CAN BE SINCERELY WRONG WITH THIS NEURO-LIMBIC TYPE

Greene & Elffers (1998, pp. 131-132) tell a story, which exemplifies this profile, about the first Emperor of China, Ch'in Shih Huang Ti (221-210 BC), who was the most powerful man in the world. While his empire was greater and more mighty than that of any other, and his conquest and leadership gave rise to a unified China, he devolved into paranoia and despite his might, became a recluse.

Ch'in Shih Huang Ti had conquered the provinces surrounding his own and created China through trickery and violence. He dismantled the ancient feudal system and, to keep his eye on the various members of the old royal families, he displaced 120,000 of them to a place within his reach.

As part of his unification and motivated by his fear, he created the Great Wall of China. He was so suspicious of organised religion that he outlawed Confucianism, which was an authoritative philosophy in the land. He even destroyed the books of Confucius' writing and executed his followers. But this was not enough to assuage his fears which were caused by the hatred he had engendered in his subjects. A contemporary of the Emperor wrote that 'Ch'in has been victorious for four generations, yet has lived in constant terror and apprehension of destruction' (Greene & Elffers, 1998, p. 131).

He lived in the most beautiful palace that had ever been built, and he had all the power he wanted, and yet his paranoia knew no bounds. Fearful of being seen by an assassin, he connected every room in the palace, sleeping in different rooms every night and beheading everyone who saw him.

In giving in to his fear and retreating deeper into the palace to protect himself, Ch'in Shih Huang Ti had slowly lost control of the empire. In the end self-imposed isolation and fears meant that political decisions often had to be made by his ministers. So in reality he was Emperor in name only. Ch'in Shih Huang Ti's fear of conspiracies led him to a position where he was constantly surrounded by conspirators, and was powerless to confront them.

In the end, Ch'in Shih Huang Ti had become so scared of human contact that when he needed to leave the palace he would travel in disguise. It was on one such occasion that he died, alone and far from his wives, his family, his friends, and his courtiers, accompanied only by a minister and a handful of eunuchs. His body was carried back to the capital with the cart packed with salted fish trailing behind it to cover up the smell of the rotting corpse. Even his death was to be hidden.

NEURO-LIMBIC TYPE SEVEN — EPICURES

The Neuro-Limbic Type Seven (NLT7) could be considered as a 'joyful person' since they are highly optimistic, imaginative, ever hopeful and orientated towards pleasure. They focus on future plans and pleasant possibilities as a way of escaping the limitations of boredom and pain.

THINKING

The NLT7 has a fascination with others, with themselves and with the natural world. They will plan optimistically for the future along with a series of alternatives in case the initial plan becomes difficult or uninteresting.

The basic assumption of the NLT7 is that the painful control of others and of events can be escaped through a fast moving mind that moves on to more pleasant options. Their attention goes to all alternative pleasurable options, to interrelationships and to pursuing happiness. They are an assertive profile because they feel that anything meaningful happens in relation to them and that something is going to happen because of them. When a NLT7 walks into a room they subconsciously think, 'Here I am! Things are going to be more lively now!' The NLT7 is convinced of their own excellence and they seek environments and people who will support their worth.

EMOTIONAL STATE

The NLT7 is formed when the chemicals released by the amygdala are interpreted by the neocortex through P2 and C1. This gives rise to the emotion of gluttony and a desire to experience in excess all the enjoyable experiences that life has to offer. Since they are focused on enjoying and experiencing life to its fullest, they try to move quickly from one thing to another. They will sample any experience, but not in depth, particularly if the experience could hold any emotional pain. A sense of absolute freedom without responsibility or commitment is the objective of this gluttony.

Since the NLT7 moves through life without any depth of experience, particularly those that may cause pain, they never learn from their mistakes. Ultimately, they create painful situations for themselves because they never develop the insight to break the patterns that would allow them to experience things more deeply.

AS A CHILD

As children, NLT7s typically report being happy and having an enjoyable childhood. These memories take on a storybook quality with very little suffering or bitterness. They were affirmed by their parents for being positive, enjoyable and optimistic, and discouraged for expressing pain or suffering. Sometimes a childhood is remembered as painful but the child's role was to be happy and optimistic. As a result the child developed a strong sense of self-worth and importance while focusing on pleasant options, optimistic outcomes, planning the future and avoiding pain and suffering (Palmer, 1988).

AT THEIR WORST

In the presence of being trapped or controlled the emotions of the NLT7 will force them to move quickly from one thing to another, sampling but never deepening any particular experience. This is particularly true if the experience could result in emotional pain. NLT7 manifests as gluttony for new, fun and enjoyable experiences. Life is like a smorgasbord and is experienced as a range of experiences rather than a single experience repeated often. At their worst, they will seek absolute freedom without responsibility or commitment.

BODY SHAPE

The NLT7 body shape is very random. Weight changes according to the gluttony of the moment. The NLT7 body size can increase or decrease very rapidly. The NLT7 can be very thin or very fat. When a NLT7 is in this space, it is very obvious to others that their weight is not right, being either too big or too thin (Diversi, 2006).

Cognitive Bias in Action:

HOW SOMEONE CAN BE SINCERELY WRONG WITH THIS NEURO-LIMBIC TYPE

This story from Greene & Elffers (1998, pp. 368-369) shows the pathology of this Neuro-Limbic Type. Marie-Antoinette married the heir-apparent to the French throne towards the end of the reign of Louis XV. The people welcomed her in anticipation of her reign. 'How fortunate,' she wrote her mother, 'to be in a position in which one can gain widespread affection at so little cost.' But she grew to take this affection for granted (Greene & Elffers, 1998, p. 368).

It was in 1774 that Louis XVI ascended the throne and the new Queen gave in to unending pleasures, extravagant gowns and jewellery, parties and fetes, without concerning herself who would foot the bill. Her search for pleasures and self-indulgence went so far that she created her own make-believe garden, where poverty and pain were absent. She had no interest in the plight of the French people, struggling under poverty and hardship. Of course, she neglected her duties to her subjects. In her egocentricity and conceit she believed it was not necessary for her to earn their respect and affection.

Once it became public knowledge about how much money Marie-Antoinette spent on jewels and dresses and masked dances, she was given the name 'Madame Deficit'. She became the focal point of the public's rapidly rising resentment.

The French Revolution started in 1789. The Queen was completely without fear. She is reported to have said, 'Let the people have their little rebellion. It will soon quiet down.' She believed that this was a minor interruption to her pleasurable life. But, of course, it wasn't. Both King and Queen were executed. Her pleasurable life came to an end without any sympathy from anyone. The unrepentant NLT7 went to the guillotine unchanged and possibly all the time planning her next party.

NEURO-LIMBIC TYPE EIGHT – THE BOSS

The Neuro-Limbic Type Eight (NLT8) could be considered the 'powerful person' as they are personally assertive and seek to control their immediate environment. The NLT8 focuses on being strong and powerful in response to an unjust world. They do this through control and dominance of their personal space and of the people within their sphere. They use confrontations with others to establish the truth, and they focus on the weaknesses of others and their own strengths in order to establish their control over their environment.

SOMATIC

The basic assumption is that any weakness will be used to control them – just as they try to use the weaknesses of others to control them. The reason that they are assertive is because they seek to protect themselves and others in order to gain respect while also hiding any weakness or vulnerability that may lead to betrayal and injustice. The focus of attention is outward and based around perceived power. NLT8 is an assertive profile in that it demands the autonomy that it seeks. They are very passionate about whatever they are doing.

EMOTIONAL STATE

The NLT8 is formed when the emergency chemicals secreted by the amygdala are interpreted by the neocortex through P2. This gives rise to the emotion of lust, as it is a desire for intensity in all things. Moderation is death, and if something is good, then they cannot have enough. With relationships they will be possessive towards friends and intimates, and will often try to take over. The lust for friendship has to do with camaraderie as they want to know that what is said is said in the spirit of friendship and they will be taken care of. Lust is a craving for satisfaction and when something desirable comes to mind, they are not particularly aware of the consequences of what they say or do. Once the goal is set, obstacles seem minimal and their task is to get what they want in the most expedient way possible. Intensity is created when the NLT8 believes that they are being taken advantage of. Intensity also creates a sense of speed and strength of will.

Since the NLT8 has a world view in which the strong survive and the weak do not, they have a deep suspicion of ambiguity or mixed messages because they see them as weak. Their desire to maintain control plays a part in their preoccupation with justice. The NLT8 applies pressure in order to discover people's real motivations, and their self-concept is as a defender of the weak.

AS A CHILD

NLT8s often report a combative childhood. In most cases the source of threat may have been physical and the NLT8 learnt that strength was respected while weakness was not. Often they perceived one parent as being strong and the other as being weak. The child was sometimes against the odds and the young NLT8 learnt to be self-reliant and to fight for justice. As a result they grew to depend on no one but themselves, to be strong or assertive and avoid vulnerability or weakness (Palmer, 1988).

AT THEIR WORST

At their worst the NLT8 will entertain an enormous lust for life. They will seek intensity in all things as the hallmark of a fulfilling life. If they enjoy something, then there can never be enough. They always want more. Moderation is death when the emotion of the NLT8 is high. Always they want more, better, faster, and louder. This sometimes leads to difficulty with people or friends who cannot 'keep up' with their energy. This intensity is used to control others through the creation of physical, material or emotional dependence. Intensity sorts out the strong from the weak. This Neuro-Limbic Type reports that most people fall into two categories – those that can't help being weak and those that can.

BODY SHAPE

The NLT8 body shape is large and muscular. Body weight is stored in the upper part of the body; their shoulders are broad and hips and bottom are generally small. Limbs are toned and the chest cavity is very thick. The face seems lean. For Eights who are not physically active, their weight is distributed in their upper abdominal region (Diversi, 2006).

Cognitive Bias in Action:

HOW SOMEONE CAN BE SINCERELY WRONG WITH THIS NEURO-LIMBIC TYPE

This Neuro-Limbic Type is exemplified in the life of Ivan the Terrible. Born in 1530, Ivan was only three when he inherited the Russian throne following his father's death. By the age of eight, he was an orphan. He was isolated and had only one friend, and was physically and emotionally abused by the Shuisky family, rivals to the throne.

It was around this time that his cruelty to both animals and people became evident. Not only was he a cruel man, it also gave him pleasure to see the pain of others. All this behaviour was driven by his anger, but was made excessive in expression by his passion and lust for life.

After his wife's death, Ivan's sense of cruelty and revenge against his perceived enemies was magnified. His moods oscillated between anger and hatred to piety and remorse. There were endless stories of his cruelty along with religious rituals that included sexual orgies, dismembering and mock piety.

In his state of mad rage, Ivan would not hesitate to burn a whole city and kill its citizens in the most bestial ways, as reported by eyewitness accounts of survivors.

Eventually Ivan killed his own son for defending his pregnant wife against his father's wrath.

Poisoned by mercury, Ivan died in a state of remorse, dressed in a monk's habit and re-christened, hoping for forgiveness of his sins.

NEURO-LIMBIC TYPE NINE — PEACEMAKERS

The Neuro-Limbic Type Nine (NLT9) is the 'peaceful person' as they have the stylised image that they are settled and relaxed. They are even-tempered, harmonious, relaxed, unflappable and unpretentious. The NLT9 focuses on being sensitive to others and their agendas as well as on keeping life comfortable and familiar. This

SOMATIC

leads to an avoidance of overt conflict and a tendency to accept the wishes of others by forgetting their own needs. Change is always postponed in order to avoid anger and separation.

The underlying assumption is that the world treats people as unimportant for what they are, and they are required to blend in as the way to experience a sense of comfort and belonging. As a consequence they will avoid conflict – not only avoiding becoming angry but also avoiding anything uncomfortable. This avoidance can manifest itself through a need to make the peace in every situation, and this will tend to be expressed as a soothing and peaceful environment. The NLT9 is a withdrawing profile as they will go into a safe and carefree inner sanctum in their minds rather than getting out of their imaginations and into action.

EMOTIONAL STATE

The NLT9 is formed when the chemicals secreted by the amygdala are interpreted by the neocortex through I1 and I2. This gives rise to much listening and absorbing but without discernment. This is referred to as sloth, and it alludes to the NLT9 being intellectually lazy. Decisions are difficult as Nines can see all sides of an issue. In particular, the slothfulness revolves around indecisiveness about personal priorities.

The NLT9 experiences anger and resentment over the feeling that they are being ignored. Since they try to avoid conflict, and any strong emotion is considered to give rise to conflict, the NLT9s try to suppress all personal emotions. They also have a strong fear of anger – their own or another person's – and of uncomfortable situations.

AS A CHILD

As children, NLT9s report that they felt overlooked or unheard. Usually they report that another sibling or a parent (or both) dominated the environment so completely that there was little room left for the NLT9. As a result the child learnt to know others' agendas better than their own. They learnt to forget themselves and to identify with others. The resentment and energy that arises at never being heard or acknowledged is diffused by the child into secondary or inessential pursuits and into a comfortable and predictable life (Palmer, 1988).

AT THEIR WORST

For the NLT9, at their worst they become very lazy about the important things that they have decided for themselves. This is particularly true if the thing that they have decided has any basis in building self-esteem or a sense of self-worth.

Their slothfulness takes the form of indecisiveness about personal priorities and positions. They avoid anger by minimising personal desire in favour of conflict minimisation. This behaviour often occurs as a feeling of being overwhelmed by life's details and distractions to the point where work on oneself is almost impossible. Finally, inertia plays a big part in keeping the NLT9 at their worst. This allows them to routinely continue doing whatever they are comfortable with to the exclusion of the tasks that may be emotionally unsettling.

BODY SHAPE

The NLT9 body shape is large and soft. Weight is distributed closer to the lower half of the body than the top half. Limbs are short and thick but not toned. The NLT9 moves very slowly and enjoys food and sleep; consequently their weight can increase very rapidly without them or others noticing too much. The NLT9 face collects extra fat along with the rest of the body (Diversi, 2006).

Cognitive Bias in Action:

HOW SOMEONE CAN BE SINCERELY WRONG WITH THIS NEURO-LIMBIC TYPE

Greene & Elffers (1998, pp. 9-11) tell the story of Michael III. Around 950 AD, Michael III became the Emperor of the Byzantine Empire. His ascension occurred after his mother, the Empress Theodora, had been banished to a nunnery, and her lover, Theoctistus, had been murdered. The conspiracy that placed Michael III on the throne had been orchestrated by his uncle Bardas. At a time when he was himself an inexperienced ruler and surrounded by intriguers, murderers and profligates, Michael needed someone experienced whom he could trust. Rather than face the difficult experience of becoming a ruler, he chose his best friend Basilius as his trusted advisor.

Basilius had absolutely no experience in government or in politics. His experience had been as the head of the royal stables, but he had proven his love and gratitude to Michael time and time again.

The two had met a few years before, when Michael had been visiting the stables just as a wild horse escaped control. A young groom from peasant Macedonian stock saved Michael's life. That groom was Basilius. It was his strength and courage that impressed Michael and that encouraged him to raise Basilius from obscurity to the position of head of the stables. Michael provided Basilius with countless gifts and favours and the two became inseparable companions. As a result of this patronage, Basilius received a formal education and was transformed into a polished courtier.

Once he was elevated to the position of Emperor, Michael ignored advice urging him to put his qualified uncle Bardas in the important position of chamberlain and chief councillor and instead installed Basilius. The Macedonian learned quickly and he was soon advising the Emperor on all matters of state. The only source of difficulty in the relationship seemed to be over money – Basilius never seemed to have enough.

When he saw the riches of the Byzantine court, Basilius became avaricious and demanded more and more money and perks. Michael repeatedly failed to be assertive in the face of these demands and pacified his trusted friend by granting his every wish.

Basilius even went so far as to convince Michael that his uncle Bardas, who was now head of the army, was a potential conspirator. He forced Michael to agree to have his uncle killed and finally, during a horse race, Basilius stabbed Bardas to death. Basilius then became the head of the army and controlled the government.

When Michael later got into financial difficulties, he asked Basilius to repay what he owed him. However, Basilius refused and, knowing that the Emperor had no real power or strength of character, he had him killed in his sleep.

Michael's inability to objectively assess the conflict implicit in the struggle of power with his friend, and to confront it, led him to his own death. Michael's life demonstrates that maintaining peace at any price is counterproductive and even catastrophic. Michael's passivity deprived the empire of a true successive monarch. Instead, the empire passed to another usurper and emotional manipulator.

APPLYING NEURO-LIMBIC TYPE INSIGHTS

Our task is to keep ourselves and those we work with in their amygdala *healthy* zone between having them energised and having amygdala moments. Too little engagement from the NLT and there is no energy. Too much NLT engagement and the individual goes into their NLT space, avoids the cerebral cortex and has an amygdala meltdown – or a *crunch*. Your task is to keep them in the middle, the *healthy* zone.

Toolbox

NLT1 (PERFECTIONIST) TOOLS

MANAGING YOURSELF AS A NLT1

- Try to model the behaviour that you want to see in others. Do not merely criticise others until they comply with your expectations.
- Appreciate that many of your comments will be taken as criticism, regardless of whether you see them that way.
- Consider the context of any criticism. While it may be appropriate for a specific behaviour, your context may be skewed and may ignore a great deal of relevant information.
- Aspire to your idealism but do not hold yourself and others to attaining it in every area of life.
- Develop realistic expectations for yourself.
- Appreciate and accept that making mistakes is part of the learning process.
- Learn what good enough means.
- Understand that people do not want to be judged. So if you insist on constantly offering criticism you will be shunned and avoided. This will seriously limit your career development.
- Do not adopt the position of moral champion; take a break from the job of policing everyone around you.
- You probably have a tendency to accept and comply blindly with the rules of other people and institutions.

(Adapted from Goldberg, 1999)

APPEALING TO NLT1 CONSUMERS

- Position the purchase as both thrifty and premium quality for money
- Allow time for careful consideration—the NLT1 views purchases as a form of investment for the family, so will want to make 'the right decision'
- Emphasise that the product is highly reliable and represents value for money

LIVING WITH NLT1S

- Be aware that the NLT1 can be stingy with what they own and what they earn, and can become personally isolated by the belief that individuals do not willingly share what they have
- Confirm moral character by adhering to a rigid system of personal improvement; this also creates the space for affection, love and support
- Be aware that the focal point of a NLT1's criticism can be just a reflection of whatever the NLT1 disapproves of in themselves
- Be aware that a NLT1 may not be giving you their whole emotional picture because they will not allow themselves to express 'inappropriate' emotions; consequentially they have a deep-rooted fear of becoming out of control and their suppressed feelings become magnified in importance.

(Palmer, 1995)

WORKING WITH NLT1S

DOS

✓ Do be neat. It counts for a great deal. This applies to both your person and your messages to the NLT1. They confuse the medium with the message or messenger.

✓ Do express yourself politely and with consideration. NLT1s believe in etiquette, so use socially polite words such as: 'please', 'thank you', and 'you are welcome'.

✓ Do be punctual. NLT1s are fixated on staying on schedule. If you make them late they are unlikely to quickly forgive or forget.

✓ Do admit your mistakes and genuinely apologise.

✓ Do play according to the organisation's rules. If you are in charge, explain how you want something done. If your superior is a NLT1, find the exact way they want it done and then do it that way.

✓ Do anticipate the problems in your own area of concern. A NLT1 will discount your contribution if you are not perceived as being able to find the likely problems in your own area of responsibility.

DON'TS

✗ Don't make generalizations. Be very, very specific about what you admit to doing wrong.

✗ Don't try to subvert the proper channels. They exist for the purpose of maintaining order and so must be adhered to.

✗ Don't disagree with a NLT1. Instead, present your argument in a 'what if' fashion.

✗ Don't offer criticism without providing a consistent objective framework for the criticism. NLT1s will want to know what rules they have violated – and they will want a copy of the rule book.

(Adapted from Goldberg, 1999)

Toolbox: NLT One

NLT2 (HELPERS) TOOLS

MANAGING YOURSELF AS A NLT2

- Turn your compassion onto yourself. Ask yourself, 'What are my real needs? Who really matters to me?' Take time to find out your own feelings, interests and desires.
- Allow people to, sometimes, solve their own problems.
- Appreciate that everyone else is not going to focus on meeting your needs. So asking for what you want may not be as humiliating as it seems.
- Ensure that you are performing the content component of your work as well as the interpersonal side.
- Learn to accept praise without discounting it.
- Learn to deal straight without manipulating. You may believe that you deserve special deals to match your special relationships, but this is actually not the case.

(Adapted from Goldberg, 1999)

APPEALING TO NLT2 CONSUMERS

- Create a relationship with the NLT2 buyer
- Position the purchase as a favourable treatment, as an indicator of the special buyer-seller relationship
- If they share efforts they are making on behalf of others, remind the NLT2 that they deserve little gifts at times; NLT2s often give themselves small impulse purchases to satisfy a fleeting fancy 'deserved' due to their efforts for others

LIVING WITH NLT2S

- Be aware that a NLT2 will look to others' wants, potentials and needs in return for approval, feeling proud of their helpfulness, and safety through being indispensable and having an 'unbreakable' special bond. Relationships then depend on what NLT2s will or will not give.
- Be aware that the NLT2 seeks to be attractive by adjusting their focus, taking on a partner's interests and sharing their tastes. They have a talent for making people feel good about themselves and can please very difficult people. Frequently a NLT2 will feel that they have many different selves, each matching the needs and desires of a specific relationship.

(Palmer, 1995).

WORKING WITH NLT2S

DOS

✓ Do provide a great deal of personal contact – face to face is best.

✓ Do be generous with your praise, approval and affection. They crave genuine admiration for their people skills and what they perceive as their own generosity. 'That is just what I needed!' 'Just the way I like it!' Imply that they have managed to satisfy your needs. A NLT2's lifeblood is emotional applause and they become vindictive when what they feel is owed them is withheld.

✓ Do speak from your own real needs without whining. NLT2s respond well to need as their need is to help others.

✓ Do be personal in your interactions. The best thing that you can say to a NLT2 is, 'I couldn't have done it without you.'

✓ Do find ways to make deposits in their favour bank and help them expand their sphere of influence.

DON'TS

✗ Don't embarrass them as they dread humiliation.

✗ Don't try to bully or lead a NLT2, as they are power mavens and will become vindictive.

✗ Don't try to reduce their socializing. That is how they energize themselves and even how they get their work done.

(Adapted from Goldberg, 1999)

NLT3 (ACHIEVERS) TOOLS

MANAGING YOURSELF AS A NLT3

- Recognise that success is not proof of virtue.
- Recognise that there is a difference between who you are and what you do, and learn to value both independently.
- Note your automatic tendency to take over, whether it is a good idea or not. Allow others to lead and see where they go.
- Take time in your schedule for other people—without an agenda or need for results!
- Develop the ability to tell the truth.
- Develop the capacity to make a personal connection with those around you.

(Adapted from Goldberg, 1999)

APPEALING TO NLT3 CONSUMERS

- Position the NLT3's purchase as efficient. The efficiency that they are looking for is given the amount of money that they have to spend, how can they make it stretch so they look their best.
- Present the good or service as helping the NLT3 to appear successful. They will want as many of these as they can afford.
- Use discounts, special rates or coupons whenever possible.
- Be aware that a NLT3 will be very interested in imitations of high quality products.
- Be aware that something of high quality that does not scream prestige is not as good as something of low quality that imitates success – particularly if it is cheaper.

LIVING WITH NLT3S

- Be aware that in relationships, the NLT3 becomes the prototype of what their mate finds attractive. They become the ideal lover or the attentive mate. Their emphasis is on form and surface. They can adopt the role model of whatever it is that their partner finds appealing, and in the process they deceive themselves that their appropriate feelings are actually genuine feelings.
- Be aware that this NLT has a tendency to view feelings as something to do. This involves seeing how others react and then pretending to have those feelings when they become appropriate. At times when, say, the emotion of love is called for then the NLT3 will adopt the facial expressions and body postures of love while their mind continues to focus on a list of things that requires doing. Since they expect to be loved for performance, the NLT3 will try very hard to do whatever the relationship requires. Unfortunately this can be a lie with no source of truth whatsoever.

(Palmer, 1995)

WORKING WITH NLT3S

DOS

✓ Do ensure that you are scheduled onto their list. They will be busy and so will need to include you amongst their things to get done.

✓ Do come straight to the point.

✓ Do deliver on what you promise. Since the NLT3 is committed, you should be as well. Doing is the area where NLT3s are most comfortable; so you must prove yourself in the area of their greatest concern.

✓ Do establish clear parameters that define success. Be explicit about what it is expected to be achieved and how performance will be measured.

✓ Do provide very clear and well defined feedback so that the NLT3 knows what is required and that their efforts are being noticed and acknowledged.

✓ Do provide short-range plans and deadlines or at least reasonable points that will provide feedback. NLT3s despise unclear expectations or responsibilities that do not have discernible boundaries.

DON'TS

✗ Don't waste a NLT3's time. Therefore be prepared and well organised for any meeting.

✗ Don't interrupt a NLT3 when they are engaged in an activity.

✗ Don't compete with a NLT3. Instead, collaborate for success together.

✗ Don't expect to receive emotional encouragement from a NLT3 for a job well done. A well-done job is the standard and need not be praised.

(Adapted from Goldberg, 1999)

NLT4 (ARTISTS) TOOLS

MANAGING YOURSELF AS A NLT4

- Do not give up. While despair shadows you, fight to see that everything is not actually a lost cause.
- Your feelings need not determine everything that you do. Learn to name them rather than just to be them. Convey emotions rather than being forced to act them out.
- Do not stew in your emotions if you can help it. Move your body instead – depression is linked to energy flow, to which movement is an appropriate means of changing it.
- Question yourself if you are ignoring a colleague's contribution because you have judged them as shallow.
- Do not confuse compromise with appropriate negotiations. The ability to collaborate and to factor in practical considerations can make your projects stronger.
- Not everything is completely personal.

(Adapted from Goldberg, 1999)

APPEALING TO NLT4 CONSUMERS

- Position the NLT4's purchase as reinforcing their own unique and special nature.
- Emphasise that the purchase is somehow completely different or un-replicable
- Be aware that NLT4s will make self-indulgent purchases to make up for the fact that no one seems to appreciate their uniqueness.
- Emphasise how what they are buying will reflect their own emotional journey.

LIVING WITH NLT4S

- Be aware that when a NLT4 feels that their heart has been touched by someone they have an impulse to follow those feelings and to abandon caution in the pursuit of having their emotional needs met. This deep requirement makes ordinary relating difficult since they want absolute emotional presence from a partner. They desire unwavering devotion, and they are highly concerned with abandonment.
- Be aware that the typical pattern of the NLT4 in relating is a push-pull pattern of attraction. They absolutely must have someone when they want them, they adore them, and they worship them. When they no longer want the individual, they reject them and become spiteful. The NLT4 distance themselves when others want them and then they start to crave attention and relationship when the partner begins to move away.

(Palmer, 1995).

WORKING WITH NLT4S

DOS

✓ Do allow the NLT4 to develop the end result. Provide them with a process, not just a rigid goal. Say, 'Paint me a picture' or 'Tell me the story,' not 'Just the facts please,' to allow the NLT4 to communicate important material.

✓ Do go out of your way to praise the NLT4 for their unique perspective and insight. While they may not need your help to feel special, they like being recognised for their uniqueness. If you want them to work hard and well, detail how a project requires their personal touch and how without their input it will fail.

✓ Do try to empathise with them rather than attempting to assist them.

✓ Do ensure that you communicate that their creative ideas have been received, understood and appreciated. This is everything to them.

✓ Do provide assurances of your commitment to them. A NLT4 will consistently be on the lookout for the possibility of abandonment.

DON'TS

✗ Don't try and use material incentives for a NLT4 to abandon their goal. This will go nowhere.

✗ Don't give them reason to feel abandoned.

✗ Don't minimise their feelings. This only makes them wrap themselves more tightly about their feelings.

✗ Don't presume that you know what will satisfy them. They must find their own motivation; all you can do is accept whatever this is.

✗ Don't try to give them an answer to their quandaries. Instead let them express themselves for however long this takes.

✗ Don't ask a NLT4 to lower their intensity. They equate this with being dishonest. A much better approach is to get them to widen their approach to include additional factors and information.

(Adapted from Goldberg, 1999)

NLT5 (ANALYSTS) TOOLS

MANAGING YOURSELF AS A NLT5

- In work you must collaborate to succeed. Try and find production-oriented people so that you can bring your ideas to life.
- Look for feedback about the effect your communications are having on others. While it may feel that you are offering helpful ideas or facts, others may perceive you as being a condescending and arrogant know-it-all.
- Express your opinion! Other people are not mind-readers.
- Risk expressing your position first. Let other people align with your ideas.
- Don't always play it safe and hide. Consider that the decision to make your opinion and feelings known might not be the best way to go.
- Get out of the habit of thinking about what you are going to say while another person is talking. Instead, listen to what they are saying.
- Assess your plans to see if you have considered the human factor at all. If you ignore it, then your projects will be less than successful.
- Recognise that there is a difference between secrecy and privacy. While it is appropriate to keep a great deal of yourself private, there is no need to keep everything secret.
- Let your colleagues know that you are actually part of the team and that you support its objectives.
- Be generous with what you have. Whenever you are, you are effectively nourishing yourself.
- Try to monitor the message that others are taking from your silences.
- Do nothing to excess – including moderation! Learn to spend a little.

(Adapted from Goldberg, 1999)

APPEALING TO NLT5 CONSUMERS

- Make information available about different products and services. Let them read this and compare aspects objectively in their own time without being pressured by a salesperson. Providing internet URLs with product details are great for this.
- Position the NLT5's purchase as cheap or cost effective. The key driver of the purchasing decision will be price. The NLT5 is very budget conscious.

LIVING WITH NLT5S

- Be aware that since their primary defence is detachment, NLT5s can find being in a relationship as dangerous, that doing without someone is easier than having them truly matter.
- Be aware that disengaging thought from feeling is a habitual manner of operating.

- Be aware that making a commitment that lasts for years disturbs private independence. It may be experienced as demanding, which causes a need to withdraw to think things through.
- Be aware that a NLT5 can be emotional when they are allowed freedom to express it in their way. They want emotional autonomy, so while you can be dependent and emotional, the NLT5 will not want to be drawn into those feelings.

(Palmer, 1995)

WORKING WITH NLT5S

DOS

✓ Do provide the NLT5 with insider information. They love it. They want that special piece of knowledge that will provide them with extra insight. Include as much supporting data as you can since the NLT5 will delight in the details. What you find as extremely trivial may be the central fact for a NLT5.

✓ Do appreciate that NLT5s find meetings very difficult. So allow them to be and feel prepared. Provide them with as much information before the meeting as you can: what is to be discussed, who will be there, what needs to be decided and what will be required of them. This final issue is the most crucial – they will want to know what it is that is required of them.

✓ If it is at all feasible, do allow the NLT5 to make decisions following the meeting rather than during the meeting.

✓ Do appreciate that a NLT5 absolutely requires privacy.

✓ Do make a private space when you are meeting with a NLT5, particularly if it is about a sensitive issue. Shut the door and hold the phone calls. Create a safe, bounded physical and emotional space in which the two of you can interact.

DON'TS

✗ Don't stray from the normal and agreed upon topics since the NLT5 may come to experience even normal questioning as cross-examinations. Be direct, precise and concise and, most importantly, do not pry.

✗ Don't try to fill every space in the conversation.

✗ Don't try to get a reaction from them. This will not occur.

(Adapted from Goldberg, 1999)

NLT6 (LOYAL SCEPTICS) TOOLS

MANAGING YOURSELF AS A NLT6

- Some NLT6s assume that their leader has all the answers and that they have none. They become completely compliant in order to avoid the constant doubting of no change authority. You must find your own inner sense of authority.
- Practise having confidence. When NLT6s look for ways to trust others, they will find them.
- Do not be afraid to play the role of devil's advocate. After all, it is what you do best anyway. You have developed formidable skill at cutting through pretense and exposing what will not work. Show where the problems and pitfalls are. Learn to give compliments; NLT6s tend to have a problem with gratitude.
- Define your own positive goals and focus on them just as much as on where you can go wrong.
- To avoid laying blame consistently, focus on the problem and not on the person.

(Adapted from Goldberg, 1999)

APPEALING TO NLT6 CONSUMERS

- Present the NLT6's purchase as safe and secure.
- Emphasise how the purchase is linked to highly respected and trustworthy institutions or brands that provide them with a sense that they are affiliated with powerful and worthy institutions.
- Emphasise the safety features of the purchase
- Provide assurances that the product or service will do what it says it will do.

LIVING WITH NLT6S

- Be aware of the NLT6 trust challenge. This can play out as being strong on ideas but weak on follow through. An initially interesting romance suddenly becomes doubtful, giving them a bind: if they proceed they will be hurt but if they do not then they will miss out. This double mindedness can present as ambivalent, unable to make a commitment, and wavering between doubt and belief even after commitment.
- In a long-term relationship, allow the NLT6 to air their concerns to build trust and to save their worries from becoming fact in their mind. With trust comes loyalty.

(Palmer, 1995)

WORKING WITH NLT6S

DOS

✓ Do strive to keep your explicit word. Nothing will help them more than their having a sense that you mean what you say, that you have integrity, and that you can be trusted.

✓ Do only commit to what you know you are capable of, and then ensure that you keep all aspects of the commitment. They focus on explicit congruence between what you say and what you do.

✓ Do make your allegiance clear. In their unconscious mind, the world is clearly split between the good (us) and the bad (them).

✓ Do disclose your self-interest as they like to know what is in it for you.

✓ Do intersperse the positives with negatives when you are communicating with them.

✓ Do restate reality. Be aware that you will need to assist a NLT6's memory and reality check.

✓ Do establish a clear plan with fall-back positions. The NLT6 does not like surprises. They want security and predictability.

✓ Do acknowledge the mistakes that you make without taking blame for what is not your fault. When the NLT6's considerations are out on the table, this is a good time for action.

✓ Do be straightforward about admitting when you are in trouble. NLT6s understand trouble; after all it is where they live.

DON'TS

✗ Don't expect to immediately earn trust. It will take a while for them to feel that they can trust you. Let them. It is very important to them to see that you keep all your agreements – particularly the small ones.

✗ Don't engage in win-lose arguments with a NLT6 about something that they have their mind made up over. There is no way that you can change their opinion. It is better to expand the discussion to include alternative ideas and additional people.

✗ Don't exaggerate. Just tell the story straight. They have a terrifying fear of being conned in some way.

✗ Don't order a NLT6 around. If you want a NLT6 to do something, share your thought processes and give reasons.

(Adapted from Goldberg, 1999)

NLT7 (EPICURES) TOOLS

MANAGING YOURSELF AS A NLT7

- Be sure to constantly ask yourself, 'What are the plausible negatives on this project?' Then find ways of dealing with them.
- Under-promise. NLT7s tend to over-promise because it gives them pleasure and they do not want to disappoint in the moment.
- Take small practical steps to bring your dreams into fruition – and then act on them.
- Learn to endure the consequences of your choices rather than simply changing paths midstream.
- Just because an idea has come into your head, it does not have to be expressed.
- Curb your tendency to make fun of people, to treat them carelessly, and to tell them to get over their problems and lighten up.
- Think about closure in advance.
- Be aware of your tendency to rationalise, to explain away failure and ethical violations without taking responsibility.
- Develop the skill of really listening rather than trying to think of something clever to say later.
- Work! Actually get your work completed rather than thinking about what else you could be doing.
- Practise mental sobriety. Do not just become drunk on ideas.

(Adapted from Goldberg, 1999)

APPEALING TO NLT7 CONSUMERS

- Encourage the NLT7 in their impulse buying by presenting the purchase as a new or fascinating product or service. The NLT7 is constantly looking for new experiences—any product or service that provides a new experience will be appreciated.
- Make the product or service, and its packaging appeal to the notion that the product or service is brand new, shiny, quirky or different.

LIVING WITH NLT7S

- Be aware that the NLT7 appears to be upbeat in relationships. Since they have difficulties staying with negative emotions, it is almost impossible for them to remain present and to feel bad. Their mind almost immediately moves onto positive options. They will try to find many different solutions and many exits before they reach the point of anger. In a relationship, it is difficult to pin them into a corner when they are trying to find a way out.
- Be aware that surface relationships can be a lot more fun than those that demand emotional engagement. But it is important for NLT7s to have relationships that are dedicated to real work.

(Palmer, 1995)

WORKING WITH NLT7S

DOS

✓ Do prepare for rapid give and take on issues. The NLT7 will talk fast and think fast. Keep in mind that this is just possibility talk, not actual commitment. If you want commitment then ensure that you get it in writing. A handshake and a smile is not sufficient.

✓ Do align with their dream. Let the NLT7 share their vision and enthusiasm with you. They will feel supported when another acknowledges their individuality, experimentation and creativity.

✓ Do ask lots of questions. The NLT7 loves hypothesizing and answering questions.

✓ Do share your problem with the NLT7 rather than internalizing it or judging them. NLT7s like being part of the process; what you see as a problem they may see as an interesting opportunity.

DON'TS

✗ Don't focus on small and picky details.

✗ Don't give the NLT7 too many options

✗ Don't let the NLT7 explain away failure and ethical violations - they need to take responsibility for their actions

✗ Don't let the NLT7 wriggle out of their commitments - encourage them to finish what they started

(Adapted from Goldberg, 1999)

Toolbox: NLT Seven

NLT8 (BOSS) TOOLS

MANAGING YOURSELF AS A NLT8

- Feeling as if someone is taking advantage of you is not the same as someone actually taking advantage of you. Check the details before you automatically retaliate.
- Choose your battles. Constantly ask yourself, 'Is this fight worth it?' Before you totally attack someone, ask yourself whether you are willing to deal with the consequences.
- For many people, your threats and tirades are not effective, no matter how much you may enjoy putting them on.
- When giving instructions, be very specific about the behaviour that will satisfy your expectations.
- Find ways to use others' talents and give them a sense of ownership and empowerment rather than just being a hired hand.

(Adapted from Goldberg, 1999)

APPEALING TO NLT8 CONSUMERS

- Present the good or service based on the motto that bigger is better. They want the biggest Ute, the loudest stereo system, the most of whatever they are purchasing.
- Don't emphasise quality, reliability or any form of restraint to make the NLT8 make a purchase. If they like something, then they will want a double serving of it.

LIVING WITH NLT8S

- Be aware that a main concern of the NLT8 is personal freedom, and they are often convinced that dependency can make them powerless. They will often confuse tenderness for dependency and so they can be inexperienced with the softer feelings of romance. The NLT8 tends to reinvigorate their relationships with conflict, activity, adventure or sex; yet they can be very sensitive to rejection in a relationship.
- Be aware that relating to a NLT8 requires confrontation. They feel they must test your limits. They have to know that it is safe to surrender control. Anger can erupt about trivial issues, since the central issue is actually power and the conflict is just a means to test who has it.

(Palmer, 1995)

WORKING WITH NLT8S

DOS

✓ Do ensure that you always turn up when you are required to.

✓ Do articulate yourself confidently. NLT8s appreciate news straight up and to the point. Do not waffle. Do not embellish.

✓ Do give the NLT8 your respect. They want respect for being a substantial figure, not a petty functionary.

✓ Do understand that if a NLT8 gives you a verbal tongue lashing, do not simply blast back. Standing up to them is different from raising the stakes, which gives the NLT8 no option but to try and annihilate them. Instead, acknowledge their power but also remind them of your own.

✓ Do provide explanations for problems in black and white terms. NLT8s have little tolerance for subtlety or philosophical context.

✓ Do you need this fight? If not, close the deal without that element. Ask yourself, 'Is this clause essential to the deal?' If it is, then explain to the NLT8 that it is a deal breaker and be prepared to back it up.

✓ Instead of holding on to your anger and resentment, do realise that they will always prefer that you tell them straight away when they are making mistakes or making you mad.

DON'TS

✗ Don't complain about the results. They do not want to hear your excuses—they want results.

✗ Withhold important information about the organisation or how they fit into it.

✗ Don't present wishy-washy information that changes as the argument evolves as this will be seen as a sign of weakness.

✗ Don't react passionately to cutting remarks by a NLT8 as this will be seen as emotional vulnerability and pounced on.

(Adapted from Goldberg, 1999)

NLT9 (PEACEMAKERS) TOOLS

MANAGING YOURSELF AS A NLT9

- Don't ask what you need to do next, rather ask what you need to finish next. Then go about finishing it.
- Write a mission statement for each of your projects to clarify where you are going and why. Do the same for your life.
- Learn to tolerate the discomfort of desire. Follow your passions and set personal goals for yourself.
- Don't leave less desirable options in play. Play them or eliminate them. Do not let decisions that can be made drag on.
- Ask yourself in each issue, 'Is it actually your issue, or have you unnecessarily taken on someone else's problem as your own?'
- Narrow your focus.
- State what you have to say without qualifying it or undermining it. When you hear yourself equivocating, stop. Learn to be specific and direct. And do not feel obliged to repeat yourself.
- Don't ignore your employee's requests for a decision. Sometimes they do in fact require real guidance.
- Don't give everything away. Own some of the credit, the authority, or the influence.

(Adapted from Goldberg, 1999)

APPEALING TO NLT9 CONSUMERS

- Present the goods or service as one that eases the pain of life by making the journey smoother.
- Position the purchase as a comfortable decision.

LIVING WITH NLT9S

- Be aware that the NLT9 seems to know other people's wishes much more clearly than they know their own. It is easier for them to step into someone else's shoes and to see through their eyes but difficult to decide for themselves. Having your own position means having to defend it, and this is so very rarely worth the effort or the risk of alienating those you love. The indecisiveness of a NLT9 can be a challenge for partners who are seeking leadership, since the NLT9 can so clearly see the arguments of both sides and so can come to no categorical conclusion.
- While the NLT9 may not know what they want they do know what they don't want. They don't want anything that will make them uncomfortable and so while they do not proffer positive options they will make their own desires felt by rejecting other options. If they feel they are being forced into a decision, the NLT9 will become stubborn. They control through non-action.

(Palmer, 1995)

WORKING WITH NLT9S

DOS

✓ Do understand that the NLT9 never makes fixed commitments as they are always filled with contingency. Confirm the decisions and then the follow up details that you want them to follow.

✓ Do establish very clear performance goals. They tend to get fuzzy and forgetful when it comes to agreements, so it is good to have them in writing. It is best if the NLT9 does the writing.

✓ Do listen for the NLT9 to convince themselves that they are not important, as this is one reason that they do not follow up very well. They need to be reminded that their assignments are important, that they themselves are important, and that other people will be disadvantaged if they do not do their job well.

✓ Do realise that asking a NLT9 for their opinion is one way to get them on board.

✓ Do provide NLT9s with regular meetings. NLT9s will not assert themselves to claim the time they need, but they do very well when they have your undivided attention.

DON'TS

✗ Don't mistake their silence for agreement.

✗ Don't take a yes for an answer either; they may not even know they do not mean it. Find out what they really think is possible.

✗ Don't present with any hint of pomposity or pretension. NLT9s hate this. They are naturally humble and want you to be as well.

✗ Don't allow disruptions to distract you when you meet with NLT9s. They will feel they are unimportant if you are distracted by a phone call or other interruptions.

(Adapted from Goldberg, 1999)

Toolbox: NLT Nine

SUMMARY OF CHAPTER 9: YOUR CAUSALITY PERSONALITY

- In the longer term, the chemicals that determine the Neuro-Limbic Types (NLTs) are physically damaging and lead to death.
- When the NLT is triggered it either moves against what is concerning them (P2), complies with the rules (P1), or moves away from what is concerning them (I1).
- Every one of us has access to one P2, one P1 and one I1 NLT.
- The NLT provides our Neuro-Rational Type with the motivation and energy to live a meaningful life.
- The task is to convert the Neuro-Limbic Type into a Neuro-Rational Type that can manifest noble qualities.

Principle #3:

Know Your Genius, and When and How to Use it

Key Concepts in this Section

- Memes as a map of consciousness
- Master personalities linked with higher attractor fields generate more energy
- We will all want to spend time where we are able to express our noble personality
- Individual nobility is driven by the tension generated by the meme
- Causality (Child) vs Adult Consciousness
- First-Order and Second-Order Judgements
- The Nine Levels of Consciousness
- Holons of Knowledge
- The Spiral Up
- The Spiral Down
- The Crusader
- The Bard
- The Chancellor
- The Commander
- The Architect
- The Navigator
- The Treasurer
- The Judge

Chapter 10

The Transition from Childhood to Adulthood

CAUSALITY CONSCIOUSNESS (CHILD) VERSUS ADULT CONSCIOUSNESS

During the development of our six Intelligences throughout our childhood we learn vital information that will help us navigate our way through the material world. This learning all takes place in the first order of causality consciousness. This is where we learn to react without even thinking (so that we can survive, since seconds can mean the difference between life or death in the game of survival).

But while all this development is taking place, where is the adult mind, essence, spirit or soul of the individual? Is our mind, spirit or soul developing at the same rate? Does such a thing as adult *mind* even exist or are we simply reacting like a child to the circumstances that find us?[1]

YOUR ADULT SELF EXISTS ONLY BECAUSE OF FREE WILL

Broadly speaking, there are two schools of thought about the mind (which we will define for the moment as your essence, spirit or soul) and matter (which we will define for the moment as your physical brain). At one extreme is materialism, which denies the existence of the mind and hence of free will. According to this school of thought the existence of a Higher Self is impossible.

The alternative position suggests the mind exists and is separate from the brain and, most importantly, it has the capacity to influence the brain. While there are many graduations in between these two positions, they are basically variations on the same theme.[2]

Before we go further we will spend a moment looking more closely at the

---

1   Before embarking on an exploration of the eight different Neuro-Rational Types it is necessary to have some understanding of current thinking on the mind and the meaning of consciousness.

2   We explore the eight schools of thought regarding consciousness later in the chapter..

implications of the materialist point of view.

THE MATERIALISM SCHOOL OF THOUGHT: LIFE AS A CHILD IN CAUSALITY CONSCIOUSNESS

Materialism posits that the brain is the determining factor of personal consciousness and that the mind is nothing more than brain states. This school of thought suggests that our subjective experience of reality is a mere by-product of the brain's physical activity. It is based on the concept that each different region of the physical brain has its own mental function. This model of the brain suggests that we ought to be able to find physical centres for the production of emotions and consciousness. As the philosopher Owen Flanagan puts it, "Mental processes are just brain processes," and understanding what those brain processes are, and how they work, tells us all there is to know about what mind is.

Materialism is built on classical physics and the rise of modern science which is largely attributable to Newton. Classical physics holds that the reality of the physical world is constituted of infinitesimal particles in a sea of space. Causation (in this scheme and at its very simplest) is about one particle's acting on its immediate neighbour which in turn acts on its neighbour, until something happens. Wholly deterministic natural laws govern the behaviour of matter.

This mechanistic but logical view—stimulus in, behaviour out—evolved into today's neurobiological model of how the mind works: neurotransmitter in, behaviour, thought or emotion out.

Unfortunately, this approach reduces human beings to automatons. The idea that the body and brain can be described without anything like a mind involved has important implications. For example, materialism would suggest that the notion that a person is morally responsible for their actions is quaint, if not scientifically naive. A machine cannot be held responsible for its actions. If our minds are unable to affect our behaviour, then surely we are no more responsible for our actions than a robot is.

So, under this model, our journey for Truth would be nothing more than a figment of our imagination, inspired by some past stimuli.

If the mysteries of the mind are reducible to physics and chemistry, then according to the neurobiologist Robert Doty:

Mind is but the babbling of a robot, chained ineluctably to crude causality.

Materialist thinkers have greatly influenced much of our modern thought and include highly influential names such as Hobbes, La Mettrie, Marx, Watson, B. F. Skinner, and Daniel Dennett. Their argument has become the consensus position of mainstream science: that mind, is, in essence, nothing but matter. Our subjective experience of that mind as something other than this is just an illusion. The argument is simply that the mind is entirely and completely derived from the brain's matter. It would seem to me that this is a world view with little hope and awe which destroys the idea of us being more than just a body—which is the most powerful and interesting part of the human condition. In fact, it condemns all of us to sad, grey lives of pointlessness.

BUT WE ARE MORE THAN A CHILD

NeuroPower argues a position described as Cartesian dualism which suggests that there is a higher adult tier of consciousness found in the mind which is quite separate to the brain but which influences the brain.[3] [4]

If you are to be more than the habitual survival patterns learned during the first six steps of development, it's helpful to believe that the mind exists quite separately from the brain and that the mind does have the capacity to exert influence over the body.

The French philosopher Descartes is one of the first on record to have suggested this dualist position. He argued the existence of two parallel yet separate domains of reality: *res extensa*, or the extended substance of the material world, and *res cogitans*, the thinking substance of the subjective mind whose essence is thought.

Descartes believed that all living things, including all 'brute animals' were just 'automata' or 'moving machines' that act, 'according to the disposition of their organs', just as a clock which is only composed of wheels and weights, is able to tell the hours and measure the time more correctly than we can with all our wisdom.

Descartes regarded the human brain as a machine, subject to mechanistic, deterministic rules, and the body as an automaton.

Mind, then, he defined as what the brain lacked. Mind was the observer, the witness, the Higher Self, the spirit, the soul, the part of you that knows there is a higher part of you. Of course, not everyone agrees.

THE GREAT DIVIDE

Right now there is a significant divide between the world of mind and the world of matter; that is, between the realm of the immaterial mind (which, according to the conventions of science, is probably illusionary) and the realm of the material brain (which is definitely real).

So prevalent is the materialistic position that it has become synonymous with science itself and I believe stands as the greatest barrier to the possibility of the

---

3   This perceived duality dissolves at very high levels of cognitive, emotional and spiritual development.

4   While materialists would argue that the mind is a function of the brain I have found it helpful for them to suspend judgement and see it as being separate to it from a therapeutic perspective.

scientific community raising its level of awareness and consciousness and ultimately, its understanding of how the world actually works. This is ironic because the physics on which materialism is based are about 100 years out of date.

One of the questions that plague materialists is how exactly an immaterial mind could act on something as fully tangible as a body. Physicist John Eccles suggests:

> *The essential feature of dualism is that the mind and brain are independent entities ... and that they interact by quantum physics.*

THE IMPACT OF QUANTUM PHYSICS ON THE MIND

In the early 1900s, quantum physics turned all previous physics on its head. Scientists have grappled with the strangeness of quantum thinking ever since and are still scratching their heads.

> *It is often stated that of all the theories proposed in this century, the silliest is quantum theory. In fact, some say that the only thing that quantum theory has going for it is that it is unquestionably correct.*
> **The physicist Michio Kaku (1995)**

This 'new' universe is one where quantum rule and the act of observation seems to have the power to determine physical 'reality'. For the quantum scientist the existence of 'mind' is required because the experiments show that reality coalesces around the act of observation. Let me explain.

In the quantum world, subatomic particles have no definite position until they are measured: the electron orbiting the nucleus of an atom is not the point-like particle we usually imagine but instead a cloud swathing the nucleus. Qualities such as the location, momentum, and other characteristics of particles can be described only by probabilities; nothing is certain until it is observed.

According to quantum physics it is the observer who decides which aspect of nature is to be probed, and reads the answer nature gives. The mind of the observer helps choose which of an uncountable number of possible realities comes into being. Placing attention on a specific question (is the electron here or there?) and making an observation (the electron is here!) corrals the wave of probability into a well-behaved quantum of certainty.

In other words, registering the observation in the mind of the observer somehow influences reality in the material world: the mental event collapses the wave function.

Pagels (1982) stated that, "There is no meaning to the objective existence of an electron at some point in space ... independent of any actual observation. The electron seems to spring into existence as a real object only when we observe it!"

THE QUANTUM ZENO EFFECT

In the Quantum Zeno Effect, physicists believe the questions one puts to nature have the power to influence the dynamic evolution of a system. Put another way, repeatedly spaced observations of a quantum property can freeze it in place forever.

In 1990, researchers at the American National Institute of Standards and Technology measured the probability that beryllium ions would decay from a high-energy to a low-energy state. As the number of measurements per unit of time increased, the probability of that energy transition fell; the beryllium atoms stayed in their initial, high-energy state because the scientists kept asking them, 'So, have you decayed yet?'

It would seem that the questions we ask determine the reality we see. So the truth we now know is based on the questions that we have asked ourselves in the past and the subsequent answers that we found. On a quantum level, repeated and closely spaced observations of a quantum property can freeze that property in place forever, or at least for much longer than it would otherwise stay if unwatched.

Neurobiologist Stapp (1993) states:

If the mere choice of which question is asked can influence the behaviour
of a system ...one's (own) behaviour could be influenced in this way
by focusing one's attention, if focusing attention corresponds
to specifying which question is posed.

OUR BRAIN FOLLOWS THE SAME RULES AS THE QUANTUM WORLD

If we apply this to the brain, neurobiologists have found that only stimuli that we focus on have the power to alter the neural structure of our brain. Interestingly, experiments have shown that the effort of directed attention alone can produce psychological changes in the brain equivalent to physically doing the activity.

THE INFLUENCE OF ATTENTION ON THE BRAIN

Neural researchers Recanzone, Merzenich and deCharms found that the patterns of activity of neurons in sensory areas can be altered by patterns of attention. They found that when adult owl monkeys were trained to pay attention to certain sounds, their auditory cortex expanded. When they were distracted by another task, and so were paying little or no attention to the tones piped into their ears, no such expansion occurred. Inputs that the monkeys failed to pay attention to, fail to produce long-term cortical changes while closely attended behaviours and inputs did. The monkey's physical brain changed when it changed its mind's focus of attention.

PRACTICE MAKES PERMANENT, BUT WHAT KIND OF PRACTICE?

Pascual-Leone, et al. (1995) had volunteers perform a five-finger piano exercise and a comparable group merely think about it. The ones thinking about it were to focus their attention on each finger in turn, essentially playing the simple piece in their head. The actual physical practice produced changes in each volunteer's motor cortex, as expected. But to the same degree the mental rehearsal did too. Pure mental imagery triggered synaptic changes at the cortical level. Physicists Merzenich and deCharms (1996) stated:

> *Experience coupled with attention leads to physical changes in the structure and future functioning of the nervous system ...*

> *This leaves us with a clear physiological fact ... moment by moment we choose and sculpt how our ever-changing minds will work, we choose who we will be the next moment in a very real sense, and these choices are left embossed in physical form in our material selves.*

Quantum physics suggests that our mind has the power to determine our physical health, emotional wholeness and level of insight. Of all the stimuli entering our brain, what our mind chooses to pay attention to will determine the physical neural trees in our brain.

Quantum physics requires the existence of a mind because reality does not coalesce from the probable to the actual until it is observed. Since our brain consists of quantum particles, it is itself coalesced around the observed fact. The mind is necessary to observe the quantum occurrences that make up the brain.

If events occur without our mind focusing on them, our brain does not register or respond to these stimuli. Furthermore, if we focus our attention on events in our imagination, this is the equivalent to physically doing the activity.

Mental force affects the brain by altering the wave functions of the atoms that make up the brain's ions, neurotransmitters, and synaptic vesicles. By a direct action of the mind, the brain is made to behave differently. How can a non-physical mind not made up of physical reality have an impact on the real world? Physicists have demonstrated that quantum effects[5] are not only real, but are even non-local in their range and capacity to have impact.

In infancy, at the first level of awareness, our mind focuses attention on reacting to external stimuli in a way that will best ensure our survival. When we do this, we are living according to the universe of causality. Because, at this level of consciousness, this is what your mind observes, this world of causality is manifested. For many, this reactive, habitual, survival-based behaviour of first-level awareness is never challenged. (This is complicated by the fact that the brain's fear system is controlled

---

5   The impact of the mind on the physical world.

by the amygdala which is much faster than the cortex or the mind. This is discussed further in Chapter 9 of this book.)

QUANTUM PHYSICS SUGGESTS WE ALL CREATE OUR WORLDS

There are two ways we can focus our attention: reactively or proactively. Charting the course and history of human development, social researchers and authors Cowan & Beck (1996) found that less than 1 per cent of the human population are engaged in proactively pursuing life in a manner that is responsibly free. The other 99 per cent of us simply react emotionally to life as it buffets against us—we are like a ship in a storm.

> *One of my favourite roles is coaching executive teams on leadership. One such group in NSW was running a government instrumentality that was going through difficult times.*
>
> *The organisation had been in its heyday about forty years earlier. The executive team saw themselves as a group of problem-solvers getting to work each day to solve the problems that popped up. Because this was their focus of attention, they were constantly pushed and pulled in a hundred different directions. The leadership team had no clear vision. The organisation was slowly falling apart with increased politics, conflict, waste and lack of engagement. The first step in the process of turning this group around was to explore the reality of quantum physics. Their focus of attention on solving problems was actually 'creating' problems. Once they accepted that their role was to focus the energy and attention of the organisation on an alternative reality—a vision—they had taken their very first step of leadership and many of the problems vanished.*

THE REACTIVE APPROACH TO LIFE (CAUSALITY, CHILD STATE)

In the ordinary course of a day many of us are unaware of our option to engage our mind's free will to influence the linear world of causality. Many of our movements are non-mindful and occur without direct conscious control. Habitual patterns of action are based on needs satisfaction (emotions) and survival and are heavily influenced by the chemicals produced by the amygdala.

I suspect that this primitive externally stimulated chemical reaction may explain more of our behaviour than we care to admit. When we are not consciously and mindfully engaged in the activity of creating our life we are in fact living reactively, emotionally and habitually. (These habitual patterns are detailed in Chapter 9.) It is our survival mechanisms that represent our greatest impediments to physis (growth) and our search for insight, wholeness and constructive somatic expression.

What's more, when a primitive chemical emotional reaction is set within your body, your mind's focus on the emotion ensures the manifestation of a tangible, two-dimensional personality. The emotion that arises as a result of an external event gives rise to reactive and habitual behaviour. The mind then justifies the reactive behaviour with a mental model of what has happened that is based on a highly partial understanding of truth. This reactive personality is trapped at the level of causality. Here's an example:

> Let's imagine that you are cut off in the traffic by another driver. Your immediate childish emotional reaction is anger and your physical reaction is to honk the horn and abuse the driver. In this situation, if your passenger were to ask why you were so angry, you may justify your behaviour with homilies about the importance of road rules and the rudeness of some people. In this situation, the causality personality has only emerged because the mind was allowed to focus on the rage and on manifesting this emotion with behaviour in the material world. In this situation you are a victim in the world of causality because no matter what happens you act habitually, which is outside your control. But there is an alternative.

THE BEHAVIOURAL DIFFERENCE BETWEEN MATERIALISM AND THE QUANTUM EFFECT ON PERSONALITY

The difference between leading a childish reactive and a proactive adult life is profound. Indeed, writers such as David Chalmers (1996) and Julian Jaynes (1976) espouse two separate states for conscious experiences that are substantially based on whether the individual experiencing consciousness is experiencing it from the 'materialist' position or from the 'quantum' approach. Chalmers refers to these two states as first-order and second-order judgements. In this model, second-order assessments incorporate all the inputs of the first-order judgements yet adhere to the 'quantum' view of life that enables the mind to exert influence over the brain. According to quantum physics there is an opportunity for the mind to throw a spanner in the brain's works and so escape causality.

TAKING THE PROACTIVE ADULT APPROACH TO LIFE IN ORDER TO MANIFEST YOUR HIGHER SELF

The alternative to being a reactive child is to adopt a proactive adult approach to life. This quantum shift assumes that your mind has the ability to influence the material world. This represents an embrace of physis and its drive to completeness.

In his groundbreaking work *Power versus Force*, Dr David Hawkins (1995) looks at the power of noble human qualities to influence the material world. He describes these qualities as the mind's powerful force-fields of intention. He refers to noble qualities, such as justice, enlightenment, peace and hope, as *attractor fields*. **These powerful attractor fields of intention have the ability to draw people to them and powerfully shape their behaviour and the material world in which they live. Hawkins' proposition is that true power to shape reality lies in our ability to proactively focus our attention on these powerful attractor fields.** The profound implications for our lives of attractor fields of intention are discussed in depth in

First-Order Reactions (Child)

First-order judgements are aware of emotional/thinking 'events' and react to them. This makes a 'materialistic' or causal connection between the stimuli and the responses. While the individual is aware of the contents of an experience, they are not aware of the experience itself. Chalmers equates this approach to that of a zombie that has all the aspects of being human but lacks the capacity for second-order thinking.

Let's imagine that this zombie is driving in traffic and is cut off by a rude driver. In this situation the zombie is aware of its environment and the sudden changes made to it by the rude driver. The zombie will respond to its environment from the stimulus in its environment (the rude driver) and its habitual responses (emotional or behavioural). In this case its emotional response is anger and its behavioural response may be to honk the horn and hurl abuse. The alternative to being one of the living dead is found in making second-order judgements.

Second-Order Responses (Adult)

Second-order thinking is also aware of the emotional/thinking 'events' but considers them prior to making a judgement. The fundamental difference is that second-order consciousness is consciously aware of the stimuli that are occurring in the environment and determines its behaviour independently of this.

In the example of the rude driver, while a second-order thinker would become angry they would be aware of the source of the anger and that it is their habitual response, but have the option of choosing a range of other creative responses.

Free will only exists in second-order thinking. First-order thinking is trapped in a materialist world that is causally closed and prevents the individual emotionally and behaviourally from escaping the constraints of their environment.

Chapter 19.

The alternative to the quantum approach is to focus our mind's attention on our reactive emotional patterns that maintain reliance on the force of personality to survive. Force of this nature leads to seeing all other humans as either competition or food.

Your personality can manifest around your reactive, emotional reactions, that is, fight, flight or freeze (these are the Neuro-Limbic Types locked in causality) or alternatively around your responsive noble Higher Self, your second-order Master Neuro-Rational Type (NRT).

Your Master personality can manifest a noble quality which forms a powerful attractor field. Each of these noble qualities has a corresponding emotion and a mental framework, which, if given mental attention, will manifest into a noble Higher Self.

When these eight Master Neuro-Rational Types are arranged in similar pairs, each pair has a particular world view which aligns with what has been described by Ken Wilber as the *Four Faces of Truth* outlined in Appendix 6.

A Closer Look at the Nature of the Mind's Adult Development and Adult Consciousness

What is adult consciousness? What does it mean for the mind to be aware of experience? Take, for example, our consciousness of colour. How would you convey the awareness of a colour to someone who has never had a similar experience? How would you convey the experience of shape, of size and textured light that constitutes visual experiences?

Consider the awareness of a comatose patient. They lie in a deep coma, unable to interact with the environment in any manner (with the possible exception of instinctual motor skills such as having their eyes follow a light). We could consider the coma patient is not conscious because they are neither aware of, nor able to influence their environment.

But if there were another patient in the same room who was aware of their environment but who had suffered a stroke that rendered them incapable of memory recall, would they be conscious? While they would have the capacity to interact with their immediate environment, they would have a very limited sense of awareness about the elements that constitute their environment. So if their condition were explained to them it would be as if they were discussing it for the first time. In this case, their awareness would extend only to the immediate environment with little or no capacity to develop an understanding of cause and effect. They would be considered conscious—but not to a very high degree. This suggests that the mind's consciousness is not just an on/off switch but it is variable—it has a volume control. If this were the case, and *NeuroPower* argues that it is, an individual's level of consciousness would have a significant impact on their adult personality and so it is important to explore this area more fully.

The nature of adult consciousness fascinates psychologists, theologians and philosophers alike. Julian Jaynes, in his impactful work *The Origin of Consciousness in The Breakdown of the Bicameral Mind* (1976, pp. 10-18) postulates that there are eight general schools of thought. To give readers context in this area of philosophy, his descriptions are briefly summarised below, with some of my additional analysis and comments. The ninth point summarises the *NeuroPower* perspective on consciousness.

1. THE HELPLESS SPECTATOR SCHOOL:

This school argues that consciousness does nothing at all, and can do absolutely nothing. Animals are evolving nervous systems and their mechanical reflexes increase in complexity as they evolve. At a certain unspecified point, sufficient nervous complexity is reached to create consciousness. Every conscious experience is no more than a result of the complex wiring of the brain and its reflexes to external stimuli. 'We are conscious automata' according to Huxley (Huxley: Jaynes, 1990, p. 10).

- Consciousness cannot impact on either the body or the environment.
- There can be no development in consciousness as it is intimately connected to the physical stimuli presented to it.
- Consciousness does not actually exist as an active agent in the world.

This position is the endpoint of a purely evolutionary perspective and is a version of the materialist position, which I believe is a bleak and inaccurate school of thought.

2. THE EMERGENT EVOLUTION SCHOOL:

Just as the property of wetness cannot be derived from the properties of hydrogen and oxygen alone, so consciousness formed at some stage in evolution is not reducible to its constituent parts.

The Biology of Consciousness

Scientists agree that consciousness is an emergent property of the human mind, but there has been significant debate about the precise timing, location and dynamics of the neurological correlates of conscious perception. Recent research using intra-cerebral electrophysiological recordings suggests that there is no one single marker or 'seat' of consciousness—instead, activity is spread throughout the brain. This suggests that consciousness is more related to dynamic interactions in the brain than specific local activity (Gaillard et al, 2009).

- Consciousness is no longer merely a brain by-product, but a result of evolution.
- Consciousness can influence both the brain and the body.
- Conscious development is a function of evolutionary development.

This position acknowledges the existence of consciousness and simply argues it cannot be dissected to be understood.

3. BEHAVIOURISM SCHOOL:

This asserts that consciousness is nothing at all. All actions and interactions are reduced to simply stimulus and response. Nothing more exists.

- Not only is there no conscious development, there is no capacity for consciousness to exist at all.

This is the clearest articulation of the materialist position and aggressively argues that *mind* simply does not exist which, once again, I believe is fundamentally and obviously inaccurate.

4. CONSCIOUSNESS AS A PROPERTY OF MATTER SCHOOL:

The series of subjective states that we experience in introspection has a property fundamental to all interacting matter. The relationship of consciousness to what we are conscious of is not fundamentally different from the relationship of a tree to the ground in which it is rooted, or even of the gravitational relationship between two bodies. This is the broadest concept of consciousness.

- Consciousness is derived from existence, and is an awareness of the role and relationship our existence has in the world.
- As our awareness grows, our understanding of our impact in the environment grows.

This suggests an energy or awareness without intention. While this position may be partially accurate, without a role for intention it has missed the point.

5. CONSCIOUSNESS AS A PROPERTY OF PROTOPLASM[6] SCHOOL:

Consciousness is not in matter as such, but it is the fundamental property of every living thing. It is seen in the irritability that a single celled organism displays to stimuli, to the actions of amoebas hunting food, right up to humans foraging.

- It is a function of our consciousness that we identify with and imagine the feelings of other organisms.

I believe this position is accurate but too general to be useful to our discussion of human potential.

---

6   The living matter of all vegetable and animal cells and tissues.

6. CONSCIOUSNESS AS LEARNING SCHOOL:

Consciousness became linked to associative memory or learning. If an animal could modify its behaviour on the basis of its experience, it must be conscious.

While the point is accurate, awareness of the environment is itself not sufficient to constitute consciousness. Learning and consciousness are two distinct concepts in that you can have memory and learning in the materialism school without consciousness.

7. CONSCIOUSNESS AS THE RETICULAR ACTIVATING SYSTEM SCHOOL:

This theory puts consciousness as a function of the brain that can be scientifically identified. Consciousness is merely a function of different systems that operate in the nervous system, and one that evolved at some point in development.

This is effectively the same position as the helpless spectator theory. The reticular activating system has turned out to be one of the older parts of the brain, not the seat of consciousness at all.

8. CONSCIOUSNESS AS A METAPHYSICAL IMPOSITION SCHOOL:

While the majority of theories assume that consciousness has evolved as a biological function, this theory denies that such an assumption is even possible and posits that an external force created consciousness in humanity. Alone of all species we try to understand ourselves. The difference between ourselves and our nearest animal kin is vast and is attributable to human consciousness.

- Consciousness is not a function of our environment or our experience. It is both external to us, and something that is given to us. It is not earned.

I believe this is true but partial. We need to know more than this if we are to understand and even develop our consciousness.

9. THE NEUROPOWER SCHOOL OF CONSCIOUSNESS:

NeuroPower embraces a ninth position that draws together many of the idea fragments and themes of the other eight positions. Developmental psychology is the study of the growth and development of the mind—the study of the internal and external expansion of consciousness. Psycho-emotional development presumes that consciousness goes through stages of growth and can exist at different degrees of development. These developmental stages are reflected in both an individual and a society.

- Consciousness has a 'volume knob' of awareness that is turned up as an individual or a society develops. The 'loudness' of this knob is tracked by psycho-emotional development.

Spiral Dynamics[7] is one psycho-emotional model that is widely used in the

---

7 Based on the lifelong work of psychologist Clare Graves and research conducted on more than 50,000 people.

Table 10.1   Developmental Models

Age and Stage (Piaget)	Individual Development	Social Equivalent
0 to 2 years Sensorimotor	An infant progresses from reflexive, instinctual action at birth to the beginning of symbolic thought. The infant constructs an understanding of the world by coordinating sensory experiences with physical actions.	Nomadic Tribes—The tenuous nature of existence does not allow the focus of attention to rise from anything other than through instinctual behaviour.
2 to 7 years Preoperational	The child begins to represent the world with words and images; these words and images reflect increased symbolic thinking and go beyond the connection of sensory information and physical action.	As people start congregating together, they form City States in ancient Samaria and in Ancient Greece—Athens and Sparta. These City States can start to establish formal centres of learning.
7 to 11 years Concrete operational	The child can now reason logically about concrete events and classify objects into different sets.	As City States collude or become amalgamated, they form Empires. Consider the Empires of Ancient Greece and Rome. The wealth and power they wrought for themselves enabled them to disperse the knowledge that they accumulated for themselves.
11 to 15 years Formal operational	The adolescent reasons in more abstract and logical ways. Thought is more idealistic.	In our Modern Nation States we have sufficient resources to strive for idealistic conditions for all members of our nation.

commercial environment and which has been validated quantitatively by US researchers Clare Graves, Don Beck and Christopher Cowan. This model details the progression and development of the individual's internal focus of attention and the corresponding external persona and behavioural characteristics as the individual moves from a basic thought to a more complete and complex higher level of thought.[8]

The NeuroPower framework argues that the physiological and socio-emotional development of an individual is a fractal representation of sociological development. The process of growth development experienced by an individual follows the same pattern as the growth and development of a society at large. Individual awareness

---

8   The NeuroPower framework argues that if an individual integrates this level of mutual complexity with emotional wholeness and constructive somatic expression, Spiral Dynamics is an accurate model to describe the different levels of consciousness.

expands through a clear series of steps and stages, each of which builds on the previous one.

Various developmental models have empirically established broad categories of growth through which children move. One of the founders of childhood development, Jean Piaget, postulated that we move through four stages of understanding the world. Each of these stages is age-related and consists of distinct ways of thinking that involve qualitatively different styles of cognitive processing. Social development follows a broadly similar path. These similarities are shown in Table 10.1

INTRODUCING THE TERM 'MEME'

Spiral Dynamics refers to each of these basic stages of adult development as *memes*. The term meme was first introduced by Richard Dawkins (*The Selfish Gene, 1976*) who abbreviated the Greek root, *mimeme*, to describe a unit of cultural information. Examples of memes include: a particular political ideology, a fashion trend, language usage, musical forms, or even architectural styles. Memes are born when an individual reacts to an experience (Csikszentmihalyi, 1990).

These memes are equivalent to core intelligences that lie below our values, beliefs and ethical structures. There are a number of memes, each reflecting the development of increased cognitive capacity and higher levels of consciousness if appropriately integrated emotionally and somatically. This model of consciousness convincingly argues that what biochemical genes are to the DNA, memes are to our psycho-cultural DNA. Genes are the information units of our physical nature derived from genetic contributions inherited from our species. Similarly, memes are information units in our collective consciousness that transport their views across our minds and influence everything we see as important. It is as if these memes hypnotise us into seeing the world in a particular way.

In particular, these memes influence the questions of existence that surround and support the values, beliefs and ethical structures of that level of consciousness or with that world view. They contain behavioural instructions that are passed from one generation to the next. These are social artefacts and value-laden symbols that glue together social systems. The memes stack on one another so that the higher memes encompass the lower and express them with greater degrees of integration.

There is a tendency for the memes to move from group focus to personal focus: see Diagram 10.4. Like an intellectual virus, a meme reproduces itself through concepts such as dress styles, language trends, popular cultural norms, architectural designs, art forms, religious expressions, social movements, economic models, and moral statements about how living should be done.

Personal development can therefore be defined as involving the awakening of, guidance of, and learning to express memes in healthy forms at appropriate times. The problems that individuals perceive they are facing are often problems embedded in the meme, or level of consciousness, at which the person exists. This even suggests that personal development may be synonymous with the development of consciousness.

As you can imagine, many of the conflicts both at work and at home are conflicts between individuals at different memes. Interestingly, the same individual can coexist in numerous memes at the same time. Their relationships could be at one meme while financially they are at another. It is valuable to identify which memes have the greatest influence in the most significant areas of your life so that you can be aware of inevitable internal conflicts and you can deal with them in a constructive way.

The school of thought that embraces this view of evolving consciousness argues that the objective of life is to focus your attention on answering the questions of existence of the meme that underpins your current world view. Until these questions are answered, you are locked at that level of partial awareness. Psychologist Clare Graves observed:

> When a person is centralized within one state of existence (meme), he or she has a psychology that is particular to that state. His or her feelings, motivations, ethics and values, biochemistry, degree of neurological activation, learning system, belief systems, conception of mental health, ideas as to what mental illness is and how it should be treated, conceptions of and preferences for management, education, economics, and political theory and practice are all appropriate to that state.

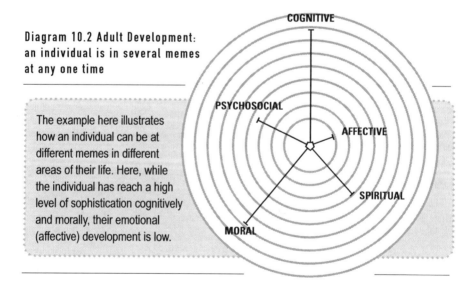

Diagram 10.2 Adult Development: an individual is in several memes at any one time

The example here illustrates how an individual can be at different memes in different areas of their life. Here, while the individual has reach a high level of sophistication cognitively and morally, their emotional (affective) development is low.

COGNITIVE
PSYCHOSOCIAL
AFFECTIVE
SPIRITUAL
MORAL

Your adult responses and world view will be built meme by meme on the answers found at each level of consciousness. Graves' research suggests that there are nine major memes through which people move in sequence.

The first six memes are referred to as the *First Tier* for a number of reasons; the primary reason is that they are exclusionary and not integratory in nature. The last three memes are referred to as the *Second Tier* and they experience vastly different cognitive, spiritual and emotional aspects from those in the First Tier.

These memes are not rigid levels but represent fluid internal waves, where there is a great deal of internal overlap and interweaving. Every individual lives at a number of memes simultaneously.

Development of consciousness is a messy business, yet it also follows a linear sequence where each stage builds on the previous one. While each meme contains intrinsic validity, the higher memes represent more complexity and are able to resolve more complex issues.

Interestingly, each time we move forward in the spiral, the complexity in the world increases, and our cognitive capacity to handle it also seems to increase. A good metaphor for Spiral Dynamics is that each and every meme represents a different form of mental software that gets uploaded into our mind when our dominant world conditions change. At each phase of development, a higher-order structure—more complex and therefore more integrated and unified—is built on the lower, less complex beliefs. Our philosophical towers are built on philosophical foundations.

As we have seen, the different memes give rise to different questions of existence. Each meme is a world unto itself and faces distinct issues that need to be resolved, each with its own sense of morality and priority. The process of moving through each meme is referred to as building a holon[9] of knowledge.

HOLONS OF KNOWLEDGE

Holons organise into a natural hierarchy or a simple order of increasing wholeness. The whole at one level becomes a part of the next and the entire structure can be referred to as a holarchy. Each emergent level in the holarchy includes and yet transcends its former levels. Such nested hierarchies are developmental in nature. All human and social organisations and institutions can be referred to as holarchies. For example, organisations include departments/divisions that include service/production branches that include work sectors that include work teams that include individual workers.

As an adult moves through the spiral, their identity emerges by first differentiating from the preceding, lower meme. This higher-order holarchy becomes more

---

9   Arthur Koestler first developed a theory of holons to describe the relationship between entities in biological and social hierarchies. The intention was to bring together the insights and strengths of both reductionist and holistic approaches to analysing social events.

Diagram 10.3 Focus of Attention of the Memes*

CORAL: COMPLETENESS
Whole. Total perspective.

Second Tier

TURQUOISE: ENCOMPASSING TRUTH
Holistic. World is one big system.

YELLOW: INDIVIDUAL INTEGRATED KNOWLEDGE
Integrative. Life is a series of natural order, flexibility, spontaneity and functionality.

C2

I1

GREEN: COLLECTIVE HARMONY
Communal Connection. Human bonding. Ecological sensitivity. Spirit freed from dogma and greed.

I2

ORANGE: PERSONAL SUCCESS
Personal Success. Analyse and strategise to prosper. Achievement orientated. Life is a game.

P2

BLUE: SUBLIMATION OF INSTINCTS
Instinctual Control. Instincts suppress for 'worthy cause/higher order'. Sacrifice for purpose. Meaning and direction. Structure, order and discipline.

First Tier

RED: EXPRESSION OF INSTINCTS
Personal Identity. Individual expression. Satisfy immediate personal inclinations. Powerful, impulsive, egocentric, heroic.

C1

PURPLE: COMMUNAL SURVIVAL
Communal Living. Drive towards collective survival. Focuses on performing rituals to ensure perpetuity. Animistic and magical world.

BEIGE: INDIVIDUAL SURVIVAL
Survival. Instinctual drive towards personal survival. Focuses on ensuring immediate needs met, food, water, warmth, sex and safety.

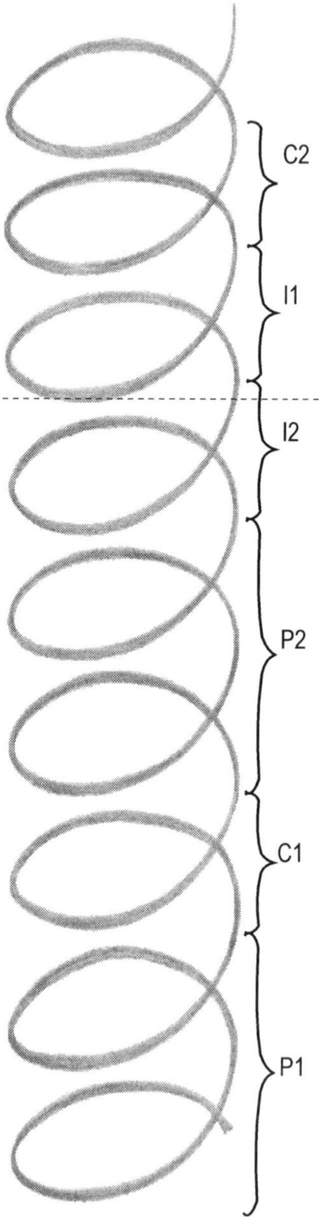

P1

---

* Refer to *Description of the Nine Levels of Adult Development* in this chapter.

organised and self-regulating and eventually the new identity becomes stabilised and incorporates all the knowledge of the preceding memes. A fully developed personality depends on lower memes being healthy. This broadly describes what happens when we move from one level of consciousness to the next.

According to the US philosopher and writer Ken Wilber, 'Reality is composed neither of things or processes, neither wholes nor parts, but whole/parts, or holons— all the way up, all the way down.'

UNDERSTANDING HOLONS EXPLAINS BEHAVIOUR OF PEOPLE, TEAMS AND ORGANISATIONS

All holons, according to Wilber, have common patterns or tenets. Knowledge of these patterns can help us to better understand people, teams and organisations. All holons have two basic drives: *agency* (P2) and *communion* (P1). These drives are aimed at maintaining both their wholeness and their partness. Agency is the drive towards autonomy, the desire for independence, and the will to preserve its own wholeness in the face of pressure from the environment that would otherwise destroy it. This can also be seen as the drive to survive, to achieve or accomplish tasks

Diagram 10.4 Development Progression

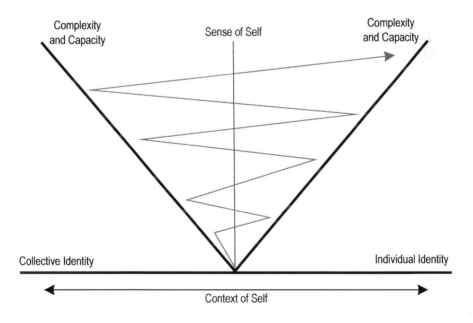

(Wilber, 2000).

Communion is the drive to maintain partness, to be part of a larger whole. This is often described as the drive or the need for interdependence, for losing oneself into, bonding, or relating with another. So at each level of consciousness or meme an individual or group has an inner drive to be both separate and a part of the larger group (Wilber, 2000). See Appendix 8 for a more complete explanation.

The primary drives of agency and communion are expressed internally (I2) and externally (I1). This can be seen clearly from a biological perspective. The separate organs of the lung or the heart represent internal agency, while internal communion can be seen in the combinations of different organs to make up the respiratory system. Without internal communion, the individual will die; without internal agency, none of the systems will function and the organism will die.

The external agency of an individual represents the work they do to provide for themselves, the manner in which their labours provide for their needs. The external communion is their role within the context of an organisation, and within the broader society as a whole. The individual's external agency is positioned within the external communion to provide for the external agency needs of other people. For example, a carpenter (their form of external agency) is hired to build a house (the contractor is the manner of external communion) to provide for the internal agency needs of another individual.

These are the two basic drives of holons—the drive to maintain a uniqueness, to be whole in oneself and the drive to be part of a larger whole. They can be recognised in the desire of an organisation to be successful, with its own brand and identity, and yet its need to align with industry standards, as well as economic, political, social and natural environments. This dynamic between individual freedom and the pressure of the larger collective is composed of contradictory tensions commonly described in organisational behaviour literature. If a holon cannot maintain its agency (self-preservation) while becoming integral to a larger whole (communion) it will break down or dissolve into lower-level sub-holons. For example, a human body breaks down into systems (like the respiratory system) and then to organs (like the lungs), then to tissues, molecules and then atoms. A cancer cell is an example of a cell in dissolution that is breaking down healthy life into lower-order complexity. In the same way, if a team or organisation cannot fulfil its purpose or is too dysfunctional it will either disband, break up or dissolve into smaller, less functional groups and clusters (Wilber, 2000).

The movement through the spiral is like the growth and development of a child. As we learn and develop, our world becomes more complex and less focused purely on ourselves. Just as a child's focus and morality change as it moves through the spiral, so too does an individual's sense of morality and their focus of attention as they move through the spiral. Childhood development of each IC is a fractal representation of societal development. For example, the development of P1 is a fingerprint of the social development in the first and second memes (answering questions of individual and communal survival).

One of my favourite quotes is from embryologist Ernst Haeckel who, in describing human life, famously said 'ontogeny recapitulates phylogeny'. He meant that the development of an individual organism evolves in a similar manner to that of the entire species. Just as physical development in the womb follows the same process as child development, individual development follows the same process as societal development. Although modern science has refuted the literal and universal form of Haeckel's theory, I still find it thought-provoking when considering human emotional development.

The following discussion plots the development of both individual and social concerns through the spiral of humanity and indicates how a person's public persona changes.

Description of the Nine Levels of Adult Development

1. LIVING AT THE BEIGE MEME (PERSONAL SURVIVAL)

The first meme focuses on immediate physical survival. This meme represents the status of most animals on earth—there is no cognitive awareness given to any long-term horizon. Life expectancy, together with the focus of attention, is centred purely on the current moment. Today is all that exists. Existence is maintained primarily through instinctual and habitual responses.

The conditions of this meme equate to P1 development in a child. There is neither a sense of time, nor a capacity to think about anything but the most pressing and immediate issues. The vast majority of humanity never experience this meme in their adult life. If they do, it is only because of severe life conditions that threaten their survival in a fundamental way. This may occur after an earthquake that destroys social infrastructure, or in the midst of war. In this meme it is the natural order and natural law that prevail, and they are centred on the satisfaction of human biological needs.

The Boxing Day tsunami of 2004 reduced a large number of people to the Beige meme. They struggled to survive through the day, with their homes destroyed, families dead and all social infrastructure washed away.

Cowan & Beck roughly estimate 0.1 per cent of the world's population operate out of this meme[10] (Cowan & Beck, 1996).

---

10 The mathematically inclined will notice that the total of these percentages is more than 100. This is because around 10 per cent of the population is in more than one meme at one time.

The questions of existence here centre on ensuring personal physical survival and the ability to provide for one's physical needs. Therefore, morality focuses on what is good for personal survival, with bad equal to personal death. As individuals start to leave this meme, they begin to form into tribal groups for mutual protection.

2. LIVING AT THE PURPLE MEME (COLLECTIVE SURVIVAL)

As these tribal groups grow in size, they provide greater protection for each member. This frees up considerable cognitive ability to think about issues that do not just focus on today's survival. At this meme humans begin to become distinct from animals. The focus of this meme is on communal survival.

In this meme individuals connect events into cause and effect sequences, but they always attribute the effect to unseeable natural forces and the actions of powerful spirits. It is a tribal meme in that it places great significance on family, clan and tribal groups. The individual is willing to die for the greater good of the community. Therefore, people are either of us or of others; there is a strong sense of in-group/out-grouping. The focus of attention is on the survival of those who are of us. Individuals in this meme do not question traditions as they are inherited in the very nature of things.

The conditions of this meme still align to those of P1 development in a child. While there is now a greater sense of time and a greater understanding of the world, there is very little sense of differentiated self. That is, the individual and the group are still largely formlessly entwined in the one entity. That is why at this meme it is vitally important to identify what tribal grouping another individual comes from, because that will contextualise their perceived place in the world.

Each part of the environment has a separate 'guardian spirit', and may require a different form of appeasement to ensure group survival. Further, each tree in the forest may be individually recognised and appreciated, but there will be no understanding of the forest as a whole.

An example of this meme is found amongst some of the tribal groups in such places as Papua New Guinea. The ethos of the meme is contained within the Papuan 'one talk' system that functions in most small rural communities. Within the 'one talk' system ownership is communal and there is no real concept of personal property. Another example of characteristics of this meme is the ritualistic behaviours of professional sports people when they will act in a certain way 'to maintain their winning streak'.

An estimated 10 percent of the world's population is operating out of this meme (Beck & Cowan, 1996).

The questions of existence focus on what actions or behaviours will ensure that the tribe survives. In answering the questions of this meme, the individual develops the ability to seamlessly fit into social norms and behaviours of different 'tribal' groups (for example, professional bodies, trades, or just the company culture). The sense of morality is an extension of the collective: what is good for the community is good—period. What is bad for the community is bad—period.

A person begins to expand their consciousness into the next meme when they acknowledge the importance of the tribe while exerting greater and greater personal influence, recognising they are distinct from their tribal group. This does not negate the capacity to exist communally, but represents the beginning of the capacity to express individual influence in coexistence with the tribe.

3. LIVING AT THE RED MEME (PERSONAL IDENTITY AND EXPRESSION)

Just as a child begins to separate its awareness of itself from its primary caregiver in the C1 stage of development, so the individual explores the world for themselves in the Red meme. The focus of this meme is egocentric expression. It is letting go of the communal, fear-based controls of Purple meme to free individual energy. While it may be, at times, raw, impulsive and wild, it is also liberating and creative. This meme resists power exercised over it. Negative expression is in the form of emotions like rage, impulsivity and wild abandon. Positive expression contributes to a sense of personal control, lets a group break from constraining traditions and energises an entire society to expand their horizons.

Individuals operating in this meme tend to locate the cause of difficulties and failures outside of themselves, to physical things. (Not spiritual ones as is the case with Purple.) There is no time horizon in Red. Things either occur now or they never will! There is no capacity for delayed gratification—just like a child developing their C1.

The French Revolution is an excellent example of the Red meme exploding into history. While the leading individuals in the revolution may have been at higher memes, the vast majority of the population of Paris revelled in their first experiences of free expression. That is why the streets of Paris ran red with the blood of victims of the revolution and with wine spilt by drunken revellers. (While there were significant presences from other memes in the revolution, the fact that it—quickly became a riotous affair expresses more Red chaos than Blue the next meme, which engenders order).

An estimated 20 percent of the world's population is operating out of this meme (Beck & Cowan, 1996).

The questions of existence focus on personal expression, being the biggest and having the most of whatever it is you are chasing. Everything must be seen to be heroic, larger than life, and have an immediate payoff. In answering the questions of existence at this meme, you develop the ability to express yourself and the essence of your individuality.

In Red, relationships tend to be short and intense rather than long and deep. Any interaction tends to be a test of strength and of will, so relationships take second seat to impulsive actions. The morality, at this meme, focuses on individual power and expression. Actions that facilitate it are perceived as good, while those that do not are not.

A person begins to expand their consciousness into the next meme when they begin to question the existence of their life, and start to have faith in a higher order or underlying purpose. At this point, the person moves towards a collective world view again. Done healthily, the person will maintain their power and self-expression of Red.

4. LIVING AT THE BLUE MEME (SACRIFICE FOR THE GREATER GOOD)

The Blue meme unfolds as an individual accepts that there is a higher order than themselves and that this order orders the universe. While this could be a religious order, it is just as likely to be any external form of code of conduct based on absolute and unvarying principles of 'right' and 'wrong'. There is a sense that this code must be adhered to. Behaviour is externally regulated, and violating the code or rules has severe, perhaps everlasting, repercussions. Following the code brings rewards for those that maintain it.

As a consequence, life in the Blue meme has meaning, direction and purpose with outcomes determined by an all-powerful other or order. There are also rigid social hierarchies. The existence of one correct code of conduct means that there is only one right way to do things and only one right way to think about everything.

The focus of this meme is on finding the truth and through this truth, meaning and purpose in life. Here there is an attention to consequences and deferred gratification rather than Red's egocentric impulsiveness. Other people become increasingly relevant as beings with rights and worth, but not all are equal. This meme binds impulses within rather than wildly expressing them outwardly. There is now a capacity to recognise and bond with abstract ideas (instead of Purple's clans or Red's instant payoff). This allows individuals to delay gratification.

This meme creates an orderly Newtonian world, offering great satisfaction to those discovering their rightful place and staying within it. Individuals here find peace of mind, have a clear hope for the future, and an abiding faith that there is meaning and purpose in living.

The Blue meme is reminiscent of P2 development in that instinctive drives are suppressed. With a sense of personal power and awareness from Red, the unquestioning collective experience of Purple is now assessed against an external structure and system that represents the core of Blue idealism.

An estimated 40 per cent of the world's population is living in this meme (Beck & Cowan, 1996).

This meme brings a sense of purpose and destiny to an individual's life, along with a capacity to delay satisfaction and work for a long-term objective. Relationships tend not to be either deep or personal, as any deviation from the prescribed behaviour results in expulsion from the collective. Morality, then, is what aligns with the collective sense of 'right', and anything or any person that questions or brings into doubt that 'rightness', is wrong.

A person begins to expand their consciousness into the next meme when they start to question the absoluteness of the prescribed behaviour and begin to see multiple options and possibilities. If this is done healthily, they will maintain their discipline and purpose.

5. LIVING AT THE ORANGE MEME (PERSONAL SUCCESS)

In the Orange meme, the social equivalent of P2 development is completed as the movement is back towards individual accomplishment and achievement. The self 'escapes' from the 'herd mentality' of Blue, and seeks truth and meaning in individualistic terms—typically in the scientific sense. The world is a rational and well-oiled machine with natural laws that can be learned, mastered and manipulated for one's own purposes. This meme is highly achievement oriented, especially towards materialistic gains.

The focus of this meme is discerning the right strategic approach in order to enjoy the best of life. With it there is new hope for individual achievement. It carries a sense of personal power derived from Red, but also contains the sense of purposefulness of Blue. While it contains Red's desire to do as the self wishes, it is now tempered by Blue's recognition of the rules and a compulsion to strive for the completion of a cause that gives life meaning. There is a striving for autonomy and independence. It seeks out the 'good life' and material abundance. Blue thought, 'There is only one way,' but Orange takes a multiplistic view—many things are possible, but one is best. Many things can happen at once and attention can be shifted between them, rather than the step-by-step approach of Blue.

For people in this meme, relationships and social interactions are focused on achievement rather than connection. What is right are those actions that facilitate personal success. An estimated 30 percent of the world's population is living in this meme.

The best example of the Orange meme in its raw form is in the New York futures exchanges, where traders buy and sell in a frenzy of unbridled capitalism. Hong Kong is another great example of an entire city built around the drive and energy of the Orange meme (Beck & Cowan, 1996).

A person begins to expand their consciousness into the next meme as they begin to accept and embrace the opinions of others and to value people for themselves rather than for what they can do for them. Only after they have found the personal power to attain what they want from life can the individual form connections with others as equals.

6. LIVING AT THE GREEN MEME (COMMUNAL CONNECTION)

The focus of this meme is on community and connectedness. It is communitarian, egalitarian and consensual. The community grows by combining different perspectives and approaches; artificial divisions are seen to take away from everyone. There is a belief that bad attitudes and negative beliefs will fade away when we look inside another person and uncover the richness within them. Sharing positive emotions can enrich association. The group starts to take on a life of its own, building on the communal memes of the past. It is more open than the family, kinship-dependent tribes of Purple, lacks the doctrinaire structures of Blue, is not as objective-focused as Orange, and is not fixated on self-expression as Red meme is.

The defining boundaries are against those who exhibit too much independence and try to climb out of niches assigned by the group. The Green meme seeks consolidation of the soul and the forces of nature through respect and even awe, but not mystical superstition or prescriptive rules.

An estimated 10 per cent of the world's population is living in this meme (Beck & Cowan, 1996).

A good example of this meme is found in some of the hallowed halls of universities. The whole notion of 'political correctness' springs from the Green meme—everyone's position is equally valid and should not be tainted by preconceived opinions.

Political correctness attempts to break down the Core Beliefs in our society. This represents the Green meme's desire to have the true essence of everybody actually heard, and not just preconceived snapshots and judgements made about them. The Green morality focuses on what breaks down barriers and facilitates communication. Everything that does not must be eliminated.

The skills learned through this meme focus on building deep and true connections with other people. This is the adult equivalent to childhood development of I2. A person begins to expand their consciousness into the next meme as they appreciate that while all people are loved and have valid views, not all views and opinions are equally constructive, and that natural hierarchies exist within society and nature.

7. LIVING AT THE YELLOW MEME (LIVING RESPONSIBLY FREE)

As the individual begins to see that the prevailing world order is the result of the existence of different levels of reality (memes), they begin to appreciate that all opinions are not equally valid. Egalitarianism is complemented by natural degrees of ranking and excellence. At this meme knowledge and competency are understood to supersede power, status or group sensitivity.

The focus of this meme is on 'being' rather than 'doing', in whatever form that takes for the individual. This is the first meme based in second-order thinking. The shift in conceptual space is greater than the sum of all the previous levels and is combined with a massive increase in degrees of behavioural freedom. The interactive universe becomes more intriguing than autonomy or even community. Acceptance and harmony are peripheral to happiness. What others think is not critical, only interesting.

In second-order thinking there is a dropping away of fears and anxieties from the previous levels, thus enhancing the individual's ability to take a contemplative approach to life and rationally review situations. As fear drops away, the quantity and quality of good ideas and solutions to problems increase dramatically. This quality of thinking penetrates to the core of an issue. Individuals in this meme act from a personal and personalised code of ethics, derived from their own reasoned choosing. This ethical position is not entrapped by rigid rules based in external dogma or mandates of authority.

The insight of the Yellow meme addresses, socially, the same issues I1 addresses for the individual, in that underlying patterns begin to be appreciated and brought to conscious awareness.

Yellow respects those in all the other memes. Morality, with a sense of good and bad, revolves around what is valuable to enhance the various hierarchies and natural spirals. What facilitates development is considered good; what hinders the healthy expression of various memes is bad.

An estimated one per cent of the world's population is living in this meme (Beck & Cowan, 1996).

The individual begins to move into the next meme if they start embracing a sense of spirituality in their integrated viewpoint.

8. LIVING AT THE TURQUOISE MEME (HOLISTIC)

The focus of this meme is on holons. It is a purpose-driven collective/communal meme. It encompasses but is not limited to the harmony-drive of Green, nor is it dogma-centred as in Blue, nor linked by mystical forces and kinship as with Purple. The sense of community is very broad. It centres on life itself, not just humans. The planet is seen as a single unit. It may also act with more urgency than Yellow to resolve problems and issues since the doubts about the value of self-sacrificial investments of time and energy may inhibit actions. Feelings and knowledge become integrated. Individuals learn not only through observation and participation, but also through the experience of simply being. The individual in this meme trusts intuition and instinct, allowing the mind to process with both the conscious and unconscious selves as co-participants. There is a sense of reconnection with aspects of themselves stifled or supplanted by powerful forces in the subsistence existence of first-order thinking. This activates greater resources within the person's mind and brain.

This view of the world sees life as interlinked causes and effects, and interacting fields of energy. Universal order, but in a living, conscious fashion, is not based on external rules (Blue) or group bonds (Green). The individual now experiences a level of bonding and communication beyond any previous meme. 'Seeing-everything-at-once' before doing anything specific, dominates the thinking process. Those thoughts and actions that enhance the health of the entire biosphere become the actions that are considered to be good, and those that do not are considered to be bad. An estimated 0.1 per cent of the world's population is living in this meme (Beck & Cowan, 1996).

The eight Master Neuro-Rational Types described in the following chapters manifest in the First Tier and through to the Yellow meme, but are very rarely seen at Turquoise because the issues that manifest at Turquoise require the individual to have a level of containment that is only possible when the Master and the Mirror are integrated and the individual can draw equally on all six Intelligences. *NeuroPower* refers to this as the *NeuroPower* Type which is the subject matter in Chapter 21.

ADULT DEVELOPMENT THROUGH THE SPIRAL

NeuroPower plots an individual's movement through these memes from the perspective of the eight Master Neuro-Rational Types. It also maps the transition from the Neuro-Limbic Type (which can only operate at Purple or Red memes) to the higher order cognitive levels of Blue meme and above.

What is significant is that a Master Neuro-Rational Type will look vastly different in different memes. For instance, a Bard focusing on the questions of existence in the Purple meme will look and sound totally different from a Bard focusing in Yellow. These two Bards will appear as though they have nothing in common. One will be focused on mysticism, and the other will be integrating all knowledge regardless of its origin. Likewise, a Judge Master personality in the Red meme will bear almost no resemblance to a Judge in the Blue meme.

The profound changes that occur in the movements between memes cannot be understated. They represent vast changes both internally and externally. Of course, this is often confusing to the people who share their life, and can be a source of a great deal of conflict.

APPLYING MEMETIC INSIGHTS

In any communication, it's important to make sure that the key messages are accessible, comprehensible and appealing for the target audience. A comprehensive understanding of Spiral Dynamics and memes is invaluable in this process, because where an individual is in the meme stack will determine both their focus of attention (i.e. their questions of existence) and the cognitive level of complexity they can understand. Communicating effectively means being able to accurately assess the audience's meme and matching it in terms of both message content, and delivery source or *channel*.

The table on the next page will help you frame your communications to match the meme of your target audience.

Meme	Appropriate sourcing	Elements of appropriate message design
Beige	• Caretaker • Provider	• Biologic senses – touch, taste, smell, see, hear • Physical contact rather than symbols
Purple	• Caring chieftain • Shaman or elders • From within tribe/clan group • From spirit realm • From word of ancestors • Traditional ways	• Traditional rites, rituals, ceremonies • Includes mystical elements and superstitions • Appeals to extended family, harmony and safety • Recognises blood-bonds, the folk, group • Familiar metaphors, drawings, and emblems • Minimal reliance on written language
Red	• Person with recognised power • Straight-talking boss • One with something to offer • Respected (feared) other • Proven tough entity	• Demonstrate 'What's in it for me, now?' • Offer 'Immediate gratification if...' • Challenges and appeals to machismo/ strength • Heroic status and legendary potential • Flashy, to-the-point, unambiguous, strong • Simple language and fiery images/graphics
Blue	• Rightful proper authority • Higher authority in the way • Down the chain-of-command • According to the book's rules • Person with position power • Revered Truth keepers	• Duty, honour, country images of discipline • Self-sacrifice for higher cause and purpose • Appeal to traditions and established norms • Use class-consciousness and knowing one's place • Propriety, righteousness, and responsibilities • Insure future rewards and delayed gratification • Assuage guilt with correct consequences
Orange	• One's own right-thinking mind • Successful mentors and models • Credible professionals • Prosperous elite contacts • Advantageous to the self • Based on proven experience • Findings of science	• Appeal to competitive advantage and leverage • Success motivations and achieving abundance • Bigger, better, newer, faster, more popular • Citations of experts and selected authorities • Experimental data and tried-and-true experience • Profit, productivity, quality, results, win • Demonstrate as best of several options

Toolbox: Communicating Through the Memes

Meme	Appropriate sourcing	Elements of appropriate message design
Green	• Consensual community norms • Enlightened friend/ colleague • Outcome of participation • Resultant of enlightenment • Observation of events • Participative decision • Team's collective findings	• Enhance belonging, sharing, harmony of groups • Sensitive to human issues and care for others • Expand awareness and understanding of inner self • Symbols of equity, humanity and bonding • Gentle language along with nature imagery • Build trust, openness, exploration, passages • Real people and authentic emotional displays
Yellow	• Any information source • Competent, more knowing person • May adopt BEIGE through GREEN • Relevant, more useful data • Merge hard sources and hunches • Conscious and unconscious mind • Disregards status or prestige	• Interactive, relevant media, self-accessible • Functional 'lean' information without fluff • The facts, the feelings and the instincts • Big picture, total systems, integrations • Connect data across fields for holistic view • Adapt, mesh, blend, access, sense, gather • Self-connecting to systems and others usefully
Turquoise	• Experience of discovery • Learning in communal network • Holistic conception of reality • Any being in TURQUOISE sphere • Systems across the planet • Resonance with First Tier • High-tech and high-touch for experiential knowing	• Multi-dimensional chunks of insight • Use multi-tiered consciousness to access • Renewed spirituality and sacrifice to whole • Ecological interdependent and interconnections • Macro (global) solutions to macro problems • Community beyond nationalities or partisanship

Moving from Childhood to Adulthood

Sooner or later, for many of us, the world of causality is not enough and we grow weary of our material, childish, reactive, sad grey lives. This is when we ask the question, 'Why am I here?' 'What is the unique contribution that I can make in this world?' The shift from child to adult consciousness often starts with a dull ache of discontentment with life, a sense that there is a large part of you that is not having the opportunity to be expressed.

John was 36. He was in a senior executive role, was paid very well, lived in an impressive house in a sought-after suburb, drove an expensive European car and holidayed internationally every year. He had everything he could possibly need in the material world, yet he felt as if he was fundamentally living the wrong life. His dis-ease intensified until he left his highly paid job to open his own art shop. He described the move as answering a call from his soul.

Linda was a Matron at the Children's Hospital. She was respected by her employees and enjoyed her work. Even though everything seemed right, something inside her felt she was in exactly the wrong place. It made no sense to her because everything she had always wanted, she now had – a family, a nice group of friends, a solid income, a comfortable house, a reliable car and a challenging and rewarding job. Slowly the discomfort became stronger until she found it almost impossible to get in the car to go to work. The very things that used to engage her now annoyed her. She felt some part of her wanted to be a Uniting Church Minister. This seemed like a strange and unlikely transition for Linda but she went and talked to her Minister about it anyway. To her amazement he endorsed her candidature and five years later she was an ordained Minister.

I can understand John and Linda. I built my consultancy until it was everything I had dreamt of, yet I felt a basic frustration that every day I was there I was wasting my life. I ignored it at first but the dissatisfaction wouldn't leave. My dis-ease intensified until I had a complete nervous breakdown. I didn't choose to become depressed. I felt as if my whole life was a farce and that my true call – which was working with personality and transformation – needed to be answered. Eventually I was physically such a mess that the pain of leaving for both me and the consultancy wasn't that great really. So I left. My health steadily improved and within six months my passion, confidence and enthusiasm were back.

I have dozens of stories just like these where perfectly happy people have this sense that they are being called to their true 'life vocation'. It's as if the first half of their life has been spent learning the ropes, but their real journey begins after they answer their call. This call has a few characteristics that are worthy of a closer look.

Firstly, it is almost always a call to use their energy in a way that will serve others. In other words, it is a call to empower, inspire or in some way improve the world. Secondly, the call always aligns with the individual's natural strengths or innate gift. It is a call to use their *Genius* or their ace area. It is their bliss. It is the activity that makes their soul sing.

Finally, the call is incredibly strong – so strong that the individual finds it impossible to ignore.

During this second phase we bring our external lives into alignment with our internal life purpose. We also develop the ability to observe ourselves both at child and adult consciousness. We discover that adult awareness gives us access to a multitude of noble qualities and a Genius that enables us to manifest outcomes in the material world.

FOUR ASPECTS OF SELF REVIEWED

You may recall that *NeuroPower* recognises four different aspects of self that constitute human personality (see Diagram 10.4). The Lower Self is hardwired into our body's defence mechanisms and represents our amygdala-driven, survival-based personality. From the perspective of the Lower Self the world is a threatening place and the only options are to fight, run away or to comply. These responses are emotionally ingrained into our behaviours. In acting out of them we are little more than any of our fellow mammals (like the family pet cat or dog) since we are operating with the same cognitive equipment as any mammal. Above all, the Lower Self represents the drive and actions of an animal trying to survive. This personality will attempt to resolve the issues of its existence from a perspective where other people are either friend, food or foe. It is a highly habitual method of acting and results in a force-based reaction from the world. (See Chapter 9, Exploring Your System 1 Emotional Reactivity for a more in-depth discussion of this part of self.) You can map your three Core Belief types on the diamond as shown. (For more detail on how your NLT and NRT work together see Appendix 1.)

The Master personality is the adult aspect of self about which our self-identity is formed. This is who we understand ourselves to be and it represents the gifted part of ourselves of which we are both aware and proud. Our Master

Diagram 10.5 The Personality Diamond
(The four manifestations of personality within each individual)

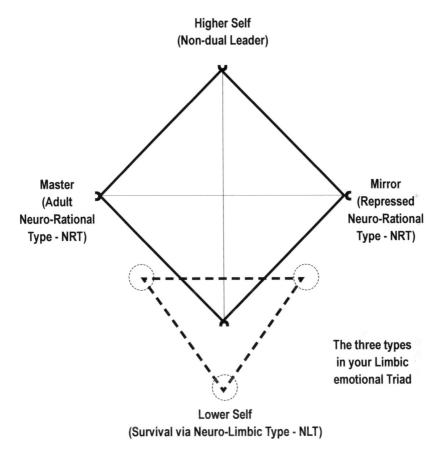

Higher Self
(Non-dual Leader)

Master
(Adult
Neuro-Rational
Type - NRT)

Mirror
(Repressed
Neuro-Rational
Type - NRT)

The three types
in your Limbic
emotional Triad

Lower Self
(Survival via Neuro-Limbic Type - NLT)

determines how we articulate ourselves. But the actions of the Master need not be noble. The nobility, which is found in the Higher Self, comes about based on the intentions with which the Master's Genius is used. Free will represents the decision by the adult Master to base actions either on the perspective of the Lower Self or on the perspective of the Higher Self. If the Master is held hostage by the perspective of the Lower Self, then the individual will use their Genius for selfish and destructive motivations, and so the drive of physis will be impeded. There are eight Geniuses in the Master profiles: conquering new territory (Crusader), assigning meaning (Bard), building bridges of understanding (Chancellor), problem-solving (Commander), seeing congruence (Architect),

Being Individual

While perusing any standard text, you are not likely to encounter any reference to the gender differences in brain organisation, let alone to the individual differences. But such differences do exist and we are only now beginning to understand them. From the aerial view of all humanity represented by a composite, we are gradually moving to the understanding of the neural foundations of individuality. (Goldberg, 2005, pp. 42-43)

planning (Navigator), creating order (Treasurer) and energising (Judge).

When the actions of the Master are based on life-affirming values, they result in the expression of the noble quality. The particular noble quality that is manifested will be based on the questions of existence that are confronting the Master, that is, the meme they are in. Expression of nobility is beneficial for human life and brings about wholeness and health as the Master takes actions aligned with truth. When the Higher Self is being expressed, the individual is fully engaged answering the questions of existence that they currently face. It is a state often referred to as a 'peak experience'.

The Mirror balances the Master. It represents all the disowned aspects of self that are not included within the Master. It also contains a perspective of the world that is completely different from that of the Master, an aspect of truth that is sometimes very uncomfortable for the Master aspect of self to hear. The Mirror also controls a great deal of the behaviour of the Master since it contains all the individual unexpressed needs. It is the tension between the Master and the Mirror that creates the energy for intellectual, emotional and somatic development. When the Master and Mirror finally integrate, a higher *NeuroPower* Type forms.

The Eight Master Neuro-Rational Types at a Glance[11]

Within each meme each adult Neuro-Rational Type has a noble quality which is a partial aspect of pure consciousness. In order to create an integrated body of understanding, the individual needs to harness and reconcile aspects from each of the Neuro-Rational Types. *NeuroPower* describes eight specific Neuro-Rational Types or Master profiles and the unique Geniuses associated with each

---

11 The following descriptions are based on Blue meme consciousness for each Neuro-Rational type.

of these. These eight Geniuses, if used with life-affirming intentions, result in eight noble qualities at each developmental level of consciousness and represent eight partial aspects of pure consciousness. The following is a brief introduction to each of the Master Neuro-Rational Types as they manifest in the Blue meme.

CRUSADER

The noble quality of the Crusader is integrity. This integrity is built on a strict code of conduct that contains five major elements. These are: being overwhelmingly honest, ensuring that both explicit and implicit commitments are kept, responding with emotional consistency to people, resolving issues with integrity, and fighting for what they believe is true. When Crusaders adhere to their internal code of conduct, people respond to their integrity by being honest.

To imagine a Crusader think of William Wallace from the film *Braveheart*.

BARD

The noble quality of the Bard is inspiration. This inspiration is built on finding the unique contribution an individual can play and finding their true course and purpose in life. By believing that each person has a special gift and contribution to make in life, this noble quality seeks to empower others to pursue their 'destiny'. It brings out a sense of hopefulness in the lives of those around them.

Bards are often driven by a strong desire to bring healing in many different forms. The Bard seeks to empower people by focusing them on their gifts and seeing them flourish.

To imagine a Bard, think of Anthony Robbins, with his personal development books like *Awakening the Giant Within,* designed to enable individual empowerment.

CHANCELLOR

The noble quality of the Chancellor is diplomacy. This flows from embracing the opinions of others in a respectful and non-judgemental way. Their empathy encourages others to become more tolerant of each other. The Chancellor empowers others by helping them see how they fit into the team.

Chancellors often seek to build bridges of understanding between people. Their desire is both to make connections themselves and to have other people realise their commonality.

To imagine a Chancellor, think of the ex-Prime Minister of the United Kingdom, Tony Blair.

COMMANDER

The noble quality of the Commander is courage. This courage enables them to face the problems that exist and do what is necessary to resolve them. This noble quality often finds the Commander standing up for what they believe is right and standing by their actions without fear of reprisals or consequences. Their courage will draw out confidence from those around them.

The capacity to face issues directly means that Commanders are excellent at problem-solving.

To imagine a Commander, think of Keanu Reeves in *The Matrix*.

ARCHITECT

The noble quality of the Architect is discernment. The Architect simultaneously considers the future, present and past in making any decisions. Consequently their world view is that the environment presents itself as a set of general forces that need to be harnessed if a problem is to be resolved. Discernment enables the Architect to perceive misalignment between what people say and do.

The Architect will seek to develop capabilities that are aligned with their life's purpose.

To imagine an Architect, think of Albert Einstein and his paradigm-shifting intellectual capacity.

NAVIGATOR

The noble quality of the Navigator is responsibility. Fulfilling the roles and responsibilities that they have in life is very important to the Navigator. They will stand up for what they believe is correct, and they will support and protect their colleagues. Their noble quality brings out a sense of security and stability amongst those around them.

To imagine a Navigator, think of Sir Winston Churchill and his famous speech, 'We will fight them on the beaches ...'

TREASURER

The noble quality of the Treasurer is objectivity. This means rationally considering the facts before making a decision. It allows the Treasurer to consider all events as a learning experience, and to document that learning so that others can benefit from it. The Treasurer acknowledges and appreciates learning and expertise in people around them. Their objectivity and rational inquiry brings out calmness in others.

Creating order from chaos is very important to the Treasurer.

To imagine a Treasurer, think of Clint Eastwood.

JUDGE

The noble quality of the Judge is drive. This enthusiasm comes from the optimistic and driven nature of the Judge type. Consequently they are able to take on large workloads and are constantly looking for challenging opportunities to test their skills and abilities. The strategy of the Judge is to attain a fit between their internal capabilities and the external possibilities. This enthusiasm brings out the energy in others.

The Judge has an in-built sense of urgency, and so they like to roll up their sleeves and get started—less talk, more action.

To imagine a Judge, think of Richard Branson whose energy has created the ubiquitous Virgin business.

The following table summarises the eight adult Master personalities, their Geniuses and the benefit each Genius brings to the team with which they work.

Neuro-Rational Type & Genius	Genius	The Value this Neuro-Rational Type Brings to the Team
Crusader Pathfinding C2 P2 I1	The Crusader's Genius is pathfinding, an ability to conquer new territory. This means that they thrive on danger or unknown territory, or creating new frontiers. As long as the crusade aligns with the stated vision, Crusaders will undergo enormous short-term pain for long-term gain. They will be the ones who blast through to achieve the results. This makes Crusaders excellent for starting up businesses or projects, for rejuvenating dead concepts or creating new visions.	• Excellent for leading the charge on any new project or idea. • Excellent for energising great teams of people who need courage, reassurance and energy. • Excellent for pushing the boundaries and dislodging people out of their comfort zone. • Keeps people accountable.
Bard Assigning Meaning C2 P2 I2	The Bard's Genius lies in their ability to develop meaning for situations or events and in their ability to integrate information and to heal. This means creating a passion for the future, giving life meaning, healing old psychological wounds and integrating knowledge in a powerful way.	• Can heal old psychological wounds so that people can get on with the present. • Can get an amazing amount done quickly. • Can create passion and enthusiasm for new direction and give hope. • Can give any pursuit meaning and purpose – a sense of being worth it.
Chancellor Building Bridges C1 P2 I2	The Chancellor's Genius comes from their ability to build bridges between people. As a consequence they develop powerful interpersonal strategies and so can achieve their objectives with very little disruption. The Chancellor has the ability to influence entire organisations without anybody triggering resistance.	• Able to navigate their way through highly political environments. • Can achieve any set of key objectives with the least exposure, cost or risk. • Excellent for promoting the work of the team or organisation to other stakeholders outside the organisation. • Excellent for negotiation.

Neuro-Rational Type & Genius	Genius	The Value this Neuro-Rational Type Brings to the Team
Commander Problem-Solving C1 P1 I2	The Commander's Genius is their ability to effectively solve problems that are complex, undefined and constantly changing. They are excellent at managing large groups of people in high-stress, dangerous or crisis situations. The Commander is practical and creative and can solve anything 'on the hop'. The Commander is the natural leader when the 'right' emergency action is needed and there is no time.	• Will take over any situation requiring strong authoritarian and practical leadership and management. • Excellent with medical emergencies, disaster clean-ups and hostage situations. • Can cope with the blood and guts of the battlefield or any emotionally charged situation where calm, 'people centred' but authoritarian leadership is required. Perfect when there are many people, many tasks and literally hundreds of problems cropping up moment by moment. • Great for doing the fix-it jobs to keep the show going.
Architect Seeing Congruence C2 P1 I2	The Architect's Genius lies in their ability to bring the people, the processes and the vision all into line. This congruence is the basis of good organisational development skills. This means checking that the vision is relevant and understood by the team, checking the processes are practical and are able to support team members, and that these practical processes are followed. While practical, Architects have the ability to think conceptually, with abstract ideas or philosophies that are complex and ungrounded. Their Genius is the ability to bring abstract vision to concrete reality.	• The ability to bring the abstract reality to practical reality. • Can create organisational congruence where systems, vision and people are all aligned. • Can create clear and practical systems and practices that are suitable to the situation and that work. • Are by their very nature an organisational change agent. • Will lead a group forward – after a disaster.
Navigator Planning C2 P1 I1	The Navigator's Genius lies in their ability to 'see' what is ahead and to prepare for it now. This means creating the right systems, anticipating the problems, researching all relevant data and ensuring blind panic is turned into beneficial and useful planning. They also understand the importance of every team member playing a central yet different role.	• Fantastic for creating strategic plans – all the scenarios and details are considered. • Excellent for planning and establishing new ventures. • Excellent for consulting on and preparing for imminent disasters. • Excellent for ensuring the chain of supply is maintained and all the details are considered. • Excellent role clarification with the team or organisation.

Neuro-Rational Type & Genius	Genius	The Value this Neuro-Rational Type Brings to the Team
Treasurer Creating Order C1 P1 I1	The Treasurer's Genius lies in their ability to create order, systems and stability. This means keeping a calm head in emergencies, grounding new opportunities or settling down situations, people and teams when there is too much ambiguity. In transition, the Treasurer creates clarity and certainty.	• Can de-emotionalise and depersonalise highly charged situations. • Create clarity, certainty and assurance that things are in control. • Excellent at keeping an audit trail.
Judge Energising and turning talk into action C1 P2 I1	The Judge has the Genius of turning talk into action by demanding absolute clarity and focusing on what can be done NOW to get things on the road.	• Excellent for energising a team. • Brilliant resource at the beginning of a project for sourcing suppliers, products or people. • Excellent for new projects or processes where trial and error is necessary to get the right answer. • Will create a 'task oriented', problem-solving team environment by taking the emphasis off the people and placing it on the task at hand.

Before we can move from one meme to the next, we must answer the questions of existence relating to that meme from each of Wilber's *Four Faces of Truth*. Together the eight Neuro-Rational Types represent all four perspectives. The journey towards truth involves integrating the noble quality of each Neuro-Rational Type in the specific order of transformation. Only when we can embrace all eight noble qualities, and the four aspects of truth that they represent, can the individual answer the questions of existence at that level of consciousness. Only then they will be able to transform their personal experience into a higher, more complete and more complex level of awareness (a holon of knowledge). This is the process of adult transformation. Each Neuro-Rational Type path of transformation at each meme has been charted in Appendix 7.

Diagram 10.6 Personal Integration Process

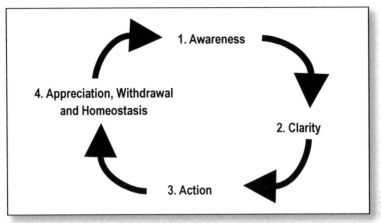

THE SPIRAL UP: THE CYCLE OF ADULT TRANSFORMATION

Every moment of every day we are either in the process of actively integrating our experiences of life into a cohesive experience of wholeness and understanding of truth or we are in the process of reactively rejecting the integration of truth. Our awareness is either growing as we accept a broader and more complex macro-sphere of the world, or it is shrinking and we are rejecting it. There is a generic process that describes this movement. The process of transforming experiences into a holon of knowledge follows an elegant, efficient and sequential process.[12]

The *NeuroPower* transformation process consists of four stages and eight steps. They are listed in Table 10.7.

ADULT AWARENESS

Awareness is enhanced when a new insight becomes the focal point of our interest. This awareness is a form of experiencing. It is a meaning-making stage in which new understanding is adopted and integrated into the sense of self.

The **Awareness** stage has three specific steps, each of which confront us with new insights that are fundamentally different from our Neuro-Rational Type's world view. The first step occurs when the issue initially enters our perceptions

---

12 Variations on this transformation are widely known. Elisabeth Kubler-Ross in *On Death and Dying.* New York: Macmillan, 1970, found that patients receiving the news of their imminent death had the potential to go through five emotional stages: denial, anger, bargaining, depression and finally acceptance. The Gestalt process also outlines a similar phased approach: sensation, awareness, mobilisation, action, final contact, satisfaction and withdrawal.

Table 10.7 Spiral Up

Stage	Step
Awareness	I
	C
	P
Clarity	C
Action	I
	C
	P
Assessment	C

and we become clear that a need or an issue exists. It is only when we integrate new insight from our weaker I Intelligence Circuit that we can understand this new issue more completely and that the work of integration begins. This challenges the perceived truth around which we have built our lives. As such, it both confronts us with our personal deficiencies and makes us aware that the issue we are confronting is our own to resolve.

The second step of Awareness involves using our creativity to broaden our perspective. This stage prepares us for the most difficult step in the first stage.

The third step is to embrace the world view of our Mirror through our processing (P) Intelligence. This is a very difficult stage because our conscious Master habitually represses the unconscious Mirror because it has been perceived as unacceptable. The completion of this stage creates greater internal alignment, strength and energy.

This release of energy enables us to start focusing on connecting this newfound awareness to constructive somatic expression. This is the **Clarity** stage of the integration process.

CLARITY

During the **Clarity** stage, various options are considered and a clear action plan is developed. The person actively reaches out towards different possibilities, seeking to overcome obstacles, as they attempt to creatively find answers. There is one step in the Clarity stage and it involves embracing the C Intelligence.

ACTION

The third stage is **Action**. Having developed a successful course of action in the Clarity stage, it is now time to move ahead with the most complete distillation of focused attention that is possible.

There are three steps in the Action phase requiring integration of I, C and P centres sequentially.

After the results of the Action stage start to become clear, it is time to move into the fourth and final stage, **Assessment**.

ASSESSMENT: APPRECIATION, WITHDRAWAL AND HOMEOSTASIS

The eighth and final step involves reflecting on the results of the Action stage and relaxing into a sense of complete satisfaction or homeostasis. The stage of Appreciation is akin to the feeling of a mother cradling her new-born baby, which, mere moments beforehand, had been a part of her. This is because the individual will have integrated the knowledge of an entire level of development and will have returned to their home state. The work for this issue has been done.

THE SPIRAL DOWN

Just as there is a generic process for embracing a greater level of insight and wholeness and constructive somatic expression, there is also a path for rejecting insight, avoiding wholeness and somatically expressing in an unconstructive way. The result of following this path of rejecting truth and living in an increasingly delusional world, is to refuse wholeness and embrace a fractured persona. In this situation the Genius of the type is often being used with negative intention.

(There are four stages with seven steps in the spiral down listed in Table 10.9.)

The objective of the integration process is to adopt a more complex and a more whole perspective of truth. When this natural process is resisted, uncomfortable truths are actively rejected and are not integrated within the sense of self. This process follows four stages of rejecting and displacing truth. How an individual moves through this process will depend on their individual Neuro-Rational Type.

Diagram 10.8 Personal Disintegration Process

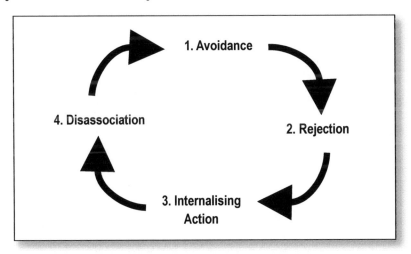

Table 10.9 Spiral Down

Stage		Step
Avoidance	C	Delusion
	P	Introjection
	C	Deflection
Rejection	I	Boundary Breakdown
	C	Projection
Internalising Action	P	Internalising Action
Disassociation	C	Disassociation

For all Neuro-Rational Types, however, the first stage is **Avoidance**. The spiral down begins with **Delusion**, which is the inappropriate use of creativity to justify the person's position. With Delusion the individual avoids experiencing the negative reality of either themselves or their environment. In this way their true feelings are diluted, disregarded or even neglected. In Introjection, a movement of the P Intelligence Circuits, either the social rules the individual learned as a child or the cultural stereotypes, become the overarching determinant of their action. This step prevents the individual from taking appropriate 'here and now' action to meet their own needs.

The third step is **Deflection**, which involves turning from direct contact with another person or situation. This is another effective way to block awareness, by making it vague, bland or polite. Instead of choosing direct contact with the situation, the individual uses abstract language or watered-down descriptions, or avoids eye contact. Again, creativity is used to diminish the unwelcome nature of reality.

If the individual continues to spiral down they move to the Rejection stage. There are two steps in this stage, both of which focus on the rejection of personal responsibility for taking constructive action. The first is through **Boundary Breakdown**, where the individual fails to differentiate between themselves and either another person or an external environment. Any threat to a part of this relationship or environment then becomes a threat to the individual. While a healthy individual's boundary awareness has a survival function, in the spiral down it loses definition.

In the second step of **Rejection** the individual projects the truth of the situation onto others. **Projection** erroneously uses creativity to deceive the individual by placing the ownership of a disowned element of their personality onto another. The unwanted parts of self are attributed to external objects or people. The projector may be unaware that they are rejecting others. Instead they believe that they are being rejected themselves. In this state an individual is experiencing himself or herself as being powerless to change the situation.

The third phase, **Internalising Action**, occurs in one of two ways. Firstly, the individual does to themselves what they want to do to or with someone else. In this

Prefrontal Impact

Compared to other primates, it is the nature of our larger prefrontal cortex that has largely set us apart. We can use our prefrontal cortex to improve the quality and flexibility of thinking on existing simpler and faster processing by other more job-specific parts of our brain. This effectively means the prefrontal cortex holds the key to self-control and any of our more noble actions. It exerts the self-control to hold back from a second round of chocolate or the courage to go forward despite the dangers (Goleman, 2006).

case the persona becomes divided into two aspects, the one who 'does' and the aspect that is 'done unto'. For example, instead of expressing anger externally the individual turns it on themselves. The other form of Internalising Action is when you do to yourself what you want or wanted to have done for you by others. For example, an individual may give themselves the attention, love and care that was not provided to them by their parents.

The fourth phase, **Disassociation**, is when the individual experiences themselves as a spectator or commentator on themselves and their life. This occurs through a movement of the C Intelligence. This creativity gets in the way of effective action to resolve personal needs and disturbs the development of wholeness or authentic connection to the truth of the situation.

This describes the process of integration and disintegration for each of the eight Neuro-Rational Types. The individual transformation paths for each of the Neuro-Rational Types are described in more depth in the following chapters.

EXPLORING EACH OF THE ADULT MASTER NEURO-RATIONAL TYPES IN MORE DEPTH: THE FORMAT OF THE NEXT EIGHT CHAPTERS

The next eight chapters will discuss each of the Master personalities in more depth. Each chapter has been designed to allow readers to refer to just the Neuro-Rational Type chapter of interest in isolation without having to refer back to other material in the book. This means there is some common background text in each chapter. Certainly the chapters follow a common format.

These chapters will start with a detailed description of each Master personality and provide an overview of their journey through life at the different levels of consciousness.

The issues surrounding character development and the difficulties these cause are also briefly discussed.

The practical steps of integration are then described. This description contains a brief overview of the work needed to be done at each step. On a less positive note, each chapter also details the downward spiral for each type as they avoid doing that work. You will notice that for each type this follows a distinct and precise path.

The next section of each chapter will discuss an area that is of particular interest for those in the Orange meme—that is, how each type creates wealth and how their unconscious motivation affects how they spend their money. This section also includes tips on how each type should manage themselves, how they manage others, and the consequences of this in the workforce.

This section also looks at the *Genius* of the Neuro-Rational Type. Applying a Genius often brings forth a *Flow* experience. Flow occurs when an individual applies their Genius such that they stretch themselves but without becoming overwhelmed. *Flow* is a state of peak performance, where all endeavour becomes effortless and is accompanied by a concentrated absorption of living in the moment. In this state of awareness, individuals become utterly absorbed in what they are doing, paying undivided attention to the task at hand. There is a merging of self and actions (Csikszentmihalyi, 1978).

The last section of each chapter looks at the body composition of each Neuro-Rational Type, their fitness and dietary behaviours, and gives a description of the common physical appearance of the Neuro-Rational Type.

The eight Neuro-Rational Types will be addressed in the following order: Crusader, Bard, Chancellor, Commander, Architect, Navigator, Treasurer and Judge.

Chapter 11

The Crusader
An In-Depth Look at the Crusader

God grant me the serenity to accept the things I cannot change,
the courage to change the things I can and the wisdom to know the difference.
Anonymous

What we've got to thank Crusaders for:

Clear rules

Code of conduct

High manufacturing standards

On time, on budget

High precision specialist medical equipment

High performance cars

Total Quality Management (TQM) movement

Business excellence

THE CRUSADER PROFILE

Whoever thinks a faultless piece to see, thinks that ne'er there was,
nor is, nor e'er shall be.

Alexander Pope

OVERVIEW

Crusaders are passionate, disciplined and dependable protectors of morality, justice and honesty. They are the defenders of what is true and correct. With a clear sense of what is 'right', Crusaders work long hours doing many of the tasks that the rest of us take for granted – cleaning, maintenance work, completing checks and audits, checking the quality is right, rechecking figures, finalising work schedules, fine-tuning project plans or lesson outlines or doing whatever it takes to get it right or as close to perfect as possible.

Crusaders respect rules, quality management and the accepted procedures. They respect authority and the established protocol. Serious, stern-looking and always ready to correct others, Crusaders are by nature frugal, independent, reliable, conservative and task-oriented. They teach us the true meaning of honour and, in a team, foster commitment from others.

> I went to a hardware shop to buy some special cleaner – I was buying a number of things. When I got home and looked at the docket I realised I'd got six bottles of this cleaner but they'd only charged me for one. I felt really awkward about this, and very quickly decided that I would just have to go back and pay the girl for the other five bottles. Needless to say, the girl was quite surprised, which to be truthful quite amazed me, because I like to think everyone would do something similar. I think as I've got older I've realised too, in some way, disbelief that not everyone does this. And that some people may think you're a bit strange for doing it. But I couldn't live with myself if I hadn't.

FOCUS OF ATTENTION

Crusaders (the White Knight archetype) fight for what is true and right. This can mean fighting for the underprivileged, the disadvantaged, the marginalised or the underdog. Crusaders demonstrate to others what ethics, justice, integrity, excellence, magnanimity, benevolence and compassion really mean.

LEVELS OF CONSCIOUSNESS AS DEFINED BY USA PSYCHOLOGIST CLARE GRAVES AND SPIRAL DYNAMICS' AUTHORS COWAN & BECK

The following table outlines the broad character development of the Crusader

Table 11.1 The Crusader Levels of Development

Level of Consciousness and the noble quality embraced at this level	Common Crusader characteristics at this level of consciousness
Level 1 (Beige) A state of nature and instincts.	Competitive, aggressive, physically abusive, angry, punitive. Closed down and off from human nobility.
Level 2 (Purple) Mysterious and frightening. *(Noble quality to be embraced at this level: Ethical)*	Religious Crusaders who maintain the rituals to the letter of the law – those with us are civilised and those against are barbarians needing to be saved from themselves; cruel to be kind; the ends justify the means.
Level 3 (Red) Raw displays of power – dictators, tough love, predators. *(Noble quality to be embraced at this level: Seeks Justice)*	Top-down style. Self-doubt is disallowed and all questioning is quashed. They are closed-minded and will not compromise or negotiate.
Level 4 (Blue) Everything is controlled by God and is purposeful. Obey God. Do it right. Feel guilt. *(Noble quality to be embraced at this level: Seeks Integrity)*	Perfectionist, opinionated and sarcastic. They reprimand others for not living up to God's standards.
Level 5 (Orange) The world is a game and I want to win. *(Noble quality to be embraced at this level: Striving for Excellence)*	Work harder than everyone else to justify rewards, assume rewards will be given to those who perform to the highest standards. Nit pick, focus on details – everything MUST be right for 'me' to succeed. Bring others down if they make mistakes. They discover their gift and how to use it for personal gain.
Level 6 (Green) We need to join together and grow personally through community. *(Noble quality to be embraced at this level: Magnanimity)*	Crusaders drop the idea that they are right and that others are wrong and instead see that they are in no position to judge things objectively. Instead, they watch that the community has integrity and that all people are focused on the community's best interests. They become defenders of the community's values. At this point the Commander Mirror is integrated into the personality. They learn to use their gift for the community.
Level 7 (Yellow) We need to explore ways of being responsibly free. *(Noble quality to be embraced at this level: Benevolence)*	New ideas are encouraged and new frontiers are explored with compassion and vulnerability from the Commander and the ability to solve the problems that the new ideas bring up.
Level 8 (Turquoise) The world is composed of delicately balanced interlocking forces, shaped by attractor fields of intention and nobility. Uses natural flows. Actively grows consciousness. The Non-dual Leader manifests at this level.	The world is seen as a series of cycles and life is seen as a quest. The individual understands the spiral of life and the streams of intra-level progression and addresses the current problems of existence that arise in their own journey so that the spiral can keep developing.
Level 9 (Coral)	TOWARDS ENLIGHTENMENT

over a lifetime from Level One – the lowest level of consciousness – through to essence at Level Nine.

KEY CHARACTER DRIVERS

There are three key Intelligences that drive the Crusader:

C2 – Vision

P2 – Passion

I1 – Data

THE SUBTYPES

Each of the eight types is made up of three Intelligence Circuits (ICs). The Crusader has C2 Vision, P2 Passion and I1 Data. As we adapt to our life circumstances we tend to favour one of the three. This subtly changes the personality and gives rise to subtypes. All Crusaders will be able to relate to all three of the subtypes at some time in their life.

THE VISIONARY CRUSADER

The Visionary Crusader fights to keep ideas and ideologies pure. This subtype does this by firstly keeping themselves pure through daily exercises or rituals that require a high degree of self-discipline. Then through meditation, reading, study or training, the Visionary Crusader keeps their eye on the original and 'pure' doctrine, practice or procedure to ensure it is kept authentic.

The Visionary Crusader is very prone to attachment – which denies the constant fluid state of the universal system. While attachment is important for keeping promises, being true to your word and being a person of integrity, it also has some downsides.

In Eastern religions this attachment is considered the source of all suffering. Attachment focuses energy outside the individual and on another person, ideology or object. When the object of the attachment is removed the Visionary Crusader's

---

I have learned through bitter experience the one supreme lesson: to conserve my anger, and as heat conserved is transmuted into energy, even so our anger controlled can be transmuted into a power which can move the world.

Mahatma Gandhi
Former Indian
Spiritual/Political Leader

> *The Government should alter its policy and avoid forcing more people to fight for justice through the courts.*
>
> Malcolm Fraser
> Former Australian Prime Minister

focus tends to remain on the lost lover, the lost opportunity, the lost reward, the disappointment.

This subtype should also watch that they don't become over-intellectual and ungrounded, addicted to spirituality as a way of escaping day-to-day responsibilities; or they may become involved in psychotic episodes where the Visionary Crusader becomes totally unpredictable and manic or simply overwhelmed by life.

Ideals

I think the world would be a good place if everyone was considerate of other people: honesty, justice, and respect for yourself as well as others. I live in an ideal world where people are nice to each other. I go out of my way to be friendly to people.

THE POWERFUL CRUSADER

With P2 as their most dominant driver, the Powerful Crusader subtype fights for compliance, getting it right and completing the long list of 'shoulds' associated with any role or any task to be undertaken.

This subtype is particularly focused on compliance and ruling with an iron fist. When in full swing the Powerful Crusader leaves no room for others to express their creativity or individuality – there is a right way to complete the task, and everyone's role is to learn to do it the RIGHT WAY. This subtype is really where the Crusader gets its name from because it is the Powerful Crusader who goes on crusade. This subtype needs to be careful that they don't become what John Bradshaw calls a human doing rather than a human being – constantly pushing themselves to achieve and produce as a means of securing approval and feeling OK about themselves.

Being Disciplined

I was very disciplined about my study in University. I got an OP2 (Overall Position) at school through discipline and sheer determination. I was going to do well no matter what. I'm very disciplined about things I think are worthwhile, and other things I don't think are so important, I'm probably not so disciplined about, depending on my vision and the vision changes. I suppose the vision is that I'm good at everything I do.

Powerful Crusaders tend to push themselves so hard that they suffer from chronic fatigue or burnout because their bodies simply can't keep up. They also need to watch that they don't become dominating and controlling bullies wanting to know everything that everyone is doing and constantly trying to micro-manage and control everyone's lives for their own personally desired outcome. At all times this subtype needs to check that it is using, rather than abusing, power.

Being 'Forceful'

I work in a hospital and at times I can be very forceful. If someone else is at risk, and you're seeing the consequences of your behaviour, you get very protective of your patients. I want to make sure other people are following the standards as what they do impacts other people. When I see that happen, I take these responsibilities seriously. I do fear that other people perceive that I am too dominating, when I actually feel like I come across meek and mild.

THE WISE CRUSADER

With I1 as their most dominant driver the Wise Crusader focuses on completing tasks so that the things they create look like the 'idealised' version of their creation. Christmas dinner, for example, must have the entire colour, decoration and food one would expect the ideal Christmas dinner to have. Home must be spotless; cars should be clean and serviced. Educationally, Wise Crusaders value education and resist being promoted past their perceived level of training.

This subtype is often called the perfectionist. As I1 rises to very high levels, Wise Crusaders can become fascinated with clairvoyance, the third eye, mysticism and psychic intuition. While this is an expansive area of study, the Wise Crusader needs to watch that they keep grounded and carefully analyse the dreams, visions and insights that they find so fascinating and don't escape into the mystical world completely.

Being passionate

I am passionate about cooking. When people come over for dinner I want to cook the best possible meal, and I want it to look just right. I want it to present well. It has to coordinate and most importantly it has to BE good. I take great delight watching other people enjoy it.

Brand

I love buying good quality clothes. The brand of the clothes is probably very important to me – but really as notification of quality rather than a label shown so you can see it.

ARCHETYPES RELATED TO THE CRUSADER

When people discuss archetypes, many of the characters they use will fall into the same category as the Crusader, much the same way that there may be fifty-seven species of fern but regardless of the species, it still belongs to the fern family.

By way of example, some of these are:

- The Perfectionist
- The Olympian
- The Soldier
- The Rescuer
- The Reformer
- The Advocate
- The Warrior
- Theseus – Athenian Bull Slayer
- The School Ma'am
- The Attorney
- The Mentor, Tutor
- Arjuna (in the Bhagavad-Gita)
- The Queen
- The Defender
- The Amazon
- The Crime Fighter
- The Revolutionary
- The Pioneer
- The Celibate Nun/Monk
- The Sheriff
- The Hero/Heroine
- The Explorer
- The Environmentalist
- The Magistrate
- Ulysses
- The Settler
- The Soldier of Fortune
- The Legislator
- The Mercenary
- The Pilgrim
- Hidesata (in Japanese legend)
- The Lobbyist
- The Gunslinger
- The Entrepreneur
- Bernado del Caprio (19th Century Spanish hero)

CHILDREN'S STORIES/NURSERY RHYMES

- *The Princess and the Pea*
- Sir Lancelot, the White Knight

THE MIRROR

While the Crusader is moral, principled and idealistic, the Crusader's Mirror, the Commander, is sexy, impulsive and laid back with a youthful sexual charm, an easy humour and a love of parties. When the Mirror is in control the Crusader loves having fun, breaking the rules, being disorderly, talking loudly, behaving badly and generally doing all the things the Crusader abhors. The Mirror is particularly likely to get the Crusader into trouble when a little alcohol is applied.

When a young Mirror Commander appears on the scene they will charm people through overt seduction and physical contact. This matures to empathetic listening, warmth, an acceptance of all people and an incredibly generous spirit that is always available to help in a crisis at any time, day or night.

When integrated into the personality, the Commander gives the Crusader patience, acceptance, warmth, generosity and the ability to solve problems patiently. It even gives them the ability to enjoy life and amuse themselves.

CHARACTER FORMATION

The formation of personality has three major influences:

1. Firstly, the physiological genetic makeup of the individual that predisposes them to accessing particular energies and not accessing others.

2. Secondly, the culture of the environment in which the child grows up that sanctions some energies over others and so encourages the child to focus on some energies and suppress others.

3. And finally, the individual's psychological and physiological response to trauma or pain that usually occurs during childhood and that alters the way they relate to the six ICs. When we experience emotional pain or trauma we can 'turn off' the emotion by turning off the energy. One theory of personality development suggests that, if in time we turn off three of the energies, we derive our energy from the remaining three. These three in turn combine to form type.

Regardless of what caused us to focus on just three of the thinking functions rather than all six, as human beings we can take three thinking function energies that are available to all humans and combine them to create a higher form of consciousness. We are, if you like, human transformers of thinking into consciousness. This higher level of consciousness takes the form of a Neuro-Rational Type – in this case the Neuro-Rational Type of the Crusader.

CHILDHOOD EXPERIENCES

The Crusader's profile can be the result of growing up in an environment where good behaviour, self-control and high standards are emphasised above personal enjoyment or spontaneous pleasure. This can create children who develop massive super-egos or internal critics and play the role of good little girl or good little boy. Over the years the internal critic or super-ego develops strength and clarity, and insists on talking the Crusader through everything they think and do.

'Shoulds' in childhood

I'm very much into the 'shoulds'. When I was younger and growing up, maybe if I did something the right way, if I was polite, you know, that's OK. If I did something the wrong way, I'd get in trouble or I'd

*get told off. So I developed a whole lot of 'shoulds'; you should do this,
I should do that.*

DEFICIENT FIRST INTELLIGENCE (P1)

Thought to be formed in the womb and during early childhood, P1 provides the infant with a feeling of stability, of being wanted and of having the right to be here. Described by Lowen (1958) and Reich (1949) as the Schizoid Character, the Crusader constantly feels that they have to continually add significant value to validate their existence. According to Lowen:

> *The Schizoid defence is an emergency mechanism for coping with a danger to life and sanity. In this struggle all mental faculties are engaged in the fight for survival. Survival depends upon absolute control and mastery of the body by the mind.*

This lack of grounding causes the Crusader to have deep-seated issues around the body, survival, roots, nourishment, trust, health, home, family and prosperity.

TRAUMA AND PAIN

While every individual has their own unique story to tell, in my experience if the formation of the personality has resulted from emotional trauma, the Crusader's trauma is centred around their legitimate role or place in the world (P1). It often has to do with the child's experience and subsequent interpretation of the love they receive from their primary caregivers. This usually occurs during childhood and early adolescence when the child is making sense of love and defining their social role. If we compare theories of child development, this correlates with Piaget's 'sensory-motor' stage, Erikson's 'trust vs. mistrust' stage, Maslow's 'physiology' phase, and Kohlberg's 'punishment / obedience' phase.

During this time if the child is traumatised, belonging is withheld from the child, or provided in highly conditional ways, the child can misinterpret this in two ways. Firstly, the child interprets that because they are not receiving the love they desperately need, they are, as an individual, not valuable. This pushes them to look for ways that they can become valuable, namely by producing or doing things, rather than just being themselves. This moves the child's energy away from learning about relating, interpersonal communication and reciprocating love towards learning about how they can turn feeling into action that will achieve outcomes that will be acknowledged and valued. If the child is further criticised for the things being created, they work until it is virtually impossible to find fault with it. This creates a focus on taking on causes that are bigger than an individual, creating things that are beyond criticism and focusing on the inanimate rather than the living as a strategy to receive love. This reinterpretation of belonging, closing down of the heart and active avoidance of criticism creates an important cornerstone of the basic character structure of the Crusader.

A second way in which trauma can shape personality at this age, is by pushing the child to create inappropriate associations with belonging. For example, if the child is verbally abused, they may associate verbal abuse with belonging. If the child is isolated and rarely touched or given any hint of affection, this becomes programmed as being 'real belonging' and the personality will then repeat this pattern with their own children or indeed with anyone belonging. For the Crusader the task of healing involves a mature understanding of belonging. The question Crusaders must ask themselves is, 'Is this tough love?' or 'Is this an inappropriate association that needs to be re-examined and reconfigured?'

THE QUEST FOR INTEGRATION: AWARENESS (I), CREATIVITY (C) AND POWER (P)

For each of us, like trees in the forest, there is a part of us that wants to grow and develop. (The Greeks referred to this force or desire as physis.) All of us want to be all that is within our potential. This constant desire to grow, which we share with all sentient beings, is what encourages us to move from one whole level of consciousness to another. We seek to answer the questions of existence at each level and to continue to expand and grow. The reality is, however, that often we get stuck. Rather than move to the next level of consciousness, we tend to let our avoidance of pain keep us in a time warp. This can be eschewed by following the seven steps of integration. Each step is a constructive step forward. Each step builds on the previous and requires a surrender of ego.

While we all have seven steps in the sequence of integration, the order of the steps is different for each Neuro-Rational Type. The unique process of integration that creates the bridge for you to move to the next level of consciousness is the real work of life. The work is simple, but not easy. In fact, for each of us the path of disintegration is much easier, but also more complex, as our ego justifies its compulsions, addictions, habitual responses and belief in their rightness. The path of disintegration is strewn with revenge, hopelessness, intolerance, bullying, procrastination, irresponsibility, withdrawal and distraction. It may be hard, but in contrast, the path of integration is a noble and profound journey requiring integrity, inspiration, diplomacy, courage, discernment, responsibility, objectivity and finally, celebration.

A day spent judging another is a painful day. A day spent judging yourself is a painful day.

Buddha

Healing in Action

SPIRALLING UP FOR THE CRUSADER — PERSONAL TRANSFORMATION AND THE PATH TO LIFE[1]

For the Crusader, transformation starts by acting with integrity. This is the noble quality of the Crusader and assures their personal commitment to their own life. If they have no commitment to their own life, it drains the very will to survive. This integrity is core to their being. It is absolutely essential that they know this and can recognise it if they wish to make this journey because it is their integrity that is their beacon at every step. Their integrity will keep them travelling in the right direction. In practice the quest for integration follows these eight steps:

AWARENESS

1. HEALING THE HEART

Personal security and renewed self-confidence enable the Crusader to risk connecting with people and risk rejection. This opening of the heart enables the first miracle of transformation – healing and integration. The healing of some of the past hurt and pain of childhood integrates some of the various personas they have adopted through life and ensures they are accepted. In taking this action, the Crusader accesses the noble quality of inspiration. This inspires the Crusader with a sense of optimism about the future and fills them with gratitude for their life.

2. BUILDING BRIDGES OF UNDERSTANDING

The healing that has taken place during the first phase of transformation enables the Crusader to begin building bridges between the various parts of themselves that have fought for what they believe is right. This is the Chancellor phase of diplomacy, and it takes this noble quality of diplomacy to create an integrated sense of what is right and to find the commonality between the different perspectives. During this phase the Crusader focuses

---

1   Based on a Crusader in the Blue meme.

their energy as they build bridges between their internal orphaned aspects of self.

3. COURAGE

With their energy behind them the Crusader now steps out with courage to begin fulfilling their vision. This is where the Crusader starts a new job or relationship, begins a new business or moves town. They step forward with courage and address the issues that have been concerning them but until now have been ignored.

CLARITY

4. DISCERNMENT

Having taken the first step with courage the Crusader now focuses on the systems and processes required to take the right action. During this time the Crusader develops a strategic yet practical plan that will guide them through the crusade. These systems and processes also check they are 'walking the talk' as they apply the noble quality of discernment to ensure that all aspects of their life are aligned.

ACTION

5. LIVING RESPONSIBLY

Living with honour requires that your word is your bond and your promises will be kept. To achieve this requires a careful assessment and management of risks and the balance between responsibility and authority. This is the work of this phase. As the Crusader does this work, workmates, friends and family have their sense of certainty and confidence about what the Crusader is doing reinforced, and they will follow them to the ends of the earth and back again.

6. LEARNING

With clarity regarding their plan and the action required, the Crusader now focuses on securing timely and appropriate information or personal or professional learning. It takes the noble quality of objectivity for the Crusader to make an accurate assessment of what knowledge they need to incorporate into their life. During this time Crusaders buy books, attend courses, update databases, tidy up the financial system, conduct competitor analysis, review the pricing or conduct benchmarking. The majority of the book-learning and understanding during the transformation cycle takes place during this phase.

7. ENTHUSIASM AND CELEBRATION

With the risks in hand and a loyal and focused team, the Crusader is ready to motivate and focus themselves and their team on breaking the glass ceiling and powering through. This involves accessing the noble quality of drive. This is a time of boundless energy, optimism, success, recognition and fun. The serious nature of the Crusader is broken by laughter, a quick mind and a love of stories, parties and celebration.

ASSESSMENT   ## 8. ASSESSING THE NEW QUESTIONS OF EXISTENCE

The final step is now taken into a brand new world – one with entirely new questions of existence. Since this integration process occurs in the Blue meme, the Crusader will have integrated this aspect of consciousness. Now they will be faced with an entirely new set of questions of existence. In the Orange meme they will be based around the need to succeed and be recognised as successful. The Assessment occurs as the Crusader takes stock of their current situation, of the lessons they have learned about life in general and their own abilities in particular, and then begins to apply their Genius of pushing the boundaries to achieve excellence.

For all the types there will be times when their development is arrested or even reversed. It's hard to believe that these honourable Crusaders can feel and behave in the ways described below. Crusaders refer to these times as their 'dark night of the soul'.

SPIRALLING DOWN FOR THE CRUSADER – THE PATH TO DEATH

The spiral downward is triggered by any event, thought, association or deed interpreted through the perspective of the Lower Self. It is this interpretation that many Christians would refer to as a separation from the divine part of ourselves and as 'sin'.

For the Crusader the downward spiral is triggered when they do not act with integrity. When this happens, the Crusader disappoints their divine self, and in an attempt to bolster their conscience, the ego looks to others for signs of their continued commitment to them. For the Crusader in this state, the obvious personal commitment of others becomes a sign to them that they (the Crusader) are still worthy and that they will not be rejected as bad, and therefore unlovable. The self talk at this stage is that they are the only ones living with integrity. This can quickly deteriorate into the downward spiral of disintegration, which has seven steps.

AVOIDANCE

1. BULLYING

If the commitment of others to the Crusader despite their lack of integrity is not forthcoming, the Crusader will begin to bully and blame others. This bullying comes in the form of cutting words, strong emotions, mood highs and lows and a focus on personal attacks. The Crusader delusionally convinces themselves that they are 'in the right' and that others need 'reprimanding' to justify their own position. At this stage the Crusader develops and tells elaborate stories that blame others for their own lack of integrity.

2. ARROGANCE AND ISOLATION

If things continue to get worse, the Crusader will begin to isolate themselves and only associate with those who can supply them with important or powerful information. They only accept information that will support their course of self-delusion. Crusaders can cut off all contact with the outside world becoming hermits, reading and refusing to communicate because, frankly, no one is up to their standard. During this phase Crusaders study the laws, rules and fine print that will help them defend themselves if their transgression ever comes to trial. Crusaders also talk endlessly about how things should be done properly (Introjection).

3. INFLEXIBILITY

As the Crusader spirals down, so too does their flexibility. Adherence to plans becomes a clear focus and their management style becomes totally closed to any new suggestions. They either become abrupt, disconnected and autocratic or very polite and talkative and deflect any authentic contact. During this phase the Crusader's personal hygiene may deteriorate and they become fascinated with tools, weapons or equipment that can help them defend themselves against a vicious world that hates them.

REJECTION

4. PROCRASTINATION

Isolated, angry and unwilling to take responsibility for their own behaviour or the situation that it created, Crusaders now look for the inconsistencies in the behaviour of others and in the systems they are following. What they come to see is their own inconsistencies, which they falsely interpret as belonging to either the other person or the environment with which they have merged. This is their first line of defence against anyone who says they are to blame. During this time the Crusader's professional performance declines as the procrastination increases.

5. VICTIM

At this point the Crusader has spiralled down to the point that they feel isolated and betrayed and they can't figure out why they have been victimised. Tears, storytelling and seduction all manifest at this stage. They perceive that they have no future, no friends and no courage. This phase often ushers in heavy drinking and drug-taking 'to get through it all'. All their own faults, victim mentality and lack of awareness are projected onto everyone and everything else.

INTERNALISING
ACTION

6. POLITICS

With some people around them now engaged in accepting the victim role portrayed by the Crusader, the Crusader is ready to play these people off against those who refused to remain committed to them. This phase can see the Crusader lie, exaggerate, change alliances and shamelessly compete for attention. No lie is too big. No political game is too ambitious. The police, supervisors, parents, wives, children and lifelong associates can all be dragged into this if they are necessary to win the political game and exact their revenge. Eventually the hate turns into self-hatred and the Crusader cruelly punishes themselves.

DISASSOCIATION

7. DISASSOCIATION

Finally, the Crusader, completely disassociated, sees themselves as the great healer, a God-like creature sent to earth to teach, preach and help the poor and misguided. This is often accompanied by visions and messages from God or outer space.

This spiralling down can be stopped immediately at any stage of the downward spiral if the Crusader observes their own behaviour, recognises the pattern, and consciously moves to the transformation spiral rather than the disintegration spiral. For the Crusader, this means getting back in touch with their integrity, apologising for their transgression, and healing the wounds they have caused.

The Crusader's Quest for Creating Wealth

Crusaders are fascinated with commerce and see themselves as a provider or protector for their family and loved ones. They have a highly developed sense of morality and of what is true and correct.

Crusaders always look ahead and put money away for a rainy day. They are not interested in putting on airs and graces and using their money to impress others; instead, they are by nature frugal, independent, reliable, conservative and safe.

Crusaders have a natural interest in tradition and genealogy. They like to know their heritage and keep 'special' family heirlooms.

Crusaders are sure of their own mind, suspicious of 'get-rich-quick-schemes', conservative and disciplined.

HOW CRUSADERS BECOME WEALTHY

Crusaders are brilliant at pushing themselves and their teams to produce the very best quality. They are totally committed to constantly refining systems and personally checking that the quality is A1.

Crusaders make big money when they start their own businesses and are involved in manufacturing tangible product development or the provision of top-end services to markets that can afford them.

Crusaders lead the professional services' army of doctors, medical specialists, lawyers, management consultants, senior government and military personnel.

DEEP UNCONSCIOUS MOTIVATION

The Crusader's energy comes from being appreciated for their ability to solve problems creatively and stick with people through thick and thin.

In their business affairs, Crusaders will want to have total hands-on involvement with all their investments. They will want transparent accounting practices and believe in paying tax so that the community can be sustained.

> *I regard this as a pretty good summary of what life is all about.*
> *I am a humanist. I don't believe in any higher power than the*
> *best expressions of the human spirit, and those are to be found*
> *in personal and social relationships. Evaluating my own life*
> *in those terms, I've had some mixed results. I've hurt some*
> *people and disappointed others but I hope that, on balance, I've*
> *given more than I've taken.*
>
> Fred Hollows,
> *a gifted opthalmologist whose crusade was to drive eye-saving*
> *anti-glaucoma programs into developing nations.*

MONEY MANAGEMENT APPROACH

Crusaders prefer to invest in tangible real estate rather than intangible stocks and shares. They prefer residential homes, in the middle price bracket, that are well positioned and are solidly built. New homes or novel homes are not as interesting to them as solidly built family homes that have been well-maintained and owner-occupied. Crusaders like to own their own homes.

Crusaders are very suspicious of professionals who give financial advice and instead prefer to 'nut things out' for themselves.

Crusaders will often attend seminars on wealth creation because they feel comfortable being anonymous and can take home the principles and apply them in their own time and in their own way.

Often Crusaders are unappreciated by their peers and colleagues for the high value they add to a project. This, together with their own highly critical nature, means that it often happens that Crusaders are underpaid and under-rewarded when they work for others.

THE CRUSADER'S MONEY HABITS

Crusaders can get so bogged down in solving all the day's problems and getting everything perfect that they can lose sight of the original financial objectives of a project.

Crusaders can pour too much energy and money into legals, paperwork and documentation. The greatest opportunities are often overlooked because they are too new or too innovative. If they are to invest, the Crusader prefers to invest in tried and tested blue chip companies (often ex-government privatisations) with a long-term focus rather than speculative projects. Every now and then the Crusader will break all his or her own rules and give money to friends or family to help them out. This causes the Crusader deep stress if the money is not returned in the agreed time. This can lead to significant interpersonal conflict.

Crusaders can become obsessed with having to have the best ingredients, systems or equipment when sometimes far cheaper options would get the job done just as effectively.

Crusaders are very prone to burn out themselves and everyone working with them with constant criticism and negativity. This costs money because it lowers the commitment of the team and the level of discretionary effort they are willing to put in to achieve the objectives.

Because Crusaders are protectors by nature, they tend to find it hard to take advice from anyone and instead rely on their own financial counsel, which is often very conservative and limited.

WHAT CRUSADERS DO WITH THEIR WEALTH

Crusaders live largely conservative lives even when wealthy. They prefer to live in homes that accurately reflect their social standing and level of income.

They have a fascination with tradition and family values, so celebrating weddings, Christmas, birthdays and anniversaries is important to them and they will enjoy festive activities in traditional style.

Wealthy Crusaders spend most of their time supporting their family and enjoy activities like looking after children/grandchildren, driving with friends and family, working with community groups and refining their daily routine.

Wealthy Crusaders are passionate, committed and loyal idealists looking for quality in everything they contribute to, buy or sell.

WEALTH CREATION FORMULA FOR CRUSADERS

Crusaders need to accept that while there are rogues in the financial services industry there are also many that they can trust and work with. Crusaders need to spend the time to find such a person and agree to accept that person's advice.

Crusaders must get over having to be right and having to win with every investment. The money game is a game and not every kick will yield a goal.

Crusaders tend to believe that rather than spending time on developing their financial plan they will simply work harder and things will turn out OK. Crusaders need to realise that working hard will get them only so far. In addition to this, they need to develop and manage their own financial plan.

Perfectionism is self-abuse in the highest order.

Ann Wilson Schaef
Author, Women's Rights Activist and Psychotherapist

Crusaders need to realise that while they are perfectionists, other people, who are not, often see their contribution as painful and unnecessary. This makes it hard for Crusaders to earn the money they deserve, particularly when they are the very last ones to ever ask for a raise. This is why the majority of wealthy Crusaders created their wealth by starting their own business and encouraging others to dance to their tune rather than the other way around.

The transition from working for somebody to running their own business simply requires Crusaders to have the confidence that they can do it and the belief that they deserve success. Crusaders need to think through what being rich really means to them.

Crusaders often have very negative scripts related to being wealthy which need to be reframed so that they believe that becoming wealthy is OK. If they don't believe this, Crusaders will ambush their own attempts to achieve financial success.

Frugal

I always love a bargain but I always look for a quality product. The quality is more important than the bargain. When shopping for clothes I always look for a good fabric, whether it's got double stitching, whether it fits well in that the cut is flattering. I always look at the wash label whether it's washable or dry cleanable, whether this is practical in terms of – it's fine if it's dry cleanable if it's a coat but, any shirts or pants, you'd be paying a fortune in dry cleaning otherwise.

Understanding Crusaders

CRUSADERS BEST MANAGE THEMSELVES BY:

- Not letting themselves get locked into one vision and becoming inflexible
- Not misinterpreting team members' rejection of the vision as being a rejection of them and their leadership
- Not pushing people so hard they burn out
- Not pushing everyone to work at the Crusader's fast pace and instead giving them time to think things through

AS TEAM MEMBERS, CRUSADERS MAKE THE BEST CONTRIBUTION WHEN:

- They are given a vision that is big enough to be worthy of their energy, commitment and enthusiasm
- They have a role that requires re-energising or motivating teams of people
- They have new and interesting challenges that require decisive decision-making and quick action

WHEN MANAGING CRUSADERS:

- Provide regular written feedback about what they are doing well and what you would like them to do differently and explain why
- Give them at least one project that stretches them into unfamiliar territory
- Give them projects with an element of competition, so that their effort can be acknowledged

HOW CRUSADERS WILL BEHAVE DURING MEETINGS:

- Will need clarity around why the meeting is required, why all the participants are required and how the team's effectiveness will be measured
- Will want there to be tangible action as a result of discussion – even if the decision is not to make a decision, the outcome must be said and noted
- Will tend to run roughshod over sensitive members of the meeting

PERSONALITY STRENGTHS THAT HELP THE CRUSADER TO FURTHER THEIR DEVELOPMENT:

- Able to break through virtually any barrier to achieve results
- Passionate and inspirational
- Fantastic at debating that the extra effort to make it better is worthwhile

PERSONALITY WEAKNESSES THAT CAN STAND IN THE WAY OF THE CRUSADERS DEVELOPMENT:

- Insensitive
- Totally task-oriented
- Can suffer from burnout
- Can link ego with vision and become inflexible

OPPORTUNITIES FOR CRUSADERS TO DEVELOP:

- Need to learn how not to offend
- Need to learn how to change direction quickly
- Need to learn how to connect with people
- Need to learn how to value themselves in ways other than just outcomes

THREATS TO A CRUSADER'S DEVELOPMENT:

- Can create many enemies who retaliate
- Can get bored when there are no new conquests and will go looking for trouble
- Can lose 'connection' with people and become lonely
- Can become too outcome-focused, judge themselves as not adding value, suffer from self-imposed disappointment and get frustrated and depressed

FAMOUS CRUSADERS

- Frank Lowy (Westfield Holdings)
- Vanessa Redgrave
- Estee Lauder (Cosmetics Manufacturer)
- Mary Poppins
- Elizabeth II (The Queen of England)
- Malcolm Fraser (Ex-Australian Prime Minister)
- Emily Post
- Carl Benz (Founder of Mercedes Benz)
- Katharine Hepburn
- Fred Hollows (Fred Hollows Foundation)
- Henry David Thoreau
- Sir Joh Bjelke-Peterson (former Queensland Premier)
- Martin Luther
- Edward Deming (founder of TQM)
- Charles Dickens
- Judith Lucy (Comedienne)
- George Harrison
- Plato
- Mahatma Gandhi
- John Paul II
- Celine Dion
- Colin Powell
- Margaret Thatcher

CRUSADERS AT WORK

Crusaders enjoy the big picture They are brilliant at painting very clear pictures of how things could be in the ideal world. Being vision-centred they cope with change easily as long as it aligns with their vision. Their energy and enthusiasm are heightened when focused on a project they are committed to and believe in.

> **Dependable**
>
> *On a report card, or anything I've ever done where there's some form of assessment, they've always said I'm a very responsible person – being answerable to whatever you're called to do or told to do. People would never check up on me. If I said I was going to do it, I'd do it.*

For the Crusaders, no vision means no energy. They are keen to cooperate if their vision and ideas are valued; if not, their willingness to contribute diminishes quickly. These wunderkind human beings can achieve the impossible, bringing to life dreams that others would consider unachievable. If a Crusader decides a project should go ahead, it will usually happen. The Crusader is excellent at getting projects off the ground and insisting on quality.

They are highly motivated to achieve their vision in what they believe is right. Efficiency fades when Crusaders are required to change tack halfway through a project. They will not willingly adhere to processes or procedures implemented by others. Their opinions are based on values rather than analysis or logic. They would rather beat their own path. When assigned a project, they will be very determined to see their vision take shape. Often they will seek to hand over a project if it is too small They will either work on a project to meet a deadline or, if it does not fit the vision, will tend to be attracted to a newer project or idea that does. They suffer boredom when there is nothing to strive for.

Colleagues may bore them easily if they do not share their vision. They like people who value their ideas and also tolerate their highs and lows. They don't respect people who allow logic to stifle creativity. Crusaders are most comfortable with like-minded people. A Crusader's confidence rises and falls. When they have a vision and an outlet for its expression they ooze confidence.

A Crusader must be able to express their vision and creativity. They are natural energisers, motivated and enthusiastic, but can become depressed and frustrated when their vision is repressed. They are excellent at delegating, and will make clear the implications of achieving or not achieving the objective.

> *If I asked someone to go and get something for me I'd always make a concerted effort to always tell them how much I'd appreciated it.*

They tend not to naturally empathise with others. They are more interested in winning the battle than being loyal to those who don't share their vision. They cope with aggression either by arguing the point or by escaping to the creative vision part of their mind. They often respond with aggression.

Their ability to analyse is often clouded by their ability to judge. They will make quick decisions generally based on preconceptions and attitudes, and when asked to make a decision regarding a new topic, they will spend a lot of time looking for facts to substantiate their decision.

Crusaders cope with stress by daydreaming or focusing on how things could be, rather than how they are. They will place themselves under a lot of stress to achieve their vision. Crusaders enjoy competition and generally win. Their assets are their convincing speech, excellent arguments and factual recall to back them up. They are fluent communicators and accomplished negotiators with excellent memories. They like power and are sometimes ruthless with it.

A Crusader's humour is often weird or bizarre, and anything taboo or offensive amuses them. They will always want things done properly. They will unconsciously exaggerate at times to win a point.

Crusaders are zany and in their passion to express possibilities, they will paint pictures, sometimes ignoring reality and the current truth. Crusaders are at their most formidable when turning an organisation or situation around, swaying large numbers of people and working as up-front, blast-through change agents or conquerors of new territory.

Some ships are ships, and some ships are watches. Our luxury yachts are as finely built as a Swiss watch. We don't need to advertise as our name is known internationally as the best luxury yacht in the world.

John Rothwell
CEO, Austal Ltd

LEADERSHIP STYLE OF THE CRUSADER

Each Neuro-Rational Type, due to its combination of thinking functions, has a different leadership style. These leadership styles tend to be expressions of the underlying world view of each personality. The most effective leaders use a variety of styles, choosing the appropriate style, timing and intensity to manage each situation.

The leadership style most closely aligned to the profile of the Crusader is a *Mentoring* style. The author's experience shows that the Mentoring style has a medium-positive effect on the overall climate of the organisation. The primary focus of the Mentoring style is the vision of the moral crusade which is to be achieved through personal performance.

Some of the attributes of the Mentoring leadership style are as follows:

- **Clarity.** The visionary (strong C2 element) nature of the Mentoring leader generates motivation because people come to see clearly how their work fits into the larger vision of the organisation. For the Crusader leader clarity is how the individuals are performing in relation to their personal best.

- **Inspire commitment.** Their visionary focus allows them to frame the individual tasks in the context of the overall vision (I1 articulated vision). Therefore, people can see how their work matters and why it is important. It brings significance to

Table 11.2 The Leadership Style of the Crusader

Situation	Explanation
1. The leader's modus operandi	One-to-one mentoring to help set high standards
2. The style in a phrase	'Do it again until you get it right'
3. Underlying emotional intelligence competencies	Self-discipline, a sense of justice, fairness
4. When the style works best	When change is being driven by moral crusade
5. Overall impact on climate	Medium positive

The Mentoring Style

Fred Hollows, the famous eye surgeon, was a Crusader (Powerful Crusader subtype). Head of the Eye Department at a Sydney hospital in 1966, he learned of the great incidence of eye disease among Australian Aborigines. Because he always believed strongly in equality, he set about establishing the first Aboriginal Medical Centre, later launching a nationwide program in Australia, then he moved his crusade to Africa. Hundreds of thousands of people benefited as he worked for excellence and affordability among the needy.

Dr Hollows was able to inspire people to follow his moral crusade – doctors and other staff volunteered and people donated millions of dollars. He was indomitable. He said, 'I believe in helping people help themselves ... When I've seen an opportunity I haven't sat down and called a committee meeting. We've gone and done it'. He was known as the 'wild colonial boy' partly because of his wild temper. One biographer politely said that he could be 'very gruff when things weren't going as he thought they should and this made him some enemies. But his family and friends loved him deeply' (Leary online, 2002 ABC, Privacy Policy).

True to the Mentoring style, Fred Hollows was dynamic and totally focused on the detail and excellence of the work they did – driven by the moral crusade. And in the process he trampled on some toes.

In their compelling book Memories of Fred, Pat Fiske and Michael Johnson offer the following recollections which demonstrate Dr Hollows' leadership style. Pat Fiske, cycling, running and climbing mate and director of the film about Fred's life and work, For all the World to See, said, 'He often gave me hell, as he did others. I had a love-hate relationship with him. There were times when I was so angry and frustrated during arguments when he would just cut me off with his shouting and self-certainty, stifling any chance of debate ... But I got heaps out of the friendship – he was dynamic, exciting to be with and always had you on wood. He had a powerful sense of self, a self-confidence that swept you along with him ... He made you feel an important member of the team. I treasure many happy memories.'

Paul Torzillo, medical student and Volunteer Driver Aboriginal Medical Service 1970s, said, 'Fred loved being a doctor and was proud of the profession. He was concerned with competence and professionalism and imprinted their importance on me for the rest of my career. I was always amazed at Fred's ability to interact with all comers. Even more amazing is how highly regarded he was, very often by people who didn't particularly share his political views! He was often challenging and provoking and frequently insulting – I think it was this ability to engage people which helped him recruit so many people to work with him ... Fred was absolutely serious and committed to the indigenous cause. Fred enjoyed being around blackfellas, he liked their company, found them interesting and enjoyed the time.'

Adapted from the Fred Hollows Foundation online www.hollows.org

We shall never have friends if we expect to find them without fault.

Thomas Fuller
English Preacher, Historian and Scholar

the employees' daily activities and so increases their sense of commitment.

- **Very high standards.** With a strong sense of vision, the leader defines standards that underpin the overall objectives. The Crusader is focused on detail and excellence of output. The emphasis is on results on – creating things of a very high standard. Key words are 'excellence', 'best in class' and 'best of breed'.

- **Feedback.** In providing feedback (assisted by I1), the single objective is whether the performance has furthered the vision. Therefore, determinates of positive or negative feedback are fixed and not subject to whims. The Mentoring style is one-to-one and always fair.

- **Objectives.** These are clear and stated up front, as are the rewards for performance.

It's important that everyone in the team contributes equally and performs their role to the best of their ability. When I was a team leader, I wanted the people I was in charge of to learn from me so that they could be proud of themselves and I could be proud of them. I tried to treat them as equals. I tried to make every experience a learning experience. I would never try to withhold information from them and I would try to encourage them in their career. I always tried to compliment them on a job well done. When managing difficult staff that didn't play by these rules of mutual respect, I had to have very strong self-control and not behave in a way that was reactionary to whatever they were doing. At great expense to myself, I still tried to treat them fairly and equally. In doing so, I think I became quite discouraged that some people had no interest in making an effort in getting along with other people, or being respectful, when personal differences were evident.

I struggled with doing the right thing by these people. I might not have liked them, or really honestly wanted to respect them, but I believed it was important that everyone had a right to be respected and treated well. Internally, I struggled greatly with the fact that they weren't treating me well. I suppose in one way I was hurt, in that no matter how hard I tried, they treated me with great disrespect, with absolutely no concern for my feelings even though I was constantly thinking of ways of working in with their requests.

SCHOOL OF STRATEGIC THOUGHT

The natural differences are not limited to leadership styles alone; they also extend to a natural inclination towards different strategic thought. These differences have been researched by Mintzberg, Ahlstrad and Lampel (1998). For the Crusader, their approach to strategy belongs in the positional school. This suggests that only a few key strategies (or positions in the economic marketplace) are desirable.

THE GENIUS OF THE CRUSADER – PATHFINDING

The Genius of the Crusader is in pathfinding, an ability to conquer new territory. This means they thrive on danger or unknown territory, or creating new frontiers. As long as the crusade aligns with the stated vision, Crusaders will undergo enormous short-term pain for long-term gain. They will be the ones who blast through to achieve the results. This makes Crusaders excellent for starting up businesses or projects, for rejuvenating dead concepts or creating new visions. Buckingham and Clifton (2001) describe this strength as follows:

- Excellence in standards, as opposed to mediocrity.
- The stance is that it takes just as much effort to transform something strong into something superb as it does to take something mediocre to something above average, so why waste time on the latter.
- The person focuses on strengths, be that their own or another's. They can discern where strengths are being met (or underused) and focus on encouraging, challenging and developing them to reach excellence.
- Because of this focus on sorting, they are seen as discriminating. This person prefers the company of people who appreciate their strengths and who have developed their own strengths.
- They avoid people who see them as deficient and try to round out their own or other people's talents. Instead, they prefer to focus on what they can do well and take that to excellence. They consider their positive attitude as more fun, more productive, even though demanding.

Buckingham and Clifton (2001, p. 108) offer several examples of the person who pushes the boundaries to conquer new territory. First is a man who had been an aerobics teacher. Because he believed it was destructive for people to focus on their deficits, he gave them permission to forget about them and concentrate on building up the parts of their bodies that they liked – and everybody, including the teacher, felt this was a better use of their time and energy.

The second example, Amy, a magazine editor, shows a different application of the same leadership style. When she came to work on articles submitted by her staff, she did not waste time on work she considered poorly written. She would return it to the writer and ask them to start again. What she did enjoy was perfecting already good work which just needed the master's touch to make it brilliant.

The third example is a marketing executive who is happy because his boss allows him to focus on, use and develop his areas of strength in team building; rather than expect him to be a good all-rounder, the boss has found someone else to do the strategic work and leaves him to concentrate on his innate abilities. This makes him feel secure and motivated.

BODY COMPOSITION

The Crusader body shape is naturally lean. Limbs are long and height is above average. Even in overweight Crusaders, the face is thin. The Crusader does not have a well defined waist and their hips are narrow. Crusaders who spend a lot of time in the Red or Orange meme have larger frames than those in Blue, Green or Yellow. In rare instances, body composition is too thin or too overweight; this is due to individual Crusaders adopting unhealthy eating behaviours; however, they genuinely think this is the way to healthily or correctly eat according to their individual set of values. Overfatness develops initially in the upper abdominal region, where continual fat gain is distributed evenly throughout the torso, arms and legs (Diversi, 2006).

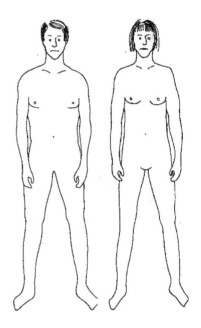

FITNESS PREFERENCES

The Crusader is naturally an active type, not perturbed by incidental exercise. The Crusader enjoys cardiovascular exercise and will often use physical means for transport and enjoyment. To be classified as exercise by the Crusader, the activity must be at a moderate to high intensity; heart rate must be increased and sweating must be evident (Diversi, 2006).

EATING PREFERENCES

The Crusader has a good relationship with their body, has a good sense of the future and is happy with delayed gratification. The Crusader eats for purpose and

> *The curious paradox is that when I accept myself just as I am, then I can change.*
>
> *Carl Rogers*
> *American Psychologist*

rarely eats more or less than they need for nourishment. They are strong believers in a balanced diet, variety and enjoy all types of food in small amounts. Crusaders are quite good cooks; they can cook without recipes but prefer to use them for quality control (Diversi, 2006).

DIETING PREFERENCES

The Crusader rarely diets. They are very suspicious of fad diets and an individual who spends most of their time in their Crusader rather than their Neuro-Limbic Type, would never follow one. The Crusader decides what type of eating style suits them and their values. They stick to this eating style as it is the right thing to do. When they discover health problems, they will seek out information that they feel confident is correct and have the self-discipline to stick to it (Diversi, 2006).

Applying Crusader Insights as an Effective Communicator

When Negotiating with Crusaders

The effective communicator is able to align their narrative and the point they want to make with the Archetype of the audience. That is, they use the same language, approach and behaviour with the Archetype of the person they are presenting to.

When negotiating with Crusaders the way you position information is very important. While Crusaders are attracted to messages centred around due process and quality, the two other themes which are most convincing to them are: *'Show me that you are willing to do what it takes to make this vision happen'* and *'Show me this idea is the best way forward.'*

These are discussed in more detail below.

'Show me that you are willing to do what it takes to make this vision happen'

There are two groups who access their P2 and C2 by nature – the Bards and the Crusaders. This segment makes up approximately 12.25% of the general population. When negotiating with this group:

- Present with passion and commitment for a clear and exciting vision
- As a leader, incorporate being motivational and inspirational of your people and your stakeholders
- Present your vision as being right and that the endpoint will justify all the hard work to achieve it
- Compare how the organisation is performing relative to the rest of the market
- Provide benchmarking comparisons
- Maintain reputation and community standing; the 'person' is as influential as their message
- Show respect for institutions, laws and precedents, and show that the organisation is 'doing the right thing'
- Show tangible evidence that the leader and their team are absolutely committed to achieving the vision and the leader supports bonus payments or incentives on this basis

'Show me this idea is the best way forward'

There are two types who access the P2 and I1 functions by nature – the Crusader and the Judge. This segment makes up approximately 37 per cent of the general population. When negotiating with this group:

- Do not show indifference, lack of passion, coldness or apathy
- Sell the benefits of new ideas particularly if these benefits can be quantified
- Keep the discussion tangible and concrete with specifics
- Do not present intuitive and unproven concepts, models, abstract ideas, hunches, intuitions or possibilities
- Show that there is a valid code of conduct and that there is a right and wrong way of doing things
- Show that leaders are approaching tasks the RIGHT way
- Demonstrate that you are following the rules, respecting the status quo, paying taxes, doing jury duty and being fair
- In your communication, be precise, passionate, action-oriented and respectful of institutions and roles/positions
- Demonstrate that their leaders are strong yet approachable, and will protect those within their responsibility
- Articulate goals, set milestones and show that these goals are achieved
- Demonstrate that the leadership is passionate to do whatever it takes to keep the energy and focus maintained

The Crusader at a Glance

Strengths

- Keeps team members accountable
- Integrity
- Brings out honesty in others

Code of Conduct

- Always keeps sensitive information that has been shared in confidence to themselves
- Acts ethically in their dealings with others
- Spends time to make sure they are in agreement about their role and your own role
- Corrects others – clearly, constructively and professionally
- Speaks directly to the person with whom they have an issue without unnecessarily involving other unrelated people
- Provides other team members with a sense of purpose

First Step of Integration

- Focuses on unconditional love and compassion for self

First Step of Disintegration

- Descends into competition with, and bullying of, others

Exemplars

- Margaret Thatcher
- Queen Elizabeth II
- Estee Lauder

Our struggle has reached a decisive moment. We call on our people to seize this moment so that the process towards democracy is rapid and uninterrupted. We have waited too long for our freedom. We can no longer wait. Now is the time to intensify the struggle on all fronts. To relax our efforts now would be a mistake which generations to come will not be able to forgive. The sight of freedom looming on the horizon should encourage us to redouble our efforts.

It is only through disciplined mass action that our victory can be assured. We call on our white compatriots to join us in the shaping of a new South Africa. The freedom movement is a political home for you too. We call on the international community to continue the campaign to isolate the apartheid regime. To lift sanctions now would be to run the risk of aborting the process towards the complete eradication of apartheid.

Our march to freedom is irreversible. We must not allow fear to stand in our way. Universal suffrage on a common voter's role in a united democratic and non-racial South Africa is the only way to peace and racial harmony...

I have fought against white domination and I have fought against black domination. I have cherished the ideal of a democratic and free society in which all persons live together in harmony and with equal opportunities. It is an ideal which I hope to live for and to achieve. But if needs be, it is an ideal for which I am prepared to die.

Nelson Mandela

Chapter 12

The Bard

An In-Depth Look at the Bard

Merlin: **Love is a force.**

Young King Arthur: **Is it very powerful?**

Merlin: **Yes. Some would say the greatest power in the Universe.**

Merlin
MAGICIAN

What we've got to thank Bards for:

Creating a sense of magic

Healing and inspiration

Creating a sense of purpose out of pain

Empowering people to use their gift

Coaching people to achieve their best

Making the impossible come true

Creating spaces with an 'other-worldly' feel such as theme parks and restaurants

THE BARD PROFILE

One's own self is well hidden from one's own self: of all mines of treasure, one's own is the last to be dug up.

Nietzsche
German Philosopher

OVERVIEW

Bards have the unique ability to see the potential in others and create environments that empower them or enable them to reach their full potential. They have a natural fascination with their own quest for meaning, the purpose of life and the deeper and more mystical parts of life.

> *I've sung for thousands and held every one of them in my hand, even the Policemen. I've preached to stone faces and watched the tears start. I've had at least one person from each of my former Churches go into Ministry and one other tell me he had 'joined up' because he'd heard me being crazy once on a Christian Radio Show.*
>
> *When I was about nine years of age, my best friend and I put on a concert. We created instruments from cardboard, made a stage of sorts, created costumes and sold tickets to the neighbours. I was in another world ... wished I could have stayed there.*

Bards can inspire with their amazing ideas and big dreams, their zest for life and their optimism, energy, passion and warmth. For the Bards everything is interdependent, so their home and work lives will merge as will their various business ventures, their ideas and their philosophies. This can sometimes mean that relatively small issues are combined to create large, complex and difficult situations. When this happens the Bards can see that any movement will impact on so many areas that they can become paralysed for fear of 'upsetting the apple cart'.

Regardless of their training or level of professional development, Bards have the ability to create teams of people all working to the same objective, all for their own personal reasons. The Bards will take the role of listener, friend, supporter and adviser for each team member.

Bards are very sensitive and can intuitively 'pick up' the feelings of others. This can mean that the internal emotions of Bards are greatly affected by the people around them. By nature Bards will avoid long-term exposure to trauma, stress, crisis and conflict because of the enormous emotional stress it causes them.

Healing

Just to prove you don't have to be an angel to do miraculous things, I have been the instrument of the spontaneous healing of illnesses, chronic conditions, psychological trauma, dementia, but so far not Athlete's foot.

When I focus on the problem and not get emotionally involved I can prescribe the correct homeopathic remedy. I feel involved but objective and it's great to see people relaxed and comfortable about what's happening.

FOCUS OF ATTENTION

Bards focus on creating a safe environment where everyone can reach their full potential. At their best, Bards are modest, confronting, inspirational, visionary, liberating, empowering and healing.

Creating a safe environment

When I was a boy we used to go on holiday to a seaside place with lots of sand dunes. I would spend all day running across the dunes with my plastic raincoat tied around my neck as a cape. I was Aqua Boy and it was my job to keep all the people in the caravans safe from the... I don't know... things they needed to be safe from. Nothing's changed.

My home is my castle. I love to create an environment where when we come back to it, even if we've been away just a short time, it's restful and refreshing. It's a haven. That's so important to me.

KEY CHARACTER DRIVERS

There are three key Intelligences that drive the Bard:

C2 – Vision

P2 – Passion

I2 – Heart

LEVELS OF CONSCIOUSNESS AS DEFINED BY US PSYCHOLOGIST CLARE GRAVES AND SPIRAL DYNAMICS' AUTHORS COWAN & BECK

Table 12.1 outlines the broad character development of the Bard over a lifetime from Level One – the lowest level of consciousness – through to essence at Level Nine.

Table 12.1 The Bard Levels of Development

Level of Consciousness and the noble quality embraced at this level	Common Bard characteristics at this level of consciousness
Level 1 (Beige) A state of nature and instincts.	Competitive, aggressive, physically abusive, angry, punitive.
Level 2 (Purple) Mysterious and frightening. *(Noble quality to be embraced at this level:* **Modesty***)*	The Bard feels instantly at home at this phase and involves themselves in the telling of the old stories or even in inventing their own. They have a natural talent for leading the rituals and maintaining the magic.
Level 3 (Red) Raw displays of power – dictators, tough love, predators. *(Noble quality to be embraced at this level:* **Confrontation***)*	This power is initially misinterpreted by the Bard as being from God but is eventually 'owned' and then managed by the Bard as they realise it really comes from them. The tough love is expressed through passion and enthusiasm and if this doesn't work, through withdrawal and coldness. People who will not conform are removed from their life.
Level 4 (Blue) Everything is controlled by God and is purposeful. Obey God. Do it right. Feel guilt. *(Noble quality to be embraced at this level:* **Inspiration***)*	For the Bard, this is the first time the Mirror (Treasurer) takes over. Life becomes orderly and controlled and God is seen as creating order through control. The Bard reads the holy books, studies the rules and the scriptures, gets the appropriate qualifications, and helps to audit the behaviour of others so that they can better follow the way and keep the order.
Level 5 (Orange) The world is a game and I want to win. *(Noble quality to be embraced at this level:* **Visionary***)*	The Bard Master returns to discover that other Bards are in the active creation of life. The dominant idea at this phase is that the winners are the ones that create a world in which they can personally win. The Bards create their world – be it a church parish, a new business, a family or community where they are the clear leaders and the clear winners because they make the rules. They discover their gift and how to use it for personal gain.
Level 6 (Green) We need to join together and grow personally through community. *(Noble quality to be embraced at this level:* **Liberating***)*	The Mirror Treasurer is integrated into the personality as the Bard admits that constantly creating reality with a weighted hand is too exhausting. Instead, the Bard recognises the cycles of life and instead of fighting them uses them to help build a community based on principles and values that reflect the whole community rather than just the Bard. They learn to use their gift for the community.
Level 7 (Yellow) We need to explore ways of being responsibly free. *(Noble quality to be embraced at this level:* **Empowerment***)*	The Bard becomes a spiral Wizard, seeing where the community's spiral needs attention and moving seamlessly between levels of development and the six energies and eight gifts so that the community is strong and the work of the community is achieved.
Level 8 (Turquoise) The world is composed of delicately balanced interlocking forces, shaped by attractor fields of intention and nobility. Uses natural flows. Actively grows consciousness. The Non-dual Leader manifests at this level.	The world is seen as a series of cycles and life is seen as a quest. The individual understands the spiral of life and the streams of intra-level progression and addresses the current problems of existence that arise in their own journeys so that the spiral can keep developing.
Level 9 (Coral)	TOWARDS ENLIGHTENMENT

Once you have mastered time, you will understand how true it is that most people overestimate what they can accomplish in a year - and underestimate what they can achieve in a decade.

Anthony Robbins,
Motivational Speaker

THE SUBTYPES

Each of the eight types is made up of three Intelligences. The Bard has C2 Vision, P2 Passion and I2 Heart.

As we adapt to our life circumstances we tend to favour one of the three. This subtly changes the personality and gives rise to subtypes. All Bards will be able to relate to all three of the subtypes at some time in their life.

THE VISIONARY BARD

Visionary Bards are future centred, often with visions that are not logically connected to their current line of thinking.

The Visionary Bard will tend to have close friends with whom they are open and honest, and they will generally keep their personal thoughts and ideas from others.

They tend to daydream or focus on what could be, rather than what is. They are sensitive to stress and prefer low-stress situations where they can relax and express their imagination without fear of ridicule or misunderstanding.

Their spiritual world will not work to a pattern and will not be disciplined. A Visionary Bard often has bizarre or taboo thoughts and ideas which may even offend themselves. They have a brilliant imagination and can visualise well and tap into the wisdom of heaven.

THE POWERFUL BARDS

Powerful Bards have strong opinions about most things and will want issues resolved. They filter thoughts through their opinions and beliefs. Powerful Bards will tend to make decisions quickly, often based on the principle of the matter, will argue well, and are motivated by a belief in the value of what they are doing. The Powerful Bard's motivation comes from believing that what they are doing is important and in line with their philosophy of life.

One of the greatest challenges for Powerful Bards is to control their anger and to understand that others can have their own ideas that may not agree with theirs. They like to be acknowledged for a job well done, and it is important to them to live up to their own very high self-expectations. The Powerful Bard is highly competitive and a high achiever.

THE SENSITIVE BARDS

Sensitive Bards are very attuned to how others are feeling – they are true empathisers, putting people first at all costs. They have an intuitive ability to sense what is happening around them.

The Sensitive Bards are naturally shy although they may hide it well. They will be extremely sensitive to the needs of others, often to their own detriment. They do not want to offend or upset others, and will tend to say nothing when they are upset or angry unless they are compelled to. Sensitive Bards need to be careful that their unexpressed anger does not turn to resentment. Resentful Bards will go to great lengths to get even. When doing this, they will use great subtlety so that no one can read their behaviour.

Sensitive Bards will think in terms of people, not facts, and intuitively sense how others are feeling. They will place relationships at the very top of their priority list and they make very sensitive partners. They will be caring and loving parents and the glue that binds a family.

Unconditional Love

My friend and I worked for eleven years to keep an elderly lady we came to love, out of a nursing home. She lived in nauseating squalor; we fixed it time and again. She would get terribly depressed and not get out of bed (for anything) for days. She had a heart of gold and severe bi-polar disorder. The illness would make her turn on us time and time again. The last time it happened, it destroyed the life I had then. I rang her a while back, just to say, 'I love you.' What else?

We lived for a time in the rainforest and during this period had a friend live with us. He was often unreliable, dirty, messy and uncommunicative, but generous to a fault. He lived with us for five years, drove me batty at times but if he needed a place to live I'd welcome him back anytime.

ARCHETYPES RELATED TO THE BARD

When people discuss archetypes, many of the characters they use will fall into the same category as the Bard, much the same way that there may be 57 species of fern but regardless of the species, it still belongs to the fern family.

By way of example, some of these are:

- The Guru
- The Spiritual Adviser
- The Caregiver
- The Evangelist
- The Preacher
- The Healer
- The Property Developer
- The Therapist

- The Counsellor
- The Kindergarten Teacher
- The Prophet
- The Monk
- The Motivational Speaker
- The Minister
- The Hypnotist

- The Soothsayer
- The Entrepreneur
- The Shaman
- The Fortune Teller
- The Magician
- The Actor
- The Entertainer

CHILDREN'S STORIES/NURSERY RHYMES

- Merlin the Magician
- Santa Claus
- Wendy from Peter Pan
- The Fairy Godmother

THE MIRROR

While the Bards see themselves as gentle, visionary, passionate people with an ability to heal the past and create a better world, their Mirror, the Treasurer, is obsessed with order, details, stability and security. Bards can be confusing because while their language is passionate, optimistic and nurturing, their behaviour, which is influenced by the Mirror Treasurer, suggests they are penny-pinching, controlling and almost obsessive-compulsive.

At home, the Mirror may express itself through constantly monitoring the household's financial position on a spreadsheet, isolating investments into a number of different funds, each having different risks, keeping friendships separated, feeling comfortable only when things are totally clean and ordered, and insisting on folded clothes, clean cars, ironed shirts, neatly stacked books and spotless tables and desk tops.

At work, the Mirror unobtrusively shadows the noisy, energetic and inspirational Bard, ensuring meetings are minuted, costs are managed and itemised, information is filed and budgets are micro-managed.

Young Mirror Treasurers are quiet and gently question the Bard's qualifications,

---

If you can dream it, you can do it. It's kind of fun to do the impossible.

Walt Disney
Walt Disney was the man behind Mickey Mouse, Donald Duck and other cartoon favourites. He created one of the largest amusement parks in the world and brought many of our favourite fairy tales to life.

---

level of knowledge and professional credibility. This often encourages the Bard to undertake study to achieve formal qualifications for the work they are doing.

As the Mirror matures, the strength and volume of the Mirror Treasurer's concerns become harder for the Master Bard to ignore, and the Bard's authenticity and practical abilities are constantly questioned. This usually leads to the Bard beginning the process of learning the 'nitty gritty' detail of the work they have been getting others to do for them.

When the Mirror is fully integrated into the personality, the Mirror Treasurer gives humour, flexibility, structure, intellectual rigour, depth and grounding to the already visionary, passionate and intuitive Bard.

CHARACTER FORMATION

The formation of personality has three major influences:

1. Firstly, the physiological genetic makeup of the individual creates a predisposition towards accessing particular energies and not accessing others.

2. Secondly, the culture of the environment in which the child grew up sanctioned some energies over others and so encouraged the child to focus on some energies and suppress others.

3. And finally, the individual's psychological and physiological response to trauma or pain that usually occurs during childhood alters the way they relate to the six Intelligences. When we experience emotional pain or trauma we can 'turn off' the emotion by turning off the energy. One theory of personality development suggests that if in time we turn off three of the energies we derive our energy from the remaining three. These three in turn combine to form type.

Regardless of what caused us to focus on just three of the Intelligences rather than all six, as human beings we can take three Intelligences that are available to all humans and combine them to create a higher form of consciousness. We are, if you like, human transformers of thinking into consciousness. This higher level of consciousness takes the form of a Neuro-Rational Type – in this case the Neuro-Rational Type of the Bard.

CHILDHOOD EXPERIENCES

For the Bard the character forms around the imbalance of C1 and the highly developed I2 and C2.

DEFICIENT SECOND INTELLIGENCE (C1)

Many Bards often also have a deficient C1. When this is the case Bards are out of touch with their feelings and sensations in their body. Their movements may be jerky rather than fluid and feelings may be intellectualised.

An often-noted characteristic of the Bard is their unwillingness and/or inability to enjoy themselves. In my experience this can usually be traced back to the first twenty-four months of the Bard's life during what Piaget calls the child's sensory-motor stage. This same stage aligns with Erikson's trust versus mistrust phase, Maslow's safety phase and Kohlberg's instrumental hedonism phase. During this time if there is tactile and sensory deprivation it gives rise to restricted physical and emotional movement in adult life.

A deficient C1 gives rise to stiff joints and a rigid musculature that has trouble yielding to softness and feeling. This reduces the level of chi energy in the body and lowers the metabolic rate and reduces the emotions. This also gives rise to inflexibility and fear of change, both of which are bard characteristics. This deficiency also prevents the individual from wanting or accepting pleasure of any type, and as pleasure is moved into their rejected self they are very harsh with others who appear to be having a good time.

DEFICIENT FIFTH INTELLIGENCE (I1)

The temptation for Bards is to stream their energy straight to their C2 and escape the mundane nature of the world of reality. This is due to a deficient I1. While this is not true of all Bards, all Bards do have an excessive C2 and so therefore have a hard time seeing, accepting and understanding reality, preferring to make their own worlds conceived in their own minds.

THE QUEST FOR INTEGRATION: AWARENESS (I), CREATIVITY (C) AND POWER (P)

Awareness – Having eyes that see (I1)

For the Bard, integration begins when the Bard is willing to see the world more as it actually is rather than constantly trying to escape from it and create their own imaginary worlds in their own minds.

For Bards, integration can mean seeing their life as it really is for the first time. This may include who they have married, where they actually live, how heavy they really are or how thin they really are. It also means being willing to look at household finances, as they really are, lifestyle and character. Finally, for Bards to develop I1 awareness, they must take time to see the repeating patterns in relationships, jobs, purchases and lifestyle and challenge the 'magic think' that is behind the behaviour that keeps getting manifested. Madness was once defined as doing the same thing over and over and expecting to get different results. This is what the Bard will do unless this awareness is awakened.

Developing earth-bound creativity (C1)

Bards are spectacularly creative, but often not in practical, hands-on ways. This is the second aspect of healing for the Bard – to get in touch with their body and the practical creativity they have within them. This can involve painting, drawing, cooking, dancing, in fact, any kind of self-expression that's fun. The key here is not to focus on the end result but instead to focus on the process. The process must be fun.

Reconnecting with the root Intelligence (P1)

The foundational Intelligence is the key to healing the original wound around which the type has formed. P1 healing strategies can include reconnecting with the body, physical activity, weights, running etc, lots of touch (for example, massage) and yoga. Much to many Bard's frustration, the process of developing the P1 is not complex or sophisticated. It is about doing whatever possible to reinforce the idea that it is safe for Bards to be alive and nurture their body. It's about reclaiming the Bard's right to be here. Many issues can be resolved if the Bard can link with their family heritage and traditions.

Healing in Action

SPIRALLING UP FOR THE BARD – PERSONAL TRANSFORMATION AND THE PATH TO LIFE[1]

For the Bard, the spiral upwards starts with unconditional love, generosity and inspiration. This energy is often channelled into creating a safe and 'other worldly' environment. In this space people are encouraged to be 'who they are' with complete freedom and can effectively deal with their hurts and disappointments with life. In practice, the quest for integration follows the ensuing eight steps:

AWARENESS   ## 1. INTEGRITY

For Bards, their journey towards integration starts when they are willing to step out into the real world rather than in their field of dreams and in their mind's eye. This is very hard for Bards who want to assume everyone is generous, things will work out all right, legal suits will not be mounted, diseases will be healed and other people will forgive. While inspirational, these views are often not in touch with reality and awareness for Bards is about coming to terms with the reality. The first step in the journey requires Bards to ensure everything they are doing is being done with honour and honesty and that there is an absolute focus on reality – not just potential. This requires that the Bard act with the noble quality of integrity, ensuring that their words and their deeds are in alignment.

2. DRIVE

Once they have learned how to see clearly, despite their own rose-coloured glasses, Bards are ready to drive forward their own life by focusing on asking themselves the hard questions, getting clarity on what action they need to take personally and getting on with it. This is a time of boundless energy, optimism, success, recognition and fun. The deep and mysterious nature of the Bard is broken by laughter, a quick mind and a love of stories, parties and celebration.

3. LEARNING

The Bard now focuses on securing timely and appropriate

---

1   Based on a Bard in the Blue meme.

information, or personal or professional learning. As they take an objective perspective on their own life, the Bard will come to appreciate what knowledge they are currently lacking. During this time Bards buy books, attend courses, update databases, tidy up the financial systems, conduct competitor analysis, review pricing or conduct benchmarking. The majority of the book learning and understanding during the transformation cycle takes place during this phase.

CLARITY

4. RESPONSIBILITY

With personal integrity and honour in place the Bard looks to their long-term plans and the key milestones ahead. In accessing the noble quality of responsibility, the Bard takes a careful assessment of the balance between responsibility and authority that they have in their life at this point. They then step out to rectify any imbalance. In the short term this clarity focuses on how they can give back to their community. For the Bard, living responsibly requires that they effectively play their role in the family, at work and in their community. Amongst other things, this requires a careful assessment and management of risks. As the Bard does this, workmates, friends and family have their sense of certainty and confidence about what the Bard is doing reinforced and they see the genuineness and committed nature of the Bard in fulfilling their role.

ACTION

5. RIGHT ACTION — THROUGH DISCERNMENT

The Bards now focus on the systems and processes required to improve efficiency and ensure they take the right action. This involves accessing the noble quality of discernment to ensure that all aspects of their life are aligned. During this time the Bards develop a strategic yet practical plan that will guide them through the rest of their journey. These systems and processes also ensure they are 'walking the talk'.

6. COURAGE

With their community or workplace behind them the Bards now step out with courage to fulfil their vision. The noble quality of courage enables the Bard to face internal or external opposition and to still move forward in their life. This is where the Bards start a new job or relationship, begin a new business or move town. They step forward with courage and certainty and never look back.

7. BUILDING BRIDGES OF UNDERSTANDING – THROUGH DIPLOMACY

The healing that has taken place during transformation enables the Bard to begin building bridges with people with humility, honesty and diplomacy. During this phase the Bard earns the reputation of being open and honest and accepting and building bridges between people from all walks of life. In this phase Bards look to create an opportunity for everyone they know to be able to grow and develop and to use their gift. This involves the noble quality of diplomacy to find the commonality between what people are doing and their innate gifts and to find ways to bring the latter into every aspect of their life.

ASSESSMENT

8. ASSESSING THE NEW QUESTIONS OF EXISTENCE

The final step is now taken into a brand new world – one with entirely new questions of existence. Since this integration process occurs in the Blue meme, the Bard will have integrated this aspect of consciousness. Now they will be faced with an entirely new set of questions of existence; in the Orange meme they will be based around the need to succeed and be recognised as successful. The Assessment occurs as the Bard takes stock of their current situation, of the lessons they have learned about life in general and their own abilities in particular and then begins to apply their Genius of meaning to develop the noble quality of being Visionary.

For all the types, however, there will be times when their development is arrested or even reversed. It's hard to believe that these inspirational Bards can feel and behave in the following ways. Bards refer to these times as their 'dark night of the soul'.

SPIRALLING DOWN FOR THE BARD — THE PATH TO DEATH

The spiral downward is triggered by any event, thought, association or deed interpreted through the perspective of the Lower Self. It is this interpretation that many Christians would refer to as a separation from the divine part of ourselves and as 'sin'.

For Bards, the spiral down is triggered by deceit of either themselves or others. This offends and traumatises the Bard who is dedicated to authenticity and honesty and can't believe what they've done. This can quickly deteriorate into the downward spiral of disintegration which has seven steps.

AVOIDANCE

1. INSECURITY AND MANIPULATION

The first phase of disintegration sees the Bard feeling insecure about their important relationships because of the deceit they have enacted. To get the reassurance they believe they need, they use manipulation and persuasion to reassure others that they were not lying and that their honour and good character are still intact. They can't believe the feedback they receive because they are delusional. This phase can see the Bard lie, exaggerate, change alliances and shamelessly compete for attention. No self-deception is too big. No political game is too ambitious. Supervisors, parents, wives, children and lifelong associates can all be dragged into this if they are necessary to ensure the Bard's good name is maintained and their key relationships are kept strong.

2. BELIEVING THEY ARE A VICTIM AND BECOMING DEPENDENT ON OTHERS

If the relationships cannot be saved, the Bard will have spiralled down to the point that they feel isolated and betrayed and they can't figure out why they have been victimised. Tears, story telling, and seduction all manifest at this stage. They perceive that they have no future, no friends and no courage. This phase often ushers in heavy drinking and drug-taking 'to get through it all' particularly if this is how their family coped with stress.

3. CONFUSION AND PROCRASTINATION

Isolated, angry and unwilling to take responsibility for their own behaviour or the situation that it created, Bards now look for the inconsistencies in the behaviour of others and in the systems they are following. Bards use deflection as their first line of defence against anyone who says they are to blame, which ensures they avoid contact with anyone who could open their eyes to the situation. During this time the Bard's professional performance subsides as the procrastination increases.

REJECTION

4. INFLEXIBILITY AND CONTROLLING BEHAVIOUR

As Bards spiral down, so too does their flexibility. Adherence to plans becomes a clear focus and their management style becomes totally closed to any new suggestions. Bard's boundaries break down during this phase as they merge with either their environment or those they are responsible for. Any criticism of their team, project or environment results in the Bard becoming abrupt, disconnected and autocratic. During this phase the Bard's attention to personal hygiene may subside and they become fascinated with tools, weapons or equipment that can help them defend themselves against a vicious world that hates them.

5. ARROGANCE AND ISOLATION

If things continue to get worse, Bards will begin to isolate themselves and only associate with those who can supply them with important or powerful information. Bards can cut off all contact with the outside world, becoming hermits, reading and refusing to communicate because, frankly, no one is up to their standard. During this phase Bards study the laws, rules and fine print that will help them defend themselves if their transgression ever comes to trial. They prefer all their communication to be done in writing. The Bard now projects their own deceit, lack of commitment and all other disowned flaws onto others.

INTERNALISING ACTION

6. COMPETITION AND BULLYING

If the spiral down continues, the Bard will begin to bully and blame others. This bullying comes in the form of cutting words, strong emotions, mood highs and lows and a focus on personal attacks. At this stage the Bard starts punishing themselves for their lack of results through impossible workloads, poor diet, or unreasonable physical stress.

DISASSOCIATION

7. COMPLETE INTOLERANCE AND PUNITIVE BEHAVIOUR

Finally, the downward spiral continues with the Bard becoming intolerant of all other positions, becoming self-righteous with degrees of a Messiah complex. The Bard decides they are the only ones doing what should be done and that others need to be punished to teach them a lesson. This is done behind the scenes by the Bard who is by now totally disassociated and is pulling the strings and creating chaos, hurt and confusion among their targets.

The spiral down has reached its last dimension before the Bard slips into a whole new self-delusion and deceit and falls into one of the nine Neuro-Limbic Types.

The Bard's Quest for Creating Wealth

HOW BARDS BECOME WEALTHY

Bards are brilliant at inspiring teams to create what seems to others to be the impossible. If the Bards can inspire and motivate others to work with them to achieve their unbelievable dream, they are considered to be brilliant. If they can't, they may be seen by others as weird.

Bards make big money when they can find a dream that they believe is worthy of their lifelong effort and can build a team that is inspired and motivated by the dream. The key for the Bards is to get both the dream and the team rather than one or the other.

I'm not a paranoid deranged millionaire. Goddamit, I'm a billionaire.

Howard Hughes
Aviator and film producer

DEEP UNCONSCIOUS MOTIVATION

The Bard's energy to earn wealth comes from wanting to create a secure home. The Bard's home certainly is their castle and their unconscious desire is to be able to minimise their contact with others by being able to work alone at home in a safe and secure environment. To achieve this, however, Bards need to use their highly developed personal interaction and diplomacy skills.

MONEY MANAGEMENT APPROACH

Bards put most of their energy and focus into increasing their current income. They tend to spend most of what they earn, and often then some.

Bards feel comfortable with investment in their principal place of residence and often overcapitalise on this property to create a special and magical home environment.

Bards often have a few highly leveraged investment properties that are negatively geared for tax purposes. They tend to hang on to these, however, rather than buying and selling properties, and see the overheads and maintenance as a form of enforced saving. As the properties accumulate, however, this can add an additional financial burden on their financial position and they sometimes need to fire-sale properties to ease the negative cashflow burden.

Bards respond best to an investment program which is organised by their financial adviser and deducts a set amount of money monthly. These can be very tax-effective if put in place by a good tax adviser.

Bards tend to have high levels of consumer debt, mostly on credit card. Family crises and the myriad of holidays, cars and clothes push the debt higher and force them to look for ways to increase their income so that the credit limit can get ever larger. Often Bards find themselves moving backwards in their mid 40s with high, non-deductible interest payments on credit cards that have never been fully paid off in more than ten years.

The Bard's ability to generate income is the highest of all the profiles. The problem is that they spend even more than they earn and often walk a financial tightrope.

Bards make the majority of their decisions to spend money emotionally and believe that money is there to be enjoyed rather than stored.

THE BARD'S MONEY HABITS

Bards will tend to abdicate rather than delegate financial issues to their financial adviser. This can result in misunderstandings and conflict between them. This failure to take responsibility can also result in misaligned financial objectives, poor investment strategies, and poor tax planning.

Bards will be drawn to investments that are new and that offer huge returns. Bards are also interested in supporting entrepreneurs, inventors, and people committed to

Imagine that men are from Mars and women are from Venus. One day long ago the Martians, looking through their telescopes, discovered the Venusians. Just glimpsing the Venusians awakened feelings they had never known. They fell in love and quickly invented space travel and flew to Venus.

John Gray
Author - 'Men Are From
Mars, Women Are From Venus'

their vision. While this kind of investment is ideal for the person promoting the new venture, it is not necessarily the best way to make money.

Bards enjoy creating homes with a 'special atmosphere'. This often involves the purchase of expensive brand-name furniture, properties with views and quality fittings and fixtures, all of which is expenditure with very low if any return on the very high level of investment required.

Bards will spend much of their discretionary income on training programs, personal development, books, tapes, CDs and conferences. Many of these are about collecting insight for the sake of it rather than focusing learning on key areas. This can be a very costly exercise with no returns.

When under stress, Bards will tend to be very cautious and will often experience 'paralysis by analysis'. This can mean that the best opportunities for investment are often missed as the Bards attend to their dreams while the real-life opportunity evaporates.

WHAT BARDS DO WITH THEIR WEALTH

Because the Bard's unconscious focus is on creating security, they tend to invest their wealth in a range of unrelated investments and put their eggs in many different baskets. Rather than one business, or one property, the Bard would prefer to invest in a number of different businesses or properties, in different states or internationally.

Bards prefer to live in highly secure and protected environments. This often means high-rise apartments, on the water, high on a hill or in a prestigious closed-gate community. Often Bards will 'invest' in antiques, rare artwork, collections, jewellery, furniture and cars.

Bards have a fascination with the mystical, healing, human interaction, the meaning of life, and authenticity and will invest heavily in activities related to these areas.

Wealthy Bards spend most of their time reading, writing, interacting with close friends, pondering the mysteries of life and expressing their thoughts through writing, music or art.

They are passionate, sagelike, wise, caring individuals who help others through difficult periods and expect the best of their friends and colleagues.

WEALTH CREATION FORMULA FOR BARDS

Bards must be willing to look at the cold hard facts of their financial situation, addressing areas such as the percentage of their current level of income that goes towards servicing non-tax deductible consumer debt and the realistic equity (net of all debts) they have in their investments including their home (using conservative values for all properties).

Bards need to set definite and realistic financial goals that they want to achieve over a specific period, for example, the next five years. The goals must be Specific, Measurable, Ambitious, Realistic and Tangible (SMART).

Bards need to find a financial adviser they can trust – someone who is wealthy themselves who they can relate to and don't feel they need to bluff or impress.

Bards must look at where their money is going and develop a system which tracks how much is being spent on restaurant bills, taxis, unnecessary impulse buys and consumer debt. They can then devise a weekly budget, which includes some discretionary spending money, and try disciplining themselves to stick with it. When Bards set themselves a task they rarely fail. They fail in money because they just don't want to have to think about it or deal with it.

Bards need to develop an investment plan that aligns with their financial goals. The basis of this is that money is taken out of their accessible income/pay packet before they get a chance to spend it, and is invested.

Bards need to discipline themselves to learn about how the money system works. This may be a boring and tedious area for them but it is important that they learn how passive wealth creation works because one day they will want to do something other than actively create money to spend on yesterday's debt.

Bards need to get themselves into the position of being able to take risks by

---

In motivating people, you've got to engage their minds and their hearts. I motivate people, I hope, by example – and perhaps by excitement – by having productive ideas to make others feel involved.

Rupert Murdoch
Media Mogul

---

having a safety zone of money or investment that is surplus to their needs. Bards who are 'down to the wire' financially all the time will not have the ability to cope with financial rough patches. By having a financial buffer they are putting fun back in the quest and are taking it away from being a matter of financial life and death which is dependent upon every one of their investments performing well.

UNDERSTANDING BARDS

Bards best manage themselves by:

- Disciplining themselves to attend to detail
- Not letting themselves get locked into one vision and instead remaining flexible and open to new ideas
- Disciplining themselves to make the hard decisions when dealing with staff and giving negative feedback
- Ruthlessly staying in touch with reality

As team members, Bards make the best contribution when:

- They are required to integrate or bring together different systems, paradigms or ideas
- They are given freedom to define their task, timeframe and deliverables
- They can encourage, motivate and nurture team members as socio-emotional leaders
- The system for measuring their effort is clear and stakeholder feedback is sought

When managing Bards:

- Provide them with clear timeframes, deliverables and available resources
- Have them break the project into phases and insist they report back to you in writing at each phase end, with an analysis and next action
- Ensure they don't start integrating elements that are not part of the project
- Help them work through detailed issues around legal implications, financial details and process specifics
- Firm up their recommendations with detail you may have to insist they – research some more and come back with specifics

How Bards will behave during meetings:

- Will want to see everyone participating and making a contribution
- Will reassure the offended, disgruntled or angry
- Will want to talk about frameworks, paradigms and visions
- Will want the meeting to run to time
- **Personality strengths that help the Bards to further their development:**
- Is able to create reality
- Can see the big picture
- Is inspirational and motivational

Personality weaknesses that can stand in the way of the Bard's development:

- Are not happy with anything that's not perfect
- Don't focus on detail, which often trips them up
- Find it difficult to motivate practical, hands-on people

Opportunities for Bards to develop:

- Need to ground themselves and get in touch with reality
- Need to be 'present' in the here and now
- Need, in difficult times, to learn how to take life one step at a time

Threats to the Bard's development:

- Can become so out of touch their skills and thoughts are irrelevant
- Can have major trip-ups because they are focused on past and future rather than the here and now
- Can be overwhelmed and 'break down' in times of crisis if there is no obvious way out

FAMOUS BARDS

- Walt Disney (created Disneyland)
- Rupert Murdoch (Chairman of News Corp)
- Peter J. Daniels (Author)
- Anthony Robbins (Motivational Speaker)
- David Hawkins (Author)
- Merlin the Magician (mythical character)
- Harold Hughes (1930s US Media Mogul)
- Michael Parkinson (UK TV Interviewer)
- Peter Beattie (former Queensland Premier)
- David Fritz (US Author)
- Dr John Gray (Author of *Men are from Mars, Women are from Venus*)
- Gandalf (mythical Wizard from the Lord of the Rings)
- Jeannie (character from *I Dream of Jeannie*)
- Samantha (character from *Bewitched*)
- Barry Humphries (entertainer)
- George Lucas (Star Wars)
- Jim Henson (creator of *The Muppets*)
- Napoleon Hill (Author)
- Luciano Pavarotti (great tenor)
- Jimeoin (Comedian)
- John Singleton (advertising mogul)
- Siimon Reynolds (Author)
- Joseph Campbell (Author)
- Al Gore (An Inconvenient Truth)

BARDS AT WORK

Bards are extremely loyal to close friends, family and selected acquaintances. They tend to be largely misunderstood by others. Bards are highly sensitive, very empathetic and understanding of others. They will be supportive of others as long as they demonstrate an interest and willingness to pursue the Bard's vision.

At first tier, Bards have a changing temperament. They can be endearing one minute and moody the next. They can become quite depressed once a project has been completed and they have no vision for the future. Similarly, if things are moving too slowly they can easily become bored. They are very spontaneous and creative and more than willing to experiment.

Bards respond well to people who are balanced, predictable and disciplined and at first tier they will generally put people into two boxes – those to be trusted and those not to be trusted. They are very likely to exaggerate. They are highly competitive and enjoy being recognised for their achievements. Bards thoroughly enjoy creating magic and, as storytellers, they are dedicated to communicating the essence rather than the detail.

Creating Magic

I can't imagine life without magic. How dull! Every kid, and adult, should watch the movie 'Never Ending Story'. Reality is too hard and boring. I like to create magic and fantasy even if it's only in my head. At least it makes the day more interesting.
Starts when I wake up, sometimes before. Couldn't be without it, wouldn't want to.

The Bard is neither analytical nor objective. Responses are based on their values and beliefs, gut reaction and vision.

At first tier, Bards will feel stress which drives them to either work harder, become more intense, talk faster or become abrupt. If confronted with aggression they will either argue, be lost for words or take it as a personal attack. They have long memories. A Bard is most formidable when leading groups to over-achieve, resolving complex personal problems and giving life meaning.

Hard work

If it's what I want to do, I'll work round the clock until I fall over. If it's not what I want to do, I'll hide behind the clock till some other bugger does it.

If I can see the reason or point to what I'm doing I'll work endlessly. If I can't engage with it or it doesn't capture my interest, I'm without energy and the whole thing is a pain in the neck.

THE LEADERSHIP STYLE OF THE BARD

Each Neuro-Rational Type, due to its combination of thinking functions, has a different leadership style. These leadership styles are a function of the centre of focus of the Neuro-Rational Types, and tend to be expressions of the underlying world view of the personality.

A groundbreaking survey of 3871 executives selected from a database of more than 20,000 executives[2] found distinct leadership styles which consistently appear in organisations. Daniel Goleman (2000) attributes these different leadership styles to different emotional intelligences. These emotional intelligences equate to the Six social Cognitive Needs.

Each leadership style has a different impact on the work environment and on organisational performance. The most effective leaders use a variety of styles, choosing the appropriate style, timing and intensity to manage each situation.

---

2   Survey was originally analysed by Kelner, S., et al. (1996).

Table 12.2 The Leadership Style of the Bard

Situation	Explanation
1. The leader's modus operandi	Develops people for the future
2. The style in a phrase	'Try this'
3. Underlying emotional intelligence competencies	Developing others, empathy, self-awareness
4. When the style works best	To help an employee improve performance or develop long-term strengths
5. Overall impact on climate	Positive

The leadership style identified by Goleman's research that is most closely aligned to the profile of the Bard is the *Coaching* style.

The author's experience supports the insightful research reported by Goleman. In most situations, the Coaching style is one of the most effective leadership styles as it drives up many aspects of corporate climate. The primary focus of the Coaching style of leadership is developing the unique capacities and abilities of the co-workers.

Some of the attributes of this leadership style are:

- By identifying the unique strengths of an individual and tying them to their personal and career aspirations, the Coaching style **increases loyalty and engagement**.

- **Empowering.** By identifying the unique strengths of an individual (a combination of C2 and I2) the Coaching leader draws commitment from employees.

- **Feedback.** Coaching leaders provide plenty of feedback and instruction. It requires constant dialogue, so employees know their boss is watching them and cares about what they do. This helps to increase flexibility and creates an environment where risk-taking can occur.

- **Conceptualisation.** The constant dialogue ensures people know what is expected of them and how their work fits into the larger vision or strategy of the organisation.

- **Delegating.** This leadership style is the best at delegating. They give challenging assignments, even if this results in short-term failure for long-term learning. The message that is implicit is, 'I believe in you, I am investing in you, and I

The Coaching Style

Daniel Goleman (2000) tells the story of Lawrence, production manager of the manufacturing division of a large company. When sales dropped, he decided in collaboration with the CEO, to close the unit and reassign the staff. When the team leader of the unit, James, heard about this, he bypassed his boss and requested a meeting with the CEO. When Lawrence learned of this, he met with James. But instead of berating him, Lawrence coached him: first he talked over the reasons for closing the unit and James' career path. Then he coached him on how to make a good impression in his meeting with the CEO. A Bard leader can see the potential in each of their team members and will want to see them grow and flourish. They will not dismiss a worker if they feel their intentions are good, so they will give them a second (and third) chance to succeed.

expect your best efforts.' Often employees will rise to the challenge with their heart, mind and soul.

The Coaching style works well in almost any business environment. It is most effective when the employee desires to be coached and is already aware of their weaknesses. If employees are resistant to change then it is ineffective. It is also ineffective as a method of leadership if the individual using it is inept at providing feedback that motivates, and instead creates fear and apathy.

> *Giving people a second chance*
> *It wouldn't occur to me not to – I've been forgiven so many times.*
> *We all make mistakes, how can I expect to be forgiven if I don't forgive. Life is short. Relationships are everything. Forgive, forget and move on.*

SCHOOL OF STRATEGIC THOUGHT

The natural differences are not limited to leadership styles alone; they also extend to a natural inclination towards different strategic thought. These differences have been researched by Mintzberg, Ahlstrad and Lampel (1998). For the Bard, their approach to strategy belongs in the Entrepreneurial school. This suggests that strategy formation results from the insights of a single leader and stresses intuition, judgement, wisdom, experience and insight. The 'vision' of the leader supplies the guiding principles of the strategy.

THE GENIUS OF THE BARD — ASSIGNING MEANING

The Bard's Genius lies in their ability to develop meaning for situations or events, to integrate information and to heal. This means creating a passion for the future, giving life meaning, healing old psychological wounds and integrating knowledge in a powerful way.

The *Genius* which most aligns with the Bard is what Buckingham and Clifton term *developing*.

Buckingham and Clifton (2001, p. 95) describe the Bard as the *developer* as a person who, when they see others, see only their potential.

That means:

- They do not see others as they are, but rather as they can be. In fact, everyone is seen as 'a work in progress, alive with possibilities'.

- It is the possibility of each person's potential growth which they find attractive.

- Their interactions with each individual are focused on seeing them reach success.

- They look for ways to challenge people to help them grow, and they watch carefully for signs of growth.

- People seek this person out for help and encouragement because they know that the Bard genuinely wants to see them reach their potential and will be as fulfilled as the person they help.

Buckingham and Clifton (2001) cite the example of John, an advertising executive who realised that his skills were not in production but in understanding people and their motives. He got pleasure from helping people develop strengths they had not realised they possessed. He valued the fact that he was able to find people for his team whose strengths were different from his own.

Another example of the strength of developing given by Buckingham and Clifton (2001) is of a nurse who changed the life of a chronically debilitated patient from suicidal to active and productive by helping her recognise and use strengths she had not realised she possessed. The Bard gets as much pleasure from the successes of the people they help as do the people themselves.

Use the biggest ad on the page. It costs four times more, but gets eleven times the response.

Simon Reynolds
Advertising Entrepreneur and Business Leader Mentor

BODY COMPOSITION

The Bard body composition is large, particularly in Bards who spend much time at the Orange meme or in the powerful Bard subtype. Bards often associate size with power. The limbs are relatively short and thin when compared with the torso. Bards do not realise their weight is a problem until they are told firmly by someone they respect but are not close to, such as their medical practitioner. Overfatness develops in the upper abdominal region initially and the abdominal region needs to become quite large prior to it being distributed to other parts of the body. The next place weight is distributed is in the legs. The shoulders generally remain rounded and thin. When Bards lose weight, they initially lose it from their legs and then face. This is followed by a reduction in weight around the abdomen. Bards look very drawn and the size of the head seems unusually large when their weight is too low (Diversi, 2006).

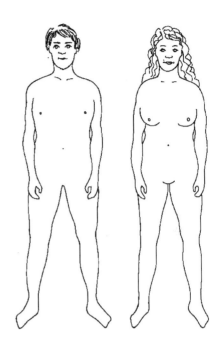

FITNESS PREFERENCES

The Bard is not very interested in fitness. They prefer arts, entertainment and reading over physical exertion. Any exercise regardless of length or intensity is justified as enough for fitness by the Bard. They are more likely to be convinced to exercise if the exercise is either for a good practical reason, is not difficult and if coercion is based on experiencing something beautiful such as swimming in a lake, walking in the rainforest or going to the beach (Diversi, 2006).

EATING PREFERENCES

The Bard loves food, particularly heavy meals such as bacon and eggs, stews, pies and other traditional English meals. If they can, they prefer to eat three hot meals per day. However, the Bard also enjoys good quality food that is presented in an appealing manner (Diversi, 2006).

DIETING PREFERENCES

The Bard does not like dieting. Regardless of their size, they rarely believe that they are overfat or that their weight is a problem. They will not follow a strict plan and always justify their behaviour as due to social occasions or expectations such as a family member's birthday or a business meeting. They like fad diets and diet products, particularly if they like the salesperson or health professional prescribing the product (Diversi, 2006).

I thought it (Star Wars) was too wacky for the general public. The secret to the film is that it's an illusion.

George Lucas
Screen writer and film maker

Applying Bard Insights as an Effective Communicator

WHEN NEGOTIATING WITH BARDS

The effective communicator is able to align their narrative and the point they are wanting to make with the archetype of the audience. That is, they use the same language, approach and behaviour with the archetype of the person they are presenting to.

When negotiating with Bards the way you position information is very important. Bards are attracted to messages centred around two main themes which are most convincing to them; *'Show me that you are willing to do what it takes to make this vision happen'* and *'Show me this solution will empower the team to achieve the objectives.'*

'Show me that you are willing to do what it takes to make this vision happen'

There are two groups who access their P2 and C2 by nature – the Bards and the Crusaders. This segment makes up approximately 12.25% of the general population. When negotiating with this group:

- Present with passion and commitment for a clear and exciting vision
- As a leader, incorporate being motivational and inspirational of your people and your stakeholders
- Present your vision as being right and that the endpoint will justify all the hard work to achieve it
- Compare how the organisation is performing relative to the rest of the market
- Provide benchmarking comparisons
- Maintain reputation and community standing; the 'person' is as influential as their message
- Show respect for institutions, laws and precedents, and show that the organisation is 'doing the right thing'
- Show tangible evidence that the leader and their team are absolutely committed to achieving the vision and the leader supports bonus payments or incentives on this basis
- Focus on teamwork, synergy and big picture strategies rather than implementation plans and processes

'Show me this solution will empower the team to achieve the objectives'

There are two groups who access their P2 and I2 by nature – the Bards and the Chancellors. This segment makes up approximately 12 per cent of the general population. When negotiating with this group:

- Is very sensitive to non-verbal communication, reading between the lines, gestures and facial expressions

- Has a huge influence on the population because they are the novelists, dramatists, television interviewers, playwrights, poets, biographers and popular journalists

- Asks questions about the meaning of actions, the purpose of the organisation, the role of leaders and the impact this all has on the organisation's stakeholders

- Sees good in everyone and assumes everyone is doing their best with the best intentions

- Has very little interest in buying and selling, or commercial occupations; and is much more interested in bringing out the best in people and enabling people to reach their full potential

- Will be, by nature, naive about the 'complexities' of law and business

The Bard at a Glance

Strengths

- Empowers teams
- Contributes inspiration
- Gives hope

Code of Conduct

- Displays an allegiance to all co-workers (above, below and beside them)
- Shows an understanding of how others are feeling
- Makes others feel valued and important
- Creates a workplace environment where colleagues feel they can try new approaches and take risks
- Looks for the unique contribution all colleagues can make to the team
- Encourages the team to be honest and open

First Step of Integration

- Focuses on personal integrity and doing the honourable thing

First Step of Disintegration

- Descends into personal insecurity and manipulation of others

Exemplars

- Walt Disney
- Howard Hughes
- Jim Henson

Chapter 13

The Chancellor
An In-Depth Look at the Chancellor

You will get all you want in life if you help enough other people get what they want.
Zig Ziglar
Motivational Speaker

What we've got to thank Chancellors for:

Diverse teams

Diplomacy

Agreements/Contracts/Treaties

Effective negotiation

Empathetic counselling

Effective conflict resolution

Fair HR practices

Customer relationship/management/service

Balanced lifestyle

Democracy

THE CHANCELLOR PROFILE

People are always blaming their circumstances for what they are. I don't believe in circumstances. The people who get on in this world are the people who get up and look for the circumstances they want, and if they can't find them, make them.

George Bernard Shaw
Irish Playwright

OVERVIEW

Chancellors are charming, enthusiastic, energetic and ambitious. They have an unmatched ability to sell ice to the Eskimos and have the Eskimos thank them, pay for their airfare and invite them back.

Regardless of their training or level of professional development, Chancellors like competition, negotiation, promoting ideas and people, and rising to the top.

It was never hard to get promoted or get selected for a job – as I had the track record of producing results and had built relationships along the way.

Chancellors are some of the most senior administrators and leaders in Australia. They live to work and rise to challenges, particularly complex people issues that others cannot nut out. Chancellors are passionate about projects with which they are involved, and manage to get everyone in the team working to achieve their objectives for their own reasons.

Chancellors can be high-profile if it is required, but prefer to work behind the scenes, enhancing their own career and credibility with each initiative.

Chancellors are excellent at creating a successful image. They rarely look concerned and appear to have the perfect lifestyle, living in the right suburbs, driving the right cars and holidaying in the right places.

I genuinely believe that we are great at building teams but often our quest to win and succeed can alienate the team. We can be very driven – I look back on my career and can reflect that whilst others may have been studying hard to get to the top, I would 'just do it' and try and outperform by delivering more or better results.

Chancellors are the ultimate diplomats. They are altruistic at heart and dedicated to authenticity and bringing out the best in others.

It is an exceptional feeling to know we can move people to greatness, alerting them to their true capabilities, and awakening them in

We should seek by all means in our power to avoid war, by analysing possible causes, by trying to remove them, by discussion in a spirit of collaboration and good will. I cannot believe that such a program would be rejected by the people of this country, even if it does mean the establishment of personal contact with the dictators.

Neville Chamberlain
Former British Prime Minister

preparation for their wonderful journey ahead.

FOCUS OF ATTENTION

Chancellors are brilliant at working in any field that requires people-to-people skills. They are particularly good at finding ingenious ways of achieving results when all else has failed. At their best, Chancellors are charming, good at negotiating and diplomatic. They strive for esprit de corps, and are kind, genuine and venerable.

If the eyes are the windows to the soul, then a smile has opened the windows. Confident body language speaks volumes in a first meeting or presentation. Much is analysed in the initial introduction. Other statements where there is continuance to build relationships would involve: 'You catch more flies with honey', and also, 'It's all in the delivery.'

KEY CHARACTER DRIVERS

There are three key Intelligences that drive the Chancellor:

C1 – Spontaneity

P2 – Passion

I2 – Heart

LEVELS OF CONSCIOUSNESS AS DEFINED BY US PSYCHOLOGIST CLARE GRAVES AND SPIRAL DYNAMICS' AUTHORS COWAN & BECK

Table 13.1 outlines the broad character development of the Chancellor over a lifetime from Level One – the lowest level of consciousness – through to essence at Level Nine.

Table 13.1 The Chancellor Levels of Development

Level of Consciousness and the noble quality embraced at this level	Common Chancellor characteristics at this level of consciousness
Level 1 (Beige) A state of nature and instincts.	Competitive, aggressive, physically abusive, angry, punitive.
Level 2 (Purple) Mysterious and frightening. (Noble quality to be embraced at this level: *Charm*)	Chancellors use their intuition to determine what people want to hear and sing from that spiritual hymn book. They know that it isn't true but work hard to convince others that their insight is real. Use their charm to become the priest/leader.
Level 3 (Red) Raw displays of power – dictators, tough love, predators. (Noble quality to be embraced at this level: *Negotiation*)	First displays of their Mirror (Navigator) where there is no willingness to genuinely negotiate. Instead, energy is put into charming and disarming and manipulating others to achieve their objectives. Use language, charm and politics to get their way – every time.
Level 4 (Blue) Everything is controlled by God and is purposeful. Obey God. Do it right. Feel guilt. (Noble quality to be embraced at this level: *Diplomacy*)	For the Chancellor this is a time of handing over to their Mirror. They become moral, masculine, absolutely committed to the group's ideals and focus on integrity, truth, strength and honesty.
Level 5 (Orange) The world is a game and I want to win. (Noble quality to be embraced at this level: *Esprit de Corp*)	The Chancellor's Master returns and focuses on winning the game. The integrity and strength from the Mirror is borrowed by the Master and increases the success of the Chancellor. In this game of life Chancellors nearly always win. They discover their gift and how to use it for personal gain.
Level 6 (Green) We need to join together and grow personally through community. (Noble quality to be embraced at this level: *Kindness*)	Chancellors grow weary of the game and the Navigator Mirror refuses to be used any longer. Now Chancellors are looking for ways that every person can be acknowledged in the community for their strengths. Integrity and honesty is as important as emotional intelligence and they learn to use their gift for the community.
Level 7 (Yellow) We need to explore ways of being responsibly free. (Noble quality to be embraced at this level: *Genuineness*)	Chancellors become a spiral Wizard, seeing where the community's spiral needs attention. They move seamlessly between levels of development, the six energies and eight gifts, so that the community is strong and the work of the community is achieved.
Level 8 (Turquoise) The world is composed of delicately balanced interlocking forces, shaped by attractor fields of intention and nobility. Uses natural flows. Actively grows consciousness. The *Non-dual* Leader manifests at this level.	The world is seen as a series of cycles and life is seen as a quest. The individual understands the spiral of life and the streams of intra-level progression and addresses the current problems of existence that arise in their own journeys, so that the spiral can keep developing.
Level 9 (Coral)	TOWARDS ENLIGHTENMENT

THE SUBTYPES

Each of the eight types is made up of three Intelligences. The Chancellor has C1 Spontaneity, P2 Passion and I2 Heart. As we adapt to our life circumstances we tend to favour one of the three. This subtly changes the personality and gives rise to subtypes. All Chancellors will be able to relate to all three of the subtypes at some time in their life.

THE CREATIVE CHANCELLOR

The Creative Chancellor will enjoy new ideas, thoughts and solutions and will be able to adapt other people's concepts, designs and processes to support their objectives. They will lose interest in old projects and people quickly, wanting instead to constantly meet new challenges. Creative Chancellors are quick-minded, sexy, funny, innovative, witty and enthusiastic.

THE POWERFUL CHANCELLOR

The Powerful Chancellor will have strong opinions about most things and will want issues resolved. They are keen to succeed and want to outperform people's expectations. They will be motivated at times and generally enthusiastic.

The Powerful Chancellor is the master strategist who is able to achieve virtually anything behind the scenes. Kings may come and go, but the Powerful Chancellor is always there behind the scenes pulling the strings.

THE SENSITIVE CHANCELLOR

The Sensitive Chancellor will be very aware of how others are feeling – a true empathiser, putting people first at all cost. They do not want their opinions to offend and so often suppress their thoughts. The Sensitive Chancellor will not necessarily need to tie up all the loose ends, but rather will constantly stay on the emotional pulse of the person or people they are with.

Meeting new people

Meeting new people is like a movie preview. You may have read the title. You may have read the reviews, but it is only when you immerse yourself, do you find truth, understanding and appreciation.

ARCHETYPES RELATED TO THE CHANCELLOR

When people discuss archetypes, many of the characters they use will fall into the same category as the Chancellor, much the same way that there may be fifty-seven species of fern but regardless of the species, it still belongs to the fern family.

By way of example, some of these are:

- The Messenger
- The Herald
- The Courier
- The Communicator
- The TV Journalist
- The Trickster

- The Goddess
- The Gossip
- The Networker
- The Black Widow
- The Negotiator
- The Flirt

- The Siren
- The Circe
- The Seductress
- The Enchantress

CHILDREN'S STORIES

- The story of Joseph and the Coat of Many Colours

THE MIRROR

While the Chancellor is flexible, charming, subtle, creative and intuitive, the Chancellor's Mirror is inflexible, blunt, direct, obvious and focused on reality. The Chancellor's Mirror, the Navigator, is constantly demanding perfection, structure, details and proof of accomplishment. From the Feng Shui perspective, the Chancellor is described as pure female energy and the Chancellor's Mirror, the Navigator, is described as pure male energy. Male energy in this context is characterised as being unyielding, confronting and bullish and looks for opportunities to express these strengths.

Mirror Navigators have a very clear idea where they should be living, to whom they should be married and their income and lifestyle. The challenge is that these expectations are all below the awareness of the Chancellor, so even though they work hard and achieve all their objectives, if these don't line up with the unconscious requirements of the Mirror, the Chancellor will not find the satisfaction for which

One of the most important things is, to not get a big head over your successes.

Ian Thorpe
Olympic gold medallist in swimming

they are searching. The answer lies in discovering this unconscious vision and informing the Master so that it can be updated or replaced.

CHARACTER FORMATION

The formation of personality has three major influences:

1. Firstly, the physiological genetic makeup of the individual creates a predisposition towards accessing particular energies and not accessing others.

2. Secondly, the culture of the environment in which the child grew up sanctioned some energies over others and so encouraged the child to focus on some energies and suppress others.

3. And finally, the individual's psychological and physiological response to trauma or pain, that usually occurs during childhood, alters the way they relate to the six core Intelligences. When we experience emotional pain or trauma we can 'turn off' the emotion by turning off the Intelligence. One theory of personality development suggests that if in time we turn off three of the Intelligences we derive our energy from the remaining three. These three in turn combine to form type.

Regardless of what caused us to focus on just three of the Intelligences rather than all six, as human beings we can take three Intelligences that are available to all humans and combine them to create a higher form of consciousness. We are, if you like, human transformers of thinking into consciousness. This higher level of consciousness takes the form of a Neuro-Rational Type – in this case the Neuro-Rational Type of the Chancellor.

DEVELOPMENTAL ISSUES

For the Chancellor the character forms around the imbalance of deficient P1, the deficient I1 and the deficient C2.

DEFICIENT FIRST INTELLIGENCE (P1)

Thought to be formed in the womb and during early childhood, P1 provides the infant with a feeling of stability, of being wanted and of having the right to be here. Both Chancellors and Bards are low or deficient in this energy and this lack of grounding provides Chancellors with deep-seated issues around the body, survival, roots, nourishment, trust, health, home, family and prosperity. Their interest in connecting and merging with others is, in part, a lifelong quest to heal themselves of the constant fear and feeling of 'not being worthy' that they carry around with them, deeply hidden yet ever present.

DEFICIENT FIFTH INTELLIGENCE (I1)

The temptation for the Chancellor is to stream their energy straight to the heart Intelligence and escape the mundane nature of the world of reality. This is due to a deficient I1. While this is not true of all Chancellors, Chancellors also have an excessive second Intelligence; therefore, they have a hard time seeing, accepting and understanding reality, preferring to use their heart to have fun and merge with people whose world view and emotional state seem appealing.

DEFICIENT SIXTH INTELLIGENCE (C2)

Many Chancellors also have a deficient sixth Intelligence. When this is the case Chancellors become spiritually cynical, adopt rigid belief systems and become apathetic and obsessed with the issues of the lower Intelligences, namely, materialism, greed and the domination of others.

THE QUEST FOR INTEGRATION: AWARENESS (I), CREATIVITY (C) AND POWER (P)

Awareness – Having eyes that see (I1)

For the Chancellor, integration begins when they are willing to see the world much more like it actually is rather than constantly trying to escape from it by merging with others. This can mean seeing for the first time who they have married, where they actually live, and how heavy or thin they really are. It also means being willing to look at household finances, as they really are, at their lifestyle and at their real character. For Chancellors to develop I1 awareness, they must take time to see the repeating patterns in relationships, jobs, purchases and lifestyle and challenge the automatic adoption of others' value systems and priorities. The Chancellor must discover that approval is not more important than truth. Madness was once defined as doing the same thing over and over and expecting to get different results. This is what the Chancellor will do unless this awareness is awakened.

Developing spiritual creativity (C2)

The Chancellor performs well in the real world, with real-world problems and issues. However, if they are unable to use their own C2 they become fixed in their ways and find it impossible to objectively assess their belief system or learn new approaches or new ideas. For the Chancellor, healing may take the form of establishing real spiritual connection, learning and studying new ideas and practices, developing spiritual discipline, meditating or even undergoing psychotherapy where the Chancellor examines their belief systems and their inner observer or inner witness (self-observation skills).

Reconnecting with their P1

The root Chakra is the key to healing the original wound around which the type has formed. Root Chakra healing strategies can include reconnecting with the body, physical activity, weights, running etc, lots of touch (for example, massage) and Hatha yoga. Much to many a Chancellor's frustration, the process of developing the P1 is not complex or sophisticated; it is about doing whatever possible to reinforce the idea that it is safe for the Chancellor to be alive and nurture their body. It's about reclaiming the Chancellor's right to be here.

Healing in Action

SPIRALLING UP FOR THE CHANCELLOR — PERSONAL TRANSFORMATION AND THE PATH TO LIFE[1]

For the Chancellor, this starts with using their understanding of others to build bridges between people. During this phase the Chancellor earns the reputation of being open and honest and accepting and building bridges between people from all walks of life. In this phase Chancellors look to create an opportunity for everyone they know to be able to grow and develop and to use their Genius.

In practice, the quest for integration follows the following eight steps:

AWARENESS   1. TURNING TALK INTO ACTION — THROUGH DRIVE

Once they have engaged their Genius to build bridges the Chancellor is ready to focus on asking themselves the hard questions, getting clarity on what action they need to take personally and getting on with it. This is a time of boundless

---

1   Based on a Chancellor in the Blue meme.

I didn't come into politics to change the Labour Party. I came into politics to change the country.

Tony Blair
Former British Prime Minister

energy, optimism, success, recognition and fun. The constant talking and bonding of the Chancellor is broken by laughter, a quick mind and a love of stories, parties, celebration and the hard work of securing some quick wins (other than relationships) from personal effort.

2. INTEGRITY

For the Chancellors, the second step on their journey towards integration starts when they are willing to step out and do what they know is right and have integrity rather than just being popular. This is very hard for the Chancellor who wants to be popular even with those who stand for values that the Chancellor does not believe in. This step in the journey requires the Chancellors to ensure that everything they are doing is being done with integrity and that there is an absolute focus on reality – not just relationships. This requires that the Chancellor act with the noble quality of integrity, ensuring that their words and their deeds are in alignment, even when this involves being unpopular.

3. RESPONSIBILITY

With personal integrity in place Chancellors look to their long-term plans and the key milestones ahead. In the short-term this clarity focuses on how they can give back to their community. For the Chancellor, living responsibly requires that they effectively play their role in the family, at work and in their community, carefully assessing the balance between responsibility and authority so that they can effectively play their various roles in life. Amongst other things, this requires a thorough consideration and management of risks. As the Chancellor does this, workmates, friends and family have their sense of certainty and confidence about what the

Chancellor is doing reinforced and they see the genuineness and committed nature of the Chancellor in fulfilling their role.

CLARITY

4. LEARNING

The Chancellor now focuses on securing timely and appropriate information, or personal or professional learning. It takes the noble quality of objectivity for the Chancellor to make an informed assessment of what knowledge they need to learn. During this time Chancellors buy books, attend courses, update databases, tidy up the financial systems, conduct competitor analysis, review pricing or conduct benchmarking. The majority of the book learning and understanding during the transformation cycle takes place during this phase.

ACTION

5. COURAGE

With a significant depth of newfound information, Chancellors now step out with courage to achieve their plan. The noble quality of courage enables the Chancellor to face internal or external opposition and to still move forward in their life. This is where Chancellors start a new job or relationship, begin a new business, or break ties with those who are not aligned with their values. They step forward with courage and certainty and never look back.

6. RIGHT ACTION — THROUGH DISCERNMENT

The Chancellors now focus on the systems and processes required to improve efficiency and ensure they take the right action. This involves accessing the noble quality of discernment to ensure that all aspects of their life are aligned. During this time the Chancellors develop a strategic yet practical plan that will guide them through the rest of their journey. These systems and processes also ensure they are 'walking the talk'.

7. HEALING THE HEART — THROUGH INSPIRATION

The personal security and a renewed sense of self-confidence established in the preceding stages enable the Chancellor to create a new world that empowers those around them. This involves a complete rethinking of what is possible and what could be attained, and linking each person to the objective through the use of the noble quality of inspiration.

ASSESSMENT

8. ASSESSING THE NEW QUESTIONS OF EXISTENCE

The final step is now taken into a brand new world – one with entirely new questions of existence. Since this integration process occurs in the Blue meme, the Chancellor will have integrated this aspect of consciousness. Now they will be faced with an entirely new set of questions of existence. In the Orange meme they will be based around the need to succeed and be recognised as successful. The Assessment occurs as the Chancellor takes stock of their current situation, of the lessons they have learned about life in general and their own abilities in particular and then begins to apply their Genius of building bridges to create a sense of esprit de corps.

For all the types, however, there will be times when their development is arrested or even reversed. It's hard to believe that these charismatic and loved Chancellors could feel and behave in the following ways. Chancellors refer to these times as their 'dark night of the soul'.

SPIRALLING DOWN FOR THE CHANCELLOR - THE PATH TO DEATH: CREATING 'DIVIDE AND RULE' FEAR

The spiral downward is triggered by any event, thought, association or deed interpreted through the perspective of the Lower Self. It is this interpretation that many Christians would refer to as a separation from the divine part of ourselves and as 'sin'.

The spiral down for the Chancellor is triggered by a lack of self-esteem and personal security that leads to overt manipulation, seduction and politicking on the part of the Chancellor. This offends and traumatises the Chancellor who is dedicated to building bridges and integrity and they can't believe what they've done. This behaviour can quickly deteriorate into the downward spiral of disintegration which has seven steps.

AVOIDANCE

1. PERSONAL DELUSION AND DECEIVING OTHERS

Very quickly the Chancellor loses sight of reality and instead disappears into a world of supposition and deceit. Rather than

Go ahead, fall in love, be for somebody. But when the primary's over, let's fall in line and bring the White House back to our party.

Bill Clinton
Former US President

dealing with the causal issues, the Chancellor adopts a form of self-deception in which they avoid having to face their own manipulation and insecurity. Those closest to them become the most suspect and all kinds of conspiracy theories start to emerge in the Chancellor's mind. This delusion can convince the Chancellor that individuals have made statements or discussed them in negative or deriding ways. With a grain of truth and 98 per cent fiction the Chancellor uses their understanding of others to dream up scenarios that will lead to their failure. This paranoia leads to a complete lack of trust and further entrenches the Chancellor in creating an 'us and them', telling the 'us' one thing and the 'them' something else.

2. CONFUSION AND PROCRASTINATION

Isolated, angry and unwilling to take responsibility for their own behaviour or the situation that it created, the Chancellor now looks for the inconsistencies in the behaviour of others and in the systems they are following. This is their first line of defence against anyone who says they are to blame. During this time the Chancellor's professional performance subsides as the procrastination reaches new highs. Chancellors use a range of interpersonal techniques to align everyone else's behaviour with the way things should be done based on either family or cultural stereotypes.

3. BELIEVING THEY ARE A VICTIM AND BECOMING DEPENDENT ON OTHERS

At the third level the Chancellor will have spiralled down to the point that they feel isolated and betrayed and they can't figure out why they have been victimised. Tears, storytelling and seduction all manifest at this stage, each a means of avoiding any real contact and connection. They perceive that they have no future, no friends and no courage. This phase often ushers in heavy drinking and drug-taking 'to get through it all'.

REJECTION

4. ARROGANCE AND ISOLATION

If things continue to get worse, the Chancellor will begin to isolate themselves and only associate with those who can supply them with important or powerful information. The Chancellor becomes co-dependently attached to either someone with powerful information or with the book, institution or computer that is the source of the data. The Chancellor can cut off all contact with the outside world becoming a hermit, reading and refusing to communicate because, frankly, no one is 'worth the effort'. During this phase the Chancellor studies the laws, rules and fine print that will help them defend themselves if their gameplaying and deceit ever comes to trial. They prefer all their communication to be done in writing.

5. INFLEXIBILITY AND CONTROLLING BEHAVIOUR

As Chancellors spiral down to their Mirror Master, so too does their flexibility. Adherence to plans becomes a clear focus and their management style becomes totally closed to any new suggestions. They become abrupt, disconnected and autocratic. During this phase the Chancellor's attention to personal hygiene may decrease and they become fascinated with computers, tools, weapons or equipment that can help them defend themselves against a vicious world that hates them. Their own disowned parts of self become projected on the world at large.

INTERNALISING
BEHAVIOUR
ACTION

6. COMPLETE INTOLERANCE AND PUNITIVE

The downward spiral continues with the Chancellor becoming intolerant of all other positions and becoming genuinely self-righteous. The Chancellor decides they are the only ones doing what should be done and that others need to be punished to teach them a lesson. During this

If we see the chance for further growth in Asia, we will seize it, and I assume that will happen soon.

Juergen Schrempp
Daimler CEO

phase the tide turns and the intolerance is focused on themselves.

DISASSOCIATION 7. COMPETITION AND BULLYING

Finally, as the spiral down continues, the Chancellor will bully and blame everyone. This bullying comes in the form of cutting words, strong emotions, mood highs and lows and a focus on personal attacks. At this stage the Chancellor develops and tells elaborate stories that blame others for their own lack of confidence and deteriorating relationships. All ties with even their loved ones are severed as they step back and watch their lives play before them like a horror movie.

This is the final brutal stage of the Chancellor's downward spiral.

The Chancellor's Quest for Creating Wealth

HOW CHANCELLORS BECOME WEALTHY

Chancellors are brilliant at working in any field that requires people-to-people skills. They are particularly good at finding ingenious ways of achieving results when all else has failed.

Chancellors make big money in practically any field or area they choose. Their consistency and sense of structure coupled with their extraordinary people skills mean that they work equally well in large organisations or in small business. Chancellors earn more than any other profile because they not only have the dedication to work night and day on every project with which they are involved, but also have the ability to let others know of their contribution without looking as if they are self-promoting.

DEEP UNCONSCIOUS MOTIVATION

The Chancellor's energy comes from a desire to be totally independent and do and say whatever they want. They feel comfortable when all potential obstacles have been considered and when there is a detailed plan that is being followed. While Chancellors appear the most flexible of the profiles, they are actually very clear on the amount of money they want to earn, the level of investment they desire, the number of income streams they are working towards and the timeframes involved.

In their business affairs, Chancellors will appear to be very flexible, but in reality they have very clear expectations that they will want to see achieved. They will come up with ingenious risk minimisation plans, not so much for the project and all the other players, but for themselves. They will also want to make one all-inclusive investment and will be reticent to let another dollar leave their wallets.

MONEY MANAGEMENT APPROACH

Chancellors are attracted to real estate as they like the thrill of the chase as well as the prestige associated with owning property. They like systems and so will also attend courses, buy software or work with their financial advisers to discover how the real estate industry works and how they can benefit from it.

Chancellors like superannuation and invest consistently into it over the period of their professional careers, particularly if it is tax-effective. Chancellors don't mind taking a calculated risk. One of the reasons they can do this is because they come up with ingenious ways of being able to limit the risk they take. This means having the legals tight, the people committed and 'out clauses' if things don't go to plan.

While Chancellors may look as if they lead the high life, in reality they are actually quite frugal. They are happy to eat at home, buy good quality clothes but not necessarily expensive brands, live in a reputable suburb in a home that will appreciate and buy reliable cars that will not need constant repairs.

Chancellors resent having to spend anything that is either not a tax write-off or that will not make them money. They are masters at getting others to pay for meals, at parking in the street rather than a car park, at ringing when telephone rates are at their lowest and claiming all their expenses.

THE CHANCELLOR'S MONEY HABITS

Chancellors can sometimes over-analyse an opportunity to the point where the moment has passed. Every now and then Chancellors will be pushed too far and will explode. In this situation they are totally inflexible and can create ultimatums that lose them money.

Chancellors can become so obsessed with saving money that they become mean-spirited with the ones they love. They do this because it is part of their nature to save and live frugally. Their family can see it as being selfish, tight-fisted and unloving.

Chancellors are very prone to spending a lot of time on the detail of cost reduction. They can sometimes spend hours trying to save $5.00 in tax. Because Chancellors are quite traditional, any non-traditional opportunities that are not sanctioned by their respected tax and investment advisers will be ruled out.

When Chancellors embark on a new venture, if there is no solid profit outcome that provides wealth for them in the way they had planned, they will not be flexible enough to reconsider their vision. Instead, they will let the opportunity pass.

WHAT CHANCELLORS DO WITH THEIR WEALTH

Because the Chancellor's unconscious focus is on using money to achieve independence and social standing, wealthy Chancellors will use their time to chair committees, lead civic or not-for-profit organisations or somehow contribute to the fabric of society. Chancellors do this out of a sense of duty.

They prefer to live in conservative suburbs where real estate appreciates well, in neat and well-presented homes that are not ostentatious. They have a fascination with the finer things in life and often collect wine, antiques or some specialty items. They also enjoy having fun and will invest in 'toys' like boats and planes or holiday homes where the whole family can get together and enjoy themselves.

Wealthy Chancellors spend most of their time climbing some kind of corporate ladder, whether it be in a not-for-profit organisation, the church, the government or in the corporate scene. Chancellors find the climb more interesting than the view at the top.

Wealthy Chancellors are good fun, resourceful, enthusiastic, motivational, independent, family-oriented and always ready to give anyone a hand.

WEALTH CREATION FORMULA FOR CHANCELLORS

Chancellors are one of the wealthiest of all the types. They are totally driven to achieve and have the ability to get themselves noticed without appearing as if they are beating their own drum. Above all, people like them. They tend to get the promotions, the good contracting jobs and the leadership roles that earn more money more than the other types. They are also willing to make the sacrifices necessary to get the job and keep it.

Chancellors naturally keep an eye on the future and can protect themselves from losing too much money on any particular deal. This enables the Chancellor to be one of the biggest risk-takers, for which they keep the rewards.

One of the biggest challenges for the Chancellor is to make time away from the chase. Because they tend to get absolutely consumed by work, they may possibly ignore family and friends. When dividing their time, work will always win because the business world is less forgiving than family and friends. This can end up being a very costly approach for the Chancellors because eventually, if this is not managed, friends and family tire of the constant phone calls and the broken promises and leave, usually taking at least some of the accumulated wealth with them. Chancellors 'achieve' because that is what they do.

They enjoy the race, and the interaction and problem-solving to get there. Having said this, Chancellors have a deep inner desire to be by themselves, to not have to perform, to be a pillar of society, to be financially secure and to know what is around the corner. This being the case, often Chancellors would be better off pausing every now and then on their quest to the top, to see if they have created enough wealth to spend some time on the other parts of their lives that have been neglected.

The Chancellor works to make their family secure. Their family, however, may often just want to be with them and enjoy life. The Chancellor is much happier when they discover this and get the balance right.

UNDERSTANDING CHANCELLORS

Chancellors best manage themselves by:

- Disciplining themselves to stick to a plan until it is absolutely clear the plan needs to be aborted and a new plan is in place
- Not constantly agreeing with everyone but instead sometimes put a stake in the ground
- Focusing on principles that will guide their lives
- Rationally considering options and consciously running through the pros and cons of options on an operational rather than political basis
- Not letting themselves get so tangled up in politics that they can't get the job done (alliances have strings)

As team members, Chancellors make the best contribution when:

- They need to bring together the interests of diverse and different groups
- They need to resolve conflict
- They are required to find resources for the team or promote the good work of the team within the team or even outside the team
- They have to deal with complex emotional issues around people

Solving problems

Chancellors have large networks of contacts/acquaintances and always know someone that can help with a problem.

Mark, Sensitive Chancellor

When managing Chancellors:

- Don't let your relationship with them become political by playing games or point-scoring
- Encourage them to rationally consider their position in a non-political way to give them a 'true north'
- Encourage them to keep reminding themselves of the team's wider vision
- Encourage them to structure their activity into phases, and document and review their achievements in writing in a structured way

How Chancellors will act during meetings:

- Will be fascinated with the group dynamics and power plays
- Will be enthusiastic and encouraging to those with power
- Will be reluctant to state their position
- Will easily get sidetracked or sidetrack discussion

Personality strengths that help the Chancellor to further their development:

- Natural strategists
- Flexible, passionate
- Understand people and how to motivate them
- Can understand how others are feeling

Personality weaknesses that can stand in the way of the Chancellor's development:

- Focus on self-gain rather than the bigger picture
- Can change their own mind so much, nothing gets done
- Can create games and politics just for their own amusement
- Can let emotions cloud their thinking

Opportunities for Chancellors to develop:

- Need to discipline themselves to keep things simple
- Need to become attached to a corporate vision – not just a personal gain
- Need to be authentic and state their position – even when it's not political

Threats to Chancellor's development:

- Can fall foul of the system if not careful
- Can get totally wound up in 'winning' rather than achieving, and waste their talents
- Can be seen by others as manipulative and therefore not trustworthy

FAMOUS CHANCELLORS

- Dale Carnegie (Motivational Speaker)
- Bob Hawke (former Australian Prime Minister)
- Tony Blair (former British Prime Minister)
- Ian Thorpe (Swimmer)
- Tom Cruise (Actor)
- Neville Chamberlain (former British Prime Minister)
- Nicole Kidman (Actor)
- Richard Gere (Actor)
- Bill Clinton (Former US President)
- Whitney Houston (Singer)
- John Travolta (Actor)
- Bob Dylan (Singer/Songwriter)
- Jeurgen Schrempp (Author)
- Paul Burrell (Princess of Wales' former Butler)
- Barack Obama (US President)

CHANCELLORS AT WORK

Chancellors are often very high achievers and their greatest strength is their ability to understand the motivation of everyone they meet. They are themselves highly motivated and enjoy praise. They are most productive when they are motivated and valued for their contribution. They are capable of achieving more in less time than many others. A Chancellor is naturally enthusiastic, optimistic and committed. They thrive on new ideas, causes or directions, and can achieve virtually anything they set their mind to.

A Chancellor is willing to cooperate as long as they agree with the project or the person at the helm. They naturally have little long-term vision and will adopt the vision of others. They will then motivate others to take up the cause. They are more willing to contribute if they can run the show. If things are not going the way they would like, they either say nothing or ambush the idea. They will happily follow rules and regulations set down by others as long as they believe in them. If not, they will try to adapt or alter the plans.

They have a charismatic leadership style and seek the best in people. They are always sensitive to the needs of their fellow workers and can see their fears, strengths and weaknesses. People are attracted to their energy and passion. New processes are willingly adopted as long as they are in harmony with their beliefs and attitudes, and they cope well with change.

They are intolerant of people who disagree with them, but are more tolerant of close friends or loved ones. They resolve conflict by trying to win the argument, either overtly or covertly. They will be aggressive to anyone who is aggressive with them. They take criticism personally and will fight the person, not the issue or activity. The personalities involved, together with issues of loyalty, beliefs and their relationship to the conflict, stand central to their arguments. They are happy to take responsibility, but may worry or rely on intuition to solve problems and sometimes wait until the last minute to complete a task. A Chancellor doesn't make snap decisions. They will take the problem home, sleep on it and do what feels right.

Chancellors will be extremely supportive when a new project starts if they believe in the project and the people involved. They will use lateral thoughts and solutions to cope with stress, and will work faster and more efficiently when they are working to deadlines. Often, Chancellors rely on stress for improved productivity

A person should only be judged in the press by how effective they are in their chosen field.

John Travolta
Actor

and subsequently have periods of high then low performance. Similarly, they will have periods of stability and instability.

A Chancellor's confidence will always appear high. However they are sensitive to criticism, although they do not always appear so. They are extremely loyal until double-crossed or betrayed. They are flexible as long as they are not asked to behave in conflict with their beliefs.

A Chancellor will always let their attitudes and beliefs colour decisions. When analysing a situation, a Chancellor will look at the people and their feelings rather than the facts. They will use humour that is often 'close to the bone'. Sometimes they get themselves into trouble for using intuitive humour. They can also play games at another's expense. Chancellors are highly competitive and will work hard for approval. They need constant recognition and strive to be the best. They can appear both optimistic and pessimistic. Their enthusiasm is cyclical.

Chancellors are at their best when starting and driving a new project and achieving the impossible – because they believe in it.

THE CHANCELLOR'S MIRROR IN THE WORKPLACE

At work, when a young Mirror Navigator is unleashed, there will be episodes of shouting, abuse, ultimatums and even physical threats. These intensely emotional and angry outbursts can stay with those they interact with forever. Because the Master has no comprehension of this behaviour, however, the Chancellor will not understand why friends, family and colleagues clear the decks when things start looking stressed or the Chancellor starts getting angry.

As the Mirror Navigator matures, the intense aggression gives way to strong words or steely ultimatums, detailed planning and a focus on controlling others through procedures and due process.

When the Mirror is integrated into this personality, the Navigator brings vision, endurance and principles, and grounds the otherwise charming, funny, flexible and politically brilliant Chancellor.

At home, the Mirror Navigator manifests when the Chancellor is stressed and the strategy to create a desired outcome is failing. Once 'out' the Navigator will state the obvious, focus on the detail, demand obedience and yell and shout. The Mirror Navigator has no subtlety, grace or sophistication. Instead, the Mirror Navigator insists on total clarity, loyalty and proof and will bully it out of their target. No enemy is too big for the Mirror Navigator who knows no fear and sees nothing but clear evidence and fault.

The Affiliative Style

Daniel Goleman (2000) describes the archetypal Affiliative leader, Joe Torre, 'the heart and soul of the New York Yankees'. We are given specific examples of the ways in which Torre carefully nurtured individual team members during the stressful 1999 World Series.

A Chancellor leader will always be in touch with the personal situation of each team member and this is true of Torre. He was careful to praise and acknowledge the pain of two young men who continued to play despite their fathers' death.

Torre also praised two players whose continuance with the team was threatened by disputes with management. The Chancellor's noble quality of bridge-building was evident here: his message was for the management as much as for the two players.

Not only was this Chancellor open to others' emotions, but he also respected his own and was ready to share with his team his own deep family concern. Here we see the emotional intelligence competencies of the Affiliative style: empathy, building relationships and communication.

THE LEADERSHIP STYLE OF THE CHANCELLOR

Each Neuro-Rational Type, due to its combination of thinking functions, has a different leadership style. These leadership styles are a function of the centre of focus of the Neuro-Rational Types, and tend to be expressions of the underlying world view of the personality.

A survey of 3871 executives selected from a database of more than 20,000 executives[2] found distinct leadership styles. Daniel Goleman (2000) attributes these different leadership styles to different emotional intelligences. Each leadership style has a different impact on the work environment and on organisational performance. The most effective leaders use a variety of styles, choosing the appropriate style, timing and intensity to manage each situation.

The leadership style identified by Goleman's research (2000) that is most closely aligned to the profile of the Chancellor is the *Affiliative* style.

The author's experience supports the insightful research reported by Goleman. In most situations, the Affiliative style is one of the most effective leadership styles as it drives up many aspects of corporate climate. The primary focus of the

---

2   Survey was originally analysed by Kelner, S., et al. (1996).

Table 13.2 The Leadership Style of the Chancellor

Situation	Explanation
1. The leader's modus operandi	Creates harmony and builds emotional bonds
2. The style in a phrase	'People come first'
3. Underlying emotional intelligence competencies	Empathy, building relationships, communication
4. When the style works best	To heal rifts in a team or to motivate people during stressful circumstances
5. Overall impact on climate	Positive

Affiliative style of leadership is in developing social capital with co-workers (a P2- and I2-based approach).

Some of the attributes of this leadership style are:

- **Social capital.** The Affiliative style values individuals and their emotions more than tasks and objectives. People using this style also create a sense of belonging by taking co-workers out for a meal or spending other one-to-one time with them to see how they are feeling.

- **Loyalty.** The focus on building strong emotional bonds generates strong ties of loyalty.

- **Communication.** People who like each other talk a lot. They share ideas and they share their inspiration.

- **Flexibility.** Trust is engendered by the focus on creating a harmonious environment. This trust means the Affiliative leader does not need to impose unnecessary strictures on how employees perform their work (C1 and I2 working together).

- **Feedback.** The Affiliative leader provides plenty of positive feedback. Under some other leadership styles, individuals receive no feedback at all, or only negative feedback. Therefore, the positive words from the Affiliative leader are very motivating.

  Competition

  As the years go by, we often will learn that there are easier ways to getting results than just working hard. We don't like working in isolation and really need the emotional connection of other people. So work can be just like part of the extended family.

Competition creates a healthy respect between individuals, encouraging heroes of those who have achieved their best, and at times making reluctant heroes of those gracious in defeat.

The Affiliative style works well, but by focusing only on praise it can allow poor performance to go uncorrected. People perceive that mediocrity is tolerated. Furthermore, since constructive criticism is not provided, employees must find out how to improve on their own. When clear directives are required, the Affiliative style does not work.

The Affiliative style should be used to build team harmony, increase morale, improve communications or repair broken trust.

Relationships with people are important and I really don't like conflict and will do a lot to avoid it because it usually causes me emotional pain. I think that most matters can be resolved with a little goodwill and some discussion. Unless I consciously decide to deal with the hard emotional stuff, I will do anything to avoid it – for example, disciplining a staff member.

If you really want to know someone, put yourself in their shoes. Understanding a person's thinking and desires aids in building relationships with them and provides a wonderful opportunity to interact and impart our most endeared experiences.

SCHOOL OF STRATEGIC THOUGHT

The natural differences are not limited to leadership styles alone; they also extend to a natural inclination towards different strategic thought. These differences have been researched by Mintzberg, Ahlstrad and Lampel (1998). The Chancellor approaches strategy formation by seeing it as an overt process of influence, emphasising the use of power and politics to negotiate strategies favourable to particular interests. This lies in the power school of strategy.

A problem is solved when harmony is restored.

THE GENIUS OF THE CHANCELLOR – BUILDING BRIDGES

The Chancellor's Genius comes from their ability to build bridges between people. As a consequence they develop powerful interpersonal strategies and so can achieve their objectives with very little disruption. The Chancellor has the ability to influence entire organisations without anybody triggering resistance.

Buckingham & Clifton (2001, p. 110) describe the Chancellor's behaviour as follows:

- The Chancellor is comfortable with intimacy. Spending time with their close friends gives them great pleasure and strength – and if they do not know you, they will naturally want to get to know you.

- They are interested in the minutiae of everyone's life, and will willingly tell you theirs.

- The Chancellor knows that this is risky, but is willing to take risks because this is the cost of genuine friendship.

- They see that two people risking together is necessary for sharing together, which is necessary for genuine caring.

Buckingham and Clifton (2001) go on to give some examples of people with the genius of relating. They describe a pilot in the marines whose experience had taught him that a friend is someone you literally trust with your life.

They then describe Jamie, an entrepreneur. He does not really go looking for new friends, but if he spends time with someone, he finds himself wanting to 'invest more' to build a deeper friendship. So he shows more of himself, makes sacrifices for them, and does things to show he cares. He has ten on his staff and regards them all as very good friends.

The third example is Gavin, a flight attendant. He has a small number of close friends, but a large extended family of whom he is very fond. They get together as often as they can, and when they do, he is the catalyst – they 'hang out' together for three or four days just enjoying one another's company.

BODY COMPOSITION

The Chancellor's body composition is society's 'ideal' shape. They are not too skinny and not too fat. The shape is lean, yet toned. Limbs are not long, nor short, but relative to the height of the Chancellor. When the weight increases on a Chancellor, excess body fat is stored in the upper abdomen and around the face (Diversi, 2006).

FITNESS PREFERENCES

The Chancellor enjoys any activity, particularly with friends, colleagues or loved ones. Growing up, they excel in team sports and often remain active in sporting clubs through their adulthood. Because they look fit, they escape scrutiny from medical practitioners and others. Therefore, they may not exercise enough to maintain their heart health, so important in this type (Diversi, 2006).

EATING PREFERENCES

The Chancellor enjoys food, particularly when prepared by a loved one or when eaten with friends. They tend to prefer sweet foods to savoury foods and these are the foods that they overeat. When eating out, they like to order sweets or coffee after the meal, but will resist if they are the only taker (Diversi, 2006).

DIETING PREFERENCES

The Chancellor rarely needs to diet for aesthetic reasons. They are often placed on heart health diets which they follow with slight resistance. The Chancellor has a tendency to take nutrition and dieting advice from anyone without scientific reason and accept loose advice as gospel (Diversi, 2006).

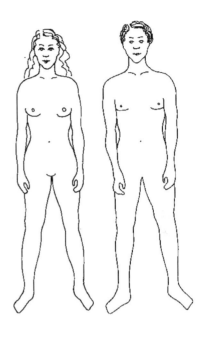

"And so, my fellow Americans, ask not what your country can do for you - ask what you

can do for your country.

My fellow citizens of the world, ask not what America will do for you, but what together

we can do for the freedom of man.

Finally, whether you are citizens of America or citizens of the world, ask of us here the

same high standards of strength and sacrifice which we ask of you. With a good conscience our only sure reward, with history the final judge of our deeds, let us go forth to lead the land we love, asking his blessing and his help, but knowing that here

on Earth God's work must truly be our own."

John F Kennedy

Applying Chancellor Insights as an Effective Communicator

When Negotiating with Chancellors

The effective communicator is able to align their narrative and the point they are wanting to make with the archetype of the audience. That is, they use the same language, approach and behaviour with the archetype of the person they are presenting to.

When negotiating with Chancellors the way you position information is very important. Chancellors are attracted to messages centred on two main themes which are most convincing to them: *'Show me how this can help us get some quick wins'* and *'Show me this solution will empower the team to achieve the objectives.'*

'Show me how this can help us get some quick wins'

There are two types who naturally access their P2 and C1 functions – the Chancellor and the Judge. This segment makes up 36 per cent of the general population. When negotiating with this group:

- Present constant initiatives that will give the organisation the edge
- Demonstrate new ideas, business ventures and people as an indication that the leadership is doing a good job
- Exhibit how the organisation has taken advantage of the opportunities created by shifts in the market (for example, competitors failing)
- Show evidence that the organisation is responsive to market trends
- Show fast activity that secures 'quick wins'
- Use strategies that are grounded and that last no longer than a few years
- Show clear milestones, responsibilities and target dates for achievement
- Be prepared to convince them on every point
- Be aware that they consider the credibility of the presenter as important as the message itself
- Demonstrate passion, success and drive

'Show me this solution will empower the team to achieve the objectives'

There are two groups who access their P2 and I2 by nature – the Chancellors and the Bards. This segment makes up approximately 12 per cent of the general population. When negotiating with this group:

- Is very sensitive to non-verbal communication, reading between the lines, gestures and facial expressions
- Has a huge influence on the population because they are the novelists, dramatists, television interviewers, playwrights, poets, biographers and popular journalists
- Asks questions about the meaning of actions, the purpose of the organisation, the role of leaders and the impact this all has on the organisation's stakeholders
- Sees good in everyone and assumes everyone is doing their best with the best intentions
- Has very little interest in buying and selling, or commercial occupations; and is much more interested in bringing out the best in people and enabling people to reach their full potential
- Will be, by nature, naive about the 'complexities' of law and business

The Chancellor at a Glance

Strengths

- Creates team cohesion
- Great at networking
- Encourages tolerance in a team

Code of Conduct

- Acknowledges and considers other opinions in a respectful and non-judgemental way
- Considers the opinions of others with an open mind
- Ensures all team members have a say in group decisions
- Seeks out, listens to and considers the opposite viewpoint on any given subject
- Offers support to colleagues who may be experiencing difficulties
- Encourages others to show their appreciation

First Step of Integration

- Focuses on asking the hard questions and seeking the truth

First Step of Disintegration

- Descends into building castles in the sky (delusion and deceit)

Exemplars

- Barack Obama
- Bill Clinton
- Tony Blair

Chapter 14

The Commander
An In-Depth Look at the Commander

Results? Why, man, I have gotten lots of results! If I find 10,000 ways something won't work, I haven't failed. I am not discouraged, because every wrong attempt discarded is often a step forward ... Of all my inventions, I liked the phonograph best ...

Thomas Edison

What we've got to thank Commanders for:

Action heroes

Innovation

Courageous acts

Breaking down unnecessary bureaucracy

Spontaneity

Action sports

New gadgets

New technology

A warrior of light is never cowardly. Flight might be an excellent form of defence, but it cannot be used when one is very afraid. When in doubt, the warrior prefers to face defeat and then lick his wounds, because he knows that if he flees he is giving to the aggressor greater power than he deserves. In difficult and painful times, the warrior faces overwhelming odds with heroism, resignation and courage.

Paulo Coelho
Author of 'Warrior of Light'

OVERVIEW

Commanders are inventors by nature and have an unquenchable thirst for knowing how things work. They love challenge, variety and new and interesting problems to solve. They get frustrated and demotivated with routine. Regardless of their training or level of professional development, Commanders like to work to a system that is efficient and practical. If 'the way it has always been done' does not achieve this, the Commander will not hesitate to redesign the system or rewrite the handbook.

Commanders are usually easygoing with a childlike curiosity and a fascinating general knowledge about just about everything. They are gregarious, party animals that enjoy having fun and forgetting the time. They are rational and systematic and can take over command in any kind of real crisis. When the pressure is on, Commanders have the ability to mobilise large teams in an efficient, sequential and effective way. When Commanders take control, all the other types stand back and let them lead.

Commanders are very fluent speakers by nature and able to think very quickly on their feet. In discussions they will be 100 percent present and enjoy pitting themselves against others in a discussion just for the sport of it.

Because they are excellent problem-solvers, Commanders will often create problems for themselves to solve when things are becoming too routine and they are bored. This cycle of creating and then solving problems seriously limits their ability to accumulate wealth.

FOCUS OF ATTENTION

Commanders are brilliant at solving problems. In a practical sense this can mean inventing a new gadget, approach or system or doing what it takes to get the show on the road. They walk beside colleagues and friends as they go through life, attending to the little things that get everyone through the day (The Good Samaritan). At their best, Commanders are reverent, disciplined, courageous, ingenious, enabling, harmonious and peaceful.

KEY CHARACTER DRIVERS

There are three key Intelligences that drive the Commander:

C1 – Spontaneity

P1 – Logic

I2 – Heart

Having fun

My 'Bucks Party' is a good example of how I like to have fun. It was held on a Saturday during the day. A group of friends and I went up to Binna Burra in the Springbrook Forest and we did a day of high ropes, low ropes, flying fox and abseiling. It was fantastic. We all had a great time. We went out for a quiet drink that evening but it was such an anti-climax after a day of testing and pushing our limits. I would much prefer to do this sort of activity than to go out drinking.

LEVELS OF CONSCIOUSNESS AS DEFINED BY US PSYCHOLOGIST CLARE GRAVES AND SPIRAL DYNAMICS' AUTHORS COWAN & BECK

Table 14.1 outlines the broad character development of the Commander over a lifetime from Level One – the lowest level of consciousness – through to essence at Level Nine.

THE SUBTYPES

Each of the eight types is made up of three thinking functions. The Commander has C1 Spontaneity, P1 Logic and I2 Heart. As we adapt to our life circumstances we tend to favour one of the three. This subtly changes the personality and gives rise to subtypes. All Commanders will be able to relate to all three of the subtypes at some time in their life.

THE CREATIVE COMMANDER

The Creative Commander will enjoy new ideas, thoughts and solutions and will be able to adapt other people's concepts, designs and processes to support their objectives. They will lose interest in old projects and people quickly, wanting instead to constantly meet new challenges. They will be quick-minded, witty and enthusiastic for the latest thought or idea.

Table 14.1 The Commander Levels of Development

Level of Consciousness and the noble quality embraced at this level	Common Commander characteristics at this level of consciousness
Level 1 (Beige) A state of nature and instincts.	Closed down and off from human nobility. One step at a time. No sense of future or past. Frozen.
Level 2 (Purple) Mysterious and frightening. *(Noble quality to be embraced at this level: **Reverence**)*	Feel they are so small in comparison to God that if they do everything God wants, God will help them. If things go bad they become the victim, or the martyr. Often create situations in which they are punished or hurt.
Level 3 (Red) Raw displays of power – dictators, tough love, predators. *(Noble quality to be embraced at this level: **Self-Control**)*	First displays of Mirror and sense of the Crusader's power. The world is broken into family/tribe and others. Family is to be protected and everyone else is to be avoided, or if the Commander cannot charm them, fought. Fierce outbursts of anger and top-down righteousness.
Level 4 (Blue) Everything is controlled by God and is purposeful. Obey God. Do it right. Feel guilt. *(Noble quality to be embraced at this level: **Courage**)*	Commanders fear that what they have been doing is not enough so they increase the level of helpfulness and use sexuality and seduction to charm others into needing them.
Level 5 (Orange) The world is a game and I want to win. *(Noble quality to be embraced at this level: **Ingenuity**)*	Commanders use their high energy, charm and innate ability to solve problems to make money. They love a crusade (Mirror) and often select new fields or cutting edge technologies to show their problem-solving skills. They become indispensable to a successful person and hang on for the ride. They discover their gift and how to use it for personal gain.
Level 6 (Green) We need to join together and grow personally through community. *(Noble quality to be embraced at this level: **Enabling**)*	Commanders complete the integration of their Mirror by 'cleaning up their act' and focusing on high-integrity behaviour. They also develop a real and deep love for themselves and stand in their own power rather than someone else's. Finally they let go of the guilt and genuinely begin to enjoy life. They learn to use their gift for the community.
Level 7 (Yellow) We need to explore ways of being responsibly free. *(Noble quality to be embraced at this level: **Harmoniousness**)*	New ideas are encouraged and projects are seen through to the end rather than through to the solving of the problem with the integrity and personal discipline of the Crusader. The focus is on ensuring all the team's energy goes towards the group's crusade, rather than being focused on the day-to-day of community life.
Level 8 (Turquoise) The world is composed of delicately balanced interlocking forces, shaped by attractor fields of intention and nobility. Uses natural flows. Actively grows consciousness. The Non-dual Leader manifests at this level.	The world is seen as a series of cycles and life is seen as a quest. The individual understands the spiral of life and the streams of intra-level progression and addresses the current problems of existence that arise in their own journeys so that the spiral can keep developing.
Level 9 (Coral)	TOWARDS ENLIGHTENMENT

The Phantom, one of the first and still one of the most popular costumed heroes of the comics, is the descendant of an English seafarer who, over 463 years ago, washed ashore in Bangalla after a pirate raid and swore an oath over the skull of his father's murderer, that he and his descendants would devote their lives to '... the destruction of piracy, greed, cruelty and injustice ...'

(The oath of the skull)

THE CONTROLLING COMMANDER

The Controlling Commander is totally committed to creating order, systems and discipline. They will want to see projects from beginning to end, have a healthy sense of humour, and be analytical and even-handed. They will be self-disciplined and stable. The Controlling Commander will want loose ends tied up. Their structure will suppress their spontaneity unless they are relaxed. They are steadfast, resolute and immovable once they have decided on a game plan.

THE SENSITIVE COMMANDER

The Sensitive Commander will be very sensitive to how others are feeling a true empathiser, putting people first at all cost. They do not want their opinions to offend and so will often suppress their thoughts. They will not necessarily need to tie up all the loose ends, but rather stay constantly focused on the emotional pulse of the person or people they are with.

The Sensitive Commander will tend to be totally different when they are with people than when they are by themselves. By themselves they will be organised, task oriented and structured; with others they will tend to be the social glue, heading off conflict and doing whatever it takes to keep everything on an emotionally even keel.

Being with people without forcing your own point of view
I have been told I am a good listener and like to hear people's stories. I find there are very valuable lessons for me from everyone I talk to and therefore give my full attention to them. Sometimes I feel that I am a bit boring after listening to other people's very interesting stories, but I have been told that I am far from it. Who knows?

ARCHETYPES RELATED TO THE COMMANDER

When people discuss archetypes, many of the characters they use will fall into the same category as the Commander, much the same way that there may be fifty-seven species of fern but regardless of the species, it still belongs to the fern family.

By way of example, some of these are:

- The Provocateur
- The Workaholic
- The Gambler
- The Follower
- The Indigent
- The Friend
- The Sidekick
- The Right Hand Man

- The Consort
- The Casanova
- The Gigolo
- The Seducer
- The Sex Addict
- The Lover
- The Good Samaritan
- The Wanderer

- The Vagabond
- The Nomad
- The Disciple
- The Indentured Servant
- The Devotee

CHILDREN'S STORIES/NURSERY RHYMES

- Huckleberry Finn
- Jack from *Jack and the Beanstalk*

THE MIRROR

While the Commander is charming, sexual, carefree and not goal-oriented, the Commander's Mirror, the Crusader, is motivated by undertaking crusades that are exciting, adventurous and worthy of their efforts and talents. As the Mirror, the Crusader demands to chase the 'big, hairy, audacious goal' or set their sights on a mountain so large that it takes everyone's breath away. The Crusader is most likely to take over when the Commander is bored or between helping people in crisis.

While the Commander's self-image is one of being easygoing, caring and practical, the Commander's Mirror is driven, ambitious and thrill-thirsty and wants to see and live the fruits of their success. The Mirror will want to see the house, the car, the clothes and the partner as a reflection of their efforts. The Crusader has a clear picture of what life will be like, what the life partner will look like, where they will live, how much they will earn and the level of respect they will receive and from whom. If this clear, yet unconscious, life vision doesn't get communicated to the Master, the Commander will pay a high emotional price, working harder and harder yet never feeling satisfied with their achievements.

I'm staggered by the question of what it's like to be a multi-millionaire.
I always have to remind myself that I am.

Bruce Willis
Actor

As the Mirror matures, the Crusader provides the Commander with energy, stamina, focus and a surprising eye for detail. When integrated into the personality, the Crusader gives the Commander vision, passion, energy, principles and the ability to inspire virtually anyone to join a righteous crusade.

The young Crusader Mirror provides the Commander with constant self-criticism about virtually everything from their hair, voice and clothes through to their job, intelligence and manner of interacting with others. The Crusader is an unforgiving and relentless Mirror yelling loudly in the Commander's mind at every turn. For the young Commander this often leads to low self-esteem until the Master grows stronger and louder and learns to discipline or drown out the Mirror, or the Mirror grows up.

CHARACTER FORMATION

The formation of personality has three major influences:

1. Firstly, the physiological genetic makeup of the individual creates a predisposition towards accessing particular energies and not accessing others.

2. Secondly, the culture of the environment in which the child grew up sanctioned some energies over others and so encouraged the child to focus on some energies and suppress others.

3. And finally, the individual's psychological and physiological response to trauma or pain that usually occurs during childhood alters the way they relate to the six core energies. When we experience emotional pain or trauma we can 'turn off' the emotion by turning off the energy. One theory of personality development suggests that if in time we turn off three of the energies we derive our energy from the remaining three. These three in turn combine to form type.

Regardless of what caused us to focus on just three of the thinking functions rather than all six, as human beings we can take three thinking function energies that are available to all humans and combine them to create a higher form of consciousness. We are, if you like, human transformers of thinking into consciousness. This higher level of consciousness takes the form of a Neuro-Rational Type – in this case the Neuro-Rational Type of the Commander.

DEVELOPMENTAL ISSUES

Deficient Third Intelligence (P2)

With a deficient P2 the Commander often finds that their personal ambition or drive is low. The impact of this is that Commanders can find themselves looking after the needs of others rather than looking after their own needs. In the personality of the Commander this often manifests in linking up with someone else and simply adopting their passion, drive or ambition for a profession or project. In relationships this is often described as co-dependency. At work this makes the Commander excellent as the second-in-charge. Unfortunately, it often also leads to others taking advantage of their availability and obvious dependency which in turn leads to the Commander giving, giving and giving and then one day, snapping and cutting the relationship because they feel taken for granted. P2 is important for defining personal boundaries and ensuring that goals are self-gratifying and that effort is recognised. (It is the seat of the ego.) Without this, Commanders are prone to organising lose/win situations, waiting too long to do anything about it and then exploding when least expected – when a last straw breaks the camel's back. A deficient P2 leads to low self-esteem and an inability to 'sell' themselves – particularly to themselves.

Deficient Fifth Intelligence (I1)

The temptation for Commanders is to stream their energy straight to the heart and escape the complicated world of reality. This is due to a deficient I1. While this is not true of all Commanders, Commanders also have an excessive C1 and therefore have a hard time seeing, accepting and understanding reality, preferring to use their heart and C1 to have fun and merge with people whose world view and emotional state seem appealing.

Deficient Sixth Intelligence (C2)

Many Commanders also have a deficient C2. When this is the case Commanders become spiritually cynical, adopting rigid belief systems and become apathetic and obsessed with the issues of materialism, greed and the domination of others.

THE QUEST FOR INTEGRATION: AWARENESS (I), CREATIVITY (C) AND POWER (P)

Awareness – Having eyes that see (I1)

For the Commander, integration begins when they are willing to see the world much more as it actually is rather than constantly trying to escape from it by merging with others. This can mean seeing for the first time who they have married, where they actually live, how heavy or how thin they really are. It also means being willing to look at household finances, as they really are, at their lifestyle and at their real character. For Commanders to develop I1 awareness, they must take time to see the repeating patterns in relationships, jobs, purchases and lifestyle and challenge the automatic adoption of others' value systems and priorities. The Commander must discover that approval is not more important than truth. Madness was once defined as doing the same thing over and over and expecting to get different results. This is what the Commander will do unless this awareness is awakened.

Developing spiritual creativity (C2)

Commanders perform well in the real world, with real-world problems and issues. However, if they are unable to use their C2 they become fixed in their ways and find it impossible to objectively assess their belief system or learn new approaches or new ideas. For the Commander, healing may take the form of establishing real spiritual connection, learning and studying new ideas and practices, developing spiritual discipline, meditating or even psychotherapy where the Commander examines their belief systems and their inner observer or inner witness (self-observation skills).

Developing P2

Commanders are good with solving the day-to-day problems that confront them. However, they need to learn how to focus their energy on doing the things that are important to them rather than others. Time management principles are an excellent place to start, using Covey's 'urgent / important matrix'. Anthony Robbins's 'moving toward and moving away from' framework is also excellent at creating clarity for Commanders. Goal management, setting objectives and reviewing daily achievements are also valuable ways to strengthen the role that would normally be played by the third Intelligence, P2. Developing P2 is particularly hard work for the sensitive Commander because as it arises so too does the possibility of the Commander being rejected for 'having their own agenda'. This is an important internal conflict for the Commander to resolve if they are to regain their self-confidence.

Healing in Action

SPIRALLING UP FOR THE COMMANDER[1]

Personal transformation and the path to life for the Commander starts with the Commander developing increased awareness of the degree to which they ignore their own needs and aspirations for the needs and aspirations of others. This requires the Commander, for the first time in their life, to practise being objective. In practice, the quest for integration follows the following eight steps:

AWARENESS

1. OBJECTIVITY

The path towards integration starts with a commitment to seeing the world they have created as objectively as possible. How balanced are their key relationships? Have these people really been given the opportunity to give as much as they receive? What are the capabilities of the Commander? What insight are they missing? Does the Commander need to develop new skills such as negotiation skills, assertiveness skills or time management? To answer these questions requires the noble quality of detachment in order to make an unbiased assessment. During this time the Commander buys books and attends courses. The majority of the book learning and self-insight during the transformation cycle takes place during this phase.

2. RESPONSIBILITY

Living with responsibility requires that your word is your bond and your promises will be kept. To do this requires a careful assessment of the balance between responsibility and authority and it also requires a careful assessment and management of risks. This is the work of the second phase. As the Commander does this their own sense of personal commitment to their own goals and aspirations increases. This is where the Commander says, 'Enough with this job, relationship, hobby – I am doing this for all the wrong reasons and I will spend my time on tasks that I

---

1   Based on a Commander in the Blue meme.

WANT rather than losing my own priorities to save others.'

3. LIVING WITH INTEGRITY

For the Commander the internal work is completed when they find their crusade. This is what they are willing to put their life on the line for. This crusade needs to be aspirational and make the world a better place. For the Commander this is about personal and life integrity and enables them to automatically see where their efforts should be going. This is the last phase where the Commander is focused internally – now the Commander begins their work in the world.

CLARITY

4. DRIVE

With the crusade clearly defined the Commander is ready to motivate and focus themselves and their team on breaking the glass ceiling and powering through. This phase engages the noble quality of drive to focus on asking themselves the hard questions, getting clarity on what action they need to take personally and then getting on with it. This is a time of boundless energy, optimism, success, recognition and fun. The serious nature of the first part of the cycle is broken by laughter, a quick mind, and a love of stories, parties and celebration.

ACTION

5. BUILDING BRIDGES OF UNDERSTANDING – THROUGH DIPLOMACY

The healing that has taken place during the first phase of transformation enables the Commander to begin building bridges with people with humility, honesty and diplomacy. During this phase the Commander builds bridges between people from all walks of life. They do this through the noble quality of diplomacy that enables them to find the common ground between themselves and the crusade that they are embarked upon.

6. CREATING AN INSPIRATIONAL ENVIRONMENT

Working with team members to achieve their crusade the Commander now focuses on creating a safe environment so that every team member can be respected for their unique contribution.

This requires the noble quality of inspiration to link each member, their personal contributions to the crusade and their personal inspiration. During this phase the Commander is obsessed with ensuring that everyone in the team knows their gift and is able to use it.

7. DISCERNMENT

The Commander focuses on the systems and processes required to take the right action. This involves accessing the noble quality of discernment to ensure that all aspects of their life are aligned. During this time the Commander develops a strategic yet practical plan that will guide them through the crusade. During this time the Commander checks they are 'walking the talk'.

ASSESSMENT

8. ASSESSING THE NEW QUESTIONS OF EXISTENCE

The final step is now taken into a brand new world – one with entirely new questions of existence. Since this integration process occurs in the Blue meme, the Commander will have integrated this aspect of consciousness. Now they will be faced with an entirely new set of questions of existence; in the Orange meme they will be based around the need to succeed and be recognised as successful. The Assessment occurs as the Commander takes stock of their current situation, of the lessons they have learned about life in general and their own abilities in particular and then begins to apply their Genius of problem-solving to develop innovative solutions and thereby active success.

For all the types, however, there will be times when their development is arrested or even reversed. It's hard to believe that these charismatic and loved Commanders could feel and behave in the following ways. Commanders refer to these times as their 'dark night of the soul'.

It would be really great if people would realise that stars are only people with the same weaknesses and flaws, not immaculate idols.

Meg Ryan
Actor

SPIRALLING DOWN FOR THE COMMANDER — THE PATH TO DEATH

The spiral downward is triggered by any event, thought, association or deed interpreted through the perspective of the Lower Self. It is this interpretation that many Christians would refer to as a separation from the divine part of ourselves and as 'sin'.

The spiral down for the Commander is triggered by a lack of self-esteem and personal security that leads to a confidence crisis and a complete shutdown.

This confuses the Commanders who are dedicated to solving problems and taking decisive action and they can't believe what they've done. Feeling alone, isolated and stupid, the Commander quickly falls into the role of victim. 'I can't do this – I'm never going to succeed, who did I think I was kidding to take on a project like this, this is way beyond my station.' This can quickly deteriorate into the downward spiral of disintegration, which has seven steps.

AVOIDANCE

1. PROCRASTINATION

Rather than looking at how they can get on with the job at hand, the Commander looks for the inconsistencies in the behaviour of others and in the systems they are following as a first line of defence against anyone who says they are not doing anything. During this time the Commander's professional performance subsides as the procrastination rises. As far as the Commander is concerned, they are OK and everything is working just fine.

2. A WORLD OF DELUSION AND INTROJECTION

The Commander, now completely out of integrity, creates a new world in their imagination with them as the only true and honest person (saviour) in the situation and the other players as weak, spineless and evil people needing to be confronted for the good of the world and for ultimate justice. The now delusional Commander hits out as hard as they can (with others and themselves) to, in their words, have the 'courage' to do the right thing. The right thing, however, is simply the Commander's introjection of the childhood values or the current social rules or cultural stereotypes. The Commander will position themselves as the victim 'doing the right thing' yet being persecuted.

3. POLITICS

With some people now engaged in the victim role portrayed by the Commander, the Commander is ready to play these people against those who refused to remain committed to them through manipulation. During this phase the Commander uses deflection to diminish the impact of any feedback. This phase can see the Commander lie, exaggerate, change alliances and shamelessly compete for attention. No lie is too big. No political game is too ambitious. The police, supervisors, parents, wives, children and lifelong associates can all be dragged into this if they are necessary to win the political game and deflect the truth.

REJECTION

4. BULLYING

If this commitment is not forthcoming the Commander will begin to bully and blame others. This bullying comes in the form of cutting words, strong emotions, mood highs and lows and a focus on personal attacks. At this stage the Commander develops and tells elaborate stories that blame others for their own lack of confidence and energy. The Commander's boundaries also break down which means that they merge with colleagues or the environment.

5. PUNITIVE REVENGE

For the Commander, the downward spiral continues as they superimpose arguments of high-minded moralism and self-righteousness on their petty bullying. At this point of disintegration Commanders are unbelievably vicious and constantly do the very things they are claiming others are doing. Commanders have been known to even physically beat up their opponents, throw television sets, break special gifts or take the law into their own hands.

INTERNALISING
ACTION

6. INFLEXIBILITY

As the Commander spirals down so too does their flexibility. Adherence to plans becomes a clear focus and their management style becomes totally closed to any new suggestions, is abrupt, disconnected and autocratic. During this phase the Commander becomes fascinated with tools, weapons or equipment that can help them defend themselves (even if it means sometimes hitting first) against a vicious world that hates them. This is a dangerous time for Commanders who can use the weapons against themselves, sometimes taking their own life.

DISASSOCIATION 7. ISOLATION AND DISASSOCIATION

If things continue to get worse, the Commander will begin to isolate themselves. In this isolation the Commander disassociates from all that is happening around them and all that they are doing to others. Commanders can cut off all contact with the outside world becoming hermits, reading and refusing to communicate. As the ability to disassociate from their world increases so too does their ability to inflict great pain on those who they believe have wronged them. They do this in a cold and calculated way. Commanders, in the final stage of disintegration, have conducted some of the grisliest murders, where victims were cut up etc. During this phase they also study the laws, rules and fine print that will help them defend themselves if their transgression ever comes to trial. All the while the Commander is quite content with their personal image of themselves as a very reasonable person. After all, it is the world's fault, not theirs.

This is the final brutal stage of the Commander's downward spiral.

The Commander's Quest for Creating Wealth

HOW COMMANDERS BECOME WEALTHY

Commanders are brilliant at solving problems. In a practical sense this can mean inventing a new gadget, approach or system or doing what it takes to get the show on the road. Commanders make big money when they are contracted to solve system-related problems. The bigger the problems they solve, the more money they make. They make excellent project managers, inventors, emergency rescue team leaders and paramedics.

Commanders also have a passion for teaching and passing on their practical knowledge. Their sessions are easy to understand, structured, yet interesting and entertaining for students. Each student's question is, after all, another problem to be solved. I1 in Mirror mode likes to see investments on a daily basis whereas I2 prefers shares.

DEEP UNCONSCIOUS MOTIVATION

A Commander's energy comes from their desire to be respected, admired and financially secure. They wish to be considered pillars of the community, reliable and loyal, with excellent technical abilities in their chosen field. For them, money buys them prestige. A Commander likes to see cash.

In their business affairs, Commanders will align themselves with people who they believe can help them in the immediate future. They don't trust others easily and so tend to work in loose teams rather than join forces with them.

MONEY MANAGEMENT APPROACH

Commanders tend to not have a formal wealth creation plan. They wait until they have a lump sum of money and then decide what they are going to do with it.

While single or young, the temptation of a Commander is to rent rather than own their own premises because they don't want to commit to one place and need to be convinced to adopt a money-making focus.

Commanders tend to like trading in commodities. They enjoy this because of the thrill of the chase and the immediate results this can bring. This suits their episodic style of thinking. A Commander will only trust people who they have worked with for a long time and who have earned their trust in many and various situations. When married, with a clear role that requires them to create stability within the household and if advised by one of their trusted associates, they can be persuaded to invest in the sharemarket, with any stock that they believe has the potential to do well but prefer to invest in their primary residence.

The simple act of paying attention can take you a long way.

Keanu Reeves
Actor

THE COMMANDER'S MONEY HABITS

The Commander's principal focus is on increasing their annual income rather than their asset base. When demoralised, Commanders can spontaneously spend large sums of money entertaining themselves. This can mean excessive expenditure on alcohol, gadgets, trips, air travel, car hire, sporting match tickets and tools of all kinds. The rest of the time, Commanders can be very frugal, spending only on the necessities of life and putting the rest in the bank. They would like to have an advanced financial plan but may not have the confidence to develop one themselves.

The greatest opportunities to invest are usually taken up by the Commander. If they have the available cash, they often invest in high-risk ventures and their wealth tends to swing wildly from being substantial to insubstantial. What they say and what they do, don't line up. This gives the Commander the impression that they have very little control over their financial position and so they don't tend to apply the thought and analysis they need to, to grow their money. While their Master may say invest in small episodic things, their Mirror will invest in big risky things.

Being in financial crisis is not threatening or concerning to Commanders. To them it just creates another series of problems to solve. This lack of financial fear means that they often can't even see the point of saving. A Commander can become so obsessed with solving a problem that they go into hibernation until it is solved. For self-employed Commanders, this can mean weeks with no active income.

Commanders are very prone to making spontaneous small purchases of tools and equipment and a wide variety of other possessions as an avenue of escape. They often use these purchases as a special reward for themselves for all the hard work they have done. When they do this they are lured by branded items and machinery that is either novel or very efficient. All these preferences mean that Commanders will pay a premium for many of their purchases.

Because Commanders are the most philanthropic of all the types, they often give their hard-earned money away to friends and family.

When Commanders investigate a new venture, if there is no emotional link with the people involved in the venture, they will be reticent to become involved.

*The retailer Gerry Harvey has been quoted as saying, '**People have traditionally said to their kids "Don't go and work in a shop. You're going to be a doctor or a dentist or a lawyer or an artist ... just don't go work in a shop."'***

*His response is: '**You're wrong, you should work in a shop because there is more opportunity there.'***

WHAT COMMANDERS DO WITH THEIR WEALTH

Because they focus on problem-solving, Commanders will often invest in companies that have gone wrong and need fixing, or in companies that are breaking new territory.

They prefer to live in safe and solid houses that are interesting in some way. They often have ingenious plans for their homes that include automated doors, gates, lighting, sprinkler systems and a range of gadgets.

They have a fascination with boats, cars, computers, toys, aircraft, tools, software, motors, electronics, energy, and the natural laws of nature.

New technology

I get really excited about new technology if it offers better ways of doing things that I already do. I don't like technology just for technology's sake but will become an instant advocate if I can see how it adds value to the way I work in speed or efficiency. I do like to have the very best of whatever it may be. Cheap tools are of no interest to me, as I cannot rely on them in case of an emergency. Multi-function tools are very appealing.

Wealthy Commanders spend most of their time getting out and about, meeting new people, travelling, and experiencing the world at first hand.

Wealthy Commanders are practical, fun-loving, nature-loving, childlike enthusiasts who have friends from one end of the globe to the other, all of whom look forward to seeing them and joining their party.

WEALTH CREATION FORMULA FOR COMMANDERS

Commanders need to decide that they are going to set and achieve their financial objectives, that it is possible for them to do it, and that the prestige and benefit of discipline will outweigh the disadvantages.

The Commander needs to clarify in their own mind what they are striving for. Techniques like putting the picture of the dream house on the fridge, buying the block of land or test-driving the desired car are important to make the vision real.

Once the objective is set, the Commander needs to develop a financial plan that automatically takes funds from their account and distributes them as agreed. This needs to be done in consultation with their preferred financial adviser(s).

Commanders are very good at judging good and bad investments, stocks and real estate if they understand how the system works and have the confidence to listen to their own advice. The recommendation for Commanders then is two-fold: learn the system and follow your hunches. One technique that can work very well is for the Commander to ask himself or herself, 'What would I advise someone else to do in this situation?' And then take their own advice.

Commanders do much better financially when they take a longer-term view of their financial position. They do well to remember that a five-year plan usually takes a while to complete – often enough – five years!

UNDERSTANDING COMMANDERS

Commanders best manage themselves by:

- Taking time to plan ahead and set agendas and priorities, rather than always taking things as they come
- Accepting that people are as important as functions and that most people need to understand why initiatives are being taken
- Disciplining themselves to be on time for meetings and deadlines
- Being organised

As team members, Commanders make the best contribution when:

- They are trouble-shooting and problem- solving
- They have complex issues/problems to solve
- They are in a deadline-driven environment where the situation needs a cool and calm head

Armies are like hungry children, the more food that is put on the table, the more they will eat. But it's up to the parents to be responsible, to provide the correct nourishment to develop the child in a well-balanced and appropriate way. Sometimes the child does not always know best. I have no problem with that system.

Lieutenant-General Peter Cosgrove,
when asked about Government funding for the Australian Defence Force

When managing Commanders:

- Always provide a clear, hard deadline

- Explain why an initiative needs to be taken and the exact role you want them to play

- Don't expect them to automatically focus themselves on the right actions

How Commanders will act during meetings:

- Will listen and watch what is going on until they perceive the discussion is going round in circles and will then step in

- Will be calming in heated or difficult meetings

- Will want to know what the group is solving

- Will easily lose interest and sidetrack the discussion if not managed

Personality strengths that help the Commander to further their development:

- Excellent at creating thinking outside the box

- Excellent in times of crisis

- Excellent at solving problems: big, small, vague or complex

Acting with courage
I don't feel like I am very courageous. I just do what needs to be done to get the job done. I can quickly assess a situation and solve the problem at hand using the tools available. I am very good in a crisis and as a first aid officer in a previous job, I was able to handle very nasty situations that had others passing out and throwing up. I just saw that a colleague was hurt and I was the one that needed to be there for him. No big deal. I just needed to get the job done.

Personality weaknesses that can stand in the way of the Commander's development:

- Tends to see people as cogs, rather than people
- Can wind down and sleep in times of low stress
- Has great difficulty understanding why others are feeling the way they are

Opportunities for the Commander to develop:

- Needs to keep the big picture in mind
- Needs to reconnect and allow passion back into their lives
- Needs to discipline themselves to read and learn before a crisis occurs

Threats to the Commander's development:

- Can lose connection – feel life is pointless and enter into self-defeating behaviour
- Can get distracted, experimenting and never getting anywhere
- Can get bogged down and develop skills that are learned only through personal experience, not based on best practice

FAMOUS COMMANDERS

- Gerry Harvey (Co-founder, Harvey Norman)
- Bruce Willis (Actor)
- Mel Gibson (Actor)
- Kevin Spacey (Actor)
- Samwise Gamgee (*Lord of the Rings*)
- Steven Bradbury (Gold Medallist Skater)
- Craig Lowndes (V8 Supercar Driver)
- Indiana Jones (Movie Character)
- Meg Ryan (Actor)
- Elvis Presley (Singer)
- Benny Andersson (ABBA)
- Layne Beachley (World Champion Surfer)
- Lote Tuquri (ARU Player)

THE COMMANDER AT WORK

The Commander balances structure with spontaneity and has an excellent ability to intellectually process data or ideas. They work efficiently and always to a plan, although it may not always be written down. The Commander can be relied upon to get things done. Once a plan is in place they become highly enthusiastic, productive and very conscientious. The Commander can adapt what they have seen elsewhere and apply this vision to their situation. Their strength is in creating the right process.

They are extremely cooperative, willing to contribute and very supportive of others, especially if they are as efficient as the Commander. They like to take responsibility for a team, to organise activities and to solve problems.

Commanders cope well with change. They love new ideas and are happy to adopt them as long as there's a problem to solve. They are often more flexible in thought than in deed.

They resolve conflict by finding a solution or workable plan if someone becomes angry the Commander will use logic to justify their position. They will not usually become angry in response, except in extreme cases, where they can purge built-up anger on someone who is unlikely to fight back.

Commanders are mostly tolerant of others as long as they are efficient, friendly and want to achieve. They are generally highly determined individuals who expect the same level of determination and creativity from those around them.

They are not motivated simply by the desire to be successful and can be considered self-paced rather than competitive. They are more interested in experimenting than point scoring. Their confidence soars when they are showing their ability to solve problems laterally.

As leaders, they enjoy new ideas and new initiatives. They are organised, structured and keen to keep people working efficiently while making time to listen. Often their judgement may be clouded by their desire to keep things systematic.

They are quick-witted, enthusiastic communicators and are renowned for their clever use of puns. They will generally sense how their listeners respond to them and seek their feedback. Commanders love spontaneity both at work and at home. They enjoy surprises and 'spur of the moment' decisions.

Commanders are very loyal to people until they are crossed. They are extremely sensitive but are selective as to when they show it. They are generally optimistic; they may, however, become depressed or bored if there is not enough urgency. They like it when there are problems to solve.

Table 14.2 The Leadership Style of the Commander

Situation	Explanation
1. The leader's modus operandi	Forges consensus through participation
2. The style in a phrase	'What do you think?'
3. Underlying emotional intelligence competencies	Collaboration, team leadership and communication
4. When the style works best	To build buy-in or get consensus, or to get input from valuable employees
5. Overall impact on climate	Positive

They have a good memory for solutions and how to deal with people, but don't easily retain facts. They are unlikely to exaggerate and will deceive only if they feel they have been deceived. A Commander has an excellent ability to negotiate.

A Commander is a formidable problem-solver, organiser and performer during times of crisis, and can mobilise entire teams with unquestioned authority.

LEADERSHIP STYLE OF THE COMMANDER

Each Neuro-Rational Type, due to its combination of thinking functions, has a different leadership style. These leadership styles are a function of the centre of focus of the Neuro-Rational Types, and tend to be expressions of the underlying world view of the personality.

A ground-breaking survey of 3871 executives selected from a database of more than 20,000 executives[2] found distinct leadership styles which consistently appear in organisations. Daniel Goleman (2000) attributes these different leadership styles to different emotional intelligences. Each leadership style has a different impact on the work environment and on organisational performance. The most effective leaders use a variety of styles, choosing the appropriate style, timing and intensity to manage each situation.

The leadership style identified by Goleman's research that is most closely aligned to the profile of the Commander is the ***Democratic*** style.

The research suggests that the Democratic style has a highly positive impact on corporate climate. The primary focus of the Democratic style of leadership is in collective decision-making and action (a P1- and I2-based approach).

---

2   Survey was originally analysed by Kelner, S., et al. (1996).

The Democratic Style

Daniel Goleman (2000) describes the actions of a leader with a Democratic style. She was a principal of a Catholic school which had to be closed when enrolment diminished.

She took the view that the problem was for everyone to solve, and she saw herself as the leader of that problem-solving process. Rather than 'awfulising' or evaluating, she simply threw herself into the situation, was present from moment to moment and spontaneously solved all the thousands of problems, big and small, that came across her desk. She held repeated meetings with staff, and later parents and the community. First, she explained the situation and listened while they talked. Then in true Commander problem-solving style, she asked for their ideas and solutions. After two months of much talking, consulting and listening, it was clear to all that the school should close and the children be transferred to another Catholic school in the district. All proceeded calmly and methodically, which demonstrated the strengths of the Commander.

Goleman contrasts this with another school that had to close. This principal did no consulting at all, but just made the announcement. His action was met by protests, litigation and negative media attention.

As we have seen, the Commander is a natural leader in a crisis or in a situation where there is no ideal outcome.

Some attributes of this style are:

- **Consensual decision-making.** By spending time finding out the opinions and ideas of other people, the Democratic leader builds trust, respect and commitment from the workforce.

- **Flexibility.** Since employees have a say in the decisions that affect their goals and how they perform their work, flexibility and responsibility are both encouraged.

- **High morale.** Listening to the concerns of the workers allows the leader to know what to do to keep morale high.

- **Realistic.** People operating in a Democratic system tend to be very realistic about what can and cannot be accomplished since they have a say in setting their own goals and the standards of success.

The Democratic style does not work well when the employees are not competent or informed enough to offer sound advice. In times of crisis consensus is totally inappropriate.

This is the birthright of our nation. Surely it is better if we own our major food brands so that the profit remains in this country to create employment and fund research and development.

Dick Smith
Entrepreneur

The Democratic style should be used when a leader is uncertain about the best direction to take and requires new ideas and guidance from able employees. It is also useful in generating fresh ideas for executing a vision, even if that vision is strong.

SCHOOL OF STRATEGIC THOUGHT

The natural differences are not limited to leadership styles alone; they also extend to a natural inclination towards different strategic thought. These differences have been researched by Mintzberg, Ahlstrad and Lampel (1998). For the Commander, their approach to strategy emerges as people (acting either individually or collectively) come to learn about a situation as well as their organisation's capability to deal with it. It is the learning school of strategy formation.

THE GENIUS OF THE COMMANDER – PROBLEM-SOLVING

The Commander's Genius is their ability to effectively solve problems that are complex, undefined and constantly changing. They are excellent at managing large groups of people in high-stress, dangerous or crisis situations. The Commander is practical and creative, and can solve anything 'on the hop'. The Commander is the natural leader when the 'right' emergency action is needed and there is no time.

Buckingham and Clifton (2001, p. 112) call this the restorative *theme of strength*. The Commander simply loves solving problems, and indeed, finds them energising[3].

Buckingham and Clifton (2001) describe how this Genius is manifested:

- This person enjoys the process of problem-solving and naturally analyses the

---

3   If you remember back to Principle #1, an individual's Intelligence is made up of thinking, feeling and somatic components. Each person will tend to be stronger in one rather than the other two. The preference is then manifested in the Neuro-Rational Type. In this instance, practical problems are preferred by the strongly somatic type, while conceptual problems are preferred by the thinking type, and personal problems by the feeling type.

symptoms first, then identifies the problem, then finds a solution.

- Each problem-solver will have their own preference for practical, conceptual, or personal problems, and for familiar or new situations.

- All problem-solvers enjoy bringing things back to life, be it a person, thing, process or company. Saving things give them a real sense of satisfaction.

Buckingham and Clifton (2001) cite the following examples of problem-solving:

> **Nigel,** a software designer, recalls his childhood enjoyment of fixing things using his woodworking tools. As an adult, he gets the same pleasure from his software programming, where he writes then tests a program, and if it has a fault, he enjoys fixing it until it works well.

> **Jan,** an internist, recognises that problem-solving is a natural part of her day-to-day life. She loves fixing things in the surgery, be it the actual sewing or sitting by a dying patient and helping them die with dignity, and also helping the family deal with it. She also recognises that with her own young family she has to resist the urge to fix things when they need to learn to do it themselves.

BODY COMPOSITION

The Commander works best in a large body and is the largest of all types. The Commander female sits well at a BMI of 24-31kg/m^2 where the male Commander sits well at a BMI 27- 36kg/m^2. (Traditional healthy weight range is between 25 and 30.) The Commander face is round and chubby, regardless of body weight. Although over traditional acceptable BMI values, the Commander at these levels is healthy when full body composition is taken, as these BMI values correspond with relatively healthy body fat percentages in Commanders. The Commander's weight is distributed away from the abdominal region; the chest cavity is very thick and the bottom and hips are large. Their arms become thick before their legs (Diversi, 2006).

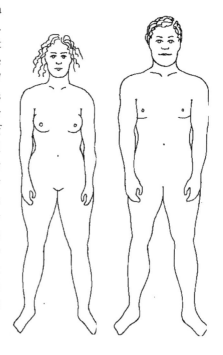

EXERCISE PREFERENCES

Commanders much prefer strength training to cardiovascular work. They are also quite partial to fighting exercise and training including boxing, kickboxing and any of the martial arts. They do well under personal trainers who are hard on them and challenge their strength. Unfortunately, many Commanders have lower back problems that can interfere with exercise and training. Growing up, Commanders are excellent at both team and individual sports. This allows them to keep their weight down until adulthood, and exercise (particularly cardiovascular exercise) is the key to keeping their weight down (Diversi, 2006).

EATING PREFERENCES

The Commander does not need to eat a lot of food to keep their weight on. However, the Commander loves food more than any other type so other types inaccurately presume that they are 'overweight' because of their eating behaviours. They love trying new food, taste testing and a good home-cooked meal. They like all types of food – sweet, savoury and fatty – but prefer the complex carbohydrates such as bread, rice, noodles, pasta and animal proteins such as meat to vegetables and salad (Diversi, 2006).

DIETING PREFERENCES

Commanders are very good at dieting. They can follow very restrictive diets much better than any other type as they are an expert in self-control. They do not do well on meal plans or diets that allow them too much choice or where they have to make most of the decisions (Diversi, 2006).

Applying Commander Insights as an Effective Communicator

When Negotiating with Commanders

The effective communicator is able to align their narrative and the point they are wanting to make with the archetype of the audience. That is, they use the same language, approach and behaviour with the archetype of the person they are presenting to.

When negotiating with Commanders, the way you position information is very important. Commanders are attracted to messages centred on two main themes that are most convincing to them: *'Show me that this will solve the next problem that comes up'* and *'Show me this is practical.'*

'Show me that this will solve the next problem that comes up'

There are two groups who access their C1 and P1 by nature, the Commanders and the Treasurers. This segment makes up 36 per cent of the general population. When negotiating with this group:

- Present the 'here and now' and how well the organisation is able to respond quickly to whatever situation arises
- Present your argument in terms of new opportunities, new ideas, new projects and in all the divergent pieces of the organisation
- Assume a very short attention span
- Present your information through pictures, captions, simple flow charts and graphs
- Do not present abstract ideas or concepts or spatially-based dynamic models
- Emphasise experiential learning where they can set the pace
- Mention any links to the Internet
- Deliver your information in gulps
- Be aware that they will often not delineate between the different pieces if they all arrive together; for example, if a dividend arrives at the same time as a court summons, the dividend will be tarred with the same brush
- Be aware that they see vision as ungrounded and largely a waste of time
- Provide immediate answers, immediate results and immediate priorities because they withstand very low levels of delayed gratification
- Do not deliver too much strategy and not enough action

'Show me this is practical'

There are two groups who access their P1 and I2 by nature – the Commander and the Architect. This segment makes up approximately 12 per cent of the general population. When negotiating with this group:

- As a leader, demonstrate decisive leadership with an open mind and high energy
- As an aside, explain, predict or control nature, cycles and reality
- As a leader, anticipate trends and proactively manage the situation
- Demonstrate competence and constant improvement, and that the leadership has a focus on this
- Be aware that they are highly critical of themselves and everyone else
- Do not be inconsistent which they read as deceit
- Deliver a strong argument rather than just rely on the credibility of the person making the statement – the rationale for the argument must be logically pieced together step by step
- Make their interaction with the organisation be a learning experience for them
- Provide constant reassurance that their leaders do have the competence to achieve the objectives; this counteracts their own constant self-doubt that failure is just around the corner
- Present your point without typos, grammatical errors or logistical oversights because under stress they become perfectionists
- Communicate in compact, short, logical statements – they respond badly to 'waffle'
- Provide the rationale for every initiative to satiate their search for the 'why' of the situation
- Provide communication with graphs, models, icons and pictures

The Commander at a Glance

Strengths

- Brings out confidence in others
- Courage
- Brings commitment to a team

Code of Conduct

- Stands up for what they believe is right
- Stands by their actions without fear of reprisals or consequences
- Acts justly and fairly in all dealings with colleagues
- Solves problems as they arise without fuss and drama
- Encourages the team to innovate or adapt if necessary to ensure a quality result
- Encourages other team members to be courageous in thought and deed

First Step of Integration

- Focuses on being objective

First Step of Disintegration

- Descends into personal confusion and procrastination

Exemplars

- Bruce Willis
- Meg Ryan
- Keanu Reeves

Chapter 15

The Architect
An In-Depth Look at the Architect

If you don't know what you are doing, darling, do it neatly.

Advice given to the author by his mother during his early maths experience at school

What we've got to thank Architects for:

Systems and practices suitability

Leadership credibility

Alignment of what we say and do

Philosophy

Sociology

The Stone Masons

Buddhism

Strategic thinking

THE ARCHITECT PROFILE

The price of wisdom is above rubies.

Job 28:18

OVERVIEW

The Architect's mind is able to see the big picture and the sequential order of activity required to achieve a given outcome. By nature they think in terms of flow charts. Although they usually feel most comfortable supporting the leadership rather than taking a high profile, they have no hesitation in stepping up to the line and outlining the most efficient way of achieving the desired outcomes if the leadership seems to be hesitating.

Even though Architects are rational and calm, they are ambitious and driven to achieve whatever goals they have set themselves. All their activity must be another step towards achieving their objectives and must be focused on learning about a new topic as well as the 'how to' of the topic so that the knowledge becomes a capability. For the Architect, work is work and play is work. Every day they expect to get closer to the planned outcomes.

Regardless of their training or level of professional development, this type likes systems and systems thinking. This can mean computer systems; information systems; or geological, engineering, organisational or agricultural systems. The mind of the Architect is instantly able to see where the system is failing to produce the required output and what needs to be done to put it right.

The Architect is particularly good at the development of effective strategies that require the construction of a series of actions to achieve a stated outcome that takes into account potential contingencies.

Very emotionally detached, the Architect rarely gives positive feedback to those living or working with them. Others sometimes think of them as removed or distant and sometimes find it difficult to understand why they run hot and cold.

> *I feel deeply and passionately about many things but don't seem to show it. When I was young I avoided giving offence by masking my feelings and I took that into adulthood. Now when I look back I feel sad and wish I had dramatised my emotions for my own family, especially my*

I don't go by the rule book. I lead from the heart, not the head.

Diana Spencer
Princess of Wales

Any intelligent fool can make things bigger, more complex, and more violent. It takes a touch of genius – and a lot of courage – to move in the opposite direction.

Albert Einstein
Physicist

pleasure when they did beautiful things for me that really touched me deeply. I said thank you in my own quiet way but it must have always disappointed them.

FOCUS OF ATTENTION

Architects are brilliant at strategic systems thinking and inventing. This means that without even having to think about it too hard, they will instantly see why the system isn't working and what can be done about it. At their best, Architects are contemplative, independent, discerning, capable, unifying, strategic and insightful.

KEY CHARACTER DRIVERS

There are three key Intelligences that drive the Architect:

C2 – Vision

P1 – Logic

I2 – Heart

LEVELS OF CONSCIOUSNESS AS DEFINED BY US PSYCHOLOGIST CLARE GRAVES AND SPIRAL DYNAMICS' AUTHORS COWAN AND BECK

The table on the following page outlines the broad character development of the Architect over a lifetime from Level One – the lowest level of consciousness – through to essence at Level Nine.

THE SUBTYPES

Each of the eight types is made up of three Intelligences. The Architect has C2 Vision, P1 Logic and I2 Heart. As we adapt to our life circumstances we tend to favour one of the three. This subtly changes the personality and gives rise to subtypes. All Architects will be able to relate to all three of the subtypes at some time in their life.

Table 15.1 The Architect Levels of Development

Level of Consciousness and the noble quality embraced at this level	Common Architect characteristics at this level of consciousness
Level 1 (Beige) A state of nature and instincts.	Closed down and off from human nobility. One step at a time. No sense of future or past. Frozen.
Level 2 (Purple) Mysterious and frightening. *(Noble quality to be embraced at this level: Contemplation)*	The Architect interprets God through nature and through natural cycles. God is natural, powerful and daunting. Nature is to be admired and life valued. Understand God by understanding nature and the seasons.
Level 3 (Red) Raw displays of power – dictators, tough love, predators. *(Noble quality to be embraced at this level: Independence)*	The Architect hesitates but the Judge Mirror doesn't. At this phase the Architect is creating systems that imitate nature's systems. If these systems are not followed, the Judge Mirror is quick to condemn and bully others into submission. Discipline can be harsh and the Judge is remorseless while the Architect stays detached.
Level 4 (Blue) Everything is controlled by God and is purposeful. Obey God. Do it right. Feel guilt. *(Noble quality to be embraced at this level: Discernment)*	Obey the world's natural laws and you will prosper; disobey and the natural laws of life will deal with you harshly. This is the view of the Architect at this phase. Everything in life is a linear cause and effect relationship – understand the relationship and you can predict the future. If you can't do the time – don't do the crime.
Level 5 (Orange) The world is a game and I want to win. *(Noble quality to be embraced at this level: Capability)*	The Architect focuses on formal education to give them the credibility that they see others don't have. Once they have an acknowledged area of expertise, the Architect uses this with hard work, usually within large corporations, to further their career. They are more interested in gaining/earning the respect of others and receiving an honest reward for their work than simply making a fortune. Their Judge Mirror constantly wants more money, more recognition and more respect and this drives the Architect to work long hours and do what it takes.
Level 6 (Green) We need to join together and grow personally through community. *(Noble quality to be embraced at this level: Unification)*	The Architect sees community as a natural system and wants the community to grow and prosper. The Architect is particularly committed to ensuring that all community members can learn whatever they want and receive the respect, rewards and recognition they deserve. Always quick to point out inconsistency between the community's stated and actual mission, vision and values, the Architect keeps the community on track and focused on the corporate vision, on maintaining practical and usable systems and on the communication systems within the community. They learn to use their gift for the community.
Level 7 (Yellow) We need to explore ways of being responsibly free. *(Noble quality to be embraced at this level: Strategy)*	The Architect has an excellent conceptual mind and uses this to work with new ideas, frameworks and visions for tomorrow's community. The Architect becomes the community 'bullshit detector' ensuring resources are used wisely and models are logical, integrated and practical.
Level 8 (Turquoise) The world is composed of delicately balanced interlocking forces, shaped by attractor fields of intention and nobility. Uses natural flows. Actively grows consciousness. The Non-dual Leader manifests at this level.	The world is seen as a series of cycles and life is seen as a quest. The individual understands the spiral of life and the streams of intra-level progression and addresses the current problems of existence that arise in their own journeys so that the spiral can keep developing.
Level 9 (Coral)	TOWARDS ENLIGHTENMENT

THE VISIONARY ARCHITECT

The Visionary Architect focuses on the future. They will often have thoughts that are totally unrelated to what they are processing. Their ability to use their imagination allows them to plan long-term. It's the irrational leap that makes discovering brand new processes or ways to solve problems possible. The Visionary Architect may appear confusing to those around them – at work, they will be structured and conservative and at play, they will be vigorous and spontaneous. The Visionary Architect lives between the ideal and the practical worlds, and is constantly travelling between the two.

THE CONTROLLING ARCHITECT

The Controlling Architect will want to see projects through from beginning to end, has a healthy sense of humour, is balanced, analytical and even-handed. They will be self-disciplined and stable. The Controlling Architect will want loose ends tied up.

Their logic will suppress their spontaneity unless they are relaxed. The Controlling Architect will suppress their vision until they are tired or under the influence of alcohol. This structure will also control their natural mood swings and keep them stable and emotionally balanced.

THE SENSITIVE ARCHITECT

The Sensitive Architect will be very perceptive to how others are feeling – a true empathiser, putting people first at all costs.

They do not want their opinions to offend and so often suppress their thoughts. They will not necessarily need to tie up all the loose ends, but rather constantly stay focused on the emotional pulse of the person or people they are with.

The Sensitive Architect will tend to be totally different when they are with people than when they are by themselves. By themselves, they will be organised, task oriented and structured. With others they will tend to be the social glue, heading off conflict and often working hard to keep the peace.

ARCHETYPES RELATED TO THE ARCHITECT

When people discuss archetypes, many of the characters they use will fall into the same category as the Architect, much the same way that there may be fifty-seven species of fern but regardless of the species, it still belongs to the fern family.

By way of example, some of these are:

- The Engineer
- The Builder
- The Schemer
- The Ambassador
- The Diplomat
- The Go-between
- The Patriarch
- The Parent
- The Change Agent

CHILDREN'S STORIES

- *Little Red Riding Hood*

THE MIRROR

While the Architect is strategic, that is, bringing the desired future into reality by creating systems that align with the vision and engaging the team to use them, the Architect's Mirror, the Judge, is constantly criticising the Architect for not getting enough done, not achieving, not articulating their position and not being particularly intelligent. The Mirror Judge is the loudest of all the Mirror Masters and constantly wants to be heard. The Mirror Judge is always ready for a fight.

The Architect's Mirror Judge will always want to have their say. Terse comments to coffee shop staff about the quality of the food or service, sharp words of criticism about low performing or unattractive people, quips about hair style, weight, ethnicity, laziness, heritage, religion or acumen made by Architects are evidence of their Mirror.

Mirror Judges are very strong, verbal and one-eyed. They can be opinionated, vindictive walking arguments, ever ready to tip their frustration, anger and opinions over anyone who is within earshot. The young Mirror Judges love to spend their energy on physical activities, dancing, sport, running community causes or events or driving themselves hard. As they mature, the Mirror Judges learn how to focus this energy in a constructive way and provide energy to the Architect.

When fully integrated into the personality, the Mirror Judge balances the Master Architect's strategic focus and detached approach to life with unlimited passion, clear judgement and unqualified loyalty to those they love.

CHARACTER FORMATION

The formation of personality has three major influences:

1. Firstly, the physiological genetic makeup of the individual creates a predisposition towards accessing particular energies and not accessing others.

2. Secondly, the culture of the environment in which the child grew up, sanctioned some energies over others and so encouraged the child to focus on some energies and suppress others.

3. Thirdly, the individual's psychological and physiological response to trauma or pain that usually occurs during childhood alters the way they relate to the six core energies. When we experience emotional pain or trauma we can 'turn off' the emotion by turning off the energy. One theory of personality development suggests that if in time we turn off three of the energies we derive our energy from the remaining three. These three in turn combine to form our type.

Regardless of what caused us to focus on just three of the Intelligences rather than all six, as human beings we can take three Intelligences that are available to all humans and combine them to create a higher form of consciousness. We are, if you like, human transformers of thinking into consciousness. This higher level of consciousness takes the form of a Neuro-Rational Type – in this case the Neuro-Rational Type of the Architect.

DEVELOPMENTAL ISSUES

Deficient Third Intelligence (P2)

With a deficient P2 the Architect often finds that their personal ambition or drive is low. The impact of this is that Architects can find themselves looking after the needs of others rather than looking after their own needs. In the personality of the Architect this often manifests in linking up with someone else and simply adopting their passion, drive or ambition for a profession or project. In relationships this is often described as co-dependency. At work this makes Architects excellent as the second in charge. Unfortunately, it often also leads to others taking advantage of their availability and obvious dependency which in turn leads to Architects giving, giving and giving and then one day, snapping and cutting the relationship because they feel taken for granted.

> In my life when my partner had a great need and I hated to see them suffer, I have sacrificed my own needs entirely in order to do the noble thing and see them happier. I regret to say that later I became resentful of the situation which is so disadvantageous for me.

The Intelligence is important for defining personal boundaries and ensuring that goals are self-gratifying and that effort is recognised. (It is the seat of the ego.) Without this, Architects are prone to organising lose/win situations, waiting too long to do anything about it and then exploding when least expected – when a last straw breaks the camel's back. Deficient P2 leads to low self-esteem and an inability to 'sell' themselves – particularly to themselves.

Deficient Fifth Intelligence (I1)

The temptation for Architects is to stream their energy straight to C2 and escape the mundane nature of the world of reality. This is due to a deficient I1. While this is not true of all Architects, all Architects do have an excessive C2 and so therefore have a hard time seeing, accepting and understanding reality, preferring to make their own worlds, conceived in their own minds.

Deficient Second Intelligence (C1)

Many Architects often also have a deficient C1. When this is the case Architects are out of touch with their feelings and sensations in their body. Their movements may be jerky rather than fluid and feelings may be intellectualised.

THE QUEST FOR INTEGRATION: AWARENESS (I), CREATIVITY (C) AND POWER (P)

Awareness – Having eyes that see (I1)

For the Architect, integration begins when the Architect is willing to see the world much more as it actually is rather than constantly trying to escape from it and create their own little worlds in their own heads. For the Architect, integration can mean seeing their life as it really is for the first time. This may include who they have married, where they actually live, how heavy or how thin they really are. It also means being willing to look at household finances, lifestyle and character, as they really are. Finally, for the Architect to develop I1 awareness, they must take time to see the repeating patterns in relationships, jobs, purchases and lifestyle and challenge the 'magic think' that is behind the behaviour that keeps getting manifested. Madness was once defined as doing the same thing over and over and expecting to get different results. This is what the Architect will do unless this awareness is awakened.

To get another view of a troubling situation, I may talk to God but I also like to talk to a trusted person who is high in I1. I used to do this unconsciously, then later did it consciously. Now I'm trying to do it myself. I always find this angle refreshing and sometimes challenging.

Developing earth-bound creativity (C1)

Architects are spectacularly creative, but often not in a practical, hands-on way. This is the second stage of healing for the Architect – to get in touch with their body and the practical creativity they have within them. This can involve painting, drawing, cooking, dancing; in fact, any kind of self-expression that's fun. The key here is not to focus on the end result but instead to focus on the process. The process must be fun.

Developing P2

Architects are good at seeing when systems or processes are not useful, practical or appropriate. However, they need to learn how to focus their energy on doing the things that are important to them rather than just urgent. Time management principles are an excellent place to start, using Covey's 'urgent/important' matrix. Anthony Robbins' 'moving toward and moving away from' framework is also excellent at creating clarity for Architects. Goal management, setting objectives and reviewing daily achievement is also a valuable way to strengthen the role that would normally be played by the third Intelligence. Developing P2 is particularly hard work for the sensitive Architect because as it arises so too does the possibility of the Architect being rejected for 'having their own agenda'. This is an important internal conflict for the Architect to resolve if they are to regain their self-confidence.

Healing in Action

SPIRALLING UP FOR THE ARCHITECT – PERSONAL TRANSFORMATION[1]

Personal transformation and the path to life for the Architect starts with developing their ability to discern what needs to be done to achieve the individual's or organisation's vision. This enables the principles of total quality management to be 'lived' as the systems and processes are refined each time they are used. This

---

1   Based on an Architect in the Blue meme.

ultimately creates teamwork based on clear, practical and efficient systems. It creates simplicity, credibility and effectiveness. When applied to the Architect personally, this ensures that who they are, what they do and how they do it are all in alignment.

In practice, the quest for integration follows the following eight steps:

AWARENESS

1. RESPONSIBILITY

With personal 'congruence' in place, the Architect looks to their long-term plans and the key milestones ahead. In the short term this clarity focuses on how they can give back to their community. For the Architect, living responsibly requires that they effectively play their role in the family, at work and in their community. Amongst other things, this requires a careful consideration and management of risks and an assessment of whether there is a correct balance between responsibility and authority in their various roles in life. As the Architect does this, workmates, friends and family have their sense of certainty and confidence about what the Architect is doing reinforced and they see the genuineness and committed nature of the Architect in fulfilling their role.

2. LEARNING

The Architect now focuses on securing timely and appropriate information, or personal or professional learning. During this time the Architect buys books, attends courses, updates databases, tidies up the financial systems, conducts competitor analysis or reviews pricing and conducts benchmarking. The majority of the book learning and understanding during the transformation cycle takes place during this phase.

3. TURNING TALK INTO ACTION – THROUGH DRIVE

When the Architect reaches the third phase they engage the noble quality of drive to focus on asking themselves the hard questions, getting clarity on what action they need to take personally and then getting on with it. This is a time of boundless energy, optimism, success, recognition and fun. The constant analysis of the Architect is broken by laughter, a quick mind and a love of stories, parties, celebration and the hard work of securing some quick wins (other than relationship) from personal effort.

CLARITY

4. INTEGRITY

For the Architect, the next step on their journey towards integration starts when they are willing to step out and do what they know is right and has integrity, rather than just wait and respond to the action of others. This is very hard for the Architect who wants to be philosophical about life. This step in the journey requires the Architect to ensure everything they are doing is being done with integrity and that there is an absolute focus on reality – not just theory.

ACTION

5. CREATING AN INSPIRATIONAL ENVIRONMENT

Working with team members to achieve their crusade the Architect now focuses on creating a safe environment so that every team member can be respected for their unique contribution. This requires the noble quality of inspiration to link each member's individual contributions to the crusade and their personal inspiration. During this phase the Architect is obsessed with ensuring that everyone in the team knows their gift and is able to use it.

6. BUILDING BRIDGES OF UNDERSTANDING – THROUGH DIPLOMACY

The healing that has taken place during transformation enables the Architect to begin building bridges with people with humility, honesty and diplomacy. This noble quality of diplomacy involves the Architect being open and honest and accepting and building bridges between people from all walks of life. In this phase the Architect looks to create an opportunity for everyone they know to be able to grow and develop and to use their gift.

7. COURAGE

With a significant depth of newfound passion, the Architect now steps out with courage to achieve their plan. This is where the Architect starts a new job or relationship, begins a new business, and breaks ties with those who are not aligned with their values. They step forward with courage and certainty and never look back.

ASSESSMENT   **8 ASSESSING THE NEW QUESTIONS OF EXISTENCE**

The final step is now taken into a brand new world – one with entirely new questions of existence. Since this integration process occurs in the Blue meme, the Architect will have integrated this aspect of consciousness. Now they will be faced with an entirely new set of questions of existence; in the Orange meme they will be based around the need to succeed and be recognised as successful. The Assessment occurs as the Architect takes stock of their current situation, of the lessons they have learned about life in general and their own abilities in particular and then begins to apply their Genius of congruence to develop capability.

For all the types, however, there will be times when their development is arrested or even reversed. It's hard to believe that these charismatic and loved Architects could feel and behave in the following ways. Architects refer to these times as their 'dark night of the soul'.

SPIRALLING DOWN FOR THE ARCHITECT - THE PATH TO DEATH

The spiral downward is triggered by any event, thought, association or deed interpreted through the perspective of the Lower Self. It is this interpretation that many Christians would refer to as a separation from the divine part of ourselves and as 'sin'.

> *I really know the meaning of the word 'grounded'. When I'm stressed, just half an hour working in my garden gives me a sense of completeness or calm and eventually I usually think through the issue or at least settle down. Camping on the ground in a tent has the same effect.*

The spiral down for the Architect is triggered by a lack of personal congruity and can quickly deteriorate into the downward spiral of disintegration, which has seven steps.

AVOIDANCE

1. BELIEVING THEY ARE A VICTIM AND BECOMING DEPENDENT ON OTHERS

At the first level the Architect spirals down to the point that they feel isolated and betrayed and they can't figure out why they have been victimised. Tears, storytelling, and seduction all manifest at this stage. They perceive that they have no future, no friends and no courage. The delusional Architect rejects any sense of personal responsibility. This phase often ushers in heavy drinking and drug-taking 'to get through it all'.

2. GAME-PLAYING AND DIVIDE AND RULE

At the second phase, lack of self-esteem and personal security lead to overt manipulation, seduction and politicking. This will often be justified as 'necessary' to reach an optimally desired outcome that conforms with the social rules from their family or from society in general. This activity offends and traumatises the Architect who is dedicated to being task oriented, and they can't believe what they've done. This can quickly deteriorate into the next step of the downward spiral of disintegration.

3. DECEIVING OTHERS

By the third phase the Architect loses sight of reality and works hard to deflect any feedback to the contrary. Those closest to them become suspected of conspiring against them. This can convince the Architect that individuals have made statements or discussed them in negative or deriding ways. With a grain of truth and 98 per cent fiction the Architect uses their understanding of others to dream up scenarios that will lead to the Architect's failure. This paranoia leads to a complete lack of trust and further entrenches the Architect in creating an 'us and them' and telling the 'us' one thing and the 'them' something else. The Architect uses their knowledge about others to foster their suspicions and to justify avoiding others.

4. COMPLETE INTOLERANCE AND PUNITIVE

The downward spiral continues and the Architect becomes intolerant of all other positions and genuinely self-righteous. The Architect decides they are the only ones doing what should be done and that others need to be punished to teach them a lesson. This is done behind the scenes with the Architect pulling the strings and creating chaos, hurt and confusion among their targets. As the Architect's boundaries break down they take the position that the institution is 'theirs to defend' and that the end justifies the means.

5. COMPETITION AND BULLYING

As the spiral down continues, the Architect will bully and blame everyone. This bullying comes in the form of cutting words, strong emotions, mood highs and lows and a focus on personal attacks. At this stage the Architect develops and tells elaborate stories that blame others for their own lack of confidence and deteriorating relationships. They project their own motives onto everyone else.

6. ARROGANCE AND ISOLATION

If things continue to get worse, the Architect will begin to isolate themselves and only associate with those who can supply them with important or powerful information. The Architect can cut off all contact with the outside world becoming a hermit, reading and refusing to communicate because, frankly, no one is 'worth the effort'. During this phase the Architect studies the laws, rules and fine print that will help them defend themselves if their game playing and deceit ever come to trial. They prefer all their communication to be done in writing. As they spiral down the Architect's desire to hold others accountable is internalised and they begin writing down every phone call, discussion and interaction.

Many African leaders refuse to send their troops on peace-keeping missions abroad because they probably need their armies to intimidate their own populations.

Kofi Annan
Secretary-General of the United Nations

DISASSOCIATION   7. INFLEXIBILITY AND CONTROLLING BEHAVIOUR

As the Architect spirals down so too does their flexibility. Adherence to plans becomes a clear focus and their management style becomes totally closed to any new suggestions. They become abrupt, disconnected and autocratic. During this phase the Architect may become obsessed with computers, tools, weapons or equipment that can help them defend themselves against a vicious world that hates them.

This is the final stage of the Architect's downward spiral.

The Architect's Quest for Creating Wealth

HOW ARCHITECTS BECOME WEALTHY

The Architect is brilliant at strategic systems thinking and inventing. This means that without even having to think about it too hard, they will instantly see why the system isn't working and what can be done about it.

Architects make big money when they use their intellect to improve the way a system works. This system can be as simple as the way to make scones and as complex as the structure of a multinational organisation. In this way systems thinking and prototype development go hand in hand, which is why Architects make such good inventors.

The task for the Architect is to decide which industry they want to work in and develop technical expertise about the key systems that drive the industry. With this insight and technical prowess the Architect will have the ability to diagnose system inefficiencies and make suggestions that can make them and their clients big money.

DEEP UNCONSCIOUS MOTIVATION

The Architect's energy comes from their desire to be recognised by their peers and to be rewarded financially for their contribution. Recognition takes the form of additional responsibilities and job title, increased resources, additional staff or equipment.

In their business affairs the Architect will be fiercely independent, trust no one, and always suspect the worst of people. They have very high personal standards that they rarely meet and their expectations of others are just as high and just as often rarely met.

MONEY MANAGEMENT APPROACH

Broadly speaking, the Architect prefers to spend their money rather than save. They realise this and feel comfortable with their approach. The Architect has little interest in having hands-on control of their investments. Instead, they usually want somebody else to take responsibility for it all.

Investment-wise, they tend to avoid any form of financial planning and, when under stress, often make impulsive decisions rather than spend the time to analyse the opportunities and decide rationally on the best course of action.

Architects are so focused on work that very few of them spend very much time planning for their wealth creation. They often assume that surplus money will come with the increased wage that will accompany their anticipated next promotion.

Architects don't like spending their money on showy possessions or major purchases. Their cars, for example, are selected because they are well-engineered, modest European vehicles that run fuel-efficiently and are functional.

Architects put a financial priority on paying off their house while sustaining life insurance and a solid superannuation plan. They feel comfortable with a share portfolio that is made up of blue chip stocks.

We must use time wisely and forever realise that the time is always ripe to do right.

Nelson Mandela
South African statesman who was released from prison to become the nation's first democratically elected president in 1994

THE ARCHITECT'S MONEY HABITS

The Architect is constantly looking for manufacturing perfection and so is therefore drawn to the very best consumer products. These purchases – including clothes, ornaments, accessories and travel goods – are branded and very expensive with no return on the investment made.

The greatest money-making opportunities are often shot down by the Architects as they see the problems with the concept, the process, the system or the approach. The Architect is often left behind looking at the system's shortfalls when the investment opportunity has come and gone.

Every now and then the Architect will become passionate about helping a friend, a charity or a social justice issue and spend large amounts of money with no return.

The Architect can become so obsessed with finding the loopholes and looking for the problems that their entrepreneurial spirit is lost and they settle for a secure and constant wage rather than making the income they deserve.

Architects are very prone to becoming bitter and twisted as they see those who are far less talented, capable or technically skilled than they are, taking entrepreneurial risks and reaping financial rewards.

Because Architects commit their lives to developing their capabilities, they can invest heavily in projects that will yield poor financial return but will enable them to learn a new skill or develop a new insight. If they are not aware of this they put the poor returns down to the dangerous nature of investment and become even more cautious.

When Architects embark on a new venture, if there is nothing new for them to learn they may refuse to invest their money or effort even if the project looks good and the financial return on the investment is solid.

WHAT ARCHITECTS DO WITH THEIR WEALTH

Because the Architect's unconscious focus is on social justice, wealthy Architects are philanthropic, giving to specific people, situations or projects that they see as needing their support.

They usually prefer to live in the country where they are able to work with nature and animals and systems rather than with people.

They have a fascination with how things work and so will spend money on anything that can bring them additional capabilities or insight into the way the world works.

Wealthy Architects spend most of their time thinking, walking, reading, talking, creating new ideas or inventions and enjoying nature. Wealthy Architects are also well read and well travelled, interested in everything, and have a great sense of humour.

Our prime purpose in this life is to help others. And if you can't help them, at least don't hurt them.

Dalai Lama
Spiritual leader of Tibet

WEALTH CREATION FORMULA FOR ARCHITECTS

Architects need to decide on a financial vision and continually reaffirm it. This is an area of strength for the Architects but more often than not, they are just too focused on other things to take the task seriously. The Architect's biggest fear is to stop working and so they just refuse to think about what will happen when their professional journey comes to an end. The Architect simply has to stop, analyse the situation and create a strategy, and they can dramatically turn around their financial situation.

The Architect must constantly remind themselves of their financial goals. This is important because often the Architect has as many visions and aspirations as there are days in the week. Finance may not be terribly exciting, but it does bring the security they want.

Architects need to build strong alliances with advisers they trust and who have themselves successfully built wealth. An Architect will enjoy talking through their financial alternatives/options with their adviser. They need to encourage themselves to consider innovative investments and not just blue chip options. This can put some of the fun back into the investment game.

Architects will need to persuade rather than coerce themselves into taking the time and effort to develop and stick to an investment plan. Another tactic that works well for Architects is to let themselves be influenced through discussion and case studies. They need to enjoy the process of assessing which adviser has the most logical arguments and can support their case with examples. Architects need to be results-oriented in regards to finance and investment. It is very easy for Architects to want to use investment to develop their capabilities at the expense of investment return. Their investments are there for one reason – return.

UNDERSTANDING ARCHITECTS

Architects best manage themselves by:

- Disciplining themselves to value the loyalty and passion of their team as much as their functional contribution

- Learning to control their sharp tongue – the cutting remarks and the closed-door comments

- Learning to manage their frustration with constant changes to the brief or situation

- Learning to appreciate that while changing systems may make the organisation more efficient in the long term, in the short term it will cause drama, confusion and inefficiency

- Learning to sandwich negative evaluations or feedback between encouraging statements

As team members, Architects make the best contribution when:

- They are able to trouble-shoot systems, organisational structures or processes to enhance efficiency and reduce user frustration

- New models, paradigms or approaches are required

- They can head up a team looking at new prototypes

- The brief is broad, even vague, but the outcome is specific

When managing Architects:

- Clearly structure any interaction with them, exploring why you want to meet, what you want to cover, and the logical meeting structure you have chosen

- Rather than ad hoc feedback, wait until formal reviews or agreed times and then provide the feedback, starting with their role and working back to specific incidents or cases

- Request that they keep you in the loop either in writing or verbally and on an agreed and regular basis

How Architects will act during meetings:

- Will enjoy exploring new models, abstract ideas/philosophy

- Will see instantly where systems are not working and will make practical suggestions as to how they should change

- Can be confrontational and appear aggressive if other team members have not thought through their ideas

I'm always wiser after I've walked away from a discussion. I seem to need reflective time alone for the penny to drop, so it's important for me to try to remember to say, 'I'll get back to you'.

Personality strengths that help the Architect:

- Can integrate the impractical vision with practical structures
- Can understand complex conceptual models
- Can integrate people with systems

One of my most successful projects, as a teacher and Architect, was when I had the vision to benefit 1000 students in one event. I handpicked the staff, trained and encouraged them, and then supported their efforts. It all came together and we shared the great feedback and celebrated at the end.

Personality weaknesses that can stand in the way of the Architect furthering their development:

- Prone to low self-esteem because their visionary ideas are not practical and not valued by themselves

- Find it difficult to understand why people are feeling a particular way

- Can't help it; they are change agents – even when they don't want to be

I enjoy a good conversation, sharing ideas and so keep having small dinner parties. But I'm constantly disappointed by them. Instead of enjoying the cut and thrust of opinions, I usually find myself watching out that everyone is comfortable and no one's feelings are getting trampled on and that everyone's opinions are heard. I don't get a chance to be heard myself. Lately I've joined some groups dedicated to discussion where I don't feel responsible for anyone else's welfare and I'm joining in rather than watching them.

Opportunities for Architects to develop:

- Need to get in touch with the passion of life
- Need to learn how to change vision midway
- Need to see people as 'alive' – not just objects

No sociologist ... should think himself too good, even in his old age, to make tens of thousands of quite trivial computations in his head and perhaps for months at a time. One cannot with impunity try to transfer this task entirely to mechanical assistants if one wishes to figure something, even though the final result is often small indeed.

Max Weber
Sociologist

Threats to Architect's development:

- Can become bored and mechanical if there is no crisis
- Can reach a 'block' when a project's parameters are changed
- Can turn everything and everyone in life into a machine which can then turn around and impersonally run them over

FAMOUS ARCHITECTS

- Princess of Wales, Diana Spencer
- HM Queen Elizabeth I
- Albert Einstein (Scientist)
- Leonardo da Vinci (Artist)
- Hippocrates (Philosopher)
- Joseph Banks (Botanist)
- Karl Marx (Philosopher)
- Max Weber (Sociologist)
- Abraham Lincoln (former US President)
- Kofi Annan (former Secretary-General United Nations)
- Dalai Lama (Spiritual Leader)
- Nelson Mandela (former South African President)

ARCHITECTS AT WORK

Architects thrive on generating new ideas and concepts and are able to picture their vision very clearly. Their strength lies in creating ideas and plans, and they are most productive once a game plan has been established. They have an excellent ability to think issues through. They are very determined and controlled and will want to have a vision to work towards. They will not be openly competitive but will certainly work longer and harder than most to achieve their vision.

Architects can be very disciplined and expect the same from others. They work efficiently and to a plan, systematising everything they can. They are highly tolerant and patient with people as long as they are efficient and want to achieve. They enjoy people who have vision.

Probably my worst quality is that I get very passionate about what I think is right.

Hillary Clinton
Former US Secretary of State

As leaders, they like structure, discipline and organisation. They are easily able to provide their staff with an understanding of the organisation's vision but probably will not see it necessary for routine work. They willingly contribute to making a team work together or getting a project organised. They are extremely supportive of staff, care about them as individuals and take responsibility for making their team feel positive and enthusiastic about their work when they themselves are excited by the vision. They are excellent delegators and have the skill of matching tasks with people. They can easily identify potential in people and can also be strict when required especially if they suspect incompetence or laziness.

Architects are very loyal as long as people fit in with their vision. They are mostly respectful of others. Generally they are able to see people for what they are and will often not enjoy being around highly opinionated people.

They resolve conflict by facing people in the direction of their vision and encouraging them to find a workable solution. They don't like people to be unhappy so they will seek to find solutions to any conflict to ensure everyone is happy. If someone is angry with them they will both feel the impact of the emotion and use logic to justify their position. Seldom will they become angry in response, but when they do they tremble with rage. They will often appear to look blank.

Architects cope well with change as long as it is heading somewhere. An Architect will want everyone to be happy about any changes that are being considered. If under stress, they work through the experience. They will most likely escape into their vision, check everyone is coping and then generate a way to solve the stress. Architects are both analytical and objective. Their internal conflict lies between cold hard logic and wanting people to be happy. They are more zany than spontaneous, and like the bizarre and oddball. They enjoy outrageous and illogical humour. They can easily see a person's weaknesses and may play on them.

They can become depressed or bored if they are unable to express their vision, or if this vision is not valued by friends or work colleagues. They are generally optimistic if they are being shown support. They are mostly balanced, stable individuals, although at times they may be influenced by the company they keep. They may deceive where necessary to achieve their plans or visions.

An Architect has an excellent understanding of the negotiation process and can gauge their opponents' thoughts and personal weaknesses and use them to

HM Elizabeth 1 was born in 1533 to Henry VIII and Anne Boleyn. Although she entertained many marriage proposals and flirted incessantly, she never married or had children. Elizabeth, the last of the Tudors, died at seventy years of age after a very successful forty four year reign.

their advantage. An Architect is most formidable when working long and hard to achieve their vision, organising large teams in crisis situations and creating order from chaos.

My physical environment is very important to me. I am not happy unless the place where I live is pleasant and comfortable. I like it to be harmonious rather than glitzy. I like to have several places for relaxation, eating, work with hobbies, so that I have choices depending on how I feel. And it is a must to have plants somewhere and music.

THE ARCHITECT'S MIRROR IN THE WORKPLACE

At work, the Architect's Mirror – the Judge – is critical, energetic and driven and this explains the Architect's energy and determination. When angry about someone's behaviour, the Architect will criticise the behaviour, the system or the situation in a diplomatic way. When the Master Architect is tired, inebriated or overly stressed, however, the same trigger will see the Judge use the situation to destroy the person by a personal attack on their intentions, capability and intellectual capacity.

At home, the Mirror Judge is argumentative, fickle and frustrated. Partners find young Mirror Judges vindictive, aggressive and insensitive – waiting for the moment that their partner is at their weakest to attack with their judgement of the situation. This judgement invariably includes a pronouncement of someone's stupidity. At home, the Mirror Judge will adopt soapboxes and stand on them at every opportunity.

LEADERSHIP STYLE OF THE ARCHITECT

Each Neuro-Rational Type, due to its combination of Intelligences, has a different leadership style. These leadership styles are a function of the centre of focus of the Neuro-Rational Types, and tend to be expressions of the underlying world view of the personality.

A groundbreaking survey of 3871 executives selected from a database of more than 20,000 executives[2] found distinct leadership styles which consistently appear in

---

2   Survey was originally analysed by Kelner, S., et al. (1996).

organisations. Daniel Goleman (2000) attributes these different leadership styles to different emotional intelligences. Each leadership style has a different impact on the work environment and on organisational performance. The most effective leaders use a variety of styles, choosing the appropriate style, timing and intensity to manage each situation.

The leadership style identified by Goleman's research that is most closely linked to the profile of the Architect is the *Pacesetting* style.

The research suggests that the Pacesetting style has a negative overall impact on corporate climate. The primary focus of the Pacesetting style of leadership is on setting a high standard and doing things better and faster. This has a number of ramifications as a leadership style.

The Pacesetting Style

Daniel Goleman (2000) tells the story of Sam, a competent technician who was made leader of an R&D team in a pharmaceutical company. Following the Pacesetting style, he made himself a model of excellent practice, helping the team when necessary. His team members were competent and the project was completed in record time.

While the Architect leader is confident that everyone in their team is competent, everything is fine.

But Sam was promoted to manager of the whole division and when he felt unsure that his team was competent, he took over and micro-managed the details. He ended up bogged down and ineffective as a leader.

When the Architect's confidence in his team members' competence is broken, they reassess everything the person has done historically, to judge whether the lapse of competence is episodic or more widespread. They may test the person's competence by verbally grilling them, micro-managing them or by demanding reports detailing process and outcomes.

The Architect needs to remember that competence is just one element in a highly functioning team. There are many examples of highly functioning teams that have low personal competence but high organisational capability. This is achieved through effective communication, team synergy, and the application of the many 'soft skills' that make teams tick.

Table 15.2 The Leadership Style of the Architect

Situation	Explanation
1. The leader's modus operandi	Sets high standards for performance
2. The style in a phrase	'Do as I do, now'
3. Underlying emotional intelligence competencies	Conscientiousness, drive to achieve, initiative
4. When the style works best	To get results from a highly motivated and competent team
5. Overall impact on climate	Negative

These are:

- **Performance standard.** The Pacesetting leader sets an extremely high performance standard and exemplifies these standards. There is an obsessiveness about doing things better and faster.

- **Feedback.** Poor performers are quickly highlighted and more is demanded from them. If they do not adjust and improve, this form of leadership seeks to replace them with people who can. No feedback is given on how people are doing unless the Pacesetter jumps in and takes over when they think that people are lagging.

- **Guidelines are rarely clearly articulated.** Others are expected to know what to do. An underlying thought process is, 'If I have to tell you, you're the wrong person for the job.' Thus work becomes about second-guessing the leader, while people also feel that they are not trusted to work in their own way or to take the initiative.

- **Work becomes task focused** and routine as flexibility and responsibility evaporate.

- **Commitment is reduced** because individuals have no sense of how their personal efforts fit into the big picture.

Despite these drawbacks, the Pacesetting style does work well when all the employees are self-motivated, highly competent, and need little direction or coordination. Given a talented team to lead, the Pacesetting approach gets the task accomplished.

Furthermore, it is extremely appropriate during the entrepreneurial phase of a company's life cycle.

SCHOOL OF STRATEGIC THOUGHT

The natural differences between Neuro-Rational Types are not limited to leadership styles alone; they also extend to a natural inclination towards different strategic thought. These differences have been researched by Mintzberg, Ahlstrad and Lampel (1998). For the Architect, the environment is the central actor in the strategy making process. The environment presents itself as a set of general forces, and the individual must respond to these factors or be 'selected out'. This is the environmental school of strategy.

THE GENIUS OF THE ARCHITECT — SEEING CONGRUENCE

The Architect's Genius is about seeing congruence. This Genius lies in their ability to bring the people, the processes and the vision all into line. This congruence is the basis of good organisational development skills. This means checking that the vision is relevant and understood by the team, checking the processes are practical and are able to support team members, and that these practical processes are followed. While practical, Architects have the ability to think conceptually, with abstract ideas or philosophies that are complex and ungrounded. Their Genius is the ability to bring abstract vision to concrete reality.

Buckingham and Clifton (2001, p. 115) explain that rather than a skill that can be learned, this is a 'distinct way of thinking, a special perspective on the world'. This type of thinking follows the following process:

- The strategist sees patterns in an apparently complex situation.

- The patterns prompt the person to think of possible actions.

- They then play out in their head a number of scenarios in turn, each time asking, 'what if…?', considering possible results and potential problems.

- Next, the strategist selects the path which is most likely to lead to success, avoiding conflict, confusion or failure.

- The chosen path becomes their strategy, and they act according to their plan.

Buckingham and Clifton (2001) offer the following examples of people with the signature strength of being strategic:

The first example is a manager who naturally sees well into the future and automatically prepares for it, as opposed to his colleagues, who see only the current situation, which controls and limits their focus of action.

The second example is a television producer who loved logic problems as a child and still loves to watch repercussions playing out in her work situations. She believes this ability helps her in interviews to notice every word and even small details such as tone of voice of the other person. Then she plays out the clues she has, and so frames her questions, based on the hunches she has imagined.

The third example is an HR executive who uses his ability to anticipate the actions of the unions to devise contingency plans that give him an immediate response to their every action.

Body Composition

The Architect body composition is quite feminine and soft. Weight is distributed towards the lower half of their body, and the lower part of the abdomen, hips and legs are larger when compared to other parts of their body. Their upper torso is relatively thin. Shoulders are narrow and roll forward, while the chest cavity is thin. Architects are not very toned or muscular, even when thin. Their muscle feel is soft and delicate (Diversi, 2006).

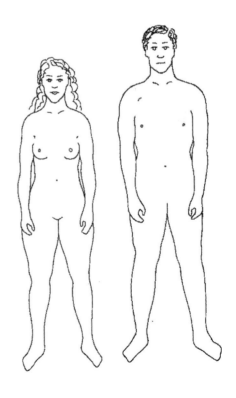

FITNESS PREFERENCES

The Architect prefers not to partake in physical or incidental exercise. Exercise takes away from time that they need to be caregiving, looking after their house or working. When they do exercise, the Architect initially only does so at low intensity and enjoys exercise such as aqua aerobics, yoga, Pilates or gentle sailing. When they are forced to increase the level of intensity by a personal trainer, tough partner or friend, they thoroughly enjoy the experience but won't keep it up without that support (Diversi, 2006).

EATING PREFERENCES

The Architect enjoys preparing food for others. While doing this, they often pick at the unprepared meal and can also snack throughout the day. Therefore, it appears that the Architect does not eat very much, because meals are small. They like to reward themselves with food for jobs well done (Diversi, 2006).

DIETING PREFERENCES

The Architect seems to always be on a diet, particularly women Architects. They enjoy the idea of fad diets where the fad diet's promises align with their goals. They also like to have support through a dietitian, personal trainer or other health practitioner and will have regular contact with this person. They often do not see that they are not following the suggestions provided and make changes very slowly when compared to other types (Diversi, 2006).

Next, let us talk about the human being as a social animal. Even if we do not like other people, we have to live together. Natural law is such that even bees and other animals have to live together in cooperation. I am attracted to bees because I like honey - it is really delicious. Their product is something that we cannot produce, very beautiful, isn't it? I exploit them too much, I think. Even these insects have certain responsibilities, they work together very nicely. They have no constitution, they have no law, no police, nothing, but they work together effectively. This is because of nature. Similarly, each part of a flower is not arranged by humans but by nature. The force of nature is something remarkable. We human beings, we have constitutions, we have law, we have a police force, we have religion, we have many things. But in actual practice, I think that we are behind those small insects.

14th Dalai Lama

Applying Architect Insights as an Effective Communicator

When Negotiating with Architects

The effective communicator is able to align their narrative and the point they are wanting to make with the archetype of the audience. That is, they use the same language, approach and behaviour with the archetype of the person they are presenting to.

When negotiating with Architects, the way you position information is very important. Architects are attracted to messages centred on two main themes, which are most convincing to them: *'Show me that you are willing to do what it takes to make the vision happen' and 'Show me this is practical.'*

'Show me that you are willing to do what it takes to make the vision happen'

There are two types who access their C2 and P1 – the Architect and the Navigator. This segment makes up 15 per cent of the general population. When negotiating with this group:

- Minimise any activity that is not contributing to the future objective or vision of the organisation

- Be aware that they have high expectations about what can be achieved and is often disappointed with the time required to reach milestones

- Be aware that they tend to fix a particular objective, milestone or vision in their mind and not update it – even when the situation or environment changes

- Provide a clear plan to achieve the clear vision, and demonstrate that there is order and organisation, together with systems, processes and guidelines

- Be aware that they are idealistic by nature and want to see the organisation striving to achieve as close to perfection as possible

- Demonstrate that the organisation is responding to future trends, new markets, potential crises and staff trends

- Present market positioning and strategic analysis

- Present with models, abstract charts, ideas, themes and concepts

'Show me this is practical'

There are two groups who access their P1 and I2 by nature – the Architect and the Commander. This segment makes up approximately 12 per cent of the general population. When negotiating with this group:

- As a leader, demonstrate decisive leadership with an open mind and high energy

- As an aside, explain, predict or control nature, cycles and reality

- As a leader, anticipate trends and proactively manage the situation

- Demonstrate competence and constant improvement, and that the leadership has a focus on this

- Be aware that they are highly critical of themselves and everyone else

- Do not be inconsistent which they read as deceit

- Deliver a strong argument rather than just rely on the credibility of the person making the statement – the rationale for the argument must be logically pieced together step by step

- Make their interaction with the organisation a learning experience for them

- Provide constant reassurance that their leaders do have the competence to achieve the objectives; this counteracts their own constant self-doubt that failure is just around the corner

- Present your point without typos, grammatical errors or logistical oversights because under stress they become perfectionists

- Communicate in compact, short, logical statements – they respond badly to 'waffle'

- Provide the rationale for every initiative to satiate their search for the 'why' of the situation

- Provide communication with graphs, models, icons and pictures

The Architect at a Glance

Strengths

- Has discernment
- Is strategic
- Brings out competence in others

Code of Conduct

- Ensures all team members 'walk the talk'
- Aligns the activity of the group with the vision of the organisation
- Ensures systems are practical and understood by the people using them
- Considers the wider organisational impact of key decisions or changes made in their area
- Puts forward suggestions to improve work practices and work flows
- Encourages the team to take a strategic approach and focus on undertaking right action

First Step of Integration

- Focuses on taking personal responsibility and having confidence in themselves

First Step of Disintegration

- Descends into being a victim which leads to co-dependence

Exemplars

- Dalai Lama
- Lady Diana Spencer
- Albert Einstein

Chapter 16

The Navigator
An In-Depth Look at the Navigator

You cannot depend on anybody. There is no guide, no teacher, and no authority. There is only you – your relationship with others and with the world – there is nothing else.

Krishnamurti

What we've got to thank Navigators for:

Risk management

Large-scale engineering projects

Computer programming

Beautiful photography

Institutions

Political and environmental stability

Clear lines of responsibility

The completion of thankless and dangerous tasks

THE NAVIGATOR PROFILE

If you have built castles in the air, your work need not be lost; that is where they should be. Now put the foundations under them.

Henry David Thoreau
American author, poet, philosopher

OVERVIEW

The Navigator's mind is structured and visionary. These opposites create a person with a clear vision and the discipline and structure to achieve it. Regardless of their training or level of professional development, the Navigator is super-dependable and likes to be a respected contributor to the community and a pillar of society.

Very emotionally detached, Navigators are inflexible when discussing plans, directions, approaches and logistics. If they are not given warning, however, they can cope with flexibility and ambiguity, and perform brilliantly 'on the hop'. This seems contradictory, but is achieved because they flip to their Mirror.

Navigators tend to get one vision in mind and be totally inflexible with regard to either the vision or its implementation. This can sometimes mean that the Navigator is committed and focused on implementing visions that are no longer relevant.

Navigators enjoy the very best quality in things and particularly enjoy collecting anything that will appreciate in value.

Navigators are very focused when there is a clear vision, executing enormous mind over matter, suppressing unwanted emotions and disciplining themselves and the people around them. They will follow the systems to the letter of the law. Any shortcutting or variance from the approved process will be quickly stopped and the perpetrator reprimanded. The Navigator's way is the right way and they will want an audit trail to demonstrate compliance. This character trait makes them good inspectors.

While Navigators see themselves as dependable and respectable, if they have no vision and no plan to follow, they freewheel and become obsessed with experiencing life. This means experiencing every possible form of physical sensation including the tasting of every kind of food and wine, flying, boating, fishing, canoeing, partying and holidaying. All this activity subsides when the Navigators are once again inspired with a new vision and plan and set about implementing it.

I don't think there's any reason on Earth why people should have access to automatic and semi-automatic weapons unless they're in the military or in the police.

John Howard
Former Australian Prime Minister

FOCUS OF ATTENTION

The Navigator is brilliant at steadfastly working in a stable and controlled way towards achieving a goal. They focus on creating stability in their own lives and the lives of those for whom they are responsible while managing the risks associated with any given endeavour. At their best, Navigators are faithful, protective, responsible, effective planners, principled, explorative and honourable.

KEY CHARACTER DRIVERS

There are three key Intelligences that drive the Navigator:

C2 – Vision

P1 – Logic

I1 – Data

LEVELS OF CONSCIOUSNESS AS DEFINED BY US PSYCHOLOGIST CLARE GRAVES AND SPIRAL DYNAMICS' AUTHORS COWAN & BECK

The table on the following page outlines the broad character development of the Navigator over a lifetime from Level One – the lowest level of consciousness – through to essence at Level Nine.

THE SUBTYPES

Each of the eight types is made up of three Intelligences. The Navigator has C2 Vision, P1 Logic and I1 Data. As we adapt to our life circumstances we tend to favour one of the three. This subtly changes the personality and gives rise to subtypes. All Navigators will be able to relate to all three of the subtypes at some time in their life.

Table 16.1   The Navigator Levels of Development

Level of Consciousness and the noble quality embraced at this level	Common Navigator characteristics at this level of consciousness
Level 1 (Beige) A state of nature and instincts.	Closed down and off from human nobility. One step at a time. No sense of future or past. Frozen.
Level 2 (Purple) Mysterious and frightening. *(Noble quality to be embraced at this level: Faithfulness)*	Believes God is a punitive and aggressive God with paternal protection in exchange for absolute obedience. Because the Navigator can never be absolutely obedient there is a constant fear of God's revenge and anger.
Level 3 (Red) Raw displays of power – dictators, tough love, predators. *(Noble quality to be embraced at this level: Protectiveness)*	Control is maintained through strong self-discipline and the discipline of others. Brute strength is important. Fierce argument about what is right is accompanied by outbursts of anger if others don't do what they are supposed to do. The anger is justified because others have behaved so badly. Love is expressed through commitment and protection.
Level 4 (Blue) Everything is controlled by God and is purposeful. Obey God. Do it right. Feel guilt. *(Noble quality to be embraced at this level: Responsibility)*	Some force predestines life, and God, karma or natural justice punishes bad behaviour. Focuses on integrity, saying what you mean, doing what you say, not playing political or emotional games and being personally disciplined and ensuring others are too. Personal stamina, strength, courage and straight-forwardness are held high as a role model.
Level 5 (Orange) The world is a game and I want to win. *(Noble quality to be embraced at this level: Role Excellence)*	This is where the Navigator's Mirror first expresses itself. While the Navigator is talking about integrity the Chancellor Mirror may be acting in a highly political way – spending time with the right people, making the right career moves and playing the system for all it's worth. This is a period of intense internal conflict for the Navigator as the Master and Chancellor Mirror fight it out internally. They discover their gift and how to use it for personal gain.
Level 6 (Green) We need to join together and grow personally through community. *(Noble quality to be embraced at this level: Principled)*	Finally the Mirror is integrated into the personality and the insight of the Chancellor is used to nurture and support others rather than for personal gain. Both the strong male energy of the Navigator and the female energy of the Chancellor Mirror can be observed by the Navigator and managed. They learn to use their gift for the community.
Level 7 (Yellow) We need to explore ways of being responsibly free. *(Noble quality to be embraced at this level: Conquering)*	The Navigator becomes interested in systems theory and in how systems develop and require maintenance. Their focus is on creating systems that can best prepare the world for what is ahead and creating stability and clarity at all levels within the spiral.
Level 8 (Turquoise) The world is composed of delicately balanced interlocking forces, shaped by attractor fields of intention and nobility. Uses natural flows. Actively grows consciousness. The Non-dual Leader manifests at this level.	The world is seen as a series of cycles and life is seen as a quest. The individual understands the spiral of life and the streams of intra-level progression and addresses the current problems of existence that arise in their own journeys so that the spiral can keep developing.
Level 9 (Coral)	TOWARDS ENLIGHTENMENT

THE VISIONARY NAVIGATOR

The Visionary Navigator is future centred, often with visions that are not logically connected to their current line of thinking. Their creativity allows them to plan long term and imagine the future. It's the irrational leap that makes it possible to discover brand new processes or ways to solve problems. Because their vision is uncontrollable, it will conflict with the structure and order of their logic. The Visionary Navigator may appear confusing to those around them because at work they will be structured and conservative and at play they will be vigorous and spontaneous.

> *Managing risk is critical because if you can be certain you've covered off the risks and integrated them squarely in your plan, you can put your heart and soul into the project with confidence that you won't be sideswiped from a blind spot down the track.*

THE CONTROLLING NAVIGATOR

The Controlling Navigator will want to see projects through from beginning to end, will have a healthy sense of humour, and be balanced, analytical and even-handed. They will be self-disciplined and stable. They will want loose ends tied up. Their personal self-control will suppress their vision unless they are relaxed, or until they are tired or under the influence of alcohol. Their structured mind will also control their natural mood swings and keep them stable and emotionally balanced.

THE WISE NAVIGATOR

For the Wise Navigator, the researching of information is far more important than following the process or coming up with ideas of their own. They would prefer to wait and obtain all the facts before making a decision. For the Wise Navigators, all the ends do not have to be tied up. They will always want to know the facts supporting opinions. They enjoy reading and going to libraries, researching and learning about everything.

ARCHETYPES RELATED TO THE NAVIGATOR

When people discuss archetypes, many of the characters they use will fall into the same category as the Navigator, much the same way that there may be fifty-seven species of fern but regardless of the species, it still belongs to the fern family.

By way of example, some of these are:

- The Saviour
- The Messiah
- The Attila
- The Avenging Angel
- The Mad Scientist
- The Samurai
- The Serial Killer
- The Spoiler
- The Patriarch
- The Progenitor
- The Parent
- The Adonis
- The Emperor
- The Leader
- The Ruler
- The Chief

CHILDREN'S STORIES/CHARACTERS

- The Little Engine That Could
- Bill Steam Shovel (from Mr Squiggle)

THE MIRROR

While the Master Navigator is structured, logical, detail oriented and inflexible, the Navigator's Mirror Master – the Chancellor – is lateral, passionate, intuitive and infinitely flexible. This means that while the Navigator appears to be rigid and unmoving on most issues because they argue in an unyielding way, their final behaviour often speaks of spontaneity and varies according to the opportunity at hand.

The Mirror Chancellor is a relatively quiet Mirror and often finds it hard to make itself heard over the volume of the Master Navigator. This means that the Navigator usually misses the insight offered by the Mirror.

At home, the Mirror gives softness to the Master Navigator and motivates spontaneous romance, a fantastic sense of humour, an interest in family and a desire to emotionally engage family and friends in events and good times.

The young Mirror Chancellor is flirtatious, game playing, ruthless, deceitful and ambitious. As the Mirror matures, however, we see this behaviour develop into an acute understanding of politics and an ability to see and act on opportunities.

When the Mirror is fully integrated into the personality, it balances the Navigator's formidable strength, clarity, vision and process with humour, flexibility, an understanding of how to engage people in strategic action and a non-judgemental acceptance and warmth for all people.

When the vision is clear, necessary and big enough to be challenging, with a clear deadline and set of outcomes, reasons why it works, and reasons why it's worth it, I get a great sense of determination for conquering the impossible.

CHARACTER FORMATION

The formation of personality has three major influences:

1. Firstly, the physiological genetic makeup of the individual creates a predisposition towards accessing particular energies and not accessing others.

2. Secondly, the culture of the environment in which the child grew up, sanctioned some energies over others and so encouraged the child to focus on some energies and suppress others.

3. And finally, the individual's psychological and physiological response to trauma or pain that usually occurs during childhood alters the way they relate to the six core energies. When we experience emotional pain or trauma we can 'turn off' the emotion by turning off the energy. One theory of personality development suggests that if in time we turn off three of the energies we derive our energy from the remaining three. These three in turn combine to form type.

Regardless of what caused us to focus on just three of the thinking functions rather than all six, as human beings we can take three thinking function energies that are available to all humans and combine them to create a higher form of consciousness. We are, if you like, human transformers of thinking into consciousness. This higher level of consciousness takes the form of an Neuro-Rational Type – in this case the Neuro-Rational Type of the Navigator.

THE QUEST FOR INTEGRATION: AWARENESS (I), CREATIVITY (C) AND POWER (P)

Re-opening the heart (I2)

The journey towards integration for the Navigator begins with the opening of the heart. The most difficult part of the integration journey for the Navigator is the first step – to accept and love themselves not for the role they play, but instead for who they are. This self-love and self-acceptance means accepting the many different human parts of themselves, or characters – even the ones that are selfish, childlike or demanding. This inner family is made up of many different characters that first of all need to be identified and then integrated with an open heart.

Developing earth-bound creativity (C1)

Navigators are visionary, but often not in a practical, hands-on way. This is the second stage of healing for the Navigator – to get in touch with their body and the practical creativity they have within them. This can involve painting, drawing, cooking, dancing – in fact, any kind of self-expression or exploration that's fun.

Developing P2

Navigators are good at planning and shouldering responsibility. However, they need to learn how to focus their energy on doing the things that are important to them personally rather than constantly sacrificing themselves for the sake of the role. Time management principles are an excellent place to start. Covey's 'urgent/important matrix', for example, provides practical and effective ways to prioritise personal activity. Anthony Robbins' 'moving towards and moving away from' framework is also excellent at creating clarity for Navigators. Goal management, setting objectives and reviewing daily achievement are also valuable ways to strengthen the role that would normally be played by the third Intelligence.

Developing the P2 is particularly hard work for the Navigator because as it strengthens so too does the awareness that the Navigator is often being taken for granted by those using them as a crutch. If the Navigator starts stepping away from these people, it will mean that they are not fulfilling their responsibilities in their central role as father/mother, husband/wife, employer/employee, etc. This is an important internal conflict for the Navigator to resolve if they are to move from being controlled externally through the roles they play to being driven internally by their own principles, priorities and life plans.

Healing in Action

SPIRALLING UP FOR THE NAVIGATOR — PERSONAL TRANSFORMATION AND THE PATH TO LIFE[1]

Spiralling up and the path to life for the Navigator through personal transformation begins when they are willing to step out and do what they know is right and honourable rather than just playing the role they have been employed or engaged to fill. This is challenging for the Navigator because the role requires them to play, their natural focus of attention is to play it well, regardless of the task.

The Navigator's greatest fear is to have their role removed from them because this would imply a lack of performance, commitment and personal discipline, all of which the Navigator prides themselves on. When the Navigator can make this stand they discover, much to their surprise and relief, that there is much more to them than simply the role they play.

In practice, the quest for integration follows the following eight steps:

AWARENESS

1. DISCERNMENT

With a stronger sense of identity outside their role, the Navigator can begin the task of looking at their life and determining what roles are not congruent with their true self. This requires the noble quality of discernment to ensure that they can reveal the misalignment between their true self and their current life. This means the Navigator may have to say goodbye to relationships that are role-based rather than soul-based, jobs that are not central to their interests, and commitments that have been made many years ago that are no longer appropriate or relevant.

2. COURAGE

With a renewed sense of self, the Navigator must now step out with courage to stand independently and explore life. The noble quality of courage enables the Navigator to face the internal or external opposition that is involved in this last phase and to still move forward in their life. This is where Navigators travel, explore new cities, start a new job or relationship, begin a new business and break ties with those who are not aligned with their values. To move forward they must step forward with courage and never look back.

---

1   Based on a Navigator in the Blue meme.

3. BUILDING BRIDGES WITHIN

During this phase the Navigator discovers the many parts of themselves that have developed as they have played the myriad roles they have taken on. For integration to continue, however, discovery is not enough. The Navigator must discover and integrate these different aspects of self into a single integrated personality before the process can continue. This involves accessing the noble quality of diplomacy to find the common ground between the different aspects of personality within the Navigator. This consolidation provides the Navigator with renewed energy, passion, confidence and zeal.

CLARITY

4. CREATING AN EMPOWERING ENVIRONMENT

Working with team members to achieve their goals the Navigator now focuses on creating a safe environment so that every team member can be respected for their unique contribution. This requires the noble quality of inspiration to link each team member, their personal contributions to the goal and their personal inspiration. During this phase the Navigator is obsessed with ensuring that everyone in the team knows their gift and is able to use it.

ACTION

5. INTEGRITY

During this phase, the Navigator steps out and identifies their BHAG – that is, their big, hairy, and audacious goal. This is very hard for the Navigator who wants to be supported by an organisation and fulfil a clear role with clearly articulated responsibilities. This step in the journey requires the Navigator to ensure they are on the right crusade – that is, a crusade that is worthy of their life work – and they move towards it with the noble quality of integrity.

6. DRIVE

With the risks in hand and a loyal and focused team, the Navigator is ready to engage the noble quality of drive in order to focus themselves and their team on breaking the glass ceiling and powering through. This is a time of boundless energy, optimism, success, recognition and fun. The serious nature of the Navigator is broken by laughter, a quick mind and a love of stories, parties and celebration.

7. LEARNING

Finally the Navigator focuses on securing timely and appropriate information, or personal or professional learning. It takes the noble quality of objectivity for the Navigator to make an informed assessment of what knowledge they need to learn. During this time Navigators buy books, attend courses, update databases, tidy up the financial systems, conduct competitor analysis, review pricing or conduct benchmarking. The majority of the book learning and understanding undertaken by the Navigator during the transformation cycle takes place during this final phase.

ASSESSMENT

8. ASSESSING THE NEW QUESTIONS OF EXISTENCE

The final step is now taken into a brand new world – one with entirely new questions of existence. Since this integration process occurs in the Blue meme, the Navigator will have integrated this aspect of consciousness. Now they will be faced with an entirely new set of questions of existence in the Orange meme based around the need to succeed and be recognised as successful. The Assessment occurs as the Navigator takes stock of their current situation, of the lessons they have learned about life in general and their own abilities in particular and then begins to apply their Genius of creating certainty to produce role excellence.

For all the types, however, there will be times when their development is arrested or even reversed. It's hard to believe that these charismatic and loved Navigators could feel and behave in the following ways. Navigators refer to these times as their 'dark night of the soul'.

Spiralling Down for the Navigator - the Path to Death

Creating divide and rule using fear

The spiral downward is triggered by any event, thought, association or deed interpreted through the perspective of the Lower Self. It is this interpretation that many Christians would refer to as a separation from the divine part of ourselves and as 'sin'.

The spiral down for the Navigator is triggered by not effectively playing the role they have been engaged to play. This fills them with shame and personal disgust.

As Navigators spiral down so too does their flexibility. Adherence to plans becomes a clear focus and their management style becomes totally closed to any new suggestions. They become abrupt, disconnected and autocratic.

> *If I think you're off the mark, overlooking key aspects, or I perceive you to be attacking me, then I'll politely hear you out, and at decision time the answer's 'No' without explanation because I'm pessimistic that it will be useful anyhow. Internally I feel like I'm very flexible. But if I can't be bothered with new thought that hasn't closed off a number of issues that I don't state then I'm sure that comes across clearly as inflexible.*

AVOIDANCE

1. ARROGANCE, ISOLATION AND DELUSION

If things continue to get worse, the Navigator will begin to isolate themselves and only associate with those who can supply them with important or powerful information. Navigators can cut off all contact with the outside world becoming hermits, reading and refusing to communicate because, frankly, no one is 'worth the effort'. During this phase Navigators study the laws, rules and fine print that will help them defend themselves if their game playing and deceit ever comes to trial. During this phase they prefer all their communication to be done in writing. Amazingly, during this phase Navigators believe everything is fine and on track.

2. COMPETITION AND BULLYING

As the spiral down continues, Navigators will bully and blame everyone else rather than take responsibility for their actions. This bullying comes in the form of cutting words, strong emotions, mood highs and lows and a focus on personal attacks. At this stage the Navigator develops and tells elaborate stories that reinforce the idea that others are not doing the 'right thing'. The 'right thing' is the introjected rules the Navigator learned as a child, the rules from society or cultural stereotypes.

3. COMPLETE INTOLERANCE AND PUNITIVE

BEHAVIOUR

The downward spiral continues with the Navigator becoming intolerant of all other positions and becoming genuinely self-righteous. The Navigator decides they are the only ones doing what should be done and that others need to be punished to teach them a lesson. At this stage they are masters of deflection to avoid any meaningful feedback.

REJECTION

4. PERSONAL DELUSION AND DECEIVING OTHERS

As Navigators spiral down even further, they lose sight of reality and disappear into a world of supposition and deceit. Those closest to them become the most suspicious and all kinds of conspiracy theories start to emerge in the Navigator's mind. This delusion can convince the Navigator that individuals have made statements or discussed them in negative or deriding ways. During this phase the Navigator's boundaries break down and they merge with the people they are protecting.

5. DIVIDE AND RULE

As the Navigator loses touch with reality they begin actively setting individuals and teams against each other by using the trust others have in them in a devious way. Trusted allies are pitted against others, hopes are dashed and bridges of understanding burnt as the Navigator uses lies to divide and rule. All the negative behaviour of the Navigator is projected onto others.

INTERNALISING

6. BELIEVING THEY ARE A VICTIM AND BECOMING DEPENDENT ON OTHERS' ACTION

By now the Navigator will have spiralled down to the point that they feel isolated and betrayed and they can't figure out why they have been victimised. Tears, storytelling, and seduction all manifest at this stage. They perceive that they have no future, no friends and no courage. This phase often ushers in heavy drinking and drug-taking 'to get through it all' as the Navigator begins to punish themselves.

DISASSOCIATION

7. CONFUSION AND PROCRASTINATION

Isolated, angry and unwilling to take responsibility for their own behaviour or the situation that it created, Navigators now look for the inconsistencies in the behaviour of others and in the systems they are following. This is their first line of defence against anyone who says they are to blame. During this time the Navigator's professional performance subsides as the procrastination reaches new highs. The Navigator sees all this play out in front of them as if it is a horror movie with them as the main character.

This is the final stage of the Navigator's downward spiral.

The Navigator's Quest for Creating Wealth

HOW NAVIGATORS BECOME WEALTHY

The Navigators are brilliant at steadfastly working in a stable and controlled way towards achieving a goal. Early in their careers, they may, in their search for excitement and experience, try a radical approach and this can be so rewarding that it will set them up for life.

Navigators make big money when they get the right vision and the right formula and provide the strength and conviction for their team to follow it to its logical end. Many of the other types stop short of achieving their visions because the going gets tough and the vision is discarded, whereas the Navigator never gives up hope and completes the task.

DEEP UNCONSCIOUS MOTIVATION

The Navigator's energy comes from the desire to learn about people and their motivation and interests, and to be able to relax and be spontaneous. If their role allows them to do this they will feel valued and secure.

In their business affairs Navigators will be structured, legalistic and detailed in the negotiation and discussion yet paradoxically flexible, quick-witted and trusting if crisis hits and action is required.

MONEY MANAGEMENT APPROACH

Navigators like to have hands-on control of any investment they make. The more control they have the more comfortable they feel. They feel particularly comfortable with commercial real estate with long-term leases and set rent reviews.

Navigators can also feel comfortable with stocks and shares, options and commodities if they have a trusted financial adviser. In choosing such an adviser, Navigators are interested in the credibility of the firm and the person and their family. Often Navigators will use the same stockbroking firm as their parents used, or one that an old school friend or someone recommended. Once selected, this adviser is trusted implicitly.

THE NAVIGATOR'S MONEY HABITS

The Navigators are systematic and detailed about all business negotiations until it comes to members of the family or friends in need. At this point the Navigators will open their wallets and can be taken advantage of and lose significant money.

The greatest opportunities are usually simply not even considered unless they are in line with the one vision being chased and the plan being implemented.

> The concept of me freewheeling seems abominable to me especially considering I'm always ready to do the impossible, protect and cover off the gaps. But if there are no gaps, my role is unclear. If somebody else is already dealing with an issue, and for me to get involved risks duplicating or competing with the solution, I generally butt out, respecting their space. Alas I can see how that might be seen as freewheeling.

Every now and then Navigators complete their vision and go into a vacuum before the next vision starts. This can be very expensive as the Navigators relax and become dedicated to experiencing everything they have missed while completing their last project. The cost of trips, games, tools, books and computer programs all adds up as the Navigator chases constant excitement.

Navigators can become so obsessed with one vision that the external environment can change and their vision is no longer relevant. This can be financially disastrous if consumers no longer want the product or if the main road no longer passes by the property on which the restaurant is to be built.

Navigators are very prone to becoming myopic and refusing to even consider another way of completing a task even if the current method is inefficient and costing more than it should.

When Navigators consider a new venture, detail about the venture is critical to them. In particular, they will want to know clearly what the venture is about, with written plans outlining responsibilities, the specific details of the finance, where the project will be located, the timeline and costings (which have been verified by an independent professional), why each party is to be involved and what is expected of the Navigator. Without this level of detail the project management will be considered hopeless and the project avoided at any cost.

WHAT NAVIGATORS DO WITH THEIR WEALTH

Because the Navigator's unconscious focus is on connecting with the people they love and creating an environment where everyone can feel safe and secure, Navigators will spend money on setting up family trusts, investing in family businesses, going banker for family members and funding children through multiple university degrees.

They prefer to live in neat, orderly and plain homes of classic style rather than houses that are opulent or fashionable or impractical. They will buy cars that are durable and reliable rather than comfortable or flashy.

Navigators love throwing a family party, particularly weddings, anniversaries and birthday parties. They have a particular way of ensuring that these are not over the top, but do reflect the conservative and classic style they embody. Navigators are also partial to initiating and maintaining get-togethers where the group performs a ritual process. These can help bind communities together, particularly when times are tough.

They have a fascination with tradition, the community, their family and its history. They enjoy visiting, reading and discovering what has happened in the past all over again.

Wealthy Navigators spend most of their time either in the pursuit of creating their next vision or experiencing life to the maximum. They particularly enjoy hunting, fishing, horse riding, motor biking, hot air ballooning and weaponry.

Wealthy Navigators are pillars of the community whose strength and single-mindedness keep everyone and everything together, and they can be relied on for their commitment, integrity, straightforwardness, and genuine family and community focus.

Your most unhappy customers are your greatest source of learning.

Bill Gates
Microsoft Founder

Nothing at last is sacred but the integrity of your own mind.

Ralph Waldo Emerson
US writer and leading exponent of transcendentalism

WEALTH CREATION FORMULA FOR NAVIGATORS

Navigators tend to get it very right or very wrong and not much in between. The key to reducing these extremes is for them to appoint a financial adviser and develop a balanced portfolio that builds at a constant rate regardless of the success or failure of the current project.

Once there is a plan in place it is important for the Navigator to protect this in a family trust or a separate entity that is protected from the various ventures undertaken by the Navigator.

Navigators need to be careful not to rely upon reputation and tradition alone to guide their appointment of their financial adviser. They may even have to consider having different advisers for different kinds of investment rather than relying on one adviser to look after everything.

While Navigators are fastidious with so many parts of their lives, they tend to allocate too little time to issues around their long-term wealth creation, opting instead to abdicate responsibility to their financial adviser and putting all their energy into their current project. This pattern needs to stop and Navigators instead need to give the same energy and passion to developing a wealth vision and plan to achieve it as they do to the rest of the activities in their lives.

Navigators also tend to help out friends, family and even community members when they go through tough times. While this is very community-minded, at retirement some Navigators are left with a number of significant informal debts that have not been appropriately documented because at the time the money was used for a crisis. The Navigator needs to tidy these up and keep a track of them rather than becoming furious and then doing nothing about it.

Between projects Navigators spend a fortune entertaining themselves. Navigators don't realise this and put it down to letting off some steam. Instead, once they see this pattern they can look for more inexpensive ways to keep themselves excited between projects.

Navigators need to be willing to be more flexible at the beginning of projects when they are still conceptual. Many times a Navigator has missed out on a major investment opportunity because the visionary who was seeking investment was too vague. Walt Disney, Colonel Sanders and even Ray Crock (McDonalds) would not have secured money from a Navigator. This is the Navigator's Achilles' heel and it can be resolved if the Navigators simply think each and every investment through for themselves and don't let themselves get 'sucked in' to being the hero and saving others without thought.

UNDERSTANDING NAVIGATORS

Navigators best manage themselves by:

- Remembering to be flexible and open to change
- Disciplining themselves to listen to those with poor reasoning and thinking skills
- Valuing all team members and the roles they play
- Giving positive feedback – face-to-face with staff
- Controlling their angry outbursts

As team members, Navigators make the best contribution when:

- They can manage and plan a project from concept through to implementation
- Difficulties can be confronted head on and dealt with rationally
- Resources and timeframes are defined and information is complete
- Consistency is required

When managing Navigators:

- Constantly encourage them to be flexible and not locked into one vision
- Encourage them to encourage their team members – help them give positive verbal feedback
- Remind them of the valuable role each team member plays
- Ensure all your key resources to them are written down in a structured format

I certainly want loose ends cleared up. In a meeting that's great, finalising the decision with a clear owner of who will action what deliverables when. In the social setting I'm really having to nip myself to just let it go.

How Navigators will act during meetings:

- Navigators don't like ambiguity or deception so often play the role of 'keeping the bastards honest'

We, the parliaments of the nation, are ultimately responsible, not those who gave effect to our laws. And the problem lay with the laws themselves. As has been said of settler societies elsewhere, we are the bearers of many blessings from our ancestors; therefore we must also be the bearer of their burdens as well. Therefore, for our nation, the course of action is clear: that is, to deal now with what has become one of the darkest chapters in Australia's history.

In doing so, we are doing more than contending with the facts, the evidence and the often rancourous public debate. In doing so, we are also wrestling with our own soul. This is not, as some would argue, a black-armband view of history; it is just the truth: the cold, confronting, uncomfortable truth - facing it, dealing with it, moving on from it.

Until we fully confront the truth, there will always be a shadow hanging over us and our future as a fully united and fully reconciled people. It is time to reconcile. It is time to recognise the injustices of the past. It is time to say sorry. It is time to move forward together.

Kevin Rudd
Former Australian Prime Minister

- Once the vision is established, Navigators will want specifics agreed upon – who, what, when, where and how
- They will be polite but not sensitive to the foibles of other team members – they will play blunt politics
- Will want the purpose of the meeting clearly defined with a clear agenda and timeframe
- Will easily lose interest and sidetrack the discussion if not managed

Having the agenda for a meeting, document or whatever is critical to having the interaction useful. Decisions and information are not meaningful in and of themselves. They're only meaningful in terms of how it fits into the tasks and directions. So having a meeting without an agenda is like a ship in a stormy sea landing on a beach, delivering nothing of any value to the right place except by fluke.

Personality strengths that help the Navigator to further their development:

- Can balance the future vision with immediate practicalities
- Very structured, analytical and task-oriented
- Excellent at maintaining complete systems

Personality weaknesses that can stand in the way of the Navigator's development:

- Can get very stressed juggling between vision and implementation
- Can often misread people and intentions
- Can be inflexible if midpoint change is required

Opportunities for Navigators to develop:

- Need to learn how to be able to change track midpoint
- Need to learn how to reinject passion and meaning into projects
- Need to learn how to read people more accurately

Threats to Navigator's development:

- Can 'close down' and refuse to budge off the agreed plan, even when change is required
- Can get bored and uninterested in their own life and try to create interest in risky activity
- Can misinterpret situations so badly that they can become ostracised or marginalised

FAMOUS NAVIGATORS

- John Howard (former Australian Prime Minister)
- Bill Gates (Microsoft Founder)
- George Bush (US President)
- Michael Jeffery (former Australian Governor General)
- Sir Winston Churchill
- Sir Edmund Hilary (Explorer)
- Billy Joel (Singer)
- HRH Prince Charles
- Madeline Albright (former US Secretary of State)

We are again reminded that the freedom to be here in the first place with our families and friends and our comrades in arms is such a special thing.

Michael Jeffery
Former Australian Governor General

NAVIGATORS AT WORK

A Navigator is analytical, logical and has creative vision. However, their talent for creative vision is usually suppressed by a strong sense of logic. They tend to have two definite minds one very practical, and one focused on the creative world. Their greatest challenge is understanding these two opposite sides of their thinking. They balance a desire to be illogical and zany with being logical and conservative.

They are highly disciplined individuals, with a willingness to be consistent. If they are consistently required to suppress their creativity over a long period of time, they may become depressed or bored for no apparent reason.

Navigators tend to exaggerate only when storytelling or sharing their vision. A Navigator will be most motivated when they have a clear plan to write or follow. They have an excellent ability to process and can see a project from beginning to end. At work, their energy and enthusiasm will increase when they have a clear understanding of the overall organisation's direction.

They will seek to understand their responsibilities within an organisation and knowing these, will take them very seriously. If the parameters are vague, they will take these responsibilities less seriously.

They are more confident when they know a system and how it works, and their loyalty to structure and accepted procedures is foremost.

They are keen to achieve but never at the expense of others. They will achieve legitimate power through providing logical and factual solutions and strong leadership.

A Navigator does not play games, preferring everyone to work together to achieve the vision. A Navigator is highly disciplined and expects the same level of discipline from others. They are tolerant of others but become frustrated by an unstructured and undisciplined approach.

When confronted with aggression, they will tend to look at statements issued rather than at the individuals involved, but will match the intensity of the aggression. A Navigator will sometimes cope with stress by escaping into their own world. They enjoy escaping from reality and a voyage into their world of creativity relieves tension.

They do not cope well with changes in course, unless they are driving the change themselves. It is important that at all times they are able to visualise the end result.

As leaders, Navigators are very structured and logical. They will seek to share an organisation's vision with staff and ensure they can achieve it. They will delegate only when job responsibilities are clear and understood. A Navigator is determined and will work methodically to achieve a specific goal, often becoming impatient with others who do not have a similar discipline.

Navigators have an exceptional memory for facts and are always willing to offer analytical and factual interpretations to problems. A Navigator is

The whole imposing edifice of modern medicine, for all its breathtaking successes, is, like the celebrated Tower of Pisa, slightly off balance. It is frightening how dependent on drugs we are all becoming and how easy it is for doctors to prescribe them as the universal panacea for our ills.

HRH Prince Charles

calm, sincere and stable with periods of zaniness to contradict their normal behaviour. They will mostly appear set in their ways and conservative; however, their creativity will often generate periods of spontaneous rebelliousness and sometimes perceived offensive behaviour.

A Navigator is at their most formidable when creating long-term strategies or when implementing operational procedures.

THE NAVIGATOR'S MIRROR IN THE WORKPLACE

At work, the Chancellor Mirror will express itself in humour, a willingness to change track when new opportunities present themselves and an almost involuntary involvement in the politics of the organisation.

Perhaps the best contribution of the Mirror at work, for Navigators in a leadership position, is the Mirror's insistence that their employees are genuinely engaged in understanding, supporting and implementing the strategic direction.

The Mirror Chancellor is also responsible for the willingness of the Navigator to move jobs and take career advancement opportunities, even if it means moving to another company, city, profession or country.

THE LEADERSHIP STYLE OF THE NAVIGATOR

Each Neuro-Rational Type, due to its combination of thinking functions, has a different leadership style. These leadership styles are a function of the centre of focus of the Neuro-Rational Types, and tend to be expressions of the underlying world view of each personality.

A groundbreaking survey of 3871 executives selected from a database of more than 20,000 executives[2] found distinct leadership styles which consistently appear in organisations. Daniel Goleman (2000) attributes these different leadership styles to different emotional intelligences. Each leadership style has a different impact on the work environment and on organisational performance. The most

---

2   Survey was originally analysed by Kelner et al. (1996).

Table 16.2 The Leadership Style of the Navigator

Situation	Explanation
1. The leader's modus operandi	Mobilises people towards a vision
2. The style in a phrase	'Come with me'
3. Underlying emotional intelligence competencies	Self-confidence, empathy, change catalyst
4. When the style works best	When changes require a new vision, or when a clear direction is needed
5. Overall impact on climate	Most strongly positive

effective leaders use a variety of styles, choosing the appropriate style, timing and intensity to manage each situation.

The leadership style identified by Goleman's research that is most closely linked to the profile of the Navigator is the *Authoritative* style.

The author's experience supports the insightful research reported by Goleman. The Authoritative style is the most effective leadership style as it drives up every aspect of corporate climate. The primary focus of the Authoritative style of leadership is vision, either for a team or the wider organisational collective. This has a number of beneficial ramifications as a leadership style as follows:

- **Role focus.** The Navigator is focused on the role and the team.

- **Clarity.** The visionary (strong C2 element) nature of the Authoritative leader generates motivation because people come to see clearly how their work fits into the larger vision of the organisation.

- **Inspire commitment.** Their visionary focus allows them to frame the individual tasks in the context of the overall vision (I1 articulated vision). Therefore, people can see how their work matters and why it is important. It brings significance to the employee's daily activities and so increases their sense of commitment.

- **Strong standards.** With a strong sense of vision, leadership can define standards that underpin the overall objectives. This assists all decision-making and creates confidence in those decisions.

The Authoritative Style

Daniel Goleman (2000) relates the tale of Tom, director of marketing in a floundering chain of pizza restaurants.

In the Authoritative style of a Navigator, he assumed the leadership role that had been missing in the company.

His clarity and specificity of thinking showed him that the real objective was to supply their customers' need for convenient-to-get pizza. This should be the bottom line. Managers should be encouraged to use their creativity to make their pizzas convenient. This became part of their mission statement.

The finances of the company were turned around by the clear vision of the Authoritative leader.

Managers used their imagination to find new convenient places to sell their pizza, and they began to guarantee faster delivery times.

The leader specified the desired outcome and the team rose to the challenge with the freedom to respond however they wished. Such is the strength of the Authoritative style of leadership.

- **Feedback.** In providing feedback, the single objective is whether the performance has furthered the vision (assisted by I1). Therefore, determinates of positive or negative feedback are fixed and not subject to whimsy.

- **Standards.** These are clear and stated up front, as are the rewards for performance.

- **Flexibility.** It is encouraged, as the desired result is stated and the specific methodology is not articulated. These leaders encourage others to take calculated risks, and give freedom to innovate and experiment. The Navigator leader creates stability, which allows the team members to move out of their lower selves and use their noble qualities.

The Authoritative style works well in almost any business environment. But when a company is 'adrift' and a new course needs to be charted it is most effective.

This style is not effective when a leader is working with a team of experts or peers who are more experienced. In these circumstances they may see the Authoritative leader as pompous or out-of-touch. Furthermore, if the leadership style becomes overbearing, then it can undermine effective teamwork.

SCHOOL OF STRATEGIC THOUGHT

The natural differences are not limited to leadership styles alone; they also extend to a natural inclination towards different strategic thought. These differences have been researched by Mintzberg, Ahlstrad and Lampel (1998). For the Navigator, strategy formation is a cognitive process that takes place in the mind of the strategist. Strategies emerge as the strategist filters the maps, concepts and schemes shaping their thinking.

THE GENIUS OF THE NAVIGATOR — PLANNING

The Navigator's Genius lies in their ability to 'see' what is ahead and to prepare for it now. This means creating the right systems, anticipating the problems, researching all relevant data and ensuring blind panic is turned into beneficial and useful planning. They also understand the importance of every team member playing a central yet different role. Because the Navigator likes their world to go to plan, they plan everything very thoroughly. In order to maintain a sense of stability and control, they set up processes and structures for all aspects of their life. When they plan, they break large projects into a series of short-term tasks, with dates, time lines, and specific and detailed items. Others may be surprised by the time and effort the Navigator gives to their organisation, routine and detailed planning, but this is how they can be totally reliable and disciplined, creating a sense of certainty about making the plan come together (Buckingham et al., 2001).

Buckingham and Clifton (2001, p. 96) tell the story of Les, a hospitality manager, who effected this signature strength in his life. Already aware that he was disciplined, he attended a training course that taught him how to use a Palm Pilot each day to plan all aspects of his life. This made him reliable, predictable and able to keep his word to family and employees alike.

Another example of this discipline in planning cited by Buckingham and Clifton (2001, p. 96) is Deidre, an office manager. Because she likes to manage her time, each day she writes a list of her tasks. And she is very disciplined in seeing that they get done. For example, she may have up to ninety items on one day's list of which she will do 95 per cent. She manages this because she politely but firmly ensures that no one wastes her time.

Body Composition

The Navigator is a thin shape. The Navigator has strong, masculine features and has the potential to increase muscular bulk and appear toned. This is true for both women and men.

The Navigator is never overweight growing up, or in early adulthood, but can increase their weight, particularly in the lower abdominal region, in their adulthood.

Male Navigators often desire to increase their muscle mass as a young male. Female Navigators have a tendency to dramatically increase their weight at the beginning of menopause; the weight tends to be distributed evenly (Diversi, 2006).

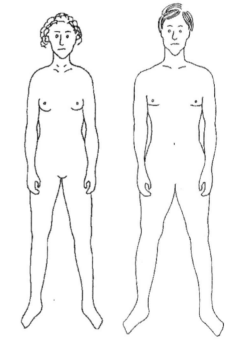

EXERCISE PREFERENCES

Navigators excel in individual sport. They enjoy the discipline of training and the structure of individual competition. For fitness, they like adventure sports, hiking, 'male' sports and running (Diversi, 2006).

EATING PREFERENCES

The Navigator sees food as something they have to eat to live. They often skip meals, eat quick convenience foods or snack foods in place of real meals. They live life in a very structured way and don't mind eating the same food every day.

Navigators eat what they believe is healthy, often low fat, low sugar; however, they tend not to eat enough vegetables or fruit (Diversi, 2006).

DIETING PREFERENCES

A Navigator will follow a prescribed diet to the letter if they believe it is the responsible thing to do. They become frustrated when they do everything asked of them, or everything they think is correct, and still suffer from health problems (Diversi, 2006).

Applying Navigator Insights as an Effective Communicator

When Negotiating with Navigators

The effective communicator is able to align their narrative and the point they are wanting to make with the archetype of the audience. That is, they use the same language, approach and behaviour with the archetype of the person they are presenting to.

When negotiating with Navigators, the way you position information is very important. Navigators are attracted to messages centred on two main themes which are most convincing to them: *'Show me that you are willing to do what it takes to make the vision happen'* and *'Show me this idea is accurate with concrete data to support your position.'*

'Show me that you are willing to do what it takes to make the vision happen'

There are two types who access their C2 and P1 – the Navigator and the Architect. This segment makes up 15 per cent of the general population. When negotiating with this group:

- Minimise any activity that is not contributing to the future objective or vision of the organisation

- Be aware that they have high expectations about what can be achieved and is often disappointed with the time required to reach milestones

- Be aware that they tend to fix a particular objective, milestone or vision in their mind and not update it – even when the situation or environment changes

- Provide a clear plan to achieve the clear vision, and demonstrate that there is order and organisation, together with systems, processes and guidelines

- Be aware that they are idealistic by nature and want to see the organisation striving to achieve as close to perfection as possible

- Demonstrate that the organisation is responding to future trends, new markets, potential crises and staff trends

- Present market positioning and strategic analysis

- Present with models, abstract charts, ideas, themes and concepts

'Show me this idea is accurate with concrete data to support your position'

There are two types who access their P1 and I1 – the Navigator and the Treasurer. This segment makes up 39 per cent of the general population. When negotiating with this group:

- Prefers not to practise and instead prefers to get started
- Likes to see a quick, logical and sensible approach to solving problems and crises
- Enjoys reading about and using tools, IT, equipment and machinery
- Will not read between the lines and instead needs all implicit information to be articulated before it is considered
- Likes information to be complete and comprehensive before a final decision is needed
- Prefers to read information rather than talk through issues
- Likes communication with in-depth analysis, charts, tables, graphs, concrete examples, photographs and details

The Navigator at a Glance

Strengths

- Planning
- Responsibility
- Brings a sense of security to a team

Code of Conduct

- Stands up for what they know is right
- Displays supportive/protective behaviour for their colleagues
- Creates a sense of security and stability within the team
- Effectively plans work with clear milestones and systems of reporting
- Identifies and manages the risks associated with completing individual or team objectives
- Works at giving other team members confidence

First Step of Integration

- Focuses on 'walking the talk'

First Step of Disintegration

- Descends into arrogance and isolation

Exemplars

- John Howard
- HRH Prince Charles
- George W Bush

Chapter 17

The Treasurer
An In-Depth Look at the Treasurer

When all is said and done,
there has been more said than done.

What we've got to thank Treasurers for:

Objectivity

Order and organisation

Rational argument

Curiosity

Specialist technical knowledge

Written records

Audit trails

The Treasurer Profile

OVERVIEW

The Treasurer's mind is highly intellectual, analytical and detailed, with an excellent memory for facts. This personality has an outstanding ability to analyse situations and has a calm and detached approach to life. Treasurers are not judgemental, are slow to anger and are naturally intrigued by money, scorecards and balance sheets. They have an inbuilt fascination with the game of life.

Regardless of their training or level of professional development, the Treasurer likes order and organisation. Their mind naturally separates their life into different compartments. The way they interact with a colleague at work and at home therefore can be quite different, with work issues kept at work and leisure issues kept for leisure time.

Very self-sufficient emotionally, Treasurers love excitement, activity and crisis. The Treasurer's core competency lies in the ability to break any situation into bite-sized pieces that can be addressed. A complex project, for example, may be broken into strengths to gain leverage from and weaknesses to be addressed, or it may be broken into short-, medium- and long-term issues. Even in the midst of a terrible crisis, the situation is still just a situation that needs to be tidied up.

FOCUS OF ATTENTION

Treasurers are brilliant at sorting out mess: minimising tax, systemising contracts, structural analysis and categorising detailed information. At their best Treasurers are self-reliant, controlled and detached; they master systems, and are holistic, expert and wise.

KEY CHARACTER DRIVERS

There are three key Intelligences that drive the Treasurer:

C1 – Spontaneity

P1 – Logic

I1 – Data

LEVELS OF CONSCIOUSNESS AS DEFINED BY US PSYCHOLOGIST CLARE GRAVES AND SPIRAL DYNAMICS' AUTHORS COWAN AND BECK

The table on the following page outlines the broad character development of the Treasurer over a lifetime from Level One – the lowest level of consciousness – through to essence at Level Nine.

Table 17.1 The Treasurer Levels of Development

Level of Consciousness and the noble quality embraced at this level	Common Treasurer characteristics at this level of consciousness
Level 1 (Beige) A state of nature and instincts.	Closed down and off from human nobility. One step at a time. No sense of future or past. Frozen.
Level 2 (Purple) Mysterious and frightening. *(Noble quality to be embraced at this level: Self-Reliance)*	Reads magic books, focuses on hidden or secret information and becomes an expert on important esoteric knowledge. Learns specific poems, spells or liturgy.
Level 3 (Red) Raw displays of power – dictators, tough love, predators. *(Noble quality to be embraced at this level: Discipline)*	Control is maintained through systems and the creation of constant chaos (the first hints of the Bard Mirror) that the Treasurer has to tidy up. These messes usually come in the way of high-risk gambles that often don't pay off. When these gambles fail the Treasurer's cool logic and absolute control is needed to get through. Love is expressed through commitment and protection.
Level 4 (Blue) Everything is controlled by God and is purposeful. Obey God. Do it right. Feel guilt. *(Noble quality to be embraced at this level: Objectivity)*	The Treasurer learns to manage their need to control and focuses instead on creating order from genuine chaos. This is a time to focus on being tidy, green and neat, on appropriate codes of conduct, honour, morality and a place for everything and everything in its place. The Treasurer epitomises a clean and tidy law-abiding citizen.
Level 5 (Orange) The world is a game and I want to win. *(Noble quality to be embraced at this level: Specialist)*	The caution is put to one side and instead the Treasurer focuses on mastering a highly specialised field of knowledge. This phase focuses on personal discipline, goals, technology, symbols of success and material rewards. The game is won through superior knowledge and technical Wizardry. They discover their gift and how to use it for personal gain.
Level 6 (Green) We need to join together and grow personally through community. *(Noble quality to be embraced at this level: Systems Mastery)*	This is where the Treasurer integrates the Mirror Bard and focuses on friends and family and on creating an environment that enables each individual to give their best and live without confusion, fear or uncertainty. The Mirror Bard focuses on symbols, rituals, healing, fun and free expression. They learn to use their gift for the community.
Level 7 (Yellow) We need to explore ways of being responsibly free. *(Noble quality to be embraced at this level: Expertise)*	The Treasurer becomes the educated optimist, seeing the cycles and being able to anticipate when and where changes will take place. The Treasurer's skill is to prepare others in the community for what is ahead in a clear, organised and constructive way.
Level 8 (Turquoise) The world is composed of delicately balanced interlocking forces, shaped by attractor fields of intention and nobility. Uses natural flows. Actively grows consciousness. The *Non-dual* Leader manifests at this level.	The world is seen as a series of cycles and life is seen as a quest. The individual understands the spiral of life and the streams of intra-level progression and addresses the current problems of existence that arise in their own journeys so that the spiral can keep developing.
Level 9 (Coral)	TOWARDS ENLIGHTENMENT

THE SUBTYPES

Each of the eight types is made up of three Intelligences. The Treasurer has C1 Spontaneity, P1 Logic and I1 Data. As we adapt to our life circumstances we tend to favour one of the three. This subtly changes the personality and gives rise to subtypes. All Treasurers will be able to relate to all three of the subtypes at some time in their life.

THE SPONTANEOUS TREASURER

Although the Spontaneous Treasurer is able to follow through with projects, their spontaneity will always be pulling them away from structures and procedures. They will like new projects, new people, new thoughts and new ideas. They will probably be good with their hands, hop from topic to topic in conversation and have a witty, albeit dry, sense of humour. This spontaneity will sometimes conflict with their logic.

THE CONTROLLING TREASURER

The Controlling Treasurer will want to see projects through from beginning to end and will have a healthy sense of humour, be balanced, analytical and even-handed. They will be self-disciplined and stable. They will want loose ends tied up. Their logic will suppress their spontaneity unless they are relaxed.

THE WISE TREASURER

For this subtype, the researching of information is far more important than either following the plan or coming up with ideas of their own. They would prefer to wait and obtain all the facts before making a decision. For the Wise Treasurer, all the ends do not have to be tied up. They will always want to know the facts supporting opinions. They enjoy reading and libraries, researching and learning about everything.

If I stopped making records or performing, I'd probably still be famous for a while being me. But I'd rather have something to show for myself.

Kylie Minogue
Australian pop star

ARCHETYPES RELATED TO THE TREASURER

When people discuss archetypes, many of the characters they use will fall into the same category as the Treasurer, much the same way that there may be fifty-seven species of fern but regardless of the species, it still belongs to the fern family. By way of example, some of these are:

- The Spy
- The Double Agent
- The Sleuth
- Sherlock Holmes

- The Warrior
- The Crime Fighter
- The Gambler
- The Private

Investigator
- The Midas
- The Miser

CHILDREN'S STORIES/CHARACTERS

- Brains (*The Thunderbirds*)
- Robin (*Batman and Robin*)
- Bert (*Ernie and Bert*)

THE MIRROR

While the Treasurer is structured, analytical, detached and focused on the detail, the Treasurer's Mirror Master – the Bard – is idealistic, optimistic, passionate and committed to bringing the best out in people and creating a better future. As a Mirror, the Bard is usually encouraging, motivating and future-centred. However, this Mirror will ask the big hard questions of the Treasurer, such as 'What value am I really adding? Is this environment at home or at work supporting the individuals I care about? Is this hard work really amounting to anything? Am I supporting my family? Am I genuine, ethical and fair? And what have I tangibly created recently?'

At home, the Mirror will take a deep and real interest in family members and will spend hours of time worrying about the issues they are facing and walking beside them as these issues are resolved.

I don't believe in pessimism. If something doesn't come up the way you want, forge ahead. If you think it's going to rain, it will.

Clint Eastwood
Actor

Young Bard Mirrors are quiet and often get marginalised by the control-focused Master Treasurer. When this happens, Treasurers have no sense of the important emotional role those close to them play in their lives and they treat them as objects to move and manage, rather than people to value, learn from and admire.

As the Bard Mirror matures, it becomes more assertive and insists the Treasurer be more generous with time, money and affection.

The Mirror Bard will insist that all resources earned and hoarded by the Treasurer go towards helping family and friends.

When the Bard Mirror is integrated into the Treasurer profile, it gives the structured and detached Treasurer a caring and nurturing side, personal passion and the desire and ability to create a better future.

CHARACTER FORMATION

The formation of personality has three major influences:

1. Firstly, the physiological genetic makeup of the individual creates a predisposition towards accessing particular energies and not accessing others.

2. Secondly, the culture of the environment in which the child grows up, sanctions some energies over others and so encourages the child to focus on some energies and suppress others.

3. And finally, the individual's psychological and physiological response to trauma or pain that usually occurs during childhood alters the way they relate to the six core energies. When we experience emotional pain or trauma we can 'turn off' the emotion by 'turning off' the energy. One theory of personality development suggests that if in time we turn off three of the energies we derive our energy from the remaining three. These three in turn combine to form type.

Regardless of what caused us to focus on just three of the Intelligences rather

---

Never speculate, never endorse beyond your surplus cash fund, make the firm's interest yours ... concentrate, put all your eggs in one basket and watch that basket; expenditure always within revenue; lastly, be not impatient, for, as Emerson says, 'no one can cheat you out of ultimate success but yourself'.

Andrew Carnegie
American Industrialist

---

than all six, as human beings we can take three Intelligences that are available to all humans and combine them to create a higher form of consciousness. We are, if you like, human transformers of thinking into consciousness. This higher level of consciousness takes the form of a Neuro-Rational Type – in this case the Neuro-Rational Type of the Treasurer.

THE QUEST FOR INTEGRATION: AWARENESS (I), CREATIVITY (C) AND POWER (P)

Re-opening the heart (I2)

The journey towards integration for the Treasurer begins with the opening of the heart. The most difficult part of this journey for the Treasurer is the first step. This requires them to accept themselves not for what they know but for who they are. This self-love and self-acceptance means accepting the many different parts of themselves – even the ones that are selfish, childlike or stupid. This inner family is made up of many different characters that first of all need to be identified and then integrated with an open heart.

Deficient Sixth Intelligence (C2)

The Treasurer also has a deficient C2. Until this is remedied the Treasurer is spiritually cynical, adopts rigid belief systems, and becomes apathetic and obsessed with the issues of the other Intelligences, namely, materialism, greed and the control of others.

Developing P2

Treasurers are good with solving the day-to-day problems that confront them. However, they need to learn how to focus their energy on doing the things that are important to them rather than just urgent. Time management principles are an excellent place to start, using Covey's 'urgent/important' matrix. Anthony Robbins' 'moving towards and moving away from' framework is also excellent at creating clarity for Treasurers. Goal management, setting objectives and reviewing daily achievement are also valuable ways to strengthen the role that would normally be played by the third Intelligence. Developing P2 is particularly hard work for the Wise Treasurer because as it strengthens, their focus changes from learning to achieving, which contradicts much that the Treasurer holds as important. This is an important internal conflict for the Treasurer to resolve if they are to regain their self-confidence.

Healing in Action

SPIRALLING UP FOR THE TREASURER — PERSONAL TRANSFORMATION AND THE PATH TO LIFE[1]

Personal transformation and the path to life for the Treasurer starts with securing timely and appropriate information, or personal or professional learning. During this time Treasurers buy books, attend courses, update databases, tidy up the financial systems, conduct competitor analysis, review pricing or conduct benchmarking. The majority of the book learning and understanding during the transformation cycle takes place during this first phase.

In practice, the quest for integration takes the following eight steps:

AWARENESS

1. COURAGE

With a head full of information the Treasurer must draw on their personal courage to courageously break down the walls that have kept them safe. The noble quality of courage enables the Treasurer to face whatever internal or external opposition has kept them from taking the action they need to take. This may mean taking the job they have been avoiding, getting married, having a family, admitting mistakes or being honest with family and friends. The work to be done at this phase is to break down the barriers and face their greatest fears so that they can move forward.

2. DISCERNMENT

Having taken action to proactively face their fears the Treasurer must now assess which parts of their life must be cut to achieve congruence and alignment. This involves the noble quality of discernment in order to find which elements

---

1   Based on a Treasurer in the Blue meme.

of their life are out of alignment. This may mean ending relationships, community or family roles, or taking on roles that have been promised but not delivered. The hurly burly of life often means that who we say and think we are and who we really are, are two different things. During this phase of alignment the Treasurer brings these two worlds into perfect alignment.

3. VISION

The Treasurer now focuses on unconditional love and generosity through the noble quality of inspiration. It is through this noble quality that the Treasurer discovers their sense of personal meaning and starts to heal the different elements of themselves. This healing releases energy that is inspirational, channelled into creating a safe and 'other worldly' environment. In this space the Treasurer can be 'who they are' with complete freedom and they can begin to live their vision.

CLARITY

4. BUILDING BRIDGES OF UNDERSTANDING

The internal healing that has taken place during the first phase of transformation enables the Treasurer to begin building bridges with people with humility, honesty and diplomacy. During this phase the Treasurer earns the reputation of being open and honest as they use the noble quality of diplomacy to find their common ground with the people around them. They spend their time building bridges between people from all walks of life. In this phase Treasurers look to create an opportunity for everyone they know to be able to grow and develop and to use their gift.

ACTION

5. DRIVE

Once they have learned how to connect with others, the Treasurer engages the noble quality of drive to focus on asking themselves the hard questions, getting clarity on what action they need to take personally and then getting on with it. This is a time of boundless energy, optimism, success, recognition and fun. The shy and detached nature of the Treasurer is broken by laughter, a quick mind and a love of stories, parties and celebration.

6. INTEGRITY

For the Treasurers, their journey towards integration continues when they are willing to live with the noble quality of integrity and this involves them stepping into the real world. This is very hard for the Treasurer who would prefer to watch others crusade for what is right and just than fight for it with their own wisdom and energy. They'd rather stay detached. To move forward the Treasurer must be willing to put their detachment to one side and focus on being a person of integrity.

7. RESPONSIBLY FULFILLING THEIR ROLE

With their crusade in place, Treasurers look to their long-term plans and the key milestones ahead. In the short term this clarity focuses on how they can give back to their community. For the Treasurer, living responsibly requires that they effectively play their role in the family, at work and in their community. Amongst other things, this requires a careful assessment and management of risks and an assessment of whether there is a correct balance between responsibility and authority in their various roles in life. As the Treasurer does this, workmates, friends and family have their sense of certainty and confidence about what the Treasurer is doing reinforced and they see the genuineness and committed nature of the Treasurer in fulfilling their role.

ASSESSMENT

8. ASSESSING THE NEW QUESTIONS OF EXISTENCE

The final step is now taken into a brand new world – one with entirely new questions of existence. Since this integration process occurs in the Blue meme, the Treasurer will have integrated this aspect of consciousness. Now they will be faced with an entirely new set of questions of existence; in the Orange meme they will be based around the need to succeed and be recognised as successful. The Assessment occurs as the Treasurer takes stock of their current situation, of the lessons they have learned about life in general, and their own abilities in particular and then begins to apply their Genius of order to develop Mastery of Systems.

For all the types, however, there will be times when their development is arrested or even reversed. It's hard to believe that these wise Treasurers can feel and behave in the following ways. Treasurers refer to these times as their 'dark night of the soul'.

SPIRALLING DOWN FOR THE TREASURER – THE PATH TO DEATH

The spiral downward is triggered by any event, thought, association or deed interpreted through the perspective of the Lower Self. It is this interpretation that many Christians would refer to as a separation from the divine part of ourselves and as 'sin'.

For the Treasurer, the spiral downward is triggered if they give inaccurate information when requested for it. They usually provide this inaccurate information because they have either simply made a mistake or can't fully understand the subject matter. This obvious uninformed response triggers the Treasurer, because they see themselves as intelligent and accurate and can't forgive themselves for getting it so wrong. When the Treasurer gets something wrong or doesn't immediately know the needed information, their central narrative and world view is challenged and their immediate self-criticism and desire to disappear from the scene and further scrutiny can quickly deteriorate into the downward spiral of disintegration that has seven steps.

AVOIDANCE

1. INFLEXIBILITY AND CONTROLLING BEHAVIOUR

As Treasurers spiral down, so too does their flexibility. Adherence to plans becomes a clear focus and their management style becomes totally closed to any new suggestions. They become abrupt, disconnected and autocratic. During this phase the Treasurer's personal hygiene may subside and they become fascinated by tools, weapons or equipment that can help them defend themselves against a vicious world that hates them. At this first step of spiral down the Treasurer refuses to believe anything is wrong.

2. COMPLETE INTOLERANCE AND PUNITIVE

BEHAVIOUR

The downward spiral continues with the Treasurer

becoming intolerant of all other positions and becoming self-righteous. The Treasurer decides they are the only one doing what should be done and that others need to be punished to teach them a lesson. During this phase the Treasurer argues that if everyone just did the 'right thing' everything would be fine. However, in this case, the right thing is based on introjected rules or social norms.

3. COMPETITION AND BULLYING

If the spiral down continues, the Treasurer will begin to bully and blame others. This bullying comes in the form of cutting words, strong emotions, mood swings and a focus on personal attacks. At this stage the Treasurer develops and tells elaborate stories that blame others for their own lack of integrity and uses deflection to avoid dealing with their own avoidance.

REJECTION

4. MANIPULATIVE PERSUASION

The next phase of disintegration sees the Treasurer feeling insecure about their important relationships. The Treasurer's desire to get these relationships back on track leads to an intensive effort to connect which in time leads to co-dependence. To get the reassurance they believe they need, they use manipulation and persuasion to reassure people that they were not bullying others and that their objectivity and good character are still intact. This phase can see the Treasurer lie, exaggerate, change alliances and shamelessly compete for attention. No self-deception is too big. No political game is too ambitious. Supervisors, parents, wives, children and lifelong associates can all be dragged into this if they are necessary to ensure the Treasurer's good name is maintained and their key relationships are kept strong.

5. PERSONAL DELUSION

The Treasurer is now in unfamiliar territory and rather than remake their perception map, they become delusional and see only what they want to see. The Treasurer creates an idealised image of themselves in their mind and they happily refuse to accept anything that may violate this idea. Even though others can see they have lost touch with reality, the Treasurer's self-identity of being detached and objective remains and they can make very poor major life decisions during this phase of disintegration. At this stage the Treasurer often falls into 'magic think' where they over-estimate their mind's power to influence outcomes. This often leads them to making rash, high-risk decisions about gambling, the stock market, relationships or the use of their assets. All these weaknesses are projected onto family, friends or colleagues.

6. CONFUSION AND PROCRASTINATION

The Treasurer now looks for the inconsistencies in the behaviour of others and in the systems they are following. This is their first line of defence against anyone who says they are to blame for the poor decisions they have made. During this time the Treasurer's professional performance subsides even further as the procrastination increases. Rather than engaging in constructive behaviour, the Treasurer now gives themselves the little financial rewards they believe they deserve.

DISASSOCIATION

7. DISASSOCIATION

Finally, the Treasurer decides that they have been the real victim or loser in this situation and that the only way forward is good old-fashioned hedonistic fun: drugs, gambling, alcohol. At this stage the disassociation is complete.

The Treasurer's Quest for Creating Wealth

HOW TREASURERS BECOME WEALTHY

Treasurers are brilliant at sorting out mess, minimising tax, systemising contracts, structural analysis and categorising detailed information.

Treasurers make big money when they work with a team on big projects and use their superior analytical skills to increase margins by a small amount. In this way, what other types would see as almost unperceivable savings or margin increases, when multiplied across the entire project or by the total number of purchases, produce massive profits.

Treasurers are not interested in using money for prestige or to impress. Instead, they are most interested in spending less than they earn and saving as much as possible on day-to-day expenses to achieve their financial objectives.

DEEP UNCONSCIOUS MOTIVATION

A Treasurer's energy comes from bringing meaning to the lives of loved ones and creating an empowering environment that is safe and compassionate. Deep down they want to see themselves as the financial source for the team with whom they work and the family and friends they support. Treasurers use money as a way of developing and managing relationships. In their business affairs the Treasurer will consolidate their interests into one major entity with multiple income streams and a group of investors. Their energy comes from achieving corporate results that provide the investors with a good return on their investment.

MONEY MANAGEMENT APPROACH

Treasurers are the most financially aware group and intuitively understand how the stock market works. They are comfortable with share trading stocks of all kinds, not only blue chips. Usually, they like to have at least one-fifth of their portfolio in shares because they are relatively liquid and can be converted into cash if the need arises.

Of all the groups, the Treasurers buy and sell their shares the most, actively punting on companies or market trends. They enjoy the research and the processes involved in the transaction as well as the returns. Of all the personalities, they also have read the most about investment and share trading systems and like to use either paper or computer systems to help them decide the most likely trading strategies to use.

Once they know the system intimately, their decisions almost become intuitive, requiring far less analysis.

Treasurers like residential and commercial real estate because it provides them

---

We have looked at all the other bank programs, and there weren't many specifics there either. The difference is we have accounted for this above the line. That puts pressure on us.

David Murray,
Former CEO Commonwealth Bank of Australia
when speaking about failing to provide adequate
information about activities

Bond: 'Do you expect me to talk?'
Blofeld: 'No Mr Bond, I expect you to die.'

with lots of hands-on activity. Choosing the tenant, collecting the rent, improving the property, and the processes behind buying and selling property all appeal to the Treasurer.

Treasurers are the most advanced in their ability to manage their investments tax-effectively.

Treasurers are the highest users of life insurance and believe that it is important to safeguard their family financially in case of ill-health or death.

Treasurers often enjoy collecting stamps, coins, artwork etc., as a hobby that doubles as a good investment.

THE TREASURER'S MONEY HABITS

The Treasurer can become so detached and obsessed with minimising spending that excellent opportunities are overlooked because some small expenditure is required that the Treasurer just doesn't feel comfortable with.

The greatest opportunities are not always exciting and sometimes Treasurers just can't get themselves interested in the investment – even if it all stacks up.

Every now and then Treasurers can go on a wild spending spree and either buy completely unnecessary 'gadgets' or splurge on satisfying their lust for excitement and the chance to 'win it big'. This includes expenditure on gambling, racing, travel, unnecessary tools, new computers, new programs, dubious stock market investments, and large but exciting property investments.

Treasurers can become so obsessed with getting every financial detail right that they miss out on the big deals. For example, they may miss out on making $100,000 profit because their energy was totally tied up in balancing the books, sorting out the tax or trying to save $100.

Treasurers are very prone to making impulse decisions to take on big, complex and interesting projects without making the required analysis beforehand. Instead, for the really big projects, Treasurers tend to bypass their analytical skills and go with their gut reaction and put more store in the people involved than verifying the facts at hand. This often leads to disastrous results.

WEALTH CREATION FORMULA FOR TREASURERS

Because Treasurers segment their life into different compartments they don't see how failure in one area can have an impact on other areas. This blind spot can mean that they don't anticipate how failure in one venture will negatively impact on the other ventures. This lack of integration is excellent for surviving hard times but can cost Treasurers a lot of money.

When Treasurers embark on a new venture, if there is no urgency for results, they can sometimes become obsessed with deep analysis with no action. This is sometimes referred to as analysis paralysis and can lead to investigation that is far more costly than necessary – which never leads anywhere. Instead, it is costly analysis for the sake of it.

WHAT TREASURERS DO WITH THEIR WEALTH

Because the Treasurer's unconscious focus is on providing money for their community of dependants, once wealthy, Treasurers are philanthropic. They give their time and money to relevant charity groups, and support their family by going banker to their needs or purchasing things for them.

They prefer to live in modest, secure housing that can keep others out if necessary, which requires a minimum of maintenance and that is close to friends and family. They have a fascination with technology and will want the latest gadgets, computers, cars or tools of their trade.

Wealthy Treasurers spend most of their time responding to the needs of their family and friends and trying out their latest 'toy'. They are stable, caring, fun-loving, excitement-seeking people with a fascination with life and an interest in almost everything.

UNDERSTANDING TREASURERS

Treasurers best manage themselves by:

- Disciplining themselves to keep an eye on the bigger picture – where are we headed and why are we doing this?

- Remembering that people are not cogs. They need to understand why they are doing things and they need to be valued for their contribution; not being fired is not good enough

- Remembering that tasks, budgets and people are interconnected; if action is taken in one area the emotional/financial fallout will bleed into other areas

It sounds vain, but I could probably make a difference for almost everyone I ever met if I chose to involve myself with them either professionally or personally.

Kevin Costner
Actor

We recognise that the world is a risky place and we have to manage it without running away from it.

Paul Batchelor
Former AMP CEO

As team members, Treasurers make the best contribution when:

- They can work on specific elements of a project and report back to the group with the outcomes
- They don't have to manage complex people issues
- They are dealing with specifics rather than vague concepts
- They are auditing/checking/receiving or analysing data

When managing Treasurers:

- Check that their activity is in line with the wider vision and ensure they refresh their focus regularly
- Encourage them to encourage their team. They won't do it by nature
- Ensure anything you want to communicate to them that is important is written down
- Insist on face-to-face meetings so that things can be discussed – otherwise everything will be done by email

How Treasurers will act during meetings:

- Will need ideas/feelings/reactions to be said, in order for them to be taken on board and will want clear decisions
- Will want specifics/real practical information, sequentially presented; keep it short, relevant and stay on topic
- Will want realism about resources and timeframes
- Will want to see continuity, only changing the segments that are not working

Personality strengths that help Treasurers to further their development:

- Consistent and reliable
- Able to make order from chaos
- Excellent cool heads in a crisis

Personality weaknesses that can stand in the way of a Treasurer's development:

- Inability to work without a clear structure
- Can lose heart and connection with people
- Can lose energy and interest when there is no pressure

Opportunities for Treasurers to develop:

- Need to look at the big picture and keep activity focused on the important rather than the urgent tasks
- Need to develop their ability to deal with ambiguity
- Need to learn how to value and empathise with others

Threats to the Treasurer's development:

- Can't see the big picture
- Will freeze when faced with ambiguous situations
- Can treat people like machines and destroy their spirit

FAMOUS TREASURERS

- Clint Eastwood (Actor)
- James Bond (Movie Character)
- David Murray (CBA CEO)
- Paul Batchelor (former AMP CEO)
- Kevin Costner (Actor)
- Kylie Minogue (Singer)
- Mark Webber (Formula 1 Driver)

TREASURERS AT WORK

Treasurers are practical and productive individuals. They are conscientious and can be relied upon to complete tasks systematically. They are dedicated and responsible, and are cooperative and supportive as long as others are working within the accepted guidelines. They tend to be critical of others whom they suspect may be working against those guidelines.

The Treasurer does not want to play power games or create friction, and is accomplished at gaining the maximum personal benefit from organisation-based infrastructure. Their tolerance is generally high as long as people are doing their best and are not trying to challenge procedures, and they respect those who understand and follow those procedures.

They approach tasks in a methodical manner, and once started on a project will persist until it is completed. They accept change willingly as long as there is a point to the change. New ideas and projects appeal to them but they become frustrated if there is no structure or plan to follow. Their challenge is to achieve set goals.

A Treasurer will want to exert influence over illogical or unstructured people. They are very disciplined, especially with themselves, and their expectation will be that staff and colleagues are similarly disciplined. They will not naturally delegate, but will want 'to do it right themselves'.

They do not enjoy competition in the workplace. Their motivation lies more in achieving specific tasks than competing with others. They are more likely to compete with themselves by setting their own performance criteria and then striving to achieve these expectations.

The Treasurer needs to be able to see their own success rather than feel it. They often aspire to being a small cog in a big wheel rather than a big cog in a small wheel. They are much more interested in the here and now than the future so will tend to take the vision of others and make it practical.

A Treasurer has an excellent ability to process complex, detailed data. Once a project is started they will persist until it is completed. They approach tasks in a methodical and patient manner. They will memorise facts and figures with no difficulty. They enjoy being able to store information and retrieve it efficiently. A Treasurer is willing to supply facts and provide analytical solutions and lateral suggestions. As their name suggests, they are excellent at analysis.

The Treasurer copes with stress in the same way they cope with everything else. They will consider the facts, analyse them and take a logical course of action. Their ability to think laterally enables them to find solutions to problems.

They tend to resolve conflict by focusing on the task and what needs to be achieved, rather than the individuals involved. Again, their skill for providing lateral solutions and ideas enables them to dissipate conflict effectively. Their judgement can be relied upon because it is balanced and even-handed.

A Treasurer is generally quiet and unassuming. They have a calming effect upon others and can be relied upon to bring stability to those around them.

Relaxation for a Treasurer, however, is often a high-energy, high-stress activity. At play, the Treasurer will show their competitive side, pitting their physical prowess against the opposition. Treasurers enjoy sport and make good team members.

They are most confident when they understand exactly what is happening around them. As a leader, they will be firm but fair. They will create rules and procedures and ensure others adhere to them. They are capable of reprimanding or dismissing staff.

A Treasurer has a practical, down-to-earth communication style. They will systematically discuss facts and topics and will tend to keep the discussion balanced and in perspective. A Treasurer will have an excellent ability to spell, punctuate and edit. Their written and verbal communication will be structured and information based.

Despite a keenness for structure, a Treasurer can be spontaneous. They will enjoy starting new projects but will insist on working to an ordered and structured timetable.

What you see is what you get with a Treasurer. They are unlikely to deceive or exaggerate. A Treasurer is principally a conservative and loyal individual. They don't respond well to being pressured, preferring to work at their own pace. They have an excellent eye for detail. They are often able to highlight issues that others may overlook.

Treasurers are at their most formidable when they are sorting, categorising, analysing and problem-solving.

THE TREASURER'S MIRROR IN THE WORKPLACE

At work, the Treasurer's Mirror – the Bard – can be seen in patient listening, reflective and supportive comments given during tough times, support for the underdog and an interest in creating an inclusive and supportive work environment where everyone is respected, valued and allowed to reach their potential.

LEADERSHIP STYLE OF THE TREASURER

Each Neuro-Rational Type, due to its combination of Intelligences, has a different leadership style. These leadership styles are a function of the centre of focus of the Neuro-Rational Types, and tend to be expressions of the underlying world view of the personality. The most effective leaders use a variety of styles, choosing the appropriate style, timing and intensity to manage each situation.

The leadership style most closely aligned to the profile of the Treasurer is the *Tactical* style.

Table 17.2 The Leadership Style of the Treasurer

Situation	Explanation
1. The leader's modus operandi	Act based on accurate and verifiable information
2. The style in a phrase	'Prove it'
3. When the style works best	In highly technical or specialised environments
4. Overall impact on climate	Positive

The author's research suggests that the Tactical style has a positive overall impact on corporate climate. The primary focus of the Tactical style is on accurate and verifiable information. This has a number of ramifications as a leadership style.

These are:

- Employee's **insight is highly valued,** and the Tactical leader is a keen interviewer.

- **Individuals are included** in bringing about the strategic plan on a 'need to know' basis.

- Tactical leaders enjoy making many small decisions that keep the business functioning smoothly (P1 and C1 interaction).

- Being neither pushy nor a fast mover, pushy people and sometimes fast movers are ignored or removed. The Tactical leader will make up their mind for themselves (strong P1 element).

- **Feedback is minimal.** The Tactical leader will brief individuals or small teams, but tend not to let everyone know what is happening. Since employees do not know the corporate vision, this lack of communication can create a political environment.

This form of leadership may lead to confusion and procrastination as key decisions are held up and bottlenecks are created.

Key performers may leave because decisions take too long and they do not feel particularly valued by the leader.

Tactical leadership works well in highly technical or specialised business environments when the people being led are professionally autonomous and work in self-managed teams. It can also work where individuals are isolated and require infrequent briefings.

Despite these drawbacks, the Tactical style does work well when all the employees are self-motivated, highly competent, and need little direction or coordination. Given a talented team to lead, a leader using the Tactical approach gets the task accomplished. This leader tends to be highly respected by their employees. While they may feel unsure of the direction of the company, workers know that they will have a high degree of job security if they are polite, reasonable, and put forward informed and logical arguments to corporate issues.

SCHOOL OF STRATEGIC THOUGHT

The natural differences between Neuro-Rational Types are not limited to leadership styles alone; they also extend to a natural inclination towards different strategic thought. These differences have been researched by Mintzberg, Ahlstrand and Lampel (1998). For the Treasurer, the simple informal steps of the design school become an elaborate sequence of steps represented by the planning school of strategic thought. It focuses on formal procedure, formal training, formal analysis, and lots of numbers. When you produce every component part as specified, assemble them according to the blueprint, strategy will result.

THE GENIUS OF THE TREASURER — CREATING ORDER

The Treasurer's Genius lies in their ability to create order, systems and stability. This means keeping a calm head in emergencies, grounding new opportunities or settling down situations, people and teams when there is too much ambiguity. It means being analytical. In transition, the Treasurer creates clarity and certainty.

Buckingham and Clifton (2001, p. 86) describes the behaviour of the person using this strength as follows:

- When they are presented with someone's theory, their reaction is to demand proof.

- The only acceptable truth is based on objective facts.

- They see themselves as objective and dispassionate, because data is value free. Others recognise their logic and intellectual rigour.

- As they analyse, they look for patterns, causes and effects in relation to the proposition or situation and so reveal any flaws in the other person's argument or the real facts of the situation.

Buckingham and Clifton (2001) report the self-analyses of the thinking of several Treasurers:

> **Jose,** a school system administrator, reveals that he can see patterns and structures in conceptual situations. When considering applying for a grant, he is able to search through his mental images to see which eligibility criteria it will match, even which form to use, how to write the proposal, and how it will look in the form.

> **Jack,** a human resources manager, describes how he supports his statements with facts and logic. The example he gives is handling a complaint that another company pays more than his does. First he

finds out where the person got their information, then he asks specific questions, such as the geographical location of the other company, the type of work the company does, and the number of people in the sample. All this is done to ensure that the other person's argument is rigorous and based on facts.

Leslie, a school principal, uses objective facts to track the performances of different groups of students. She analyses the data – the building they were in, their attendances, which teachers they had, and what were the teaching styles. In this way she is able to objectively see the real picture without any personal bias.

Body Composition

The Treasurer body composition is lean. They are not muscular and women Treasurers tend to be petite. They carry their weight around their hips; however, their bottom is not large. Their shoulders are moderate; not narrow, yet not broad. Their legs are relatively short (Diversi, 2006).

EXERCISE PREFERENCES

Many Treasurers enjoy physical activity and sport of all kinds. They do enjoy being active and if they are not involved in organised sport will enjoy walking and keeping themselves physically active (Diversi, 2006).

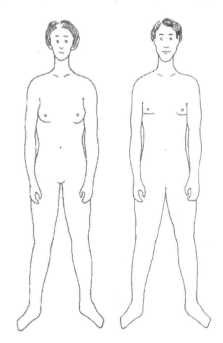

EATING PREFERENCES

The Treasurer eats to live and what they eat is dependent on a number of things including cost, health and convenience.

The Treasurer prefers to eat at home rather than eating out. They generally eat how they were taught as a child, according to what they deem as facts they have gathered through their life, again relating to cost, convenience or family favourites.

They often do place restrictions on their diet; however, these are not seen as a restriction to the Treasurer, they are just part of the equation that is life. The Treasurer does not binge eat but can miss meals if they are doing other tasks (Diversi, 2006).

DIETING PREFERENCES

The Treasurer is quite disciplined and rarely needs to diet. They often have bowel problems and will follow special diets to help with this. They subconsciously eat appropriate portion sizes and do enjoy a treat, particularly dessert after dinner (Diversi, 2006).

Applying Treasurer Insights as an Effective Communicator

WHEN NEGOTIATING WITH TREASURERS

The effective communicator is able to align their narrative and the point they are wanting to make with the archetype of the audience. That is, they use the same language, approach and behaviour with the archetype of the person they are presenting to.

When negotiating with Treasurers the way you position information is very important. Treasurers are attracted to messages centred around two main themes which are most convincing to them: *'Show me this idea is accurate with concrete data to support your position'* and *'Show me that this will solve the next problem that comes up.'*

'Show me this idea is accurate with concrete data to support your position'

There are two types who access their P1 and I1 — the Treasurer and the Navigator. This segment makes up 39 per cent of the general population. When negotiating with this group:

- Prefers not to practise and instead prefers to get started

- Likes to see a quick, logical and sensible approach to solving problems and crises

- Enjoys reading about and using tools, IT, equipment and machinery

- Will not read between the lines and instead needs all implicit information to be articulated before it is considered

- Likes information to be complete and comprehensive before a final decision is needed

- Prefers to read information rather than talk through issues

- Likes communication with in-depth analysis, charts, tables, graphs, concrete examples, photographs and details

'Show me that this will solve the next problem that comes up'

There are two groups who access their C1 and P1 by nature, the Treasurers and the Commanders. This segment makes up 36 per cent of the general population. When negotiating with this group:

- Present the 'here and now' and how well the organisation is able to respond quickly to whatever situation arises

- Present your argument in terms of new opportunities, new ideas, new projects and in all the divergent pieces of the organisation

- Assume a very short attention span

- Present your information through pictures, captions, simple flow charts and graphs

- Do not present abstract ideas or concepts or spatially-based dynamic models

- Emphasise experiential learning where they can set the pace

- Mention any links to the Internet

- Deliver your information in gulps

- Be aware that they will often not delineate between the different pieces if they all arrive together; for example, if a dividend arrives at the same time as a court summons, the dividend will be tarred with the same brush

- Be aware that they see vision as ungrounded and largely a waste of time

- Provide immediate answers, immediate results and immediate priorities because they withstand very low levels of delayed gratification

- Do not deliver too much strategy and not enough action

The Treasurer at a Glance

Strengths

- Rational inquiry
- Understanding
- Brings out objectivity in others

Code of Conduct

- Encourages colleagues to develop their technical knowledge and skills
- Creates clear audit trails related to activity or key decisions
- Learns from mistakes and documents this learning so that other team members can benefit
- Shows respect for colleagues' knowledge or expertise
- Rationally considers the facts before making key decisions
- Encourages others to show team members respect

First Step of Integration

- Focuses on personal courage and spontaneity

First Step of Disintegration

- Descends into being inflexible and controlling others

Exemplars

- Clint Eastwood
- Kylie Minogue
- Kevin Costner

Chapter 18

The Judge
An In-Depth Look at the Judge

RULE #1: 'With your partner in life - appear interested.'
Warren Clarke

What we've got to thank Judges for:

Clarity

Search for truth

Energy

Enthusiasm

Getting things done

The 'Devil's Advocate' position

Stamina

Determination

OVERVIEW

The Judge's mind is fast, efficient, clear, certain and razor sharp. It can remember details and likes to keep discussion concrete, ideas practical and tasks specific. It is driven by a constant desire to complete large amounts of work. While quality is important, Judges enjoy following efficient systems that enable them to do two days' work in one day. Constantly changing, refining and improving systems is an annoyance to Judges who would prefer to 'get on with it' rather than spend two days refining a system that could save one day's work.

Regardless of their training or level of professional development, the Judge likes working quickly and efficiently in an area of personal interest where they are recognised and rewarded financially. Their passion is being able to successfully complete projects where all the key stakeholders are happy and there is written acknowledgement of the contribution made by the Judge or their team.

Very emotionally passionate, Judges see strong relationships as being central to achievement and will protect those they are responsible for, defend those they respect and confront those they believe are wrong. They believe in the importance of institutions like the church, schools, and the legal system. They do not, however, have an abiding trust in their leaders and so constantly ask the hard questions to 'keep the bastards honest'. They often join social clubs or groups and conduct community work because they enjoy meeting new people and doing the right thing.

A Judge has great clarity with regard to their opinions on most issues and likes to put their case forward even if the topic doesn't come up. They are energetic, enthusiastic, focused and quick working and have an excellent eye for ensuring all the details are right and the ends are tied up.

Judges have a natural interest in commerce and the process of making money. They are natural small business owners and tend to find themselves in charge of logistics organisation, be it for sales, weddings, charity balls, fundraising or banquets. Judges thrive on activity, deadlines, logistics, organising teams, and multi-tasking.

I'm not interested in wanting to score points. I know that's ironic because a lot of people view what I do as just that. But what's driving me is the knowledge that the great interview is the one where everybody is talking about what the guest said.

Andrew Denton
TV Presenter

FOCUS OF ATTENTION

Judges are brilliant at building and maintaining customer loyalty because they genuinely want the right outcome for the customer and go the extra mile in making sure the customer is not only happy but wants to do further business with them. At their best, Judges are obedient, loyal, enthusiastic, driven, entrepreneurial, motivational, enlivening and cathartic.

KEY CHARACTER DRIVERS

There are three key Intelligences that drive the Judge:

C1 – Spontaneity

P2 – Passion

I1 – Data

LEVELS OF CONSCIOUSNESS AS DEFINED BY US PSYCHOLOGIST CLARE GRAVES AND SPIRAL DYNAMICS' AUTHORS COWAN AND BECK

The table on the following page outlines the broad character development of the Judge over a lifetime from Level One – the lowest level of consciousness – through to essence at Level Nine.

THE SUBTYPES

Each of the eight types is made up of three Intelligences. The Judge has C1 Spontaneity, P2 Passion and I1 Data. As we adapt to our life circumstances we tend to favour one of the three. This subtly changes the personality and gives rise to subtypes. All Judges will be able to relate to all three of the subtypes at some time in their life.

When I saw her I just wanted to put her across my knee and spank her for being such a naughty, naughty girl.

Richard Branson
(talking about Courtney Love,
who abused Virgin staff on a transatlantic flight)

Table 18.1 The Judge Levels of Development

Level of Consciousness and the noble quality embraced at this level	Common Judge characteristics at this level of consciousness
Level 1 (Beige) A state of nature and instincts.	Competitive, aggressive, physically abusive, angry, manic.
Level 2 (Purple) Mysterious and frightening. *(Noble quality to be embraced at this level: Loyalty)*	Clarity regarding what is and is not allowed and quick and loud condemnation of anyone not aligning with the prevailing attitude. Rituals have to be done right. People need to be able to understand what is happening and articulate their belief.
Level 3 (Red) Raw displays of power – dictators, tough love, predators. *(Noble quality to be embraced at this level: Enthusiasm)*	Straight down the line on any topic. You are either right or wrong. Any topic is up for debate but at the end of the day it's 'my way or the highway'. The Judge has the gift of energy and learns to use this together with their Mirror Architect's ability to instantly see what doesn't line up – or the other person's Achilles heel. This is an all out brawl, yelling, shouting and plenty of humour, threats and all or nothing approach to everything.
Level 4 (Blue) Everything is controlled by God and is purposeful. Obey God. Do it right. Feel guilt. *(Noble quality to be embraced at this level: Drive)*	Do it right. Don't kid a kidder, do it right or get blasted. The Judge knows if it isn't right through the insight of the Mirror Architect. When the Judge is riled, expect bursts of anger and the dispensation of their own justice. They don't hesitate to set things straight on God's behalf.
Level 5 (Orange) The world is a game and I want to win. *(Noble quality to be embraced at this level: Entrepreneurialism)*	The Judge discovers their ability to breathe energy into projects and their self-esteem builds. Their Mirror insists on learning new capabilities and this coupled with their energy enables them to develop extraordinary generalist and specialist skills. They discover their gift and how to use it for personal gain.
Level 6 (Green) We need to join together and grow personally through community. *(Noble quality to be embraced at this level: Motivation)*	The Judge becomes concerned that their gain is at the expense of others and they focus instead on building a congruent and meaningful life for themselves while working with rather than bullying others. They use their extraordinary verbal skills to cut down other bullies or controlling community members. They create optimism and fun in the community.
Level 7 (Yellow) We need to explore ways of being responsibly free. *(Noble quality to be embraced at this level: Enlivenment)*	The Judge makes clear decisions about what the community needs and feeds these memes, people or projects with energy – focusing on the virtues rather than the vices of each situation. New ideas are explored enthusiastically and integrated with older ideas by the Architect Mirror.
Level 8 (Turquoise) The world is composed of delicately balanced interlocking forces, shaped by attractor fields of intention and nobility. Uses natural flows. Actively grows consciousness. The *Non-dual* Leader manifests at this level.	The world is seen as a series of cycles and life is seen as a quest. The individual understands the spiral of life and the streams of intra-level progression and addresses the current problems of existence that arise in their own journeys so that the spiral can keep developing.
Level 9 (Coral)	TOWARDS ENLIGHTENMENT

If you feel you have a film that's valid, you stick your ass on the line.

Nick Nolte
Actor

THE CREATIVE JUDGE

The Creative Judge will enjoy new ideas, thoughts and solutions and will be able to adapt other people's concepts, designs and processes to support their objectives. They will lose interest in old projects and people quickly, wanting instead to constantly meet new challenges. They are quick minded, witty and enthusiastic for the latest thought.

THE POWERFUL JUDGE

The Powerful Judge will have strong opinions about most things and will want issues resolved. They are keen to succeed and want to outperform people's expectations.

At times they will tend to soapbox their ideas even though others may not wish to hear. Certainly one of their greatest challenges is to voice their opinions and ideas in such a way as not to offend their audience and not tread on emotional toes. The Powerful Judge will be excellent for creating change and will not be daunted by negative feedback. It is recommended, however, that they find themselves an intuitive person they can trust, and be guided by their ability to read other people's reactions, and therefore know when they are going too far.

THE WISE JUDGE

For the Wise Judge, the researching of information is far more important than either following the plan or coming up with ideas of their own.

They would prefer to wait and obtain all the facts before making a decision. For the Wise Judge, all the ends do not have to be tied up. They will always want to know the facts supporting opinions. They enjoy reading, the Internet, researching, and learning about the world.

ARCHETYPES RELATED TO THE JUDGE

When people discuss archetypes, many of the characters they use will fall into the same category as the Judge, much the same way that there may be fifty-seven species of fern but, regardless of the species, it still belongs to the fern family.

By way of example, some of these are:

- Bully
- Hedonist
- Gourmet
- Chef
- Critic

- Examiner
- Mediator
- Arbitrator
- Liberator
- Anarchist

- Revolutionary
- Political protester
- Nonconformist
- Scribe
- Journalist

CHILDREN'S STORIES/NURSERY RHYMES

- Basil Brush
- Oscar the Grouch
- Mr Squiggle
- Miss Piggy

THE MIRROR

While the Judge is dedicated to fast-paced, fast-talking, argumentative action, the Judge's Mirror Master – the Architect – looks for the strategic intent of the activity and is motivated by learning new capabilities, that is, the 'how to' of the 'what'. This thirst for new capabilities often draws the Judge to projects that will teach them new skills even if the projects seem strangely unrelated to the Judge's current skills, interests or preferences.

As a Mirror Master, the Architect is constantly critiquing the behaviour and pointing out the inconsistencies of the spontaneous and energetic Judge. This constant questioning demoralises the Judge who, in response, learns to ignore the constant criticism and usually adopts the attitude of think less and do more.

At home, the Mirror Architect is cunning and strategic, pointing out to the Judge's friends and family the inconsistencies between what is said and done, and what is promised and forgotten, providing interpretations for inconsistent behaviour.

The young Mirror Architect is strong and speaks rarely but when they do speak, they do so with great authority, which puts the Master Judge off balance. The Mirror Architect focuses on truth, honesty and teasing out weaknesses so they can be dealt with strategically. The Mirror is not interested in keeping the peace if the Judge is speaking rubbish.

As the Mirror Architect matures, they learn that not all inconsistency is bad, not everything can be solved in advance and that passion rather than logic is OK.

When fully integrated, the Master Judge's passion, energy and focus on action are balanced by the Mirror Architect's strategic outlook and philosophy, drive to learn new capabilities and ability to align all action with the vision and genuine needs and wants of the people involved.

CHARACTER FORMATION

The formation of personality has three major influences:

1. Firstly, the physiological genetic makeup of the individual creates a predisposition towards accessing particular energies and not accessing others.

2. Secondly, the culture of the environment in which the child grew up, sanctioned some energies over others and so encouraged the child to focus on some energies and suppress others.

3. And finally, the individual's psychological and physiological response to trauma or pain that usually occurs during childhood alters the way they relate to the six core energies. When we experience emotional pain or trauma we can 'turn off' the emotion by turning off the energy. One theory of personality development suggests that if in time we turn off three of the energies we derive our energy from the remaining three. These three in turn combine to form type.

Regardless of what caused us to focus on just three of the Intelligences rather than all six, as human beings we can take three Intelligences that are available to all humans and combine them to create a higher form of consciousness. We are, if you like, human transformers of thinking into consciousness. This higher level of consciousness takes the form of a Neuro-Rational Type – in this case the Neuro-Rational Type of the Judge.

THE QUEST FOR INTEGRATION: AWARENESS (I), CREATIVITY (C) AND POWER (P)

Re-opening the heart (I2)

The journey towards integration for the Judge begins with the opening of the heart. The most difficult part of this journey for the Judge is the first step. The very first step is for the Judge to accept themselves not for what they achieve but for who they are. This self-love and self-acceptance means accepting the many different parts of themselves – even the ones that are selfish, childlike or demanding. This inner family is made up of many different characters which first of all need to be identified and then integrated with an open heart.

Deficient Sixth Intelligence (C2)

Most Judges also have a deficient C2. When this is the case Judges become spiritually cynical, adopting rigid belief systems, and become apathetic and obsessed with the issues of the lower Chakras, namely, materialism, greed and the domination of others.

Deficient First Intelligence (P1)

Thought to be formed in the womb and during early childhood, P1 provides the infant with a feeling of stability, of being wanted and of having the right to be here. Described by Lowen in his book *Language of the Body* (1958) and Reich, *Character Analysis* (1949) as the Schizoid Character, the Judge constantly feels that they have to continually add significant value to validate their existence. According to Alexander Lowen:

The Schizoid defence is an emergency mechanism for coping with a danger to life and sanity. In this struggle all mental faculties are engaged in the fight for survival. Survival depends upon absolute control and mastery of the body by the mind.

This lack of grounding provides the Judge with deep-seated issues around the body, survival, roots, nourishment, trust, health, home, family and prosperity. Their interest in healing is, in part, a lifelong quest to heal themselves of the constant fear and feeling of 'not being worthy' that they carry around with them, deeply hidden yet ever present.

Healing in Action

SPIRALLING UP FOR THE JUDGE – PERSONAL TRANSFORMATION AND THE PATH TO LIFE[1]

Personal transformation and the path to life for the Judge is focused on asking themselves the hard questions, getting clarity on what action they need to take personally and getting on with it. The personal transformation of the Judge begins when they determine to become the driver of their own life. By nature Judges have boundless energy, optimism, enthusiasm and fun. Before they can begin the transformation process, they must question in what way they have breathed life into the difficult and joyful parts of their life.

In practice, the quest for integration follows the eight steps listed below:

AWARENESS

1. BUILDING BRIDGES OF UNDERSTANDING

The first step for the Judge is to actively build bridges with the various aspects of their personality. Often during childhood the Judge will have adopted a range of quite different personalities as a technique for gaining attention. These different personalities can all cohabit in the Judge because the Judge doesn't let them communicate. Instead, the Judge simply acts differently around different people or in different circumstances. The first step of integration for the Judge is to create dialogue between these different aspects of self. This involves accessing the noble quality of diplomacy. This noble quality involves bringing the different aspects of personality together so that the common ground can be found.

This can be done using a range of therapeutic techniques including two-chair therapy and self-discussion techniques. During these processes the different aspects of self get to meet each other and dialogue.

2. PERSONAL VISION

Once the Judge has met the different characters that make up their internal family, they can focus in this next stage on unconditionally loving and integrating each one into one congruent profile. This involves accessing the noble quality of

---

1   Based on a Judge in the Blue meme.

inspiration in order to find the personal meaning that links the different aspects of self and to draw them together towards a common cause. This is often channelled into creating an environment where the Judge can be true to themselves without fear of rejection. In this space the Judge focuses on being 'who they are' and on becoming their ideal self with complete freedom.

3. DISCERNMENT

Having taken action to proactively integrate their aspects of self and therefore their energy, the Judge must now assess which parts of their life must be cut to achieve congruence and alignment. This may mean ending relationships, community or family roles, or taking on roles that have been promised but not delivered. The hurly burly of life often means that who we say and think we are and who we really are, are two different things. During this phase of alignment the Judge brings these two worlds into perfect alignment. This requires accessing the noble quality of discernment in order to discover misalignment and the path to resolving it. With this work complete the Judge is ready to start focusing on their external world.

CLARITY

4. COURAGE

With their energy effectively harnessed the Judge now steps out with courage to achieve their goals. The noble quality of courage is needed so that the Judge can face the world openly and honestly with the integrated sense of self that they have created. This is where the Judge starts a new job or relationship, begins a new business or moves town. They step forward with courage and certainty and never look back.

ACTION

5. LEARNING

The Judge is now focused on securing timely and appropriate information, or personal or professional learning. It takes the noble quality of objectivity for the Judge to make an accurate assessment of what knowledge they need to learn. During this time they buy books, attend courses, update databases, tidy up the financial systems, conduct competitor analysis, review pricing or benchmark. The majority of the book learning and understanding during the transformation cycle takes place during this phase.

6. RESPONSIBILITY

With personal vision, discernment, courage and learning in place, Judges look to their long-term plans and the key milestones ahead. In the short term this clarity focuses on how they can give back to their community. For the Judge, living responsibly requires that they effectively play their role in the family, at work and in the community. As they access the noble quality of responsibility they consider the balance between their authority and their personal responsibilities. Amongst other things, this requires a careful assessment and management of risks. As the Judge does this, workmates, friends and family have their sense of certainty and confidence about what the Judge is doing reinforced and they see the genuineness and committed nature of the Judge in fulfilling their role.

7. ACCEPTING THE CRUSADE

For the Judge, their seventh step on their journey towards integration can take place when they are willing to align themselves with a crusade that has integrity. This involves accessing the noble quality of integrity to ensure that they do what they say they will, and that they align to the crusade that they say they will align with. This stage is very hard for the Judge who would prefer to have not one substantial crusade but instead many little crusades or multiple projects all happening spontaneously and simultaneously. They'd rather stay free. To move forward the Judge must be willing to put their spontaneity to one side and focus on finding a crusade or vocation worthy of their life's work.

ASSESSMENT

8. ASSESSING THE NEW QUESTIONS OF EXISTENCE

The final step is now taken into a brand new world – one with entirely new questions of existence. Since the integration process outlined here has focused on the Blue meme, the Judge will have integrated this aspect of consciousness. Now they will be faced with an entirely new set of questions of existence in the Orange meme. These will be based around the need to succeed and be recognised as successful. The Assessment occurs as the Judge takes stock of their current situation, of the lessons they have learned about life in general and their own abilities in particular and then begins to apply `their Genius of energy to become successfully entrepreneurial.

For all the types, however, there will be times when their development is arrested or even reversed. It's hard to believe that these honourable Judges can feel and behave in the following ways. Judges refer to these times as their 'dark night of the soul'.

SPIRALLING DOWN FOR THE JUDGE – THE PATH TO DEATH

The spiral downward is triggered by any event, thought, association or deed interpreted through the perspective of the Lower Self. It is this interpretation that many Christians would refer to as a separation from the divine part of ourselves and as 'sin'.

The spiral down starts when the Judge begins to bully and blame others. This bullying comes in the form of cutting words, strong emotions, mood highs and lows and a focus on personal attacks. At this stage the Judge develops and tells elaborate stories that blame others for their own lack of integrity. The Judge is avoiding reality by deluding themselves into believing that others are to blame for their problems. This can quickly deteriorate into the downward spiral of disintegration that has eight steps.

AVOIDANCE BEHAVIOUR	**1. COMPLETE INTOLERANCE AND PUNITIVE**

As the Judge spirals down they become intolerant of all other positions and become self-righteous. Their self-righteousness will be based on the rules they absorbed during childhood. The Judge decides they are the only ones doing what should be done and that others need to be punished to teach them a lesson. This is done behind the scenes with the Judge pulling the strings and creating chaos, hurt and confusion among their targets. While this is happening, the Judge genuinely believes they are doing the right thing.

2. INFLEXIBILITY AND CONTROLLING BEHAVIOUR

As the Judge spirals down, so too does their flexibility. Adherence to plans becomes a clear focus and their management style becomes totally closed to any new suggestions. They become abrupt, disconnected and autocratic, vigorously arguing that others should do the 'right thing'. In this case the Judge is talking about introjected, child-sourced, social or cultural rules. In this way, they have cut themselves off from others to reduce any likelihood that they receive insight. During this phase the Judge's attention to personal hygiene may deteriorate and they become fascinated with tools, weapons or equipment that can help them defend themselves against a vicious world that hates them.

3. ARROGANCE AND ISOLATION

If things continue to get worse, the Judge will begin to isolate themselves and associate only with those who can supply them with important or powerful information. The Judge can cut off all contact with the outside world, becoming a hermit, reading and refusing to communicate because, frankly, no one is up to their standard. During this period the Judge deflects any comments aimed at bringing awareness to the table.

The Judge creates a closed environment that safely seals them off from everyone who may disturb their disintegrated grasp on reality. During this phase the Judge studies the laws, rules and fine print that will help them defend themselves if their transgression ever comes to trial. They prefer all their communication to be done in writing.

REJECTION

4. BELIEVING THEY ARE A VICTIM AND BECOMING DEPENDENT ON OTHERS

As their relationships deteriorate, the Judge will have spiralled down to the point that they feel isolated and betrayed and they can't figure out why they have been victimised. They can't see that their suffering is of their own making. During this time the Judge merges with their work, partner or colleagues as a defence mechanism. Tears, story-telling and seduction all manifest at this stage. They perceive that they have no future, no friends and no courage. This phase often ushers in heavy drinking and drug-taking 'to get through it all'.

5. CONFUSION AND PROCRASTINATION

Isolated, angry and unwilling to take responsibility for their own behaviour or the situation that it created, the Judge now looks for the inconsistencies in the behaviour of others and in the systems they are following. This method of projection is their first line of defence against anyone who says they are to blame. During this time the Judge's professional performance subsides as the procrastination increases. The Judge adopts a highly dysfunctional interpretation of reality wherein they find everything and anyone else to blame for their own inadequacy.

INTERNALISED
ACTION

6. DELUSION AND DECEPTION

The Judge is now in unfamiliar territory and rather than remake their perception map, they become delusional and see only what they want to see. The Judge creates an idealised image of themselves in their mind and they happily refuse to accept anything that may violate this idea. Even though others can see they have lost touch with reality, the Judge's self-identity of being right remains as they make very poor major life decisions. During this phase the Judge 'treats' themselves with presents, special treats or purchases for a job well done. They give themselves rewards they've been looking for from others.

DISASSOCIATION

7. DISASSOCIATION

Finally, as the Judge totally disassociates from their life, they play politics and power games, and sever the relationships people have with others through gossip, lies and innuendo.

The Judge's Quest for Creating Wealth

HOW THE JUDGE BECOMES WEALTHY

The Judge is brilliant at building and maintaining customer loyalty because they genuinely want the right outcome for the customer and go the extra mile in making sure the customer is not only happy but wants to do further business.

The Judge makes big money when they are involved in sales and customer service. The bigger the contracts and the number of customers, the more money Judges make because they are genuinely admired and appreciated by the people they serve.

DEEP UNCONSCIOUS MOTIVATION

A Judge's energy comes from a desire to connect with others in a stable environment where they do not have to perform to feel they are making a contribution that is valued by others.

In their business affairs the Judge will want to follow all the rules, pay the tax, have simple and transparent accounting policies, spend the extra money to keep customers happy and charge what they believe they are worth, not a dollar less or more.

MONEY MANAGEMENT APPROACH

Judges feel very uncomfortable with the stock market because it is too risky and totally out of their control. They do, however, feel comfortable with government bonds and treasury notes and often invest in ex-mutuals or government organisations like GIO, Telstra, Commonwealth Bank and AMP.

Judges talk about minimising tax but see tax-effective strategies as sneaky and dodging their community responsibility. They prefer to make more money and pay more tax than consider what may be a 'risky' tax scheme.

Judges don't trust anyone when it comes to money, not even themselves. They tend to not take the advice of investment specialists and prefer to attend seminars, think through the issues themselves and then do nothing about it.

Of all the investments, the one that they feel most comfortable with is residential real estate because they can see it and touch it. However, they are usually unhappy with the rate of return this investment offers, and the constant maintenance of the properties causes them stress.

Judges feel they have little control over their ability to create wealth and as a result of this tend to focus very little attention on learning about financial issues or wealth creation practices, concentrating instead on working hard and maximising their current year's income.

Judges feel most comfortable with their money in a bank account. They can see that this doesn't bring them the return they want, but at least it is safe.

THE JUDGE'S MONEY HABITS

Judges are focused on providing for and protecting their family members. This leads to concentrating on satisfying the specific day-to-day financial needs of the family rather than investing in projects for future income.

Because the Judge is committed to providing for their family, they are very sceptical of long-term projects with an unproven track record and step away from excellent investment opportunities because they will require capital to be tied up for more than twelve months.

Every now and then, the Judge will be confronted with an investment opportunity that they want to be a part of but for some reason they don't feel comfortable with. The comfort will usually return after some time but usually the investment opportunity will have passed while they passively sat by attending to the immediate needs of others rather than their important longer-term financial interests. They can become so obsessed with simplicity, honour, loopholes and security that their only form of wealth creation is their savings in a bank account.

A Judge is very prone to judging the potential of a project more by the people involved and their social standing than the analysis of the figures. This often means that they back projects that enjoy a high profile and are good for the community and for the leaders of the project but not so good for return on investment.

When a Judge considers embarking on a new venture, if there is no guarantee of the project's success, they will walk away rather than risk their family's security. This means that they walk away from many excellent investments with good return that are low-risk.

A Judge may not splurge on huge outlays but they do believe in pampering themselves. This usually takes the form of small luxuries that they believe they need, to get over a bad day or a bad experience. Over a period of twelve months these little indulgences can add up to a significant sum of money that could be invested more wisely for better long-term returns.

WEALTH CREATION FORMULA FOR JUDGES

The first step for Judges is to realise that it is not too late for them to start creating wealth. In fact, their approach to life is ideal for matters regarding money management and if they can get over their fear and start playing the game they can become very wealthy.

As Judges tend to see themselves as powerless in the financial world, they can spend their time blaming banks, the tax department, life's experiences, their family or their own disorganisation rather than sorting it out and making the decisions they need to make. The Judges who do accumulate wealth are the ones who have insight into their excuses and nip these in the bud, break through their fear and get the show on the road.

Like all types, the Judge needs to find a technical expert they can relate to. A Judge tends to work best with advisers who get paid by the hour rather than as a percentage of the money invested because it reassures the Judge that their advice is unbiased. They also like advisers who are not ostentatious with their wealth. While they will find reasons why they don't trust most advisers, this passes if they can build trust and a friendship with the person. Finding this person and building a rapport with them is a critical platform from which the Judge can begin the serious wealth creation program.

WHAT JUDGES DO WITH THEIR WEALTH

Because the Judge's unconscious focus is on security, wealthy Judges will invest in a balanced portfolio with a good proportion of their wealth in guaranteed investments.

They prefer to live in homes that reflect the position they hold within the community. These homes are selected in the most appropriate areas where the family will be safe, where their investment is secure and where the home is conveniently situated near facilities the family will need (for example, schools, work, universities or hospitals).

Judges have a fascination with nature and the way nature works, and so often will take up gardening or an art form that allows them to express themselves.

Wealthy Judges spend most of their time supporting their family and the community. They are not big financial givers but instead give of themselves and their time to community groups, charities and civil groups.

I enjoy giving the time and any expertise but not giving the money.

I'm not a white-bread politician. I'm not in that groove. I'll do things according to my own style.

Mark Latham
Former Australian politician
vowing to watch his language but not change his style

If you find you're digging yourself into a hole, stop digging.

John Burley
multi-millionaire, business owner and wealth creation expert

CREATIVE JUDGE

Wealthy Judges are fun, witty, organised and efficient, dedicated to making the world a better place through their own passion, hard work and commitment to people.

UNDERSTANDING JUDGES

Judges use their personality to best manage themselves by:

- Learning to be more sensitive with reprimands, requests and feedback
- Disciplining themselves to confirm the bigger picture before they get started on the operation at hand
- Disciplining themselves to see the value in people with whom they disagree
- Disciplining themselves to slow down for people who need more time to think things through

As team members, Judges make the best contribution when:

- A team needs to be rejuvenated and re-energised
- A 'roll up the sleeves and get started' approach is required
- Vast amounts of activity are required, and outputs are needed
- Things need to be brought to a head
- There is clarity, unity, purpose and direction, and the Judge is given the OK to make things happen

When managing Judges:

- Provide clear and written feedback, both positive and negative, on their activity
- State specifically what behaviour you want to see and what you don't want to see
- Provide feedback 'on the spot' or immediately after the meeting
- Give negative feedback in short two-minute sessions
- Write down feedback on reports given – positive and negative
- Always be pacey, to the point and specific

How Judges will act during meetings:

- Will tend to shoot from the hip and polarise their support very quickly
- Will want clear decisions made and outcomes from the meeting
- Will argue their point passionately and creatively
- Will want public recognition for the work they do
- Will be insensitive to the feelings of others
- Will praise those they feel have done a good job
- Will not want complexity, vagueness or sluggish thoughts

Personality strengths that help the Judges to further their development:

- Ability to drive new projects
- Can drive a team hard
- High achiever
- Never miss a deadline, never late
- Very focused on doing what it takes to achieve the goal

Personality weaknesses that can stand in the way of the Judge's development:

- Misreads people
- Can 'burn out' themselves and others
- Fractures world into 'good' and 'bad'
- Can be very insensitive
- Can be too egocentrically linked to outcomes

Opportunities for the Judge to develop:

- Needs to keep deadlines and expectations in perspective
- Needs to learn how to relax
- Needs to see the continuum, not the poles
- Needs to learn how far to push people

Threats to the Judge's development:

- Can create needless conflict
- Can create enemies
- Can become too political
- Can provoke people to revolt

I wouldn't say I invented tacky, but I definitely brought it to its present high popularity.

Bette Midler
Actress and Singer

FAMOUS JUDGES

- Richard Branson (Billionaire)

- Nick Nolte (Actor)

- Bette Midler (Actress & Singer)

- Karen Walker (Character – *Will and Grace*)

- Fran Drescher (Character – *The Nanny*)

- Kramer (Character – *Seinfeld*)

- John Burley (Author)

- Andrew Denton (Interviewer)

THE JUDGE AT WORK

At work, the Judge's Mirror can be seen in the constant questions regarding how the behaviour of others either aligns or doesn't align with their personal philosophy, their past behaviour or the project objectives. It is the Judge's Mirror that makes the quiet sarcastic remarks about double standards, faulty processes and flawed strategy. The Mirror Architect is also constantly looking for opportunities to learn new skills and capabilities and understand systems or organisations at all levels.

LEADERSHIP STYLE OF THE JUDGE

Each Neuro-Rational Type, due to its combination of Intelligences, has a different leadership style. These leadership styles are a function of the centre of focus of the Neuro-Rational Types, and tend to be expressions of the underlying world view of the personality.

A survey of 3871 executives selected from a database of more than 20,000 executives[2] found distinct leadership styles. Daniel Goleman (2000) attributes these different leadership styles to different emotional intelligences. Each leadership style has a different impact on the work environment and on organisational performance. The most effective leaders use a variety of styles, choosing the appropriate style, timing and intensity to manage each situation.

The leadership style identified by Goleman's research that is most closely linked to the profile of the Judge is the **Coercive** style.

---

2   Survey was originally analysed by Kelner et al. (1996).

Table 18.2 The Leadership Style of the Judge

Situation	Explanation
1. The leader's modus operandi	Demands immediate compliance
2. The style in a phrase	'Do what I tell you'
3. Underlying emotional intelligence competencies	Drive to achieve, initiative, self-control
4. When the style works best	In a crisis, to kickstart a turnaround, or with problem employees
5. Overall impact on climate	Negative

The author's experience supports the insightful research reported by Goleman. In most situations, the Coercive style has the most negative overall impact on corporate climate. The primary focus of the Coercive style of leadership is on extreme top-down decision-making. It is focused on achieving the immediate results at all cost (a strong P2 element).

Some of the characteristics of this leadership style are:

- Coercive leaders **demand immediate compliance** with orders, but do not bother explaining the reasons behind them. If they are not followed, then the leaders tend to resort to threats.

- Rather than delegating authority, they **seek tight control** of any situation and monitor it studiously.

- **Feedback is minimal**. If given at all, it tends to focus on what people did wrong rather than what they did well. By rarely using praise and freely criticising employees, they start to erode people's spirits and the pride of satisfaction they take in their work.

- **Flexibility and responsibility are lost**. Since the decisions are made from the top, flexibility and creativity die and people feel so disrespected that responsibility evaporates.

- This style does **not give feedback** building the individual's sense that their job fits into a grand, shared mission.

Despite these drawbacks, the Coercive style is beneficial in extreme circumstances, such as during a turnaround or when a hostile takeover is looming. It can be used to break failed business habits and shock people into new ways of working. But the long-term impact is detrimental if another style of leadership is not used once the emergency has passed.

SCHOOL OF STRATEGIC THOUGHT

The natural differences between Neuro-Rational Types are not limited to leadership styles alone; they also extend to a natural inclination towards different strategic thought. These differences have been researched by Mintzberg, Ahlstrand and Lampel (1998). The Judge proposes a model of strategy that seems to attain a fit between internal capabilities and external possibilities. It equates to the design school, and is the home of the SWOT approach (Strengths, Weaknesses, Opportunities and Threats).

THE GENIUS OF THE JUDGE – ENERGISING AND TURNING TALK INTO ACTION

The Judge has the Genius of turning talk into action by focusing on what can be done NOW to get things on the road. That is, the Genius of the Judge is in the application of their energy and activating projects with energy.

Buckingham and Clifton (2001, p. 84) describe the Judge's behaviour as follows:

- Their focus is on action, getting things started, getting things done.

- They are impatient with analysis and debate and once a decision is made they cannot wait to start. The absence of detail does not slow them down.

- This person learns by experience. They act, look at the result and learn from it. This is a reactive rather than a proactive stance.

- They believe we are judged only by what we actually do.

Buckingham and Clifton (2001) tell the story of Jane, a Benedictine nun who dealt with an energy shortage on their 140-acre block of land, using her signature strength of energising. Instead of researching, planning or strategising, she followed a hunch that they should drill for their own gas. She immediately contracted a firm to drill, only to discover that she had spent $70,000 just to find that there was gas there. It would be useless unless she spent another $30,000 to test the reliability of the supply. Fortunately she was successful.

The Coercive Style

Daniel Goleman (2000) gives an example of a CEO who was brought into a failing company because of his reputation for turning companies around.

He proceeded to do the cost cutting and firing that was long overdue, and the company was momentarily saved.

But because of the aggressive, belittling, abusive personality of the Coercive leader, morale suffered. Most of the senior staff left or were fired and people only reported good news for fear that the CEO would 'shoot the messenger' of bad news. In the end, the board had to fire the CEO and find another person to rescue the company.

The Judge has to remember that 50 per cent of the population do not care about outputs – they're only interested in the process. So if you get the job done at the expense of the relationship and the respect of 50 per cent of the team, it is too high a price to pay. They will all 'dig in' on the next project. So slow down, connect with people and remember that whereas a broom doesn't mind sweeping the floor, the person behind the broom does. And sometimes let them do it their own way in their own time.

A second example of the Energiser given by Buckingham and Clifton is an entrepreneur who prefers taking action to discussing risks. He realises that some of the people with whom he works see his impatience to get going as dismissing the risks. But while taking into account major risks, which he calls hitting the wall, he is ready to gamble upon minor risks, which he calls bumping the wall. The advice he relies on is how great a risk he is taking, how high the odds.

BODY COMPOSITION

The body composition of the Judge is slightly above average, neither lean nor fat. Where appropriate BMI is between 22 and 27kg/m² for women, and 24 and 29kg/m² for men. They naturally have good muscle tone, particularly in their legs.

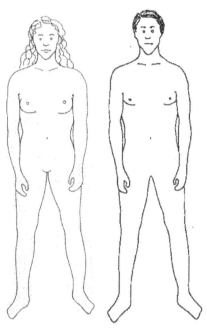

They tend to have slightly broader shoulders than other types; however, their hips and bottom tend to be narrow. Overfatness first develops in the upper abdominal region, followed by the arms, face, and finally the legs and hips (Diversi, 2006).

EXERCISE PREFERENCES

A Judge needs to be pushed to their limit when exercising. They prefer to be sedentary or very active, and not in between. Growing up, the young Judge performs well at both individual and team sports (Diversi, 2006).

EATING PREFERENCES

The Judge loves food and alcohol. They prefer salty and savoury foods to sweet foods if given the choice. The Judge loves entertaining, eating out and cooking. When making a meal, they tend not to follow a recipe too closely and love adapting these where possible (Diversi, 2006).

DIETING PREFERENCES

The Judge enjoys instant gratification and is therefore attracted to fad diets that promote instant weight loss. They will follow one fad diet this week, be off the diet next week and follow another fad diet the week after (Diversi, 2006).

And, as I say, the starting point might be to recognise that the
problem starts with us non-Aboriginal Australians.
It begins, I think, with the act of recognition. Recognition that it
was we who did the dispossessing. We took the traditional lands
and smashed the traditional way of life. We brought the disasters.
The alcohol. We committed the murders. We took the children
from their mothers. We practised discrimination and exclusion.
It was our ignorance and our prejudice. And our failure
to imagine these things being done to us. With some noble
exceptions, we failed to make the most basic human response and
enter into their hearts and minds. We failed to ask – how would
I feel if this were done to me? As a consequence, we failed to see
that what we were doing degraded all of us.

Paul Keating
Former Australian Prime Minister

Applying Judge Insights as an Effective Communicator

When Negotiating with Judges

The effective communicator is able to align their narrative and the point they are wanting to make with the archetype of the audience. That is, they use the same language, approach and behaviour with the archetype of the person they are presenting to.

When negotiating with Judges the way you position information is very important. Judges are attracted to messages centred around two main themes which are most convincing to them: *'Show me how this can help us get some quick wins'* and *'Show me this idea is the best way forward.'*

'Show me how this can help us get some quick wins'

There are two types who naturally access their P2 and C1 functions – the Judge and the Chancellor. This segment makes up 36 per cent of the general population. When negotiating with this group:

- Present constant initiatives that will give the organisation the edge

- Demonstrate new ideas, business ventures and people as an indication that the leadership is doing a good job

- Exhibit how the organisation has taken advantage of the opportunities created by shifts in the market (for example, competitors failing)

- Show evidence that the organisation is responsive to market trends

- Show fast activity that secures 'quick wins'

- Use strategies that are grounded and that last no longer than a few years

- Show clear milestones, responsibilities and target dates for achievement

- Be prepared to convince them on every point

- Be aware that they consider the credibility of the presenter as important as the message itself

- Demonstrate passion, success and drive

'Show me this idea is the best way forward'

There are two types who access the P2 and I1 functions by nature – the Judge and the Crusader. This segment makes up approximately 37 per cent of the general population. When negotiating with this group:

- Do not show indifference, lack of passion, coldness or apathy

- Sell the benefits of new ideas particularly if these benefits can be quantified

- Keep the discussion tangible and concrete with specifics

- Do not present intuitive and unproven concepts, models, abstract ideas, hunches, intuitions or possibilities

- Show that there is a valid code of conduct and that there is a right and wrong way of doing things

- Show that leaders are approaching tasks the RIGHT way

- Demonstrate that you are following the rules, respecting the status quo, paying taxes, doing jury duty and being fair

- In your communication, be precise, passionate, action-oriented and respectful of institutions and roles/positions

- Demonstrate that their leaders are strong yet approachable, and will protect those within their responsibility

- Articulate goals, set milestones and show that these goals are achieved

- Demonstrate that the leadership is passionate to do whatever it takes to keep the energy and focus maintained

The Judge at a Glance

Strengths

- Drive and energy for activating tasks and getting things done
- Passion
- Brings out drive in others

Code of Conduct

- Looks outside the organisation for innovative ideas that can be applied internally
- Seeks out challenging opportunities to test their skills and abilities
- Manages their time effectively so that they get all things done for which they are responsible
- Celebrates with a sense of satisfaction when a project is completed or a key milestone is reached
- Meets daily challenges with enthusiasm and energy
- Uses questions to clarify team member points of view, team objectives and procedures

First Step of Integration

- Focuses on empathising with others and building bridges with them

First Step of Disintegration

- Descends into being intolerant and punitive

Exemplars

- Richard Branson
- Andrew Denton
- Bette Midler

Chapter 19

Exploring Your Emotional Reactivity

Perhaps the simplest thing we can do to manage our emotional reactivity is to engage our higher mind in recalling a positive and secure situation. For example, we can quieten our prejudice-creating amygdala (low road) through thinking or talking about how tolerant we are which in turn triggers our neural prefrontal area. Some now famous Israeli experiments conducted by neurobiologists showed how participants' prejudices dampened when they felt more secure. Whereas talking about groups they felt emotional about, such as Arabs or ultra-orthodox Jews, had evoked prejudices only minutes before, thinking about their loved ones enabled participants to become far more tolerant and open to spending time with them (Lieberman et al., 2005).

The amygdala does have an important role to play. It exists at a functional level to assist us to make snap judgements and help us to avoid pain and to survive. While it is useful in making life and death judgements, it may be less useful in higher order

Wisdom of the Phylum (or Subphylum, 'Class')

This form of knowledge is expressed as a set of processes in the brain (to a substantial degree genetically encoded and transmitted), which are automatically triggered by certain stimuli or situations. This type of wisdom captures millions of years of experience of mammalian evolution and is expressed in humans as basic emotional responses to certain stimuli, as well as basic perceptual discriminations.

Wisdom of the Species

This form of wisdom is expressed as a culturally encoded and transmitted set of categories enabling us to parse the world in a species-adaptive way. This type of wisdom captures thousands of years of human experience and is expressed as language and other symbolic systems at our disposal.

Wisdom of the Group

This type of knowledge is the collection of skills and competencies possessed by a group of individuals with shared background (such as all the members of the same profession), which allows them to perform complex tasks, daunting to most people, in a relatively effortless fashion.

(Goldberg, 2005, pp. 97-98)

issues. It fails at reasoning anything that takes longer than a moment's thought to recall a similar situation. So amygdala-based decisions are often illogical yet feel certain despite being based on little information. The amygdala is designed to give an instant 'take' on the reality or 'truth' of a situation. But this introduces a very controversial question: what is truth? This is an unexpectedly complex question that we will address using a surprising methodology that accesses the body's somatic wisdom.

THE RELATIVITY OF TRUTH

If you know something is true, how can you be sure? Imagine if there were some way we could test different ideas, theologies or philosophies and put them into some kind of truth hierarchy. If we could do that we could measure the relative truth of everything we read, hear or see and we'd have a way of evaluating it before we let it influence our opinions and potentially our lives.

Amazingly, one group of scientists has discovered a test like this. In his groundbreaking work, *Power vs Force* (1995), Dr David Hawkins traces the development of researchers' understandings of the measurement of relative truth. It all started in 1976 when Dr George Goodheart scientifically proved that the human body contained somatic knowledge that was independent of the conscious mind. It was such an unbelievable claim that at the time it split the scientific and medical world and created a new science – kinesiology, accessing knowledge from the body.[1]

Dr Goodheart showed that in blind tests, certain indicator muscles in the body reacted in a uniform way depending on whether the stimulus was benign or malignant. Surprisingly, this would occur regardless of the conscious knowledge of

---

1 The implied meaning of accessing knowledge from the body came after the originating studies about muscles and their movement and how that manifested in physical health, either anabolic or catabolic. Thus, the new science created was kinesiology, the study of the movement of muscles and their corresponding influences, physiologically. It was subsequent to his pioneering work that the science evolved into the recognition and accessing of what was then considered somatic knowledge.

A Kinesiology Test That You Can Try

1. In a typical example of muscle testing, you're given an herb to hold. Have the subject stand erect, right arm relaxed at their side. Have the left arm held out parallel to the floor, elbow straight, holding the herb. (Which arm is used does not matter, only their relative positions matter.)

2. Face your subject and place your left hand on their right shoulder to steady them. Then place your right hand on the subject's extended left arm just above the wrist.

3. Tell the subject you are going to try to push their arm down as they resist with all their strength.

4. Now push down on their arm fairly quickly, firmly and evenly. The idea is to push just hard enough to test the spring and bounce in the arm but not so hard that the muscle becomes fatigued. It is not a question of who is stronger, but of whether the muscle can 'lock' the shoulder joint against the push. If the herb is something you need, you'll be able to resist the downward pressure and hold your arm rigid. If not, you won't.

It is important that there is no physical problem with the muscles of the arm and that the subject is in a normal, relaxed state of mind. They must also not be receiving any extraneous stimuli (this means the tester must not smile or otherwise interact with the subject). Initially the subject will 'test strong' and the arm will remain locked. If the test is repeated in the presence of a negative stimulus, like the artificial chemical supplement, the muscle will not be able to resist. It will immediately collapse to the subject's side.

(Adapted from Hawkins, 1995)

the subject. That is, even if the person being tested had no conscious knowledge of the topic being tested, their indicator muscles would react in a uniform manner. This suggested that somehow the body 'knew' the answers to questions that the mind didn't.

But one of Goodheart's kinesiology tests took the theory to the next level of abstraction. It involved placing an unhealthy chemical sweetener in one envelope and a healthy natural supplement in another. When in the presence of these envelopes, the kinesiology results of individuals tested showed that their muscles strengthened around the healthy supplement and weakened around the chemical sweetener.

On this occasion, not only did test subjects not need any conscious acquaintance with the substance being tested, the artificial sweetener would cause the deltoid[2]

---

2   The deltoid sits at the very top of the arm and helps to fix the arm to the shoulder area.

to weaken whether placed on the tongue, held in its package adjacent to the solar plexus or hidden in a plain envelope where neither the presenter nor the subject were consciously aware of it. This test has since been validated in psychology departments of universities hundreds of times over in double-blind studies (using the scientific method), and in mass demonstrations involving entire lecture audiences. The subjects universally tested weak in response to unmarked envelopes containing artificial sweetener, and strong in response to identical placebo envelopes (Hawkins, 1995).

These test responses occurred irrespective of the subject's physical strength. Researchers found the same results when testing frail old women or strong young men. In one documented case study an audience of a thousand people were given five hundred envelopes containing artificial sweetener along with five hundred identical envelopes containing organic vitamin C. The audience was divided into dyads and alternated in testing each other. When the audience opened their envelopes, in every case they found that their own muscles had gone weak in response to the artificial sweetener and strong in response to the vitamin C.

In the 1970s, Dr John Diamond (1979) developed a new specialty called **behavioural kinesiology**. This field was based on the idea that the indicator muscles would strengthen or weaken in the presence of positive or negative *emotional and intellectual stimuli*. This would mean that a smile would make an individual test strong while the statement, 'I hate you,' would make them test weak.

Diamond proved that certain abstract symbols caused all subjects to test weak while others caused all subjects to test strong. He also showed that virtually all classical music and most pop music (including 'classic' rock-and-roll) caused a universally strong response while the hard-core, heavy metal and punk genres produced a universally weak response. Behavioural kinesiology could even be tested with just the image of a substance or person, not even with their physical presence (Hawkins, 2005).

For example, one of John Diamond's favourite tests was to hold up an apple grown with pesticides and ask the audience to look directly at it while being tested. The audience would all test weak. Then an organically grown apple, free of contaminants would be held up. As the audience focused on the apple their muscles would test strong. This test would have the same results regardless of whether the audience knew which apple was which.

The results of behavioural kinesiology tests proved to be predictable, repeatable and universal – even where no rational link existed between the stimulus and the response (Hawkins, 1987).

Another discovery of behavioural kinesiology was that subjects listening to tapes of known deceivers, such as Lyndon Johnson perpetrating the Tonkin Gulf hoax, universally tested weak. Conversely, subjects listening to recordings of demonstrably

Dr Hawkins' Method for Using Kinesiology to Test Relative Truth

Two people are required. To determine the suitability of a test subject, press down quickly with two fingers on the wrist of the horizontally extended arm of the subject while also asking them to resist. A suitable subject is able to resist the pressure and keep the arm extended parallel to the ground.

Keep the testing situation impersonal; refrain from smiling or making personal comments. Keep the environment free of noise, background music or distractions such as pets or children. Remove metal objects such as eyeglass frames from the test subject's body. Also remove watches or jewellery, including necklaces. Be aware that certain stimuli, such as a tester's perfume or after-shave lotion may affect the test results. To improve concentration, have the test subject close their eyes.

(If subjects repeatedly go weak regardless of the question, evaluate the examiner's voice. The occasional voice that makes others go weak disqualifies its owner as a tester under ordinary conditions.)

Do a trial run with the subject. Ask them to think of someone they love, then press down with two fingers on the wrist of the arm extended out to the side, parallel to the ground. A normal subject will be quite strong and able to resist firmly. Next, have the party think of someone they fear or has resentment towards (you can always use Adolph Hitler, who makes everybody go weak even if they have never heard of him). A normal subject will go very weak and be unable to resist downward pressure on their wrist. Run through a few more contrasting pairs of stimuli to establish consistency of response and develop a rapport between the tester and subject. Some suggested stimuli with predictable responses are:

Test Weak	Test Strong
• Hate	• Love
• Adolph Hitler	• Mahatma Gandhi
• Rap music	• Classical music

After establishing that the test subject reacts reliably and is in a normal state, proceed with the topic under investigation by making declarative statements. Questions should always be posed as a declaration of fact. It is useless to ask questions about the future, as the test results will have no reliability. Always preface the investigation with the statement, 'It is safe for me to make inquiry into... (whatever the specific topic is).' (Yes/No?)

The line of questioning itself can be checked by stating, 'This is the correct form for the question.' (Yes/No?) Each time a question is stated, the test subject is told to resist and the tester presses down quickly with two fingers on the test subject's extended wrist.

To calibrate the relative truth of a question, ask, 'On a scale of 1 to 600 where 600 represents enlightenment, this......calibrates at......' The scale is relative only and Dr Hawkins originally chose the numbers and the range arbitrarily.

true statements universally tested strong.

In order to perform a behavioural kinesiology test, the questions need to be asked in a binary fashion. In other words, the question needs to be asked in a way that elicits a yes or no answer. It seemed to Diamond that the somatic knowledge of the body appeared to operate similarly to the binary coding of computer programming.

You may like to test this for yourself. The procedure takes two people to perform a kinesiological test. We will refer to the second person, the one being tested, as the subject (Kendall, 1979: Hawkins, 1987).

USING KINESIOLOGY TO TEST THE RELATIVITY OF TRUTH

Dr David Hawkins built on the work already done with somatic knowledge and kinesiology to generate a simple procedure to calibrate relative truth. Dr Hawkins numerically represented relative truth as being between the numbers 1 and 1000. The numbers represent the logarithm (to the base 10) of the power of the respective levels of truth – the lower the number, the lower the relative truth.

The concept of relative truth is a complex one. Consider the relative truth of the following statement: 'The world is a big place.' On one level this statement is true – the world is indeed a big place. On another level this statement is not true – Earth is tiny in comparison to the solar system and all but non-existent when we consider a galactic scale. This relative truth measurement is one of comparison. The truth of the statement is also relative in terms of perspective. The magnitude of the world is not so great for a businessperson capable of flying around it in a supersonic jet. In contrast, a peasant farmer who cannot afford shoes let alone an airplane ticket will perceive the world as being vast beyond comprehension. Which is right? Dr Hawkins dedicated twenty years of research to refine a process for answering this kind of question.

CREATING THE MAP OF CONSCIOUSNESS

Using his simple, scientifically validated kinesiological testing technique, Dr Hawkins and his team spent twenty years developing a map of human consciousness using somatic intelligence[3] as his guide.

---

3   Here, somatic refers exclusively to *body* or *bodily*. Hawkins himself testifies that the paradigm shift came for him when he realised that the source of the information was non-local (non-linear) and not, as the specialists and professionals were suggesting, *from the body* or *cellular memory*. In the above text, while the phrase *somatic intelligence* accords with the *NeuroPower* model of the Intelligence Centres and somatic knowledge/ intelligence as part of the triad of the Intelligence Centres, from Hawkins' perspective the intelligence exists *outside* (non-linear) the soma yet localises (linear, possibly through the

This map was generated from millions of tests, involving a wide spectrum of people. In all these cases, the same results were found. These tests were conducted on subjects whose mental capacity ranged from what is considered normal to severely ill psychiatric patients. They were tested in Canada, the United States, Mexico, and throughout South America and Northern Europe. The subjects came from all nationalities, ethnic backgrounds and religions. They ranged in age from children to elders in their nineties, and covered a wide spectrum of physical and emotional health. In all cases, without exception, the results provided statistically valid responses and were scientifically validated using the guidelines and principles of all scientific research studies.[4]

The subjects themselves were selected at random and tested in a wide array of physical and behavioural settings. They were tested on the top of mountains and down by the seashore, at holiday parties and during the course of everyday work. At the time of the testing, some of the subjects were experiencing joy and others were experiencing sorrow, yet these variables had no effect on test results, which instead were found to be universally consistent irrespective of physical, emotional and environmental factors.

The results of this process were absolutely staggering because they mapped a clear framework that contextualised both consciousness and relative truth.

Hawkins' central theory was built on the idea that there were energy fields that lay under truth. These energy fields encompassed thought, emotion and behaviour at a range of different levels. Furthermore, these energy fields influenced not only the individual, but also the world views and spiritual beliefs of every individual on earth. Hawkins says it best:

> The resultant map of relative value scales of consciousness seemed to indicate levels of relative power, and each represented a perspective, a point of view and its perceptual field. Each calibrated level represented a process in consciousness, a predominant orienting emotion, as well as a way of life. Each level implied a different way of not only seeing life but of experiencing it. An array of attitudes, beliefs, practices, philosophies, mental mechanisms, psychological sets, as well as healthy and unhealthy psychological defences characterised each level of consciousness. (Hawkins, 2005, p. 81)

---

medium of the Chakra and the respective brain/mind interface) it for the purposes of communication using the soma. Thus, while this statement is correct (tests as true at a 400-500 level), it does not reflect the level of truth that Hawkins worked at to formulate the Map.

4   For peer-reviewed test results, refer to *Qualitative and Quantitative Analysis and Calibration of the Level of Human Consciousness*, David R Hawkins, MD, PhD Institute for Advanced Spiritual Research.

His research showed that the range of 1 to 600 represented the domain of the vast majority of human experience. The levels from 600 to 1000 described the realm of non-ordinary evolution – of enlightenment, sages, and the highest spiritual states.

One of the most controversial aspects of the study was the finding that as the calibrated level of truth rose, so too did the capacity to influence vast populations. Thoughts, emotions and behaviour that calibrated below 200 were shown to be harmful to the individual and to society generally. (This form of relative truth was referred to as force.) Every aspect of truth above 200, Hawkins referred to as power.

From 200 to 600 the influence was shown to be positive. The power of the thoughts, emotions and behaviours that calibrated above 600 was enormous.

Hawkins identified that the critical point of consciousness was around 200, which is the level of courage. All thoughts, emotions, behaviours and associations below that level of calibration resulted in the person testing weak. All attitudes, thoughts,

Table 19.1 Dr David Hawkins' Map of Consciousness

Expression	Calibration	Emotion
Shame	20	Humiliation
Guilt	30	Blame
Apathy	50	Despair
Grief	75	Regret
Fear	100	Anxiety
Desire	125	Craving
Anger	150	Hate
Pride	175	Scorn
Courage	200	Affirmation
Neutrality	250	Trust
Willingness	310	Optimism
Acceptance	350	Forgiveness
Reason	400	Understanding
Love	500	Reverence
Joy	540	Serenity
Peace	600	Bliss
Enlightenment	700-1000	Ineffable

Hawkins, 1987, *Power vs Force*, pp. 52-53

feelings and associations above that level of calibration resulted in the person testing strong. He identified this as the line between power-based and force-based thoughts, emotions and behaviours and the invisible line that divides force from power.

He found that consciousness levels below 200 were motivated primarily by survival. (Although at the very bottom levels even the desire for survival was missing.) The levels of fear (100) and anger (150) were characterised by egocentric impulses arising from the drive for personal survival.

At the level of pride (175) the survival motive often expanded to consider the survival of others as well. And as consciousness crossed the 200-point, the wellbeing of others became increasingly important.

By the 500 level, the happiness of others emerged as the essential motivating attractor. The high 500s were characterised by interest in spiritual awareness for both oneself and others, and by the 600s the good of humankind and the search for enlightenment became the primary goal. From 700 to 1000 life became dedicated to the salvation of all of humanity.

To understand the concept, Hawkins suggests that we consider the struggle for freedom from colonialism between Mahatma Gandhi and the British Empire. The motivations of Mahatma Gandhi calibrate at 700 (you may like to test this yourself to validate the statement). The position of the British Empire was below the critical level of 200 and so it represented an imposition of force. Hawkins argues that Gandhi won his struggle because at a metaphysical level his thoughts, ideas, emotions and behaviours were far more powerful than the British Empire.

INTRODUCING CHAOS THEORY

To appreciate how our understanding of consciousness has progressed, it is interesting to consider some significant developments in physics. In the early 1960s the computer revolution and the development of computational mathematics enabled vast amounts of data to be graphically depicted, revealing consistent systems (Lorenz, 1963). Using this approach theoreticians were able to understand data that had previously been considered incoherent, or non-linear. New patterns emerged that previously had not been possible to see with classical (linear) physics. Analysis of this 'incoherent' data revealed hidden energy patterns, attractors or attractor fields that lay behind apparently random natural phenomena (Hawkins, 1987).

INTRODUCING ATTRACTOR FIELDS

Like the attractor fields discovered in chaos theory, Hawkins' map of consciousness revealed new patterns that historically had been hidden. These influences acted on an individual's consciousness in exactly the same way as attractor fields operated in the physical world.

His research and calibration of truth showed that profoundly powerful and hitherto unseen forces organised human behaviour into recognisable patterns. These unseen forces (attractor fields) could radiate either high or low energy. The relevance and credibility of data in the individual's mind were found to be determined by the predominant attractor field influencing the individual or the collective group at the time. Like attractor fields, these patterns could be identified, described and scientifically tested. But Hawkins went even further.

Hawkins believed there was a giant attractor field organising all human thoughts, emotions and behaviours. Within this macro field were smaller attractor fields generating less energy and power. He used his theory of these fields to explain the undeniable patterns of thought, emotion and behaviour that are consistent across cultures and time throughout human history. He argued that the interactions between the lesser attractor fields could explain the rise and fall of all civilisations throughout history.

Hawkins' map of consciousness correlated with Rupert Sheldrake's concept of 'morphogenetic fields' and with Karl Pribram's holographic model of brain-mind functions. It also aligned with the theory of Nobelist Sir John Eccles who argued that the brain acted as a receiving set for energy patterns or attractor fields and that these attractor fields were converted by the brain from consciousness to thought. He believed the brain was the aerial link between the external attractor field and the brain's human manifestation of thought, emotion and behaviour (Hawkins, 1995).

CHAOS REVEALED AS HOAX

A good example of how an attractor field can be revealed in what appears to be chaos can be found in the kitchen sink. When you turn on the tap a little of the water drips out very regularly. If you turn on the tap a little more, while the drips speed up, it is still at a regular pace. If you turn it on a little more, the drips sound irregular, like rain dripping off a roof. If you measure the time between the drops and make a list of these numbers, you have the classic example of a chaotic time series. They appear to be completely random. But are they?

In what has become a textbook example of attractor field measurement, US physicist Rob Shaw subjected the dripping tap to serious study and created one of the most widely used methods of studying chaotic information.

His method involved placing a microphone in the sink where the drop would hit it and having this trigger an electronic beep. This enabled him to enter the precise time intervals of the drips into his computer and mathematically model the results.

When the simulated dripping tap was modelled by the computer, the water drop would get bigger and bigger until its mass reached a critical value and the drop would fall off the tap. When this computer model was run it produced results that were almost identical to the experimental data from the actual tap. Had there not been an underlying pattern (attractor field) influencing the drips, the computer model would not have been able to so accurately simulate the timing of the real dripping tap.

This study went on to produce a simple method of revealing the existence of underlying order within apparent chaos.

This method involved:

Step 1: Take the sequence of numbers that represent the time between drops in an initial study.

Step 2: Make a copy of this column of numbers.

Step 3: Remove one number from the top of this second column and move the entire column up one space.

Step 4: Plot the two lines of numbers on a graph from Step 1 with Step 3 and notice the pattern that has emerged.

Step 1: Original Time between Drops (seconds)	Step 2	Step 3
4		4.1
4.1	4.1	4.5
4.5	4.5	3
3	3	2.7
2.7	2.7	

If the data from the sequence of numbers were really random the dots would be all over the place. Instead, they lie along a smooth curve. The smooth curve clearly indicates the attractor field.

ATTRACTOR FIELDS, M-FIELDS AND SPIRAL DYNAMICS

Another way to interpret the way attractor fields work is by applying Rupert Sheldrake's (1981) notion of morphogenetic fields, or M-fields. Hawkins makes the point that these invisible organising patterns act like energy templates which establish forms on various levels of life. Sheldrake would argue that it is the discreteness of M-fields that enables identical representations of a species to exist (Sheldrake: Hawkins, 1987).

Sheldrake's M-fields work biologically in exactly the same way as Hawkins' attractor fields work consciously and social psychologists Cowan and Beck's memes[5] work sociologically in their model of Spiral Dynamics. All three are descriptions of energy fields that create patterns out of what seems to be chaos. They could be described as underlying forces that create predictable thought patterns, images, emotions and behaviours. This would suggest that most of our views of the world are formed, not by facts, personal experience or insight at all, but rather by attractor fields that organise our thoughts into a predictable pattern.

Hawkins uses the case of the runner Roger Bannister to make his point. He was the first to break the four-minute mile. Before he did this it was commonly believed to be a physical impossibility. Once Bannister broke that misconception, a new attractor field was revealed and many more runners suddenly began to run sub-four-minute miles. Hawkins would argue that the attractor field determined reality and not the other way around.

Attractor field theory would argue that this is the hidden process that is occurring when an individual adopts a new paradigm. A new paradigm is simply a different attractor field. Sheldrake believed that he proved this with his laboratory rat experiment. He found that teaching a new behaviour to one rat in one laboratory made it easier to train the same behaviour to other rats in other laboratories. Attractor field theory would explain this by suggesting that once the new attractor field is born, all rats have equal access to it and so the behaviour becomes a *remembering* or *receiving* rather than an *inventing* (Hawkins, 1987).

BIFURCATION AND PERSONALITY

In Hawkins' map of consciousness there are distinct levels that represent very different perspectives on reality. Corresponding to each perspective of reality are different ways of thinking, different emotions and different ways of behaving.

---

5   A cultural unit (an idea or value or pattern of behaviour) that is passed from one generation to another by non-genetic means (as by imitation); 'memes are the cultural counterpart of genes'.

These differences can be explained through mathematical bifurcation models. A bifurcation point is one around which observed patterns fundamentally change. At this bifurcation point the substance moves from one underlying attractor field to another. If the next attractor field is unable to be recognised by the observer the behaviour will appear, to the observer, to be chaotic. Of course, to the trained eye it is not chaotic at all – it's just a different kind of order that reflects a different attractor field.

If, for example, you were to heat gas in a glass container, there are models to predict how the gas will behave. But when the heat is increased to a certain point these models become ineffective. Experimenters may know, for example, that for a particular gas, temperatures between 20 and 30 degrees centigrade will see the gas hold true to the mathematical model of the gas permutation attractor field. As the temperature rises above 30 degrees, however, this gas will start to behave in a completely different manner from that which the mathematical model has predicted. Using attractor field theory, it would be interpreted that the gas has simply moved from one attractor field to a higher attractor field. If we apply this theory to your consciousness, we could argue that your thoughts, ideas and emotions are forming around an attractor field. Perhaps the inherent drive that propels us to grow into that which we all can be (as we noted in Principle #1, the Greeks referred to this as *physis*) acts like a Bunsen burner ever raising the temperature until we settle on a specific bifurcation point.

ENERGY, PERSONALITY AND CONTAINMENT

The concept of energy, which is one of the great unifying concepts of physics, was formulated in the nineteenth century, yet to this day it is not entirely clear what energy is. Many scientists argue that energy is the principle of change. The more energy there is, the more change can take place. In this sense, it is a causative principle that exists in any process. The energetic flow is organised into forms by attractor fields. Using this model, matter would be considered to be energy that is bound within attractor fields.

This concept is best explained by considering the movement of energy within a heating and cooling system. At very high temperatures atoms don't exist in the system. Electrons fly off the nuclei and you get plasma, which is a soup of atomic nuclei and electrons with its own distinctive properties.

If you cool the plasma to a certain temperature, atoms begin to form. Electrons start circulating around nuclei, and you get a gas of atoms. But at this point the temperature is still too high for any molecules to form. If you cool it down further, you get molecules. If you cool the system down even further, more complex molecules materialise but they are still gaseous. Cool it down further, and these molecules turn into a liquid that can form drops and have quite complex and ordered arrays of molecules. Cool it further still and you get a crystal that is a highly ordered, formal arrangement of atoms and molecules. All substances increase in complexity as you lower the temperature and reduce the energy.

Lowering the temperature manifests less random kinetic particle motion; there is less chaos and an increase in complexity of structure as the cooling process takes place. Consider the cooling of steam into water and the cooling of water into ice crystals, snowflakes or frost. As this formative process occurs, thermal chaos is reduced. The lower the ambient temperature, the more the energy has been transferred to the physical substance. As the energy drops, more energy is *contained* in the substance. Let's now apply this to consciousness.

The concept of *containment* is central to Eastern spiritual practice and is a central plank of Freudian psychiatric practice. It is an important principle because it enables us to understand *why* some attractor fields contain more energy and power than others.

The reason that one truth (an attractor field) that calibrates at a high level has more power than another truth (an attractor field) that calibrates at a lower level is due to the greater complexity and energy that the higher attractor fields contain. Low-power, low-calibrating attractor fields are simple. High-power, high-calibrating attractor fields are complex.

In other words, the greater the level of relative truth (high-calibrating attractor field) from which a person is operating, the greater the amount of conscious energy they have the ability to contain. The more energy they can contain, the more psychological, interpersonal and spiritual power they have at their disposal (Power as opposed to Force).

For example, using Hawkins' map of consciousness, the Constitution of the United States calibrates at 700. Going through the document sentence by sentence reveals that its power originates from one core attractor field. This attractor field states that all men are equal by virtue of the divinity of their creation and as such their human rights are intrinsic to their creation.

This power arises from the complexity contained in the meaning associated with an attractor field that supports the significance of life itself. It appeals to the higher side of humanity, to that part of human nature that we call noble. It appeals to that which uplifts, dignifies and ennobles.

For the human being, operating from a high-power attractor field like this will energise, empower and support them by providing high-level life purpose and meaning. Meaning is so important to us as humans, that when life loses meaning, depression, hopelessness and then suicide commonly follow. If we dedicate our life to enhancing the lives of others by connecting them to higher attractor fields of meaning and purpose this power will manifest in their lives as life-enhancing energy, empowerment and support (Hawkins, 1995).

MASTER PERSONALITIES LINKED WITH HIGHER ATTRACTOR FIELDS WHICH GENERATE MORE ENERGY

While the energy of human thought is tiny, it is measurable. Research by Hawkins (1987, p. 234) showed that a thought that calibrates from an attractor field at 100 will typically measure between log $10^{-800\text{ million}}$ to $10^{-700\text{ million}}$ microwatts. In contrast, a loving thought that calibrates at 500 measures approximately log $10^{-35\text{ million}}$ microwatts. Higher attractor fields enable the brain to physically generate higher levels of energy. This means that one individual calibrating at 700 will have the same impact on the world as 70 million who calibrate below 200.

Consider the following scales arrived at by Hawkins:

One Individual at X Level of Consciousness	Counterbalances	Y Individuals below 200
700	Counterbalances	70 million
600	Counterbalances	10 million
500	Counterbalances	750,000
400	Counterbalances	400,000
300	Counterbalances	90,000

Hawkins, 1987, p. 234

This helps to explain why the motivation of Mahatma Gandhi (700) was able to triumph over the British Empire (175) and achieve independence for India. Similar to the Constitution of the United States, Gandhi held that all men are equal by virtue of the divinity of their creation. When individuals tapped into the same attractor field as Gandhi (700) they were energised, supported and empowered with meaning that gave them purpose and power.

ATTRACTOR FIELDS, MEMES AND CALIBRATIONS

The most widely used map of consciousness is Cowan and Beck's *Spiral Dynamics*. Each meme identified in *Spiral Dynamics* is itself an attractor field. *Spiral Dynamics* expresses how individuals and societies develop and grow in their complexity as they mature. While Hawkins' map of consciousness primarily focuses on the emotional aspect of the attractor field, *Spiral Dynamics* primarily focuses on the cognitive

Meme	Calibration Range	Emotional Theme	Thought and Behaviour
Beige	50-60	Apathy	Survival
Purple	150-170	Anger	Appease the Gods
Red	200-250	Courage	Demonstrate personal independence
Blue	310-330	Willingness	Sacrifice personal needs for the sake of a higher goal
Orange	350-400	Reason	Focus on personal success
Green	500-510	Love	Accept that all people are equal and have an important contribution to make
Yellow	600-630	Peace	Responsibly free
Turquoise	660-670	Bliss	Integral awareness and understanding of the world
Coral	700-760	Ineffable	Enlightenment

Meme Focus	Personal Interpretation and Expression reflecting work from Hawkins (1995)
PERSONAL SURVIVAL Beige (50-60)	**Apathy:** The world and the future look bleak. Pathos is the theme of life. It is a state of helplessness; its victims, needy in every way, lack the resources and the energy to help themselves.
TRIBAL SURVIVAL Purple (150-170)	**Anger:** This can lead to either constructive or destructive action. It is most often expressed as resentment and revenge stemming from frustrated want. The individual is suppressed in order to appease greater powers.
PERSONAL EXPRESSION Red (200-250)	**Courage:** Life begins to be seen as exciting, challenging and stimulating. The individual realises that they have some personal control over their world which encourages a willingness to try new things.
HIGHER ORDER Blue (310-330)	**Willingness:** This is a willingness to suppress personal words and dreams for the greater good. At this level the individual has overcome inner resistance to participating in a wider campaign to improve life for everyone.

Meme Focus	Personal Interpretation and Expression reflecting work from Hawkins (1995)
PERSONAL SUCCESS Orange (350-400)	**Reason:** This allows engagement in their life on their own terms. There is an emphasis on the individual's ability to create success through rational problem-solving, analysis, and strategic action. Emotional calm, perception is widened and there are ample opportunities to succeed.
COLLECTIVE HARMONY Green (500-510)	**Love:** Characterised by the development of a love that is unconditional, unchanging and permanent because its source is within a person whose love is not dependent on external factors.
INTEGRATING TRUTH Yellow (600-630)	**Peace:** The distinctions between subject and object begin to blur. Perception is sometimes reported as occurring in slow motion.

and cognisant and behavioural aspects of consciousness. The two systems can be synthesised thus:

If we were to state this truth less egocentrically we would say that every moment of every day we are being influenced and motivated from the attractor fields that encompass human consciousness. Our thinking, feeling and acting reflects the field which is the expression of our consciousness. This, in turn, influences the thoughts, emotions and behaviours of others. This means that our moment-by-moment decisions create both our experience of the world and contribute to the experience of those around us. Every decision that manifests a high attractor field (for example, love) is the expression of our personal awareness and thus a higher level of nobility, which in turn is increasingly benevolent for humankind. Every decision that manifests a lower attractor field (for example, hate) is the expression of a lower level of awareness that reduces not only our own nobility but also our potential for benevolent coexistence in the world we share with others.

DEVELOPING HIGHER CONSCIOUSNESS: EVERY GREAT JOURNEY STARTS WITH THE FIRST STEP

We are human; and, as with all human endeavours, every time we try something new we have to start at the bottom and work our way up.

As we discussed in earlier chapters, consciousness works as a holarchy or nested hierarchy (nesting is exemplified in Russian matryoshka dolls), which means that the higher attractor fields embrace and encompass lower attractor fields. In other words, we can't just start at the top. This helps to explain the emotional shift that we experience when we fall from an area of our life in which we have high levels of competence (for example, Blue, Orange, Green or Yellow based knowledge, emotional expression and/or behaviour) to areas where we have low levels of competence (Beige, Purple or Red). At first, as we master the new endeavour, we re-experience what it is like to be at these lower memes – with all the emotional and mental turmoil that that brings. Then as we mature, we begin to tap into higher attractor fields and the anxiety and emotional turmoil subside.

This can't and shouldn't be avoided. Instead, the best approach seems to be (just as Susan Jeffers (1987) suggests in her best-selling book *Feel the Fear and Do It Anyway*) to feel the fear of the lower meme – and do it anyway. (By 'doing it' we are referring to the work of holding the tension and manifesting human nobility. This concept is explained on the following pages.)

WE WILL ALL WANT TO SPEND TIME WHERE WE ARE ABLE TO EXPRESS OUR NOBLE PERSONALITY

Consider the example of a professional who is highly experienced and adept in business life (let's assume they are at the Green meme of consciousness) but is far less experienced socially (let's assume they are at the Red meme of consciousness).

At work, when manifesting their nobility, if they were at the Green meme, they would operate from a genuine quality of love. They may have taken younger colleagues under their wing to guide them and provide professional development. They would be accepted by their team as caring and they would be a valued member of the organisation.

Socially, however, it may be a very different story. If they haven't mastered their social skills and are still at the Red meme they would feel stress and anxiety as they try to express themselves in their interactions. Many of their emotions at this meme would be strong and raw as they try to interact and get through it as best they could.

In this context it is to be expected that this individual would want to spend more time and energy at work where they feel more competent, loving and accepted than at social functions where they are stressed and anxious. Unsurprisingly, this individual is likely to be considered a workaholic because this is where they want to spend time – and in this case they want to do that because this is where they are most in touch with their higher nobility.

THE QUESTIONS OF EACH MEME

The meme (attractor field) creates the questions of existence that dominate our thoughts and emotions. These questions are embedded in the attractor field and become all consuming for us, as individuals, to answer.

The way we try to answer these questions is by using our brain. Luckily, our brains are equipped with thinking functions that love to spend time solving exactly these kinds of problems. But as we struggle to comprehend the questions and then formulate answers we experience what we describe as inner conflicts or tensions. It makes our brain hurt.

Within us these tensions emanate from the different thinking functions of our brain, that is, between the functions that process and the functions that interpret the world.

Processing Tensions	Information Tensions
Sequential Processing (P1): How can I maintain my family connection in this situation? What do my associates say about this dilemma?	**Factual Information (I1):** Does this image represent the archetypal image I desire? What information should I find out to help my decision? What is the real situation? (That can be seen, measured and sensed.)
Priority Processing (P2): How can I use this situation to my advantage? How can I benefit from this situation?	**Intuitive Information (I2):** Am I connecting with those around me in this situation? How do I authentically feel about this? Am I being honest with myself? How will this impact on my connection with others?

Every minute of every day we face internal tension between the different functions that define the problem. Whether our actions are ones of power or ones of force will depend upon how we manage these internal polarities.

How often do we have an important decision to make and find ourselves going around and around in circles asking ourselves the same questions and not being able to make a decision? This state, called the 'infinite regress', sees us struggle for hours, days or even years with the same questions and with no resolution. This may sound bad, but there is an even worse alternative.

If we fail to maintain the internal tension we can choose to collapse into one of the polarities. This leads to momentary resolution and relief but reduces the possible calibration of the attractor field that we can access to below 200.

When this happens our personality collapses into a neurotic state. This neurotic state will be made up of one of the P1 or P2 processing functions, the I1 information function, and in some situations one other colluding function. When a personality forms solely around one of P1, P2 or I1 it represents one of Karen Horney's[6] moving towards, moving against or withdrawing 'neurotic' personalities.

These collapsed fragmented personalities represent socialised expressions of force. They align with force-based attractor fields, and create disharmony and disempowerment, and they remove noble action.

In essence, we have two ways of dealing with the internal tension and conflict that we feel when trying to resolve the issues of existence at each meme.

Firstly, we can collapse into one of the polarities (thinking functions) of our Master profile and project the inner tension we feel onto the external world making the conflict everyone else's problem. Alternatively, we can *contain* the tension internally and seek to have it resolved by accessing a higher attractor field.

The principle here is summarised in the often-used quote of Albert Einstein's that no problem can be solved at the level it was created. In this case we need to be able to access a higher attractor field to solve the problems of existence manifesting at the meme at which we are currently living. We can do this in one of two ways: by accessing the Intelligence that Jung referred to as the transcendent function (C2) or by accessing the Intelligence that Nietzsche referred to as the Dionysian man (C1).

We have access to the higher attractor field through our two creative functions that are also hardwired into our personalities. These transformational functions are the two forms of creativity, C2 and C1.

The C2 (Transcendent) (Apollonian man) function can be activated through awe which contextualises the situation; or through mental, physical and emotional exercises.	**The C1 (Dionysian man) function** can be activated through flexibility, spontaneity and social fun; or through mental, physical and emotional exercises.

When we do this, that is, hold the tension and introduce either C1 or C2 into our thinking, an extraordinary thing happens. We experience a personal conversion from internal tension to the manifestation of one of the fifty-six noble qualities at one of the seven levels of consciousness.

THE MASTER PERSONALITY AND CONSCIOUSNESS

The noble qualities of each Master personality represent a method of expressing

6   US psychiatrist Karen Horney (1945) proposed that much of our neurotic interpersonal behaviour can be traced back to these three interpersonal reactions.

the positive aspects of the meme in which they are embedded. In this manner, the noble quality allows for the resolution of the issue at hand. The noble quality sits above the meme and helps to bridge the gap to the next meme.

According to the Jewish Kabbala, containment is the key to opening the portal to God himself. This could be interpreted as the portal that sits between the individual and Hawkins' greater attractor field.

INDIVIDUAL NOBILITY IS DRIVEN BY THE TENSION GENERATED BY THE MEME

There exists an innate tension within each meme. This tension is picked up and embraced by the individual. (This aligns with Sir John Eccles' theory that the mind operates as an antenna that receives the tension and energy existing within the meme or the sub-attractor field with which it is entrained (Eccles: Hawkins, 1987). The personality tries to resolve this tension through the thinking functions and if the individual can integrate this tension with creativity then human nobility is manifested.

The tensions of the memes are summarised below:

Meme	Tension
Purple	How do I appease God(s)?
Red	How do I get what I want when I want it?
Blue	How are my actions aligning with the greater cause?
Orange	How do I become what others would consider to be successful?
Green	How am I expressing myself and allowing others to express themselves fully?
Yellow	How am I integrating life and creating a life that is responsibly free?

Humanity, 'like any other energetic system is dependent on the tension of opposites' (Jung, 1954: Huskinson, 2004). Here, these internal opposites are the four Intelligences – P1, P2, I1 and I2 – which provide the basis of personality.

This suggests that all growth, all human nobility and all transformation can take place only through the effective unification of the internal tensions we all feel as we ascend through the memes.

This is vastly different from the philosophy of a society that encourages instant gratification of internal tension by collapsing into one of the polarities, projecting the

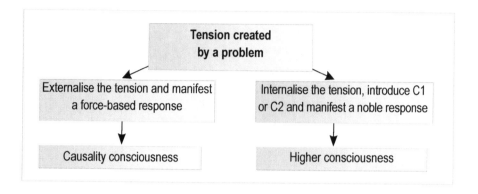

issues externally and then temporarily resolving them through sophisticated forms of avoidance or denial.

This sophisticated avoidance or denial can take the form of consumerism (everything will be resolved when I buy this new product/service), drugs (perhaps I can momentarily escape the tension), projection (it is my boss's, partner's or parent's fault), by compliance (roles at work, at home, at service organisations) and a range of other games, neuroses and rackets that successfully distract us from the hard work of containment, reconciliation and unification. To be fully human is to be fully awake and fully formed. This can happen only when we are actively addressing the questions of existence embedded in the meme from which we are currently operating. This takes courage, willingness, acceptance and love and results in personal peace and even bliss. We shall expand on this in Chapter 21, where we explore further how to

DIAGRAM 19.2 THE CHOICE BETWEEN COLLAPSE AND CONVERSION

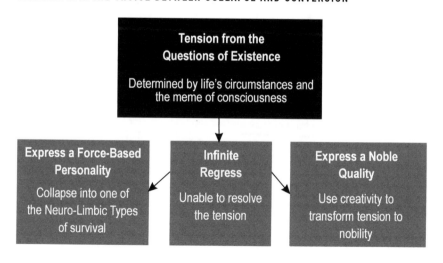

convert the Low Row (Force) to the High Road (Power).

THE CHOICE BETWEEN COLLAPSE AND CONVERSION

Why is it that containment and conversion of tension into a noble quality results in integrating life's lessons whereas prematurely collapsing results in a force-based response and a perpetuation of the problem? When we contain the tension embedded within any problem, and use creativity to resolve it, we make a second-order judgement about the situation based on nobility and insight. In contrast, when we collapse into one of the polarities, we adopt a simplistic resolution to the presenting issue that is force-based and that leads to actions that are detrimental to life. Furthermore, the source of the tension does not become integrated into our understanding of the world or our sense of Self. Instead of learning from life's events, we adopt Core Beliefs that act as perceptual filters, which remove our ability to constructively answer the question or problem at hand.

When we make a decision, we can use two approaches. Firstly, we can rely on affect (an emotionally-driven causal and first-order approach) or we can approach the situation with containment and conversion (a cognitive, noble approach that exercises second-order judgement). The cognitive approach to decision-making involves containing the tensions embedded within the various memes and the different functions and converting them through the use of creativity. The result of adopting this approach is the manifestation of a noble quality. These noble qualities are discussed in more detail in Chapter 20.

When we are unable, unwilling or too undisciplined to make the mental effort to contain the tension that is required in order to make a cognitive decision, we tend to use relatively simple cues to arrive at conclusions, or relatively simple positions to justify our subsequent decisions (an affect decision). The personality that forms from an affect-based decision is called the Neuro-Limbic Type (NLT) and the perceptual filters we use to interpret the world are referred to as *Core Beliefs*.

WHY COLLAPSE PREVENTS INTEGRATION

There are vast differences between the characteristics of a decision based on nobility (built through cognition) and those of an affect-driven decision. These characteristics arise from the different aspects of the brain that are used in the decision-making process. The cognitive process is centred in the neocortex (which allows us to think about thinking) while Core Beliefs arise from the amygdala (which acts like an internal watchdog scanning the environment for threats). Core Beliefs help us to react to danger and remove our ability to creatively consider options. This means that all of us share common traits when we are accessing our Core Beliefs.

The following list outlines common characteristics of Core Beliefs:

- The same conclusion and results are consistently arrived at because they are based on a chemical or instinctual reaction;

- Focusing on one Core Belief can alter the intensity with which another Core Belief is held;

- The perceptions of the Neuro-Limbic Types are not closely related to facts;

- The world views of Neuro-Limbic Types are strongly (but irrationally) held; and

- The decision-making process of a Neuro-Limbic Type tends to be subconscious and the cognitive mind is used to later justify rather than question these perceptions.

In contrast, when we attempt to resolve our disparate internal drives through a cognitive process, the decisions tend to be:

- Able to integrate complex issues;

- Relatively stable;

- Relatively resistant to challenges from other ideas or messages; and

- Creative or innovative in some way.

Summary of Chapter 19: Choosing the High Road (Power) or the Low Road (Force)

- The human body is a somatic warehouse of knowledge that can be accessed to reveal the level of truth contained within a statement.

- There are attractor fields that are embedded in the memes and that have associated emotional overlays, mental frameworks and somatic consequences.

- Actions can be either based on force, which is detrimental to life, or based on power, which is supportive of life. Power always wins over force.

- The questions of existence (problems) embedded within a meme are translated to our consciousness through the Intelligences and then become a source of internal tension.

- We can respond to tension through either collapsing into it and producing a force-based response or containing the tension and converting it through creativity into a noble quality that is power-based.

Principle #4:

Explore How You Can Hardwire Character and Wisdom into Your Personality

CHARACTER IS AN ACT OF COGNITION.
WISDOM IS THE RESULT OF A CHARACTER-FILLED LIFE.

Chapter 20

The NeuroPower Inventory of Human Character

Have you ever observed a situation and drawn an initial conclusion, only to think about what you saw a little more and then make a rather different assessment of the situation? At a neurobiological level that first spontaneous emotional response from the amygdala happens so fast that as the amygdala triggers its reactions which in turn triggers other brain areas, the cortical centres are still analysing the situation. The brain's emotional and cognitive centres confirm and fine-tune the amygdala's quick-fire reactions to add an emotional dimension to the perception which becomes our first impression, known as priming.

We also have the circuitry to change that first impression. The success of muting that first impression is directly linked to the level of activity in some prefrontal areas. The success of intentionally replacing that first impression is directly proportional to the level of involvement from the Anterior Cingulate Cortex (ACC).

The mental strategy we take in a reappraisal determines the prefrontal circuit the brain uses. For example, there is a circuit for reappraising through taking an objective, clinically detached approach, such as that used by health professionals when dealing with patients in trauma; there is another circuit for taking a 'hope for the best' and 'it could be worse' approach (Ochsner, 2004); if we verbalise our feelings we can also hush the amygdala (Hariri et al., 2000). By changing the meaning of what we perceive, we also alter its emotional impact (Ochsner, 2006). This hints to us the power of words and our narrative in managing our amygdala.

This highlights that we don't have to be a victim to our feelings, that our brains are wired to enable us to be able to choose the noble path.

Throughout history people who have adopted this approach have made the world a better place through noble action – some would say even saintly. In recent history, individuals like Mother Teresa, Winston Churchill, Diana Princess of Wales, Nelson Mandela and Fred Hollows are just a few of those who have touched the lives of millions of people with a power that is extra-ordinary. This power of human nobility is within reach of every human being. But if this is the case, why does it seem to manifest in so few?

The manifestation of human nobility is not a matter of chance. It takes containment, awareness, self-discipline and creativity to unify and transform the disparate elements of self into a coherent and powerful attractor field that can reorganise the very fabric of reality. This requires the hard thinking, emotional work and physical discipline that most of us try to avoid. (If we do successfully avoid this hard work, we become at best neurotic and at worst evil – destroying the lives of our closest and dearest friends and family.)

Every day we have the choice of using our internal conflict or tension to manifest either human nobility or pure selfishness. One path leads to life, the other to death. This chapter explores the path to life through the expression of human nobility and defines the central forty-eight noble qualities that are the birthright of each and every human being.[1] But if we are to chase nobility, we will need to first define exactly what it is. This has been undertaken at first and second order and at each of the memes.

REMEMBER FIRST-ORDER NOBILITY?

Table 20.1 summarises the noble qualities of first-order judgements. As we said in Principle #1, as children work through each phase of their psychological development, they begin the difficult process of integrating the *aspects* of thinking, feeling and somatic (physical) elements of each IC in the following order: P1, C1, P2, I2, I1 and C2. These single ICs are capable of presenting as personalities in their own right and, as such, are capable of first-order judgements (as defined by the philosopher David Chalmers) and first-order nobility.

Table 20.1 Noble Qualities of First-order Judgements

P1	**TRIBAL LOYALTY:** *Thinking* – Learned logic; *Feeling* – Calmness; *Somatic* – Associated with physical strength and compliance with established tribal rules.
C1	**SPONTANEITY:** *Thinking* – Lateral; *Feeling* – Childlike; *Somatic* – Body sensations and pleasure.
P2	**VITALITY:** *Thinking* – Focused on attaining end results; *Feeling* – Enthusiasm, *Somatic* – High energy.
I2	**EMPATHY:** *Thinking* – Understanding others; *Feeling* – Compassion; *Somatic* – Sensation of connection to others.
I1	**LOVE OF LEARNING:** *Thinking* – Pattern recognition and a focus on data; *Feeling* – Curiosity; *Somatic* – Withdrawal and objectification.
C2	**AWE:** *Thinking* – Creative Vision; *Feeling* – Appreciation; *Somatic* – Daydreaming, meditation or prayer.

---

1   Noble qualities in the Turquoise meme are not defined in this edition.

In Chalmers' description, first-order awareness responds to environmental stimuli and makes assessments that lead to immediate behaviour that is based on what the individual perceives will meet their immediate internal desires. This consciousness lacks a crucial sense of self-awareness. This predicates a tendency towards entrenched behavioural patterns that will repeat habitually with no potential for resolution because in consciousness terms, the individual is blind.

Many therapeutic modalities, counselling and psychiatric methodologies are designed to help guide the adult individual through the process of going back and redoing the work of aligning and reintegrating the three aspects of these ICs in a healthy and productive way.

With effective integration work, these ICs will manifest first-order noble qualities that support health and life. There are six of these: loyalty (from P1), spontaneity (from C1), vitality (from P2), empathy (from I2), love of learning (from I1) and awe (from C2). These have been summarised in Table 20.1.

SECOND-ORDER NOBILITY: THE PORTAL TO POWER

When three of these six ICs are unified, a more complex and complete second-order noble attractor field is formed. This is the manifestation of the highest possible human expression of nobility at each level of the spiral of consciousness or *meme*.

By accessing the profound insight of this second-order nobility the individual can resolve any problem, attain clarity of thought, have authentic and appropriate emotion and undertake right action.

The noble qualities manifested in this way are also the key to the individual's internal unification, understanding, growth and transformation. For the individual, the experience of manifesting a noble quality is extraordinary; and it has the ability to change what seems like an impossible situation into a clear path of action.

Chalmers suggests that second-order nobility of this nature incorporates all the inputs of the first-order nobility, but with the added capacity of the mind to exert influence over the brain. For him, this defines awareness and makes growth and change possible.

The principal difference between first-order noble qualities and second-order noble qualities revolves around this idea of conscious awareness. When experiencing the individual energies at the first order, there is little **conscious** application of the noble quality. At the second order, however, there is conscious and intentional use of the noble attractor.

Regardless of whether it is a first- or a second-order noble quality, in order to be considered noble it must have the following three characteristics.

1. **The noble quality must be able to resolve the individual's current questions of existence or internal tension**

(Questions are defined by the meme from which the problem manifests.) To be a noble quality it must calibrate slightly above the meme at which the problem is manifesting. This is what enables it to resolve the problems embedded in that meme. The noble quality energetically sits at a higher level than the meme containing the problems but below the next meme.

2. The noble quality must bring value to humanity

To be a noble quality it must be life affirming and lead to activity that improves the world and makes a positive difference to everyone with whom it comes in contact.

When the noble quality manifests in an individual's life, it must be evident in activity that makes a positive difference. It isn't just a 'nice feeling'. It must manifest constructive somatic expression – in behaviour that makes the world a better place. Nobility is not just what the individual says. It's what they DO that changes the world. Nobility must result in action that can be measured.

3. There is a yearning to act in accordance with the noble quality and when it is accessed the individual experiences a paradigm shift

In determining the positive expression of the noble qualities, we have embraced the Aristotelian notion of *eudaimonia*, which holds that a sense of wellbeing is not a consequence of virtuous action but an inherent aspect of it. That is to say, the benefits are part and parcel of the noble quality and are not a reward for its exercise. It is an exercise of the adage, 'Virtue is its own reward.'

When an individual accesses a noble quality they experience a paradigm shift. This is because, in the process of resolving the individual's current questions of existence or internal tension, the individual necessarily sees the world differently, and it is so different that it is like a Kuhnian paradigm shift[2] (Kuhn, 1962). That is, the individual can review anything and distinguish novelties of fact, theory or relationships, and draw fundamentally different conclusions. Simply, the individual sees new things when looking at old objects. The transition impacts the individual's methods and goals, and their world is qualitatively transformed and quantitatively enriched.

A second-order experience of noble qualities (*NeuroPower* describes them as noble attractors – short for noble attractor fields) has the same sense of intense concentration and absorption; but in addition to this, there is an awareness of self which is external to the actions.

---

2   The paradigm, in Kuhn's view, is not simply the current theory, but the entire worldview in which it exists, and all of the implications which come with it

Neural Scaffolding

Neural scaffolding is a term neuroscientists use to describe how reusing a neural pathway strengthens the connections, like builders strengthening scaffolding at a construction site. Habits can be hard to break because of neural scaffolding. But we can build and strengthen new neural pathways with effort and awareness (Goleman, 2006, p. 161).

The three conditions (the ability to answer the individual's current questions of existence, the ability to bring value to the community, and a paradigm shift) must be present for the quality to be considered a noble attractor. When researching each of the six first-order and the forty-eight second-order noble qualities we have evaluated them against these criteria and found they fit the requirements.

USING THE ROAD MAP

In Principle #1 we described the six first-order noble qualities and the contribution they make to nobility at the second order. In this section we catalogue and describe the second-order noble qualities that are associated with the tension between the Ps and Is at each of the memes.[3]

Conscious Nobility

A SUMMARY OF SECOND-ORDER NOBILITY

Table 19.2 summarises the second-order noble qualities. As the second-order noble qualities move through the memes they unify increasingly complex tension or problems. This is also a characteristic of all thinking as it moves up the memes – as outlined by Clare Graves and later by Cowan and Beck in their Spiral Dynamics framework.

You will recall when we covered memes earlier we started at Beige and Purple and worked our way up to Yellow, Turquoise and Coral, reflecting the order through which we develop throughout life. We will take the same approach in this chapter by examining all the eight noble qualities meme by meme.[4]

---

3   These are not supposed to be in-depth discussions of each noble quality. Instead, they provide readers with a clear definition of the noble qualities at each meme. The best way to learn about human nobility is to develop the ability to see it in action and then learn about it in real time. We could easily fill a book on each noble quality, its mental, emotional and somatic state, constructive behaviours and impact on others.

4   Beige is not described in this work because when the individual is in survival their Neuro-Limbic Type breaks in – so a Neuro-Rational Type doesn't exist at Beige.

Table 20.2 The Map of Human Nobility

Level	Crusader C2 (P2I1)	Bard C2 (P2I2)	Chancellor C1 (P2 I2)	Commander C1 (P1I2)	Architect C2 (P1I2)	Navigator C2 (P1I1)	Treasurer C1 (P1I1)	Judge C1 (P2I1)
1. Beige	Survival	Survival	Survival	Survival	Survival	Survival	Survival	Survival
2. Purple	Ethical	Modest	Charming	Reverent	Contemplative	Faithful	Self-Reliant	Loyal
3. Red	Justice Seeking	Confronting	Negotiating	Self-Controlled	Independent	Protecting	Disciplined	Enthusiastic
4. Blue	Integrity Seeking	Inspiring	Diplomatic	Courageous	Discerning	Responsible	Objective	Driven
5. Orange	Striving for Excellence	Visionary	Striving for Esprit de Corps	Ingenious	Capable	Seeking Role Excellence	Specialist	Entrepreneurial
6. Green	Magnanimous	Liberating	Kind	Enabling	Unifying	Principled	Mastering Systems	Motivational
7. Yellow	Benevolent	Empowering	Genuine	Harmonious	Strategic	Conquering	Expert	Enlivening

A RECAP ON THE PURPLE MEME

Those living in Purple find it a very uncertain and mysterious world. Life in Purple involves appeasing your God, gods or family. Individuals in this meme believe they have no underlying personal power.

Problems in Purple usually revolve around family or religious conflicts. Each of the Purple noble qualities provides a mechanism for the resolution of these conflicts.

The common theme of the Purple noble qualities is the role they play contextualising the ego of the individual. They remind us that our ability to control ourselves and our world is far less significant than our ego would have us believe. Therefore, in many situations the noble quality will attune us to a higher purpose rather than letting us continue to egocentrically think that we know how things should happen and then using our personality to try to force it to take place.

ETHICAL

ETHICAL – PURPLE MEME (CRUSADER)

Ethical: (adjective) Pertaining to or dealing with morals or the principles of morality.

Synonym: Moral.

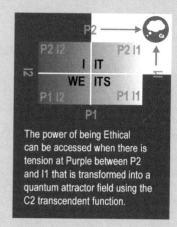

The Ethical attractor field enables the individual to embrace a set of Ethical underpinnings that provide a principled and consistent basis for decisions, rather than a prescriptive series of behavioural requirements based on rules.

This is an important attractor field for leading those in the Purple meme who cannot understand

The power of being Ethical can be accessed when there is tension at Purple between P2 and I1 that is transformed into a quantum attractor field using the C2 transcendent function.

the thinking behind justice, for example, but can understand the importance of clear values and the benefits of having defined punishment for individuals not abiding by these values.

BEING ETHICAL SATISFIES THE THREE CRITERIA OF NOBILITY

Ethics enable individuals to express their motivations to others in a clear and persuasive manner. They do this by drawing a link between their personal ethics and the ethical position of their God or Purple-meme worship figure, or the ethical position handed down to them from their family.

Being Ethical brings value to the community because the leader's clear Ethical position helps bring a sense of stability and certainty to the community.

WHAT YOU CAN EXPECT WILL HAPPEN IF YOU USE THIS ATTRACTOR FIELD

When the Ethical attractor field is manifested the individual will stand or sit with a straight back and will look very serious. They will often talk in the third person, for example, 'One must...' or 'This is the proper thing to do.' This comes from the ideological position of 'Do unto others as you would have them do unto you (according to your family, community or moral code).'

MODEST – PURPLE MEME (BARD)

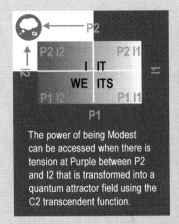

Modest: (adjective) Having or showing a moderate or humble estimate of one's merits, importance, etc; having and showing regard for the decencies of behaviour, speech, dress, etc; humble in spirit or manner; suggesting retiring mildness.

Synonyms: Humble, meek.

The power of being Modest can be accessed when there is tension at Purple between P2 and I2 that is transformed into a quantum attractor field using the C2 transcendent function.

The noble quality of being Modest fosters a profound awareness of the relative insignificance of the individual in the wider scheme of things. Modesty focuses the individual's attention on the significant aspects of life. This Modest understanding of their place in the universe gives the individual a non-egotistical self-identity

MODESTY SATISFIES THE THREE CRITERIA OF NOBILITY

Modesty contextualises the individual's existence and establishes their understanding of how they fit in the world. Modesty fosters an understanding of the greatness of the universe, and a capacity to not rely on material possessions.

Being Modest brings value to the community because it puts the everyday struggles of life into the context of the broader picture of time and space, and enables the community to appreciate the relative insignificance of their ego-based dramas. Without Modesty, the community becomes self-inflated with its own importance and its egocentric thrust for power.

WHAT YOU CAN EXPECT WILL HAPPEN IF YOU USE THIS ATTRACTOR FIELD

When the Modest attractor field is manifested the individual will appear quiet, unaggressive, and open. Modesty enables an almost complete removal of the ego and the vices associated with it. In our research we have also found a link between Modesty and an awakened awareness of the individual's good fortune or 'luckiness'. It is linked to appreciation and an awareness of God's grace. Modesty comes with a quiet and humble voice, and with an acceptance and appreciation of how things are, right here, right now.

CHARMING — PURPLE MEME (CHANCELLOR)

Charm: (verb) To attract powerfully through innate qualities.

Synonyms: Captivating, pleasing, delighting.

The Charming attractor field gives the individual the ability to engage another person in a way that permits the Charmer to be perceived as pleasant or desirable. Being Charming involves a person having an intuitive understanding of what others desire to feel, and then using this knowledge to position themselves as attractive.

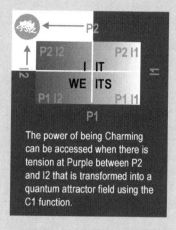

The power of being Charming can be accessed when there is tension at Purple between P2 and I2 that is transformed into a quantum attractor field using the C1 function.

CHARM SATISFIES THE THREE CRITERIA OF NOBILITY

Being Charming helps to ensure that the individual is desirable and welcome. This enables them to be accepted within their community. Without Charm the members of the community would gather together for mutual protection, but may not actually desire to spend personal time with one another.

The expression of being Charming requires that another party 'be charmed' and since it is built on an understanding of what the other party finds pleasurable, being Charming helps build connections within the community.

Our research findings consistently show that individuals in Purple like to be popular and that when P2-I2 problems in this meme are addressed using the Charming attractor field, the issue dissolves.

WHAT YOU CAN EXPECT WILL HAPPEN IF YOU USE THIS ATTRACTOR FIELD

When the Charming attractor field is manifested the individual will smile, look into the person's eyes, use humour to connect, lighten the situation, and make the person feel appreciated, respected and possibly even adored. The central component of Charm is that the person being Charmed feels important, attractive, interesting, funny and sexy. When 'Charming', the individual experiences a complete loss of a sense of self and instead focuses 100 per cent on engaging the other person.

REVERENT — PURPLE MEME (COMMANDER)

Revere: (verb) To regard with respect tinged with awe; to venerate.

Synonym: Worshipful.

For an individual in the Purple meme, Reverence fosters stillness and the ability to subsume their own needs so that they can acknowledge something bigger.

The power of being Reverent can be accessed when there is tension at Purple between P1 and I2 that is transformed into a quantum attractor field using the C1 function.

REVERENCE SATISFIES THE THREE CRITERIA OF NOBILITY

Being Reverent, usually through establishing a connection with nature, enables the individual to become aware of the power and beauty of something greater than themselves. As they become attuned to this noble quality, they develop a deep appreciation and love for the natural world. It is an appreciation for the balance, strength and synchronicity of nature.

With Reverence the individual develops a deep respect for the laws of nature and a desire for their community to align with these laws.

WHAT YOU CAN EXPECT WILL HAPPEN IF YOU USE THIS ATTRACTOR FIELD

When the Reverent attractor field is manifested the individual is struck by a sense of the beauty of the natural world and its laws, and a realisation of the importance of not interfering with the natural world just for the sake of an egocentric whim. Reverence usually leaves a person quiet and reflective and gives them access to a somatic appreciation of natural beauty. Reverence focuses on being rather than doing, accepting rather than enforcing, and on learning rather than teaching.

CONTEMPLATIVE – PURPLE MEME (ARCHITECT)

The power of being Contemplative can be accessed when there is tension at Purple between P1 and I2 that is transformed into a quantum attractor field using the C2 transcendent function.

Contemplative: (verb) To look at or view with continued attention; to observe thoughtfully; to have as a purpose, intend; to think studiously; to meditate; to consider deliberately; to be persistently thoughtful.

Synonyms: Meditative, pensive, reflective, ruminative.

The noble quality of Contemplation encourages the individual to devote considerable time to thinking about the issue at hand. Contemplation involves accessing imagination in a grounded and practical way to resolve the tension that is formed between the P1 and I2 positions.

BEING CONTEMPLATIVE SATISFIES THE THREE CRITERIA OF NOBILITY

Through Contemplation the individual develops a deeper spiritual understanding of life.

Being Contemplative brings value to the community because it ensures problems are put into perspective by identifying the *real* issues. These real underlying issues are usually the drivers beneath the presenting external issues. Contemplation enhances the spiritual nature of a community because it reduces knee-jerk limbic reactions.

WHAT YOU CAN EXPECT WILL HAPPEN IF YOU USE THIS ATTRACTOR FIELD

When the Contemplative attractor field is manifested the individual pulls back from the situation and allocates time to appreciate the wider situation and their authentic feelings about the situation. The Contemplative attractor field requires hours rather than minutes, to resolve the issue at hand. When applied it results in an evaluation of significance, an appreciation of past experience, and, finally, a path forward that is both practical and palatable for the key stakeholders involved.

FAITHFUL — PURPLE MEME (NAVIGATOR)

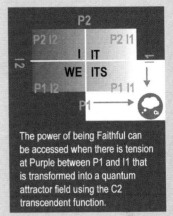

Faithful: (adjective) Strict or thorough in the performance of duty; that may be relied upon, trusted, or believed.

Synonyms: Dutiful.

The power of being Faithful can be accessed when there is tension at Purple between P1 and I1 that is transformed into a quantum attractor field using the C2 transcendent function.

The Faithful noble attractor gives the individual in the Purple meme a total and absolute confidence that the direction that they are taking is best. Their Faith can be, as George Galloway said, "... a power beyond himself whereby he seeks to satisfy emotional needs and gain stability in life" (cited in Houf, 1945). It can also be Faith in themselves, their own principles or beliefs, or their own talent and decision-making abilities.

An individual who evokes the Faithfulness noble attractor does not need to look back or question the correctness of the chosen path but instead adamantly follows what they believe to be true.

BEING FAITHFUL SATISFIES THE THREE CRITERIA OF NOBILITY

Having the inner conviction of Faith reduces the sense of uncertainty about the world. Faithful individuals learn how to transform P1-I1 doubt into faithful conviction.

Faith allows the community to join together with confidence that their plan is right and should be pursued. This creates a sense of certainty and stability. When leaders evoke this attractor field it settles down community members in times of crisis.

WHAT YOU CAN EXPECT WILL HAPPEN IF YOU USE THIS ATTRACTOR FIELD

When the Faithful attractor field is manifested the individual steps forward with absolute confidence. There is a significant difference between believing you are right and having Faith. It was once said that if there is a rope hanging between two sheer cliffs, if you have belief, you believe the rope could hold your weight; Faith, however, is stepping onto the rope. Physiologically, when someone uses this attractor field, they will look the other person in the eye, speak in absolute terms, and reiterate the thinking behind the original plan. Faith holds fast, even if the plan appears to be failing. There is a sense that, 'We're heading in the right direction. We may need to apply some tactics to deal with the issues that have emerged, but we are making progress and the central plan is absolutely right.'

SELF-RELIANT – PURPLE MEME (TREASURER)

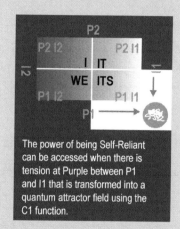

Self: (noun) A person or thing referred to with respect to individuality; one's own person.

Reliant: (adjective) Confident; trustful.

Synonym: Autonomous.

The power of being Self-Reliant can be accessed when there is tension at Purple between P1 and I1 that is transformed into a quantum attractor field using the C1 function.

Being Self-Reliant boosts the individual's ability to have the confidence to trust in their own abilities. It is about knowing they can rely on themselves to meet their own needs. When confronted with an overwhelming world, the Self-Reliant individual will withdraw into their own space and trust their own judgements. Self-Reliance involves having a confidence in their own abilities and in their own capacity to meet their own needs.

SELF-RELIANCE SATISFIES THE THREE CRITERIA OF NOBILITY

Self-Reliance reassures the individual that their own internal capacities are sufficient to deal with any situation that comes their way.

Self-Reliance brings the community a sense of optimism, and a confidence that problems can be resolved. Self-Reliance encourages people to accept and face life's problems with the knowledge that they really can be addressed.

WHAT YOU CAN EXPECT WILL HAPPEN IF YOU USE THIS ATTRACTOR FIELD

When the Self-Reliant attractor field is manifested the individual draws on their own experiences, insights, family traditions or spiritual awareness to solve the problem at hand. Self-Reliance involves looking from within rather than from outside or externally to find the solution. When this noble quality is evoked there are three distinct phases. In phase one the individual is withdrawn, remembering, recalling and accessing. In phase two the individual brings that wisdom to bear on the current situation. Finally, in phase three the individual applies the knowledge and approach with a sense of confidence.

LOYAL – PURPLE MEME (JUDGE)

> **Loyal:** (adjective) Firm, truehearted, unwavering in devotion to friend or vow or cause; being a firm ally; steadfast in allegiance or duty.
>
> **Synonym:** Truehearted.

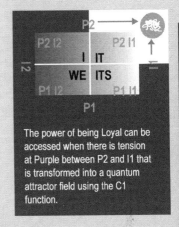

The power of being Loyal can be accessed when there is tension at Purple between P2 and I1 that is transformed into a quantum attractor field using the C1 function.

The Loyal noble attractor is expressed in both word and in deed. Loyalty involves a personal allegiance to another individual or to an organisation that overrides personal interest. The nobility of Loyalty is that self-interest is sacrificed for the sake of those to whom it is given.

BEING LOYAL SATISFIES THE CRITERIA OF NOBILITY

Being Loyal enables individuals to resolve some of the uncertainties of a mysterious Purple world in that in any situation they can quickly assess what they should do.

Loyalty builds commitment within the community. Without Loyalty, people 'move on' at the first sign of difficulty or disagreement.

WHAT YOU CAN EXPECT WILL HAPPEN IF YOU USE THIS ATTRACTOR FIELD

When the Loyal attractor field is manifested the individual recalls a commitment they have made to themselves about where their loyalty lies. Usually Loyalty is afforded to a person, but it can be linked with a role, an institution, a belief, a family or tribal group, an organisation, a political group or a vision. The noble quality of Loyalty disregards the popular view and relies instead on a personal commitment that has been made previously. Loyalty is consistent, unconditional and usually lifelong.

A RECAP ON THE RED MEME

Problems in this meme centre around self-expression, personal power or personal rights. It has an individual focus.

In Red, the common theme of all the noble qualities is that they help the individual express their individuality, their independence and their true needs and wants in a situation. These noble qualities either help the individual to do that, or enable the individual to help someone else do that, depending on where the problem lies. Red noble qualities help the individual to speak their truth with confidence and clarity.

JUSTICE SEEKING — RED MEME (CRUSADER)

Justice: (noun) The maintenance or administration of law, often involving fair punishment or reward, doing what is fair and just.

Synonyms: Fairness, even-handedness, impartiality.

The power of Seeking Justice can be accessed when there is tension at Red between P2 and I1 that is transformed into a quantum attractor field using the C2 transcendent function.

When the noble quality of Seeking Justice is manifested in the Red meme there is instant clarity about what makes a situation fair, and the just position to take when mediating between the individual and the group. The concept of Seeking Justice traditionally is divided into retributive justice and distributive justice. This noble quality deals with both issues. When a person aligns with the attractor field of Seeking Justice, they use their power to mediate justly, and to fairly apportion incentives and punishments to appropriate parties. This is a justice grounded in balancing the needs; for example, the needs of one with the needs of many, and the immediate needs with future needs.

SEEKING JUSTICE SATISFIES THE CRITERIA OF NOBILITY

The Justice Seeking noble attractor locates the locus of control within the individual and provides them with internal guidance on how to speak and behave.

The leader's drive for justice helps ensure equitable and fair decisions within the community. Colby, Kohlberg, Gibbs and Lieberman (1983) researched social moral development and found that only 20 per cent of the population develop an advanced perspective of justice and access this noble quality personally. The other 80 per cent of the population rely on the community leaders for this noble quality. Without a sense of justice in the community, decisions are made through corrupt and self-serving processes, which leads to anarchy, authoritarian rule or both.

WHAT YOU CAN EXPECT WILL HAPPEN IF YOU USE THIS ATTRACTOR FIELD

When the Justice Seeking attractor field is manifested the individual will identify where the power isn't and defend the rights of these underdogs while simultaneously emphasising the responsibilities of the perpetrator. When evoking this attractor field the user will have total clarity on what will set things right in a just and fair way.

CONFRONTING — RED MEME (BARD)

Confront: (verb) To stand or to meet facing.

Synonym: Facing up.

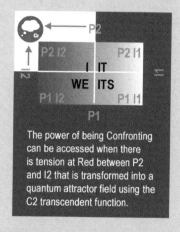

This noble attractor Confronts those aspects of the environment (in themselves or in others) that threaten freedom of expression. Being Confronting also enables the individual to face negative behaviours or attitudes. This noble attractor enables the individual to consciously face the dis-pleasurable elements of their lives and the lives of those around them, and simply state them 'warts and all'.

The power of being Confronting can be accessed when there is tension at Red between P2 and I2 that is transformed into a quantum attractor field using the C2 transcendent function.

Only once a situation has been accurately Confronted (articulated) is it possible to address it. Confrontation is the CAT scan that identifies the cancerous attitudes and beliefs that take over if not kept in check.

BEING CONFRONTING SATISFIES THE CRITERIA OF NOBILITY

Being Confrontational enables the individual to freely express themselves and to create an environment where others can also freely express themselves. Developing the capacity to articulate their opinions reduces the individual's inclination to play politics and manipulate others in order to be heard.

In creating an environment in which people are able to freely express themselves, this noble attractor creates a forum of honesty that is necessary within any community.

WHAT YOU CAN EXPECT WILL HAPPEN IF YOU USE THIS ATTRACTOR FIELD

The Confronting noble attractor is manifested from a position of unconditional love. This means that when being Confronting, the individual simultaneously connects with the person, maintains eye contact, may express their love through hugging or touching and maintains a safe environment, while simultaneously speaking with absolute clarity about the issues at hand. The person receiving the information feels both supported and put on notice.

NEGOTIATING – RED MEME (CHANCELLOR)

Negotiate: (verb) To arrange for or bring about by discussion and settlement of terms; to deal; to clear or pass (an obstacle); to get around an obstacle; to do bargaining and wheeling and dealing; to mediate between two disagreeing parties.

Synonyms: Bargaining, conferring, parleying, settling.

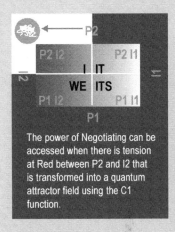

The power of Negotiating can be accessed when there is tension at Red between P2 and I2 that is transformed into a quantum attractor field using the C1 function.

Since the Red meme focuses on the expression of individual power which is in conflict with established (tribal) positions, this noble attractor gives the individual the ability to negotiate their rights in a unifying and positive way.

BEING NEGOTIATING SATISFIES THE CRITERIA OF NOBILITY

Negotiating answers Red's question of existence regarding self-expression and personal power because to effectively negotiate and find common ground between two positions requires the individual to express their own position clearly. The noble quality of Negotiation enables the individual to build bridges between two otherwise opposing positions.

Negotiation finds and builds on the points of commonality between two separate positions within the community. This noble quality enables successful resolutions to otherwise intractable disagreements. It enables bargaining to be built on points of similarity rather than points of difference, which increases understanding and collaborative interaction.

WHAT YOU CAN EXPECT WILL HAPPEN IF YOU USE THIS ATTRACTOR FIELD

When evoking this noble quality the individual will experience immediate clarity between 'must haves' and 'like to haves' in the negotiation. In other words, the aspects that are non-negotiable become immediately apparent. This self-awareness makes resolution possible because there can be compromise on other 'like to have' aspects. This noble quality fosters clarity within the individual before the negotiation takes place. It also provides the energy the individual needs to put in the effort to keep the Negotiation going until an outcome is reached that is acceptable to both parties.

SELF-CONTROLLED – RED MEME (COMMANDER)

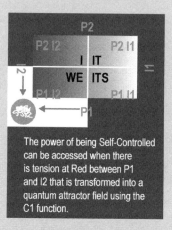

The power of being Self-Controlled can be accessed when there is tension at Red between P1 and I2 that is transformed into a quantum attractor field using the C1 function.

Self: (noun) A person or thing referred to with respect to individuality; one's own person.

Control: (verb) To exercise restraint or direction over; to command; to act with the power of controlling; to act with regulation; to act with restraint.

The nobility of Self-Control enables the individual to focus on self-expression through physical, mental and emotional control. This noble attractor is a central plank in all martial arts.

BEING SELF-CONTROLLED SATISFIES THE CRITERIA OF NOBILITY

Being Self-Controlled answers Red's question of existence regarding self-expression and personal power because it enables the individual to learn how to express their physical, emotional and mental energy by controlling their focus of attention. Through focusing all their physical, mental and emotional energy on the issue or problem at hand, the individual develops the ability to hold the internal tension and the resulting discomfort before unifying it through 'playing with the options'.

Self-Control allows the individual to effectively resolve problems and tensions within the community without becoming part of the problem or emotionally collapsing into one of the polarities of the issue. The individual's Self-Control ensures that emotional conflict within the community does not escalate but is maintained at a manageable level.

WHAT YOU CAN EXPECT WILL HAPPEN IF YOU USE THIS ATTRACTOR FIELD

When evoking the noble quality of Self-Control you can expect the individual to hold their needs and wants in a balance until the issue at hand can be resolved using C1. This noble quality fortifies the individual against physical pain, emotional pain, hunger, anger and anxiety. When an individual is using this noble quality you often see an inscrutable or blank look on their face and an unmoving body.

INDEPENDENT — RED MEME (ARCHITECT)

Independent:(adjective) Not influenced by others; not subject to another's authority or jurisdiction; autonomous; free; not dependent; not dependent or contingent on something or someone else for existence, operation, etc; not affiliated with another party.

Synonyms: Autonomous.

The power of being Independent can be accessed when there is tension at Red between P1 and I2 that is transformed into a quantum attractor field using the C2 transcendent function.

Independence gives the individual the capacity to arrive at conclusions not conditioned by collective opinions or traditional wisdom. In the Red meme, this noble quality enables the individual to express an independent point of view even if nobody else agrees with them and it is unpopular.

BEING INDEPENDENT SATISFIES THE CRITERIA OF NOBILITY

Independence answers Red's question of existence regarding self-expression and personal power because it enables the individual to arrive at their own autonomous opinion. The individual learns how to think and act in a manner that is independent of the majority and of peer group pressure. Without Independence, the individual loses touch with their own emotional, intellectual and physical needs and wants. Independence enables the individual to see, think, feel and act in a way that reflects their own, sometimes unique, point of view.

Manifesting Independence is also constructive for the wider community because it role-models for all community members what Independent thought looks and sounds like. It gives others the confidence to express their views and prevents 'groupthink', cults and tunnel vision.

WHAT YOU CAN EXPECT WILL HAPPEN IF YOU USE THIS ATTRACTOR FIELD

When evoking the noble quality of Independence the individual is polite yet very clear about their own insight, experience, knowledge, interpretation of events, view of the situation and proposed action. It is a cool rather than a hot emotion and there is a sense that they have cut themselves off from the rest of the group. It is not that they aggressively disagree with others' points of view but rather that they coolly articulate their own views even if nobody else agrees with them.

PROTECTING — RED MEME (NAVIGATOR)

Protect: (verb) To defend or guard from attack, invasion, annoyance, insult, etc.

Synonym: Defending.

Protecting enables the individual to take action to help ensure that harm does not come to those unable to look after themselves. This noble quality is a reflection of the paternal archetype. The noble quality provides the focus and energy needed to defend whoever needs protecting, be it children, the sick, the elderly, the values of an institution, or those who are disadvantaged or in need.

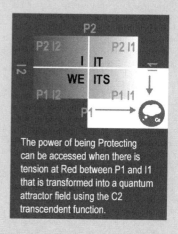

The power of being Protecting can be accessed when there is tension at Red between P1 and I1 that is transformed into a quantum attractor field using the C2 transcendent function.

BEING PROTECTING SATISFIES THE CRITERIA OF NOBILITY

Berkowitz and Lutterman (1968) defined Protecting as a social responsibility and found that it was a discernible noble trait that was admired within the general population.

By taking action to protect those weaker than themselves, those using this noble quality enable members of a community to feel safe and to experience a sense of permanence and support that reduces fear and increases Red self-expression.

WHAT YOU CAN EXPECT WILL HAPPEN IF YOU USE THIS ATTRACTOR FIELD

When evoking the noble quality of Protecting, the individual will physically and verbally stand between the threat and the person they are protecting. This can mean speaking louder than the threat, standing over the person they are protecting, physically removing the individual from the threat, or anticipating future problems and taking mitigating actions. The noble quality enables its user to be clear, absolute, unyielding and strong.

DISCIPLINED — RED MEME (TREASURER)

Discipline: (noun, verb) Training to act in accordance with rules; drill; punishment inflicted by way of correction and training; the training effect of experience, adversity, etc; a branch of instruction or learning; to bring to a state of order and obedience by training and control.

Synonym: Penalised

The power of being Disciplined can be accessed when there is tension at Red between P1 and I1 that is transformed into a quantum attractor field using the C1 function.

For the individual in the Red meme, the noble quality of being Disciplined gives them the capacity to mediate personal emotions and desires, and train or drill themselves to act in a particular way. It fosters both calmness and detachment. Discipline allows the individual to handle whatever circumstances they might find themselves in and take appropriate and rational action.

BEING DISCIPLINED SATISFIES THE CRITERIA OF NOBILITY

This noble quality enables the individual to express themselves very precisely. Establishing personal boundaries about behaviour and attitudes is the Disciplined individual's method of ring-fencing conflict; this in turn, almost surprisingly, gives everyone the personal freedom to express themselves.

Discipline enables the individual to maintain their personal resources (emotional, financial and physical) so that they do not waste or squander them. Discipline keeps panic down in times of crisis or stress. Discipline also enables the community to build a reservoir of resources (food, water, personnel) that are available in trying times.

WHAT YOU CAN EXPECT WILL HAPPEN IF YOU USE THIS ATTRACTOR FIELD

When evoking this noble quality the individual will immediately start assessing, 'To what am I disciplining myself?' The answer could be a set of values, an agreement, the terms of a relationship, a contract made to themselves, a sports or martial arts code, a profession or a set of beliefs. Issues requiring the noble quality of Discipline involve a tension between the P1 moral code and the I1 reality of what is actually happening. Discipline will unify these polarities by reconciling the behaviour with the code in a creative new way.

ENTHUSIASTIC — RED MEME (JUDGE)

Enthusiasm: (noun) Absorbing or controlling possession of the mind by any interest or pursuit; lively interest.

Synonyms: Eager, passionate, zealous, spirited.

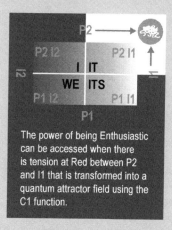

When the noble quality of Enthusiasm is engaged, the individual focuses their passion and energy on a person or project. This Enthusiasm will involve the individual in making enormous personal efforts in an endeavour about which they are particularly keen. In expressing Enthusiasm, the individual takes their personal passion and uses it to dynamise a new idea or concept.

The power of being Enthusiastic can be accessed when there is tension at Red between P2 and I1 that is transformed into a quantum attractor field using the C1 function.

ENTHUSIASM SATISFIES THE CRITERIA OF NOBILITY

Being Enthusiastic answers Red's question of existence regarding self-expression and personal power because the noble quality allows the individual to express their true feelings about an individual or circumstances.

Enthusiasm builds the energy level within the community and increases the community's capacity to act. Without Enthusiasm, there is no energy or interest to take new ideas or opportunities and bring them to life.

WHAT YOU CAN EXPECT WILL HAPPEN IF YOU USE THIS ATTRACTOR FIELD

When evoking the noble quality of Enthusiasm you can expect to experience enormous amounts of energy, a complete lack of self-control, emotional outbursts, and an almost childlike embracing of possibilities, opportunities and people. This Enthusiasm can take a tiny hint of an idea and blow it into a revolutionary breakthrough. In this context, enthusiastic behaviour can involve tears, laughter, passion, high physical energy, frantic physical activity and displays of extraordinary stamina.

A RECAP ON THE BLUE MEME

In Blue the questions of existence focus on sublimating personal drivers for a higher purpose.

All the Blue noble qualities enable the problem to be resolved in a way that aligns the subsequent perceptions and behaviours with a higher cause. This means that ultimately an alliance forms between the individual's ego and the cause.

INTEGRITY SEEKING – BLUE MEME (CRUSADER)

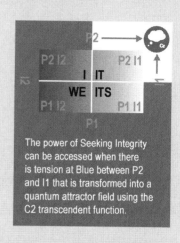

Integrity: (noun) Soundness of moral principle and character; uprightness; honesty.

Synonym: honour, uprightness

When the noble quality of Seeking Integrity manifests, the individual does what they say they will do. Integrity comes from the Latin integritas, meaning wholeness, soundness, untouched, whole and entire. It involves:

The power of Seeking Integrity can be accessed when there is tension at Blue between P2 and I1 that is transformed into a quantum attractor field using the C2 transcendent function.

1. A regular pattern of behaviour that is consistent with espoused values

2. Public justification of moral convictions, even if those convictions are not popular. That is, doing what they say they will in terms of their convictions.

Integrity fosters alignment between what the individual says and what they do – even when it may be personally beneficial for them to change their position.

SEEKING INTEGRITY SATISFIES THE CRITERIA OF NOBILITY

Seeking Integrity answers Blue's questions by focusing on sublimating personal drivers for a higher purpose. Integrity also provides the individual with the energy to search for a cause that aligns with their own world view and values.

The individual's Integrity enables others to trust and have confidence in their word. The same trust and confidence can be extended to whatever institution or cause with which the individual is aligned. Integrity helps strengthen community bonds and establishes the basis for community members to commit to a common purpose. Integrity gives the individual the energy to challenge group norms and demand community honesty.

WHAT YOU CAN EXPECT WILL HAPPEN IF YOU USE THIS ATTRACTOR FIELD

When evoking the noble quality of Integrity the individual will keep true to their promises and do what they said they would do regardless of whether or not it is convenient or if there is a better offer on the table. It resolves the tension between P2 and I1 by recalling what was said or promised, and focusing the individual on delivering on these promises (rather than seeking new opportunities, changing the position or altering the plan). Integrity helps the individual to be honest with themselves and 'come good' on what they have promised. Integrity is hardest when a new option would provide better outcomes or more personal reward. At these times this noble attractor reminds the individual that the short-term pain leads to long-term gain because Integrity leads to trust. In this case the trust includes trust from others and from within the individual themselves.

INSPIRING — BLUE MEME (BARD)

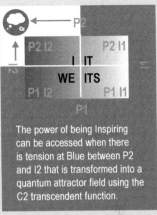

Inspire: (verb) To infuse an animating, quickening or exalting influence; to produce or arouse (a feeling or thought etc); to give rise to, occasion or cause.

Synonym: motivating, uplifting

The power of being Inspiring can be accessed when there is tension at Blue between P2 and I2 that is transformed into a quantum attractor field using the C2 transcendent function.

The Inspiring individual in the Blue meme will seek to create an environment that helps to achieve the greater purpose with which they are aligned. This noble attractor enables the individual to elevate and encourage others by reigniting their sense of personal meaning. It creates an environment where people feel hope for, and start moving towards, a better future. Being Inspirational fosters a fit between the group's higher purpose, and the role and purpose of the individual.

People often confuse inspiration and vision. Vision is where the individual paints a picture of the future. Inspiration enables the individual to combine the vision of each community member with the single wider vision of the community. Often the wider vision may need to be broadened if this is to be achieved. Inspiration enables people to achieve the wider vision for their own personal reasons.

BEING INSPIRING SATISFIES THE CRITERIA OF NOBILITY

Being Inspiring answers Blue's questions because, before the individual can link other people's sense of purpose with a greater cause, they must first find the connection between themselves and the 'higher purpose' with which they are aligned.

Inspiration reignites a sense of meaning in an individual or community. This brings about renewed commitment and a greater sense of purpose and passion. Without Inspiration people perform their roles without conviction. They merely go through the motions often with begrudging compliance rather than actively engaging with the work they are doing.

WHAT YOU CAN EXPECT WILL HAPPEN IF YOU USE THIS ATTRACTOR FIELD

When an individual manifests Inspiration they will be as interested in the vision of the person they are inspiring as the vision they are promoting. The Inspiring noble quality enables the individual to adapt their original vision so that it encompasses the vision of the person they are inspiring. Inspiration gives the individual the ability to connect at a heart level and then piggyback the shared vision on this relational foundation. It fosters commitment from the heart.

DIPLOMATIC — BLUE MEME (CHANCELLOR)

Diplomacy: (noun) The conduct of negotiations and other relations between parties; skill in managing any negotiations; artful management.

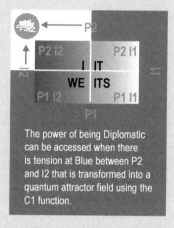

Synonym: discretion, negotiation

The noble quality of Diplomacy in the Blue meme involves bringing two conflicting parties or positions together. It involves a capacity to both understand and appreciate the positions of both parties, and an ability to find common ground.

The power of being Diplomatic can be accessed when there is tension at Blue between P2 and I2 that is transformed into a quantum attractor field using the C1 function.

This represents a more complex version of the Red meme noble quality of Negotiating because it focuses on both values and the outcome rather than just the outcome. Diplomacy can be applied to bring any two parties or groups closer.

BEING DIPLOMATIC SATISFIES THE CRITERIA OF NOBILITY

To be Diplomatic, the individual must sublimate their own immediate feelings in order to achieve a values-based outcome. Every Diplomatic interaction provides the individual with the opportunity to renegotiate not just for a win-win but also for an outcome that aligns with their values.

The capacity this noble attractor gives to blur the edges of a dispute and to find a creative way around otherwise intractable differences represents a quality of great importance to humanity, particularly in arresting war within the community or war with other communities. The capacity to find values-based solutions and build common ground between opposing parties means that daily conflicts can be transformed into agreements that support the community's values.

WHAT YOU CAN EXPECT WILL HAPPEN IF YOU USE THIS ATTRACTOR FIELD

When evoking the noble quality of Diplomacy the individual connects at a heart level first and then is able to quickly adapt their message in a way that maintains the core content but frames it somatically, cognitively and emotionally in a way that is aligned with the world view of the person with whom they are communicating. Using this noble quality enables the person to automatically mirror body language and select the somantic nuances that align with relevant attitudes and preferences. The Diplomatic noble attractor enables the individual to take an unpalatable message and frame it in such a way that the truth is conveyed while the sensibilities of the other are respected.

COURAGEOUS – BLUE MEME (COMMANDER)

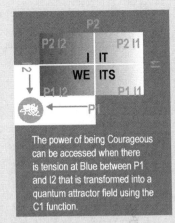

Courage: (noun) Bravery, valour, daring.

Courageous: (adjective) Having or characterised by courage; valiant, intrepid.

Synonyms: Brave, fearless.

Courage enables the individual to be true to themselves regardless of opposition from other people or internal resistance. Courage enables the individual to say and do what is required in order to solve the presenting problem.

The power of being Courageous can be accessed when there is tension at Blue between P1 and I2 that is transformed into a quantum attractor field using the C1 function.

BEING COURAGEOUS SATISFIES THE CRITERIA OF NOBILITY

Courageously expressing their convictions in the face of internal or external opposition enables the individual to live according to a higher purpose rather than being a slave to their own emotional vagaries. In Courageously taking action that may not be popular but is right, they develop the ability to sublimate their drives for a worthy cause.

Courage is valuable for the wider community because it ensures that issues are raised and dealt with and the red tape of bureaucracy is reduced. The Courageous noble attractor is required for all emergency services within the community.

WHAT YOU CAN EXPECT WILL HAPPEN IF YOU USE THIS ATTRACTOR FIELD

When evoking the noble quality of Courage the individual uses action rather than words. It has been said that you don't need to be a hero for life, but just for the fifteen seconds that matter the most. Courage creates heroes because it focuses and empowers the individual for fifteen seconds of somatic action rather than hours of cognitive rationalisation. The noble quality of Courage will enable people to say what they think or feel, and behave with a combination of spontaneity, emotional intelligence and tribal loyalty. Courage calls the individual to be who they are, warts and all, rather than shape shifting, over-intellectualising or deflecting. When Courage is the noble attractor the individual knows what they need to do; they know they need to get on with it and 'Just do it.'

DISCERNING – BLUE MEME (ARCHITECT)

Discern: (verb) To perceive by sight or some other sense or by the intellect; see, recognise or apprehend.

Discernment: (noun) Faculty of discerning; discrimination.

Synonym: Distinguishing.

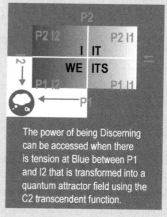

The power of being Discerning can be accessed when there is tension at Blue between P1 and I2 that is transformed into a quantum attractor field using the C2 transcendent function.

The noble quality of Discernment brings with it the ability to ensure alignment between people, processes and purpose. In the Blue meme Discernment involves assessing whether the group's expenditure of resources is moving them towards the achievement of their higher purpose. Discernment enables the individual to discover any source of misalignment between purpose and practice and to locate the cause of that misalignment.

DISCERNMENT SATISFIES THE CRITERIA OF NOBILITY

Discernment enables the individual to accurately identify a cause with which they naturally resonate. All behaviour that is not aligned with the cause is identified and able to be realigned.

Discernment brings into stark relief misalignment within the community. This occurs when people or organisations say one thing but end up doing another. If acted on, Discernment saves both resources and energy. Discernment enables the community's vision to be aligned with their processes, structure and capabilities.

WHAT YOU CAN EXPECT WILL HAPPEN IF YOU USE THIS ATTRACTOR FIELD

When evoking the noble quality of Discernment the individual gains clarity about the key elements of the jigsaw that do not line up. Somatically it lets the individual feel if something is not right. The feeling is difficult to put into words but there is a 'knowing' that something is not aligned. It could be that people are saying they are someone they are not or claiming to achieve something they haven't, that the action is not aligning with the corporate vision, that someone else's assessment does not line up with what they said, or that some new philosophy or approach does not line up with the body of knowledge they trust. Somebody experiencing Discernment will tend to be quiet and hesitant, will find it difficult to put their knowledge into words, and will experience physical discomfort and uncertainty until they have expressed the insight the Discernment has brought.

RESPONSIBLE – BLUE MEME (NAVIGATOR)

Responsible: ((adjective) Answerable or accountable for something within one's power, control or management; able to discharge obligations or pay debt; ability to meet debts or payments.

Synonyms: Accountable, answerable.

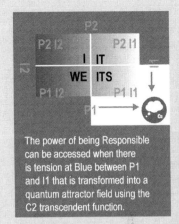

The Responsible noble attractor enables the individual to have the authority to execute their role. Once this is clear, this noble attractor provides the energy to ensure they do all that is humanly possible to achieve this.

The power of being Responsible can be accessed when there is tension at Blue between P1 and I1 that is transformed into a quantum attractor field using the C2 transcendent function.

RESPONSIBILITY SATISFIES THE CRITERIA OF NOBILITY

Modelling Responsibility within the community ensures that others will take the actions that are necessary for them to fulfil their respective roles. With too much authority but no responsibility, decisions become capricious and irresponsible. With too much responsibility and no authority, many community leaders experience burnout.

WHAT YOU CAN EXPECT WILL HAPPEN IF YOU USE THIS ATTRACTOR FIELD

When evoking the noble quality of being Responsible the individual first of all focuses on the responsibilities of their role. This is often an exploration of how team members each have their own responsibilities which they must fulfil if the wider group is to achieve its objective. Once this is clear this noble attractor enables the person to embrace wholeheartedly the action needed to fulfil the requirements of the role regardless of personal discomfort, the amount of work, personal preferences or even their capability.

RESPONSIBLE

OBJECTIVE

OBJECTIVE – BLUE MEME (TREASURER)

Objective: (adjective) Free from personal feelings or prejudice.

Synonym: Unbiased.

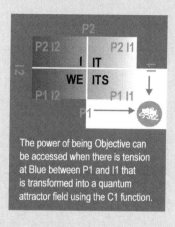

The power of being Objective can be accessed when there is tension at Blue between P1 and I1 that is transformed into a quantum attractor field using the C1 function.

The Objective noble attractor enables the individual to withdraw and make a careful assessment of the effectiveness of the current approach. This is a vital noble quality to access when questioning and researching to find the I1 reality of a situation. It fosters a willingness to consider input from all sources of information without arriving at a hasty conclusion.

Objectivity has two key aspects. First, it gives the individual the sense of being removed from expectations, assumptions or preconceived ideas; and second, it ensures the individual is not egotistically linked to any specific outcome, ideas or processes. The noble quality of Objectivity allows the individual to maintain their commitment to the higher purpose of the Blue meme, while objectively considering information, perspectives or approaches that may not completely align with that purpose.

OBJECTIVITY SATISFIES THE CRITERIA OF NOBILITY

Objectivity allows individuals to take a reserved and balanced view of situations and potential scenarios without preconceived ideas dominating their perspective.

Unbiased assessment creates an environment within the community where all points of view are respected and heard. It allows issues to be discussed and all sides to have their opinions voiced.

WHAT YOU CAN EXPECT WILL HAPPEN IF YOU USE THIS ATTRACTOR FIELD

When evoking the noble quality of Objectivity the individual feels a sense of intellectual, emotional and somatic detachment from the issue at hand. In this space the problem or issue almost becomes an object with shape, texture and colour that can be objectively analysed like a poem, rock or shoe. Objectivity enables the person to look at the problem from many different angles, from the past and future, above and below, from the positions of different stakeholders, from a wider context where it is compared to other problems, or a narrower context where it is broken down into its constituent parts. The noble quality of Objectivity tends to focus the individual on thinking and analysis. It fosters curiosity and interrogation of data. When an individual evokes this noble quality they are very interested in how the problem looks, the exact words people have used to describe it, the way people are emotionally reacting to it, and what the logical consequence will be of any particular intervention. Objectivity creates the space that is sometimes needed to let the truth emerge.

DRIVEN — BLUE MEME (JUDGE)

Drive: (verb) To push, propel or press onward forcibly; urge forward; to repulse or put to flight by force or influence; to create or produce by penetrating forcibly; to carry through vigorously to a conclusion.

Synonym: ambitious, guided, motivated

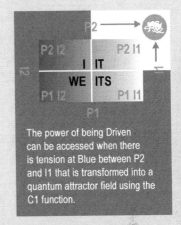

The power of being Driven can be accessed when there is tension at Blue between P2 and I1 that is transformed into a quantum attractor field using the C1 function.

The Driven noble attractor enables the individual to take all action possible to attain a desired result. In the Blue meme it gives the individual both a capacity to expend more effort than other people, and a desire to review and assess the results of the past actions in order to improve them. The noble quality of Drive is what enables the individual to pursue their objectives with sustained intensity.

DRIVE SATISFIES THE CRITERIA OF NOBILITY

Being Driven towards a higher goal channels the individual's energetic impulses towards a higher and more meaningful purpose.

The capacity to engage in focused action in order to bring a task to completion ensures that the community's goals are Driven to fruition. Drive fosters an environment in which large workloads are embraced. Without Drive, the community stagnates and does not have the capacity to move beyond its current level of development; that is, it lacks the Drive to bring opportunities to reality.

WHAT YOU CAN EXPECT WILL HAPPEN IF YOU USE THIS ATTRACTOR FIELD

When evoking the noble quality of being Driven the individual has a sense that their energy is not their own but is coming from a higher order or manifesto that is worthy of their life's commitment. This noble quality drives the individual to the very edge of their intellectual, physical and emotional capacity to achieve the Blue meme objectives that they have set themselves. This energy is the stuff of legends. Christopher Columbus, Nelson Mandela and Richard Branson have used Drive to fundamentally change our modern world, and the energy this noble quality gives can directly impact the lives of thousands and possibly millions of people. Drive asks the question 'What do you want me to achieve and how can I get started immediately?' Usually it is an emotional and somatic expression, does not take 'no' for an answer and breaks through any barrier to achieve its Blue meme objectives.

A RECAP ON THE ORANGE MEME

In the Orange meme the questions of existence focus on how to succeed personally, and how to achieve personal objectives.

The noble qualities in Orange are eight different ways of turning lemons into lemonade. These are eight different noble attractors that enable the achievement of success, however that is defined, be that money, popularity, breakthrough thinking, world peace, or any other personal goal.

EXCELLENCE SEEKING – ORANGE MEME (CRUSADER)

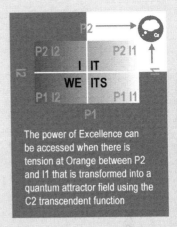

> **Excellence:** (noun) The state of excelling, achieving high quality or superiority.
>
> *Synonym:* Quality seeking.

The power of Excellence can be accessed when there is tension at Orange between P2 and I1 that is transformed into a quantum attractor field using the C2 transcendent function

The Excellence Seeking noble attractor enables the individual to set and maintain high personal standards. Without the C2 conversion of the P2-I1 tension the individual can become critical and project the frustration of their own mediocrity onto those closest to them and then curse them for it. This can be a crisis for leaders because without this inside-out approach others will fail to commit to them. This is a strong attractor field and sets the individual apart as a strong and important leader in any organisation or community.

SEEKING EXCELLENCE SATISFIES THE CRITERIA OF NOBILITY

Seeking Excellence enables the individual to succeed personally because high standards attract premium prices.

Within the community the internal standard of Excellence establishes a high benchmark and enables the community to want to strive for Excellence in all they undertake. This Excellence helps ensure that high-quality community projects are sponsored by the people which in turn leads to an improved standard of living for all community members.

WHAT YOU CAN EXPECT WILL HAPPEN IF YOU USE THIS ATTRACTOR FIELD

When evoking the noble quality of Seeking Excellence the individual automatically searches for the best of breed, and sets this as a base requirement for achievement. There is a fundamental difference between excellence and perfection. Excellence is a focus on achieving a standard that is as high as or higher than the best in its class, whereas perfection strives for something which is perfect or ideal, and is often an unachievable pursuit. Once a high standard has been set, the Excellence attractor will focus on ever-increasing incremental improvements. Every time a task is completed Excellence would like it to be a slight improvement from the time before. When this noble quality is evoked the individual automatically finds the market leader or thought leader in the particular field or endeavour, identifies the difference between that and their own performance (the delta) and starts looking at ways to close that gap. This noble quality is passionate, unwilling to accept 'near enough is good enough' and is completely satisfied to keep doing the same task again and again until it is at the required standard of excellence. It is about quality not quantity.

VISIONARY — ORANGE MEME (BARD)

Visionary: (adjective) Given to or characterised by radical, novel, revolutionary or futuristic views or schemes.

Synonym: dreamy, idealised

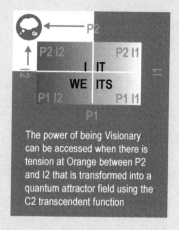

The noble quality of being Visionary allows the individual to see above and beyond the presenting problems to create audacious, future-centred solutions. It involves conveying these solutions to everyone involved, in a manner that captures and inspires them. Being Visionary means that the individual's response to adversity is not constrained by the circumstances of the situation. This noble quality allows the individual to find radical, future-centred solutions to seemingly impossible commercial problems.

The power of being Visionary can be accessed when there is tension at Orange between P2 and I2 that is transformed into a quantum attractor field using the C2 transcendent function

BEING VISIONARY SATISFIES THE CRITERIA OF NOBILITY

The Visionary noble attractor enables the individual to achieve personal success by connecting teams with a clearly articulated picture of a better future world.

Creating a unique future-centred vision that supersedes current intractable problems gives the community hope for the future.

WHAT YOU CAN EXPECT WILL HAPPEN IF YOU USE THIS ATTRACTOR FIELD

When evoking the noble quality of being Visionary the individual creates a second-order leap which is so brand new and different from the current situation that it demonstrates that many of the problems and issues of the current situation will very soon be irrelevant. Rather than an incremental movement from the current position, this noble attractor enables the individual to conceive whole new realities and then condense these vague, esoteric and somewhat formless concepts into images that feel real and more than possible. This is achieved through vision, purpose and a connection with the individual. When an individual evokes this noble quality their energy will rise, and their ideas will be stated as if they exist in the current situation. This is done with such clarity and enthusiasm that sometimes these visions appear more real than actual life at the time. The Visionary noble attractor is high energy, abstract, future-centred, enthusiastic and heart felt. It embraces and lifts up all who connect with it.

ESPRIT DE CORPS – ORANGE MEME (CHANCELLOR)

> **Esprit de corps:** (noun) A high level of collegial team spirit.
>
> *Synonym:* Team spirit.

The power of Esprit de Corps can be accessed when there is tension at Orange between P2 and I2 that is transformed into a quantum attractor field using the C1 function.

The Esprit de Corps noble attractor enables the individual to build bridges of understanding between divergent parties so that the team's performance is enhanced. A strong sense of team spirit (Esprit de Corps) involves having all members of a team feeling that their perspectives are being heard and understood. It is an attitude of 'All for one and one for all!'

ESPRIT DE CORPS SATISFIES THE CRITERIA OF NOBILITY

Research (Fisher, 1988) has found that 80 per cent of career failure for executives occurs because they are not able to develop an effectively functioning team. The Esprit de Corps attractor enables executives to attain personal success by being one of the exceptional 20 per cent who can build effectively functioning teams that can exceed their performance KPIs.

Creating synergistic teams in which the contribution of one member enhances the work of other members is also highly beneficial for the community. An effective team produces far greater results than the sum of the individuals working on their own (Goleman, 1998). This noble attractor enables the community to achieve greater results faster. Workplaces that are imbued with a sense of Esprit de Corps are highly effective and enjoyable working environments. Without it, the work environment descends into a highly competitive environment.

WHAT YOU CAN EXPECT WILL HAPPEN IF YOU USE THIS ATTRACTOR FIELD

When evoking the noble quality of creating Esprit de Corps the individual immediately evaluates the skills of their immediate team and wider networks and decides how everybody can use their skills to achieve a wider team vision or purpose. But Esprit de Corps is not all inclusive. When the noble quality is evoked it confirms the team's purpose and then selects the members who can contribute the most. Esprit de Corps is achieved in the team because each team member knows that they are highly valued and provide a critical ingredient to the team's success. When it is evoked this noble quality creates a passion within the individual to find the right people to achieve the right tasks, to build bridges between them, and finally to have them all adopt the same vision, mission and values.

ESPRIT DE CORPS

INGENIOUS — ORANGE MEME (COMMANDER)

Ingenious: (adjective) Showing cleverness of invention or construction; having inventive faculty; skilful in contriving or constructing.

Synonyms: Innovative.

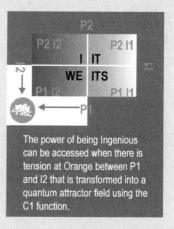

The power of being Ingenious can be accessed when there is tension at Orange between P1 and I2 that is transformed into a quantum attractor field using the C1 function.

In the Orange meme the noble quality of Ingenuity enables the individual to find innovative and original solutions to existing problems. Being Ingenious involves solving a problem in an innovative way. Ingenuity uses the resources at hand to find creative and effective solutions in real time.

BEING INGENIOUS SATISFIES THE CRITERIA OF NOBILITY

Being Ingenious enables the individual to be rewarded for their ability to 'keep the show on the road'. They learn how to take everything that they have learned in life and intuitively apply it to the problem at hand.

In finding Ingenious solutions to problems, individuals are able to keep projects on track by dismantling the road blocks. Without this noble attractor the infrastructure often breaks down. Ingenious individuals keep the telephones, trains and roads working as they respond to the many and varied daily crises that nobody saw coming.

WHAT YOU CAN EXPECT WILL HAPPEN IF YOU USE THIS ATTRACTOR FIELD

When evoking the noble quality of Ingenuity the individual, contrary to popular belief, concentrates less and 'plays' more with the presenting issue. This means trying random solutions, playing with new ideas, linking it with other activities, solving the problem in unusual places, and generally not taking the whole thing too seriously. When this noble attractor is manifested the Ingenious ideas tend to fall on people as a result of spontaneity and qualitative awareness nurtured with patience and taking a 'one step at a time' approach (rather than as a result of complex, rigorous and intellectual analysis). Ingenuity is practical, hands-on and simple and the solution is obvious once you know the answers. Once someone engages this noble quality you can expect them to relax, and use their hands in some way to either draw, repair, fiddle around with or fix the problem.

CAPABLE — ORANGE MEME (ARCHITECT)

Capable: (adjective) Having much ability; competent; efficient; qualified or fitted for.

Synonyms: Able, competent.

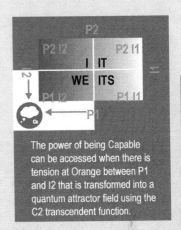

The Capable noble attractor enables the individual to achieve personal competence and corporate capability. In expressing this noble quality, the individual will develop systems and standards to ensure that they, and those around them, can capably execute their roles.

The power of being Capable can be accessed when there is tension at Orange between P1 and I2 that is transformed into a quantum attractor field using the C2 transcendent function.

BEING CAPABLE SATISFIES THE CRITERIA OF NOBILITY

As they apply this noble attractor in their professional life, the individual ensures that their abilities are current and relevant to the marketplace.

In expressing Capability the individual also ensures that others within the community have the minimum competencies to execute their functions. This noble quality fosters systems and practices which develop personal Capability which in turn leads to well run communities.

WHAT YOU CAN EXPECT WILL HAPPEN IF YOU USE THIS ATTRACTOR FIELD

When evoking the noble quality of being Capable the individual immediately focuses on the sequence of small tasks required to achieve the objective in a way that is most expedient and at the same time holds the least risk of failure. Capability is the mixture of institutional process with individual competence. This noble quality assesses both of these variables. In the organisational context this noble attractor assesses if the processes will achieve the desired result, are practical and efficient, and are understood by the people using them. It also evaluates individual competence, which is a measure of the individual's ability to follow recognised standards outlined by the relevant professional body, educational institution or trade. When this noble quality is evoked the individual is unyielding, highly evaluative, and gives highly prescriptive advice to help others (and themselves) achieve the required level of capability to get the job done well.

ROLE EXCELLENCE SEEKING – ORANGE MEME (NAVIGATOR)

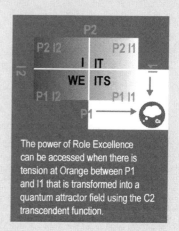

Excellence: (noun) The fact or state of excelling; superiority; eminence.

Role: (noun) The part or character which an actor presents in a play; proper or customary function.

In the Orange meme, the noble quality of Role Excellence enables the individual to have certainty about what is involved in their role and to focus on performing these functions. This noble attractor

The power of Role Excellence can be accessed when there is tension at Orange between P1 and I1 that is transformed into a quantum attractor field using the C2 transcendent function.

encourages the individual to constantly check that they are fulfilling what is required of their role and to strive to perform this role with excellence.

HAVING ROLE EXCELLENCE SATISFIES THE CRITERIA OF NOBILITY

This noble attractor enables the individual to succeed at any role they choose. It does this by supplying the energy, clarity and ambition necessary to completely embody the role.

The benefit to the community of Role Excellence is that people can have confidence that roles will be performed as they should be. Role Excellence reminds the community what is involved in playing a role, for example, being a father, a brother, a sister or a doctor. It also provides people with a sense of security and understanding of where they and everyone else fits in the wider community.

WHAT YOU CAN EXPECT WILL HAPPEN IF YOU USE THIS ATTRACTOR FIELD

When evoking the noble quality of Seeking Role Excellence the individual seeks to satisfy the role on three levels. First, they ensure that they exceed the base deliverables of the role in terms of the role's objectives. Secondly, Role Excellence draws the individual to look, sound and embrace the body language of the archetypal image of that role. Finally, Role Excellence looks to push the boundaries of the role, in an aligned and healthy way that adds value to the core objectives of the role. This noble attractor gives rise to our society's role models in every occupation.

SPECIALIST – ORANGE MEME (TREASURER)

Specialist: (noun) One who devotes themselves to one subject, or to one particular branch of a subject or pursuit.

Synonym: virtuoso

This noble attractor enables the individual to develop their knowledge about a particular field of study, or a particular subject.

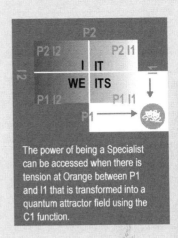

The power of being a Specialist can be accessed when there is tension at Orange between P1 and I1 that is transformed into a quantum attractor field using the C1 function.

BEING A SPECIALIST SATISFIES THE CRITERIA OF NOBILITY

This noble attractor gives the curiosity, patience and memory required to develop deep insight about a given topic. As the individual's reputation grows, this Specialist knowledge is highly valued commercially when it comes to solving associated problems or issues.

Being a Specialist also contributes to the community by providing highly sought after, specific, accurate advice built on years of study and research.

WHAT YOU CAN EXPECT WILL HAPPEN IF YOU USE THIS ATTRACTOR FIELD

When evoking the noble quality of Specialisation the individual narrows their focus, takes a highly defined area and drills down in that area to the point that they have as much data as they can accumulate on that topic. In the academic world, this noble quality has given rise to the PhD. When an individual accesses Specialisation, their first focus is on reducing the scope of the topic so that they can 'dig deep' and develop a knowledge that is comprehensive in a small area rather than a general knowledge in a wider area. When an individual accesses this noble quality, expect that they will be rigorous in excluding most areas of inquiry and instead will focus their energy on collecting all the available data in their field of inquiry. The power of this noble attractor lies in its ability to create a pinpointed focus of attention and aggregate data around that specific area.

SPECIALIST

ENTREPRENEURIAL – ORANGE MEME (JUDGE)

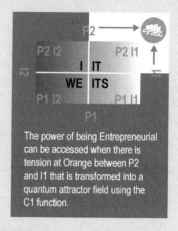

Entrepreneurial: (noun) One who is enterprising in any situation.

Synonym: pioneering, enterprising

The Entrepreneurial noble attractor enables the individual to take any circumstance and find within it the potential for a positive outcome. This noble quality pushes the individual to find numerous ways to apply an idea, concept or process to new situations and circumstances. The noble attractor also focuses

The power of being Entrepreneurial can be accessed when there is tension at Orange between P2 and I1 that is transformed into a quantum attractor field using the C1 function.

the individual on the best ways to provide service to others which results in much needed creative products or services.

BEING ENTREPRENEURIAL SATISFIES THE CRITERIA OF NOBILITY

The Entrepreneurial noble attractor enables the individual to find the hidden potential within any situation or circumstance. In seeing and realising the opportunities, the individual learns how to succeed by metaphorically turning lemons to lemonade.

Being Entrepreneurial builds the community by enabling it to take any situation and find the positive potential within it. Without this noble quality, the rate of progress and forward momentum within the community significantly slows.

WHAT YOU CAN EXPECT WILL HAPPEN IF YOU USE THIS ATTRACTOR FIELD

When evoking the noble quality of being Entrepreneurial the individual develops a hypervigilance for identifying unsatisfied needs and quickly developing ways of satisfying those needs. The Entrepreneurial noble quality opens people's eyes to a new world of opportunities and ways to earn financial reward for solving problems, alleviating emotional discomfort, creating excitement, or satisfying the limbic needs of the nine Neuro-Limbic Types (Core Belief Profiles). The Entrepreneurial attractor field imbues people with high energy, optimism, a 'can do' attitude, and confidence that no matter what the problem is, they can solve it for a price. For the Entrepreneur, the bigger the problem, the bigger the reward.

A RECAP ON THE GREEN MEME

In Green the questions of existence focus on the wider community. Attention has moved from an Orange focus of pure self-interest to also embracing others and their opinions. In Green, attention goes to accepting the opinions and positions of others without judgement, and onto building a sense of community where all belong.

The noble qualities in Green provide us with eight ways of tearing down the fences and misunderstandings that exist between people or groups of people. Internally, this means accepting the parts of us that have historically been rejected. Outside ourselves it is about accepting the common positive intentions that sit behind the ideological differences that exist between people.

MAGNANIMOUS – GREEN MEME (CRUSADER)

Magnanimous: (adjective) Praising the work of others.

Synonyms: Bighearted, generous

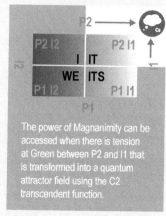

The power of Magnanimity can be accessed when there is tension at Green between P2 and I1 that is transformed into a quantum attractor field using the C2 transcendent function.

The Magnanimous noble attractor enables the individual to be generous in all things, praising others for their endeavours, being financially generous, being emotionally generous and being generous with forgiveness and flexibility.

In the Green meme the Magnanimous attractor focuses the individual on building strength and justice within the community on the principles of democracy. When the noble quality of Magnanimity is present, the individual enthusiastically praises team members for their commitment and intent rather than just the standard or quality of their output.

In the Green meme attention goes to accepting the opinions and positions of others without judgement, and to building a sense of community where all belong.

MAGNANIMITY SATISFIES THE CRITERIA OF NOBILITY

Being Magnanimous builds a sense of community where all are welcome, and allows the individual to develop meaningful personal connections with others. The Magnanimous individual creates authentic connections because they look past human utility to positive human intention.

Magnanimity has a positive impact on the community because it fosters the sharing of resources within the community.

WHAT YOU CAN EXPECT WILL HAPPEN IF YOU USE THIS ATTRACTOR FIELD

When evoking the noble quality of being Magnanimous the individual has the ability to put to one side their own needs for stability, fun, recognition, love, learning and a clear future. The Magnanimous attractor field is so strong that in the case of Joan of Arc, even when she was about to lose her own life, she put her own fear of death to one side, replacing it with prayers for her jury and killers. Magnanimity focuses the individual on the wider needs of the community and enables them to forget 'self' for the sake of the cause or the principle at stake.

LIBERATING — GREEN MEME (BARD)

Liberate: (verb) To set free, release; to disengage.

Synonym: Freeing.

The Liberating noble attractor enables the individual to remove barriers that restrict others' development and potential. Liberation enables the individual to see the potential in others and remove the obstacles that prohibit that potential being realised.

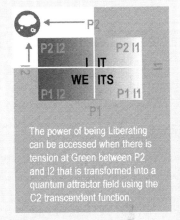

The power of being Liberating can be accessed when there is tension at Green between P2 and I2 that is transformed into a quantum attractor field using the C2 transcendent function.

BEING LIBERATING SATISFIES THE CRITERIA OF NOBILITY

Through helping others perceive and overcome the obstacles to their personal development, this noble attractor enables the individual to create strong, lifelong connections.

When leaders exhibit the noble quality of being Liberating, they enable the community to see a future that extends beyond their current limiting paradigms, precedents and plans.

WHAT YOU CAN EXPECT WILL HAPPEN IF YOU USE THIS ATTRACTOR FIELD

When evoking the noble quality of being Liberating the individual can see the ideological, emotional and physical barriers that are preventing others from realising their full potential. This means challenging out-of-date philosophies, questioning theologies and philosophies, and dismantling narratives that are outdated and are the source of the problem. Liberation has three phases. Phase 1 involves the identification of the constraining thoughts. Phase 2 involves dismantling these logic streams and narratives; this phase is initially experienced by the individual being liberated as threatening and chaotic. Phase 3 involves the replacement of the original narrow philosophies with a more embracing philosophy which allows more of the individual to shine. Often the liberated person does not realise the positive impact of the Liberation until well after the event, and can experience the Liberation process as terrifying.

LIBERATING

KIND — GREEN MEME (CHANCELLOR)

Kind: (adjective) Having a good or benevolent nature or disposition.

Synonym: generous

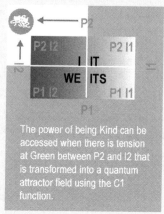

The noble quality of Kindness enables the individual to find the common humanity around which connection can be made, and builds a desire to assist the other party with whatever difficulty they may be experiencing.

The power of being Kind can be accessed when there is tension at Green between P2 and I2 that is transformed into a quantum attractor field using the C1 function.

In the Green meme attention goes to accepting the opinions and positions of others without judgement, and to building a sense of community where all belong. Kindness enables the individual to help others with little, unrecognised actions that make life easier.

KINDNESS SATISFIES THE CRITERIA OF NOBILITY

When evoking Kindness the individual learns to help another person regardless of their social standing or status. In doing so, they learn to make a real connection with them.

Kindness focuses the individual on actively addressing the needs of other people which reassures everyone they meet that they are an important part of the community.

WHAT YOU CAN EXPECT WILL HAPPEN IF YOU USE THIS ATTRACTOR FIELD

When evoking the noble quality of being Kind the individual displays a positive regard for all who come in their path. Kindness is often mistaken as something given to people who deserve it. The Kind noble attractor, however, is a value-based attitude to life, to self and to others that shows Kindness to the most as well as to the least needy. In this sense Kindness usually manifests in physical help of some sort, such as helping somebody to lift a heavy load, giving someone a drink of water when they are looking thirsty, helping somebody move house, picking up food on the way home, or smiling or waving to people you know on the street. Kindness fosters a view that every interaction can come with a gift.

ENABLING – GREEN MEME (COMMANDER)

Enable: (verb) To make able; give power, means, or ability to.

Synonym: Render capable.

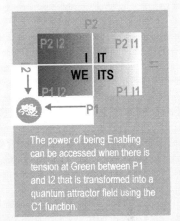

The power of being Enabling can be accessed when there is tension at Green between P1 and I2 that is transformed into a quantum attractor field using the C1 function.

The Enabling noble attractor gives the individual the ability to give another the confidence and guidance required to successfully complete a task. The Enabling attractor is practical, hands-on and fosters a 'walking beside' approach.

BEING ENABLING SATISFIES THE CRITERIA OF NOBILITY

Actively Enabling another person to complete a task develops a deep rapport between the individuals concerned. Often community members are held back by small barriers which this noble attractor can enable them to overcome. As the old saying goes, 'A friend in need is a friend indeed,' and the Enabling individual is a friend indeed.

WHAT YOU CAN EXPECT WILL HAPPEN IF YOU USE THIS ATTRACTOR FIELD

When evoking the noble quality of being Enabling the individual takes a position of standing beside others as they undergo their quest. Usually a noble quality that expresses itself through somatic action, Enabling is like a power booster. Enabling does not change the course, direction or intention of the activity. Instead, like a bionic arm, it simply takes some of the load. It could be likened to moving from the earth's gravity to the gravity on the moon in that you need less effort to achieve the same results. When an individual is Enabling they enable the other person to achieve the same results using less physical, mental and emotional effort. When somebody evokes this noble attractor they stand beside the person and are almost invisible. They stay in the role of coach and never get in the way of the real players.

UNIFYING – GREEN MEME (ARCHITECT)

Unify -fied, -fying: (verb) To form into one; make a unit of; reduce to unity.

Unity: (noun) The state or fact of being one; the oneness of a complex or organic whole or of an interconnected series; freedom from diversity or variety; oneness of mind, feeling, etc, as among a number of persons; concord, harmony, or agreement.

Synonym: Uniting.

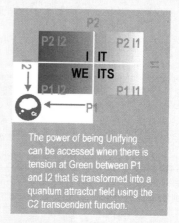

The power of being Unifying can be accessed when there is tension at Green between P1 and I2 that is transformed into a quantum attractor field using the C2 transcendent function.

Expressing the noble quality of Unifying, the individual in the Green meme will take actions that focus people on their common intent. This noble quality focuses on bringing people back to the reason they formed as a team or community (their vision) and forms them into a committed group of people. The noble quality of Unification involves bringing about agreement between different factions or elements of an organisation or group of people.

UNIFICATION SATISFIES THE CRITERIA OF NOBILITY

This noble attractor concentrates the individual on developing a thorough understanding of each person's aspirations and motivations. Unifying people around a common theme is an effective means of building a sense of community.

By drawing people together the noble quality of Unification allows the community to move forward towards a common objective. Without this noble attractor, the community will scatter, lose focus and break into factions.

WHAT YOU CAN EXPECT WILL HAPPEN IF YOU USE THIS ATTRACTOR FIELD

When evoking the noble quality of Unification the individual carefully assesses the various clashing philosophical positions being taken and looks for the common denominator. Then, in language that appeals to all parties, they weave a narrative which draws together the different positions in a way that simultaneously satisfies their desire for differentiation and the noble attractor's desire to reframe the narrative around the universally accepted core or theme. When enacted, this attractor field looks measured, open and considered, and comes with lots of nodding, smiling and constant eye contact.

PRINCIPLED – GREEN MEME (NAVIGATOR)

Principle: (noun) An accepted or professed rule of action or conduct; a fundamental, primary, or general truth, on which other truths depend; guiding sense of the requirements and obligations of right conduct.

Synonym: ethical

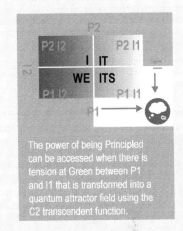

The power of being Principled can be accessed when there is tension at Green between P1 and I1 that is transformed into a quantum attractor field using the C2 transcendent function.

The Principled noble attractor enables the individual to act with a highly developed internal code of conduct that is based on values.

The Principled noble attractor focuses the individual on holding to their principles around the people with whom they are involved. It is through these genuine interactions with others that leaders can develop and articulate a suitable set of Principles that can guide their community.

BEING PRINCIPLED SATISFIES THE CRITERIA OF NOBILITY

The guiding principles that this noble attractor develops enables a deep connection and trust to develop between community members.

These principles bind a community together because they represent unchanging values in a constantly changing world. These principles also give the members of the community a sense of control as they focus their energy on their circle of control rather than their circle of concern.

WHAT YOU CAN EXPECT WILL HAPPEN IF YOU USE THIS ATTRACTOR FIELD

When evoking the noble quality of being Principled the individual aligns their values, behaviours and narrative around life-affirming principles that can be embraced by all first-tier memes. These principles must be able to hold true, regardless of the external environment, and must implicitly articulate a clear philosophy embedded in cause and effect terms. When used, this noble attractor realigns the individual to their own sense of true north.

MASTERY OF SYSTEMS — GREEN MEME (TREASURER)

Master: (noun) To conquer or subdue; to rule or direct as master.

System: (noun) A combination of parts forming a complex or unitary whole; a coordinated body of methods, or a complex scheme or plan of procedure – for example, the entire human body.

The power of having Mastery of Systems can be accessed when there is tension at Green between P1 and I1 that is transformed into a quantum attractor field using the C1 function.

The noble quality of Mastery of Systems enables the individual to know how to use and manipulate systems in the most effective manner. It also involves developing a thorough understanding of the causal relationships within an entire system.

MASTERY OF SYSTEMS SATISFIES THE CRITERIA OF NOBILITY

Staudinger and Baltes (1996) showed experimentally that social collaboration facilitates knowledge accumulation. Perhaps this noble attractor manifests within the Green meme because the knowledge accumulation required for Systems Mastery is only possible when data is drawn from all possible sources.

WHAT YOU CAN EXPECT WILL HAPPEN IF YOU USE THIS ATTRACTOR FIELD

Mastering Systems allows the individual to see that everything is in formation (in the process of being formed) and that there are underlying principles in all systems. When evoking the noble quality of having Mastery of Systems, the individual will 'helicopter' above the situation and understand how the system works. When this noble attractor is applied to a problem, the user identifies the situation as a complex integral system with inputs, outputs, information flow, energy flow, energy leaks, drivers, barriers and channels. This conceptual and philosophical analysis usually comes hand in hand with flow charts, diagrams and metaphors that enable the person to diagrammatically explore what is really happening. When applied to internal work, this enables them to identify the changes they need to make to their thoughts, emotions and behaviours (the inputs) to solve the problem at hand.

MOTIVATIONAL — GREEN MEME (JUDGE)

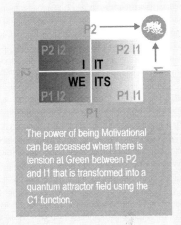

Motivation: (noun) The act or process of motivating; the state of being motivated, determined or energetic. Motivation involves being enthusiastic and communicating this to others.

Synonym: inspirational

The Motivational noble attractor arises from excitement about the potential in others rather than from self-interest. It arises out of the Green meme's focus on building relationships and helping others.

The power of being Motivational can be accessed when there is tension at Green between P2 and I1 that is transformed into a quantum attractor field using the C1 function.

BEING MOTIVATIONAL SATISFIES THE CRITERIA OF NOBILITY

The Motivational noble attractor enables the individual to connect the other person with their deeply held ambition. This Motivation creates a sense that we are all in *this* together and that *this* will not only be possible, but it will be easy if we all work together and roll up our sleeves.

The community benefits from this noble attractor because it enables its members to enthusiastically engage in the latent potential that is inherent in the current situation. Communities lacking Motivation find that the slightest problem results in the community's members becoming disheartened and giving up.

WHAT YOU CAN EXPECT WILL HAPPEN IF YOU USE THIS ATTRACTOR FIELD

When evoking the noble quality of being Motivational the individual translates intention into behaviour. This attractor field has two aspects. Firstly, it attacks entropy, laziness, intellectual sloth and the various manifestations of the Core Belief Profiles by naming them, and arguing that they are not a constructive way to behave. Secondly, the Motivational attractor weaves into the dialogue operant conditioning through positive reinforcement. This keeps going until the energy to take the action overpowers the fear, cynicism or barrier that is holding the person back. When accessing this noble attractor, the individual moves between collapsing the barriers and embracing the drivers, using humour to break down the barriers and incentives to embrace the drivers. In the best case, this noble attractor translates strategies into action, courtships into marriages, visions into companies and ideas into reality.

A RECAP ON THE YELLOW MEME

In the Yellow meme, attention goes to being rather than doing. Yellow is about being responsibly free, and having an acceptance of others' ways with the acknowledgement that not everyone has a constructive approach.

In the Yellow meme the questions of existence focus on perceiving the hierarchies of knowledge, integrating this knowledge and creating a life of personal meaning. In the Yellow meme you can actually see the intention of the person in multiple memes, and you unify the polarities in a way that is discerning. Therefore, it is a very sophisticated meme.

Each of the noble qualities of Yellow has the ability to discern the hierarchy of intentions, behaviours and outcomes embedded in a problem or situation. Often the solutions identified when evoking the Yellow meme noble attractors will have action plans that include activities in Purple, Red, Blue, Orange and Green that are directed at different aspects of the presenting problem. It may seem complex when discussed here but in practice it is instantaneous. This is made possible because the individual has access to all first-tier noble qualities and has the ability to deal with multi-variable complex problems. 'For every problem,' says Yellow, 'there is a simple solution, and this simple solution usually addresses only one aspect of the complex problem and so must be supported with a range of other solutions.' With each of the eight Yellow noble qualities you will see hierarchies within the problem and the solution will require prioritisation and situational leadership.

BENEVOLENCE – YELLOW MEME (CRUSADER)

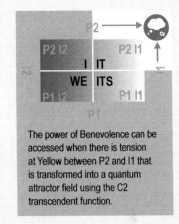

Benevolent: (adjective) Desiring to do good for others; intended for benefits rather than profit.

Synonym: Benefaction.

When expressing the noble quality of Benevolence, the individual will take actions that are beneficial for all stakeholders within their community. This noble quality focuses on righting social injustices. The nobility of Benevolence occurs when the individual is engaged in a cause that is greater than themselves and is making a meaningful difference to the lives of other people and the community at large.

The power of Benevolence can be accessed when there is tension at Yellow between P2 and I1 that is transformed into a quantum attractor field using the C2 transcendent function.

BENEVOLENCE SATISFIES THE CRITERIA OF NOBILITY

Benevolence answers questions related to creating a life of personal meaning. As the individual develops the ability to bring about significant social change, they are able to create a life of meaning for their community. Through focusing on making the world a better place for others, the individual learns to develop purpose and meaning in their own life.

Benevolence brings value to the community because it brings about significant social change not linked to personal self-interest. With a focus on benefiting society at large, significant sources of discontent can be addressed and resolved.

Having purpose and meaning in life is correlated with high levels of public interest and also personal satisfaction (Easterlin and Crimmins, 1991). Individuals report that being engaged in a project or issue that is greater than themselves and that will have a significant impact on those around them creates a feeling of being 'unstoppable'. This feeling involves having a high degree of energy, passion and enthusiasm.

WHAT YOU CAN EXPECT WILL HAPPEN IF YOU USE THIS ATTRACTOR FIELD

When evoking the noble quality of Benevolence the individual has the ability to see past the behaviour and to accurately see the positive intention of the other person (regardless of the negative impact of their behaviour). Benevolence then simultaneously holds them accountable for their behaviour while acknowledging and fanning the flames of the noble intention. Benevolence enables the individual to assess behaviours of the individual and identify the specific aspects of the behaviours that are unacceptable. This noble attractor fosters questions that will elicit the aspects of the intention that were pure so they can be nurtured, and enables the individual to let go of the aspects of the intention that were not noble. Benevolence looks for the pure intention, can see the hierarchy of intentions and resulting behaviours, lets go the aspects that don't line up, and then recreates the narrative with the individual in a way that links future behaviour with the positive intention.

EMPOWERING — YELLOW MEME (BARD)

Empower: (verb) To give power, authority or otherwise provide opportunity for others to exercise their delegated authority.

Synonym: Endow opportunity.

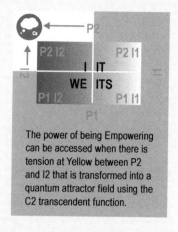

The Empowering noble attractor enables the individual to identify the unique motivations and capabilities of a person and proactively seek ways to enhance and develop them. The noble attractor brings with it an ability to perceive people's potential and an ability to create an environment

The power of being Empowering can be accessed when there is tension at Yellow between P2 and I2 that is transformed into a quantum attractor field using the C2 transcendent function.

in which that potential can flourish. It also fosters a strong personal desire to have each member of the team rise to their fullest potential.

BEING EMPOWERING SATISFIES THE CRITERIA OF NOBILITY

Being Empowering enables the individual to put people in touch with their own purpose and facilitate their own development. As they help others find personal meaning, this noble attractor helps the individual integrate their own understanding of life. For example, as the individual focuses others on discovering the relative importance of different aspects of their life, the individual learns to focus on different aspects of their own life and to integrate the knowledge they have accumulated from these different aspects of self.

Empowerment helps to bring out the higher side of other people, and it helps to create an environment that provides the opportunity for them to both experience it and also link their identity and life story to it.

WHAT YOU CAN EXPECT WILL HAPPEN IF YOU USE THIS ATTRACTOR FIELD

When evoking the noble quality of Empowering the individual gains immediate clarity on the aspects of the behaviours of the other person that are aligned with noble intentions and those that aren't. This noble attractor then provides energy to empower only the nobly motivated behaviours and skills in a way that fosters freedom, individuality and dividends that are aligned with the person's needs rather than with their wants. Doing this, the person experiences Empowerment and healing simultaneously. The individual using the Empowering noble quality is very intense, connects from the heart, looks the person in the eye, and uses personal stories to illustrate that they really can achieve the task ahead of them.

GENUINE – YELLOW MEME (CHANCELLOR)

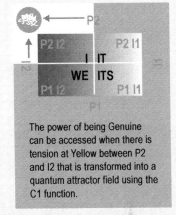

Genuine: (adjective) Being truly such; real; authentic; sincere; free from pretence or affectation.

Synonym: authentic, real

The power of being Genuine can be accessed when there is tension at Yellow between P2 and I2 that is transformed into a quantum attractor field using the C1 function.

Expressing the noble quality of being Genuine, the individual will establish deep and intimate connections with and between people. Being Genuine involves being personally sincere in interpersonal interactions, and bringing about an equivalent response from other people. Genuine connections with people foster a strong personal desire to know the other party and to be willing to share what it means to be human together.

BEING GENUINE SATISFIES THE CRITERIA OF NOBILITY

Genuineness allows the individual to make deep connections with other people and not only to accept them, but also to recognise that not all parts of them are of equal nobility. While some parts of the individual are worthy of praise and recognition, other parts are not. This noble attractor enables the individual to integrate their regard for others with discernment. Creating Genuine connections answers questions about creating a life of personal meaning through relationships that are not based on social standing or mutual benefit, but are based instead on genuine and authentic relating.

The noble quality of Genuineness creates the close and intimate bonds between people that keep a group honest. The individual's ability not only to be genuine but also to identify when others are not being genuine keeps relationships real and stops the lowest common denominator from ruling the group. Genuineness helps a community to be honest and open, and to form strong ties that are based on love and mutual respect.

WHAT YOU CAN EXPECT WILL HAPPEN IF YOU USE THIS ATTRACTOR FIELD

When evoking the noble quality of being Genuine the individual is given the ability to see the rich complexity of motivations, aspirations and intentions within a problem or person. Genuineness embraces all these factors and communicates with an honesty or candidness that can be disarming. Genuineness enables the person to understand that they're not only 'light' but they're also 'dark'. Genuineness enables the individual to accept themselves and others, warts and all, and to see situations as they really are. It enables them to let go of ideal imprints, scripts, preconceptions or assumptions that they have clung to about themselves, others and the world.

HARMONIOUS — YELLOW MEME (COMMANDER)

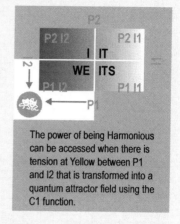

Harmony: (noun) Agreement; accord; a consistent, orderly or pleasing arrangement of parts; congruity.

Synonym: social agreement

The power of being Harmonious can be accessed when there is tension at Yellow between P1 and I2 that is transformed into a quantum attractor field using the C1 function.

The noble attractor of Harmony enables the individual in the Yellow meme to work in conjunction with another person who may not have the same vision. This noble attractor fosters the capacity to walk alongside someone and assist him or her, without necessarily sharing their destination or point of view.

BEING HARMONIOUS SATISFIES THE CRITERIA OF NOBILITY

Harmony enables the different people in the community to pursue their own objectives without conflict. Harmony creates an environment where different groups will help one another to the best of their ability. This fosters an environment of mutual collaboration and support.

WHAT YOU CAN EXPECT WILL HAPPEN IF YOU USE THIS ATTRACTOR FIELD

When evoking the noble quality of Harmony the individual can bring warring divisions, tribes, family members or aspects of the self together. The noble quality does this by firstly giving the individual immediate access to the intentions and motivations behind the philosophies or behaviours causing the disharmony and then secondly by creating the social bridge that enables both sides to self-reference and fully understand the noble intentions of the other party. The Harmony that is created is lasting and honours all the needs of all the memes because the Harmony is not based on ensuring everybody complies with a strict set of rules, but instead enables all parties at the table to see past the behaviour and through to the heart. This second-tier noble quality also enables the individual who is undertaking behaviour that is not noble, to get a glimpse of their selfishness and unreasonableness in the matter. In this way, Harmony has a regulating effect on the players at the table.

STRATEGIC — YELLOW MEME (ARCHITECT)

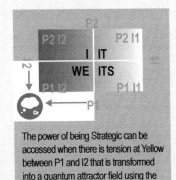

Strategy: (noun) The method of conducting operations especially by manoeuvring or planning.

The Strategic noble attractor enables the individual to find a process that will deliver the greatest output from the least resources. Being Strategic involves ensuring that the people and processes align with the Strategic expectations. This represents the Strategic attractor's desire for congruence. Strategic intent involves simultaneously considering the past, present and future when making any significant decision, and

The power of being Strategic can be accessed when there is tension at Yellow between P1 and I2 that is transformed into a quantum attractor field using the C2 transcendent function.

taking into account the *Four Faces of Truth*. It requires looking at the situation from all points of view and developing a sequential path of action that builds on the strengths and opportunities, and mitigates risks and threats. Strategic is an often used word. It defines the process of closing the gap between the current and desired positions at each meme. Yellow meme understanding of relativity enables the person using this noble attractor to use questions to ensure that the most appropriate vision is being used for the desired state, and that the most realistic assessment is being made of the current state.

BEING STRATEGIC SATISFIES THE CRITERIA OF NOBILITY

In being Strategic and drawing together elements of the past, present and future, the individual begins to integrate all aspects of their life. The individual learns how to create a life of personal meaning in a Strategic manner. To be Strategic they must ask themselves, 'What do I really want out of this life?' Strategy assists the community by ensuring community resources are applied to achieving agreed outcomes.

Strategic decision-making is highly beneficial in maximising the community's resource allocation, because ensuring there is congruence between people, processes and purpose makes the community or organisation more efficient and effective.

WHAT YOU CAN EXPECT WILL HAPPEN IF YOU USE THIS ATTRACTOR FIELD

When evoking the noble quality of being Strategic the individual is immediately traumatised by the gap or delta between the current and the desired situations. This noble attractor takes into account the level of mental complexity and the psycho-emotional development of the people who will be tasked with closing the gap, and tailors a linear process that is not only practical and efficient, but also able to be understood. This noble attractor often challenges the strategies in place because the people rolling them out don't understand them, they are not engaged, and the processes they are being asked to embrace are inefficient. In an intrapersonal context this noble attractor helps the individual see the internal delta between their current and desired self and develops an action plan that engages the various parts of self in the task of closing the gap. This noble attractor works very well alone, and enjoys flow charts, force field analysis, process design, and phased strategy development. Strategists often refer to problems as puzzles needing to be solved by placing the right pieces of the jigsaw together.

CONQUERING – YELLOW MEME (NAVIGATOR)

Conquering: (adjective) Unstoppable in overcoming major adversaries such as disease, unrest, fear or maladies.

Synonym: Custodial.

In expressing the Conquering noble attractor the individual is motivated to lead themselves or a group into new uncharted territory or experiences.

Being Conquering fosters both a sense of purpose and a capacity to move people in a desired direction. It also involves a sense of wonder for the world and a desire to experience more of it first hand.

The power of being Conquering can be accessed when there is tension at Yellow between P1 and I1 that is transformed into a quantum attractor field using the C2 transcendent function.

BEING CONQUERING SATISFIES THE CRITERIA OF NOBILITY

To effectively lead others, this second-tier noble attractor integrates much of the information the individual has learned over the course of their life. The Conquering noble quality gives leaders the energy and mental focus to identify and conquer the real or emotional demons terrorising the community.

WHAT YOU CAN EXPECT WILL HAPPEN IF YOU USE THIS ATTRACTOR FIELD

When evoking the noble quality of being Conquering the individual gains clarity on what needs to be conquered and how they should approach the task. At first-tier awareness it seems obvious that the task is to conquer the bad and support the good. At the second tier, this awareness is broadened and there is a realisation that there is good and bad within what was previously considered good, and there is good and bad in what was previously considered bad. As this awareness deepens it becomes obvious that there are no 'rights' and 'wrongs', and that instead there are only results. This noble attractor gives the individual the ability to discern the results that are supportive and the results that are unsupportive and gives them a burning desire to change the social laws, provide the physical resources and, for that matter, do whatever it takes to conquer the causal factors driving the unsupportive results.

EXPERT – YELLOW MEME (TREASURER)

Expert: (noun) A person who has special skill or deep knowledge in some particular field.

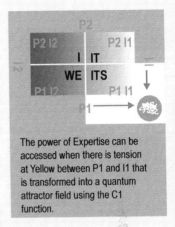

The noble attractor of Expertise enables the individual to access highly developed knowledge and skills within a particular field or body of knowledge. It involves being highly informed about the issue, and being able to integrate knowledge from other areas in a systematic manner. Being an Expert involves bringing information and procedures from disparate sources and adapting and integrating them into one cohesive whole.

The power of Expertise can be accessed when there is tension at Yellow between P1 and I1 that is transformed into a quantum attractor field using the C1 function.

BEING AN EXPERT SATISFIES THE CRITERIA OF NOBILITY

At the Orange meme, the individual builds Specialist knowledge which is broadened at the Green meme to a Mastery of Systems. When these two qualities are combined in a field of endeavour, the noble quality of Expertise is manifested. Using the Expert noble attractor, the individual clearly sees the hierarchies of knowledge and is able to create personal meaning from these. The wealth of knowledge and insight that the individual develops provides sustainable solutions to issues confronting the community.

WHAT YOU CAN EXPECT WILL HAPPEN IF YOU USE THIS ATTRACTOR FIELD

When evoking the noble quality of Expertise the individual has the energy to search for information that tells a complete story. This noble quality enables the person to see the difference between core insight and red herrings, miscellaneous data and false information. There are three principal differences between a subject Expert and a well-informed individual. First, a subject Expert understands the fundamental principles that sit behind the topic area, and they reorganise the information around this fundamental principle. They differ from someone who knows a lot about a subject because the non-expert simply relates data in an unintegrated way. Second, the Expert can apply the knowledge usefully. For example, they will understand the cause and effect linkages, the impact a topic has on an individual, and the relative merit of different approaches. They will have made creative connections that others may never have made historically, and will see connections between their particular field of endeavour and other fields of endeavour that seem unrelated (for example, between neurosurgery and carpentry, or healing and computer programming). In this way the subject Expert can relate to other experts in different fields and find much in common. Finally, the noble attractor field gives the person the desire to know everything about everybody who has known about and studied that subject. An Expert will see the subject as a story involving a whole cast of contributors all of whom should be acknowledged for their contribution.

ENLIVENING

ENLIVENING — YELLOW MEME (JUDGE)

Enlivening: (adjective) Giving vivacity, life, action, animation or spirit.

Synonym: animating, energising

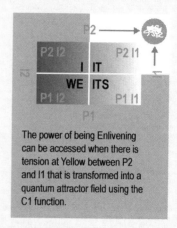

The Enlivening noble attractor enables the individual to get behind a person or project, and do what it takes to bring it to completion.

The power of being Enlivening can be accessed when there is tension at Yellow between P2 and I1 that is transformed into a quantum attractor field using the C1 function.

ENLIVENING SATISFIES THE CRITERIA OF NOBILITY

The Enlivening attractor enables the individual to perceive the hierarchical nature of truth and to breathe life into the 'most' truthful aspects of it. In breathing their energy and passion into those truths that resonate with them, the individual begins to create a life of personal authenticity. Their focus turns to being rather than doing. In focusing on truth and these higher aspects of it, the individual begins to integrate the knowledge they have developed throughout their life.

The Enlivening attractor feeds energy into those ideas and concepts that the individual believes to be supporting the community. Without Enlivenment the best ideas can become swamped by the morass of mediocre concepts.

WHAT YOU CAN EXPECT WILL HAPPEN IF YOU USE THIS ATTRACTOR FIELD

When evoking the noble quality of Enlivening the individual takes to its logical conclusion whatever theory, feeling, relational agreement, vision, proposition or idea is on the table. This noble quality, however, enables this conclusion to be reached within minutes and sometimes even seconds rather than hours and sometimes years. At the second tier this noble quality can consciously focus in on unconstructive patterns of behaviour or thoughts and provide an Enlivening awareness that may have otherwise taken years of lower awareness to recognise. When an individual manifests this noble attractor, others sometimes describe the impact it has on them as a flash of brilliance, a sudden awakening or knowing, or a realisation of a direction that needed to be taken. Enlivenment is often accompanied by the dissolving of the ego, the release of energies, and the breaking of previously held patterns of thought by somatic passion, and it is often emotionally experienced through crying, laughter or extreme physical movement. After coming into contact with this noble attractor, the individual feels relaxed, calm and back in touch with reality. The Enlivening noble attractor always comes with a clear and immediate action plan, with simple and practical actions that can be started immediately.

Chapter 21

Problems are the Seeds of our Nobility

Our deepest fear is not that we are inadequate.
Our deepest fear is that we are powerful beyond measure. It is our light not
our darkness that most frightens us. We ask ourselves – who am I to be
brilliant, gorgeous, talented, fabulous? Actually, who are you not to be? You
are a child of God. Your playing small does not serve the world. There's
nothing enlightened about shrinking so that other people won't feel insecure
around you. You are born to manifest the glory of God that is within you. It's
not just in some of us, it's in everyone. And as we let our own light shine, we
unconsciously give other people permission to do the same. As we're liberated
from our own fear, our presence automatically liberates others.

Marianne Williamson
Author and International Speaker

UNDERSTANDING THE NATURE OF PURE POWER

There is nothing more compelling than positive and focused power. This power is available to us all if we understand how to access and apply it. In Chapter 20 we explored the meaning of the noble qualities – the attractor fields which change the very fabric of reality. In this chapter we lift the bonnet on how individuals for thousands of years have manifested and applied these noble qualities to change the world – forever. For example, let's consider a nineteen-year-old peasant farm girl who changed the course of French history.

THE NOBILITY OF JOAN OF ARC

Born 6 January, 1412 in Domrémy, France, Joan of Arc lived only nineteen years and her noble power was such that she became a national heroine of France and a saint of the Catholic Church. Joan was renowned for having visions (C2), which she believed came from God. These visions were so strong and clear that they gave rise to powerful noble qualities that, as you will discover in her remarkable story, galvanised Charles VII's troops to retake most of his dynasty's former territories which had been under English and Burgundian dominance during the Hundred Years' War.

Joan of Arc came from an obscure village and rose to prominence when she was barely more than a child and she did so as an uneducated peasant. French and English kings had justified the ongoing war through competing interpretations of the thousand-year-old Salic law. The conflict had been an inheritance feud between monarchs. Joan of Arc gave meaning to appeals such as that of Squire Jean de Metz when he asked, 'Must the king be driven from the kingdom; and are we to be English?' (Devries, p. 3: http://en.wikipedia.org). In the words of Stephen Richey, 'She turned what had been a dry dynastic squabble that left the common people unmoved except for their own suffering into a passionately popular war of national liberation' (Richey: http://en.wikipedia.org, accessed 12 February, 2006). Joan did this by refusing to collapse into the I1 acceptance of the reality of the way things were. She also refused to simply play P2 politics to gain personally from the situation. Instead, she held these two polarities and used her C2 vision to create something both profound and powerful – a new sense of corporate and national ethics. She had a clear sense of the ethical path forward. Viewed from this position, the country's situation looked very different and the energy that only noble qualities generate began to infuse the situation.

At the age of sixteen and an illegitimate, peasant farm girl, Joan faced the impossible task of gaining an audience with the royal French court to share with them her passion for what needed to be done. Joan enthusiastically petitioned every high-ranking or highly regarded person she could contact (accessing her P2) and suffered clear rejection until she gained the support from two men of standing, Jean de Metz and Bertrand de Poulegny. Under their auspices she gained an interview, where she not only clearly summarised the current situation (I1 reality) but also made an apparently miraculous prediction about a military reversal near Orléans (C2 conversion). This simple prediction in and of itself, however, did not hold the power of persuasion (Oliphant, http://www.authorama.com/book/jeanne-d-arc.html, accessed 12 February, 2006).

It was only when Joan of Arc not only refused to collapse into P1 compliance, I1 withdrawal or P2 aimless aggression, but also was able to hold the tension, that true power manifested. She held the tension between P2 and I1 and then transformed this tension into the noble quality of **Integrity**. This noble attractor changed the perception of the situation so completely that it galvanised the leadership to start walking their talk. When Joan was able to manifest the noble quality of integrity it was this powerful noble attractor that enabled her to persuade her audience to embrace a path that was both clear and compelling.

But Joan's astonishing ability to convert tension into nobility and power didn't stop there. The following transcript is a letter from Joan of Arc to the King of England. It highlights how, even in writing, Joan's crusade is embedded in noble attractor fields. In her letter Joan sets up the polarities, converts them with C2 and then outlines action motivated by this noble attractor. For the readers at the time it was most compelling.

At the beginning of the letter Joan is very clear in stating that the current occupation of France by the English (I1 sees the reality of the situation) will not be tolerated and that France will enthusiastically expel the English (P2 agency). Once this tension is established, she then introduces the idea that she is receiving her instruction from no other than God Himself (accessing C2). This gives rise to a clear sense of justice. Joan outlines a path forward that is based on the idea that there is a specific ideal/just outcome that is best for all involved. No half measures here. Joan describes the exact requirements of England and also 'promises and guarantees' her own just standards of behaviour. In this situation Joan is striving for justice for both France and the other party. The focus at this stage is on achieving the desired results in the most efficient and timely manner. It is the focus of the Red meme. Note in her letter how precise her writing is and her constant focus on achieving an acceptable and just outcome for all involved if at all possible.

> King of England, do right by the King of Heaven concerning His Royal line; hand over to the Maiden the keys to all the towns which you have taken. She has come on behalf of the Royal family, and is quite ready to make peace if you are willing to do right, so long as you give up France, and make amends for occupying it.
>
> King of England, if you do not do so, I am a commander. Whenever I come across your troops in France, if they are not willing to obey I shall make them leave, willing or not. And if they are willing to obey, I will have mercy upon them. Know that if they will not obey, the Maiden is coming to wipe them out. She comes on behalf of the King of Heaven, an eye for an eye, to drive you out of France.
>
> And the Maiden promises and guarantees that she will cause such a great clash of arms there that not for a thousand years has another one so great been seen in France, if you do not do right. And believe firmly that the King of Heaven will send more force to her and good men-at-arms than you would be able to have in a hundred assaults.
>
> You, archers, soldiers, who are around Orleans, go back to your own land, in God's name. And if you do not do so, watch for the Maiden, and you will shortly contemplate your misfortunes. Do not think otherwise, for you will never hold France from the King of Heaven, from the son of Saint Mary; but rather it will be held by King Charles, the true heir, to whom God has given it, who will enter Paris with a fine contingent

of troops. If you do not believe the tidings from God and the Maiden, wherever we find you we will strike against you harshly, and you will see who will have the better right, God or you.

William de la Pole, Earl of Suffolk; John, Lord of Talbot; Thomas, Lord of Scales, Lieutenant of the Duke of Bedford, self-styled Regent of the Kingdom of France for the King of England; reply if you want to make peace or not at the city of Orleans. If you do not do so, then you will contemplate your misfortunes.

Duke of Bedford, who call yourself Regent of the Kingdom of France for the King of England, the Maiden asks and requests that you will not cause your own downfall. If you do not do right, she will ensure that the French will do the finest deed ever done in Christendom... (http://archive.joan-of-arc.org/joanofarc_ letter_Mar1429.html, accessed on 29 May, 2006)

Joan was sent to the siege of Orléans by the then uncrowned King Charles VII as part of a relief mission. She gained prominence when she overcame the disregard of veteran commanders and ended the siege in only nine days. Several more swift victories led to Charles VII's coronation at Reims and Joan had ensured that justice prevailed, with the disputed succession to the throne settled. However, immediately following the coronation of King Charles VII, the Royal army attempted further campaigns, but with less success. Joan refused to leave the field when she was wounded during an attempt to recapture Paris. Hampered by court intrigues, she led only minor companies from then on, and fell prisoner during a skirmish near Compiègne the following spring.

Guillaume de Flavy continued to hold Compiègne resolutely for his King, while Joan's constant thought during the early months of her captivity (I1 reality) was to escape and come to assist him in this task of defending the town (P2). Thinking not of her own freedom or impending doom, Joan used prayer (C2) to convert the tension between the P2 and I1 and manifest nobility. This nobility focused her on wanting to help Guillaume de Flavy in holding Compiègne for the King even if it meant she lost her life doing it.

A politically motivated trial by the English convicted her of heresy. The Duke of Bedford claimed the throne of France for his nephew Henry VI. Joan was responsible for the rival coronation. Condemning her was an attempt to discredit her King. Joan's most famous quote during the trial was to the question, 'Do you know if you are in the grace of God?' The following is her response taken verbatim from her trial.

If I am not, may God place me there. If I am, may God so keep me. I should be the saddest in all the world if I knew that I were not in the grace of God. But if I were in a state of sin, do you think the voice would come to me? I would that every one could hear the voice as I hear it.

He came for a great purpose. I was in hopes that the King would believe the sign, and that they would cease to argue with me, and would aid the good people of Orleans. The Angel came for the merits of the King and of the good Duke d'Orleans.

She held the tension between P2 and I1 until her death. Right up to her last breath she had the internal strength and ability to contain this reality and the connection with God to transform this tension into nobility. As you can see, her responses were clear and powerful.

Joan defended her crusade to the court based on the tension between the reality of the situation (using her I1), the accusation of heresy, and her own personal desire to effect change (accessing her P2). During the trial she emphasised that she was acting in the interest of freeing her country from England's occupation, deferring to God for her guidance in how she should best serve the needs of her country and its people (accessing C2). The strength of this spirit of **Magnanimity**, the Crusader's noble quality in the Green meme, is extraordinary. Her Green-meme focus here is on doing what is right for all of humanity, giving each player a part in the unfolding story and providing the option for everyone to receive dignity and God's love. Even at the very last moment of her life her internal strength which enabled her to hold the tension and her ability to convert this into nobility, powerfully affected those in her company.

Eyewitnesses described the scene of the execution on 30 May, 1431.

She listened calmly to the sermon read to her but then broke down weeping during her own address in which she forgave her accusers for what they were doing and asked them to pray for her. The accounts say that most of the judges and assessors themselves and a few of the English soldiers and officials were openly sobbing. (Williamson, 1999, http://archive.joan-of-arc.org)

In the final moments when she was about to be burned at the stake (using I1 reality), rather than collapse into the self-indulgence that comes with an inability to hold the tension, Joan held to her values (accessing her P2) and used prayer to convert this final tension to the noble quality of **Benevolence**. While it is impossible to be sure of her state of mind from the transcripts that we have, at nineteen, in her final moments, Joan of Arc may have even jumped to the second tier and manifested second-tier nobility. She demonstrated the noble quality of **Benevolence** by forgiving her sentencers, even those who had denied truth (I1) and wrongly ordered her death (P2) and encouraged them to use prayer so that they too could access C2 to unify the tension between I1 and P2 polarities and experience human nobility for themselves.

> *Tied to a tall pillar, she asked two of the clergy, Martin Ladvenu and Isambart de la Pierre, to hold a crucifix before her. She repeatedly called out 'in a loud voice the holy name of Jesus, and implored and invoked without ceasing the aid of the saints of Paradise'.* (http://en.wkikpedia.org/Joan_of_Arc, accessed 27 May, 2006)

After her death, the English raked back the coals to expose her charred body so that no one could claim she had escaped alive, then burned the body twice more to reduce it to ashes and prevent any collection of relics. They cast her remains into the Seine. (Richey, 'Joan of Arc: A Military Appreciation': DeVries in Fresh Verdicts on Joan of Arc, ed. Bonnie Wheeler, accessed 12 February, 2006). The executioner, Geoffroy Therage, later stated that he '...greatly feared to be damned for he had burned a holy woman' (Pernoud, *Joan of Arc by Herself and Her Witnesses*, p. 233).

Some twenty-four years later, after the English were driven out, Joan's aged mother, Isabelle, convinced the Inquisitor-General and Pope Callixtus III to re-open Joan's case, resulting in an appeal which overturned the original conviction by the English (Pernoud and Clin, pp. 220-221. accessed 12 February, 2006: http://en. Wikipedia.org/Joan_of_Arc). Pope Benedict XV canonised her on 16 May, 1920.

The following prayer is a testimony to the fact that Joan of Arc's nobility not only changed lives in her own lifetime but is continuing to do so to this very day. Such extraordinary noble power is very rare indeed and an inspiration to us all.

Prayer to Joan of Arc for Faith

In the face of your enemies, in the face of harassment, ridicule,
And doubt, you held firm in your faith.
Even in your abandonment, alone and without friends, you held firm in your faith.
Even as you faced your own mortality, you held firm in your faith.
I pray that I may be as bold in my beliefs as you, St. Joan.
I ask that you ride alongside me in my own battles.
Help me be mindful that what is worthwhile can be won when I persist.
Help me hold firm in my faith.
Help me believe in my ability to act well and wisely. Amen.

Even though (as it must have felt for Joan of Arc) it may feel to us as though every day's problems exist in our very own heart and soul, in fact, they exist outside us. If we believe there is a problem in life, it is because we have felt an internal tension between our P functions and our I functions. The tension may be internal, but the problem is external.

Every problem also exists within a meme.

Put simply, every problem you face, big or small, life threatening like Joan of Arc's or otherwise, exists within a meme and exists as the energetic tension between either P1 and I1, P2 and I1, P1 and I2, or P2 and I2. Pure power is the ability to resolve this tension and solve the problem.

We trigger this pure power by using either C1 or C2 to unify the tension into a non-dual reality where one of the noble qualities is manifested and acts as an attractor field. It sounds complicated, but the truly exceptional people we read about have been applying this approach, almost certainly not consciously, for thousands of years. And when they have, they have fundamentally changed the world forever. Let me give you another example.

IBM'S PROBLEM WAS BILL GATES' OPPORTUNITY

In 1980 IBM had completed building the hardware for their new desktop personal computer. There was one major problem: IBM needed to find and install an operating system. The most popular microcomputer operating system at the time was CP/M developed by Digital Research in Monterey. CP/M allowed software written for the Intel 8080/Zilog Z80 family of microprocessors to run on many different models of computer from many different manufacturers. This device-independent feature was essential for the formation of the consumer software industry because without it, software had to be rewritten for each different model of computer.

IBM approached Bill Gates who referred IBM to Gary Kildall, the founder of Digital Research. But IBM and Kildall could not reach agreement so they went back to Gates for a solution.

This situation gives us an example of a problem that existed in the Orange meme (market success). Gates felt the internal tension between the reality of the situation through his (I1) and IBM's desire to dominate a new PC market (P2 agency and market differentiation). Gates used C1 to resolve the tension by quickly contacting Tim Paterson from Seattle Computer Products and paying him $56,000 for a licence for a CP/M-compatible Operating System called QDOS ('Quick and Dirty Operating System'). Gates went back to IBM with his solution and they accepted it 100 per cent and the rest, as they say, is history.

In hindsight it all looks so easy but what was it that Gates actually did? He held the tension between the reality (accessing I1) and the potential for him to personally do something that would achieve the results they were looking for (using P2) and he used (C1) spontaneity to do something quickly before the opportunity evaporated.

This gave him access to the noble quality of **Entrepreneurship**, which in turn gave him the ability to see the potential in the situation, the ability to move quickly and the commitment to put his $56,000 where his mouth was. It seems easy now that we know how the story ends but honestly, **how would you have acted in the same situation?**

You could have said to yourself, 'IBM will work it out,' and denied the reality (I1) of the situation. You could have collapsed into P1 and decided that you didn't have the ability, money or confidence to do anything about the situation ('Who am I to solve IBM's problem?') or you could have gone and had a drink (accessing C1) and discussed the whole thing with your fellow drinkers without doing anything concrete.

Or, you could have done exactly what Gates did and turned a seemingly impossible problem into a life-changing opportunity.

Fortunately these opportunities, disguised as problems, come across our path every day.

In previous sections we have discussed the formation of personality, the process of integration, the eight adult personalities and the nine force-based personalities. We also outlined how human nobility specifically changes as the individual's level of consciousness changes. You now have the insight you need to turn every problem in life into action based on nobility. And you can achieve this by converting situational tension into power-based, non-dual, quantum level resolution.

THE LADY WITH THE LAMP

Let me give you another example. This time I'd like to introduce you to Florence Nightingale, who later came to be known as *The Lady with the Lamp*.

Unlike so many of the other nurses at the time, Florence Nightingale was able to overcome the horror, despair and pain of makeshift wards and transform them into **Self-Control** which enabled both the staff and the patients to survive and heal. This took extraordinary strength of character as you will see in the following transcripts from her correspondence.

Florence Nightingale, OM (12 May, 1820 - 13 August, 1910) was a pioneer of modern nursing. She was also a noted statistician. Inspired by what she understood to be a divine calling (first experienced in 1837 at the age of seventeen at Embley Park and later throughout her life), Nightingale made a commitment to nursing. This decision demonstrated a strong will on her part; it constituted a rebellion against the expected role for a woman of her status, which was to become an obedient wife. At the time, nursing was a career with a bad reputation, filled mostly by poorer women, 'hangers-on' who followed the armies; they were equally likely to function as cooks. Nightingale announced to her family her decision to enter nursing in 1845, which evoked intense anger and distress from her family, particularly her mother.

Florence Nightingale's most famous contribution came during the Crimean War, which became her central focus when reports began to filter back to Britain about the horrific conditions for the wounded. On 21 October, 1854, she and a staff of thirty-eight women volunteer nurses, trained by Nightingale and including her aunt Mai Smith, were sent (under the authorisation of Sidney Herbert) to Turkey, some 545km across the Black Sea from Balaklava in the Crimea, where the main British camp was based.

Nightingale arrived early in November, 1854 in Scutari (modern-day Üsküdar in Istanbul). She and her nurses found wounded soldiers being badly cared for by overworked medical staff in the face of official indifference. Medicines were in short supply, hygiene was being neglected, and mass infections were common, many of them fatal. There was no equipment to process food for the patients (http:// en.wikipedia.org, accessed on 4 June, 2006).

HOW FLORENCE NIGHTINGALE DESCRIBED OPERATIONS IN THE HOSPITAL

Barrack Hospital, Scutari, Asiatic Side, 14 November, 1854:

Then come the operations and a melancholy, not an encouraging list is this. They are all performed in the wards – no time to move them. One poor fellow, exhausted with [bleeding], has his leg amputated as a last hope and dies ten minutes after the surgeons have left him. Almost before the breath has left his body, it is sewn up in a blanket and carried away – buried the same day.

We have no room for corpses on the wards… I am getting a screen now for amputations, for when one poor fellow, who is to be amputated tomorrow, sees his comrade today die under the knife it makes an impression and diminishes his chances.

But anyway, among these exhausted frames the mortality of operations is frightful. Now comes the time of haemorrhage [bleeding] and Hospital Gangrene, and every ten minutes an orderly runs, and we have to go and cram lint into the wound till a Surgeon can be sent for, and stop the bleeding as well as we can.

So how did Florence access the pure power of human nobility?

She felt devastated at not having time to properly mourn each loss (I2 polarity) and yet was required to maintain a functional hospital for the surviving soldiers in her care (accessing P1). She resolved this tension with creative makeshift ways of adapting the ward to the situation at hand. Her Red meme focus on responding to these immediate and life-threatening issues and her ability to transform the tension between P1 and I2 with C1 gave her access to the noble quality of **Self-Control**. It was this **Self-Control** which saved the lives of possibly thousands of young soldiers. Pure power like this, when applied with focus and right intention, is life changing.

LIVING A LIFE OF POWER

The idea of going to all the effort of holding the internal tension before strategically applying C1 or C2 contradicts the current consumerist view that argues that the goal of life is to live in complete harmony without any tension whatsoever at any stage.

In fact, I would argue that there are three ways to resolve internal tension and only one of these is noble or powerful. The first simple but weak way is to collapse into one of the ICs: P1, C1, P2, I2, I1 or C2. This, at best, gives rise to first-order nobility. The second

---

How to Hardwire Character into Your Personality

Hardwiring character into your personality is a simple four-step process.

1. **Be cognitively aware** of your emotional reactions. We are neurobiologically wired to develop the ability to become aware of our emotional reaction if we so choose.

2. **Apply nobility.** Use your brain's executive function (the cerebral cortex) to analyse the situation and see what noble quality is best applied in this situation. Exactly how to do this is detailed later in this chapter.

3. **Practice makes permanent.** Repeat steps 1 and 2 until it becomes habit. That is, create a neural pathway for each situation requiring a noble quality so that each survival-based amygdala reaction triggers the cerebral cortex to dull it and override it with an action of nobility. This means that when there is a pattern identified by the amygdala, the specific ICs of the brain that underpin the noble quality (as outlined in the table of noble qualities) are activated. Wisdom results from this being automatic.

4. **Learn how to engage others.** Learn how to communicate noble character and how to engage others so that they mirror the same circuitry in their brain. Learn to lead others by expressing your noble quality through words, behaviour and emotions. When a leader in any situation applies this approach their followers mirror the same noble quality. This is made possible because their brain's open systems circuitry attunes them with the people they admire.

is to collapse into one of the Neuro-Limbic Types and use one of the nine emotions as an attractor field. This will resolve the tension but lead to unconstructive behaviour, ill-health and type-specific psychopathology. (My personal experience suggests that more than half the mental illnesses in the world can be linked back to this form of collapse.) Finally, you can resolve the tension by initially holding the tension between the Ps and the Is and then unifying them using either C1 or C2. This transforms the tension to one of the noble attractors. Tension itself, therefore, is not bad at all, but it does create a decision point for the individual facing the problem. Ultimately what the individual does with this tension will determine whether it, in a small or large way, supports or destroys their life.

FOOL'S GOLD

Consumerism uses an individual's inability to convert tension to sell products. The product is promised as the 'magic bullet' and is expected to play the role that in reality C1 or C2 should play. The pitch goes something like this: 'Do you feel tension? You don't have to. If you buy this product or service it has the ability to create a life of non-dual harmony.' The reality, of course, is that it actually fosters one of the emotions triggered by the Neuro-Limbic Types and cognitively narrows our focus to one of the Core Belief sets. Addictions to chemicals, activities, people or emotions, work, sex or food impact us in exactly the same way. Of course, they also prevent us from accessing the true power that is available to us by manifesting the noble attractor.

When the tension is converted into the noble attractor, there is no tension but it is because the individual has firstly 'held' the tension and then converted it into second-order nobility. From this point of view the collapse option is fool's gold and only conversion leads to true nobility and pure power.

THE FOUR-STEP PURE POWER PROCESS

There is a four-step process required to convert internal tension into nobility;

Step 1. Build awareness and identify the meme;

Step 2. Identify the polarities;

Step 3. Apply creativity; and

Step 4. Convert the insight into action.

We will now explore these in more depth

Diagram 21.1 The Three Options for Dealing with Internal Tension

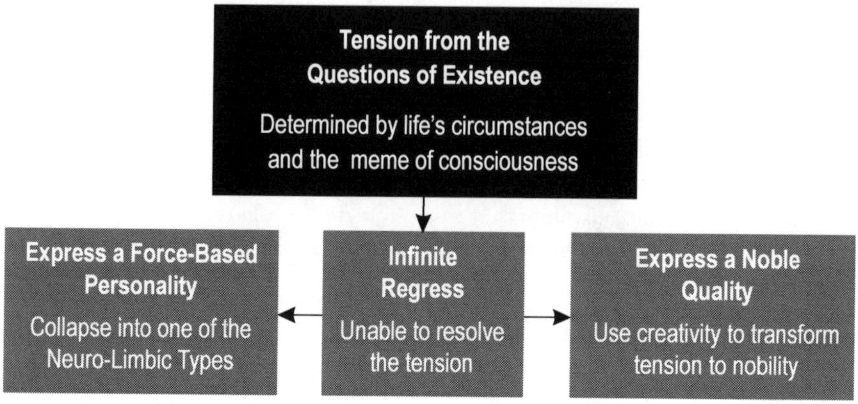

Tension from the Questions of Existence

Determined by life's circumstances and the meme of consciousness

Express a Force-Based Personality

Collapse into one of the Neuro-Limbic Types

Infinite Regress

Unable to resolve the tension

Express a Noble Quality

Use creativity to transform tension to nobility

BUT WHY DO WE HAVE PROBLEMS IN THE FIRST PLACE?

The tension provided by external problems provides the energy and the motivation to convert ambiguity and uncertainty into nobility. As the psychologist Maslow stated, 'A need satisfied no longer motivates.' Taken from this perspective, tension is not only inherent within human life; it is also essential if we are ever to live beyond causality, or first-order consciousness.

We have a choice. We can either convert our tension into something noble that enables us to grow, or we collapse. If we collapse, we create one of the force-based personalities, a Neuro-Limbic Type that leads to pain, mental illness, addictions and eventually to death.

Alternatively, when we follow the four steps outlined in the table, this converts our tension into a powerful noble attractor. **This noble attractor is pure gold and will enable us to achieve all we were created to achieve, be, do, have or experience.**

To enable you to understand exactly how this process works let us take each step one at a time and explain each step in more depth.

STEP 1. BUILD AWARENESS

As a leader, business manager, politician, counsellor, therapist, friend, parent, helper, teacher or effective human being, our first step is to develop the ability to see how and if the individual (us or somebody else) is able to maintain inner tension and hold the polarities.

If the individual's nobility is currently being expressed, your task is to

Function	Questions
Step 1. **Build awareness and identify the meme**	The conversion process begins with Awareness. This involves recognising that the external problem is creating internal tension. It is also critical at this first stage to identify the meme in which the problem sits. Essentially there are only three ways in which the individual can deal with internal tensions and you will need to be able to identify which of these options is playing out. a. Feel the tension and collapse into a Neuro-Limbic Type, discussed in Chapter 18 or a first-tier IC. When this happens, move to Step 2. b. Feel the tension and hold it. When this happens, move to Step 3. c. Feel the tension, convert the tension into nobility using C1 or C2, expressing human nobility with noble behaviour. Move to Step 4.
Step 2. **Identify the polarities**	This step involves accurately identifying the polarities of the tension. Every external problem creates internal tension between the Ps and the Is. Once you know which P (P1 or P2) and which I (I1 or I2) and you know in which meme the problem sits, you can identify the noble attractor that will resolve the problem. If collapse has occurred, the task is to rebuild the tension through targeted questioning and focusing attention on the required Intelligence Circuits. This necessitates being aware of the nature of the IC tensions.
Step 3. **Use creativity (C1 or C2) to unify the tensions and manifest a non-dual noble quality**	Use your awareness of the meme in which the problem sits and your understanding of the polarities and apply C1 or C2 to manifest the appropriate noble quality.
Step 4. **Convert insight into action**	Discern when the noble quality is being expressed, and then embed it in the narrative. You achieve this by viewing the situation from the noble quality's perspective and then retelling the story or describing the problem and its resolution from this viewpoint.

immediately encourage the individual to stay in the noble state.[1] If there is no nobility but the internal tension is being maintained, the individual will experience a term known as *infinite regression*. In this situation they are swinging between the two polarities of the problem (P1 and I1, P2 and I2, P1 and I2, or P2 and I1). In cases like this they will be locked into the problem and the meme theme as they oscillate between the two polarities. In this situation, the task is to move to Step 3 of the process and introduce either C1 or C2 creativity to the equation so that the internal tension can be unified.

Conversely, if your diagnosis is that the individual has collapsed into their Neuro-Limbic Type, you will need to best guess which profile they have collapsed into and begin the process of rebuilding their internal tension.

But how do you know their Neuro-Limbic Type? This best-guess process is easier said than done, but fortunately the Neuro-Limbic Types exhibit relatively consistent behaviour. There are a series of predictable emotions and issues around which their attention will fixate which, with a little practice, you will be able to identify.

Dr Ginger Lapid-Bogda (2004), author of *Bringing out the Best in Yourself at Work* argues that the collapse into Neuro-Limbic Types can be triggered by particular situations or language used by others. She refers to these amygdala reactions as *pinches*. When one of these trigger points is crossed, the person who has collapsed into a Neuro-Limbic Type will typically experience knots in the stomach, jolts in the head, or pangs in the chest. Along with these somatic indicators there will be thoughts along the line of, 'Why am I being treated this way? That person is wrong for acting in that manner!' There is also an emotional sensation of anger, hurt or fear. Being able to observe these *pinches* is enormously helpful in diagnosing the Neuro-Limbic Type into which the individual has collapsed.

A series of *pinches*[2] accumulates into a *crunch*. Crunches are much more obvious. A crunch is the time when most people label an event as conflict. During the crunch, our feelings become more heated, our sensitivities become heightened, and the risk of either conflict or avoidance rises. Regardless of whether the individual collapses[3] into I1 (moving away), P2 (moving against) or P1 (moving towards), the crunches experienced by yourself or others represent an excellent way of recognising if the individual has collapsed into their Neuro-Limbic Type (NLT). The Pinch-Crunch table summarises this framework.

The problem exists externally to the individual. This is critical to remember because when this is forgotten the 'self' merges with the problem and actually

---

1 The inner tension creates the energy required to manifest the noble quality.
2 Pinch-crunch comes from a larger conceptual model called *Planned renegotiation: A norm-setting OD Intervention*, developed by Jack Sherwood and John Glidewell, 1973.
3 Psychologist Karen Horney observed that people undergo internal collapse in one of three ways.

Neuro-Limbic Type	Sensitivities	Evidence of Collapse
NLT1 **Perfectionist** P1 with a colluding element of P2	• Any form of criticism, real or perceived; • Another person not following the letter of an agreement; • Not being involved with changing the rules or an agreement; • Believing they have been deceived.	• Somatic evidence of anger; • Talking in short and sharp statements; • Giving criticisms on seemingly unrelated issues; • Withdrawing into silence.
NLT2 **Helper** P1 with a colluding element of I2	• Not having their efforts appreciated; • Any sense that they themselves are not appreciated; • Not feeling like they have been heard by the other person; • Not having their needs heard by others.	• They may stew on their emotions for a long period of time; • They may become very emotional when they do say something; • They will always think through what they are going to say in advance, what has made them feel the way that they do, and what they believe that the other person has done wrong.
NLT6 **Loyal Sceptic** Pure P1 compliance	• A lack of what they believe to be truthful communication; • Authority that seems to be acting in an abusive manner; • Being under pressure.	• They may withdraw from the situation; • They could engage in intensive analysis of the situation; • They may act sycophantically alternated with bullying; • They might be highly reactive.

Neuro-Limbic Type	Sensitivities	Evidence of Collapse
NLT3 **Achiever** P2 with a colluding element of I1	• Any sense that they might fail or be perceived as failing; • Not appearing professional; • Any chance that they will not receive the praise and credit for their work; • Receiving culpability for fault that is not their own.	• They will ask brief and to the point questions; • They are unlikely to express their own feelings of being upset; • As they express themselves, their voice becomes harsh; • Their body language is unlikely to show that they are upset.
NLT7 **Epicure** P2 with a colluding element of C1	• Any task or activity that they interpret as being boring or of no significance; • Feeling that other people ignore and dismiss them; • Feeling that they are not being taken seriously; • Receiving criticism that they feel is unjust.	• They may rationalise their own behaviour; and/or • Blame others for their behaviour; • Become physically agitated; • Avoid the situation by thinking of pleasant alternatives.
NLT8 **Boss** Pure P2 aggression	• Any perceived injustice; • Not confronting an issue directly; • Others not taking personal responsibility for their actions; • A lack of candour in other people.	• They may feel extreme levels of anger that immediately prompt them to action; • They will sift and sort information in a very fast manner; • They will seek ways to avoid feeling vulnerable or out of control; • They may withdraw; • They may seek out the counsel of those whom they trust and respect; • They will discount those whom they feel are not worthy of respect.

Neuro-Limbic Type	Sensitivities	Evidence of Collapse
NLT9 **Peacemaker** I1 with a colluding element of I2	• Anything that disrupts the general peace and harmony; • Being told what they are supposed to do; • Feeling as if they are ignored; • Other people being rude; • Expressions of hostility; • Feeling as if they are being taken advantage of; • Being confronted; • Not feeling as if others are supporting them.	• They may withdraw; • They may display slight somatic expressions of anger, particularly about the face; • They may actually be unaware of their own anger; • Their anger may remain with them for extended periods of time.
NLT5 **Analyst** Pure I1	• Having information they have shared with someone shared with others; • Receiving surprises; • Someone being dishonest; • Situations that are not under control; • Tasks that they feel they cannot do.	• They may withdraw into silence; • Their withdrawal may not be physical, but mental; • They may actually express intense anger under pressure.
NLT4 **Artist** I1 with a colluding element of C2	• Receiving any form of sleight; • Feeling like they are being ignored; • Being required to act in a manner that contravenes their beliefs; • Any event that brings out a feeling of envy.	• They may withdraw into silence; • They may say something in a very blunt manner; • They may spend excessive periods of time reviewing and assessing a situation; • They will very likely hold onto feelings for long periods of time.

BECOMES the problem. That is, 'I am a failure', rather than, 'There is a problem with finances that I am currently working on'. This ability to dissociate from the problem is possible only with second-order thinking which is why it can't happen with the single ICs or with the Neuro-Limbic Types. Pure power is only available to those who can work at second-order awareness.

STEP 2. IDENTIFY THE POLARITIES

The problem may exist externally, but the tension is 'felt' internally. Humans are unique in that they are the only creatures that can use intention to change the world. But to do this we need to be able to 'see' the nature of the polarities which the problem is creating.

When this process is administered effectively and tension is accurately identified and then converted into nobility, this in turn leads to an explosion of energy and optimism. We can suddenly envisage new creative solutions, and feel the surge of positive emotion that accompanies the achievement of important goals or the knowledge that we have made a difference.

It is important to note the difference between dialogue that clarifies the tensions and dialogue that exacerbates the situation. Disabling dialogue leaves the other party paralysed with fear and doubt because it focuses not on solutions, but instead on the severity and intensity of the problem. It does this because it focuses on reinforcing the collapsed state of operating from one polarity, that is, P1, P2, I1 or I2.

As the tension between the Ps and Is is identified, the individual will tell their story about the situation with increasing clarity. This is the objective. It provides an opportunity to identify which polarities are in tension and the meme at which the problem exists.

It is important for the individual to retell the story again and again until this is clear. By the end of this second step, the individual should have clarity about the nature of the tension they are feeling and the meme in which this problem is manifesting. Once you are at this point you are ready to move on to the third step which involves introducing creativity.

STEP 3. INTRODUCE CREATIVITY TO THE STORY

So far you have identified the polarities and brought these to awareness. This creates the option to either contain the tension and resolve the issue through one of the noble qualities by introducing creativity, or to return to force and perpetuate the problem through one of the Neuro-Limbic Types. When creativity is added to the equation, the internal tension can be converted into something greater. Carl Jung correctly observed that creativity creates the opportunity for the individual to reach a new level of consciousness (Jung, cited by Huskinson, 2004).

There are two forms of creativity that will enable an individual to create nobility from tension. There is either the C1 spontaneous (Dionysian) creativity or the C2 visionary (transcending/Apollonian) creativity.

The C1 creativity is activated through a sense of spontaneity and gives rise to noble qualities that usually involve interacting with others to find the resolution. The C2 creativity is activated through an appreciation of the magnitude of the world and its awesome nature. It is activated through reflection, meditation or prayer and leads to a heightened sense of gratitude. This leads to understanding the tension within a broader context.

Each individual has their own unique ways of accessing these two forms of creativity. By introducing one of them, the person creates a 'portal' or noble quality that lies above the level of the problem's meme. It is through this portal or noble quality that the problem can be resolved.

The *NeuroPower* transformation process works because the noble quality or attractor enables the polarities to be unified at a higher level than they exist. The tension of the problem is unified and suddenly everything becomes clear and harmonious again in a non-dual reality.

When this happens it feels incredible. Suddenly the path forward becomes crystal clear. At this time it is important to discuss and embed this non-dual awareness so that the insight can be cemented.

Tips to Enhance C1 Creativity	
Work your body	Any activity that gets you in touch with your body can enhance your sense of gratitude, such as dancing, exercise, gym, craft work, sculpture, pottery, painting, sex or partying (C1).
Laugh	Use humour. The laughter itself is a release of tension and an expression of C1.
Socialise	Spend social time with some friends, enjoying good food and good wine (C1).
Stay light	Make light of the situation, for example, 'You really stuffed that up didn't you! Oh well, at least you didn't lose all your fingers.'

Putting the Problem into Perspective through C2	
Meditation	Persistent and focused attention on one issue or idea for an extended period of time.
Prayer	Prayer is generally both supplication and thanksgiving. This puts problems in perspective relative to what we have been given in life.
Reframe	Reframe the existing situation into a broader context. This can be over the course of the life of an individual or over the course of the life of an entire nation. Abraham Lincoln was fond of saying, 'This too shall pass' whenever he received troubling news about the progress of the American Civil War. Ask: • 'What is the bigger perspective?' • 'Let's helicopter above this.' • 'Let's put this situation in context.'

STEP 4. DISCERN, DISCUSS, ANCHOR AND PLAN THE PATH FORWARD

Once the noble quality is expressed it must be embedded through enabling questions which allow the individual to fully associate with the noble quality and translate the idea into action. This may involve asking how clear the individual is about the insight and solution they have put forward and then clarifying what they can do to apply this in the next twenty-four hours, one week, three months or twelve months. It may also involve asking them to retell their story, only this time embedding their new insight.

THE IDEA IN PRACTICE

Through this four-step process of conversion, using noble attractors can become a way of life, rather than an exception. In this way your life can become one which lifts all who come in contact with you as you convert torment and tension into nobility and action. In *NeuroPower* we refer to the conversion process as the four steps required to 'convert' problems into noble attractors.

Richard Branson has mastered the skill of converting problems into noble attractors. This is not to say that Branson is a saint all the time. Instead, we are simply saying, here is an ordinary man who has mastered this extra-ordinary capability, a capability that is within your reach now that you know how it works. Let us explore how Branson has used this conversion technique to change the lives of millions of people, one problem/opportunity at a time.

RICHARD BRANSON

Sir Richard Charles Nicholas Branson (born 18 July, 1950) is an English entrepreneur, best known for his Virgin brand, a banner that encompasses a variety of business organisations. The name Virgin was chosen because a female friend involved in setting up the initial record label commented, 'We're all virgins at business.' Sir Richard Branson was educated at Stowe until he was fifteen years old, and he began his entrepreneurial activities there by setting up a student magazine. When he was seventeen, he opened a Student Advisory Centre, his first charity institution (http://en.wikipedia.org/wiki/richard_branson, accessed 6 June, 2006).

In 1970 Branson was faced with a problem. He had very little capital and no real business experience and no real qualifications for a job. He knew (accessing his I1) that he could get his hands on very inexpensive records and that he could sell these at a fantastic profit for his own benefit (accessing P2). The question was how could he do it? He decided that the answer lay in using the mailing list and relationships he had built through the student magazine and Advisory Centre (using I1) in a new or innovative way (accessing his C1). This problem sat in the Orange meme, which in turn gave rise to the **Entrepreneurial** attractor. This led Branson to set up a record mail order business in 1970 and open his first record shop in Oxford Street, London shortly afterwards.

This entrepreneurial spirit also drove the formation in 1972 of the record label Virgin Records with Nik Powell and the opening of a recording studio. Branson's ability to convert business problems into opportunities, as in the example above, has enabled him to build one of the most loved business empires in the world.

It seems so easy when you read about success like this but its genesis was in the manifestation of the **Entrepreneurial** noble attractor and this is available to us all if we apply the four steps of conversion.

While the *NeuroPower* term *conversion* refers to an individual's ability to convert tension into nobility, we use the term *transformation* to refer to the creation of nobility corporately. This process is complex but enables individuals to experience the power of nobility by being part of a group or team. You will be able to understand this powerful process because you understand the process of conversion. Transformation takes the four steps of conversion and embeds it with a Sufi process to create an environment which fosters team commitment, discretionary effort, creativity and the achievement of corporate goals. Read on to find out how.

THE TRANSFORMATION PROCESS

NeuroPower refers to transformation as the series of steps which take a group through the stages of team building. Sometimes loosely described as Forming, Storming, Norming and Performing, the transformation process tracks individual resistance to change and the role of the leader to dissolve this resistance (which is based on communal collapse) into communal nobility. The history and complexity of this transformation process is fascinating and so I have included just some of the story below to enhance your ability to contextualise the approach.

It is thought that the transformation process was first identified by the Sufis thousands of years ago but it was introduced to the West by two of the mid-twentieth century founding fathers of modern psychiatry, Gurdjieff and Jung. They developed a range of physical and psychological methodologies for integrating its approach with modern psychological practice.

The transformation process as identified by the Sufis was based on the mathematical law of seven ($1/7 = 0.142857$ recurring). The Sufis believed that within any linear sequence, 1, 2, 3, 4, 5, 6, 7, 8 and 9, there was a special relationship between steps 1, 4, 2, 8, 5 and 7 at a deeper but hidden level. This sequence revealed that moving through any linear or logical sequence, from steps 1 to 9, was like the hands moving around a clock face. In this linear time, moments pass, but there is no development and no integration of knowledge. In contrast, moving through the Sufi sequence is like moving across time. There is profound development, progress and an integration of knowledge and experience.

Mathematically the sequence 1, 4, 2, 8, 5 and 7 represents infinity, indicating the timeless integration of knowledge. Gurdjieff worked extensively translating this sequence into a system of physical movements and meditations that could somatically help individuals to transform their human consciousness.

If we apply this transformation sequence to our understanding of the development of personality, could it mean that there is a hidden relationship between the sequential phases of development at causality awareness (as understood by the Sufis), (linear development) and the more advanced personalities at quantum adult consciousness (the deeper or hidden level of consciousness)?

My research suggests that the Neuro-Limbic Types that develop at the first level of causality awareness around the six phases of development (ICs) are force-based mimics of the power-based adult personalities that form at the second level.

This proposition makes sense if consciousness is structured as a holarchy and the partial personality at causality awareness is subsumed by the more complex and whole Neuro-Rational Type which brings with it a quantum level awareness. The emergent quantum level in the holarchy includes and yet transcends its former level. This takes place in a very structured and well-defined way.

For example, the first-order mimic profile (Neuro-Limbic Type One) that manifests at the first phase of development is a mimic of the profile that we refer to as the Crusader profile. The Crusader sits in the IT quadrant as outlined by Wilber in the *Four Faces of Truth* matrix.

The first-order mimic profile (Neuro-Limbic Type Two) that manifests at the second phase of development is a mimic Commander Profile. The Commander sits in the WE quadrant as outlined by Wilber in the *Four Faces of Truth* matrix.

My research shows that we can match the eight Master personalities with the eight Neuro-Limbic Types (NLTs) as follows:

NLT1 – Mimic Crusader	**NLT5** – Mimic Treasurer
NLT2 – Mimic Commander	**NLT6** – Mimic Navigator
NLT3 – Mimic Chancellor	**NLT7** – Mimic Judge
NLT4 – Mimic Bard	**NLT8** – Mimic Architect

If these eight profiles are put in the transformation sequence outlined by the Sufis, they look like this:

Phase 1: Crusader	**Phase 8:** Architect[*]
Phase 4: Bard	**Phase 5:** Treasurer
Phase 2: Commander	**Phase 7:** Judge

Integral philosophy argues that in order to move from one meme to the next, the individual must answer the questions of existence from each of the *Four Faces of Truth* (the four quadrants) (Wilber, 2000). If this were true and you were able to experience the noble quality of each Neuro-Rational Type in this order (by focusing your mind's attention on manifesting the noble quality of that type in the material world) it would build a 'holon' of experience or knowledge about that issue or topic. It would also mean that you would have addressed the questions of existence at that

---

[*] The only profile not to fit here is the Architect because there is no phase eight in first-order causality consciousness. The Architect's Genius is seeing Congruence. This is a second-order Genius that focuses on aligning the individual's life with their true purpose. As a second-order gift, it does not manifest at the first level even as a mimic. For this reason Architects are often described as being born old. It seems they were always serious, strategic and way beyond their years. Fortunately their Mirror Judge never really grows up so they enjoy parties and being young whenever they access their Mirror.

level and would begin to move naturally to the next level of consciousness. In this case, you would have experienced personal transformation through integration.

In practice this process may not be all plain sailing. One of the significant contributions made by process transformation philosophers like Gurdjieff was to identify three points along the way that are referred to as 'shock points'. These shock points are hurdles along the path of transformation that most of us cannot bridge. In the transformation sequence the shock points are points 3 and 6 and 9. (Point 9 is the end of the sequence and signifies the simultaneous beginning and end of the cycle.)

The Master profiles that correspond with these other two shock points are the Chancellor and the Navigator. If we now place these profiles in the transformation sequence, the transformation process has eight clear steps in the following order (shock points are bracketed): Crusader, Bard (Chancellor), Commander, Architect (Navigator), Treasurer, Judge.

This process has some fundamental components that make sense only when you can analyse the sequence using the Intelligence Circuits. Look at the following list and notice what change needs to take place at each step.

Step 1.	C2 P2 I1	The Crusader
Step 2.	C2 P2 I2	The Bard
Step 3.	C1 P2 I2	The Chancellor
Step 4.	C1 P1 I2	The Commander
Step 5.	C2 P1 I2	The Architect
Step 6.	C2 P1 I1	The Navigator
Step 7.	C1 P1 I1	The Treasurer
Step 8.	C1 P2 I1	The Judge

Notice that each step in the transformation process requires the movement of just one IC at a time. We can also see why steps 3 and 6 were shock points because if we simply apply the Sufi sequence, 1, 4, 2, 8, 5 and 7, without the Chancellor and the Navigator IC combinations, the transformation journey would require shifting two energies at once, between 4 and 2, and 8 and 5, which it seems is almost impossible.[4]

4　The process outlined above, however, would only be relevant if your Master profile were a Crusader. The other seven Master personalities have a different starting point and so must have a very different transformation process. These are individually outlined in each of the Neuro-Rational Type chapters in Principle #2.

THE IDEA IN PRACTICE

What is the practical use of this knowledge? This transformation process maps the way any leader can take their followers through transformation. I'll give you an example. Let's consider what it means in terms of how a group of people, that is, business or community, will react if they are told they need to change. The theory suggests that if they are engaged, a significant percentage of the community will move through the eight steps of the cycle together, at each phase addressing different issues and building momentum.

The first step in the cycle refers to the causality Neuro-Limbic Type One (NLT1), that forms around the emotion of self-righteous anger. When required to change, there is a tendency for all of us to resist with self-righteous anger, 'Because,' they say, 'there is absolutely nothing wrong with me. I am absolutely fine just the way I am.' The NLT1 (P1/P2) will endlessly justify why the current practice is the best and only practical solution for moving forward. In this situation, the leader's role is to convert the NLT1 into a Crusader profile through the introduction of C2 and I1. What this means is that the self-righteousness becomes transformed by the introduction of appreciation, vision and a healthy sense of reality. Once the perspective of the Crusader profile emerges with the associated noble attractors that manifest at the appropriate meme, the group will move to the next step in the cycle – NLT4.

At first this will be experienced emotionally as a NLT4, which will need to be transformed into the second-order profile of a Bard. The NLT4 is formed around the emotion of envy. This profile is a combination of C2 and I1. At this step, there is a strong awareness of all that is missing in life and a longing for what is not there. 'If only I had (whatever it is that is missing at the moment) my life would be better.' What is needed is for the leader to foster an authentic appreciation of present relationships while refocusing on results. This involves the introduction of I2 and P2 relationships. When this is done effectively the noble qualities of the Bard appear. When these elements are brought to the situation, there is the capacity to create a safe environment in which problems can be addressed and healing can take place. Only after the Bard profile is created can the meaning of the situation be appreciated. (At the force-based level, meaning is formed around what is missing from life rather than gratitude for what already exists.)

Once the perspective of the Bard has been achieved the first of Gurdjieff's shock points emerges. There is a strong tendency to want the progress that has been made so far to be seen and recognised. Vain glory, the emotion that drives the NLT3, emerges. The NLT3 uses the P2 from the Bard step to look for specific outcomes that will lead to measurable successes (an I1 application of this P2 drive).

Vain glory brings with it a continuous pursuit of approval that relentlessly drives the NLT3 to compete rather than cooperate. What is needed at this point is to introduce a sense of fun and flexibility, C1, and connection to others, I2.

Introducing these elements forms the perspective of the Chancellor and changes the focus from, 'How can I succeed and obtain ALL the recognition?' towards a position that seeks to find a way to make a connection with others so that the team shines. Success is achieved through genuine connections (I2 and C1) rather than through deceit, self-focus and approval seeking.

Once the Chancellor work is completed, the natural cycle of resistance continues with movement towards NLT2, comprising P1 and I2. This resistance pridefully states, 'I am completely self-sufficient, despite how very much everyone else seems to need me. I do not need anything or anyone.' The NLT2 perspective is to meet the needs of others with the expectation that they, in turn, will satisfy the NLT2's needs. What is needed is to introduce C1, through gratitude, flexibility and integrity in relationship, so that the Commander profile is formed. With the formation of the Commander, there is the capacity to courageously assess the problems preventing the accomplishment of the goals set in the Chancellor position, and to take innovative steps to resolve them. As these problems are resolved, resistance moves to NLT8.

As problems begin to be solved, and issues that once stopped progress are sequentially resolved, the natural resistance takes the form of lust. This lust emotionally reflects the NLT8, formed purely about P2, and it brings a strong desire to achieve immediate results. While there may be enormous amounts of passion, it heads off in many different directions often at the expense of teamwork. What is needed is the strategic contemplation of the Architect profile. This comes with the introduction of C2, P1 and I2. The difference between the Commander and the Architect is a movement away from solving the immediate problems towards solving future problems in a strategic fashion. As the capability to attain the future vision is developed, the second of Gurdjieff's shock points emerges.

Rather than moving directly from the Architect to the Treasurer, which represents a movement from C2 to C1 and a movement from I2 to I1, the nobility of the Navigator is needed to bridge the gap. While the Architect step focuses on setting the strategic direction and ensuring the capability to attain it, many of the team will get stuck on the worst-case scenarios and can get themselves trapped in 'awfulising' the future. This fear will focus on absolutely anything that may go wrong, and team members will constantly question the strategic direction. What is required is for the partial P1 of the NLT6 to be reinforced, C2 to be reintroduced together with a focus on the details and patterns of the situation, I1. This brings out the Navigator profile, which is the archetypal profile of leadership and which enables the real risks to be addressed, appropriately assessed and resolved. The noble qualities of the Navigator settle everyone down.

The emotion that arises after the Treasurer work is done is one of conceit; a sense that having made all these changes and having learned all this information, there is nothing more to learn. Rather than resolving issues and celebrating real successes, the NLT7 will think of all the various distractions that life has to offer. What is needed is for the leader to introduce I1 to focus the energy and enthusiasm that has been built through the transformation process on celebrating real successes and attaining specific outcomes. This occurs through the Judge profile that introduces the life force necessary to end one cycle and to begin another.

Highly effective teams experience the noble quality of each Neuro-Rational Type in this order, and carefully focus their attention on manifesting the noble quality of the appropriate Master personality in the sequence. This enables them to build a holon of experience and knowledge. It also means that they have addressed the questions of existence at that level of consciousness and begin the move to the next. In this situation, each team member will have experienced personal integration through community or team transformation.

APPLYING THE TRANSFORMATION PROCESS TO THE INDIVIDUAL

If we look at the transformation cycle detailed above and move to a higher logical level we can see that there is a definite pattern which emerges. The first step in the cycle moves from one I function to the other, the second from one C to the other and the third from one P to the other. If we continue down the process, the cycle finishes with C, I, C, P and C.

In other words, there is a higher-level generic transformation process through which all Master personalities travel which reads as follows: I, C, P, C, I, C, P and C. This has been discussed in more detail in Principle #2 in each of the Neuro-Rational Types.

The importance and the power of this transformation process cannot be understated. This sequence is the most efficient and effective way for us as human beings to answer the questions of existence at one meme. We do this by systematically embracing and embodying all eight noble qualities at that level of consciousness. This cycle clearly, concretely and eruditely articulates the road map for personal integration.

This clear process also speaks to us about the relative importance of the ingredients needed for transformation. The cycle has two parts awareness (I represents information and there is awareness of the internal and the external world), two parts action (P represents the two ways we take action either as a member of a team or by ourselves) and four parts creativity (C stands for creativity – both abstract and concrete). The cycle also clearly shows that the first step in transformation is awareness. Only with a new awareness should we engage our creativity. Contrast this to the cycle of disintegration (which is the same process but in the opposite order) where the first step is to engage our creativity to justify not doing the hard work of integration. No wonder this path leads to trauma.

Each of the eight Master personalities has a distinct view of 'truth' that represents their focus of attention. Since they start at different points, each type has a different cycle with different work to do. The movement through the transformational cycle for each of the eight personality types and the noble quality for that phase is plotted in Table 21.2 The Transformation Matrix.

As shown in this matrix, *NeuroPower* describes eight specific personalities or Neuro-Rational Types each with a noble quality. These eight noble qualities are eight partial aspects of pure consciousness. Two of the eight fall into each of the quadrants of truth outlined earlier by Wilber. Right now, you will probably fully understand just one of these eight, the one that aligns with your particular Master personality.

Reading down the column, the transformation matrix also maps how each of the eight Master personalities can logically and sequentially integrate the seven noble qualities they need in order to complete a holon of knowledge at the Blue meme, following the sequence of the transformation process. Once this journey has been made the questions of existence for that topic or area of focus for that level of consciousness (Integral refers to this as a line) will have been addressed. Once the eight perspectives of the Neuro-Rational Types have been successfully integrated the individual is ready to move to a higher level of consciousness in that area.

This proactive transformation cycle sequentially confronts an individual with a series of questions and exercises that, once addressed, enable them to move through the eight noble qualities in the sequence outlined. Along the way, in order to answer these questions, the individual must reconcile and integrate the perspectives of the eight Neuro-Rational Types. Once these have been successfully integrated the individual is ready to move to a higher level of consciousness in that area.

If during the process of integration any of the perspectives of the eight Neuro-Rational Types are ignored or denied, those ignored aspects of truth actually reappear as fresh problems at a later time and the denied perspectives will flavour and confuse the transition to the next level. (The unintegrated aspects will eat away from within and ambush any attempt to move to a higher level of consciousness.)

The transformation process is a natural consequence for those who are focusing on the high side or noble quality of themselves and others. I have also found that if you proactively engage in following the tenets of most established religious or spiritual practices, you will move through this process irrespective of your conscious knowledge of it. Despite this, it is estimated that less than 1 per cent of the population is proactively engaged in the transformation cycle.

The energy for the transformation process is driven by physis or the desire for all

Table 21.2 The Transformation Matrix[5]

The Path of Transformation through Integration (Blue Meme)

Neuro-Rational Type and Noble Quality at Blue	Crusader	Bard	Chancellor	Commander	Architect	Navigator	Treasurer	Judge
NRT Noble Quality	1. Integrity	1. Inspiration	1. Diplomacy	1. Courage	1. Discernment	1. Responsibility	1. Objectivity	1. Drive
Step 1	2. Inspiration	2. Integrity	2. Drive	2. Objectivity	2. Responsibility	2. Discernment	2. Courage	2. Diplomacy
Step 2	3. Diplomacy	3. Drive	3. Integrity	3. Responsibility	3. Objectivity	3. Courage	3. Discernment	3. Inspiration
Step 3	4. Courage	4. Objectivity	4. Responsibility	4. Integrity	4. Drive	4. Diplomacy	4. Inspiration	4. Discernment
Step 4	5. Discernment	5. Responsibility	5. Objectivity	5. Drive	5. Integrity	5. Inspiration	5. Diplomacy	5. Courage
Step 5	6. Responsibility	6. Discernment	6. Courage	6. Diplomacy	6. Inspiration	6. Integrity	6. Drive	6. Objectivity
Step 6	7. Objectivity	7. Courage	7. Discernment	7. Inspiration	7. Diplomacy	7. Drive	7. Integrity	7. Responsibility
Step 7	8. Drive	8. Diplomacy	8. Inspiration	8. Discernment	8. Courage	8. Objectivity	8. Responsibility	8. Integrity

INTERNAL   EXTERNAL

5 Based on the Blue meme. See Appendix 7 for a complete map of each Neuro-Rational Type at all memes.

living things to grow and develop to reach their full potential. If you are committed to taking the hard road, doing the hard work and staying focused on the noble qualities of the human spirit you will move through the transformation cycle.

Once you are aware of the transformational path, it is always interesting to review your life or the lives of those close to you and see how they have either unwittingly spiralled up through integration or unwittingly spiralled down. Both cycles have been outlined in each of the Master personality chapters earlier in this book.

So now you have the insight and the capability to live a life of awareness. We have introduced you to the conversion process so that daily problems can be converted into nobility. We have introduced you to the corporate transformation process so that you can lead teams or groups in a way that supports and encourages everyone in the team and we have explored the process of personal integration. With this awareness we encourage you to apply the knowledge. This information has the potential to change your life in ways that you can't imagine.

Summary of Chapter 21:
Problems are the Seeds of our Nobility

- There is a practical method that we can all use to transform tension into nobility.

- The first step is to become aware of how you deal with tension. Is it being maintained and transformed? Have you collapsed into one of the polarities?

- If collapse has occurred, the tension needs to be rebuilt again.

- Once the tension is established, introduce creativity so that the appropriate noble quality can be manifested.

- Recall, amplify and anchor the noble quality and then address your questions of existence from this state.

- This method allows problems to be solved in the physical world while achieving greater wholeness and manifesting human nobility.

- The transformation path maps the process of moving from one meme to the next through the eight noble qualities.

- Insight is the booby prize – your task is to turn this insight into your own noble action.

- Get started.

Chapter 22

Wisdom through the Four Non-dual Leader Profiles

First among the virtues found in the state, wisdom comes into view

Plato in *The Republic*

PEACE

GRATITUDE

HUMILITY

COMPASSION

The Cognitive Axioms of Adult Personality that Prevent the Manifestation of Non-duality

Ax.i.om (noun)

1. A statement or idea that people accept as self-evidently true.

2. A basic proposition of a system that, although unproven, is used to prove the other propositions in the system.

Non-duality (Various usages)

1. Non-dualism may be viewed as the belief that dualism or dichotomy are illusory phenomena. Examples of dualisms include self/other, mind/body, male/female, good/evil, active/passive, dualism/non-dualism and many others. It is accessible as a belief, theory, condition, as part of a tradition, as a practice, or as the quality of union with reality.

2. A non-dual philosophical or religious perspective or theory maintains that there is no fundamental distinction between mind and matter, or that the entire phenomenological world is an illusion (with reality being described variously as the Void, the Is, Emptiness, the mind of God, Atman or Brahman). Non-theism provides related conceptual and philosophical information.

3. Many traditions (generally originating in Asia) state that the true condition or nature of reality is non-dualistic, and that these dichotomies are either unreal or (at best) inaccurate conveniences. While attitudes towards the experience of duality and self may vary, non-dual traditions converge on the view that the ego, or sense of personal being, doer-ship and control, is ultimately said to be an illusion. As such, many non-dual traditions have significant overlap with mysticism.

WHILE CHARACTER IS SITUATIONAL, WISDOM IS ENDURING

There are Non-dual Leaders all around us, in governments, running our hospitals, building our roads and leading our social movements. They are the people we admire and follow.

We follow Non-dual Leaders because we trust them. We trust them because we are neurobiologically wired to sense they are coming from a position of nobility rather than a position of selfishness. While we might trust them, they are difficult to understand because they have integrated so much knowledge in the domain of their leadership that they live in a world of non-dual simplicity on the other side of complexity.

Exploring leaders who access non-dual consciousness is a challenge for most people because it is only possible when the explorer has the physical, cognitive, emotional and spiritual capacity to not only comprehend the complexity that comes with duality but also the awareness to understand that all experience is the non-dual wave of non-dual reality. This is the defining experience of what I describe as the Non-dual Leader. For most of us, achieving this state is easier said than done.

Methodologies for achieving this state have been outlined by the Non-dual Leaders of many of the great faiths and religions including Hinduism, Buddhism,

---

The Neurobiology of Trust

Leaders that others want to follow are trustworthy. That is, trustworthiness is the primary determinant of being a leader. The process we use to assess another's trustworthiness is largely innate, can happen outside of our awareness and uses our amygdala.

Your amygdala reads and automatically judges the trustworthiness of everybody you come in contact with. Your amygdala enables you to better perceive others by fully immersing in the other person's state of being.

If the verdict is 'untrustworthy', the right insula lights up to broadcast that message to the viscera. The face-responsive region of the fusiform gyrus also activates. If the verdict is 'trustworthy', there is a more substantial activation from the orbitofrontal cortex. Either way, the right superior temporal sulcus takes the role of an association cortex to process the judgement. The emotional systems such as the orbitofrontal cortex and the amygdala thereafter tag the subject with the verdict (Winston et al., 2002).

Taoism, Christianity, Islam and Judaism. Writings that explore this space are sometimes referred to as articulating a *Perennial Philosophy*; that is, a philosophy that is focused on not only defining a supreme identity or unity consciousness, but also on techniques for breaking down the barriers that prevent us, as sentient beings, from being able to merge with this supreme being or unity consciousness and experience a non-dual level of awareness.

The key to this is to unify the opposites that we insist on dividing the world into. This is beautifully described in the following three texts:

> Content with getting what arrives of itself
> Passed beyond the pairs, free from envy.
> Not attached to success nor failure,
> Even acting, he is not bound.
> He is to be recognized as eternally free
> Who neither loathes nor craves; For he that is freed from the pairs,
> Is easily freed from conflict.
>
> *Bhagavad Gita*

> They said to Him: Shall we then, being children, enter the Kingdom?
> Jesus said to them: When you make the two one,
> and when you make the inner as the outer
> and the outer as the inner
> and the above as the below,
> and when you make the male and the female into a single one,
> then you shall enter the Kingdom.
>
> *The Gospel of St. Thomas*

> False-imagination teaches that such things as light and shade, long
> and short, black and white are different and are to be discriminated;
> but they are not independent of each other; they are only different
> aspects of the same thing, they are terms of relation, not reality.
> Conditions of existence are not of mutually exclusive character. In
> essence things are not two but one.

> We could multiply these quotes indefinitely, but they would all point to
> the same thing: ultimate reality is a union of opposites. And since it is
> expressly the boundaries which we superimpose on reality that slice it
> up into innumerable pairs of opposites, the claim of all these traditions
> that reality is freed from the pairs of opposites is a claim that reality is
> freed from all boundaries. That reality is not-two means that reality is
> no-boundary.

> But, we ask, what will happen to our drive for progress if we see
> all opposites are one? Well, with any luck, it will stop – and with it
> that peculiar discontent that thrives on the illusion that the grass is
> greener on the other side of the fence. But we should be clear about
> this. I do not mean that we will cease making advancements of a
> sort in medicine, agriculture and technology. We will only cease
> to harbour the illusion that happiness depends on it. For when we
> see through the illusions of our boundaries, we will see, here and
> now, the universe as Adam saw it before the Fall: an organic unity, a
> harmony of opposites, a melody of positive and negative, delight with
> the play of our vibratory existence. When the opposites are realised
> to be one, discord melts into concord, battles become dances, and old
> enemies become lovers. We are then in a position to make friends with
> all of our universe, and not just one half of it.
>
> *Taken from the Lankavatara Sutra*

In Principle #1, I introduced readers to key frameworks that helped to define the human experience at first-tier levels of consciousness. Foundational to this understanding are the six neurobiological social cognitive functional networks that provide the building blocks of more complex and integrated personality that manifest at higher levels of consciousness.

These six neurobiological building blocks are accessed in different combinations to give rise to the nine childlike or Neuro-Limbic Types, the eight adult Master Neuro-Rational Types (and their corresponding Mirrors), the four Non-dual Leaders, and finally, the two Integrated Avatar Archetypes.

In Spiral Dynamics parlance this level of consciousness aligns with the Turquoise meme. Spiral Dynamic's authors, Don Beck and Christopher Cowan describe this as:

> *The focus of this meme is on holons (an integration of 'I' 'WE' 'IT' and*
> *'ITS' quadrants of Ken Wilber's integral framework). It is a purpose-*
> *driven collective/communal meme. It encompasses, but is not limited to*
> *the harmony-drive of Green, nor is it dogma-centred as in Blue, nor do*
> *mystical forces and kinship link it as with Purple. The sense of community*
> *is very broad. It centres on life itself, not just humans. The planet is seen as*
> *one single unit. It may also act with more urgency than Yellow to resolve*
> *problems and issues since the doubts about the value of self-sacrificial*
> *investments of time and energy may have inhibited actions. Feelings*
> *and knowledge become integrated. Individuals learn not only through*
> *observation and participation, but also through the experience of simply*
> *being. The individual in this meme trusts intuition and instinct allowing*

the mind to process with both the conscious and the unconscious selves as co-participants. There is a sense of reconnection with aspects of themselves stifled or supplanted by powerful forces in the substance existence of first-order thinking. This activates greater resources within the person's mind and brain.

This view of the world sees life as interlinked causes and effects and interacting fields of energy. Universal order, but in a living, conscious fashion, is not based on external rules (Blue) or group bonds (Green). The individual now experiences a level of bonding and communication beyond any previous meme. Seeing everything at once before doing anything specific, dominates the thinking process. Those thoughts and actions that enhance the health of the entire biosphere become the priority. Beck and Cowan (1996) estimated that approximately 0.1 per cent of the world's population is living in this meme. (Spiral Dynamics, 1996, p. 188)

On Hawkins' map of consciousness, the Turquoise meme calibrates as a band from 660 to 670 and links this with Bliss and an integral awareness and understanding of the world.

The Process of Hardwiring Nobility

What character are we shaping or hardwiring into our brain? We can hardwire nobility through neuroplasticity, which is the concept that repeated experiences impact the shape, size and number of neurons and their synaptic connections for that type of experience. That is, what we commonly experience creates certain neural circuitry to experience more of the same. So, if we spend time habitually stressed in a Core Belief state, perhaps holding onto long-term hurt or being repeatedly triggered in a key relationship, over the course of years it can shape our brain to experience more of the same. Similarly, repeatedly expressing nobility forms a brain with neurons shaped, sized and connected for more nobility (Goleman, 2006, p. 11).

The Role of Integration

'... there are not just one but many levels of identity
available to an individual.
These levels of identity are not
theoretical postulates but observable realities –
you can verify them in and for yourself.
Ken Wilber (1979, p. 8)

THE ROLE OF INTEGRATION, LINES, STAGES AND STATES IN OUR MULTI-DIMENSIONAL EXPERIENCE OF CONSCIOUSNESS

As sentient beings we are all drawn to wholeness. This powerful drive was referred to by the Greeks as physis and describes the in-built drive that energises us all towards the manifestation of our most integrated self. For many Mesoamerican native tribes such as the Maya Lenca, this force was identified as Ik. It is also referred to in the Christian tradition as the Holy Spirit.

In life there are many different aspects to our existence and to our development. The moral, spiritual, professional, interpersonal and intellectual parts of us can all be at different stages of development. This concept, which has been articulated by Ken Wilber and others, suggests that in a life of development these different aspects can be referred to as lines of development. In this way we may be highly developed in one area (line) and not at all developed in another.

Stages refer to definite, sequential stages of development that everyone passes through as they mature and develop. Each meme as described in Spiral Dynamics could be considered to be a different sequential stage of development. By answering the questions of existence at the previous memes the individual earns stages. Developmentally, it is impossible to skip a meme.

States, however, are quite different from stages. An individual can experience being in a state at a higher meme than they normally experience life. This can be as a result of a peak experience that overrides the stage they are in developmentally.

The Non-dual Leader exists in the Turquoise meme, which sits between a calibration of 660 to 670 on Hawkins' map of consciousness. We all have a Non-dual Leader buried within us. But this is where lines, stages and states become central to our discussion.

We may experience our Non-dual Leader in one particular line of our life. For example, at work, in a particular academic specialty, in a relationship or in a specific role we could be in the Non-dual Leader space and working at the Turquoise meme. This, however, may not extend to other areas of our life. It is useful to reflect on your life and your areas of interest and see if you can identify any Turquoise lines.

Throughout our history, great spiritual and civic leaders have developed many lines so that their psycho-spiritual development has a centre of gravity in the Non-dual Leader or Turquoise meme. I would refer to this as an individual who is a Non-dual Leader. It is a loose classification because in reality virtually no one is experiencing their non-dual self all of the time.

Unsurprisingly, most of us experience our internal Non-dual Leader episodically as a state rather than a stage. We come up with a brilliant idea, become aware of a major breakthrough, integrate previously unintegrated information or have a blinding 'flash' of brilliance. In these situations we may only experience the Non-dual Leader for moments but they can be the moments that change not only our lives but also the lives of possibly millions of others.

Fortunately, to access this non-dual state there is a map and a method, which we can now explore in more detail.

Introducing the Four Types of
Non-dual Leaders

'Just when the caterpillar thought the world was over,
it became a butterfly.'
Anonymous

THE NON-DUAL LEADER

In researching the differences between the Non-dual Leader and the Master Neuro-Rational Type, I found that there were three noticeable themes; firstly, the Non-dual Leader embraces both context and content. This comes from their limbic/ intuitive wisdom. Secondly, the Non-dual Leader realises the impossibility of their cognitive fixation, which when unlocked, liberates them to cognitively focus on living consciously in the moment rather than being distracted by a problem that doesn't exist. This is what I refer to as the resolution of the type's implicit paradox. And finally, by accessing both their limbic/intuitive and cognitive systems to deliver timely, powerful and practical applications of their noble quality, Non-dual Leaders convert problems that are embedded in duality into non-dual solutions. All this is experienced by the Non-dual Leader as effortless and for others encapsulates dignity and leadership.

The Maya Lenca refer to the Non-dual Leader as the Moloilo. The Moloilo is a non-dual being that each of the Lenca aspired to become. The following text is taken from the sacred Maya Lenca Creed, which is thought to originate from around AD 300, and explains the Non-dual Leader beautifully.

> V: 15: Aim to be a Moloilo because only a Moloilo is complete amid the emptiness. He is a master and disciple, a leader and a follower, a great lord and humble servant. He is a warrior and a maiden at once. In his heart there is abundance, his presence illuminates like a smokeless torch. A Moloilo leads himself, follows himself, talks to himself and listens to himself because truly dual is his being, a true twin he is.

> V: 34: Follow the noble road, the one that crosses the green fields and mountains, rivers, valleys, volcanoes and seas. This is the only road that goes beyond the portal of death. This is the road that takes your footsteps to the door of the grand house of your great tribe that wait your arrival to your real home once you have lived on this earth. Becoming a Moloilo is becoming eternal. A Moloilo pierces through time because it becomes the white road linking yesterday, today and eternity, thus the Moloilo becomes a white road on which our children and grandchildren may walk to return home.

In exploring each of the four types of Non-dual Leaders we will consider the nature of the wound from which the Non-dual Leader has emerged, the infant/adult/ emotional position, the impact this has on the emotional level (Lost Aspect of Love), the impact this has on the intellectual level (Implicit Paradox), the limbic integration, the egocentric derailer, the virtue to be internalised and the virtue to be manifested. All these elements and their relationship to the four Non-dual Leaders have been summarised in Table 22.2.

DIAGRAM 22.1 THE INTEGRATION PROCESS

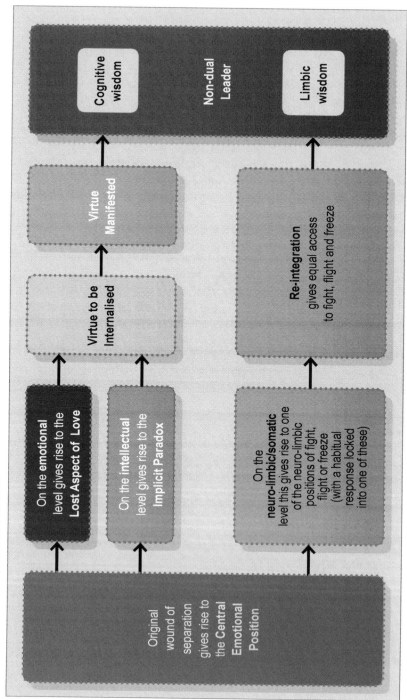

Copyright Peter Burow 2007

TABLE 22.2 THE PATH TO NOBILITY

NON-DUAL LEADER	CENTRAL EMOTIONAL POSITION (HARRIS)	INFANT CLASSIFICATION	ADULT EMOTIONAL POSITION	THE LOST ASPECT OF LOVE	THE AXIOM OR IMPLICIT PARADOX	EGO-CENTRIC POSITION 'DERAILER'	VIRTUE TO BE INTERNALISED	VIRTUE MANIFESTED
Peaceful Warrior	I'm not OK, you're not OK	Disorganised or disoriented	Unresolved, disorganised	Charity	Worthiness through purpose	Self-criticism	Compassion	Peacefulness
Grateful Healer	I'm OK, you're not OK	Avoidant	Dismissing	Affection	Freedom through security	Arrogance	Humility	Gratitude
Humble Sage	I'm not OK, you're not OK	Disorganised or disoriented	Unresolved, disorganised	Friendship	Alignment through Power	Ingratitude	Gratitude	Humility
Compassionate Leader	I'm not OK, you're OK	Resistant or ambivalent	Preoccupied	Eros	Love through beauty	Restlessness	Peacefulness	Compassion

EXPLORING THE FOUR LOVES AND PERSONALITY

The book *The Four Loves*, by C. S. Lewis, is an exploration of the experience of human love from a Christian perspective; however, I believe it is an interesting piece of work that is equally relevant to all who want to explore the dynamics of a Perennial Philosophy.

Central to Lewis' argument is the idea that disowned aspects of love can become twisted when the individual's personality rejects the aspect and then tries to compensate by creating a mimic of this aspect of love with their mind. When this happens the *man- made* version of the aspect of love can become an addiction because it is egocentric rather than spirit based. The ego-version of love then becomes a conditional love and an illusion.

> *Every human love, at its height, has a tendency to claim for itself a divine authority. Its voice tends to sound as if it were the will of God Himself. It tells us not to count the cost, it demands of us a total commitment, and it attempts to over-ride all other claims and insinuates that any action which is sincerely done for love's sake is thereby lawful and even meritorious* (Lewis, 1960, p. 15).

Lewis argues that the desire to experience love can be so compelling and important to a person that it can override their obligations as humans to be moral and just.

In our search for the experience of the four loves the unconditional allegiance which we owe only to God becomes skewed. I believe that each of us has disconnected from one of the four loves. The love from which we have disconnected then underpins and drives our quest to rediscover it through our own creation. The love from which we have disassociated becomes a weakened down, skewed version of the original, but of our own creation.

This personality-based aspect of God then becomes our demon. Lewis calls these loves natural loves and argues that they will destroy us. He argues that natural loves that are allowed to become gods do not remain loves. They are still called so, but can become in fact complicated forms of hatred (Lewis, 1960, p. 17).

Lewis also argues that the hatred that a corrupt love is transformed into is often a form of jealousy where the lover owns the object of affections and is offended at every moment spent apart.

Lewis begins his exploration of love by dividing it into three domains: need-love, gift-love, and appreciative-love.

He argues that need-love cries to God from our poverty (this bubbles up from the Neuro-Limbic Types); gift-love longs to serve, or even to suffer for, God; and appreciative-love says, 'We give thanks to thee for thy great glory.' Need-love says of another 'I cannot live without them'; gift-love longs to give him/her happiness, comfort, protection if possible, wealth; and appreciative-love gazes and holds its breath and is silent, rejoices that such a wonder should exist even if not for him/her, will not be wholly dejected by losing him/her, would rather have it so than never to have seen him/her at all (Lewis, 1960, p. 26).

By distinguishing need-love (such as the love of a child for its mother) from gift-love (epitomised here by God's love for humanity), Lewis emphasises that the natures of even these basic categorisations of love are more complicated than they, at first, seem. As a result, he formulates the foundation of his topic ('the highest does not stand without the lowest') by exploring the nature of pleasure, and then by dividing love into four categories, based in part on the four Greek words for love: affection, friendship, Eros and charity. Lewis warns his readers that just as Lucifer, a former archangel, perverted himself by pride and fell into depravity, so too can love become corrupt by presuming itself to be what it is not ('love begins to be a demon the moment he begins to be a god').

Each of us has one of the four loves as an ego-love rather than a real love. This personality-created mimic of the original love is resolved at the Turquoise meme This resolution marks the transition from the dualistic leader to the Non-dual Leader. We will now explore each of the loves in more detail.

Love at a Biochemical Level

The presence of the different loves is reflected in our bodies biochemically. Eros or lust shows itself through the sex hormones androgens and estrogens. Affection and friendship is apparent in our bodies through a concoction of relaxation and pleasure chemicals in the form of large doses of norepinephrine and dopamine, and small doses of serotonin. Charity is reflected in the body by changing levels of kindness and caregiving chemicals, namely vasopressin and oxytocin (Fisher, 2004).

Charity

(THIS IS THE DISOWNED ASPECT OF LOVE FOR THE CRUSADER AND THE COMMANDER)

Charity (agapē, αγαπη) is a love directed towards one's neighbour, which does not depend on any lovable qualities that the object of love possesses. Charity focuses on the need of subordinating the natural loves to the love of something greater. Lewis postulates the idea of love being like a garden in its effect on charity. God's love and guidance act on our natural love (that cannot remain what it is by itself) as the sun and rain act on a garden: without either, the object would cease to be beautiful or worthy. Lewis warns that those who exhibit charity must constantly check themselves that they do not flaunt and thereby warp this love ('But when you give to someone, don't tell your left hand what your right hand is doing.' Matthew 6:3), which is its potential threat.

Retrieved and adapted from http://en.wikipedia.org/wiki/The_Four_Loves

For the Crusader/Commander, whose central emotional position is 'I'm not OK, you're not OK', this lost aspect of love makes perfect sense because it enables the personality to disappear and join forces with a cause that is bigger than both themselves and the world. It can even provide a spiritual crusade to the Crusader/Commander that, as we will see later, supports their implicit paradox.

Affection

(THIS IS THE DISOWNED ASPECT OF LOVE FOR THE BARD AND THE TREASURER)

Affection (storge,στοργε) refers to fondness built on familiarity. Specifically it refers to people who have found themselves together by chance. Lewis suggests that affection is the most natural, emotive and widely diffused of loves; natural in that it is present without coercion; emotive because it is the result of fondness due to familiarity; and most widely diffused because it pays the least attention to those characteristics deemed 'valuable' or worthy of love and, as a result, is able to transcend most discriminating factors.

Retrieved and adapted from http://en.wikipedia.org/wiki/The_Four_Loves

> *Affection at its best practises a courtesy which is incomparably more subtle, sensitive, and deep than the public kind. In public a ritual would do. At home you must have the reality, which that ritual represented, or else the deafening triumphs of the greatest egoist present. You must really give no kind of preference to yourself; at a party it is enough to conceal the preference (Lewis, 1960, p. 55).*

For the Bard/Treasurer, affection is the lost aspect of love and so rather than relaxing and assuming affection, the Bard/Treasurer over-compensates by creating safe environments that will lure people to visit, through over-generosity in the case of the Bard and under-generosity in the case of the Treasurer. Both behaviours assume that affection does not manifest without active personality-based intervention. This crystallises the central emotional position 'I'm OK, you're not OK' because it assumes the other is not OK enough to have the ability to display affection autonomously.

Friendship
(THIS IS THE DISOWNED ASPECT OF LOVE FOR THE ARCHITECT AND THE JUDGE)

Friendship (philia, φιλια) describes the strong bond existing between people who share a common interest or activity. Lewis explicitly says that his definition of friendship is narrower than mere companionship: friendship in his sense only exists if there is something for the friendship to be *about*. It is the least natural of loves, states Lewis; that is, it is not biologically necessary to progeny like affection (for example, rearing a child), Eros (for example, creating a child), or Charity (for example, providing for a child). It has the least association with impulse or emotion. In spite of these characteristics, it was the belief of the ancients (Lewis himself, too) that it was the most admirable of loves because it looked not at the beloved (like Eros), but it looked towards the thing about which the relationship was formed. He argues that this frees the participants in the friendship from self-consciousness because they are looking towards something beyond or above themselves. And although the love may not be biologically necessary, it has, argues Lewis, civilisation value. The thing beyond or above them may be of monumental importance to society. But without the benefit of friendship to blunt the loneliness of *being the only person who sees this*, or the idea that two heads are better than one, many advances in society may never have been embarked upon. The relationship is by its nature selective and, therefore, exclusive.

Retrieved and adapted from http://en.wikipedia.org/wiki The_Four_Loves

For the Architect/Judge whose central emotional position which is the same as the Crusader/Commander, 'I'm not OK, you're not OK', this lost aspect of love makes perfect sense because it enables the personality to secure friendship by creating organisations, institutions or community groups to make the world a better place. As we will see later, this also underpins the Architect/Judge implicit paradox.

Eros

(THIS IS THE DISOWNED ASPECT OF LOVE FOR THE CHANCELLOR AND THE NAVIGATOR)

Eros (εροσ) is love in the sense of being in love. This is distinct from sexuality, which Lewis calls Venus, although he does spend time discussing sexual activity and its spiritual significance in both a pagan and a Christian sense. He identifies Eros as indifferent. This is good because it promotes appreciation of the beloved regardless of any pleasure that can be obtained from them. It can be counter-productive, however, and this blind devotion has been at the root of many of history's most abominable tragedies. In keeping with his warning that 'love begins to be a demon ...' he warns against the danger of elevating Eros to the status of a god.[1]

For the Chancellor/Navigator, whose central emotional position is 'I'm not OK, you're OK', this lost aspect of love makes perfect sense to focus on creating because they become OK if their appreciation of someone or something is so absolute that for a moment they can forget about their unworthiness. Once again, this supports the Chancellor/Navigator's implicit paradox, as will be explored in more depth in the next section.

But first let's explore each of the four Non-dual Leaders, their implicit paradox and how the resolution of this implicit paradox allows for the re-integration of the lost aspect of love.

---

1   Retrieved and adapted from *http://en.wikipedia.org/wiki/The_Four_Loves*

ethical

seeks justice

seeks integrity

strives for
excellence

magnanimous

benevolent

compassionate

The
Peaceful
Warrior

harmonious

enabling

ingenius

courageous

self-controlled

reverent

peacefulness

The Peaceful Warrior

(CREATIVE, POWERFUL AND SOCIAL SUBTYPES)

The Peaceful Warrior emerges from the integration of the Commander and Crusader Master Profiles. These determined, yet peaceful, people often talk of past times in their lives when they were physically and verbally aggressive and were feared by fellow workers, friends and family alike (particularly the leadership subtype). Both the Commander and Crusader in the Red meme can be pretty feisty.

The Peaceful Warrior, however, is intense, present, calm, strong, balanced and simultaneously wise and almost childlike in their innocence. They enjoy debating big picture social issues and have the disarming honesty and down-to-earth style of no-nonsense practical clarity. Consistent, stable and willing to roll up their sleeves, the Peaceful Warrior is the voice of reason when others are taking up arms, wanting revenge, seeking legal action or playing politics.

The Peaceful Warrior is naturally drawn to legal issues and practical action that may enable hungry people to eat, shut-in people to get out or disabled people to live a more fulfilling life. The Peaceful Warrior often takes on the thankless tasks that are not paid, rewarded or remembered but that can make an enormous difference in the lives of both individuals and communities. Like all the Non-dual Leaders, Peaceful Warriors are the quiet achievers impacting millions without fanfare.

Table 22.3 Non-dual Leader - The Peaceful Warrior

The Lost Aspect of Love	Infant Classification	Adult Emotional Position	Central Emotional Position (Harris)	The Axiom or Implicit Paradox	Ego-centric Position 'Derailer'	Virtue of Doing	Virtue of Being
Charity	Disorganised or disoriented	Unresolved, disorganised	I'm not OK, you're not OK	Worthiness through purpose	Self-criticism	Com-passion	Peace-fulness

The Peaceful Warrior's Axiom

THE IMPLICIT PARADOX: WORTHINESS THROUGH PURPOSE

The implicit paradox describes the unconscious cognitive question that the Master and Mirror strive to answer through the application of their strategic world view and their respective noble qualities. For the Crusader and Commander this manifests as a constant searching for an external purpose that is so great that it will lead to internal worthiness. The initial wound comes from disorganised or disoriented infant behaviour that leads in turn to an adult emotional position described as unresolved or disorganised. Harris describes this central emotional position as *I'm not OK, you're not OK.*

This central emotional position can give us deeper insight as to how and why the implicit paradox forms. The Peaceful Warrior spends a lifetime of cognitive attention trying to tame and improve a dangerous and unsure, not OK world, so that the not OK self can be redeemed.

When working with Crusaders and Commanders wishing to explore their Non-dual Leader, it can be helpful to have them meditate on the many external crusades they have been on in their lives and are still on that are driven by the internal desire to feel redeemed and worthy. Below is a list of the purposes or sacrifices Crusaders or Commanders have made to achieve worthiness – of course, the list is endless.

Sample purposes (at lower memes purpose can often be replaced by personal sacrifices):

- Sacrificing a career by staying home to look after the children
- Running the local charity
- Supporting the local church
- Feeding the hungry
- Visiting hospitals
- Looking after the homeless
- Giving to every charity
- Not buying any new clothes or going on holiday
- Not marrying
- Not having sex
- Not taking the promotion
- Not studying
- Not putting in for a pay rise or a promotion

- Staying in a regional area when you want to move to the city or vice versa
- Not having surgery
- Fasting
- Going to jail for somebody else's crime
- Being expelled
- Not having the career they want

The Non-dual Leader manifests when the Crusader or the Commander and their respective Mirrors see that *their redemption/worthiness is totally unrelated to purpose or personal sacrifice.* The Peaceful Warrior realises they have no need to be redeemed because worthiness is a false construct built on first-tier duality.

There is a realisation that worthiness is the trough of the same wave that carries conviction as its crest because in reality in a non-dual world there can be no worthiness.

Of course, the individual cannot be redeemed even if they are engaged in a purpose regardless of how noble it is. This paradox can only be resolved when the individual lets go of *self* and of overly identifying with the feelings of guilt and unworthiness and replaces them with non-dual acceptance and peacefulness. The peace of the Peaceful Warrior comes from within.

When we are working with Crusaders and Commanders we encourage them to look deeply at the mental frameworks and *unconscious deals* they have done with themselves, their families and their friends that support or underpin the *worthiness through purpose* implicit paradox. In this way the unconscious script is brought out into the open and exposed for what it is – a red herring.

The all-consuming implicit paradox is resolved by dissolving the small 's' self that needs worthiness into the large 'S' Self that is love and is itself unity consciousness. This letting go of self and movement to a non-dual reality enables the Peaceful Warrior to realign their purpose from being linked to *personal worthiness* to being an *outpouring of the love of unity consciousness.*

CHARITY

Finally, the Peaceful Warrior accepts the aspect of love that has been rejected by them – charity. C. S. Lewis describes charity as love that is directed towards a neighbour who themselves may not be worthy of that charity.

While this charity exists in any community naturally, the Crusader/Commander fears that this is not the case and engineers situations that will enable them to demonstrate charity because there is no charity in their hostile world.

They spend significant mental and emotional energy trying to manifest charity through overt and covert manipulation of meetings, timings and causes.

Luckily for both the Crusader/Commander and everyone else in their life, the dissolving of the implicit paradox enables them to move on and simply accept that charity is a core element of the love that makes up the very essence of the universe and will happen between people without their constant striving to fill the gap they perceive to be there.

MEDITATION FOR THE PEACEFUL WARRIOR

(Being the value proposition)

Purposeful worth

In the moment, right now

Adding value, seeing the value

Explaining the value

Articulating the value

Making a difference

Actively contributing

Defining the purpose

Taking the first step

Knowing when to let go

Knowing how to let go

Clarifying, transforming, defining

Knowing what isn't

Focusing

Building

Fighting good enough

Prioritising

Knowing that the act of delivering worth is a moment by moment choice

Unnecessary to measure but able to be managed

Redemption unnecessary

Beingness realised

Compassion resolving the self criticism

Peace at last

Peter Burow

modest

confronting

inspirational

visionary

liberating

empowering

healing

The Grateful Healer

self-reliant

disciplined

objective

specialist

masters systems

expert

wise

The Grateful Healer

(CREATIVE, POWERFUL AND SOCIAL SUBTYPES)

The Grateful Healer results from the integration of the Bard and Treasurer Master Profiles. These big picture, enthusiastic and high-energy people take on the big challenges, the international issues, and strive to achieve the impossible dream.

The Grateful Healer, however, is equally interested in the potential of the individual, the unique contribution they can make, and healing. They enjoy taking on the situations that seem impossible and turning them around with audacious and contagious positivity and enthusiasm. Larger than life, expressive, humorous and quirky, the Grateful Healer is well versed in their area of interest with extensive knowledge and a mind that can recall detail and contextualise it in a way that inspires and supports others.

The Grateful Healer is naturally drawn to large projects that require big teams to work together to get the job done. The Grateful Healer often takes on the tasks that have been tried and have failed in the past but that will have a significant impact on the quality of the lives of both individuals and communities. Like all the Non-dual Leaders, Grateful Healers are often the quiet achievers impacting millions without fanfare.

Table 22.4 Non-dual Leader - The Grateful Healer

The Lost Aspect of Love	Infant Classifi-cation	Adult Emotional Position	Central Emotional Position (Harris)	The Axiom or Implicit Paradox	Ego-centric Position 'Derailer'	Virtue of Doing	Virtue of Being
Affection	Avoidant	Dismissing	I'm OK, you're not OK	Freedom through security	Arrogance	Humility	Gratitude

The Grateful Healer's Axiom

THE IMPLICIT PARADOX: FREEDOM THROUGH SECURITY

The implicit paradox describes the unconscious cognitive question that the Master and Mirror strive to answer through the application of their strategic world view and their respective noble qualities. For the Bard and the Treasurer this manifests as a constant searching for external security that is so great that it will lead to complete freedom. The initial wound comes from an avoidant infant behaviour that leads in turn to an adult emotional position described as dismissing. Harris describes this central emotional position as *I'm OK, you're not OK.*

This central emotional position can give us deeper insight as to how and why the implicit paradox forms. The Grateful Healer spends a lifetime of cognitive attention trying to control a dangerous and unsure, not OK world, so that the OK self can have the freedom to be all that it is.

When working with Bards and Treasurers wishing to explore their Non-dual Leader, it can be helpful to have them meditate on the many ways they have strived to create security externally that have been driven by the internal desire to feel freedom. Below is a list of just some of the ways Bards and Treasurers strive to create external security so that they can experience true freedom – of course, the list is endless.

Sample strategies for creating security:

- Removing all desire to have anything so that financial overheads are kept to a bare minimum
- Running the local charity so that if things go bad they can always secure support
- Supporting the local church
- Making purchases that are all timeless so that they will never need to be replaced
- Breaking investments up into a number of smaller ventures to reduce the risks
- Embracing asceticism
- Being overly generous with people so that they all owe them one if things get tight
- Lending people money with a 'someday you can pay it back' clause
- Not marrying in order to reduce overheads
- Not being vain in any way so that all clothes/image purchases can be minimised
- Buying new books and not reading them – just in case in the future they cannot be afforded

- Being accredited in many different disciplines so that there can be multiple income streams
- Buying antiques as a way of combining living expenses with lifestyle and investment
- Not having surgery unless absolutely necessary in order to save money
- Fasting
- Having offshore investments
- Going into business with friends and family so that there is a ledger

The Non-dual Leader manifests when the Bard or the Treasurer and their respective Mirrors see that *their freedom is totally unrelated to security.* The Grateful Healer realises that they have no need to be secure because the concept of security is a false construct built on first-tier fear. There is a realisation that security is the trough of the same wave that carries insecurity as its crest because in reality in a non-dual world there can be no externally provided security.

Of course, the individual cannot be free even if they are secure regardless of how strong the perceived security. This paradox can only be resolved when the individual lets go of *self* and of overly identifying with the feelings of insecurity and fear and replaces them with non-dual acceptance and gratitude. The gratitude of the Grateful Healer comes from within.

When I am working with Bards and Treasurers I encourage them to look deeply at the mental frameworks and *unconscious deals* they have done with themselves, their families and their friends that support or underpin the *freedom through security* implicit paradox. In this way the unconscious script is brought out into the open and exposed for what it is – a red herring.

The all-consuming implicit paradox is resolved by dissolving the small 's' self that needs security into the large 'S' Self that is love and is itself unity consciousness. This letting go of self and movement to a non-dual reality enables the Grateful Healer to realign their freedom from being linked to personal security to being an *outpouring of the love of unity consciousness.*

AFFECTION

Finally, the Grateful Healer deals with the aspect of love that has been rejected by them – affection. C. S. Lewis describes affection as the fondness that develops between people through familiarity. While this fondness occurs between people naturally, the Bard/Treasurer fears that this is not the case and engineers situations that will foster this affection. They spend significant mental and emotional energy trying to ensure that this affection will manifest in their key relationships through overt and covert manipulation. Luckily for both the Grateful Healer and everyone else in their life, the dissolving of the implicit paradox enables the Grateful Healer to move on from this activity and simply *accept* that affection will develop between people without their constant meddling.

MEDITATION FOR THE GRATEFUL HEALER

(Live the dream)

Secure Freedom

To be and do whatever

Here and now

To feel, to think

To realise

To give

To hope, forgive and let go

To transform

To create, improve and heal

To love without constraint

To give without limits

To be in the moment

To be the present, in the present, for those present

can't be removed

Can be revealed

Is a state of being

Is unquenchable

Is beyond comprehension

Humility dissolving the arrogance

Gratitude

Peter Burow

contemplative

independent

discerning

capable

unifying

strategic

insightful

The
Humble
Sage

loyal

enthusiastic

driven

entrepreneurial

motivational

enlivening

cathartic

The Humble Sage

(CREATIVE, POWERFUL AND SOCIAL SUBTYPES)

The Humble Sage results from the integration of the Architect and Judge Master Profiles. These Non-dual Leaders are an unusual mix of enthusiasm and cynicism and have a practical *how to* approach to solving life's challenges.

The Humble Sage enjoys exploring philosophical issues and easily distils issues down to their constituent principles. Curious, logical and able to understand issues from a practical perspective as well as a theoretical framework, the Humble Sage is the voice of considered action when something strategic needs to be done.

The Humble Sage is naturally drawn to working with institutions to develop their constitutions, legal frameworks or guiding principles. The Humble Sage often takes on the administrative or *thinking* tasks that others couldn't be bothered thinking through but that make an enormous difference in the lives of both individuals and communities. Like all the Non-dual Leaders, Humble Sages are often quiet achievers who impact millions without fanfare.

Table 22.5 Non-dual Leader - The Humble Sage

The Lost Aspect of Love	Infant Classifi- cation	Adult Emotional Position	Central Emotional Position (Harris)	The Axiom or Implicit Paradox	Ego- centric Position 'Derailer'	Virtue of Doing	Virtue of Being
Friendship	Disorganised or disoriented	Unresolved, disorganised	I'm not OK, you're not OK	Alignment through Strategy	Ingratitude	Gratitude	Humility

The Humble Sage's Axiom

THE IMPLICIT PARADOX: ALIGNMENT THROUGH STRATEGY

The implicit paradox describes the unconscious cognitive question that the Master and Mirror strive to answer through the application of their strategic world view and their respective noble qualities. For the Architect and Judge this manifests as a constant searching for alignment that is so great that it will enable them to do what it takes to make the world a better place. Like the Peaceful Warrior, the initial wound comes from disorganised or disoriented infant behaviour that leads in turn to an adult emotional position described as unresolved or disorganised. Harris describes this central emotional position as *I'm not OK, you're not OK.*

This central emotional position can give us deeper insight as to how and why the implicit paradox forms. The Humble Sage spends a lifetime of cognitive attention trying to use power to tame and improve a dangerous and ever changing not OK world, so that future generations can live a better and more predictable, more controlled and better quality of life.

When working with Architects and Judges wishing to explore their Non-dual Leader, it can be helpful to have them meditate on the many ways they use power in their lives driven by the internal desire to make the world a better place. Below is a list of the ways Architects and Judges seek power to achieve hope for the future – of course, this list is just a sample to give you the idea of how the concept works.

Sample power:

- Chairman of the Board, the church, the community, the mayor to drive alignment to the strategy
- Being a teacher or principal of a school
- Always volunteering to be on committees to influence alignment to the strategy
- Aggressively hiring and firing people not aligned to the strategy
- Insisting that family members seek permission before making major life decisions and punishing when they don't
- Giving gifts to those who are 'aligned' to the strategy
- Taking up money back guarantees when products don't 'walk the talk'
- Demanding the promotion/pay rise for their strategic impact
- Always using a microphone in groups
- Facilitating groups – never an unstrategic member
- Only attend meetings where they lead the alignment to the strategy
- Writing institutional legal agreements, principles, constitutions, laws
- Judging community competitions to align with the competitions stated strategy
- Only associating with powerful or influential people who can influence alignment to the strategy
- Marrying into a powerful family

The Non-dual Leader manifests when the Architect or the Judge and their respective Mirrors see that *alignment is totally unrelated to power.* The Humble Sage realises that they have no need to vicariously control the future through strategically enforced agreements, legislation or convention because anything other than the present is a false construct built on first-tier cognition and consciousness. There is a realisation that alignment is the trough of the same wave that carries the present moment as its crest because in reality in a non-dual world there can be no alignment that is not contained in the moment.

Of course, the individual cannot influence the future for very long, regardless of how powerful they are. This paradox can only be resolved when the individual lets go of *self* and of overly identifying with the feelings of being small and making no impact on the world and replaces this with non-dual acceptance and humility. The humility of the Humble Sage comes from within.

When I am working with Architects and Judges I encourage them to look deeply at the mental frameworks and *unconscious deals* they have done with themselves, their families and their friends that support or underpin the alignment through strategy implicit paradox. In this way the unconscious script is brought out into the open and exposed for what it is – a red herring.

The all-consuming implicit paradox is resolved by dissolving the small 's' self that needs to so desperately improve the world into the large 'S' Self that is love and is itself unity consciousness. This letting go of self and movement to a non-dual reality enables the Humble Sage to realign their driving need to make the world a better place by using their own *personal power and aligned thinking* to being in the reality of experiencing the eternal now that witnesses the outpouring of the *love of unity consciousness and source of all hope.*

FRIENDSHIP

Finally, the Humble Sage deals with the aspect of love that has been rejected by them – genuine friendship. C. S. Lewis describes friendship as the strong bond that develops between people. While this friendship occurs between people naturally, the Architect/Judge fears that this is not the case and engineers situations that will foster this. They spend significant mental and emotional energy trying to ensure that friendship will manifest. Luckily for both the Humble Sage and everyone else in their life, the dissolving of the implicit paradox enables them to see that through *grace* that true and lasting friendships develop between people without their ego trying to make it happen through strategy and performance.

Meditation for the Humble Sage

(Being the change required)

Powerful alignment

Bringing the vision into the present

Realising the walk mentors the talk

Being the change needed

Describing the alignment

Aligning the self, ideas, plans and concepts

Noble alignment

Practical alignment

Powerfully articulated

Powerfully brought to life

Communicated

Fostering immediate engagement

For both the current and the future

Alignment enabling 'them and us' to become 'thus'

Nudging, pruning, trimming ideas

Getting started

Strategic conversations

Unrelenting alignment in every aspect of endeavour

Mentoring alignment

Designing

This moment is the future

From 'one day' to 'today'

Gratitude transforming the ingratitude

Humility bubbling up

Peter Burow

charming

negotiating

diplomatic

strives for
esprit de corps

kind

genuine

venerable

faithful

protecting

responsible

role excellence

The
Compassionate
Leader

principled

conquering

honourable

The Compassionate Leader
(CREATIVE, POWERFUL AND SOCIAL SUBTYPES)

The Compassionate Leader results from the integration of the Navigator and Chancellor Master Profiles. These charismatic and engaging people naturally rise to positions of leadership.

The Compassionate Leader is humorous, clear, consistent, strong, balanced and committed. These Non-dual Leaders enjoy tackling social issues and have a disarming ability to turn talk into action – clear planned action. Faithful, old-fashioned and with old-fashioned ideals, the Compassionate Leader is the voice of stability when others want to forsake the current direction or approach for the newest idea.

The Compassionate Leader is naturally drawn to positions of leadership, chairman, head of the household, Minister (political or religious), lead singer, conductor, head scientist. The Compassionate Leader often takes on the difficult tasks that involve conflict or holding people accountable and that make an enormous difference in the lives of both individuals and communities. Like all the Non-dual Leaders, Compassionate Leaders are often quiet achievers who impact millions without fanfare.

Table 22.6 Non-dual Leader - The Compassionate Leader

The Lost Aspect of Love	Infant Classifi-cation	Adult Emotional Position	Central Emotional Position (Harris)	The Axiom or Implicit Paradox	Ego-centric Position 'Derailer'	Virtue of Doing	Virtue of Being
Eros	Resistant or ambivalent	Preoccupied	I'm not OK, you're OK	Love through beauty	Restlessness	Peace-fulness	Compassion

The Compassionate Leader's Axiom

THE IMPLICIT PARADOX: LOVE THROUGH BEAUTY

The implicit paradox describes the unconscious cognitive question that the Master and Mirror strive to answer through the application of their strategic world view and their respective noble qualities. For the Navigator and Chancellor this manifests as a constant searching for an external beauty that is so great that it will lead to experiencing true love. While the initial source for the need for experiencing love sits in the P1 Intelligence Circuit and is linked to pre-birth/somatosensory/emotional issues developed in the first twelve months of life, the Master and Mirror treat this wound as real and all pervasive and apply all their spare cognitive capacity to its resolution.

When working with Navigators and Chancellors wishing to explore their Non-dual Leader, it can be helpful to have them meditate on the many external searches for beauty they have been on in their lives and are still on that are driven by the internal desire to experience true unconditional love. Below is a list of the purposes or sacrifices Navigators and Chancellors have made to experience love – of course, this list is just a sample to give you the idea of how the concept works.

Sample searches for beauty:
- Becoming infatuated with a beautiful PA, neighbour, friend or celebrity
- Becoming infatuated with a beautiful piece of art
- Becoming infatuated with a particular place that is believed to be beautiful
- Becoming infatuated with a new boss or powerful person who is considered to be beautiful
- Becoming infatuated with their children
- Becoming infatuated with youthfulness
- Becoming infatuated with fashion, plastic surgery or health
- Having sex with beautiful people
- Developing deep emotional connections with beautiful people who come across their path
- Divorcing when their partner is no longer young and beautiful
- Becoming infatuated with young, sexually attractive people from other countries
- Using their position to seduce beautiful employees
- Wearing the latest fashion to appear beautiful to others
- Refusing to dialogue with unattractive people
- Attending beauty-based events like *Miss Australia/America*
- Buying products, cars, clothes, fashion that is associated with beauty
- Mentoring, coaching, counselling, managing or guiding beautiful people with whom they become infatuated

The Non-dual Leader manifests when the Navigator or the Chancellor and their respective Mirrors see that *their appreciation of and infatuation with beauty is totally unrelated to their experience of true love*. The Compassionate Leader realises that they have no need to be hypnotised by love because true love is a false construct built on first-tier cognition and consciousness. There is a realisation that love is the trough of the same wave that carries disconnection as its crest because in reality in a non-dual world there can be no true love outside oneself.

Of course, the individual cannot experience self-love if they are infatuated by beauty regardless of how beautiful it is. This paradox can only be resolved when the individual lets go of *self* and of overly identifying with the feelings of lovelessness and replaces them with non-dual acceptance and self-love. The compassion of the Compassionate Leader comes from within.

When I am working with Navigators and Chancellors I encourage them to look deeply at the mental frameworks and *unconscious deals* they have done with themselves, their families and their friends that support or underpin the *love through beauty* implicit paradox. In this way the unconscious script is brought out into the open and exposed for what it is – a red herring.

The all-consuming implicit paradox is resolved by dissolving the small 's' self that needs worthiness into the large 'S' Self that is love and is itself unity consciousness. This letting go of self and movement to a non-dual reality enables the Compassionate Leader to realign their love from being linked to *perfect beauty* to experiencing the *outpouring of the love of unity consciousness* in the eternal moment.

EROS

Finally, the Compassionate Leader deals with the aspect of love that has been rejected by them – Eros. C. S. Lewis describes Eros as *falling in love*. While this occurs between people naturally, the Navigator/Chancellor fear that this is not the case and engineers situations that will foster this falling in love. They spend significant mental and emotional energy trying to ensure that they fall in love in as many aspects of their work, love and play as they can. Luckily for both the Compassionate Leader and everyone else in their life, the dissolving of the implicit paradox enables them to see that through *grace* people fall in love all the time – even their own family and friends.

MEDITATION FOR THE COMPASSIONATE LEADER

(Share the love)

Beautiful Love

Has no owner

Has no limit

Has no memory

Loves forever

Gives without borders

Has no envy

No control

Gives to give

Builds, grows, nourishes, connects

Fills the space

Opens, calms and reassures

Rounds the edges

Is forever in this moment

Peacefulness displacing restlessness

Compassion

Peter Burow

The Role of
the Limbic System
for the
Non-dual Leaders

NEURO-LIMBIC INTEGRATION - TOWARDS WISDOM

So far we have considered the role of integration in the formation of the Non-dual Leader, but what of the Neuro-Limbic Types? What has happened to the fight/flight/comply response of the Neuro-Limbic Types?

Possibly one of the best ways to illustrate the way the Non-dual Leader interacts with the Neuro-Limbic Type is through the lens of a significant body of research that has been undertaken by a group of academics at the Max Planck Institute for Human Development. Known as the Berlin Wisdom Paradigm, the framework has been made famous by Paul Baltes and Ursula Staudinger.[2] Their study focuses on defining wisdom.

Baltes and Staudinger define wisdom as an expert knowledge system concerning the fundamental pragmatics of life.

The fundamental pragmatics of life include knowledge and judgement about the meaning and conduct of life and the orchestration of human development towards excellence while attending co-jointly to personal and collective well-being.

Wisdom is generally considered the pinnacle of insight into the human condition and about the means and ends to a good life (Baltes et al., 2000, p. 3).

I would argue that there are three different ways that we, as humans, seek to achieve the means and ends to a good life and each one is only available to us once we have integrated our Neuro-Limbic triads.

The five factors outlined below are an attempt to quantify what it is that wise leaders do, feel and think. It is a model that tries to explain the nature of wisdom without the help of the *NeuroPower* framework of personality. For this reason after each of their criteria I have linked it back to the *NeuroPower* insights.

Specifically, Baltes and Staudinger have attempted to quantify wisdom with five key factors:

1. *Rich, factual, declarative knowledge about the fundamental pragmatics of life* (Baltes et al., 2000). In a *NeuroPower* context, this refers to the I1 Intelligence. This links with the Neuro-Limbic Types Four, Five and Nine. In this context Baltes and Staudinger's insight corresponds to I1 data about human nature (I1 Feeling NLT4), the nature of lifelong development models and frameworks such as Spiral Dynamics) social norms (I1 Thinking NLT5), critical events in life and their possible constellations and the nature of well-being both from a personal perspective and from the perspective of others (I1 Somatic NLT9).

---

2   The Berlin Wisdom Paradigm is a framework for defining wisdom extensively researched and vigorously tested by Paul B Baltes and Ursula M Staudinger who built on the earlier work of many academics at the Max Planck Institute for Human Development. *http://www.mpib-berlin.mpg.de/volltexte/institut/dok/full/Baltes/wisdomam/index.htm*

The Impact of
Different Limbic States on the Way We Think

Different moods evoke different parts of the brain and different Intelligences. For example, an elevated and upbeat mood evokes higher achievement, seeking out new information regardless of its negativity (P2), but can work poorly for detail work such as bookkeeping or reviewing a contract (Aspinwall, 1998). A serious, downbeat or negative mood can create a space which works better for withdrawing and dealing with details (I1) (Ashkanasy, Härtel, & Zerbe, 2000). Choosing the mood for the desired outcome is a helpful skill accessed by the wise.

2. *Rich procedural knowledge about the pragmatics of life* (Baltes et al., 2000). This refers to P1 and links with the Neuro-Limbic Types One, Two and Six. In this context procedural knowledge about the fundamental pragmatics of life involves strategies and heuristics for dealing with the meaning and conduct of life (P1 Somatic NLT1); heuristics for giving advice and for the structuring and weighing of life goals (P1 Feeling NLT2); and ways to handle life conflicts and life decisions, and knowledge about alternative back-up strategies if development were not to proceed as expected (P1 Thinking NLT6).

3. *Relativism of values and life priorities* (Baltes et al., 2000). In a *NeuroPower* context, this refers to P2. This links with the Neuro-Limbic Types Three, Seven, and Eight. In this context Baltes and Staudinger suggest that it refers to the acknowledgement of and tolerance for value differences and the relativity of the values held by individuals and society (P2 Feeling NLT7). In this context it is not meant to imply relativity of values and value-related priorities. On the contrary, it includes an explicit concern with the topic of virtue and the common good (P2 Somatic NLT8). And aside from the recognition of certain universal values (Kekes, 1995), value-relative knowledge, judgement, and advice is part of the essence of wisdom (P2 Feeling NLT3).

4. Lifespan contextualism refers to knowledge that considers the many themes and contexts of life (for example, education, family, work, friends, leisure, the public good of society, etc.), their interrelations and cultural variations, and in addition, incorporates a lifetime temporal perspective (past, present, future) (Baltes et al., 2000). Another feature of lifespan contextualism is the historical and social location of individual lifespan development, as well as the idiographic

or non-normative events that operate in human development (Bandura, 1982). In *NeuroPower* this refers to a practical working knowledge of the various levels of consciousness – for example, Spiral Dynamics.

5. The final criteria is the recognition of and management of uncertainty, which is based on the ideas (for example, Dawes, 1988; Gigerenzer, 1996; Nisbett & Ross, 1980; Simon, 1983; Stich, 1990) that (1) the validity of human information processing itself is essentially limited (constrained), (2) individuals have access only to select parts of reality, and (3) that the future cannot be fully known in advance. Wisdom-related knowledge and judgement are expected to offer ways and means to deal with such uncertainty about human insight and the conditions of the world, individually and collectively (Baltes et al., 2000). Using the *NeuroPower* framework this refers to the Non-dual Leader's ability to manage the process of interaction between the Neuro-Limbic and Neuro-Rational aspects of self.

When an individual has access to all these five attributes, they are considered to be *wise*. But as we can see, this has at least two implications from a *NeuroPower* perspective:

1. Firstly, the individual must be able to move between the P1, P2 and I1 almost instantaneously.

2. The individual must be able to use both the limbic Neuro-Limbic Types and the Neuro-Rational Types simultaneously and harmoniously to have both a practical *know-how* and to be able to manifest the virtues or noble qualities of the Master.

Wise Non-dual Leaders demonstrate both of these attributes.

The Three Neuro-Limbic Types
that Provide the Fuel for
the Non-dual Leaders

We mentioned earlier that, at a limbic level, we are all seeking to develop the means and ends to a good life. While this is consistent for all of us, the way we attempt to achieve this end goal can be broken into three broad strategies: the creative approach, the social approach and the power approach. Each approach summarises an innate paradigm that is distinct from the other two. This world view is so implicit for us all that many never stop to consider that there may be other options or approaches. The three world paradigms that underlie all consciousness have been listed below. Every one of us has just one of these and this makes up our instinctual or intuitive wisdom.

1. **Creative limbic wisdom:** *This is the integration of P1 Somatic, P2 Thinking and I1 Feeling (the NLTs 1, 7 and 4).*

   It is little wonder that whenever the limbic model is introduced to a group of people they all want to type themselves in this triad – the means and ends to a good life through creativity seems like a very good context to bring to the world. Creative wisdom is made up of three distinct elements: the ability to consider the ideal future outcome which is derived from NLT4; the ability to draw on and leverage from the very best and highest standards from the past which is derived from NLT1; and finally the ability to think laterally, have fun and enjoy the moment which is derived from NLT7.

2. **Socially intelligent limbic wisdom:** *This is the integration of P1 Thinking, P2 Feeling and I1 Somatic (the NLTs 3, 6 and 9).* Daniel Goleman in his 2006 book *Social Intelligence* outlines a social intelligence model that aligns with the effective integration of these three limbic positions. Broadly speaking, Goleman argues 'social intelligence is a shorthand term for being intelligent not just about relationships but also in them' (Goleman, 2006, p. 11).

   He goes on to explain that social intelligence is made up of two distinct components: social awareness and social facility. When all three Neuro-Limbic Types are integrated the individual has immediate access to this form of wisdom and sees the world limbically through this lens.

   Social awareness:

   - Primary empathy: Derived from the NLT9's ability to feel what others are feeling and sense non-verbal emotions
   - Attunement: Derived from the NLT9's ability to listen with full receptivity
   - Empathetic accuracy: Derived from the NLT9's ability to understand another person's thoughts, feelings and intentions

- Social cognition: Derived from the NLT6's knowledge of how the social world works (Goleman, 2006, p. 84)

   Social facility

- Synchrony: Derived from the NLT3's ability to interact smoothly at the non-verbal level

- Self-presentation: Derived from the NLT3's ability to present themselves effectively

- Influence: Derived from the NLT3's ability to shape the outcome of social interactions

- Concern: Derived from the NLT6's caring about others' needs and acting accordingly (Goleman, 2006, p. 84)

3. **Limbic wisdom that understands the true nature of power:** *This is the integration of the P1 Feeling, P2 Somatic and I1 Thinking (the NLTs 2, 8 and 5).* This integration creates wisdom in the area of the effective use of power. Power in this context has three vital components: alignment with powerful people, ideas and organisations which is derived from NLT2; the knowledge of powerful information which is derived from NLT5; and the ability to take action based on what the individual believes is right, which is derived from NLT8.

When the Core Beliefs are integrated as outlined above, they are very different from Neuro-Limbic Types from which they are made.

The integration gives the individual instant access to practical know-how about how to best respond to any situation.

The purpose of the integrated Limbic Type is to establish *CONTEXT*. This means that when an event takes place, the Non-dual Leader is able to draw instantly on knowledge that contextualises the tasks at hand and puts the Higher Self to work. The role of the integrated Non-dual Leader is to populate the contextualised event with *CONTENT*. All content requires context to have meaning.

The wise Leader has the ability to instantly contextualise a situation and set the Higher Self at work to then solve the puzzle within that context.

The Four Levels of the Implicit Paradox

Each of the four Non-dual Leaders has a specific implicit paradox that dissolves when they reach the Non-dual Leader state. But the process doesn't end there. The resolution of the one paradox at each meme makes way for another. This, after all, is what drives human evolution and the deep desire to be whole. The order in which each Non-dual Leader resolves these paradoxes at each meme is outlined below.

The Peaceful Warrior

The Grateful Healer

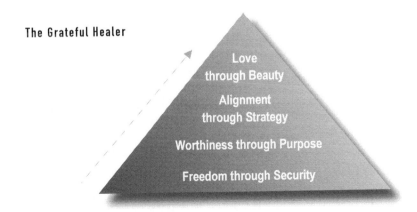

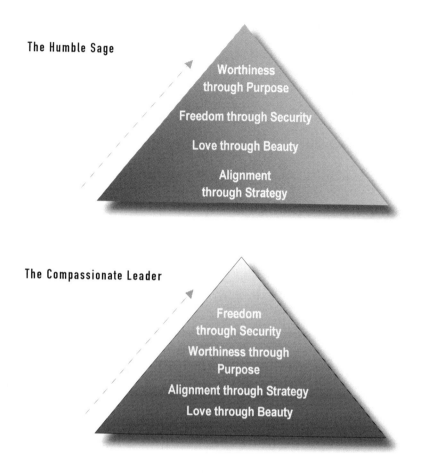

At each meme these paradoxes are addressed to the satisfaction of the individual according to the context of the meme and the limbic world view.

The task of the individual is to answer these questions at each meme so that they can move forward. If the individual does not address these paradoxical questions at each meme they will need to return to the meme so that the work can be done. If the work is not done the individual can only ever experience the Non-dual Leader as an induced state rather than an enduring stage.

For all of us this understanding allows us to contribute constructively to discussions - both ours and others - at the various memes. It shows us the underlying unspoken conundrum that is preventing the individual from being present and instead takes them into their head. It helps us guide them forward by addressing the real issue rather than ignoring or changing the implicit paradox for something more rational.

These unconscious conundrums become the stumbling blocks for progress at each meme. For the Commander/Crusader who has the potential to become The Peaceful Warrior, the derailer is CRITICISM, the residue of the survivalist central emotional position, the UNRESOLVED and DISORGANISED 'I'm not OK, you're not OK'.

For the Bard/Treasurer who has the potential to become The Grateful Healer, the derailer is ARROGANCE, the residue of the survivalist central emotional position, the DISMISSIVE 'I'm OK, you're not OK'.

For the Judge/Architect who has the potential to become The Humble Sage the derailer is INGRATITUDE, the residue of the survivalist central emotional position, the UNRESOLVED and DISORGANISED I'm not OK, you're not OK.

For the Chancellor/Navigator who has the potential to become The Compassionate Leader the derailer is RESTLESSNESS, the residue of the survivalist central emotional position, the PREOCCUPIED 'I'm not OK, you're OK'. Each of the implicit paradoxes are linked with a specific noble quality.

1. Worthiness through Purpose is dissolved through COMPASSION which leads to PEACEFULNESS.

2. Freedom through Security is dissolved through HUMILITY which leads to GRATITUDE.

3. Alignment through strategy is dissolved through GRATITUDE which leads to HUMILITY.

4. Love through Beauty is dissolved through PEACEFULNESS which leads to COMPASSION.

The four points above indicate that each Non-dual Leader state at Turquoise possesses a virtue of Being accessed by a virtue of Doing. The Non-dual Leader state is an integrated state of the personality driven by a deep inner desire to mature and be a contributor to the society in which he or she lives.

This journey is not for the faint-hearted yet for those who recognise that to live is to grow into all that we can be, the difficulties encountered are commensurate to the need to realise a life of significance.

For the Peaceful Warrior, the shift from Self-Criticism to Peacefulness requires the decision to persistently access the virtue of Compassion. This involves letting go of their judgemental I'm not OK, you're not OK position, and instead realising that in the eternal present moment, there are no past of future benchmarks or standards that need to be met, and that they are complete and worthy as they are.

For the Grateful Healer the shift from Arrogance to Gratitude requires the decision to persistently practise the virtue of Humility, the letting go of the self-serving I'm OK, you're not OK. Instead, the work to be done centres around seeing all people in the context of the unity of humankind and recognising that we all have a journey to travel and that each one of us is doing the best we can with what we know.

For the Humble Sage, the shift from Ingratitude to Humility requires the decision to persistently practise the virtue of Gratitude. In so doing, the Architect/Judge lets go of their 'I'm not OK, you're not OK' position and its preoccupation with reinforcing their sense of insignificance by creating an enduring future. Instead, the Humble Sage is at one with the love of unity consciousness, which knows no bounds and is eternally present.

For the Compassionate Leader the shift from Restlessness to Compassion requires the decision to persistently realise that the state of Peace dissolves any preoccupation with the past. The Peacefulness that the Chancellor/Navigator is to practise comes from living in the present moment with no attachment to what was once their 'I'm not OK, you're OK' focus on having to be connected with someone or something to experience meaning.

AT A HIGHER LEVEL (ACCEPTANCE AND GRACE)

At an even higher level, however, we see that peace and gratitude are simply the yin (peace) and yang (gratitude) of one overriding principle – the principle of Grace. Grace integrates and defines both peace (internal focus) and gratitude (external focus).

In the same way, we can see that compassion and humility are simply the yin (humility) and yang (compassion) of the one overriding principle – the principle of Acceptance. Acceptance integrates and defines both compassion (external focus) and humility (internal focus).

This is true at every meme.

This is relevant because the effective integration of the implicit paradoxes at each level of consciousness will be evident when the noble qualities of acceptance and grace manifest. Acceptance and grace are the indicators that the work at that level of consciousness has been done. They are the flags that the individual really has answered the underlying implicit questions of existence at that meme and will be moving forward in an effort to further integrate the Self.

For counsellors, advisers and leaders alike, the individual's awareness of acceptance and grace are the signs that the real work has been done. Conversely, when the individual demonstrates a complete lack of acceptance and grace, the work has not been done and the true gold has been substituted for fool's gold.

THE FINAL STAGE IN THE INTEGRATION OF THE HUMAN PERSONALITY

As dynamic and extraordinary as the Non-dual Leader state is, it is by no means the end of the journey and far less an end in itself. Beyond this level of awareness lies another of profound significance that has only been accessed by a select few living souls during the millennia of human life on this planet.

The fact that only a few recorded humans have attained or experienced this level of realisation is no reason for us to not pursue an understanding of it or acquaint ourselves with its ultimate power and wisdom. This consummate state is that of the Avatar and in terms of *NeuroPower* it represents the integration of all aspects of the personality, fully healed of its original wound and at total liberty from the implicit paradoxes that once held it bound. It is a state of consciousness whereby the personality has reunited with its originating essence in the ever-present bliss of pure awareness.

We have previously discussed how the wound arose through the dis-integration of the Intelligences. This resulted in the need for the long journey back to wholeness and the many pains that such a journey produces. Yet from this long and dark night of the soul arose the hope that every individual can discover the true Self and what it means to be whole again and experience life in all its fullness.

NeuroPower interprets this journey as a process of integration. This Handbook offers a description of that journey and in a sequential manner plots the work to be

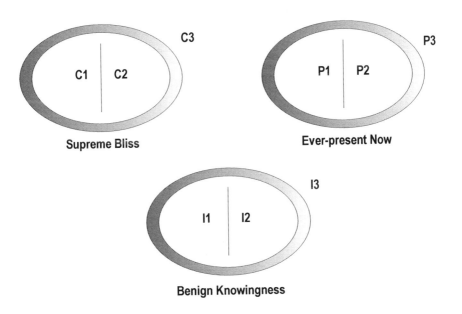

Supreme Bliss

Ever-present Now

Benign Knowingness

done. The final state of the Avatar then becomes the destination of human seeking.

It is a level of consciousness and awareness whereby C1 assimilates with C2 and the regained whole manifests as Supreme Bliss (C3). P1 assimilates with P2 and the original coherence reappears results in the dissolving of duality and the revelation of the Ever-present Now (P3). I1 assimilates with I2 and the Pure Awareness of the original state shines forth as the radiance of Benign Knowingness (I3).

So finally, the Integrated Personality of the Avatar emerges and, when the opposites are united, the original state of Unity Consciousness is once again attained (C3, P3, I3).

As Brahman constitutes a person's Self
it is not something to be attained
by that person.
Shankara
(Hindu)

That there is nothing to be attained
is not idle talk;
it is the truth.
Huang Po
(Buddhist)

Thou shalt know God without image and without
means (without path).
Eckhart
(Christian)

The real is near, you do not have
to search for it; and a man
who seeks truth will
never find it.
Krishnamurti

Final Word

Wise, Non-dual Leaders are extraordinary. They are amazingly rounded, practical, loving and enthusiastic human beings who change the experience we have of life. They do this by accessing many lifetimes of wisdom tied up in their limbic profiles and by dedicating their conscious efforts to being present and to dissolving problems in duality to non-dual wisdom. For most of us this looks like magic. But in reality they are simply more in touch with life as it actually is than the rest of us. Our problem is that we believe the illusion we create. Enlightened Leaders are simply aware of a more complete reality.

End Note

Like all Holmes's reasoning, the thing seemed simplicity itself when once it was explained.

Sir Arthur Conan Doyle

The purpose of this book has been to explore human personality, integration, consciousness and transformation by bringing together the latest findings from neuroscience with the oldest and most respected philosophies known to man. In doing this we have outlined a method that enables the individual to move from basic causality consciousness to higher consciousness through the expression of human nobility. While this may be hard because it means breaking our comfortable pattern of avoidance it's worth the effort.

I believe you and I are here to master the journey and not just reach the destination. Allow the problems you face every day to generate noble attractors that not only draw you through the spirals of consciousness but also make the world a better place. Even as you take your next breath, I encourage you to make your own journey one of nobility, meaning and significance. Embrace your nobility with all your heart, all your mind and all your strength so that you manifest the power you were born to exude. Live a life of character and hardwire this character into your brain until it is transformed into wisdom. Do this because this wisdom will positively impact the world in ways you would never believe even if you knew. Do this because only then will you understand what it is to be human and live life in all its fullness.

Appendices

To download the Appendices please visit:
http://neuropowergroup.com/wp2/neuropower-book-appendices/

50238842R00460

Made in the USA
San Bernardino, CA
17 June 2017